SPSS

SPSS® for Windows™
Base System User's Guide
Release 6.0

Marija J. Norušis / SPSS Inc.

`SPSS Inc.
444 N. Michigan Avenue
Chicago, Illinois 60611
Tel: (312) 329-2400
Fax: (312) 329-3668

SPSS Federal Systems (U.S.)
SPSS Latin America
SPSS Benelux BV
SPSS UK Ltd.
SPSS UK Ltd., New Delhi
SPSS GmbH Software
SPSS Scandinavia AB
SPSS Asia Pacific Pte. Ltd.
SPSS Japan Inc.
SPSS Australasia Pty. Ltd.

For more information about SPSS® software products, please write or call

Marketing Department
SPSS Inc.
444 North Michigan Avenue
Chicago, IL 60611
Tel: (312) 329-2400
Fax: (312) 329-3668

SPSS® for Windows™: Base System User's Guide, Release 6.0
Copyright © 1993 by SPSS Inc.
All rights reserved.
Printed in the United States of America.

2 3 4 5 6 7 8 9 0   95 94 93

ISBN 0-13-178856-6

Library of Congress Catalog Card Number: 93-084969

Preface

SPSS is a comprehensive and flexible statistical analysis and data management system. SPSS can take data from almost any type of file and use them to generate tabulated reports, charts and plots of distributions and trends, descriptive statistics, and complex statistical analyses.

SPSS® for Windows™ Release 6 brings the full power of the mainframe version of SPSS to the personal computer environment. It will enable you to perform many analyses on your PC that were once possible only on much larger machines. You can now analyze large data files with thousands of variables. The algorithms are identical to those used in SPSS software on mainframe computers, and the statistical results will be as precise as those computed on a mainframe.

SPSS for Windows provides a user interface that makes statistical analysis more accessible for the casual user and more convenient for the experienced user. Simple menus and dialog box selections make it possible to perform complex analyses without typing a single line of command syntax. The Data Editor offers a simple and efficient spreadsheet-like facility for entering data and browsing the working data file. High-resolution, presentation-quality charts and plots are included as part of the Base system.

The *SPSS for Windows Base System User's Guide* documents the graphical user interface of SPSS for Windows. Beneath the menus and dialog boxes, SPSS uses a command language, and some features of the system can be accessed only via command syntax. Appendix A lists the commands available only with command syntax. Complete command syntax is documented in the *SPSS Base System Syntax Reference Guide*.

SPSS Options

The following options are available as add-on enhancements to the SPSS Base system:

- **SPSS Professional Statistics**™ provides techniques to measure the similarities and differences in data, classify data, identify underlying dimensions, and more. It includes procedures for these analyses: cluster, k-means cluster, discriminant, factor, multidimensional scaling, proximity, and reliability.

- **SPSS Advanced Statistics**™ includes sophisticated techniques such as logistic regression, loglinear analysis, multivariate analysis of variance, constrained nonlinear regression, probit analysis, Cox regression, Kaplan-Meier and actuarial survival analysis.

- **SPSS Tables**™ creates a variety of presentation-quality tabular reports, including complex stub-and-banner tables and displays of multiple response data.
- **SPSS Trends**™ performs comprehensive forecasting and time series analyses with multiple curve-fitting models, smoothing models, and methods for estimating autoregressive functions.
- **SPSS Categories**™ performs conjoint analysis and optimal scaling procedures, including correspondence analysis.
- **SPSS CHAID**™ simplifies tabular analysis of categorical data, develops predictive models, screens out extraneous predictor variables, and produces easy-to-read tree diagrams that segment a population into subgroups that share similar characteristics.
- **SPSS LISREL**® 7 analyzes linear structural relations and simultaneous equation models.

You can expand the system yourself by incorporating programs written in C or FORTRAN. Contact SPSS Inc. for SPSS for Windows User Code documentation.

Compatibility

The SPSS for Windows Base system is designed for personal computers in the IBM PC and IBM PS/2 lines with at least 4MB of random access memory and 23MB of hard disk space, running Windows 3.1 or later. This product also functions on closely IBM-compatible hardware.

Serial Numbers

Your serial number is your identification number with SPSS Inc. You will need this serial number when you call SPSS Inc. for information regarding support, payment, a defective diskette, or an upgraded system.

The serial number can be found on the diskette labeled Installation that came with your Base system. Before using the system, please copy this number to the registration card.

Registration Card

STOP! Before continuing on, *fill out and send us your registration card*. Until we receive your registration card, you have an unregistered system. Even if you have previously sent a card to us, please fill out and return the card enclosed in your Base system package. Registering your system entitles you to:

- Technical support services
- Favored customer status
- New product announcements

Don't put it off—send your registration card now!

Customer Service

Contact Customer Service at 1-800-521-1337 if you have any questions concerning your shipment or account. Please have your serial number ready for identification when calling.

Training Seminars

SPSS Inc. provides both public and onsite training seminars for SPSS for Windows. All seminars feature hands-on workshops. SPSS for Windows seminars will be offered in major U.S. and European cities on a regular basis. For more information on these seminars, call the SPSS Inc. Training Department toll-free at 1-800-543-6607.

Technical Support

The services of SPSS Technical Support are available to registered customers of SPSS for Windows. Customers may call Technical Support for assistance in using SPSS products or for installation help for one of the supported hardware environments.

To reach Technical Support, call 1-312-329-3410. Be prepared to identify yourself, your organization, and the serial number of your system.

If you are a Value Plus or Customer EXPress customer, use the priority 800 number you received with your materials. For information on subscribing to the Value Plus or Customer EXPress plan, call SPSS Software Sales at 1-800-543-2185.

Additional Publications

Additional copies of all SPSS product manuals may be purchased separately from Prentice-Hall, the exclusive distributor of SPSS publications. To order additional manuals, just fill out and mail the Publications insert included with your system.

Lend Us Your Thoughts

Your comments are important. So send us a letter and let us know about your experiences with SPSS products. We especially like to hear about new and interesting applications using the SPSS for Windows system. Write to SPSS Inc. Marketing Department, Attn: Micro Software Products Manager, 444 N. Michigan Avenue, Chicago IL, 60611

Contacting SPSS Inc.

If you would like to be on our mailing list, write to us at one of the addresses below. We will send you a copy of our newsletter and let you know about SPSS Inc. activities in your area.

SPSS Inc.
444 North Michigan Ave.
Chicago, IL 60611
Tel: (312) 329-2400
Fax: (312) 329-3668

SPSS Federal Systems
12030 Sunrise Valley Dr.
Suite 300
Reston, VA 22091
Tel: (703) 391-6020
Fax: (703) 391-6002

SPSS Latin America
444 North Michigan Ave.
Chicago, IL 60611
Tel: (312) 329-3556
Fax: (312) 329-3668

SPSS Benelux BV
P.O. Box 115
4200 AC Gorinchem
The Netherlands
Tel: +31.1830.36711
Fax: +31.1830.35839

SPSS UK Ltd.
SPSS House
5 London Street
Chertsey
Surrey KT16 8AP
United Kingdom
Tel: +44.932.566262
Fax: +44.932.567020

SPSS UK Ltd., New Delhi
c/o Ashok Business Centre
Ashok Hotel
50B Chanakyapuri
New Delhi 110 021
India
Tel: +91.11.600121 x1029
Fax: +91.11.6873216

SPSS GmbH Software
Steinsdorfstrasse 19
D-80538 Munich
Germany
Tel: +49.89.2283008
Fax: +49.89.2285413

SPSS Scandinavia AB
Gamla Brogatan 36-38
4th Floor
111 20 Stockholm
Sweden
Tel: +46.8.102610
Fax: +46.8.102550

SPSS Asia Pacific Pte. Ltd.
10 Anson Road, #34-07
International Plaza
Singapore 0207
Singapore
Tel: +65.221.2577
Fax: +65.221.9920

SPSS Japan Inc.
AY Bldg.
3-2-2 Kitaaoyama
Minato-ku
Tokyo 107
Japan
Tel: +81.3.5474.0341
Fax: +81.3.5474.2678

SPSS Australasia Pty. Ltd.
121 Walker Street
North Sydney, NSW 2060
Australia
Tel: +61.2.954.5660
Fax: +61.2.954.5616

Contents

6 File Handling and File Transformations 127

7 Data Tabulation 155

8 Descriptive Statistics 167

23 Overview of the SPSS Chart Facility   439

24 Bar, Line, Area, and Pie Charts   461

25 High-Low Charts   511

26 Boxplots and Error Bar Charts   537

27 Scatterplots and Histograms   553

1 Overview of SPSS for Windows

SPSS for Windows provides a powerful statistical analysis and data management system in a graphical environment, using descriptive menus and simple dialog boxes to do most of the work for you. Most tasks can be accomplished simply by pointing and clicking the mouse.

In addition to the menu-driven dialog box interface for statistical analysis, SPSS for Windows provides:

- **Data Editor.** A versatile spreadsheet-like system for defining, entering, editing, and displaying data.

- **Chart Editor.** A highly visual, object-oriented facility for manipulating and customizing the many charts and graphs produced by SPSS.

- **High-resolution graphics.** High-resolution, full-color pie charts, bar charts, histograms, scatterplots, 3-D graphics, and more are now included as a standard feature in the SPSS Base system.

Getting Started

The SPSS program group, created when you install SPSS, is shown in Figure 1.1.

Figure 1.1 SPSS program group

To start an SPSS session:

1 Double-click the mouse on the SPSS icon, or select the SPSS icon and press ⏎Enter.

② The first time you start a session after installing SPSS, the Startup Preferences dialog box opens. Click on OK to accept the default settings. (See Chapter 36 for information on startup preferences.)

This opens the SPSS application window, an output window, and the Data Editor window, as shown in Figure 1.2.

Figure 1.2   SPSS application, output, and Data Editor windows

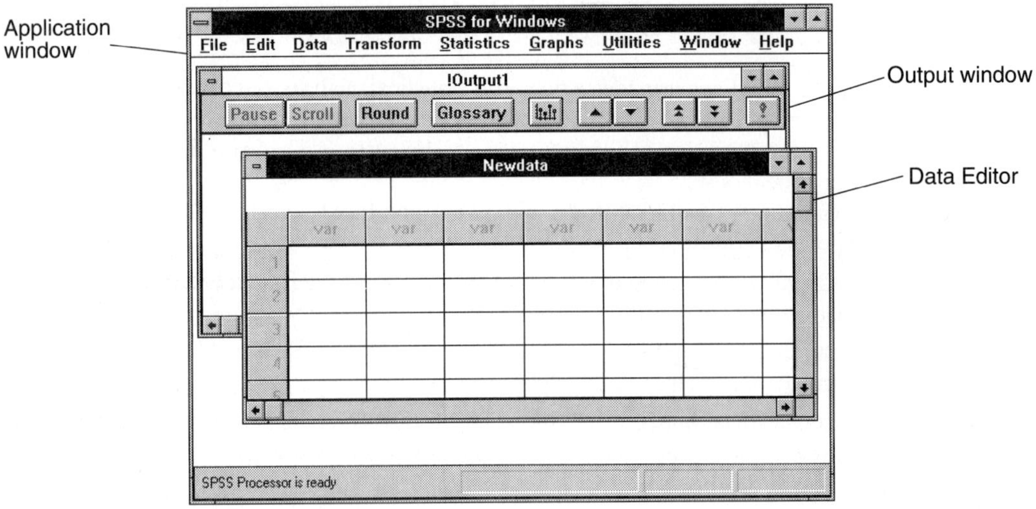

You can also begin a session with a specific SPSS file by double-clicking the icon for that file in a program group or the File Manager:

Data files. Any file with an extension of *.sav* is assumed to be a data file in SPSS format (see Chapter 2). The contents of the data file are displayed in the Data Editor window.

Chart files. Any file with an extension of *.cht* is assumed to be a bar chart, pie chart, histogram, scatterplot, or other chart created with SPSS. The chart is displayed in a chart window.

Text files. Any file with an extension of *.sps* is assumed to be a syntax file and is displayed in a syntax window. Any file with an extension of *.lst* is assumed to be an output file and is displayed in an output window.

If SPSS is not running when you select a file from a program group or from the File Manager, SPSS automatically starts and opens the file in the appropriate window. If SPSS is already running, it opens a new window containing the selected file. For data files, the selected file replaces the working data file in the Data Editor window.

SPSS Windows

There are six types of windows in SPSS:

SPSS application window. This window contains the menu bar, which you use to open files, choose statistical procedures, and select the other features of the system.

Output window. As you make selections from the menus and dialog boxes, various system information and the text-based results of your work—such as descriptive statistics, crosstabulations, or correlation matrices—appear in an output window. You can edit this output and save it in files for later use. An output window opens automatically when you start a new SPSS session. You can also open additional output windows.

Data Editor window. This window displays the contents of the data file. You can create new data files or modify existing ones with the Data Editor. The Data Editor window opens automatically when you start an SPSS session.

Chart Carousel window. All of the charts and graphs produced in your SPSS session are accessed through the Chart Carousel, which opens automatically the first time you generate a chart during the session. If you produce multiple charts, you can view them in the Chart Carousel before modifying, saving, or discarding them.

Chart window. You can modify and save high-resolution charts and plots in chart windows. You can change the colors, select different type fonts or sizes, switch the horizontal and vertical axes, rotate 3-D scatterplots, and even change the chart type.

Syntax window. You can paste your dialog box choices into a syntax window, where your selections appear in the form of command syntax. You can then edit the command syntax to utilize special features of SPSS not available through dialog boxes. You can save these commands in a file for use in subsequent SPSS sessions. You can open multiple syntax windows.

Designated versus Active Window

If you have more than one open output window, the text-based results of your work are routed to the **designated** output window. If you have more than one open syntax window, command syntax is pasted into the designated syntax window. The designated windows are indicated by an exclamation point (!) before the word Syntax or Output on the title bar. You can change the designated windows at any time (see "Icon Bars" on p. 5).

The designated window should not be confused with the **active** window, which is the currently selected window. If you have overlapping windows, the active window appears in the foreground. If you open a new syntax or output window, that window automatically becomes the active window, but it does not become the designated window until you instruct SPSS to make it the designated window.

Main Menu

SPSS for Windows is **menu driven**. Most of the features are accessed by making selections from the menus. The main menu bar contains nine menus:

File. Use the File menu to create a new SPSS file, open an existing file, or read in spreadsheet or database files created by other software programs.

Edit. Use the Edit menu to modify or copy text from the output or syntax windows.

Data. Use the Data menu to make global changes to SPSS data files, such as merging files, transposing variables and cases, or creating subsets of cases for analysis. These changes are only temporary and do not affect the permanent file unless you explicitly save the file with the changes.

Transform. Use the Transform menu to make changes to selected variables in the data file and to compute new variables based on the values of existing ones. These changes do not affect the permanent file unless you explicitly save the changes.

Statistics. Use the Statistics menu to select the various statistical procedures you want to use, such as crosstabulation, analysis of variance, correlation, and linear regression.

Graphs. Use the Graphs menu to create bar charts, pie charts, histograms, scatterplots, and other full-color, high-resolution graphs. Some statistical procedures also generate graphs. All graphs can be customized with the Chart Editor.

Utilities. Use the Utilities menu to change fonts, access the dynamic data exchange, display information on the contents of SPSS data files, or open an index of SPSS commands.

Window. Use the Window menu to arrange, select, and control the attributes of the various SPSS windows.

Help. This opens a standard Microsoft Help window containing information on how to use the many features of SPSS. Context-sensitive help is also available through the dialog boxes.

Chart Menus

The Chart Carousel and chart windows provide different sets of menus for reviewing and editing charts. These menus replace the main menu bar if the Chart Carousel or chart window is the active window. For more information on these menus, see Chapter 32.

Icon Bars

At the top of the output, syntax, and chart windows, there is an **icon bar** that provides quick, easy access to the special features of these windows. See Chapter 4 for information about the output and syntax window icon bars. See Chapter 32 for more information about the chart window icon bar.

Status Bar

At the bottom of the SPSS application window, there is a status bar that indicates the current status of the SPSS processor. If the processor is running a command, it displays the command name and a case counter indicating the current case number being processed. When you first begin an SPSS session, the status bar displays the message Starting SPSS Processor. When SPSS is ready, the message changes to SPSS Processor is ready. The status bar also provides the following information:

- **Command status.** For each procedure or command you run, a case counter indicates the number of cases processed so far. For statistical procedures that require iterative processing, the number of iterations is displayed.

- **Filter status.** If you have selected a random sample or a subset of cases for analysis, the message Filter on indicates that some type of case filtering is currently in effect and not all cases in the data file are included in the analysis.

- **Weight status.** The message Weight on indicates that a weight variable is being used to weight cases for analysis.

- **Split File status.** The message Split File on indicates that the data file has been split into separate groups for analysis, based on the values of one or more grouping variables.

Statistical Analysis with the Dialog Box Interface

There are three basic steps in performing statistical analysis with SPSS for Windows:

- Choose a data file. This can be a file you create with the Data Editor, a previously defined SPSS data file, a spreadsheet file, a database file, or a text file.

- Choose a statistical procedure from the menus.

- Choose the variables to include in the analysis and any additional parameters from the dialog boxes.

Choosing a Data File

To select a data file for analysis:

① Click on File on the main menu bar.

② Click on Open on the File menu.

③ Click on Data... on the Open submenu. This opens the Open Data File dialog box, as shown in Figure 1.3.

Figure 1.3   Open Data File dialog box

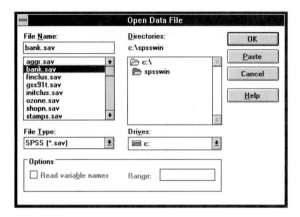

By default, SPSS looks for any files in the current directory with an extension of *.sav*. This is the default extension for SPSS data files. The various types of data files that you can open in SPSS are discussed in Chapter 2.

For now, we're going to use an SPSS data file. Although your file list may be different from the one shown in Figure 1.3, it should include an SPSS data file called *bank.-sav*. To open this data file:

④ Click on the file *bank.sav* on the list or type the filename in the File Name text box.

⑤ Click on OK or press ⏎Enter.

The contents of the data file are displayed in the Data Editor window, as shown in Figure 1.4

Figure 1.4   Data file displayed in Data Editor

	id	salbeg	sex	time	age	salnow	edlevel	work	jobcat
1	628	8400	0	81	28.50	16080	16	.25	4
2	630	24000	0	73	40.33	41400	16	12.50	5
3	632	10200	0	83	31.08	21960	15	4.08	5
4	633	8700	0	93	31.17	19200	16	1.83	4
5	635	17400	0	83	41.92	28350	19	13.00	5
6	637	12996	0	80	29.50	27250	18	2.42	4

c:\spsswin\bank.sav — 1:id — 628

Choosing a Statistical Procedure

The Statistics menu, shown in Figure 1.5, contains a list of general statistical categories. Each of these is followed by an arrow (▶), which indicates that there is another menu level. The individual statistical procedures are listed at this submenu level.

For example, to produce frequency tables:

1 Click on Statistics on the main menu bar.

2 Click on Summarize ▶ on the Statistics menu.

3 Click on Frequencies... on the Summarize submenu.

Figure 1.5   Statistics menu and Summarize submenu

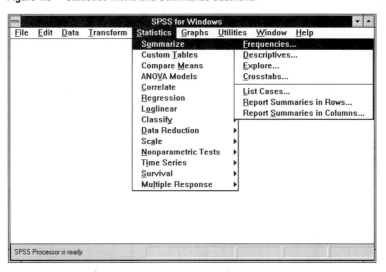

Throughout the rest of this book, we'll use the following shorthand method to indicate menu selections:

Statistics
  Summarize ▶
    Frequencies...

Main Dialog Box

When you choose a statistical procedure from the menus, a dialog box appears on the screen. Figure 1.6 shows the Frequencies dialog box.

Figure 1.6   Frequencies main dialog box

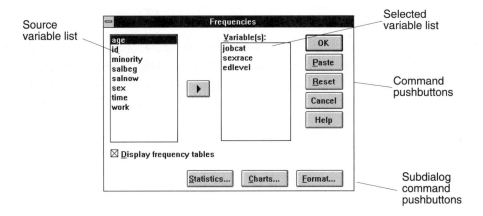

The main dialog box for each statistical procedure has three basic components:

Source variable list. A list of variables in the data file.

Selected variable list(s). One or more lists indicating the variables you have chosen for the analysis, such as dependent and independent variable lists. This is sometimes referred to as the target variable list.

Command pushbuttons. Action buttons that tell SPSS to do something, such as run the procedure, get help, or go to a subdialog box for additional specifications.

Source Variable List

The source variable list contains any variables in the data file that can be used by that procedure. There are three basic types of variables:

- **Numeric variables.** This includes any variables that use a numeric coding scheme, even if the underlying "real" values are not numeric. Date and time format variables are also considered numeric because they are stored internally as a number of seconds.
- **Short string variables.** Alphanumeric string values up to eight characters long. These are identified with a "less than" symbol (<).
- **Long string variables.** Alphanumeric string values more than eight characters long. These are identified with a "greater than" symbol (>).

Command Pushbuttons

There is a column of pushbuttons on the right side of the dialog box (see Figure 1.6). These are often referred to as **command** or **action pushbuttons** because they tell the system to do something immediately, such as run a procedure or get help. There are five standard command pushbuttons in the main dialog box:

OK. Runs the procedure. After you select your variables and choose any additional specifications, click on OK to run the procedure. This also closes the dialog box.

Paste. Generates command syntax from the dialog box selections and pastes the syntax into a syntax window. You can then customize the commands with additional SPSS features not available from dialog boxes.

Reset. Deselects any variables in the selected variable list(s) and resets all specifications in the dialog box and any subdialog boxes to the default state.

Cancel. Cancels any changes in the dialog box settings since the last time it was opened and closes the dialog box. Within an SPSS session, dialog box settings are persistent. A dialog box retains your last set of specifications until you override them. (See "Persistence of Settings" on p. 15.)

Help. Context-sensitive help. This takes you to a standard Microsoft Help window that contains information about the current dialog box.

Selecting Variables

To select a single variable, you simply highlight it on the source variable list and click on the ▶ button next to the selected variable list box. If there is only one selected variable list (as in the Frequencies dialog box), you can double-click individual variables to move them from the source list to the selected list.

You can also select multiple variables:

- To highlight multiple variables that are grouped together on the variable list, as shown in Figure 1.7, use the click-and-drag technique. Alternatively, you can click on the first one and then shift-click on the last one in the group.
- To highlight multiple variables that are not grouped together on the variable list, as shown in Figure 1.8, use the ctrl-click method. Click on the first variable, then ctrl-click on the next variable, and so on.

For example:

1. Click on the variable *jobcat* on the source variable list. It is now highlighted.

2. Click on the ▶ pushbutton. The variable *jobcat* moves from the source variable list to the selected variable list labeled Variable(s).

3. Click on the variable *salbeg* on the source variable list, hold down the mouse button, and drag the pointer down to *time*. Alternatively, click on *salbeg* and then shift-click on *time*. All the variables from *salbeg* to *time* are highlighted, as shown in Figure 1.7.

4. Click on the ▶ pushbutton. All the highlighted variables move to the Variable(s) list.

5. Click on *edlevel* on the source variable list. Then ctrl-click on *work*. The two variables are highlighted without affecting the variables between them, as shown in Figure 1.8.

6. Click on the ▶ pushbutton. The two variables move to the Variable(s) list.

Figure 1.7   Selecting a group of variables with shift-click or the click-and-drag technique

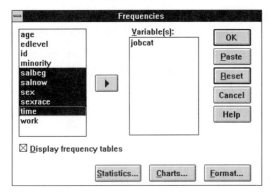

Figure 1.8   Selecting noncontiguous multiple variables with ctrl-click

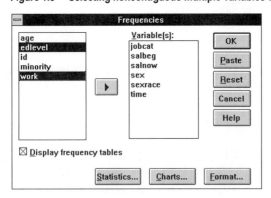

Deselecting Variables

You can also deselect variables, removing them from the selected list and putting them back onto the source list. Deselecting variables works just like selecting them. When you highlight variables on the selected variable list, the ▶ pushbutton changes direction, pointing back to the source variable list.

Running a Procedure

In many instances, all you need to do to run a statistical procedure is select your variables and click on OK. The results then appear in the output window. For example:

1 Click on Reset in the Frequencies dialog box to clear anything you have entered.

2 Click on the variable *jobcat* on the source variable list. The variable is now highlighted.

3 Click on the ▶ pushbutton. The variable moves to the Variable(s) list.

4 Click on OK. This runs the procedure and closes the dialog box. The results are displayed in the output window, as shown in Figure 1.9.

Figure 1.9   Results displayed in the output window

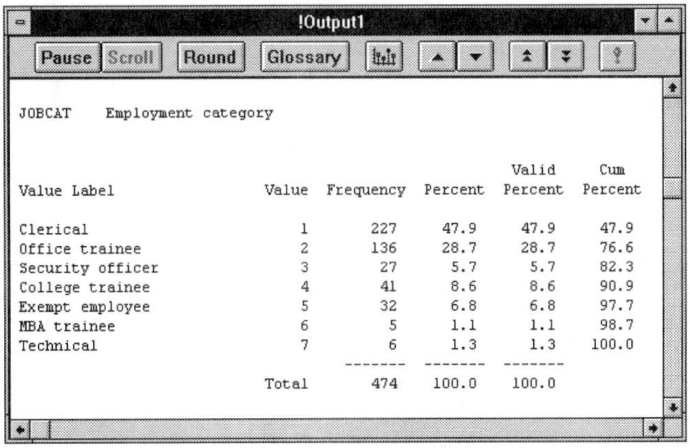

```
                                    !Output1

  Pause  Scroll   Round   Glossary


 JOBCAT    Employment category


                                         Valid    Cum
 Value Label          Value  Frequency  Percent  Percent  Percent

 Clerical                1       227     47.9     47.9     47.9
 Office trainee          2       136     28.7     28.7     76.6
 Security officer        3        27      5.7      5.7     82.3
 College trainee         4        41      8.6      8.6     90.9
 Exempt employee         5        32      6.8      6.8     97.7
 MBA trainee             6         5      1.1      1.1     98.7
 Technical               7         6      1.3      1.3    100.0
                               -------  -------  -------
                     Total       474    100.0    100.0
```

You can use the scroll bars to view portions of the output not visible in the window, or you can resize the window to show more of the output.

Subdialog Boxes

Since most SPSS procedures provide a great deal of flexibility, not all of the possible choices can be contained in a single dialog box. The main dialog box usually contains the minimum information required to run a procedure. Additional specifications are made in subdialog boxes.

In the main dialog box, pushbuttons with an ellipsis after the name indicate a subdialog box. For example, the Frequencies main dialog box has three associated subdialog boxes: Statistics, Charts, and Format.

❶ Open the Frequencies dialog box again.

❷ Click on Statistics... in the Frequencies dialog box. This opens the Frequencies Statistics subdialog box, as shown in Figure 1.10.

Figure 1.10   Subdialog box with check boxes

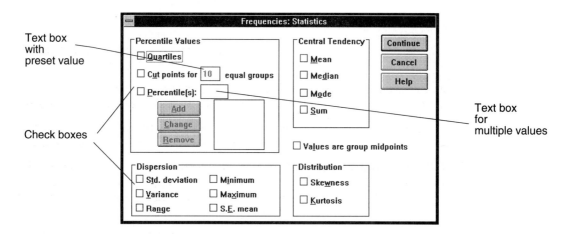

Subdialog Box Command Pushbuttons

The subdialog box contains three command pushbuttons:

Continue. Saves any changes to the settings and returns to the main dialog box.

Cancel. Ignores any changes, restores the previous settings, and returns to the main dialog box.

Help. Context-sensitive help for the dialog box.

Multiple Selections with Check Boxes

In the Frequencies Statistics subdialog box, there is a variety of summary statistics available. The **check box** next to each one indicates that you can choose one or more of these statistics in any combination. For convenience, they are grouped by type of summary measure (central tendency, dispersion), but there is no restriction on how many you can choose from each group.

To select an item, simply click on the check box next to it. An × is displayed in the check box, indicating that the item is selected. You deselect items the same way. When you click on a selected item, the × disappears, indicating that the item is no longer selected. For example:

1. Click on Mean, Median, and Mode in the Central Tendency group. An × is displayed in each check box, indicating that the item is selected.

2. Click on Mode again to deselect it. The check box is now empty again, indicating that the item is not selected.

User-defined Specifications with Text Boxes

Sometimes there are **text boxes** associated with selections that provide additional control over the specifications. There are three basic types of text boxes:

Preset text boxes. Some text boxes have a preset default value already entered. If you choose the item without entering a new value in the text box, the default value is used.

Blank text boxes. There is no default setting. If you choose an item with an associated blank text box, you must enter a value (or deselect the item) before you can continue.

Multiple-entry text boxes. If an item can have multiple values (such as percentile specifications), the text box is accompanied by a list box and a group of pushbuttons. Enter each value in the text box, click on Add, and it appears in the list box. You can also change and delete values. For example:

1. Click on Percentile(s) in the Frequencies Statistics subdialog box. An × appears in the check box and a flashing cursor appears in the text box.

2. Type in the value 25 and click on Add. The value appears in the list box.

3. Type the value 40 in the text box and click on Add. The value is added to the list.

4. Type the value 75 in the text box and click on Add. The value is added to the list.

5. Click on the value 40 on the list. The value is highlighted on the list, and it also appears in the Percentiles text box.

6. Highlight the entire value in the text box, type in the value 50, and click on Change. The new value replaces the old one on the list.

7. Click on the value 75 on the list. The value is highlighted on the list.

8. Click on Remove. The value is deleted from the list.

9. Click on Continue to save the new settings and return to the main dialog box.

Single Selections with Radio Buttons

Some selections are mutually exclusive and you can choose only one from a list of alternatives. **Radio buttons** next to each choice in a group, as shown in Figure 1.11, indicate that you can choose only one item in the group. (Radio buttons are round, while check boxes are square.)

Figure 1.11   Subdialog box with radio buttons

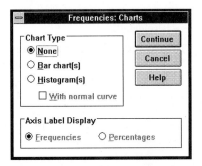

In a radio button group, there is always a default selection. To change the selected alternative, you simply click on a different radio button in the group. For example:

❶ Click on Charts... in the Frequencies dialog box. This opens the Frequencies Charts subdialog box, as shown in Figure 1.11.

❷ Click on the Bar chart(s) radio button in the Chart Type group. This selection replaces the default selection of None.

❸ Click on Continue to save the new setting and return to the Frequencies dialog box.

❹ Click on Cancel to close the Frequencies dialog box without running the procedure.

Single Selection with Drop-down Lists

In some dialog boxes, **drop-down lists** are used instead of radio buttons for single selections from a list of alternatives. The current selection appears in a box with a down arrow icon pushbutton next to it, as shown in Figure 1.12. Click on the arrow to open the drop-down list and change the selection.

Figure 1.12   Single selection from a drop-down list (Linear Regression dialog box)

Persistence of Settings

You may have noticed that the variable *jobcat* was still selected when you reopened the dialog box after running the procedure. That's because dialog box settings are **persistent** within an SPSS session. Once you click on OK or Paste, the current dialog and subdialog selections are saved. The next time you open that dialog box, those are the settings in effect.

At the subdialog box level, any changes you make are temporarily saved when you click on Continue. If, however, you then click on Cancel in the main dialog box, the subdialog selections revert to their former settings. As with the main dialog box, the subdialog box selections are persistent only after you click on OK or Paste.

The Reset button always returns all dialog and subdialog settings to the default state. You cannot undo this action. (The Cancel button has no effect on Reset.)

Dialog box settings are not persistent for different data files in the same SPSS session. If you make dialog box selections using one data file and then open a different data file, all dialog boxes are reset to the default state with no selected variables.

Order of Operations

For most procedures, you can make your dialog box selections in virtually any order. You can change the selected variable list (or any other setting) in the main dialog box after you make selections in the subdialog boxes, and you can go to subdialog boxes in any sequence. You can even make subdialog box selections before you choose any variables for analysis.

Data Editor

The Data Editor provides a convenient spreadsheet-like facility for entering, editing, and displaying the contents of your data file.

The Data Editor opens automatically when you start an SPSS session. If there isn't an open data file, you can use the Data Editor to create one. If there is an open data file, you can use the Data Editor to change data values and add or delete cases and variables.

The Data Editor has many similarities to a spreadsheet program, but there are several important distinctions:

- Cases are represented in rows.
- Variables are represented in columns.
- There are no "empty" cells within the boundaries of the data file. For numeric variables, blank cells are converted to the system-missing value (represented by a period). For string variables, a blank is considered a valid value.

Entering Data

Basic data entry in the Data Editor is simple:

① Click on the Data Editor title bar to make it the active window. (You may have to move the output window first.) The contents of the data file (*bank.sav*) are displayed. A heavy border appears around the currently selected cell (this should be the first cell in the Data Editor—row 1, column 1).

② Use the ⬅ key to move the cursor to the first empty column (the column to the right of the variable *sexrace*). Empty columns with the dimmed title *var* indicate **potential variables**.

③ Beginning with the first data cell (below the variable name) in the column, type the following:

123.4 ⏎Enter

123.45 ⏎Enter

123.456 ⏎Enter

123 ⏎Enter

As you type, the value appears in the cell editor at the top of the Data Editor window. Each time you press ⏎Enter, the value is entered in the cell and you move down to the next row. The values appear in the default numeric format, with two decimal places. Thus, 123.456 is displayed as 123.46, but the complete value is stored internally and used in any calculations.

By entering data in the column, you automatically create a variable, and SPSS gives it the default variable name *var00001*. The variable name at the top of the column is no longer dimmed, indicating that it is now a real variable rather than a potential one. Since there are no "empty" cells within the boundaries of the data file, SPSS supplies the system-missing value (represented by a period) for the new variable for all the remaining cases in the data file.

④ Select the first cell in the next column (the next potential variable). You can use the mouse to click on the cell or use the arrow keys on the keyboard to move to the cell. (Make sure the selected cell is in row 1.)

⑤ Type

223.4 ⏎Enter

By entering a value in the column, you automatically create a new variable with the default name *var00002*. Once again, SPSS supplies the system-missing value to all the remaining cases.

⑥ Select the first cell in the next column (the next potential variable). You can use the mouse to click on the cell or use the arrow keys on the keyboard to move to the cell.

⑦ Type

323.4 ⏎Enter

SPSS automatically creates another new variable, *var00003*, and assigns the system-missing value to the remaining cases. At this point, the Data Editor window should look like Figure 1.13.

Figure 1.13   Data Editor window with missing data

	work	jobcat	minority	sexrace	var00001	var00002	var00003
1	.25	4	0	1.00	123.40	223.40	323.40
2	12.50	5	0	1.00	123.45	.	
3	4.08	5	0	1.00	123.46	.	.
4	1.83	4	0	1.00	123.00	.	.
5	13.00	5	0	1.00		.	.
6	2.42	4	0	1.00		.	.
7	3.17	1	0	1.00	.	.	.

c:\spsswin\bank.sav
2:var00003

Editing Data

You can change, delete, copy, and move data values in the Data Editor.

① In the column for the new variable *var00001*, click on the second cell (row 2) or use the arrow keys to move to the cell. The highlighted value appears in the cell editor at the top of the Data Editor.

② Type

234.56 ⏎Enter

The new value of 234.56 replaces the old value of 123.45.

③ Select the first cell (row 1) for the variable *var00001* again. If you use the mouse, click on the cell. If you use the keyboard, use the arrow keys to move to the cell.

④ Select the first four values for the variable. If you use the mouse, click and drag to case 4 (row 4) in the same column. If you use the keyboard, press and hold the ⇧Shift key and use the ⬇ key to move down to the fourth row. The first four values in the column are highlighted, indicating that they are selected.

⑤ From the menus choose:

Edit
  Copy

⑥ Select the first cell for variable *var00002*.

⑦ From the menus choose:

Edit
  Paste

The four values for variable *var00001* are duplicated in the column for *var00002*.

⑧ Select the fourth cell in the column for *var00002* (row 4). This cell should contain the value 123.00.

⑨ From the menus choose:

Edit
  Copy

⑩ Select the first four cells for *var00003*.

⑪ From the menus choose:

Edit
  Paste

The value 123.00 is duplicated in all four cells for variable *var00003*, and the Data Editor window should look like Figure 1.14.

Figure 1.14   Data Editor window with copied data

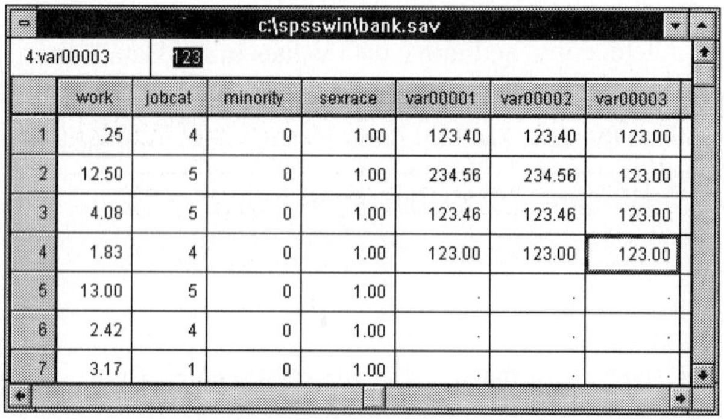

	work	jobcat	minority	sexrace	var00001	var00002	var00003
1	.25	4	0	1.00	123.40	123.40	123.00
2	12.50	5	0	1.00	234.56	234.56	123.00
3	4.08	5	0	1.00	123.46	123.46	123.00
4	1.83	4	0	1.00	123.00	123.00	123.00
5	13.00	5	0	1.00	.	.	.
6	2.42	4	0	1.00	.	.	.
7	3.17	1	0	1.00	.	.	.

c:\spsswin\bank.sav

4:var00003   123

For a complete discussion of the Data Editor, see Chapter 3.

Creating and Editing Charts

If you run a procedure that produces charts or graphs, SPSS displays the results in the Chart Carousel. You can then select the chart and edit it in a chart window.

1. Open the Frequencies dialog box again.

2. Click on Reset to clear any previous settings.

3. Click on the variable *jobcat* on the source variable list and click on the ▶ pushbutton to move it to the Variable(s) list.

4. Click on Charts... to open the Frequency Charts subdialog box.

5. Click on Bar Chart(s).

6. Click on Continue or press ⏎Enter to save the new setting and return to the Frequencies dialog box.

7. Click on the Display frequency tables check box in the Frequencies dialog box to deselect this default setting and suppress the display of frequency tables.

8. Click on OK or press ⏎Enter to run the Frequencies procedure.

9. Click on ⫼ in the output window icon bar or double-click on the Chart Carousel icon, as shown in Figure 1.15.

Figure 1.15 Opening the Chart Carousel

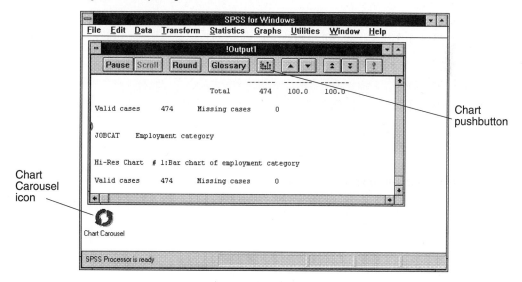

The bar chart is displayed in the Chart Carousel, as shown in Figure 1.16, which opens automatically.

Figure 1.16   Chart Carousel

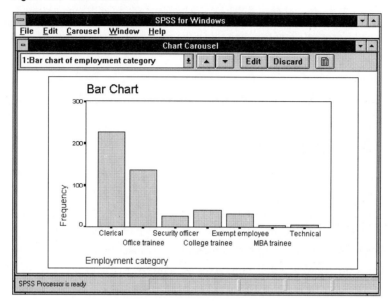

⑩ Click on Edit on the Chart Carousel icon bar or press Ctrl-E. The chart is displayed in a chart window, as shown in Figure 1.17.

Figure 1.17   Chart window

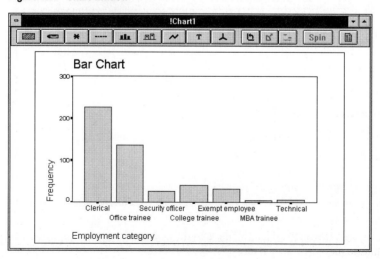

The SPSS menu bar changes when a chart window is active, providing a set of menus for editing charts. Most of the chart window menu choices can also be accessed through the icon bar on the chart window.

⑪ From the menus choose:

Attributes
  Bar Style...

This opens the Bar Styles dialog box, as shown in Figure 1.18.

Figure 1.18   Bar Styles dialog box

⑫ Click on 3-D effect in the Bar Styles dialog box.

⑬ Type 40 in the Depth text box.

⑭ Click on Apply All or press ⏎Enter and then click on Close in the Bar Styles dialog box. The chart now looks like Figure 1.19.

Figure 1.19   Bar chart with 3-D effects

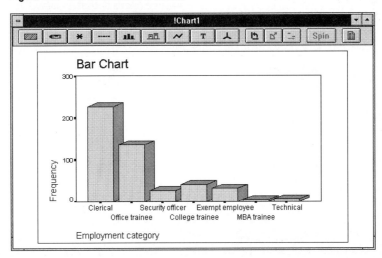

For more information on creating and editing charts and plots, see Chapter 23 through Chapter 32.

Pasting and Editing Command Syntax

The dialog box interface is designed to handle most of the capabilities of SPSS. Beneath the dialog boxes, there is a command language that you can use to access additional features and customize your analysis.

The SPSS command language consists of descriptive and usually self-explanatory commands. For example, the command to obtain frequency tables is FREQUENCIES.

After you make your dialog box selections, you can paste the underlying command syntax into a syntax window. You can then edit the resulting text like any text file and run the modified commands.

- Use the Paste pushbutton in the main dialog box to paste the command syntax into a syntax window.

- Use the Run pushbutton on the icon bar at the top of the syntax window to run the modified commands.

For example:

1. Open the Frequencies dialog box again. (If the chart window or the Chart Carousel is the active window, make the output window or the Data Editor the active window to change the menu bar.)

2. Click on Reset to clear any previous settings.

3. Click on the variable *jobcat* on the source variable list and click on the ▶ pushbutton to move it to the Variable(s) list.

4. Click on Paste.

If you don't have an open syntax window, one opens automatically. The FREQUENCIES command syntax appears in the syntax window, as shown in Figure 1.20.

Figure 1.20   Command syntax pasted to a syntax window

⑤ Using the mouse or the arrow keys, position the blinking cursor between the word *jobcat* and the period at the end of the second line.

⑥ Type in

```
(5, 7)
```

This indicates a value range for the frequency table, a specification not available in the dialog boxes. The entire command should now look like this:

```
FREQUENCIES
 VARIABLES = jobcat (5, 7).
```

⑦ Click on the Run pushbutton on the icon bar at the top of the syntax window or press Ctrl-A. This runs the command, and the frequency table for the modified command appears in the output window. The results are shown in Figure 1.21.

Figure 1.21   Results from modified command syntax

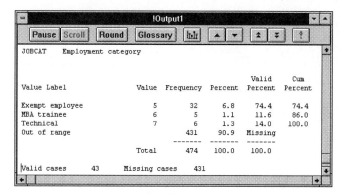

For a complete discussion on editing text files with SPSS and running commands from a syntax window, see Chapter 4.

Saving Results

Data files. You can save data files in SPSS, spreadsheet, database, or text format (see Chapter 2).

Output window results. The output window contains the text-based results of your SPSS session. You can edit this output and save it in text files for later use (see Chapter 4). Since the results are saved as text, you can easily cut and paste portions of the output to other applications, such as a word processing program.

Syntax window commands. You can edit and save the command syntax that you paste into a syntax window. You can then recall and rerun these commands in other SPSS sessions or process the commands in production mode (see Appendix C).

Charts and plots. You can save charts and plots from the Chart Carousel or from chart windows and then recall and edit them in other sessions (see Chapter 23).

Ending an SPSS Session

To end an SPSS session:

1. From the menus choose:

   File
      Exit

2. For each open window, SPSS asks if you want to save the contents before it ends the session. To end the session without saving any changes, click on No for each window. If you click on Yes or press ⏎Enter, SPSS opens the appropriate dialog box for saving each type of file (data, output, syntax, chart).

Working with Large Data Files

There is no defined limit to the number of variables that can be contained in an SPSS data file. Using command syntax, the system has been tested with up to 32,000 variables in a data file. However, there is a Windows limitation that effectively restricts the number of variables that can be accessed from dialog boxes to approximately 4500 (depending on the length of variable names). If your file contains a larger number of variables, only the first 4500 will appear on dialog box source lists. Appendix D provides a few tips on how to work with large data files.

Decimal Indicator and Windows International Settings

The decimal indicator used in the Data Editor and in results displayed in output windows is determined by the International settings in the Windows Control Panel. If you specify anything other than a period as the decimal indicator in the International settings, SPSS uses a comma as the decimal indicator.

The decimal indicator in the Windows International settings also affects the display of the system-missing value in the Data Editor and in output windows. If a period is the decimal indicator, a period is also used to represent the system-missing value. If anything other than a period is the decimal indicator, a comma is used to represent the system-missing value.

Regardless of the Windows International settings, a period must be used as the decimal indicator in command syntax and in transformation expressions.

Keyboard Movement

If you don't have a mouse, you can use the keyboard to navigate the menus and dialog boxes. The following general rules apply:

Menus

For selecting items from menus:

- [Alt] used with the underlined letter in a menu name opens that menu. For example, [Alt]-[S] opens the Statistics menu.
- [↑] and [↓] move up and down an open menu.
- [←] and [→] move between menus and submenus.
- [←Enter] selects the highlighted menu item and takes you to the corresponding submenu or dialog box.
- [Esc] cancels the selection and takes you back up one level, closing the open menu or submenu.

Dialog Boxes

For selecting items from dialog boxes:

- [Alt] used with the underlined letter in a dialog box selection makes that selection. For example, in the Frequencies dialog box, [Alt]-[C] is equivalent to clicking on the Charts... pushbutton.
- [↑] and [↓] move up and down variable lists and between group items (for example, a group of radio button alternatives).
- [Tab→] and [⇧Shift]-[Tab→] move between selections.
- [Space] selects the highlighted item.
- [←Enter] is equivalent to OK or Continue.
- [Esc] is equivalent to Cancel.

For a complete guide to navigating the system with the keyboard, see Appendix G.

2 Data Files

Data files come in a wide variety of formats, and SPSS is designed to handle many of them, including:

- Spreadsheet files created with Lotus 1-2-3, Excel, and Multiplan.
- Database files created with dBASE and various SQL formats.
- Tab-delimited and other types of ASCII text files.
- SPSS data files created on other operating systems.

Creating a New Data File

If your data are not already in computer files, you can use the Data Editor to enter the data and create an SPSS data file. The Data Editor is a simple, efficient spreadsheet-like facility that opens automatically when you start an SPSS session. For information on the Data Editor, see Chapter 3.

Opening a Data File

To open an SPSS, spreadsheet, dBASE, or tab-delimited data file, from the menus choose:

File
  Open ▶
    Data...

This opens the Open Data File dialog box, as shown in Figure 2.1.

Figure 2.1   Open Data File dialog box

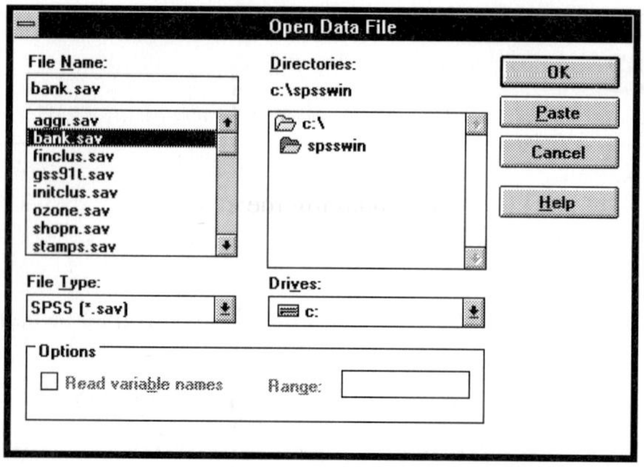

File Name. You can select a file from the list, or you can type in a filename, a directory path and filename, or a wildcard search. By default, SPSS looks for all files in the current directory with the extension *.sav* and displays them on the list.

Directories. To change the directory location, select the name of the directory on the Directories list. Directories below the current directory are denoted by closed file folder icons. Directories above the current directory are denoted by open file folder icons. The current directory is displayed above the list of directories and is also denoted by the last (lowest) open file folder icon.

Drives. To change the drive location, select a drive from the drop-down list of available drives.

Specifying File Type

Before you can open a data file, you need to tell SPSS what type of file it is.

File Type. Select one of the following alternatives from the drop-down list:

SPSS (*.sav). Data files created and/or saved in SPSS for Windows or SPSS for UNIX.

SPSS/PC+ (*.sys). Data files created and/or saved in SPSS/PC+.

SPSS portable (*.por). Portable SPSS files created on other operating systems (for example, Macintosh, OS/2).

Excel (*.xls). Microsoft Excel spreadsheet files.

Lotus (*.w*). Lotus 1-2-3 spreadsheet files, releases 1A, 2.0, and 3.0.

SYLK (*.slk). Microsoft Excel and Multiplan spreadsheet files saved in SYLK (symbolic link) format.

dBASE (*.dbf). dBASE II, III, and IV database files.

Tab-delimited (*.dat). ASCII text files with values separated by tabs.

Note: SPSS needs to know the file type, regardless of the file extension. You cannot specify a different file type simply by changing the extension of the wildcard search in the File Name text box. To change the file type, you must change the selection on the drop-down list.

Options

For Lotus, Excel, SYLK, and tab-delimited files, the following option is available:

❑ **Read variable names.** The values in the first row of the file (or cell range) are used as variable names. If variable names exceed eight characters, they are truncated. If they are not unique, SPSS modifies them. (See "Define Fixed Variables" on p. 42 for rules regarding variable names.)

For Lotus, Excel, and SYLK files, the following option is also available:

Range. User-specified range of cells to read.

- For Lotus files, specify the beginning column letter and row number, two periods, and the ending column letter and row number (for example, A1..K14).
- For Excel files, specify the beginning column letter and row number, a colon, and the ending column letter and row number (for example, A1:K14).
- For SYLK files and Excel files saved in R1C1 display format, specify the beginning and ending cells of the range separated by a colon (for example, R1C1:R14C11).

If you have defined a name for a range of cells in the spreadsheet file, you can enter the name in the Range text box.

How SPSS Reads Spreadsheet Data

An SPSS data file is rectangular. The boundaries (or dimensions) of the data file are determined by the number of cases (rows) and variables (columns). There are no "empty" cells within the boundaries of the data file. All cells have a value, even if that value is "blank." The following general rules apply to reading spreadsheet data:

- Rows are considered cases, and columns are considered variables.
- The number of variables is determined by the last column with any nonblank cells or the total number of nonblank cells in the row containing variable names. If you read variable names, any columns with a blank cell for the variable name are not included in the data file.

- The number of cases is determined by the last row with any nonblank cells within the column boundaries defined by the number of variables.

- The data type and width for each variable are determined by the column width and data type of the first data cell in the column. Values of other types are converted to the system-missing value. If the first data cell in the column is blank, the global default data type for the spreadsheet (usually numeric) is used.

- For numeric variables, blank cells are converted to the system-missing value, indicated by a period.

- For string variables, a blank is a valid string value, and blank cells are treated as valid string values.

- If you don't read variable names from the spreadsheet, SPSS uses the column letters (A, B, C,...) for variable names for Excel and Lotus files. For SYLK files and Excel files saved in R1C1 display format, SPSS uses the column number preceded by the letter C for variable names (*C1*, *C2*, *C3*,...).

Figure 2.2   Reading spreadsheet data with variable names

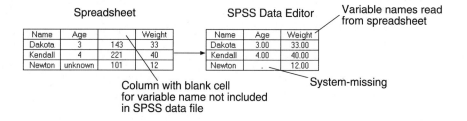

Figure 2.3   Reading Excel spreadsheet file without variable names

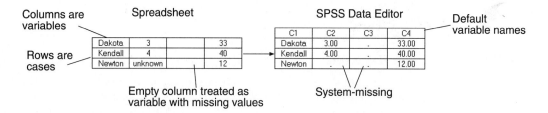

How SPSS Reads dBASE Files

Database files are logically very similar to SPSS data files. The following general rules apply to dBASE files:

- Field names are automatically translated to SPSS variable names.

- Field names should comply with SPSS variable-naming conventions (see "Define Fixed Variables" on p. 42). Field names longer than eight characters are truncated. If the first eight characters of the field name don't produce a unique name, the field is dropped.

- Colons used in dBASE field names are translated to underscores.

- Records marked for deletion but not actually purged are included. SPSS creates a new string variable, *D_R*, which contains an asterisk for cases marked for deletion.

How SPSS Reads Tab-delimited Files

The following general rules apply to reading tab-delimited files:

- Values can be either numeric or string. Any value that contains non-numeric characters is considered a string value. (Formats such as Dollar and Date are not recognized and are read as string values.)

- The data type and width for each variable are determined by the type and width of the first data value in the column. Values of other types are converted to the system-missing value.

- For numeric variables, the assigned width is eight digits or the number of digits in the first data value, whichever is greater. Values that exceed the defined width are rounded for display. The entire value is stored internally.

- For string variables, values that exceed the defined width are truncated.

- If you don't read variable names from the file, SPSS assigns the default names *var1, var2, var3,* etc.

Data Files Created in Non-Windows Applications

If you work with data files created with non-Windows (for example, DOS) applications, you might find that some special characters appear as arbitrary characters in SPSS for Windows, because of the character set used by Windows. This problem does not affect numbers, but it can affect any alphanumeric character strings, including string variable values.

For SPSS/PC+ data files, SPSS for Windows automatically converts special characters correctly—provided that the character set used by the computer on which the file was created is the same as the character set used in DOS at the time you installed Windows. (Windows creates a character-set conversion table during installation.) For data files created with other non-Windows applications (for example, Excel, dBASE), special characters are not converted.

Reading SQL Databases

In addition to dBASE database files, SPSS can read the following types of SQL databases:

- Oracle (version 5.1 or later)
- SQL Server (version 1.1 or later)
- SQL databases accessed via installed ODBC drivers

Variable Names and Labels

The complete database column name is used as the variable label. SPSS assigns variable names to each column from the database in one of two ways:

- If the name of the database column (or the first eight characters) forms a valid, unique SPSS variable name, it is used as the variable name.
- If the name of the database column does not form a valid, unique SPSS variable name, SPSS creates a name by using the first few characters from the column name and adding a numeric suffix, based on the column's position number in the SQL SELECT statement (Fields to Retrieve in the Select Table and Fields dialog box). If the first few characters of the column name are not valid characters for SPSS variable names, the prefix *col* is used with a numeric suffix.

SQL Server Databases

To read an SQL Server database into SPSS, from the menus choose:

File
  Open ▶
    SQL Server...

This opens the Open SQL Server Database dialog box, as shown in Figure 2.4.

Figure 2.4   Open SQL Server Database dialog box

Login. The database login name. This is required. SPSS does not read the environment variable *dblogin* from the login string.

Password. The password that accesses the database. Depending on how the database system is set up, this may be required or optional. As a security precaution, asterisks are displayed instead of the password you enter.

Server. A list of servers accessed by the login name and the password is displayed. You can enter a server name or choose one from the list.

Selecting a Database

After you select a server, click on Continue to open the Select Database dialog box, as shown in Figure 2.5.

Figure 2.5   Select Database dialog box

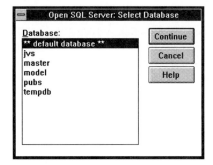

Tables and Fields

After you select the database, click on Continue to open the Select Table and Fields dialog box, as shown in Figure 2.6.

Figure 2.6   Select Table and Fields dialog box

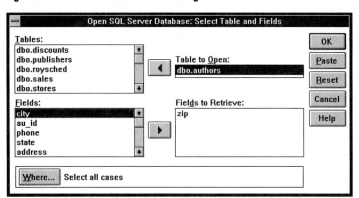

Tables. A list of tables and views in the database.

Table to Open. Select a table or view from the Tables list. You can select only one.

Fields. A list of fields in the selected table. If there is no currently selected table, the Fields list is empty.

Fields to Retrieve. Select one or more fields to retrieve. Fields are columns in the database. They are read as variables by SPSS.

Selecting a Subset of Cases

To select a subset of cases from the database, click on Where... in the Select Table and Fields dialog box. This opens the Where Cases dialog box, as shown in Figure 2.7.
   You can choose one of the following alternatives:

○ **Select all cases.** This is the default. Values are calculated for all cases, and any WHERE clause is ignored.

○ **Select where case satisfies condition.** Enter an SQL WHERE clause in the text box. (Do not include the actual word "where.") If you change the selected table in the SQL Server Select Table and Fields dialog box, the current WHERE clause is deleted.

Figure 2.7   Where Cases dialog box

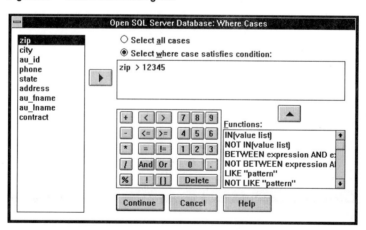

Calculator Pad

The calculator pad contains numbers and arithmetic, relational, and logical operators (see Table 2.1). You can use it like a calculator (using the mouse to point and click on keys) or simply as a reference for the correct symbols to use for various operators.

Since fairly complex expressions are possible, it is important to keep in mind the order in which operations are performed. Functions are evaluated first, followed by multiplication and division, and finally addition and subtraction. You can control the order of operations by enclosing the operation you want executed first in parentheses.

Table 2.1   Calculator pad operators

Arithmetic Operators		**Relational Operators**[*]		**Logical Operators**[†]	
+	Addition	<	Less than	And	Both relations must be true.
-	Subtraction	>	Greater than	Or	Either relation can be true.
*	Multiplication	<=	Less than or equal to	!	Not. Reverses the true/false outcome of the expression.
/	Division	>=	Greater than or equal to		
%	Modulus (remainder)[‡]	=	Equal to		
( )	Order of operations	!=	Not equal to		

[*]A relation is a logical expression that compares two values using a relational operator.

[†]A logical operator joins two relations or reverses the true/false outcome of an expression.

[‡]Available for SQL Server only.

Functions

The SQL functions available are listed below. You can paste one of these functions into the expression or type in any valid SQL function.

IN	NOT IN	BETWEEN	NOT BETWEEN
IS LIKE	IS NOT LIKE	IS NULL	IS NOT NULL
ABS	MOD[*]	POWER	SQRT

[*]Available for Oracle only.

Pasting and Editing Functions

Pasting a Function into an Expression. To paste a function into an expression:

1. Position the cursor in the expression at the point where you want the function to appear.

2. Double-click on the function on the Functions list (or select the function and click on the ▲ pushbutton).

The function is inserted in the expression.

Editing a Function in an Expression. The function isn't complete until you enter the **arguments**, represented by question marks in the pasted function. The number of question marks indicates the minimum number of arguments required to complete the function.

To edit a function:

1. Highlight the question mark(s) in the pasted function.

2. Enter the arguments. If the arguments are field (variable) names, you can paste them from the source list.

Oracle Databases

To read an Oracle database into SPSS, from the menus choose:

File
  Open ▶
    Oracle...

This opens the Open Oracle Database dialog box, as shown in Figure 2.8.

Figure 2.8   Open Oracle Database dialog box

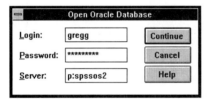

Login. The database login name. This is required. SPSS does not read the environment variable *dblogin* from the login string.

Password. The password that accesses the database. Depending on how the database system is set up, this may be required or optional. As a security precaution, asterisks are displayed instead of the password you enter.

Server. Enter the name of the server that contains the database.

Tables and Fields

After you select the database, click on Continue to open the Select Table and Fields dialog box, as shown in Figure 2.9.

Figure 2.9   Select Table and Fields dialog box

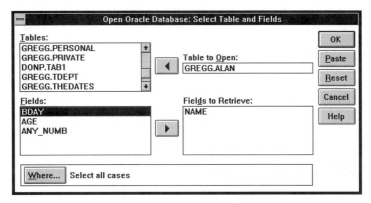

Tables. A list of tables and views in the database.

Table to Open. Select a table or view from the Tables list. You can select only one.

Fields. A list of fields in the selected table. If there is no currently selected table, the Fields list is empty.

Fields to Retrieve. Select one or more fields to retrieve. Fields are columns in the database. They are read as variables by SPSS.

Selecting a Subset of Cases

To select a subset of cases from the database, click on Where... in the Select Table and Fields dialog box. This opens the Where Cases dialog box, as shown in Figure 2.10.

Figure 2.10   Where Cases dialog box

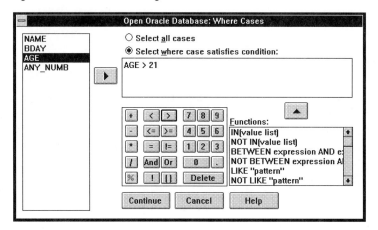

You can choose one of the following alternatives:

○ **Select all cases**. This is the default. Values are calculated for all cases, and any WHERE clause is ignored.

○ **Select where case satisfies condition**. Enter an SQL WHERE clause in the text box. (Do not include the actual word "where.") If you change the selected table in the Oracle Select Table and Fields dialog box, the current WHERE clause is deleted.

The operation of the Oracle Where Cases dialog box is the same as the SQL Server Where Cases dialog box (see "Selecting a Subset of Cases" on p. 34).

Reading SQL Databases with ODBC

If you have Microsoft ODBC (Open Database Connectivity), you can read any database that has an installed ODBC driver. To read a database using ODBC, from the menus choose:

File
  Open ▶
    ODBC...

This opens the SQL Data Source dialog box, as shown in Figure 2.11.

Figure 2.11   SQL Data Source dialog box

Select Data Source. Select the data source (network host) from the list of installed data sources. If the data source you want is not on the list, you can use the ODBC Administrator to add data sources. See your Microsoft ODBC documentation for more information.

Depending on the ODBC driver and the requirements of the database, you may have to enter a login ID and/or password before you can access the database. Figure 2.12 shows the SQL Server Login dialog box that opens if the data source is an SQL Server dialog box.

Figure 2.12   SQL Server Login dialog box accessed via ODBC

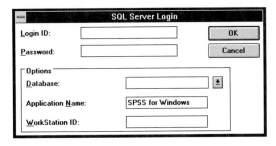

After you enter any information necessary to gain access to the database, you can select tables and fields and subsets of cases from dialog boxes similar to those described for SQL Server. The actual dialog boxes available depend on the ODBC driver and the type of database. The list of available functions in the dialog box for selecting subsets of cases is also dependent on the ODBC driver and will probably be more extensive than the list of functions provided for SQL Server and Oracle.

Note: For SQL Server and Oracle databases, it is best to use the SPSS Open Oracle and Open SQL Server dialog box interfaces rather than ODBC. SPSS converts the data directly, while ODBC first converts the data to ODBC data types and then to SPSS data types. Since not all source data types have analagous ODBC data types, the direct SPSS data conversion yields more accurate results.

Time-saving Tip

By default, SPSS automatically reads the entire data file when you click on OK in the Select Table and Fields dialog box. This may take some time if it is a large database. To avoid this potentially time-consuming data pass, there are two options:

- Change your Preferences setting for Transformation and Merge Options to Calculate values before used (see Chapter 36).

or

- Paste the command syntax into a syntax window and delete the EXECUTE command.

To paste and edit the underlying command syntax:

1. Click on Paste to paste the underlying command syntax into a syntax window.

2. Delete the EXECUTE command in the syntax window, as shown in Figure 2.13.

3. Click on Run on the syntax window icon bar.

Figure 2.13   Pasting and editing database capture syntax

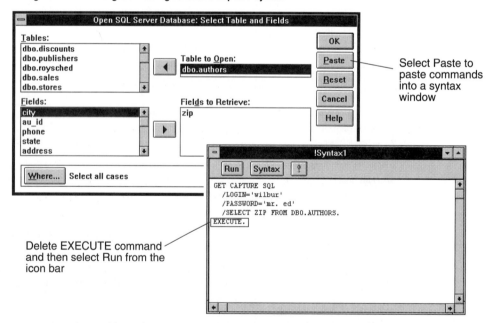

The variable names will appear in the Data Editor, but no data values will appear in the cells until SPSS runs a command that requires a data pass, such as a statistical procedure.

Reading Text Files

If your raw data are in simple text files (standard ASCII format), you can read the data in SPSS and assign variable names and data formats. To read a text file, from the menus choose:

File
  Read ASCII Data...

This opens the Read ASCII Data File dialog box, as shown in Figure 2.14.

Figure 2.14   Read ASCII Data File dialog box

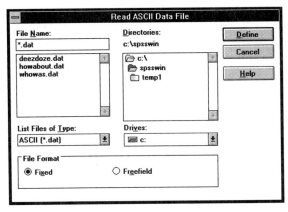

File Name. You can select a file from the list, or you can type in a filename, a directory path and filename, or a wildcard search. By default, SPSS looks for all files in the current directory with the extension *.dat* and displays them on the list.

List Files of Type. Provides a wildcard search list of default file extensions for appropriate file types. The list contains the default extension for ASCII data files, (*.dat*), and the wildcard search for all files (*.*).

Directories. To change the directory location, select the name of the directory on the Directories list. Directories below the current directory are denoted by closed file folder icons. Directories above the current directory are denoted by open file folder icons. The current directory is displayed above the list of directories and is also denoted by the last (lowest) open file folder icon.

Drives. To change the drive location, select a drive from the drop-down list of available drives.

File Format. You can choose one of the following alternatives:

○ **Fixed.** Each variable is recorded in the same column location on the same record (line) for each case in the data file. This is the default.

○ **Freefield.** The variables are recorded in the same order for each case, but not necessarily in the same locations. Spaces are interpreted as delimiters between values. More than one case can be recorded on a single line. After reading the value for the last defined variable for a case, SPSS reads the next value encountered as the first variable for the next case.

Define Fixed Variables

To define fixed-format data, select Fixed for the File Format in the Read ASCII Data File dialog box and click on Define. This opens the Define Fixed Variables dialog box, as shown in Figure 2.15.

Figure 2.15   Define Fixed Variables dialog box

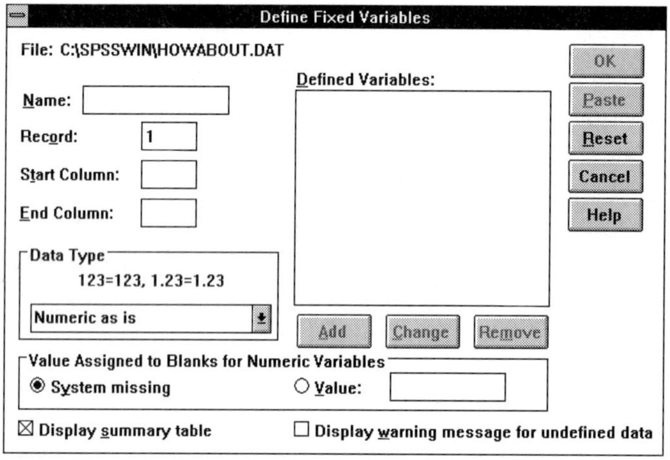

For each variable, you must specify the following:

Name. The following rules apply to variable names:

• The name must begin with a letter. The remaining characters can be any letter, any digit, a period, or the symbols @, #, _, or $.

• Variable names cannot end with a period.

• Variable names that end with an underscore should be avoided (to avoid conflict with variables automatically created by some procedures).

• The length of the name cannot exceed eight characters.

- Blanks and special characters (for example, !, ?, ', and *) cannot be used.
- Each variable name must be unique; duplication is not allowed. Variable names are not case-sensitive. The names *NEWVAR*, *NewVar*, and *newvar* are all identical in SPSS.
- The following reserved keywords cannot be used.

ALL	NE	EQ	TO	LE
LT	BY	OR	GT	
AND	NOT	GE	WITH	

Record. A case can have data on more than one line. The **record number** indicates the line within the case where the variable is located.

Start Column/End Column. These two column specifications indicate the location of the variable within the record. The value for a variable can appear anywhere within the range of columns. With the exception of string variables, leading blank spaces in the column range are ignored.

Data Type. You can choose one of the following alternatives:

⬇ **Numeric as is.** Valid values include numbers, a leading plus or minus sign, and a decimal indicator.

Numeric 1 decimal (1). If there is not an explicitly coded decimal indicator, one **implied decimal position** is assigned. For example, 123 is read as 12.3. A value with more than one explicitly coded decimal position (for example, 1.23) is read correctly but is rounded to one decimal position in output unless you change the variable definition (see Chapter 3).

Numeric 2 decimals (2). If there is not an explicitly coded decimal indicator, two implied decimal positions are assigned. For example, 123 is read as 1.23. A value with more than two explicitly coded decimal positions (for example, 1.234) is read correctly but is rounded to two decimal positions in output unless you change the variable definition (see Chapter 3).

Dollar (DOLLAR). Valid values are numbers with an optional leading dollar sign and optional commas as thousands separators. If you don't enter the dollar sign or commas, they are automatically inserted in output. Decimal positions are read but do not appear in output unless you change the variable definition (see Chapter 3). For example, $10.95 would be displayed as $11.

String (A). Valid values include virtually any keyboard characters and imbedded blanks. Leading blanks are treated as part of the value. Internally, string values are right-padded to the total width of the field defined by the Start and End columns. If the defined width is eight or less characters, it is a **short string variable**. If the defined width is more than eight characters, it is a **long string variable**. Short string variables can be used in many SPSS procedures; long string variables can be used in fewer procedures.

Date (DATE). Dates of the general format dd-mmm-yyyy. The following conventions apply:

- Dashes, periods, commas, slashes, or blanks can be used as delimiters. For example, 28-10-90, 28/10/1990, 28.OCT.90, and October 28, 1990 are all acceptable.
- Months may be represented in digits, Roman numerals, three-letter abbreviations, or fully spelled out. For example, 10, X, OCT, and October are all acceptable.
- Two-digit years are assumed to have the prefix 19.

Date format variables are displayed with dashes as delimiters and three-letter abbreviations for the month values. Internally, dates are stored as the number of seconds from October 14, 1582.

European Date (EDATE). Dates of the general format dd.mm.yyyy. The conventions for Date format also apply to European Date format. Edate format variables are displayed with slashes as delimiters and numbers for the month values.

American Date (ADATE). Dates of the general format mm/dd/yyyy. The conventions for Date format also apply to American Date. Adate format variables are displayed with slashes as delimiters and numbers for the month values.

Julian Date (JDATE). Dates of the general format yyyyddd. The following rules apply:

- If the input value contains only five digits, a two-digit year is assumed, and 1900 is added.
- Year values can be two or four digits. Two-digit year values less than 10 must contain a leading zero.
- All day values must be three digits. Leading zeros are required for day values less than 100.

Quarter and Year (QYR). Dates of the general format qQyyyy. The quarter is expressed as 1, 2, 3, or 4, and the year is represented by two or four digits. If two digits are used, 1900 is added. The quarter and the year are separated by the letter Q. Blanks may be used as additional delimiters. For example, 4Q90, 4Q1990, 4 Q 90, and 4 Q 1990 are all acceptable.

Month and Year (MOYR). Dates of the general format mm/yyyy. The Date format conventions for month and year apply.

Week and Year (WKYR). Dates of the general form wkWKyyyy. A week is expressed as a number from 1 to 53. Week 1 begins on January 1, week 2 on January 8, and so forth. The year is a two- or four-digit number. If it is a two-digit number, 1900 is added. The week and year are separated by the string WK. Blanks can be used as additional delimiters. For example, 43WK90, 43WK1990, and 43 WK 1990 are all acceptable.

Date and Time (DATETIME). Values containing a date and a time. The following conventions apply:

- The date must be written as an international date (dd-mmm-yyyy) followed by a blank and then a time value in the form hh:mm:ss.ss.
- The time conforms to a 24-hour clock. Thus, the maximum hour value is 23; the maximum minute value is 59; and the seconds value must be less than 60.
- Fractional seconds must have the decimal indicator explicitly coded in the data value.

For example, the input values 25/1/90 1 2, 25-JAN-1990 1:02, and 25 January 1990 01:02:00 are all acceptable variations for the same value.

Time (TIME). Time of day or time interval values of the general form hh:mm:ss.ss. The following conventions apply:

- Colons, blanks, or periods may be used as delimiters between hours, minutes, and seconds. A period is required to separate seconds from fractional seconds.
- Data values must contain hours and minutes. Seconds and fractional seconds may be omitted.
- Data values may contain a sign.
- Hours may be of unlimited magnitude. The maximum for minutes is 59, and seconds must be less than 60 (for example, 59.99 is acceptable).

Internally, times are stored as the number of seconds.

Day and Time (DTIME). Time interval that includes days in the form ddd hh:mm:ss.ss. The following conventions apply:

- The number of days is separated from the hours by an acceptable Time delimiter: a blank, a period, or a colon. A preceding sign (+ or –) may be used.
- The maximum value for hours is 23.
- The remainder of the field must conform to required specifications for Time format. Fractional seconds must have the decimal indicator explicitly coded in the data value.

Day of Week (WKDAY). The day of the week expressed as a character string. Only the first two characters are significant. The remaining characters are optional. For example, Sunday can be expressed as Sunday, Sun, or Su. Internally, values are stored as integers from 1 to 7 (Sunday=1).

Month (MONTH). Month of the year expressed as an integer or a character string. Only the first three characters are significant. The remaining characters are optional. For example, January can be expressed as 1, January, or Jan. Internally, values are stored as integers from 1 to 12 (January=1).

Other Formats. Using SPSS syntax in a syntax window (see Chapter 4), you can specify different widths for many of the above formats, plus numerous other formats, including:

- Comma format: commas as thousands separators
- Dot format: Commas as decimal indicators and periods as thousands separators
- Scientific notation
- Percent
- Hexadecimal
- Column binary
- Packed decimal

For a complete list of data format types, see the *SPSS Base System Syntax Reference Guide*.

Value Assigned to Blanks for Numeric Variables. For fixed-format data, you can choose one of the following alternatives for the treatment of blank numeric fields:

○ **System missing.** Blank numeric fields are treated as missing data. This is the default.

○ **Value.** Blank numeric fields receive a user-specified value. For example, blanks may represent a value of zero instead of missing data. Enter the value in the text box.

The following options are also available:

❏ **Display summary table.** Displays a summary table of defined variables, including data type and column location, in the output window.

❏ **Display warning message for undefined data.** If anything other than a number is encountered in a numeric field, the system-missing value is assigned, and a warning message is displayed in the output. To suppress the warning message, deselect this default setting.

Entering Variable Definitions

To enter a variable definition:

1. Specify the variable name, record and column locations, and data type.

2. Click on Add. The record number, start and end columns, variable name, and data type appear on the Defined Variables list, as shown in Figure 2.16.

Figure 2.16   Defined Variables

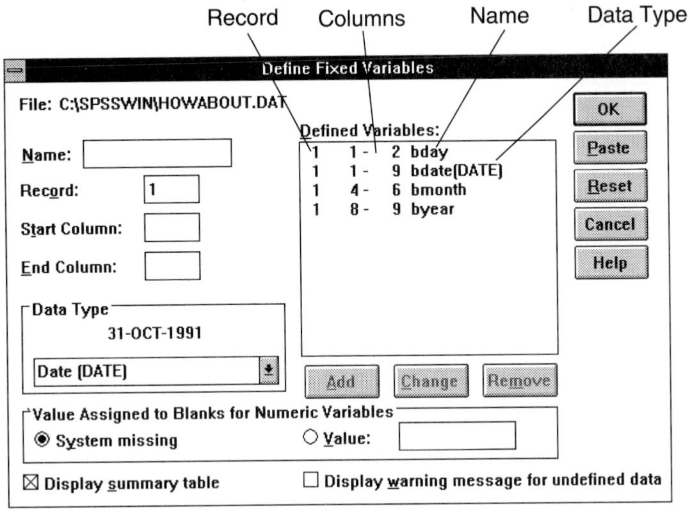

The following general rules apply:

- You can enter variables in any order. They are automatically sorted by record and start column on the list.

- You can specify multiple variables in the same or overlapping column locations. For example, in Figure 2.16, *bday* is in columns 1–2, *bmonth* in columns 4–6, *byear* in columns 8–9, and *bdate* in columns 1–9.

- You can read selective data fields and/or records. You don't have to define or read all the data in the file. SPSS reads only the columns and records you specify and skips over any data you don't define.

Changing and Deleting Variable Definitions

To change a variable definition, highlight the variable on the Defined Variables list, make the changes, and then click on Change. To delete a variable, highlight the variable on the Defined Variables list and click on Remove.

Define Freefield Variables

To define freefield format data, select Freefield for the File Format in the Read ASCII Data File dialog box and click on Define. This opens the Define Freefield Variables dialog box, as shown in Figure 2.17.

Figure 2.17   Define Freefield Variables dialog box

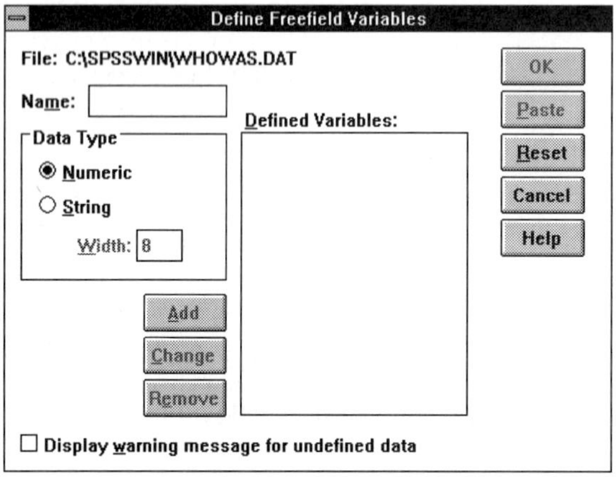

For each variable, you must specify the following:

Name. Variable names must begin with a letter and cannot exceed eight characters. Additional variable naming rules are given in "Define Fixed Variables" on p. 42.

Data Type. For freefield data, there are only two alternatives for data type:

○ **Numeric.** Valid values include numbers, a leading plus or minus sign, and a decimal indicator. Imbedded thousands separators are not allowed in data values.

○ **String.** Valid values include virtually any keyboard characters and imbedded blanks. For width, specify the *maximum* width of the string. Internally, shorter string values are right-padded to the defined width. If the defined width is eight or fewer characters, it is a short string variable. If the defined width is more than eight characters, it is a long string variable. Short string variables can be used in many SPSS procedures; long string variables can be used in fewer procedures. If a value contains blanks, the entire string must be enclosed in apostrophes or quotes.

The following option is also available:

❏ **Display warning message for undefined data.** If anything other than a number is encountered in a numeric field, the system-missing value is assigned, and a warning message is displayed in the output. To suppress the warning message, deselect this default setting.

Entering Variable Definitions

To enter a variable definition, specify the variable name and data type and click on Add. The variable appears on the Defined Variables list. If it is a string variable, the letter A and the defined width appear in parentheses next to the variable name.

While defining data in freefield format is relatively simple and easy, it is also easy to make mistakes. Keep the following rules in mind:

- You must enter variables in the order in which they appear in the data file. Each new variable definition is added to the bottom of the list, and SPSS reads the variables in that order.

- You must provide definitions for all variables in the file. If you omit any, the data file will be read incorrectly. SPSS determines the end of one case and the beginning of the next based on the number of defined variables.

- The data file cannot contain any missing data. Blank fields are read as delimiters between variables, and SPSS does not distinguish between single and multiple blanks. If a single observation is missing, the entire remainder of the data file will be read incorrectly.

- If your Windows International settings (accessed from the Control Panel) use a period as the decimal indicator, SPSS interprets commas as delimiters between values in freefield format. For example, a value of 1,234 is read as two separate values: 1 and 234.

Changing and Deleting Variable Definitions

To change a variable definition, highlight the variable on the Defined Variables list, make the changes, and then click on Change. To delete a variable, highlight the variable on the Defined Variables list and click on Remove.

Data Editor Window

When you open a data file, the data appear in the Data Editor window, as shown in Figure 2.18. You can then use the Data Editor to change variable definitions, add or delete cases or variables, and modify data values. For more information on the Data Editor, see Chapter 3.

Figure 2.18   Data Editor window

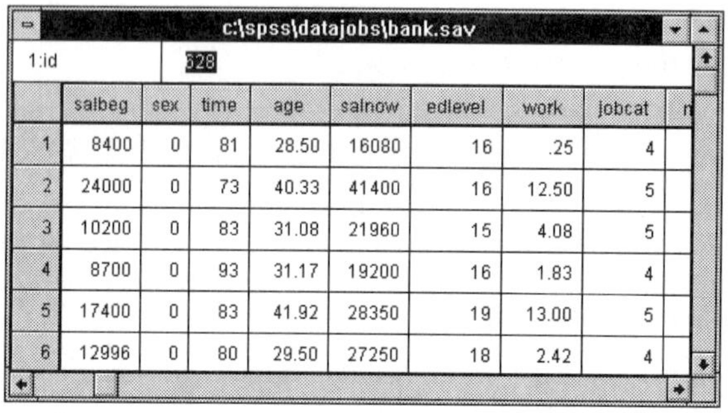

File Information

An SPSS data file contains much more than raw data. It also contains any variable definition information, including:

- Variable names
- Variable formats
- Descriptive variable and value labels

This information is stored in the dictionary portion of the SPSS data file. The Data Editor provides one way to view the variable definition information (see Chapter 3). You can also display complete dictionary information for the working data file or any other SPSS data file.

Working Data File

To display complete dictionary information for every variable in the working data file, from the menus choose:

Utilities
  File Info

The following information is displayed in the output window:

- Variable names.
- Descriptive variable label (if any).

- Print and write formats. The data type is followed by a number indicating the maximum width and the number of decimal positions (if any). For example, F8.2 indicates a numeric variable with a maximum width of eight columns, including one column for the decimal indicator and two columns for decimal positions.
- Descriptive value labels (if any) for different values of the variable. Both the value and the corresponding label are displayed.

You can also obtain dictionary information on individual variables using the Variables dialog box (see Chapter 34).

Other SPSS Data Files

To display dictionary information for SPSS data files not currently open, from the menus choose:

File
  Display Data Info...

This opens the Display Data Info dialog box, as shown in Figure 2.19.

Figure 2.19   Display Data Info dialog box

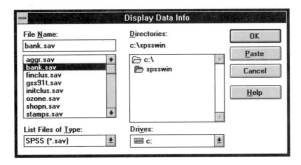

File Name. You can select a file from the list or you can type in a filename, a directory path and filename, or a wildcard search. By default, SPSS looks for all files in the current directory with the extension *.sav* and displays them on the list.

List Files of Type. Provides a wildcard search list of default file extensions for appropriate file types. The list contains the default extension for SPSS data files, (*.sav*) and the wildcard search for all files (*.*).

Directories. To change the directory location, select the name of the directory on the Directories list. Directories below the current directory are denoted by closed file folder icons. Directories above the current directory are denoted by open file folder icons. The current directory is displayed above the list of directories and is also denoted by the last (lowest) open file folder icon.

Drives. To change the drive location, select a drive from the drop-down list of available drives.

The dictionary information for the specified file is displayed in the output window.

Saving Data Files

Any changes you make in a data file last only for the duration of the SPSS session—unless you explicitly save the changes. To save any changes to a previously defined SPSS data file:

1. Make the Data Editor the active window.

2. From the menus choose:

    File
      Save Data

The modified data file is saved, overwriting the previous version of the file. *Note:* SPSS always asks if you want to save changes to a file before closing it or ending the session.

Save As New File or Different Format

To save a new SPSS data file or save the data in a different file format:

1. Make the Data Editor the active window.

2. From the menus choose:

    File
      Save As...

This opens the Save Data As dialog box, as shown in Figure 2.20.

Figure 2.20   Save Data As dialog box

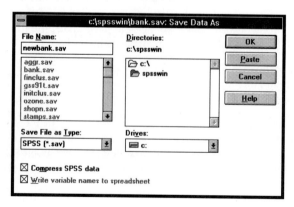

File Name. You can type in a filename, a directory path and filename, or a wildcard search. By default, SPSS provides an extension of .*sav* and displays a list of files in the current directory with that extension. If you select a filename from the list, SPSS asks if you want to replace the existing file.

Directories. To change the directory location, select the name of the directory on the Directories list. Directories below the current directory are denoted by closed file folder icons. Directories above the current directory are denoted by open file folder icons. The current directory is displayed above the list of directories and is also denoted by the last (lowest) open file folder icon.

Drives. To change the drive location, select a drive from the drop-down list of available drives.

Specifying File Type

Before you can save a data file, you need to specify a file format.

Save File as Type. Select one of the following alternatives from the drop-down list:

⬇ **SPSS (*.sav)**. SPSS 6.0 for Windows.

SPSS/PC+ (*.sys). SPSS/PC+ format. If the data file contains more than 500 variables, only the first 500 will be saved. For variables with more than one defined user-missing value, additional user-missing values will be recoded into the first defined user-missing value.

SPSS portable (*.por). Portable SPSS file that can be read by other versions of SPSS on other operating systems (for example, Macintosh, OS/2).

Tab-delimited (*.dat). ASCII text files with values separated by tabs.

Fixed ASCII (*.dat). ASCII text file in fixed format, using the default write formats for all variables. There are no tabs or spaces between variable fields.

Excel (*.xls). Microsoft Excel spreadsheet file. The maximum number of variables is 256.

1-2-3 Release 3.0 (*.wk3). Lotus 1-2-3 spreadsheet file, release 3.0. The maximum number of variables you can save is 256.

1-2-3 Release 2.0 (*.wk1). Lotus 1-2-3 spreadsheet file, release 2.0. The maximum number of variables you can save is 256.

1-2-3 Release 1.A (*.wks). Lotus 1-2-3 spreadsheet file, release 1A. The maximum number of variables you can save is 256.

SYLK (*.slk). Symbolic link format for Microsoft Excel and Multiplan spreadsheet files. The maximum number of variables you can save is 256.

dBASE IV (*.dbf). dBASE IV database files. The maximum number of variables you can save is 255.

dBASE III (*.dbf). dBASE III database files. The maximum number of variables you can save is 128.

dBASE II (*.dbf). dBASE II database files. The maximum number of variables you can save is 32.

For SPSS data files, the following option is available:

❏ **Compress SPSS data.** Compressed files occupy less disk space and usually take less time to process than uncompressed files.

For Lotus 1-2-3, Excel, SYLK, and tab-delimited files, the following option is available:

❏ **Write variable names to spreadsheet.** Variable names are written in the first row of the file.

If you save as SPSS format, the new file becomes the working data file and the new filename is displayed on the title bar of the Data Editor window. If you save as any other format, the working data file is unaffected.

Note: SPSS needs to know the file type, regardless of the file extension. You cannot specify a different file type simply by changing the extension of the wildcard search in the File Name text box. To change the file type, you must change the selection on the drop-down list.

Closing a Data File

Since only one data file can be open at a time, SPSS automatically closes the working data file before it opens another one. If there have been any changes to the data file since it was last saved, SPSS asks if you want to save the changes before it closes the file and opens the next one.

3 Data Editor

The Data Editor provides a convenient, spreadsheet-like method for creating and editing SPSS data files. The Data Editor window, shown in Figure 3.1, opens automatically when you start an SPSS session.

Figure 3.1 Data Editor window

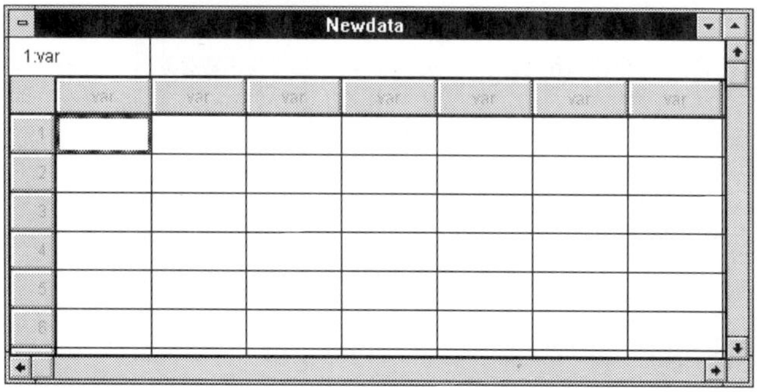

If you have previous experience with spreadsheet programs, many of the features of the Data Editor should be familiar. There are, however, several important distinctions.

- **Rows are cases**. Each row represents a **case** or an observation. For example, each individual respondent to a questionnaire is a case.

- **Columns are variables**. Each column represents a **variable** or characteristic being measured. For example, each item on a questionnaire is a variable.

- **Cells contain values**. Each cell contains a single value of a variable for a case. The cell is the intersection of the case and variable. Cells contain only data values. Unlike spreadsheet programs, cells in the Data Editor cannot contain formulas.

- **The data file is rectangular**. The dimensions of the data file are determined by the number of cases and variables. You can enter data in any cell. If you enter data in a cell outside the boundaries of the defined data file, SPSS extends the data rectangle to include any rows and/or columns between that cell and the file boundaries. There are no "empty" cells within the boundaries of the data file. For numeric variables, blank cells are converted to the system-missing value (see "Missing Values" on p. 62). For string variables, a blank is considered a valid value.

Defining Variables

When you open an existing data file (see Chapter 2), the data are displayed in the Data Editor, as shown in Figure 3.2. Any existing data definition recognized by SPSS (that is, variable names, formats, etc.) is reflected in the display. Beyond the boundaries of the defined data file, the Data Editor displays dimmed row numbers and dimmed column headings to indicate potential cases and variables.

Figure 3.2   Data file displayed in the Data Editor

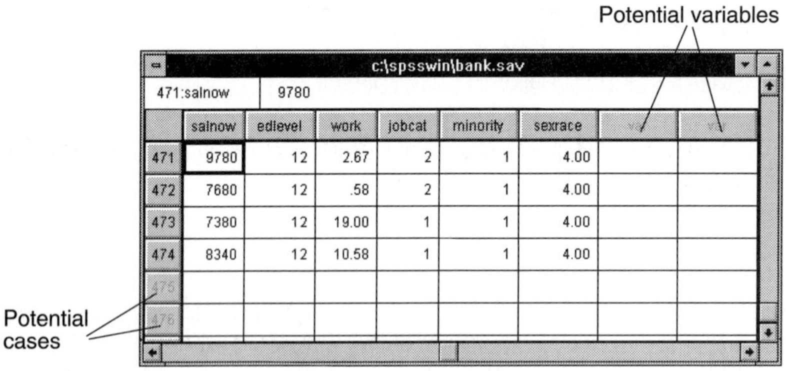

You can replace existing or default data definitions with your own specifications. You can:

- Create your own variable names.
- Provide descriptive variable and value labels.
- Use special codes for missing values.
- Assign different formats (such as string, date, and time).

To change the name, format, and other attributes of a variable:

- Double-click on the current variable name at the top of the column.

or

- Select any cell in the column for the variable, and from the menus choose:

  Data
   Define Variable...

This opens the Define Variable dialog box, as shown in Figure 3.3.

Figure 3.3   Define Variable dialog box

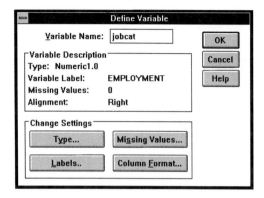

The variable name, type, label, missing values (if any), and alignment for the selected variable are displayed.

Variable Names

The default name for new variables is the prefix *var* and a sequential five-digit number (*var00001*, *var00002*, etc.). To change the variable name, simply enter the new name in the Variable Name text box. The following rules apply to valid variable names:

- The name must begin with a letter. The remaining characters can be any letter, any digit, a period, or the symbols @, #, _, or $.
- Variable names cannot end with a period.
- Variable names that end with an underscore should be avoided (to avoid conflict with variables automatically created by some procedures).
- The length of the name cannot exceed eight characters.
- Blanks and special characters (for example, !, ?, ', and *) cannot be used.
- Each variable name must be unique; duplication is not allowed.
- Variable names are not case sensitive. The names *NEWVAR*, *NewVar*, and *newvar* are all identical in SPSS.
- The following reserved keywords cannot be used.

ALL	NE	EQ	TO	LE
LT	BY	OR	GT	
AND	NOT	GE	WITH	

The following are all valid variable names: *location*, *loc#5*, *x.1*, and *over$500*.

Renamed Variables in Dialog Boxes

Source variable lists in dialog boxes are updated to reflect new variable names, but, in some cases, selected variable lists may not be updated. If a selected variable list contains an old variable name and you want to run the procedure again during the same session, you should remove the variable name from the selected variable list or an error will result.

To remove an old variable name from a selected variable list, select the variable and click on the ◄ pushbutton. This removes the variable name without placing it back on the source variable list.

Variable Type

By default, SPSS assumes that all new variables are numeric. To change the variable type, click on Type... in the Define Variable dialog box. This opens the Define Variable Type dialog box, as shown in Figure 3.4.

Figure 3.4   Define Variable Type dialog box

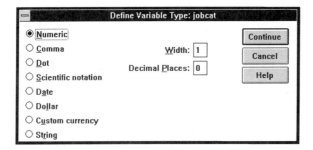

The contents of the Define Variable Type dialog box depend on the data type selected. For some data types, there are text boxes for width and number of decimals; for others, you can simply select a format from a scrollable list of examples. You can choose one of the following alternatives:

○ **Numeric.** Valid values include numerals, a leading plus or minus sign, and a decimal indicator. For width, enter the maximum number of characters, including one position for the decimal indicator. For decimal places, enter the number of decimal positions for display purposes. The maximum width for numeric variables is 40 characters; the maximum number of decimal positions is 16.

○ **Comma.** Valid values include numerals, a leading plus or minus sign, one period for the decimal indicator, and multiple imbedded commas as thousands separators. If you don't include the commas when you enter data values, they are automatically inserted. For width, enter the maximum number of characters, including the decimal point and imbedded commas. For decimal places, enter the number of decimal positions for display purposes.

○ **Dot**. Valid values include numerals, a leading plus or minus sign, one comma for the decimal indicator, and multiple imbedded periods as thousands separators. If you don't include the periods when you enter data values, they are automatically inserted. For width, enter the maximum number of characters, including the decimal indicator and imbedded periods. For decimal places, enter the number of decimal positions for display purposes.

○ **Scientific notation**. Valid values include all valid numeric values plus scientific notation indicated with an imbedded E, D, plus sign, or minus sign. For example, 123, 123E3, 123D3, 123+3, 123–3, and 123E+3 are all acceptable.

○ **Date**. Valid values are dates and/or times. Choose a format from the list.

○ **Dollar**. Valid values include a dollar sign, one period for the decimal indicator, and multiple commas as thousands separators. Choose a format from the list or enter values for width and number of decimal places. If you don't include the dollar sign or the commas when you enter data values, they are automatically inserted.

○ **Custom currency**. If you have created any custom currency formats (see Chapter 36), you can specify them as display formats. For width, enter the maximum number of characters, including any custom currency characters. For decimal places, enter the number of decimal positions for display purposes. You cannot include custom currency characters when you enter data values. They are automatically inserted after you enter the value.

○ **String**. Valid values include letters, numerals, and other characters. Enter the maximum number of characters (that is, the longest valid string value for the variable). String variables with a defined width of eight or fewer characters are **short strings**. String variables with a width of more than eight characters are **long strings**. Short string variables can be used in many SPSS procedures. The use of long string variables is severely restricted or not allowed in most SPSS procedures.

Other Formats

SPSS data files created on other operating systems or generated by command syntax in a syntax window may contain other data formats. If the selected variable uses one of these other formats, the format appears as an additional alternative at the bottom of the list. You can change the format to one of the standard format alternatives—but once you apply the change, you cannot change the variable back to its original format. Other formats recognized by SPSS include:

- Implied decimal
- Percent
- Hexadecimal
- Column binary

Input versus Display Formats

Depending on the format, the display of values in the Data Editor may differ from the actual value as entered and stored internally. Here are some general guidelines:

- For numeric, comma, and dot formats, you can enter values with any number of decimal positions (up to 16), and the entire value is stored internally. The Data Editor displays only the defined number of decimal places, and it rounds values with more decimals. However, the complete value is used in any computations.

- For string variables, all values are right-padded to the maximum width. For a string variable with a width of 6, a value of 'No' is stored internally as 'No   ' and is not equivalent to ' No '.

- For date formats, you can use slashes, dashes, spaces, commas, or periods as delimiters between day, month, and year values, and you can enter numbers, three-letter abbreviations, or complete names for month values. Dates of the general format dd-mmm-yy are displayed with dashes as delimiters and three-letter abbreviations for the month. Dates of the general format dd/mm/yy and mm/dd/yy are displayed with slashes for delimiters and numbers for the month. Internally, dates are stored as the number of seconds from October 14, 1582.

- For time formats, you can use colons, periods, or spaces as delimiters between hours, minutes, and seconds. Times are displayed with colons as delimiters. Internally, times are stored as the number of seconds.

See the *SPSS Base System Syntax Reference Guide* for more information on input and display data formats.

Decimal Indicators and International Settings

For numeric format variables, the decimal indicator can be either a period or a comma, depending on the setting in the International dialog box in the Windows Control Panel. If the International decimal indicator is anything other than a period, SPSS uses a comma as the decimal indicator. Comma, dollar, dot, and custom currency formats are not affected by the International decimal indicator setting.

Labels

To provide descriptive variable and value labels, click on Labels... in the Define Variable dialog box. This opens the Define Labels dialog box, as shown in Figure 3.5.

Figure 3.5   Define Labels dialog box

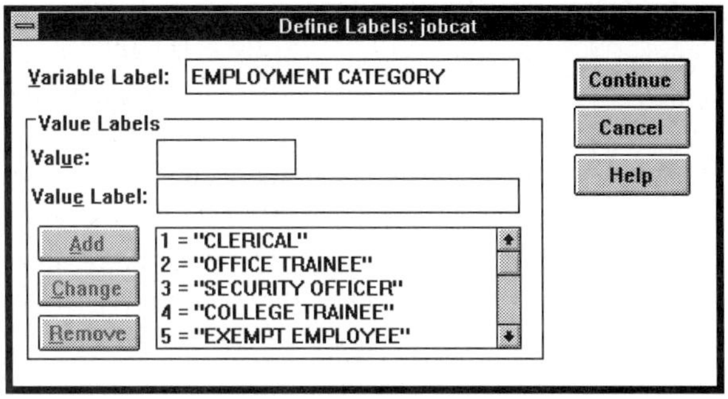

Variable Label

Variable labels can be up to 120 characters long, although most procedures display fewer than 120 characters in output. Variable labels are case sensitive; they are displayed exactly as entered.

Value Labels

You can assign a label for each value of a variable. This is particularly useful if your data file uses numeric codes to represent non-numeric categories (for example, codes of 1 and 2 for male and female). Value labels can be up to 60 characters long, although most procedures display fewer than 60 characters in output. Value labels are case sensitive; they are displayed exactly as entered. Value labels are not available for long string variables.

Assign a label. To assign value labels:

1. Enter the value in the Value text box. The value can be numeric or string.

2. Enter a label in the Value Label text box.

3. Click on Add. The value label is added to the list.

Modify a label. To modify a value label:

1. Highlight the label on the list.

2. Enter the new label (or value) in the text box.

3. Click on Change. The new label appears on the list.

Delete a label. To delete a value label:

1. Highlight the value label.

2. Click on Remove. The label is removed from the list.

You can display value labels instead of values in the Data Editor window. You can also use value label lists for data entry. (See "Display Value Labels" on p. 77.)

Missing Values

In SPSS, there are two types of missing values:

- **System-missing values.** Any blank numeric cells in the data rectangle are assigned the system-missing value, which is indicated with a period (.).

- **User-missing values.** It is often useful to be able to distinguish why information is missing. You can assign values that identify information missing for specific reasons and then instruct SPSS to flag these values as missing. SPSS statistical procedures and data transformations recognize this flag, and those cases with user-missing values are handled specially. Figure 3.6 shows how user-missing values are treated by the Frequencies procedure.

Figure 3.6   User-missing values

```
OZONE      Concern About Ozone Depletion


                                          Valid    Cum
Value Label               Value Frequency Percent  Percent  Percent

Very concerned             1.00    237     51.3     54.4     54.4
Somewhat concerned         2.00    144     31.2     33.0     87.4
Not concerned              3.00     55     11.9     12.6    100.0
Never use ozone            8.00      9      1.9    Missing                User-missing
No answer                  9.00     17      3.7    Missing                values
                                  -------  -------  -------
                          Total    462    100.0    100.0

Valid cases     436    Missing cases     26
```

User-missing Values

To specify user-missing values, click on Missing Values... in the Define Variable dialog box. This opens the Define Missing Values dialog box, as shown in Figure 3.7.

Figure 3.7   Define Missing Values dialog box

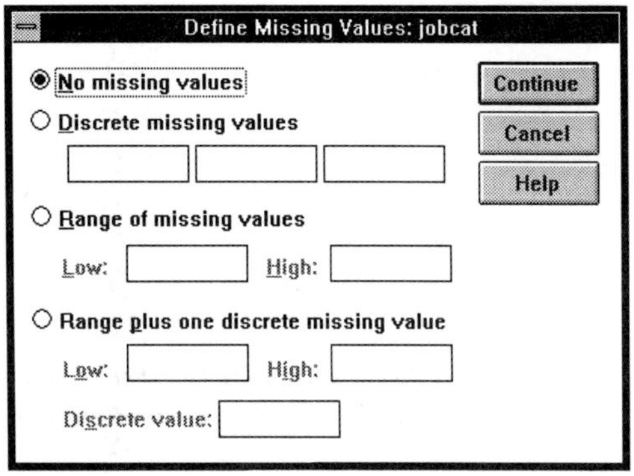

User-missing values can be assigned to variables of any format type except long string (see "Variable Type" on p. 58). You can choose one of the following alternatives:

○ **No missing values**. No user-missing values. All values are treated as valid. This is the default.

○ **Discrete missing values**. You can enter up to three discrete (individual) user-missing values for a variable. You can define discrete missing values for numeric or short string variables.

○ **Range of missing values**. All values between and including the low and high values are flagged as missing. Not available for short string variables.

○ **Range plus one discrete missing value**. All values between the low and high values and one additional value outside the range are flagged as missing. Not available for short string variables.

If you want to include all values below or above a certain value in a range but you don't know what the lowest or highest possible value is, you can enter an asterisk (*) for Low or High.

Column Format

To adjust the width of the Data Editor columns or to change the alignment of data in the column, click on Column Format... in the Define Variable dialog box. This opens the Define Column Format dialog box, as shown in Figure 3.8.

Figure 3.8   Define Column Format dialog box

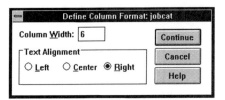

Column Width. The default column width is determined by the defined width of the variable (see "Variable Type" on p. 58). To change the column width, enter a new value. You can also change the column width in the Data Editor window. Position the mouse pointer on the border between two variable names at the top of the Data Editor window and use the click-and-drag technique to move the column border.

New column widths remain in effect as long as the data file is open or until they are changed again. They are not saved with the data file. The next time you open the file, the default column widths are used.

Text Alignment. The default alignment depends on the data type. You can choose one of the following alternatives:

○ **Left.** Text is left-aligned. This is the default for string variables.

○ **Center.** Text is centered.

○ **Right.** Text is right-aligned. This is the default for nonstring variables.

Column Width versus Variable Width

Column formats affect only the display of values in the Data Editor. Changing the column width does not change the defined width of a variable. If the defined and actual width of a value are wider than the column, the value appears truncated in the Data Editor window.

Templates

You can assign the same variable definition information to multiple variables with variable templates. For example, if you have a group of variables that all use the numeric codes 1 and 2 to represent "yes" and "no" responses and 9 to represent missing responses, you can create a template that contains those value labels and missing value specifications and apply the template to the entire group of variables.

To create, apply, or modify a template, from the menus choose:

Data
  Templates...

This opens the Template dialog box, as shown in Figure 3.9.

Figure 3.9   Template dialog box

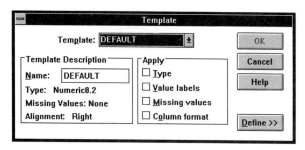

You can select and apply one of the existing templates from the Template list, modify it, or create a new template.

Applying Templates

To apply an existing template, select a template from the list and specify the template characteristics to be applied.

⬇ Template. All of the existing templates are listed. The description of the most recently selected template is displayed. SPSS comes with the following predefined templates:

Default. Numeric, eight characters wide, two decimal positions.

Months. A numeric variable with the month names as value labels for the values 1 through 12.

States. A two-character string variable with the full state names as value labels for the corresponding two-character zip code abbreviation.

Weekdays. A numeric variable with the weekday names as value labels for the values 1 through 7.

Template Description. The currently selected template name, variable type, user-missing values, and alignment are displayed.

Apply. You can apply any or all of the template characteristics to the selected variables. Choose one or more of the following alternatives:

❏ **Type**. Variable type (for example, numeric, string, or date).

❏ **Value labels**. Descriptive labels for value categories (for example, labels of *No* and *Yes* for values coded 0 and 1).

❏ **Missing values**. User-missing values (See "Missing Values" on p. 62).

❏ **Column format**. Column width and alignment for display in the Data Editor (see "Column Format" on p. 63.)

Creating and Modifying Templates

To modify an existing template or to create a new one, click on Define>>. This expands the Template dialog box, as shown in Figure 3.10.

Figure 3.10   Expanded Template dialog box

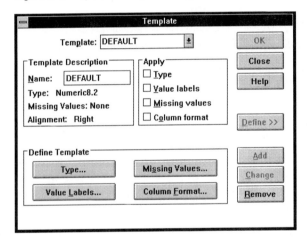

Defining a template is almost identical to defining a variable and uses the same dialog boxes for variable type, labels, missing values, and column format (see "Variable Type" on p. 58 through "Column Format" on p. 63).

Modify a template. To modify an existing template:

1. Select the template from the Template list.

2. Make the changes using the Define Template options.

3. Click on Change.

4. Click on OK to apply the template to the selected variables or click on Close to save the modified template without applying it to any variables. Any variables defined with the template but not currently selected remain unchanged.

Create a new template. To create a new template:

1. Select an existing template from the Template list. (If possible, select a template similar to the one you want to create.)

2. Use the Define Template options to create the template.

3. Enter a name for the template in the Name text box.

4. Click on Add.

5. Click on OK to apply the template to the selected variables or click on Close to save the modified template without applying it to any variables.

Saving Templates

Templates are saved in a file named *spss.tpl*. If this file is not found in the Windows directory, a new template file is automatically created.

Entering Data

You can enter data in virtually any order. You can enter data by case or by variable, for selected areas or individual cells. To enter a value in a cell:

1. Click on the cell or use the arrow keys to move to the cell. As shown in Figure 3.11, a heavy border appears around the cell, indicating that it is the active cell. The variable name and the row number are displayed in the upper left corner of the Data Editor window.

2. Type in the value. The value is displayed in the cell editor at the top of the Data Editor window. (See "Data Value Restrictions" on p. 69 for data value restrictions.)

3. Press ⏎Enter (or select another cell). The data value from the cell editor appears in the cell.

If you select a single cell, the ⏎Enter and Tab→ keys move down and right one cell, respectively. ⇧Shift-Tab→ moves left one cell. If you enter a value in a column outside the boundaries of the defined data file, you automatically create a new variable. If you enter a value in a row outside the boundaries of the data file, you automatically create a new case.

Figure 3.11   Active cell and cell editor

Variable name

Row number

Cell editor

c:\spsswin\bank.sav

4:salnow   19200

	id	salbeg	sex	time	age	salnow	edlevel	work
1	628	8400	0	81	28.50	16080	16	.25
2	630	24000	0	73	40.33	41400	16	12.50
3	632	10200	0	83	31.08	21960	15	4.08
4	633	8700	0	93	31.17	19200	16	1.83
5	635	17400	0	83	41.92	28350	19	13.00
6	637	12996	0	80	29.50	27250	18	2.42

Active cell

Entering Data in a Selected Area

You can restrict and control the flow of movement by selecting an area for data entry.

- **Select a case (row).** Click on the case number on the left side of the row or select any cell in the row and press ⇧Shift-Space. This highlights the entire row. Both the ↵Enter and Tab→ keys are restricted to movement between variables (columns) for that case.

- **Select a variable (column).** Click on the variable name at the top of the column or select any cell in the column and press Ctrl-Space. This highlights the entire column. Both the ↵Enter and Tab→ keys are restricted to movement between cases for that variable.

- **Select an area of cases and variables.** Click and drag the mouse diagonally from one corner of the area to the far corner (for example, upper left to lower right) or select a cell in one corner of the area, press and hold the ⇧Shift key, and use the arrow keys to define the area. The Tab→ key moves from left to right through the variables for each case in the selected area. The ↵Enter key moves from top to bottom through the cases for each variable in the selected area. (See Figure 3.12.)

Figure 3.12   Moving in a selected area

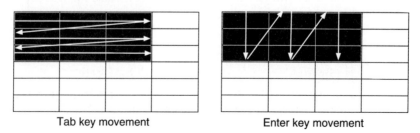

Tab key movement   Enter key movement

Data Value Restrictions

The defined variable type and width determine the type of value that can be entered in the cell.

- If you type a character not allowed by the defined variable type, the Data Editor beeps and does not enter the character.
- For string variables, characters beyond the defined width are not allowed.
- For numeric variables, integer values that exceed the defined width can be entered, but the Data Editor displays either scientific notation or asterisks in the cell to indicate that the value is wider than the defined width. To display the value in the cell, change the defined width of the variable. (*Note*: Changing the *column* width does not affect the *variable* width.)

Editing Data

With the Data Editor, you can modify a data file in many ways. You can:

- Change data values.
- Cut, copy, and paste data values.
- Add and delete cases.
- Add and delete variables.
- Change the order of variables.
- Change variable definitions.

Changing Data Values

To change a data value, you can either replace the entire value or modify part of it.

Replace a value. To delete the old value and enter a new value:

1. Click on the cell or use the arrow keys to move to the cell. The cell value is displayed in the cell editor.

2. Enter the new value. It replaces the old value in the cell editor.

3. Press ⏎Enter (or select another cell). The new value appears in the cell.

Modify a value. To modify a data value using the mouse:

1. Click on the cell. The cell value appears in the cell editor.

2. Click on the cell editor. A blinking cursor appears at the position where you clicked the mouse. To reposition the cursor, simply aim and click the mouse again.

3. Edit the data value as you would any other text (see Chapter 4).

4. Press ⏎Enter (or select another cell). The modified value appears in the cell.

To modify a data value using the keyboard:

1. Use the arrow keys to move to the cell. The cell value is displayed in the cell editor.

2. Press F2 to switch to edit mode. A blinking cursor appears at the end of the value in the cell editor. The left and right arrow keys now move between characters in the value, and the ⇧Shift key used with the arrow keys selects blocks of text.

3. Edit the data value as you would any other text (see Chapter 4).

4. Press ⏎Enter (or press F2 to switch out of edit mode and select another cell). The modified value appears in the cell.

Cutting, Copying, and Pasting Values

You can cut, copy, and paste individual cell values or groups of values. You can:

- Move or copy a single cell value to another cell.
- Move or copy a single cell value to a group of cells.
- Move or copy the values for a single case (row) to multiple cases.
- Move or copy the values for a single variable (column) to multiple variables.
- Move or copy a group of cell values to another group of cells.

Move or Copy Cell Values

To move or copy cell values:

1. Select the cell value(s) you want to cut or copy.

2. From the menus choose:

   Edit
     Cut

   or

   Edit
     Copy

3. Select the target cell(s).

4. From the menus choose:

Edit
　Paste

The pasted values appear in the cells, unless the defined variable types are not the same and no conversion is possible.

Data Conversion

If the defined variable types of the source and target cells are not the same, SPSS attempts to convert the value. If no conversion is possible, SPSS inserts the system-missing value in the target cell.

- **Numeric or Date into String**. Numeric (for example, numeric, dollar, dot, or comma) and date formats are converted to strings if they are pasted into a string variable cell. The string value is the numeric value as displayed in the cell. For example, for a dollar format variable, the displayed dollar sign becomes part of the string value. Values that exceed the defined string variable width are truncated.

- **String into Numeric or Date**. String values that contain acceptable characters for the numeric or date format of the target cell are converted to the equivalent numeric or date value. For example, a string value of 25/12/91 is converted to a valid date if the format type of the target cell is one of the day-month-year formats, but it is converted to system-missing if the format type of the target cell is one of the month-day-year formats.

- **Date into Numeric**. Date and time values are converted to a number of seconds if the target cell is one of the numeric formats (for example, numeric, dollar, dot, or comma). Since dates are stored internally as the number of seconds since October 14, 1582, converting dates to numeric values can yield some extremely large numbers. For example, the date 10/29/91 is converted to a numeric value of 12,908,073,600.

- **Numeric into Date or Time**. Numeric values are converted to dates or times if the value represents a number of seconds that can produce a valid date or time. For dates, numeric values less than 86,400 are converted to the system-missing value.

Pasting into Areas with Different Dimensions

If the target area does not have the same number of rows and columns as the source area, the pasting rules shown in Figure 3.13 apply.

Figure 3.13 Pasting into areas with different dimensions

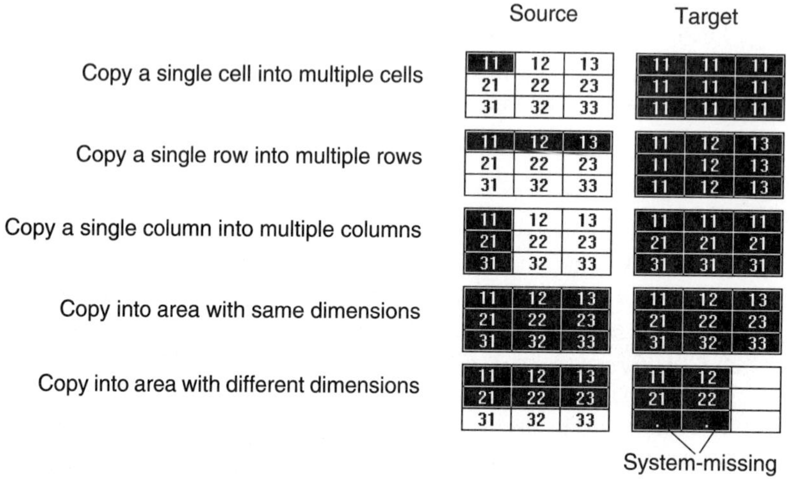

Copy a single cell into multiple cells

Copy a single row into multiple rows

Copy a single column into multiple columns

Copy into area with same dimensions

Copy into area with different dimensions

Source   Target

System-missing

Pasting Outside the Defined Data File

If you paste values outside the boundaries of the defined data file, SPSS extends the data file to include the pasted area and creates new cases and/or new variables as needed with system-missing values for new cells outside the pasted area (see Figure 3.14).

Figure 3.14 Pasting outside the defined data file

New variable
with missing values

Copy area

New cases
with missing values

Original data file boundary

New data file boundary

Paste area

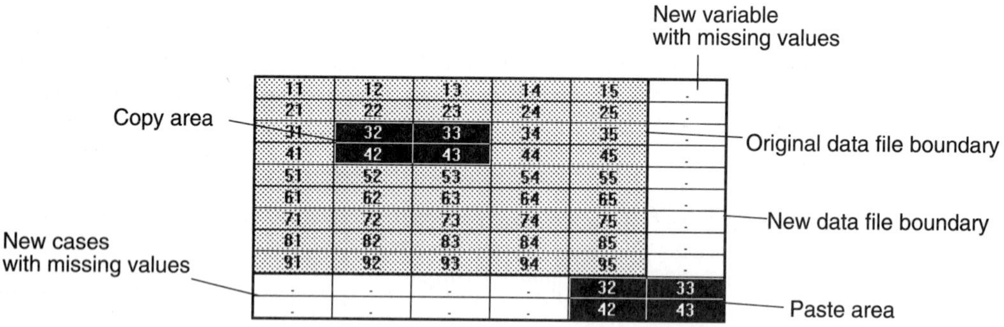

Pasting Outside the Data Editor

You can paste data from the Data Editor into a syntax or an output window or into an-other application. If you paste data values outside the Data Editor, what you see dis-played in the cell is what is pasted. For example, if the real value of a cell is 1.29 but it is displayed as 1.3, the value 1.3 is pasted. If you display value labels instead of values (see "Display Value Labels" on p. 77), the value labels are pasted, not the actual values.

Inserting New Cases

Entering data in a cell on a blank row automatically creates a new case. SPSS inserts the system-missing value for all the other variables for that case. If there are any blank rows between the new case and the existing cases, the blank rows also become new cases with the system-missing value for all variables.

Insert a new case between existing cases. To insert a new case between existing cases:

1. Select any cell in the case (row) below the position where you want to insert the new case.

2. From the menus choose:

   Data
     Insert Case

A new row is inserted for the case and all variables receive the system-missing value.

Inserting New Variables

Entering data in a blank column automatically creates a new variable with a default vari-able name (the prefix *var* and a sequential five-digit number) and a default data format type (numeric). SPSS inserts the system-missing value for all cases for the new variable. If there are any blank columns between the new variable and the existing variables, these columns also become new variables with the system-missing value for all cases.

Insert a new variable between existing variables. To insert a new variable between existing variables:

1. Select any cell in the variable (column) to the right of the position where you want to insert the new variable.

2. From the menus choose:

   Data
     Insert Variable

A new variable is inserted with the system-missing value for all cases.

Deleting Cases and Variables

Delete a case. To delete a case (row):

1. Click on the case number on the left side of the row or select any cell in the row and press ⇧Shift-Space. The entire row is highlighted. To delete multiple cases, use the click-and-drag method or use the ⇧Shift key with the arrow keys to extend the selection.

2. From the menus choose:

    Edit
     Clear

The selected cases are deleted. Any cases below them shift up.

Delete a variable. To delete a variable (column):

1. Click on the variable name at the top of the column or select any cell in the column and press Ctrl-Space. The entire column is highlighted.

    To delete multiple variables, use the click-and-drag method or use the ⇧Shift key with the arrow keys to extend the selection.

2. From the menus choose:

    Edit
     Clear

The selected variables are deleted. Any variables to the right of the deleted variables shift left.

Deleted Variables in Dialog Boxes

Source variable lists in dialog boxes are updated when variables are deleted, but, in some cases, selected variable lists may not be updated. If a selected variable list contains a deleted variable and you want to run the procedure again during the same session, you should remove the variable name from the selected variable list or an error will result.

To remove a deleted variable name from a selected variable list, select the variable and click on the ◄ pushbutton. This removes the variable name without placing it back on the source variable list.

Moving Variables

To move a variable by cutting and pasting in the Data Editor:

1. Insert a new variable in the position where you want to move the existing variable (see "Inserting New Variables" on p. 73).

2. For the variable you want to move, click on the variable name at the top of the column or select any cell in the column and press (Ctrl)-(Space). The entire column is highlighted.

3. From the menus choose:

Edit
  Cut

The selected variable is cut. Any variables to the right of the cut variables shift left.

4. Click on the variable name of the new, inserted variable or select any cell in the columns and press (Ctrl)-(Space). The entire variable is highlighted.

5. From the menus choose:

Edit
  Paste

The cut variable is pasted into the new variable space. All dictionary information for the variable is retained.

Changing Data Type

You can change the data type for a variable at any time using the Define Variable Type dialog box (see "Variable Type" on p. 58), and SPSS will attempt to convert existing values to the new type. If no conversion is possible, SPSS assigns the system-missing value. The conversion rules are the same as those for pasting data values to a variable with a different format type (see "Cutting, Copying, and Pasting Values" on p. 70). If the change in data format may result in the loss of missing value specifications or value labels, SPSS displays an alert box and asks if you want to proceed with the change or cancel it.

Finding Variables

Because variables are not always sorted in alphabetical order, it can sometimes be difficult to find a specific variable, particularly if the data file contains a large number of variables. You can use the Go To pushbutton in the Variables dialog box to find the selected variable in the Data Editor window. For more information about the Variables dialog box, see Chapter 34.

Finding Cases

To find a specific case (row) in the Data Editor, from the menus choose:

Data
  Go To Case...

This opens the Go to Case dialog box, as shown in Figure 3.15.

Figure 3.15   Go to Case dialog box

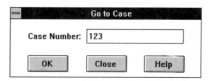

For Case Number, enter the row number for the case in the Data Editor. This value reflects the current position of the case in the data file. It is not a fixed value of a case ID variable. If you change the position of the case by inserting or deleting cases above it or by sorting the data file, the case number value changes.

Finding Data Values

Within a variable, you can search for specific data values or value labels in the Data Editor. To search for a data value:

1. Select any cell in the column of the variable you want to search.

2. From the menus choose:

   Edit
     Search for Data...

This opens the Search for Data dialog box, as shown in Figure 3.16.

Figure 3.16   Search for Data dialog box

You can search forward or backward from the active cell location. To search for a value label, value labels must be turned on (see "Display Value Labels" on p. 77).

The following option is also available:

❑ **Ignore case in strings.** By default, the search for string values in string variables and value labels ignores case. Deselect this default setting for a case-sensitive search.

Case Selection Status

If you have selected a subset of cases but have not discarded unselected cases, unselected cases are marked in the Data Editor with a vertical line through the row number, as in Figure 3.17.

Figure 3.17   Selection filter status

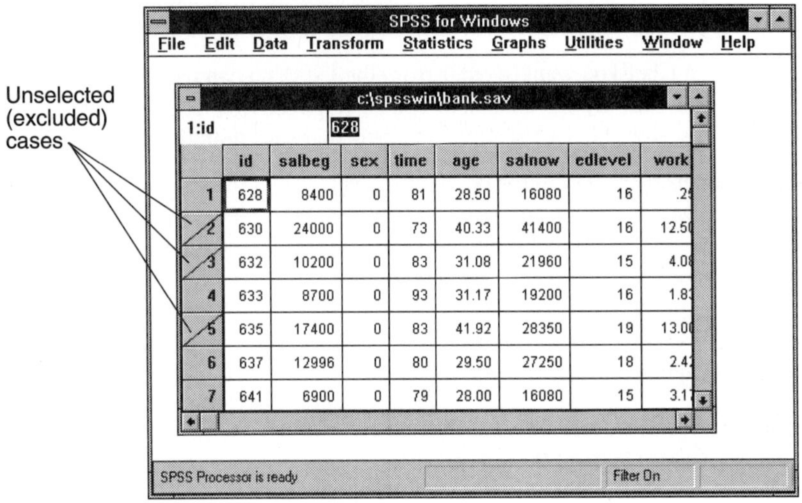

Unselected (excluded) cases

	id	salbeg	sex	time	age	salnow	edlevel	work
1	628	8400	0	81	28.50	16080	16	.2
2	630	24000	0	73	40.33	41400	16	12.5
3	632	10200	0	83	31.08	21960	15	4.0
4	633	8700	0	93	31.17	19200	16	1.8
5	635	17400	0	83	41.92	28350	19	13.0
6	637	12996	0	80	29.50	27250	18	2.4
7	641	6900	0	79	28.00	16080	15	3.1

Preferences

The Utilities menu offers several additional features to customize the Data Editor. You can:

- Display value labels instead of values.
- Control the automatic creation of new cases.
- Turn the grid lines on and off for display and/or printing.
- Change fonts for display and/or printing.

Display Value Labels

If you have defined descriptive value labels for any variables, you can display these labels in the Data Editor instead of the actual values. From the menus choose:

Utilities
  Value Labels

Data Entry with Value Labels

The Value Labels option also provides a list of value labels for data entry, as shown in Figure 3.18. To use the value label list for data entry:

1. Use the mouse or the arrow keys to select the cell. The actual value (not the label) is displayed in the cell editor.

2. Click the *right* mouse button or press ⇧Shift-F2 to display the list of value labels for that variable. If value labels have not been defined for the variable, no list appears.

3. Select the value label you want to enter from the list. You can use the arrow keys or the scroll bar to scroll through the list, or you can type the first letter of the value label to sequentially search the list for all value labels that start with that letter.

4. Double-click the *left* mouse button or press ↵Enter to enter the value that corresponds to the selected value label. When you leave the cell, the selected value label appears in the cell. (To cancel the operation and leave the original value in the cell, use the mouse to select another cell or press Esc.)

Figure 3.18   Data entry with value labels

	time	age	salnow	edlevel	work	jobcat
4	93	31.17	19200	16	1.83	COLLEGE TRAINEE
5	83	41.92	28350	CLERICAL / OFFICE TRA		EXEMPT EMPLOYEE
6	80	29.50	27250	SECURITY C / COLLEGE TR		COLLEGE TRAINEE
7	79	28.00	16080	EXEMPT EM		CLERICAL
8	67	28.75	14100	MBA TRAINE		CLERICAL
9	96	27.42	12420	15	1.17	CLERICAL

c:\spsswin\bank.sav

5:jobcat   5

Auto New Case

By default, a new case is automatically created if you move down a row from the last defined case by pressing the ↵Enter key. To turn this feature on and off, from the menus choose:

Utilities
  Auto New Case

Grid Lines

You can turn the Data Editor grid lines on and off for both display and printing. From the menus choose:

Utilities
  Grid Lines

Fonts

To change the font in which data values are displayed and printed, from the menus choose:

Utilities
  Fonts...

This opens the Fonts dialog box. Select a font, size, and style. Font changes are applied to all the data values in the Data Editor window. Fonts cannot be selectively applied to portions of the data. See Chapter 34 for more information.

Printing

To print the contents of the Data Editor:

1. Make the Data Editor the active window.

2. From the menus choose:

   File
     Print...

This opens the Print dialog box. You can print the entire data file or a selected area. For more information on printing, see Chapter 33.

Pending Transformations and the Data Editor

If you have pending transformations (see Chapter 36), the following limitations apply to the Data Editor:

- Variables cannot be inserted or deleted.
- Variable names and format type cannot be changed.
- Variables cannot be reordered.
- Templates cannot be applied to potential variables.
- If you change any data values, the changes may be overwritten when the transformations are executed. An alert box asks if you want to run the pending transformations.

Saving Data Files

Any changes you make to a data file in the Data Editor window last only for the duration of the SPSS session or until you open another data file—unless you explicitly save the changes. To save a previously defined SPSS data file:

1. Make the Data Editor the active window.

2. From the menus choose:

   File
     Save Data

The modified data file is saved, overwriting the previous version of the file.

Save As New File or Different Format

To save a new SPSS data file or to save the data in a different file format:

1. Make the Data Editor the active window.

2. From the menus choose:

   File
     Save As...

This opens the Save As Data File dialog box. See Chapter 2 for more information on saving data files.

Closing a Data File and Opening a Different One

Only one data file can be open at any time. If you have an open data file and then open a different one, SPSS automatically closes the open data file first. If there have been any changes to the data file since it was last saved, SPSS asks if you want to save the changes before it closes the file and opens the next one.

Keyboard Movement

If you don't have a mouse, you can use the keyboard to navigate the Data Editor window and select cells. Table 3.1 and Table 3.2 provide a list of the basic keyboard actions. A more complete list is provided in Appendix G.

Table 3.1   Keyboard movement

Action	Keys
Move and select one cell down	↓ or ↵Enter
Move and select one cell up	↑
Move and select once cell right or left	→ ← or Tab→ /⇧Shift+Tab→
Select first cell in case (row) or selected area	Home
Select last cell in case (row) or selected area	End
Select first case (row) for a variable (column)	Ctrl+↑
Select last case (row) for a variable (column)	Ctrl+↓
Select entire case (row)	⇧Shift+Space
Select entire variable (column)	Ctrl+Space
Extend selection	⇧Shift + arrow keys
Scroll up or down the height of the window	PgUp PgDn
Scroll left or right the width of the window	Ctrl+PgUp/ Ctrl+PgDn
Copy from selected cells	Ctrl+Ins
Cut from selected cells	⇧Shift+Del
Paste into selected cells	⇧Shift+Ins

Table 3.2   Edit Mode keyboard movement

Edit Mode	Keys
Switch to Edit Mode	F2
Move one character right or left	→ ←
Extend selection	⇧Shift + arrow keys
Move to beginning of value	Home
Move to end of value	End
Select to beginning of value	⇧Shift+Home
Select to end of value	⇧Shift+End

4 Output and Syntax Windows

In SPSS, there are two types of text windows:

Output windows. The text-based results of your SPSS session are displayed in output windows. This includes any nongraphic statistical results, such as a crosstabulation or a correlation matrix. You can edit and save the output in text files.

Syntax windows. Syntax windows are text windows that you can use to run SPSS commands with command syntax. You can generate SPSS command syntax by pasting your dialog box choices into a syntax window. You can then edit the command syntax to take advantage of features not available in the dialog box interface. You can save the commands in text files and run them again in other SPSS sessions. If you have existing command files, you can open these in a syntax window and run the commands.

You can open any text file in an output or a syntax window. However, output generated during the session is always displayed in an output window, and you can run command syntax only from a syntax window.

Output Windows

An output window opens automatically when you start an SPSS session. This output window opens a new, untitled text file. You can have more than one open output window. These windows can contain new or existing text files.

Opening a New Text File in an Output Window

To open an output window for a new text file, from the menus choose:

File
 New ▶
  SPSS Output

This opens an output window for a new text file.

Opening an Existing Text File in an Output Window

To open an existing text file in an output window, from the menus choose:

File
  Open ▶
    SPSS Output...

This opens the Open Output dialog box, as shown in Figure 4.1.

Figure 4.1   Open Output dialog box

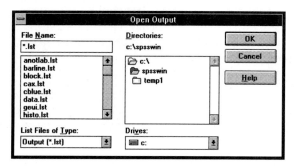

Select the file you want to open and click on OK. This opens a new output window containing the text file. The file can be a previously saved SPSS output or syntax file or a file created in another application and saved in text format.

File Name. You can select a file from the list or you can type in a filename, a directory path and filename, or a wildcard search. By default, SPSS looks for all files in the current directory with the extension *.lst* and displays them on the list.

List Files of Type. Provides a wildcard search list of default file extensions for appropriate file types. For output files, the list contains the default extension for SPSS output files (*.lst*) and the wildcard search for all files (*.*). The default extension, *.lst*, stands for **listing file**, a term used to denote a file of text-based SPSS results.

Directories. To change the directory location, select the name of the directory on the Directories list. Directories below the current directory are denoted by closed file folder icons. Directories above the current directory are denoted by open file folder icons The current directory is displayed above the list of directories and is also denoted by the last (lowest) open file folder icon.

Drives. To change the drive location, select a drive from the drop-down list of available drives.

Multiple Output Windows

If you have more than one output window open, SPSS sends output results to the **designated output window**. Although you can open multiple output windows, there can be only one designated output window. By default, the output window that opens automatically at the start of the session is the designated output window.

To designate a different output window, click on the [!] pushbutton on the icon bar at the top of the output window where you want to send the output, or make the output window the active window and choose Designate Window from the Utilities menu.

All new output is appended to the bottom of the text file in the designated output window. The window remains the designated output window until you select another. You cannot close the designated output window. There is always at least one open output window in an SPSS session.

Output Window Icon Bar

As shown in Figure 4.2, an icon bar at the top of each output window provides the following features:

Pause. Pauses the output display. By default, the display of output scrolls through the output window as it is generated. You can pause the display at any point.

Scroll. Scrolls the output display as it is generated.

Round. Rounds numbers in the highlighted area. By default, the Round pushbutton rounds numbers to integers (0 decimal positions). Use the Edit menu to specify a number of decimals for rounding (see "Round" on p. 93).

Glossary. This opens a Microsoft Help window with an index of SPSS glossary terms. Click on Search... and enter the term in the Search dialog box (see Chapter 38).

Displays the selected chart in the Chart Carousel. If a procedure generates high-resolution charts, the output window displays a message line for each chart, indicating the chart number and contents. Position the cursor anywhere on the message line for the chart you want and click on the chart icon to go directly to that chart.

Moves up and down the output window one page at a time. The start of each page is marked with a small, solid rectangle in the left margin. Page headers must be on (or page markers must be inserted manually) for this feature to work. (See Chapter 36 for information on output preferences and page headers.)

Moves up and down the output window one output block at a time. Each SPSS procedure that you run generates an **output block**. The start of each output block is marked with a small, hollow diamond in the left margin.

Makes this output window the designated output window. This pushbutton is enabled only if you have more than one output window open and is disabled for the currently designated output window.

Figure 4.2   Output window icon bar

Syntax Windows

The dialog box interface is designed to handle most of the capabilities of SPSS. Underlying the dialog boxes, there is a command language that you can use to access additional features and customize your analysis. After you make your dialog box selections, you can use the Paste pushbutton to paste this underlying command syntax into a syntax window. You can then edit the resulting text and run the modified commands from the syntax window (see "Using SPSS Command Syntax in a Syntax Window" on p. 87).

Opening a New Text File in a Syntax Window

If you don't have an open syntax window, one opens automatically the first time you use the Paste pushbutton. You can also use the menus to open a new text file in a syntax window. From the menus choose:

File
  New ▶
    SPSS Syntax

This opens a syntax window for a new text file.

Opening an Existing File in a Syntax Window

To open an existing text file in a syntax window, from the menus choose:

File
  Open ▶
    SPSS Syntax...

This opens the Open SPSS Syntax dialog box, as shown in Figure 4.3.

Figure 4.3   Open SPSS Syntax dialog box

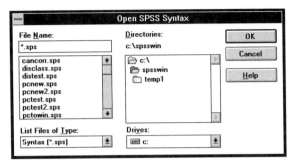

Select the file you want to open and click on OK. This opens a new output window containing the text file. The file can be a previously saved SPSS output or syntax file or a file created in another application and saved in text format.

File Name. You can select a file from the list or you can type in a filename, a directory path and filename, or a wildcard search. By default, SPSS looks for all files in the current directory with the extension .*sps* and displays them on the list.

List Files of Type. Provides a wildcard search list of default file extensions for appropriate file types. For output files, the list contains the default extension for SPSS command syntax files (*.*sps*) and the wildcard search for all files (*.*).

Directories. To change the directory location, select the name of the directory on the Directories list. Directories below the current directory are denoted by closed file folder icons. Directories above the current directory are denoted by open file folder icons. The current directory is displayed above the list of directories and is also denoted by the last (lowest) open file folder icon.

Drives. To change the drive location, select a drive from the drop-down list of available drives.

Using SPSS Command Syntax in a Syntax Window

You can use any text editor or word processing software that saves files in text format to create a file of SPSS command syntax and then open the file in a syntax window. You can also use the dialog box interface to generate the basic command syntax and then edit the commands in the syntax window.

Pasting Command Syntax from Dialog Boxes

Use the Paste pushbutton to paste your dialog box selections into a syntax window. If you don't have an open syntax window, one opens automatically the first time you paste from a dialog box.

Pasting Variable Names from the Variables Dialog Box

You can use the Variables dialog box to copy variable names and then paste them into command syntax. For more information, see Chapter 34.

Running SPSS Commands

You can run single commands or groups of commands in the syntax window.

1. Select the commands you want to run.

   Using the mouse, use the click-and-drag method to highlight the commands. Using the keyboard, press and hold the ⇧Shift key and use the up and down arrow keys to highlight the commands. The highlighted area can begin anywhere in the first command and end anywhere in the last command, as shown in Figure 4.4.

   If you want to run only a single command, you can position the cursor anywhere in the command line. If you want to run all the commands in the syntax window, you can choose Select All from the Edit menu.

2. Click on the Run pushbutton on the icon bar at the top of the syntax window (or press Ctrl-A).

Figure 4.4   Running selected commands

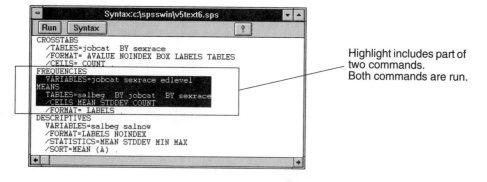

Highlight includes part of two commands.
Both commands are run.

Multiple Syntax Windows

You can have multiple syntax windows, but there is only one **designated syntax window**. If you have more than one syntax window open, the Paste pushbutton pastes command syntax into the designated syntax window. By default, the first syntax window opened is the designated syntax window. To designate a different syntax window, click on the [!] pushbutton on the icon bar at the top of the syntax window where you want to paste the commands, or make the syntax window the active window and choose Designate Window from the Utilities menu.

All new commands that you paste are appended to the bottom of the text file in the designated syntax window. The window remains the designated syntax window until you select another. If you close the designated syntax window, there is no designated syntax window until you select one. If there is no designated syntax window, a new one is automatically opened the next time you click on the Paste pushbutton.

Syntax Window Icon Bar

An icon bar at the top of each syntax window provides the following features:

Run. Runs the highlighted commands. If there is no highlighted text, SPSS runs the command line where the cursor is located.

Syntax. Opens a Help window containing a syntax chart for the command line where the cursor is located.

 Makes this syntax window the designated syntax window. This pushbutton is enabled only if you have more than one syntax window open and it is disabled for the currently designated syntax window.

Editing Text Files

You can edit text in syntax and output windows using text-editing features similar to those used in word processing software. You can:

- Insert or overtype text.
- Cut, copy, and paste blocks of text within and between text files and windows.
- Copy text to and from the Data Editor and other software applications.
- Search for and replace text strings.
- Change type fonts.

Basic Text-editing Concepts

SPSS follows the usual Windows conventions for editing text. It also provides features for copying tables in tab-delimited form (see "Edit Menu," below) and rounding numbers (see "Round" on p. 93). The following is a brief overview of some basic text-editing concepts:

- **Insertion point.** A blinking cursor (a vertical bar) in the active window indicates where text will be inserted or deleted.

- **Insert mode.** By default, new text is inserted between existing text at the insertion point. Text to the right of the insertion point moves as new text is entered.

- **Overtype mode.** To overtype text to the right of the insertion point, press the [Ins] key. The vertical bar at the insertion point changes to a rectangular cursor. To change back to insert mode, press the [Ins] key again.

- **Deleting text.** The [←Backspace] key deletes one character to the left of the cursor. The [Del] key deletes one character to the right of the cursor. Both the [←Backspace] and [Del] keys delete highlighted blocks of text (without putting the text on the clipboard).

- **Highlighting text.** To highlight entire lines of text, use the click-and-drag method with the left mouse button. To select a rectangular area of text, use the click-and-drag method with the right mouse button.

- **Cutting, copying, and pasting.** You can cut or copy highlighted text to the clipboard and paste the contents of the clipboard to another area of the same file, to another text file in another syntax or output window, to the Data Editor, or to another software application (for example, a spreadsheet or a word processing program).

Edit Menu

The following text-editing options are available with the Edit menu:

Cut. Cuts the highlighted text and puts it on the clipboard.

Copy. Copies the highlighted text onto the clipboard.

Copy Table. Copies the highlighted columns onto the clipboard in tab-delimited format. This is useful for copying output tables (for example, frequency distributions, means tables, etc.) into spreadsheet or word processing files.

Paste. Pastes the contents of the clipboard into the file at the insertion point. In insert mode, the text is inserted between existing text, and text to the right of the cursor moves over. In overtype mode, text to the right of the cursor is replaced with the pasted text. Paste is enabled only if there is something on the clipboard.

Clear. Cuts the highlighted text without putting it on the clipboard. (You cannot paste the text anywhere else.)

Select. The following options are available:

All. Selects the entire contents of the active output or syntax window.

Page. Selects the contents of the current page in the active output window.

Output. Selects the contents of the current output block in the active output window.

Command. Selects the contents of the current command in the active syntax window.

Search for Text. Searches for a text string in the active syntax or output window. This opens the Search dialog box.

Replace Text. Searches for and replaces a text string with a new text string. This opens the Replace dialog box.

Round. Rounds any numbers in the highlighted area. This opens the Round dialog box.

Add Page Break. Adds a page break at the current cursor location in the active output window.

Add Output Break. Adds an output break at the current cursor location in the active output window.

Search for Text

To search for a text string in a syntax or output window, from the menus choose:

Edit
  Search for Text...

This opens the Search for Text dialog box, as shown in Figure 4.5.

Figure 4.5   Search for Text dialog box

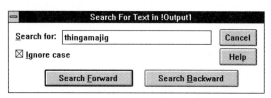

Search Forward. Searches forward from the cursor location to the end of the file.

Search Backward. Searches backward from the cursor location to the beginning of the file.

The following option is also available:

❑ **Ignore case.** By default, SPSS searches for any occurrence of the specified text string, regardless of case. If you want to restrict the search to occurrences that match the case as entered, deselect this default setting.

Replace Text

To search for a text string and replace it with another text string, from the menus choose:

Edit
  Replace Text...

This opens the Replace Text dialog box, as shown in Figure 4.6.

Figure 4.6   Replace Text dialog box

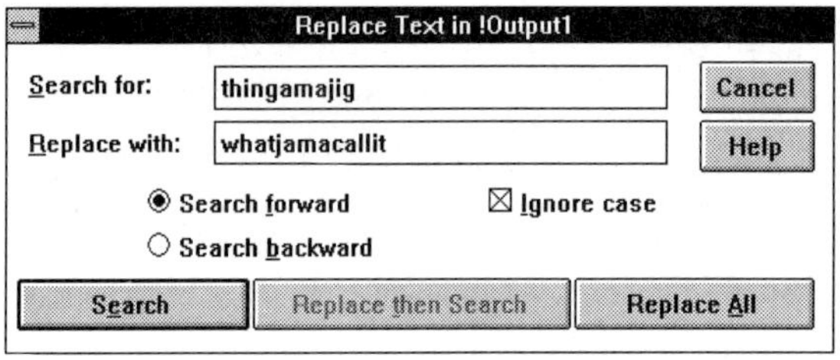

Search. Finds the next occurrence of the text string.

Replace then Search. Replaces the current occurrence of the text string and searches for the next one. If an occurrence of the text string is not currently highlighted in the syntax or output window, click on Search to find and highlight the text string.

Replace All. Replaces all occurrences of the text string from the cursor location to the end (or beginning) of the file.

For search direction, you can choose one of the following alternatives:

○ **Search forward.** Searches forward from the cursor location to the end of the file.

○ **Search backward.** Searches backward from the cursor location to the beginning of the file.

The following option is also available:

❑ **Ignore case.** By default, SPSS searches for any occurrence of the specified text string, regardless of case. If you want to restrict the search to occurrences that match the case as entered, deselect this default setting.

Round

To round or truncate highlighted values in a syntax or output window, from the menus choose:

Edit
  Round...

This opens the Round dialog box, as shown in Figure 4.7.

Figure 4.7   Round dialog box

Number of decimals. Enter an integer value from 0 to 9. The default value is 0.

Round. Rounds values in the highlighted area to the specified number of decimals.

Truncate. Truncates values in the highlighted area at the specified number of decimals.

You can also round values in an output window with the Round pushbutton on the icon bar. This rounds numeric values based on the number of decimals currently specified in the Round dialog box. By default, it rounds values to integers.

Type Fonts

To change the font type, style, and size of text in a syntax or output window:

1. Make the syntax or output window the active window.

2. From the menus choose:

    Utilities
      Fonts...

This opens the Fonts menu, which contains a list of the available fixed-pitch fonts. Font changes are applied to all the text in the active window. Fonts cannot be selectively applied to portions of the file. (See Chapter 34 for more information on fonts.)

Copying and Pasting Output into Other Applications

You can copy and paste SPSS output into other applications, such as a word processing program, in several ways:

- Highlight the text you want, select Copy from the Edit menu, paste it into the other application, and then apply a fixed-pitch font to the block of text for proper alignment. If the output contains box characters (such as the line-drawing characters in crosstabulations), these characters are converted to typewriter characters.

- Highlight a block of tabular output, such as a frequency table, select Copy Table from the Edit menu, paste the text into the other application, and then adjust the tab stops (if necessary). This is effective only for aligned columns of text. If the output contains any box characters, those characters are ignored.

- Select a fixed-pitch, TrueType font (for example, Courier New) for the output display, select Copy from the Edit menu, select Paste Special from the other application's Edit menu, and then select Picture from the Paste Special dialog box. All text is correctly aligned, and any box-drawing characters are preserved. However, since the text is treated as a picture, you cannot edit the contents.

Note: Paste Special may not be available for some applications. This feature enables the application to paste the contents of the clipboard as a "picture" in Windows metafile format.

Saving Text Files

New syntax and output files and changes to existing text files are not saved unless you explicitly save them. To save changes to an existing text file:

1. Make the syntax or output window containing the file the active window.

2. From the menus choose:

    File
      Save SPSS Output

    or

    File
      Save SPSS Syntax

The modified text file is saved, overwriting the previous version of the file.

Save As New File

To save a new syntax or output text file or to save changes to an existing file as a new file:

1. Make the syntax or output window containing the file the active window.

2. From the menus choose:

    File
      Save As...

3. This opens the Save Output SPSS Output As dialog box for output windows, as shown in Figure 4.8, or the Save SPSS Syntax As dialog box for syntax windows. Enter a name for the file in the Save As dialog box and click on OK.

Figure 4.8   Save As Output dialog box

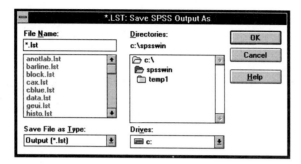

File Name. You can type in a filename, a directory path and filename, or a wildcard search. By default, SPSS provides an extension of .*lst* for output files or .*sps* for syntax files and displays a list of files in the current directory with that extension. If you select a filename from the list, SPSS asks if you want to replace the existing file.

List Files of Type. Provides a wildcard search list of default file extensions for appropriate file types. For output files, the list contains the default extension for SPSS output files (*.*lst*) and the wildcard search for all files (*.*). For command syntax files, the list contains the default extension for SPSS syntax files (*.*sps*) and the wildcard search for all files (*.*)

Directories. To change the directory location, select the name of the directory on the Directories list. Directories below the current directory are denoted by closed file folder icons. Directories above the current directory are denoted by open file folder icons The current directory is displayed above the list of directories and is also denoted by the last (lowest) open file folder icon.

Drives. To change the drive location, select a drive from the drop-down list of available drives.

Saving Selected Areas of Text Files

To save a selected area of a syntax or output file, highlight the area you want to save before choosing Save or Save As from the File menu. An alert box will ask if you want to save the selected area only. Click on Yes to save the selected area, or click on No to save the entire file.

5 Data Transformations

In an ideal situation, your raw data are perfectly suitable for the type of analysis you want to perform, and any relationships between variables are either conveniently linear or neatly orthogonal. Unfortunately, this is rarely the case. Preliminary analysis may reveal inconvenient coding schemes or coding errors, or data transformations may be required in order to coax out the true relationship between variables.

With SPSS, you can perform data transformations ranging from simple tasks, such as collapsing categories for analysis, to creating new variables based on complex equations and conditional statements.

Computing Values

To compute values for a variable based on numeric transformations of other variables, from the menus choose:

Transform
  Compute...

This opens the Compute Variable dialog box, as shown in Figure 5.1.

Figure 5.1   Compute Variable dialog box

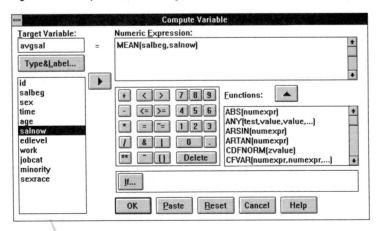

Target Variable. The name of the variable that receives the computed value. The target variable can be an existing variable or a new one. New variable names must begin with a letter and cannot exceed eight characters. (See Chapter 2 for complete variable naming rules.) By default, new computed variables are numeric (see "Variable Type and Label" on p. 104 for information on computing new string variables).

Numeric Expression. The expression used to compute the value of the target variable. The expression can use existing variable names, constants, arithmetic operators, and functions. You can type and edit the expression in the text box just like text in a syntax or output window (see Chapter 4). You can also use the calculator pad, variable list, and function list to paste elements into the expression.

Calculator Pad

The calculator pad contains numbers, arithmetic operators, relational operators, and logical operators (Table 5.1). You can use it like a calculator (using the mouse to point and click on keys) or simply as a reference for the correct symbols to use for various operators.

Table 5.1   Calculator pad operators

Arithmetic Operators		Relational Operators		Logical Operators	
+	Addition	<	Less than	&	And. Both relations must be true.
–	Subtraction	>	Greater than			
*	Multiplication	<=	Less than or equal to	|	Or. Either relation can be true.
/	Division	>=	Greater than or equal to		
**	Exponentiation	=	Equal to	~	Not. Reverses the true/false outcome of the expression.
( )	Order of operations	~=	Not equal to		

Arithmetic Operators

Since fairly complex expressions are possible, it is important to keep in mind the order in which operations are performed. Functions are evaluated first, followed by exponentiation, then multiplication and division, and finally addition and subtraction. You can control the order of operations by enclosing the operation you want executed first in parentheses. You can use the ( ) key on the calculator pad to enclose a highlighted portion of the expression in parentheses.

Relational Operators

A relation is a logical expression that compares two values using a relational operator. They are primarily used in conditional transformations (see "Relational and Logical Operators in Conditional Expressions" on p. 104).

Logical Operators

You can use logical operators to join two relations or reverse the true/false outcome of a conditional expression. They are primarily used in conditional transformations (see "Relational and Logical Operators in Conditional Expressions" on p. 104).

Functions

The function list contains over 70 built-in functions, including:

- Arithmetic functions
- Statistical functions
- Distribution functions
- Logical functions
- Date and time aggregation and extraction functions
- Missing-value functions
- Cross-case functions
- String functions

The following sections provide descriptions of some of the more commonly used functions. A complete list of functions is provided in the *SPSS Base System Syntax Reference Guide*.

Arithmetic Functions

ABS(numexpr). Absolute value. If the value of variable *scale* is −4.7, ABS(scale) results in a value of 4.7, and ABS(scale − 5) results in a value of 9.7.

RND(numexpr). Round to the nearest integer. If the value of *scale* is 4.7, RND(scale) results in a value of 5, and RND(scale + 5) results in a value of 10.

TRUNC(numexpr). Truncate to an integer. If the value of *scale* is 4.7, TRUNC(scale) results in a value of 4, and TRUNC(scale + 5) results in a value of 9.

MOD(numexpr,modulus). Remainder of the first argument (numexpr) divided by the second argument (modulus). If the value of *year* is 1983, MOD(year, 100) results in a value of 83. The two arguments must be separated by a comma.

SQRT(numexpr). Square root. If *scale* is 4.7, SQRT(scale) results in a value of 2.17, and SQRT(scale − 0.7) results in a value of 2.

EXP(numexpr). Exponential. *e* is raised to the power of the argument (numexpr). If the value of *scale* is 2, EXP(scale) results in a value of 7.39.

LG10(numexpr). Base 10 logarithm. If the value of *scale* is 4.7, LG10(scale) results in a value of 0.67.

LN(numexpr). Natural or Naperian logarithm (base e). If the value of *scale* is 10, LN(scale) results in a value of 2.3.

ARSIN(numexpr). Arcsine. The result is expressed in radians.

ARTAN(numexpr). Arctangent. The result is given in radians.

SIN(radians). Sine. The argument must be specified in radians.

COS(radians). Cosine. The argument must be specified in radians.

All arithmetic functions except MOD have a single argument enclosed in parentheses. MOD has two arguments that must be separated by a comma. Arguments can be variables, constants, or expressions.

Statistical Functions

SUM(numexpr,numexpr,...). Sum of the values across the argument list. For example, SUM(var1, var2, var3) computes the sum of the three variables.

MEAN(numexpr, numexpr,...). Mean of the values across the argument list. For example, MEAN(var1, var2, 5) computes the mean of the two variables and the constant 5.

SD(numexpr, numexpr,...). Standard deviation of the values across the argument list. For example, SD(var1, var2, var3**2) computes a standard deviation based on the values of *var1* and *var2* and the squared value of *var3*.

VARIANCE(numexpr,numexpr,...). Variance of the values across the argument list.

CFVAR(numexpr,numexpr,...). Coefficient of variance of the values across the argument list.

MIN(value,value,...). Minimum value across the argument list.

MAX(value,value,...). Maximum value across the argument list.

All statistical functions have at least two arguments enclosed in parentheses. Arguments must be separated by commas. Arguments can be numeric variables, constants, or expressions.

Logical Functions

RANGE(test,lo,hi...). True if the value of the first argument is within the inclusive range(s) defined by the remaining arguments. The first argument (test) is usually a variable name. The other arguments are pairs of values defining ranges. You can have more than one pair of low and high values. For example, RANGE(year, 1900, 1949, 1960, 1999) is true if the value of *year* is between 1900 and 1949 or between 1960 and 1999, and it is false for the values 1950 through 1959.

ANY(test,value,value...). True if the value of the first argument matches the value of any of the remaining arguments on the list. The first argument (test) is usually a variable name, as in ANY(year, 1951, 1958, 1986, 1987).

Random Number Functions

NORMAL(stddev). Each case is assigned a pseudo-random number from a normal distribution with a mean of 0 and a user-specified standard deviation.

UNIFORM (max). Each case is assigned a pseudo-random number from a uniform distribution with a minimum of 0 and a user-specified maximum.

Distribution Functions

SPSS provides a variety of cumulative, inverse cumulative, and random number generator distribution functions. Cumulative distribution functions (CDF) are available for continuous, discrete, and noncentral distributions. Inverse cumulative distribution functions (inverse CDF) are available only for continuous distributions. Random number generator distribution functions (RNG) are available for continuous and discrete distributions. Table 5.2 lists the types of distribution functions available.

Table 5.2 Distribution functions

Continuous[*]	Discrete[†]	Noncentral[‡]
Beta	Bernoulli	Beta
Cauchy	Binomial	Chi-square
Chi-square	Geometric	F
Exponential	Hypergeometric	Student's t
F	Negative Binomial	
Gamma	Poisson	
Laplace		
Logistic		
Lognormal		
Normal		
Pareto		
Student's t		
Uniform		
Weibull		

*CDF, inverse CDF, and RNG

†CDF and inverse CDF

‡CDF only

See the *SPSS Base System Syntax Reference Guide* for a complete list of distribution functions and the required arguments.

Nested Functions

A function can be used as an argument in another function, as in

```
MEAN(RND(var1),TRUNC(var2))
```

or even

```
MEAN(RND(SD(var1)),TRUNC(SQRT(var2)))
```

Missing Values with Functions

Functions and simple arithmetic expression treat missing values in different ways. In the expression,

```
(var1+var2+var3)/3
```

the result is missing if a case has a missing value for *any* of the three variables. However, in the expression,

```
MEAN(var1, var2, var3)
```

the result is missing only if the case has missing values for *all* three variables. For statistical functions, you can specify the minimum number of arguments that must have nonmissing values. To do so, type a period and the number after the function name (before the argument list), as in

```
MEAN.2(var1, var2, var3)
```

In this example, at least two of the three variables on the argument list must contain a nonmissing value for the function to return a nonmissing result.

Pasting and Editing Functions

Pasting a Function into an Expression. To paste a function into an expression:

1. Position the cursor in the expression at the point where you want the function to appear.

2. Double-click on the function on the Functions list (or select the function and click on the ▲ pushbutton).

The function is inserted in the expression. If you highlight part of the expression and then insert the function, the highlighted portion of the expression is used as the first argument in the function.

Editing a Function in an Expression. The function isn't complete until you enter the **arguments**, represented by question marks in the pasted function. The number of question marks indicates the minimum number of arguments required to complete the function. To edit a function:

1. Highlight the question mark(s) in the pasted function.

2. Enter the arguments. If the arguments are variable names, you can paste them from the source variable list.

Conditional Expressions

You can use **conditional expressions** (also called logical expressions) to apply transformations to selected subsets of cases. A conditional expression returns a value of true, false, or missing for each case. If the result of a conditional expression is true, the transformation is applied to that case. If the result is false or missing, the transformation is not applied to the case.

To specify a conditional expression, click on If... in the Compute Variable dialog box. This opens the If Cases dialog box, as shown in Figure 5.2.

Figure 5.2   If Cases dialog box

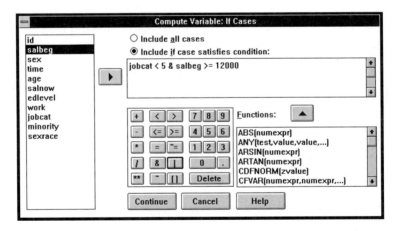

You can choose one of the following alternatives:

○ **Include all cases**. This is the default. Values are calculated for all cases, and any conditional expressions are ignored.

○ **Include if case satisfies condition**. Enter the conditional expression in the text box. The expression can include variable names, constants, arithmetic operators, numeric and other functions, logical variables, and relational operators.

Calculator Pad and Function List

These are identical to those described for the Compute Variable dialog box. See "Calculator Pad" on p. 98 and "Functions" on p. 99.

Relational and Logical Operators in Conditional Expressions

Most conditional expressions contain at least one relational operator, as in

```
age>=21
```

or

```
salary*3<100000
```

In the first example, only cases with a value of 21 or greater for *age* are selected. In the second, *salary* multiplied by 3 must be less than 100,000 for a case to be selected.

You can also link two or more conditional expressions using logical operators, as in

```
age>=21 | educat=1
```

or

```
salary*3<100000 & jobcat~=5
```

In the first example, cases that meet either the *age* condition or the *educat* condition are selected. In the second, both the *salary* and *jobcat* conditions must be met for a case to be selected.

Variable Type and Label

By default, new computed variables are numeric. To compute new string variables or assign descriptive variable labels, click on Type & Label.... in the Compute Variable dialog box. This opens the Type and Label dialog box, as shown in Figure 5.3.

Figure 5.3   Type and Label dialog box

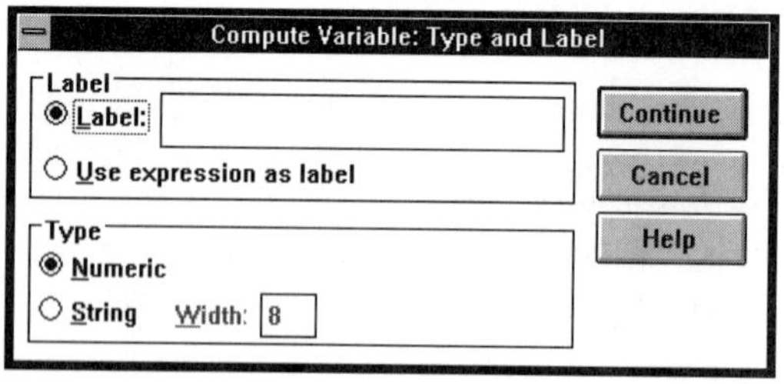

Label. Descriptive variable label. You can choose one of the following alternatives:

○ **Label**. Enter a label up to 120 characters long.

○ **Use expression as label**. The first 110 characters of the expression are used as the label.

Type. Variable format type. You can choose one of the following alternatives:

○ **Numeric**. This is the default setting.

○ **String**. Alphanumeric string.

Width. Enter the maximum width. A width specification is required for string variables.

Syntax Rules for Expressions

Items selected from the calculator pad, function list, and source variable list are pasted with correct syntax. If you type an expression in the text box or edit part of it (such as arguments for a function), remember the following simple syntax rules:

- String variable values must be enclosed in apostrophes or quotation marks, as in NAME='Fred'. If the string value includes an apostrophe, enclose the string in quotation marks.

- The argument list for a function must be enclosed in parentheses. You can insert a space between the argument name and the parentheses, but none is required.

- Multiple arguments in a function must be separated by commas. You can insert spaces between arguments, but none is required.

- Each relation in a complex expression must be complete by itself. For example, age>=18 & age<35 is correct, while age>=18 & <35 generates an error.

- A period (.) is the only valid decimal indicator in expressions, regardless of your Windows international settings.

Random Number Seed

Computations or conditional expressions that include random numbers (for example, the NORM and UNIFORM distribution functions) use the SPSS pseudo-random number generator, which begins with a **seed**, a very large integer value. Within a session, SPSS uses a different seed each time you generate a set of random numbers, producing different results. If you want to duplicate the same random numbers, you can reset the seed value. From the menus, choose:

Transform
  Random Number Seed...

This opens the Random Number Seed dialog box, as shown in Figure 5.4.

Figure 5.4   Random Number Seed dialog box

The seed can be any positive integer value up to 999,999,999. SPSS resets the seed to the specified value each time you open the dialog box and click on OK.

To duplicate the same series of random numbers, you should set the seed *before* you generate the series for the first time. Since SPSS resets the seed as it generates a series of random numbers, it is virtually impossible to determine what seed value was used previously unless you specified the value yourself.

Counting Occurrences

To count occurrences of the same value(s) across a list of variables within cases, from the menus choose:

Transform
  Count Occurrences...

This opens the Count Occurrences dialog box, as shown in Figure 5.5.

Figure 5.5   Count Occurrences dialog box

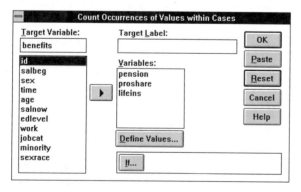

Target Variable. The name of the variable that receives the counted value. The target variable can be an existing numeric variable or a new one. New variable names must begin with a letter and cannot exceed eight characters. (See Chapter 2 for complete variable naming rules.) The target variable must be numeric.

Target Label. Descriptive variable label for the target variable. The label can be up to 120 characters. If the target variable already exists, the current label (if any) is displayed.

Variables. The selected numeric or string variables from the source list for which you want to count occurrences of certain values. The list cannot contain both numeric and string variables.

Defining Values to Count

To specify the values to count, highlight a variable on the selected variables list and click on Define Values... in the Count Occurrences dialog box. This opens the Values to Count dialog box, as shown in Figure 5.6.

Figure 5.6   Values to Count dialog box

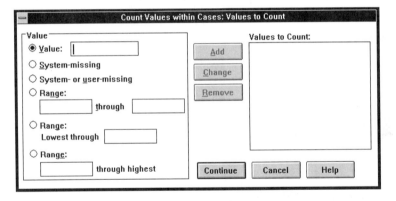

You can specify a single value, a range, or a combination of the two. To build a list of values to count, make selections from the Value alternatives and click on Add after each selection. Each occurrence of any value on the list across the variable list is counted.

Value. You can choose one of the following alternatives:

○ **Value**. Counts occurrences of the value you have specified.

○ **System-missing**. Counts occurrences of the system-missing value. This appears as SYSMIS on the Values to Count list. Not available for string variables.

○ **System- or user-missing**. Counts occurrences of any missing values, both system-missing and user-missing values. This appears as MISSING on the Values to Count list.

○ **Range**. Counts occurrences of values within the specified range. Not available for string variables.

○ **Range: Lowest through n.** Counts occurrences of any value from the lowest observed value to the specified value. Not available for string variables.

○ **Range: n through highest.** Counts occurrences from the specified value to the highest observed value. Not available for string variables.

All range specifications include any user-specified missing values that fall within the range.

Selecting Subsets of Cases

You can count occurrences of values for selected subsets of cases using conditional expressions. To specify a conditional expression, click on If... in the Count Occurrences dialog box. This opens the If Cases dialog box, as shown in Figure 5.2. (See "Conditional Expressions" on p. 103 for a description of this dialog box and instructions on how to specify conditional expressions. See "Calculator Pad" on p. 98, "Functions" on p. 99, and "Syntax Rules for Expressions" on p. 105 for additional information.)

Recoding Values

You can modify data values by recoding them. This is particularly useful for collapsing or combining categories. You can recode the values within existing variables or you can create new variables based on the recoded values of existing variables.

Recode into Same Variables

To recode the values of an existing variable, from the menus choose:

Transform
  Recode ▶
    Into Same Variables...

This opens the Recode into Same Variables dialog box, as shown in Figure 5.7.

Figure 5.7   Recode into Same Variables dialog box

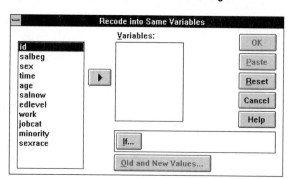

The source variable list contains the numeric and string variables in the data file. Select one or more variables for recoding. If you select multiple variables, they must all be the same type. You cannot recode numeric and string variables together.

Defining Values to Recode

To define the values to recode, click on Old and New Values... in the Recode into Same Variables dialog box. This opens the Old and New Values dialog box, as shown in Figure 5.8.

Figure 5.8   Old and New Values dialog box

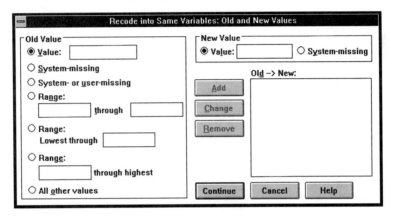

For each value (or range) that you want to recode, specify the old value and the new value, and then click on Add. You can recode multiple old values into a single new value. You cannot, however, recode a single old value into multiple new values.

Old Value. The current values for the variable that you want to recode into new values. You can choose one of the following alternatives:

○ **Value.** Enter a single value. String values are automatically enclosed in apostrophes or quotes when they appear on the value list. If you enter quotation marks or apostrophes, they are considered part of the string value.

○ **System-missing.** The system-missing value. This appears as SYSMIS on the value list. Not available for string variables.

○ **System- or user-missing.** All missing values, including user-missing values. This appears as MISSING on the value list.

○ **Range.** Enter an inclusive range of values. Not available for string variables.

○ **Range: Lowest through n.** Any value from the lowest observed value to the specified value. Not available for string variables.

○ **Range: n through highest**. Any value from the specified value to the highest observed value. Not available for string variables.

○ **All other values**. Any remaining values not previously specified. This appears as ELSE on the value list.

New Value. The recoded value. You can choose one of the following alternatives:

○ **Value**. Enter a value. String values are automatically enclosed in apostrophes or quotes when they appear on the value list. If you enter quotation marks or apostrophes, they are considered part of the string value.

○ **System-missing**. The system-missing value. This appears as SYSMIS on the value list. Not available for string variables.

You can use the same new value with multiple old value specifications. This is particularly useful for combining noncontiguous categories that can't be defined in a range.

Recode Order

Recode specifications are automatically sorted on the value list, based on the old value specification, using the following order:

- Single values
- Missing values
- Ranges
- All other values

If you change a recode specification on the list, SPSS automatically re-sorts the list, if necessary, to maintain this order.

Selecting Subsets of Cases

You can recode values for selected subsets of cases using conditional expressions. To specify a conditional expression, click on If... in the Recode into Same Variables dialog box. This opens the If Cases dialog box, as shown in Figure 5.2. (See "Conditional Expressions" on p. 103 for a description of this dialog box and instructions on how to specify conditional expressions. See "Calculator Pad" on p. 98, "Functions" on p. 99, and "Syntax Rules for Expressions" on p. 105 for additional information.)

Recode into Different Variables

To create new variables based on the recoded values of existing variables, from the menus choose:

Transform
  Recode ▶
    Into Different Variables...

This opens the Recode into Different Variables dialog box, as shown in Figure 5.9.

Figure 5.9   Recode into Different Variables dialog box

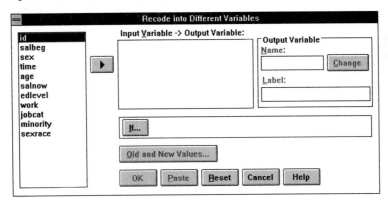

The source variable list contains the numeric and string variables in the data file. Select one or more variables for recoding. If you select multiple variables, they must all be the same type. You cannot recode numeric and string variables together.

Input Variable –> Output Variable. Selected variables from the source list appear in the input variable column. (The word Input changes to Numeric or String depending on the type of variables selected.) A question mark in the output variable column indicates that a name needs to be supplied for the output variable. You must provide output variable names for all selected input variables.

Output Variable. The new variable that receives the recoded values.

  Name. An output variable name is required for each input variable. Highlight the input variable on the selected variable list and then type a name for the corresponding output variable. Variable names must start with a letter and cannot exceed eight characters. (See Chapter 2 for complete variable naming rules).

  Label. Optional descriptive variable label, up to 120 characters long.

After entering the output variable name and the optional label, click on Change to put the name on the output variable list, next to the corresponding input variable name.

Defining Values to Recode

To define the values to recode, click on Old and New Values... in the Recode into Different Variables dialog box. This opens the Old and New Values dialog box, as shown in Figure 5.10.

Figure 5.10   Old and New Values dialog box

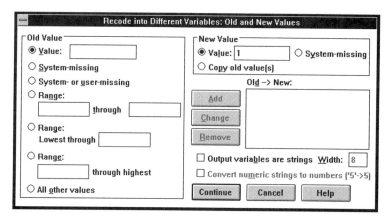

For each value (or range) that you want to recode, specify the old value from the input variable and the new value for the output variable, and then click on Add. You can recode multiple old values into a single new value. You cannot, however, recode a single old value into multiple new values.

Old Value. The values for the input variable that you want to recode for the output variable. You can choose one of the following alternatives:

○ **Value**. Enter a value. String values are automatically enclosed in apostrophes or quotes when they appear on the value list. If you enter quotation marks or apostrophes, they are considered part of the string value.

○ **System-missing**. The system-missing value. This appears as SYSMIS on the value list. Not available for string variables.

○ **System- or user-missing**. All missing values, including user-missing values. This appears as MISSING on the value list.

○ **Range**. Enter an inclusive range of values. Not available for string variables.

○ **Range: Lowest through n**. Any value from the lowest observed value to the specified value. Not available for string variables.

○ **Range: n through highest**. Any value from the specified value to the highest observed value. Not available for string variables.

○ **All other values**. Any remaining values not previously specified. This appears as ELSE on the value list.

New Value. The recoded value for the output variable. You can choose one of the following alternatives:

○ **Value**. Enter a value. String values are automatically enclosed in apostrophes or quotes when they appear on the value list. If you enter quotation marks or apostrophes, they are considered part of the string value.

○ **System-missing**. The system-missing value. This appears as SYSMIS on the value list. Not available for string variables.

○ **Copy old value(s)**. Retains the input variable value.

You can use the same new value with multiple old value specifications. This is particularly useful for combining noncontiguous categories that can't be defined in a range.

For string variables, there are two additional parameters:

❏ **Output variables are strings**. Select this item if your new output variables are string variables. This is required for new string variables.

Width. Enter an integer between 1 and 255 for the maximum width of the string.

❏ **Convert numeric strings to numbers**. Valid values are numbers with an optional leading sign (+ or –) and a single period for a decimal point. Alphanumeric strings are assigned the system-missing value.

Missing Values

Any unspecified old values for the input variable are undefined for the new output variable and are assigned the system-missing value. To make sure unspecified old values for the input variable receive a nonmissing value for the output variable, do the following:

1. For the old value, select All other values.

2. For the new value, select Copy old value(s).

3. Click on Add.

ELSE –> COPY appears on the value list. Any unspecified values for the input variable are retained for the output variable.

Selecting Subsets of Cases

You can recode values for selected subsets of cases using conditional expressions. To specify a conditional expression, click on If... in the Recode into Different Variables dialog box. This opens the If Cases dialog box, as shown in Figure 5.2. (See "Conditional

Expressions" on p. 103 for a description of this dialog box and instructions on how to specify conditional expressions. See "Calculator Pad" on p. 98, "Functions" on p. 99, and "Syntax Rules for Expressions" on p. 105 for additional information.)

Ranking Data

To compute ranks, normal and savage scores, or classify cases into groups based on percentile values, from the menus choose:

Transform
  Rank Cases...

This opens the Rank Cases dialog box, as shown in Figure 5.11.

Figure 5.11   Rank Cases dialog box

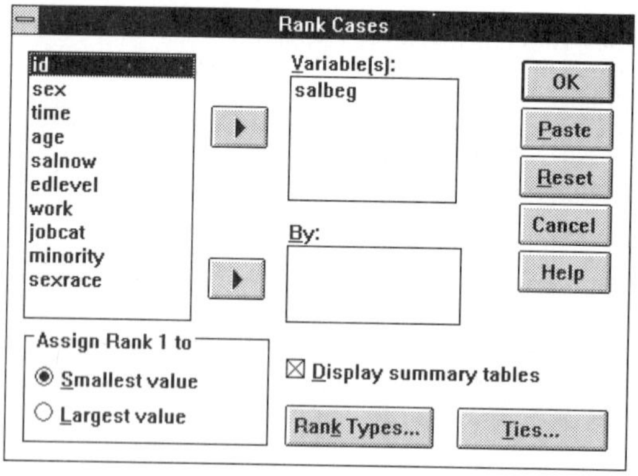

The numeric variables in the data file are displayed on the source variable list. Select one or more variables for which you want to compute ranks. To obtain the default simple ranking in ascending order with the mean rank assigned to ties, click on OK. SPSS creates a new variable that contains the rankings. The original variable is unaffected.

Optionally, you can organize rankings into subgroups by selecting one or more **grouping variables** for the By list. Ranks are computed within each group. Groups are defined by the combination of values of the grouping variables. For example, if you select *sex* and *minority* as grouping variables, ranks are computed for each combination of *sex* and *minority*.

Assign Rank 1 to. There are two options for the order in which values are ranked:

○ **Smallest value.** Assigns ranks by ascending order, with the smallest value receiving a rank of 1. This is the default.

○ **Largest value.** Assigns ranks by descending order, with the largest value receiving a rank of 1.

SPSS automatically creates a new variable name and a descriptive variable label for each variable ranked and each ranking method (see "Ranking Method," below). The following option is available for displaying a summary table of new variable names:

❑ **Display summary tables.** Displays a table of new variable names and labels that describe the variable ranked, ranking method, and any grouping variables. This is displayed by default. Deselect this item to suppress the summary table.

Ranking Method

Simple ranks are computed by default. To choose other ranking methods, click on Rank Types... in the Rank Cases dialog box. This opens the Rank Types dialog box, as shown in Figure 5.12.

Figure 5.12 Rank Types dialog box

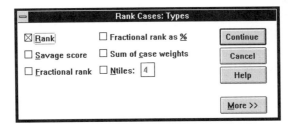

You can select multiple methods. A separate ranking variable is created for each method. You can choose one or more of the following methods:

❑ **Rank.** Simple rank. This is the default.

❑ **Savage score.** Scores based on an exponential distribution.

❑ **Fractional rank.** Each rank is divided by the number of cases with valid values or by the sum of any weighting variables (see Chapter 6).

❑ **Fractional rank as %.** Each rank is divided by the number of cases with valid values and multiplied by 100.

❑ **Sum of case weights.** The value of the variable is a constant for cases in the same group.

❑ **Ntiles.** A user-specified number of percentiles, each with approximately the same number of cases.

Proportion Estimates and Normal Scores

To create new ranking variables based on proportion estimates and normal scores, click on More>> in the Rank Types dialog box. The dialog box expands, as shown in Figure 5.13.

Figure 5.13   Expanded Rank Types dialog box

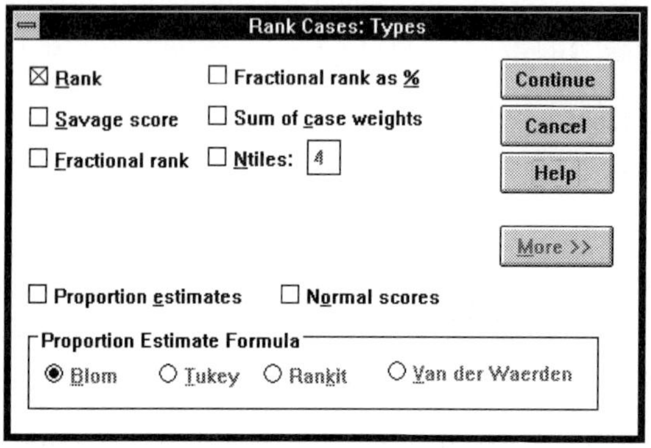

You can choose one or both of the following:

❏ **Proportion estimates**. The estimate of the cumulative proportion (area) of the distribution corresponding to a particular rank.

❏ **Normal scores**. The new variable contains the Z scores from the standard normal distribution that correspond to the estimated cumulative proportion. For example, if the estimated cumulative proportion is 0.50, the normal score is 0.

Proportion Estimate Formula. You can choose one of the following formula methods:

○ **Blom**. Blom's transformation, defined by the formula $(r - 3/8)\,/\,(w + 1/4)$, where w is the number of observations and r is rank, ranging from 1 to w (Blom, 1958). This is the default.

○ **Tukey**. Tukey's transformation, defined by the formula $(r - 1/3)\,/\,(w + 1/3)$, where w is the sum of case weights and r is the rank, ranging from 1 to w (Tukey, 1962).

○ **Rankit**. Uses the formula $(r - 1/2)\,/\,w$, where w is the number of observations and r is the rank, ranging from 1 to w (Chambers et al., 1983).

○ **Van der Waerden**. Van der Waerden's transformation, defined by the formula $r/\,(w + 1)$, where w is the sum of case weights and r is the rank, ranging from 1 to w (Lehmann, 1975).

Rank Ties

By default, cases with the same values for a variable are assigned the average (mean) of the ranks for the tied values. To choose an alternate method for handling ties, click on Ties... in the Rank Cases dialog box. This opens the Rank Ties dialog box, as shown in Figure 5.14.

Figure 5.14   Rank Ties dialog box

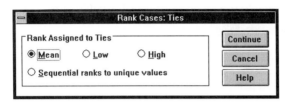

Rank Assigned to Ties. You can choose one of the following alternatives for assigning ranks to tied values:

○ **Mean**. Average rank assigned to tied values. This is the default.

○ **Low**. Lowest rank assigned to tied values.

○ **High**. Highest rank assigned to ties.

○ **Sequential ranks to unique values**. Ranks are assigned from 1 to D, where D is the number of unique values. Cases with the same value receive the same rank.

Table 5.3 shows the effects of each method on a group of data values.

Table 5.3   Alternatives for ranking ties

Value	Mean	Low	High	Sequential
10	1	1	1	1
15	3	2	4	2
15	3	2	4	2
15	3	2	4	2
16	5	5	5	3
20	6	6	6	4

Creating Consecutive Integers from Numeric and String Values

When category codes are not sequential, the resulting empty cells reduce performance and increase memory requirements for many SPSS procedures. Additionally, some procedures cannot use long string variables, and some require consecutive integer values for factor levels.

To recode string and numeric variables into consecutive integers, from the menus choose:

Transform
  Automatic Recode...

This opens the Automatic Recode dialog box, as shown in Figure 5.15.

Figure 5.15   Automatic Recode dialog box

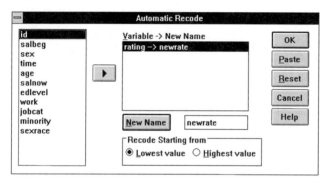

The variables in the working data file are displayed on the source variable list. Select one or more variables for which you want to recode values into consecutive integers. SPSS creates new variables containing the recoded values. The original variables are not affected. Any existing variable or value labels are retained for the new variables. If the original value doesn't have a value label, the original value is used as the value label for the recoded value.

Variable –> New Name. You must specify a new variable name to receive the recoded values for each selected variable. To specify a new variable name, highlight the original variable on the selected list, enter the new variable name in the text box, and click on New Name. The new variable name is displayed next to the original variable name. Variable names must begin with a letter and cannot exceed eight characters. (See Chapter 2 for complete variable naming rules.)

Recode Starting from. There are two alternatives for the order in which new values are assigned:

○ **Lowest value.** Assigns values by ascending order, with the lowest value receiving a recoded value of 1. This is the default.

○ **Highest value.** Assigns values by descending order, with the highest value receiving a recoded value of 1.

String values are recoded in alphabetical order, with uppercase letters preceding their lowercase counterparts. Missing values are recoded into missing values higher than any nonmissing values, with their order preserved. For example, if the original variable has 10 nonmissing values, the lowest missing value would be recoded to 11, and the value 11 would be a missing value for the new variable.

Time Series Data Transformations

SPSS provides several data transformations that are useful in time series analysis:

- Generate date variables to establish periodicity, and distinguish between historical, validation, and forecasting periods.
- Create new time series variables as functions of existing time series variables.
- Replace system- and user-missing values with estimates based on one of several methods.

A **time series** is obtained by measuring a variable (or set of variables) regularly over a period of time. Time series data transformations assume a data file structure in which each case (row) represents a set of observations at a different time, and the length of time between cases is uniform.

Generating Date Variables

The observations in a time series occur at equally spaced intervals. The actual date of each observation does not matter in the analysis but is useful for establishing periodicity, labeling output, or specifying a portion of the time series that you want to analyze.

To generate date variables, from the menus choose:

Data
  Define Dates...

This opens the Define Dates dialog box, as shown in Figure 5.16.

Figure 5.16   Define Dates dialog box

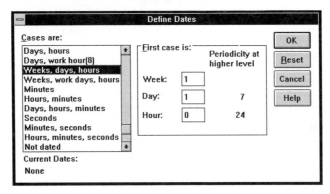

Cases Are: Defines the time interval used to generate dates.

First Case Is: Defines the starting date value, which is assigned to the first case. Sequential values, based on the time interval, are assigned to subsequent cases. All values must be positive integers.

Periodicity at higher level. Indicates the repetitive cyclical variation, such as the number of months in a year or the number of days in a week. The value displayed indicates the maximum value you can enter.

For each component that is used to define the date, SPSS creates a new numeric variable. The new variable names end with an underscore. A descriptive string variable, date_, is also created from the components. For example, in Figure 5.16, four new variables would be created: week_, day_, hour_, and date_.

If date variables have already been defined, they are replaced when you define new date variables. Variables with the following names are removed from the working data file and replaced with the new date variables: year_, quarter_, month_, week_, day_, hour_, minute_, second_, and date_.

Table 5.4 and Table 5.5 indicate the range of valid starting values for each date component.

Table 5.4 Dates involving years, quarters, and months

Cases Are:	Year	Quarter	Month
Years	0–9999		
Years, quarters	0–9999	1–4	
Years, months	0–9999		1–12
Years, quarters, months	0–9999	1–4	1–12

Table 5.5 Dates involving weeks, days, hours, minutes, and seconds

Cases Are:	Week	Day	Hour	Minute	Second
Days		0–9999			
Weeks, days	0–9999	1–7			
Weeks, work days (5)	0–9999	1–5			
Weeks, work days (6)	0–9999	1–6			
Hours			0–9999		
Days, hours		0–9999	0–23		
Days, work hours (8)		0–9999	0–7		
Weeks, days, hours	0–9999	1–7	0–23		
Weeks, work days, hours	0–9999	1–5	0–7		

Table 5.5 Dates involving weeks, days, hours, minutes, and seconds (Continued)

Cases Are:	Week	Day	Hour	Minute	Second
Minutes				0–9999	
Hours, minutes			0–9999	0–59	
Days, hours, minutes		0–9999	0–23	0–59	
Seconds					0–9999
Minutes, seconds				0–9999	0–59
Hours, minutes, seconds			0–9999	0–59	0–59

The following alternatives are also available:

Not dated. Removes any previously defined date variables. Any variables with the following names are deleted: *year_, quarter_, month_, week_, day_, hour_, minute_, second_,* and *date_.*

Custom. Indicates the presence of custom date variables created with command syntax (for example, a four-day work week). This item merely reflects the current state of the working data file. Selecting it from the list has no effect. (See the *SPSS Syntax Reference Guide* for information on using the DATE command to create custom date variables.)

Creating Time Series Variables

You can create new time series variables based on functions of existing time series variables. (Any variable measured regularly over a period of time is a **time series variable**.)

To create new time series variables, from the menus choose:

Transform
  Create Time Series...

This opens the Create Time Series dialog box, as shown in Figure 5.17.

Figure 5.17 Create Time Series dialog box

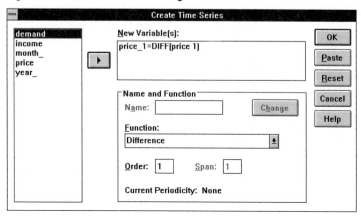

The numeric variables in the working data file are displayed on the source variable list.

New Variable(s). Displays new variable names and the functions based on existing variables that will be used to create them.

Name and Function. You can change the name and/or function used to create new time series variables. Enter a new name and/or select a different function and click on Change.

Name. Default new variable names are the first six characters of the existing variable used to create it, followed by an underscore and a sequential number. To override the default name, enter a new name. Variable names cannot exceed eight characters (see Chapter 3 for complete variable naming rules).

⬇ **Function**. You can choose one of the following alternatives:

Difference. Nonseasonal difference between successive values in the series.

Order. The number of previous values used to calculate the difference. Since one observation is lost for each order of difference, system-missing values appear at the beginning of the series. For example, if the difference order is 2, the first two cases will have the system-missing value for the new variable.

Seasonal difference. Difference between series values a constant span apart. The span is based on the currently defined periodicity. To compute seasonal differences, you must have defined date variables that include a periodic component (such as months of the year). See "Generating Date Variables" on p. 119 for information on creating date variables and changing the periodicity.

Order. The number of seasonal periods used to compute the difference. The number of cases with the system-missing value at the beginning of the series is equal to the periodicity multiplied by the order. For example, if the current periodicity is 12 and the order is 2, the first 24 cases will have the system-missing value for the new variable.

Centered moving average. Average of a span of series values surrounding and including the current value.

Span. The number of series values used to compute the average. If the span is even, the moving average is computed by averaging each pair of uncentered means. The number of cases with the system-missing value at the beginning and at the end of the series for a span of n is equal to $n/2$ for even span values and $(n-1)/2$ for odd span values. For example, if the span is 5, the number of cases with the system-missing value at the beginning and at the end of the series is 2.

Prior moving average. Average of the span of series values preceding the current value.

Span. The number of preceding series values used to compute the average. The number of cases with the system-missing value at the beginning of the series is equal to the span value.

Running median. Median of a span of series values surrounding and including the current value.

Span. The number of series values used to compute the median. If the span is even, the median is computed by averaging each pair of uncentered medians. The number of cases with the system-missing value at the beginning and at the end of the series for a span of n is equal to $n/2$ for even span values and $(n-1)/2$ for odd span values. For example, if the span is 5, the number of cases with the system-missing value at the beginning and at the end of the series is 2.

Cumulative sum. Cumulative sum of series values up to and including the current value.

Lag. Value of a previous case, based on the specified lag order.

Order. The number of cases prior to the current case from which the value is obtained. The number of cases with the system-missing value at the beginning of the series is equal to the order value.

Lead. Value of a subsequent case, based on the specified lead order.

Order. The number of cases after the current case from which the value is obtained. The number of cases with the system-missing value at the end of the series is equal to the order value.

Smoothing. New series values based on a compound data smoother. The smoother starts with a running median of 4, which is centered by a running median of 2. It then resmoothes these values by applying a running median of 5, a running median of 3, and hanning (running weighted averages). Residuals are computed by subtracting the smoothed series from the original series. This whole process is then repeated on the computed residuals. Finally, the smoothed residuals are computed by subtracting the smoothed values obtained the first time through the process. This is sometimes referred to as T4253H smoothing.

Missing Values

If the original time series contains missing values, the following rules apply:

- **Difference and Seasonal difference**: If either of a pair of values involved in a difference computation is missing, the result is set to system-missing in the new series.
- **Centered moving average, Prior moving average, Running median**: If any value within the span is missing, the result is set to system-missing in the new series.
- **Cumulative sum**. Cases with missing values are assigned the system-missing value in the new series.

- **Lag and Lead:** If the lag or lead case value is missing, the result is set to system-missing in the new series.
- **Smoothing:** Cases with missing values are not allowed, and all cases in the new series are assigned the system-missing value.

Replacing Missing Values

Missing observations can be problematic in time series analysis, and some time series measures cannot be computed if there are missing values in the series. To circumvent problems with missing values, you can replace missing values with estimates computed with one of several methods.

To create new time series variables that replace missing values in existing series, from the menus choose:

Transform
  Replace Missing Values...

This opens the Replace Missing Values dialog box, as shown in Figure 5.18.

Figure 5.18   Replace Missing Values dialog box

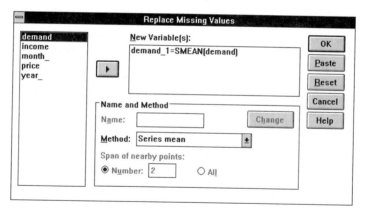

The numeric variables in the working data file are displayed on the source variable list.

New Variable(s). Displays new variable names and the functions based on existing variables that will be used to create them.

Name and Method. You can change the name and/or method used to create new time series variables. Enter a new name and/or select a different method and click on Change.

Name. Default new variable names are the first six characters of the existing variable used to create it, followed by an underscore and a sequential number. To override the default name, enter a new name. Variable names cannot exceed eight characters (see Chapter 3 for complete variable naming rules).

⬇ **Method**. You can choose one of the following alternatives:

Series mean. Replaces missing values with the mean for the entire series.

Mean of nearby points. Replaces missing values with the mean of valid surrounding values.

    Span of nearby points. You can select one of two alternatives:

○ **Number**. The number of valid values above and below the missing value used to compute the mean. The default is 2. Missing values near the beginning or end of the series will not be replaced if there are not enough valid values for the specified span. For example, if the second case has a missing value and the span is 2, the missing value for the case will not be replaced.

○ **All**. Replaces missing values with the mean for the entire series. (This is equivalent to Series mean.)

Median of nearby points. Replaces missing values with the median of valid surrounding values.

    Span of nearby points. You can select one of two alternatives:

○ **Number**. The number of valid values above and below the missing value used to compute the median. The default is 2. Missing values near the beginning or end of the series will not be replaced if there are not enough valid values for the specified span. For example, if the second case has a missing value and the span is 2, the missing value for the case will not be replaced.

○ **All**. Replaces missing values with the median for the entire series.

Linear interpolation. Replaces missing values using a linear interpolation. The last valid value before the missing value and the first valid value after the missing value are used for the interpolation. If the first or last case in the series has a missing value, the missing value is not replaced.

Linear trend at point. Replaces missing values with the linear trend for that point. The existing series is regressed on an index variable scaled 1 to n. Missing values are replaced with their predicted values.

Pending Transformations

To run pending transformations, from the menus choose:

Transform
  Run Pending Transforms

By default, data transformations are executed immediately. If you have a large number of transformations or you are working with a large data file, you can save processing time by changing your Preferences settings to delay the execution of transformations until SPSS encounters a command that requires a data pass (see Chapter 36). If you choose to delay the execution of data transformations, they are automatically executed as soon as you run any statistical procedure that requires a data pass. You can also run pending transformations at any time without running any statistical procedure.

6

File Handling and File Transformations

Data files are not always organized in the ideal form for your specific needs. You may want to combine data files, sort the data in a different order, select a subset of cases, or change the unit of analysis by grouping cases together. SPSS offers a wide range of file transformation capabilities, including the ability to:

- **Sort data**. You can sort cases based on the value of one or more variables.
- **Transpose cases and variables**. SPSS reads rows as cases and columns as variables. For data files in which this order is reversed, you can switch the rows and columns and read the data in the correct format.
- **Merge files**. You can merge two or more data files together. You can combine files with the same variables but different cases, or files with the same cases but different variables.
- **Select subsets of cases**. You can restrict your analysis to a subset of cases or perform simultaneous analyses on different subsets.
- **Aggregate data**. You can change the unit of analysis by aggregating cases based on the value of one or more grouping variables.
- **Weight data**. Weight cases for analysis based on the value of a weight variable.

Sorting Data

Sorting cases (sorting rows of the data file) is often useful—and sometimes necessary—in conjunction with merging files (see "Combining Data Files" on p. 129), split-file processing (see "Sorting Cases for Split-File Processing" on p. 147), and generating summary reports (see Chapter 22).

To reorder the sequence of cases in the data file based on the value of one or more sorting variables, from the menus choose:

Data
  Sort Cases...

This opens the Sort Cases dialog box, as shown in Figure 6.1

Figure 6.1   Sort Cases dialog box

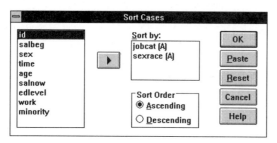

The variables in the data file appear on the source variable list. Select one or more sort variables. If you select multiple sort variables, the order in which they appear on the Sort list determines the order in which cases are sorted. For example, based on the Sort list in Figure 6.1, cases will be sorted by the value of *sexrace* within sorted categories of *jobcat*. For string variables, uppercase letters precede their lowercase counterparts in sort order (for example, the string value "Yes" comes before "yes" in sort order).

Sort Order. There are two alternatives for sort order:

○ **Ascending**. Sort cases by ascending order of the values of the sort variable(s). This is the default.

○ **Descending**. Sort case by descending order of the values of the sort variable(s).

Transposing Cases and Variables

SPSS assumes a file structure in which cases are represented in rows and variables are represented in columns. Sometimes, however, data are recorded in the opposite fashion. You might, for example, find this to be the case with spreadsheet data. To switch the columns and rows in the data file, from the menus choose:

Data
 Transpose...

This opens the Transpose dialog box, as shown in Figure 6.2.

Figure 6.2   Transpose dialog box

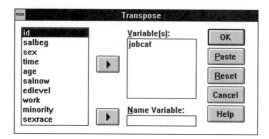

The variables in the data file appear on the source variable list. Select one or more variables. The selected variables become cases, and all cases become variables.

Name Variable. By default, SPSS assigns the new variable names *var001*, *var002*, and so on to the transposed data. Optionally, you can use the values of an existing variable in the untransposed file as the variable names for the transposed file. If the name variable is numeric, the new variable names begin with the letter *V* followed by the numeric values. If values exceed eight characters, they are truncated. If values are not unique, SPSS creates unique variable names by adding a sequential number to the end of the value. A table of the new variable names is displayed in the output window.

Missing Values in Transposed Data Files

Any user-missing values are converted to the system-missing value when the data file is transposed. If you want to retain the original data values in the transposed file, before transposing the file, change the variable definition so that there are no user-missing values (see Chapter 3).

Combining Data Files

With SPSS, you can combine data from two files in two different ways. You can:

- Merge files containing the same variables but different cases.
- Merge files containing the same cases but different variables.

Merging Files That Contain Different Cases

The Add Cases procedure merges two data files that contain the same variables but different cases. For example, you might record the same information for customers in two different sales regions and maintain the data for each region in separate files. The variables can be in any order in the two files. Variables are matched by name. The procedure also provides a facility to match variables that contain the same information but different variable names in the two files.

The Add Cases procedure adds cases to the working data file from a second, external SPSS data file. So, before you can merge the files, one of them must already be open.

To add cases to the working data file from an external SPSS data file, from the menus choose:

Data
  Merge Files ▶
    Add Cases...

This opens the Add Cases Read File dialog box, as shown in Figure 6.3.

Figure 6.3   Add Cases Read File dialog box

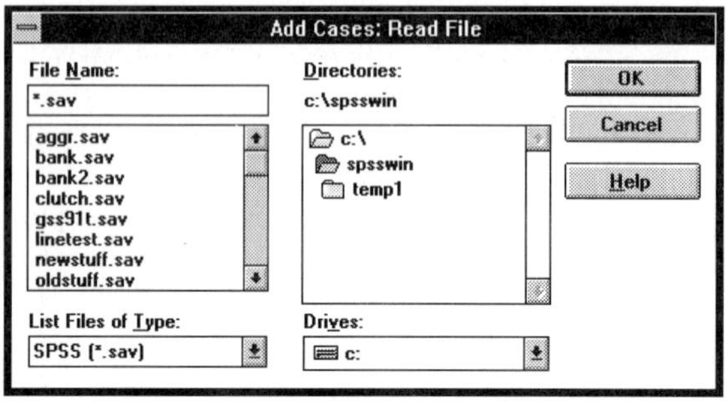

File Name. Enter the name of the external data file that you want to merge with the working data file. The file must be an SPSS or SPSS/PC+ data file. You can select a file from the list or you can type in a filename, a directory path and filename, or a wildcard search. By default, SPSS looks for all files in the current directory with the extension *.sav* and displays them on the list.

List Files of Type. Provides a wildcard search list of default file extensions for appropriate file types. The list contains the default extension for SPSS data files (**.sav*) and the wildcard search for all files (**.**).

Directories. To change the directory location, select the name of the directory on the Directories list. Directories below the current directory are denoted by closed file folder icons. Directories above the current directory are denoted by open file folder icons. The current directory is displayed above the list of directories and is also denoted by the last (lowest) open file folder icon.

Drives. To change the drive location, select a drive from the drop-down list of available drives.

Select the external data file you want to merge with the working data file and click on OK. This opens the Add Cases From dialog box, shown in Figure 6.4.

Figure 6.4   Add Cases From dialog box

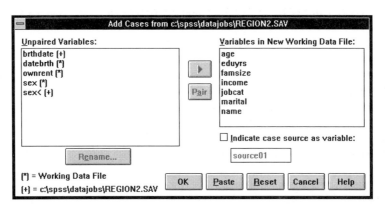

Unpaired Variables. Variables to be excluded from the new, merged data file. Variables from the working data file are identified with an asterisk (*). Variables from the external data file are identified with a plus sign (+). By default, this list contains:

- Variables from either data file that do not match a variable name in the other file. You can create pairs from unpaired variables and include them in the new, merged file (see below).

- Variables defined as numeric data in one file and string data in the other file. Numeric variables cannot be merged with string variables. For example, in Figure 6.4, *sex* is a numeric variable in the working data file, but it is a short string variable in the external data file.

- String variables of unequal width. The defined width of a string variable must be the same in both data files.

Variables in the New Working Data File. Variables to be included in the new, merged data file. By default, all the variables that match both name and data type (numeric or string) are included on the list. You can remove variables from the list if you don't want them included in the merged file.

The following option is also available:

❑ **Indicate case source as variable.** Creates an **indicator variable** that indicates the source data file for each case in the merged file. For cases from the working data file, the value of this variable is 0; for cases from the external data file, the value of this variable is 1. The default name of the variable is *source01*. You can enter a variable name up to eight characters long. The name cannot be the same as one of the variables on the list to be included in the merged file.

Selecting Variables

If the same information is recorded under different variable names in the two files, you can create a pair from the Unpaired Variables list. Select the two variables on the Unpaired Variables list and click on Pair. (Use the ctrl-click method to select noncontiguous pairs of variables.) Both variable names appear together on the same line on the list of variables to be included in the merged file, as shown in Figure 6.5. By default, the name of the variable in the working data file is used as the name of the variable in the merged file.

Figure 6.5   Selecting variable pairs

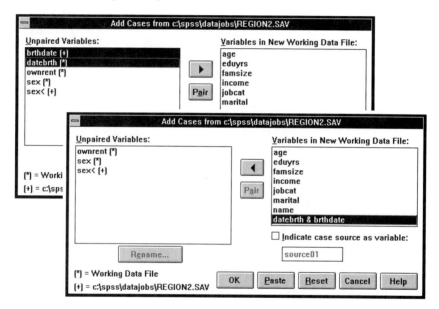

To include an unpaired variable from one file without pairing it with a variable from the other file, select the variable on the Unpaired Variables list and click on ▶. Any unpaired variables included in the merged file will contain missing data for cases from the file that does not contain that variable. For example, the variable *ownrent* exists in the working data file but not in the external data file. If this variable is included in the merged file, cases from the external file will contain the system-missing value for this variable in the merged file.

Removing Variables

To remove a variable from the list of variables to be included in the merged file, select the variable on the list and click on [◄]. The variable is moved to the Unpaired Variables list. The variable name is displayed twice on the Unpaired Variables list, once for the working data file and once for the external file. To move the variable back to the list of variables to be included in the merged file, select both variable names on the Unpaired Variables list and click on Pair.

Renaming Variables

You can rename variables from either the working data file or the external file before moving them from the Unpaired Variables list to the list of variables to be included in the merged data file. Renaming variables enables you to:

- Use the variable name from the external file rather than the name from the working data file for variable pairs—for example, to use *brthdate* instead of *datebrth* for the variable pair in Figure 6.7.
- Include two variables with the same name but of unmatched types or different string widths. For example, to include both the numeric variable *sex* from the working data file and the string variable *sex* from the external file, one of them must be renamed first.

To rename a variable on the Unpaired Variables list, highlight the variable and click on Rename... in the Add Cases From dialog box. This opens the Rename dialog box, as shown in Figure 6.6. The new variable name can be up to eight characters long. (See Chapter 3 for complete variable naming rules.)

Figure 6.6   Rename dialog box

Both the original variable name and the new name are displayed on the Unpaired Variables list. If the new variable name is the same as the other variable in the pair, only one variable name appears on the list of variables to be included in the merged file, as shown in Figure 6.7.

Figure 6.7   Selecting renamed variables

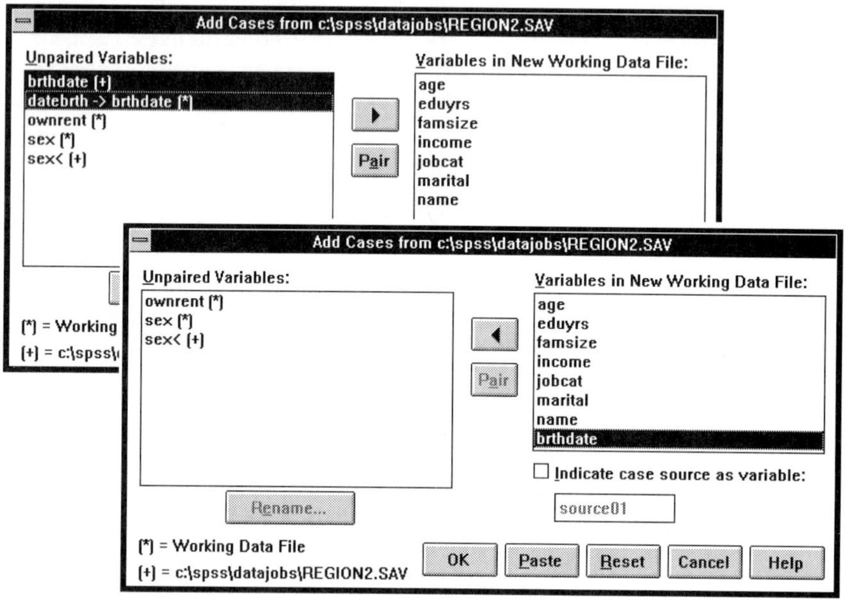

To undo variable renaming, simply go back to the Rename dialog box and delete the new variable name.

Dictionary Information

Any existing dictionary information (variable and value labels, user-missing values, display formats) in the working data file is applied to the merged data file. If any dictionary information for a variable is undefined in the working data file, dictionary information from the external data file is used.

If the working data file contains any defined value labels or user-missing values for a variable, any additional value labels or user-missing values for that variable in the external file are ignored.

Merging Files That Contain Different Variables

With the Add Variables procedure, you can:

- Merge two SPSS data files that contain the same cases but different variables.
- Use a table lookup file to add data to multiple cases in another file.

The two data files to be merged must meet the following requirements:

- Files must be in SPSS or SPSS/PC+ format.
- Cases must be sorted in the same order in both data files.
- If one or more key variables are used to match cases, the two data files must be sorted by ascending order of the key variable(s).

The Add Variables procedure merges the working data file with an external SPSS data file. Both files must be sorted in the same case order, so before you can merge the files, you must complete any necessary sorting. One of the files must already be open when you start the procedure (see "Sorting Data" on p. 127).

To add variables to the working data file from an external SPSS data file or to use data from a table lookup file, from the menus choose:

Data
  Merge Files ▶
    Add Variables...

This opens the Add Variables Read File dialog box, as shown in Figure 6.8.

Figure 6.8   Add Variables Read File dialog box

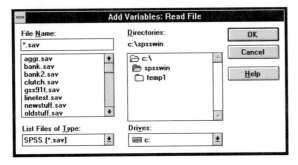

File Name. Enter the name of the external data file that you want to merge with the working data file. The file must be an SPSS or SPSS/PC+ data file. You can select a file from the list or you can type in a filename, a directory path and filename, or a wildcard search. By default, SPSS looks for all files in the current directory with the extension *.sav* and displays them on the list.

List Files of Type. Provides a wildcard search list of default file extensions for appropriate file types. The list contains the default extension for SPSS data files (*.sav*) and the wildcard search for all files (*.*).

Directories. To change the directory location, select the name of the directory on the Directories list. Directories below the current directory are denoted by closed file folder icons. Directories above the current directory are denoted by open file folder icons. The current directory is displayed above the list of directories and is also denoted by the last (lowest) open file folder icon.

Drives. To change the drive location, select a drive from the drop-down list of available drives.

Select the external data file you want to merge with the working data files and click on OK. This opens the Add Variables From dialog box, as shown in Figure 6.9.

Figure 6.9   Add Variables From dialog box

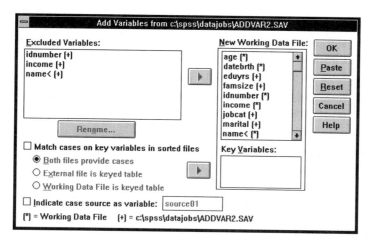

Excluded Variables. Variables to be excluded from the new, merged data file. By default, this list contains any variable names from the external data file that duplicate variable names in the working data file. If you want to include the variable with the duplicate name in the merged file, you can rename it and add it to the list of variables to be included (see "Renaming Variables" on p. 138). Variables from the working data file are identified with an asterisk (*). Variables from the external data file are identified with a plus sign (+).

New Working Data File. Variables to be included in the new, merged data file. By default, all unique variable names in both data files are included on the list.

The following options are also available:

❑ **Match cases on key variables in sorted files.** If some cases in one file do not have matching cases in the other file (that is, some cases are missing in one file), use **key variables** to identify and correctly match cases from the two files. You can also use key variables with table lookup files. The key variables must have the same names in both data files. Both data files must be sorted by ascending order of the key variables, and the order of variables on the Key Variables list must be the same as their sort sequence. Key variables are included in the new, merged file.

Cases that do not match on the key variables are included in the merged file but are not merged with cases from the other file. Unmatched cases contain values for only the variables in the file from which they are taken; variables from the other file contain the system-missing value.

You can choose one of the following alternatives for the key variable matching method:

○ **Both files provide cases**. Cases in one file correspond to cases in the other file on a one-to-one basis. This is the default. The key variables should uniquely identify each case. If two or more cases have the same values for all the key variables, SPSS merges those cases in sequential order and issues a warning message.

○ **External file is keyed table**. The external data file is a table lookup file.

○ **Working data file is keyed table**. The working data file is a table lookup file.

A **keyed table** or **table lookup file** is a file in which data for each "case" can be applied to multiple cases in the other data file. For example, if one file contains information on individual family members (for example, sex, age, education) and the other file contains overall family information (for example, total income, family size, location), you can use the file of family data as a table lookup file and apply the common family data to each individual family member in the merged data file.

The following option is also available:

❏ **Indicate case source as variable**. Creates an indicator variable that indicates the source data file for each case in the merged file. For cases from the working data file that are missing from the external file, the value of this variable is 0; for cases from the external data file that are missing from the working data file and cases present in both files, the value of this variable is 1. The default name of the variable is *source01*. You can enter a variable name up to eight characters long. The name cannot be the same as one of the variables on the list to be included in the merged file.

Selecting Key Variables

Key variables are selected from the Excluded Variables list. The key variables must be present in both data files. By default, any variables in the external file that duplicate variable names in the working data file are placed on the Excluded Variables list. For example, in Figure 6.10, *idnumber* and *name* are the key variables.

To select a key variable, highlight the variable on the Excluded Variables list, select Match cases on key variables in sorted files, and click on the ▶ pushbutton next to the Key Variables list. You can select multiple key variables. Both files must be sorted by ascending order of the key variables, and the order of variables on the Key Variables list must be the same as their sort sequence.

Key variables must have the same variable names in both data files. If the names differ, you can rename the variable in one file to match the variable name in the other file (see "Renaming Variables," below).

Figure 6.10 Selecting key variables

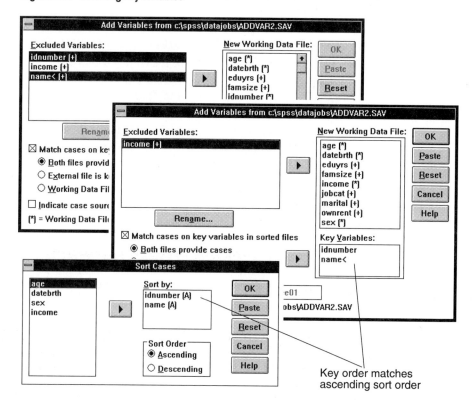

Key order matches
ascending sort order

Renaming Variables

There are several reasons for renaming variables before merging two files that contain different variables:

- You want to include a variable from the external file that has the same name as a variable in the working data file but contains different data.
- You want to select a key variable that does not have the same name in both data files.
- You don't like a variable name and want to change it.

To rename a variable, highlight the variable on the Excluded Variables list and click on Rename... in the Add Variables From dialog box. This opens the Rename dialog box, as shown in Figure 6.11. The new variable name can be up to eight characters long. (See Chapter 3 for complete variable naming rules.)

Figure 6.11   Rename dialog box

Both the original variable name and the new name are displayed on the Excluded Variables list. If you move the renamed variable to the New Working Data File list or the Key Variables list, only the new variable name is displayed, as shown in Figure 6.12.

To undo variable renaming, simply go back to the Rename dialog box and delete the new variable name.

Figure 6.12   Selecting renamed variables

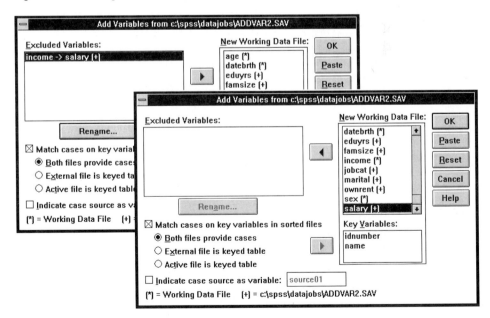

Applying a Data Dictionary

An SPSS data dictionary can contain extensive data definition information, including:

- Data type (numeric, string, etc.) and width
- Display format
- Descriptive variable and value labels
- User-missing value specifications

To apply the data dictionary information from another SPSS data file to the working data file, from the menus choose:

Data
  Apply Dictionary...

This opens the Apply SPSS Dictionary dialog box, as shown in Figure 6.13.

Figure 6.13   Apply SPSS Dictionary dialog box

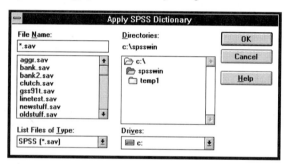

File Name. Enter the name of an SPSS or SPSS/PC+ data file. You can select a file from the list or you can type in a filename, a directory path and filename, or a wildcard search. By default, SPSS looks for all files in the current directory with the extension *.sav* and displays them on the list.

List Files of Type. Provides a wildcard search list of default file extensions for appropriate file types. The list contains the default extension for SPSS data files (*.sav*) and the wildcard search for all files (*.*).

Directories. To change the directory location, select the name of the directory on the Directories list. Directories below the current directory are denoted by closed file folder icons. Directories above the current directory are denoted by open file folder icons. The current directory is displayed above the list of directories and is also denoted by the last (lowest) open file folder icon.

Drives. To change the drive location, select a drive from the drop-down list of available drives.

Dictionary information is applied based on matching variable names. The variables don't have to be in the same order in both files, and variables that aren't present in both files are unaffected. The following rules apply:

- If the variable type (numeric or string) is the same in both files, all the dictionary information is applied.
- If the variable type is not the same for both files, or if it is a long string (more than eight characters), only the variable label is applied.
- Numeric, dollar, dot, comma, date, and time formats are all considered numeric, and all dictionary information is applied.
- String variable widths are not affected by the applied dictionary.
- For short string variables (eight characters or less), missing values and specified values for value labels are truncated if they exceed the defined width of the variable in the working data file.
- Any applied dictionary information overwrites existing dictionary information.

Weighted Files

The following rules apply to weighted files (see "Weighting Cases" on p. 153):

- If the working data file is weighted and the file containing the dictionary is unweighted, the working data file remains weighted.
- If the working data file is unweighted and the file containing the dictionary is weighted by a variable that exists in the working data file, the working data file is weighted by that variable.
- If both files are weighted but they are not weighted by the same variable, the weight is changed in the working data file if the weight variable in the file containing the dictionary also exists in the working data file.

The status bar at the bottom of the SPSS application window displays the message Weight on if weighting is in effect in the working data file.

Aggregating Data

You can aggregate cases based on the value of one or more grouping variables and create a new data file containing one case for each group. For example, you can aggregate county data by state and create a new data file in which state is the unit of analysis. To aggregate cases, from the menus choose:

Data
  Aggregate...

This opens the Aggregate Data dialog box, as shown in Figure 6.14.

Figure 6.14   Aggregate Data dialog box

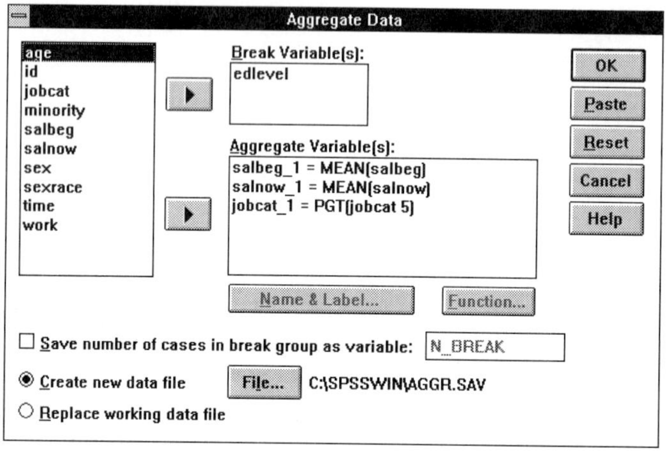

The variables in the data file appear on the source variable list. You must select at least one break variable and define at least one new variable based on an aggregate variable and an aggregate function. SPSS automatically creates a new file with the default name *aggr.sav* unless you specify a different filename.

Break Variable(s). Cases are grouped together based on the values of the break variables. Each unique combination of break variable values defines a group and generates one case in the new aggregated file. All break variables are saved in the new file with their existing names and dictionary information. The break variable can be either numeric or string.

Aggregate Variable(s). Variables are used with aggregate functions (see "Aggregate Functions" on p. 143) to create the new variables for the aggregated file. By default, SPSS creates new aggregate variable names using the first several characters of the source variable name followed by an underscore and a sequential two-digit number. For example, *salbeg* on the source list becomes *salbeg_01* on the Aggregate Variable(s) list. The aggregate variable name is followed by an optional variable label (see "New Variable Names and Labels" on p. 145) in quotes, the name of the aggregate function, and the source variable name in parentheses. Source variables for aggregate functions must be numeric.

To create a variable containing the number of cases in each break group, select:

❑ **Save number of cases in break group as variable.** You can create a variable containing the number of cases in each break group. The default variable name is *N_BREAK*. Enter a new name to override the default. Variable names must begin with a letter and cannot exceed eight characters.

To specify the filename and location of the aggregated data file, choose one of the following alternatives:

○ **Create new data file.** By default, a file called *aggr.sav* is created in the current directory. To change the file name or directory, click on File... (see "Aggregate Filename and Location" on p. 145).

○ **Replace working data file.** Replaces the working data file with the new aggregated data file. This creates a temporary aggregated file unless you explicitly save the file.

Aggregate Functions

New variables in the aggregated file are created by applying aggregate functions to existing variables. By default, the mean of values across cases is used as the value of the new aggregated variable. To specify a different aggregate function, highlight the variable on the Aggregate Variable(s) list and click on Function... in the Aggregate Data dialog box. This opens the Aggregate Function dialog box, as shown in Figure 6.15.

Figure 6.15   Aggregate Function dialog box

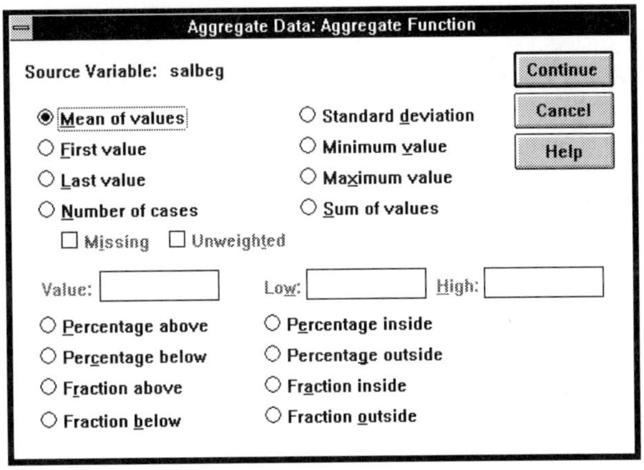

For each variable, you can choose one of the aggregate functions described below. When a function is performed, the resulting value is displayed on the Aggregate Variable(s) list in the Aggregate Data dialog box.

○ **Mean of values.** Mean across cases in the break group. This is displayed as MEAN.

○ **First value.** First nonmissing observed value in the break group. This is displayed as FIRST.

○ **Last value.** Last nonmissing observed value in the break group. This is displayed as LAST.

○ **Number of cases.** Number of cases in the break group. This is displayed as N. You can also choose one or both of the following:

❑ **Missing.** Number of missing cases in the break group. This is displayed as NMISS.

❑ **Unweighted.** Number of unweighted cases in the break group. This is displayed as NU.

If you select both Missing and Unweighted, the result is the number of unweighted missing values in the break group. This is displayed as NUMISS.

○ **Standard deviation.** Standard deviation across cases in the break group. This is displayed as SD.

○ **Minimum value.** Minimum value across cases in the break group. This is displayed as MIN.

○ **Maximum value.** Maximum value across cases in the break group. This is displayed as MAX.

○ **Sum of values.** Sum of values across cases in the break group. This is displayed as SUM.

○ **Percentage above.** Percentage of cases in the break group greater than a user-specified value. This is displayed as PGT.

○ **Percentage below.** Percentage of cases in the break group less than a user-specified value. This is displayed as PLT.

○ **Fraction above.** Fraction of cases in the break group greater than a user-specified value. This is displayed as FGT.

○ **Fraction below.** Fraction of cases in the break group less than a user-specified value. This is displayed as FLT.

○ **Percentage inside.** Percentage of cases in the break group with values within the inclusive range defined by Low and High. This is displayed as PIN.

○ **Percentage outside.** Percentage of cases in the break group with values outside the inclusive range defined by Low and High. This is displayed as POUT.

○ **Fraction inside.** Fraction of cases in the break group with values within the inclusive range defined by Low and High. This is displayed as FIN.

○ **Fraction outside.** Fraction of cases in the break group with values outside the inclusive range defined by Low and High. This is displayed as FOUT.

New Variable Names and Labels

SPSS provides default variable names for the variables in the new aggregated data file. To specify a different variable name and an optional descriptive label for a new variable, highlight the variable on the Aggregate Variable(s) list and click on Name & Label... in the Aggregate Data dialog box. This opens the Variable Name and Label dialog box, as shown in Figure 6.16.

Figure 6.16   Variable Name and Label dialog box

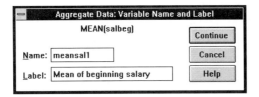

The aggregate function name, the original variable name, and any related value specifications are displayed for reference purposes. To specify a different aggregate function, return to the main dialog box and click on Function... (see "Aggregate Functions" on p. 143).

Name. Variable names must begin with a letter and cannot exceed eight characters. (See Chapter 3 for complete variable naming rules.)

Label. Optional, descriptive variable label, up to 120 characters long.

Aggregate Filename and Location

By default, SPSS creates a new aggregated data file named *aggr.sav* in the current directory. To specify a different filename or directory or to replace the working data file with the aggregated data file, click on File... in the Aggregate Data dialog box. This opens the Output File Specification dialog box, as shown in Figure 6.17.

Figure 6.17   Output File Specification dialog box

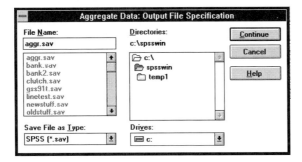

File Name. You can type in a filename, a directory path and filename, or a wildcard search. By default, SPSS provides an extension of *.sav* and displays a list of files in the current directory with that extension. If you select a filename from the list, SPSS asks if you want to replace the existing file.

Save File as Type. Provides a wildcard search list of default file extensions for appropriate file types. The list contains the default extension for SPSS data files (*.sav*) and the wildcard search for all files (*.*).

Directories. To change the directory location, select the name of the directory on the Directories list. Directories below the current directory are denoted by closed file folder icons. Directories above the current directory are denoted by open file folder icons The current directory is displayed above the list of directories and is also denoted by the last (lowest) open file folder icon.

Drives. To change the drive location, select a drive from the drop-down list of available drives.

Split-File Processing

To split your data file into separate groups for analysis, from the menus choose:

Data
  Split File...

This opens the Split File dialog box, as shown in Figure 6.18.

Figure 6.18 Split File dialog box

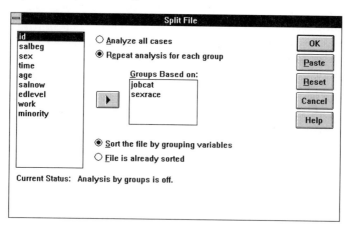

The numeric and short string variables in the data file appear on the source variable list. Select Repeat analysis for each group and choose one or more variables to use as grouping variables. The maximum number of grouping variables is eight. You can use numeric, short string, and long string variables as grouping variables. A separate analysis is performed for each subgroup.

If you select multiple grouping variables, the order in which they appear on the Groups list determines the manner in which cases are grouped. For example, based on the Groups list in Figure 6.18, cases will be grouped by the value of *sexrace* within categories of *jobcat*.

Turning Split-File Processing On and Off

Once you invoke split-file processing, it remains in effect for the rest of the session unless you turn it off. You can choose one of the following alternatives for the status of split-file processing:

○ **Analyze all cases**. Split-file processing is off. All cases are analyzed together. Any split-file grouping variables are ignored. This is the default.

○ **Repeat analysis for each group**. Split-file processing is on. A separate analysis is performed for each subgroup.

If split-file processing is in effect, the message Split File on appears on the status bar at the bottom of the SPSS application window.

Sorting Cases for Split-File Processing

The Split File procedure creates a new subgroup each time it encounters a different value for one of the grouping variables. Therefore, it is important to sort cases based on the values of the grouping variables before invoking split-file processing. You can choose one of the following alternatives for file sorting:

○ **Sort the file by grouping variables**. This is the default. If the file isn't already sorted, this sorts the cases by the values of the grouping variables before splitting the file for analysis.

○ **File is already sorted**. If the file is already sorted in the proper order, this alternative can save processing time.

Selecting Subsets of Cases

You can restrict your analysis to a specific subgroup based on criteria that include variables and complex expressions. You can also select a random sample of cases. The criteria used to define a subgroup can include:

- Variable values and ranges
- Date and time ranges
- Case (row) numbers
- Arithmetic expressions
- Logical expressions
- Functions

To select a subset of cases for analysis, from the menus choose:

Data
  Select Cases...

This opens the Select Cases dialog box, as shown in Figure 6.19.

Figure 6.19   Select Cases dialog box

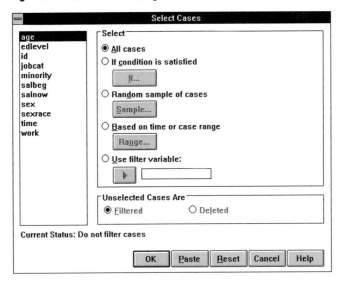

Select. You can choose one of the following alternatives for case selection:

○ **All cases**. Use all cases in the data file. This is the default. If filtering (see below) is in effect, you can use this option to turn it off.

○ **If condition is satisfied**. You can use conditional expressions to select cases. A **conditional expression** returns a value of true, false, or missing for each case. If the result of a conditional expression is true, the case is selected. If the result is false or missing, the case is not selected. (For information on how to use conditional expressions, see "Selecting Cases Based on Conditional Expressions" on p. 150.)

○ **Random sample of cases**. You can select a percentage or an exact number of cases. (For more information on random samples, see "Selecting a Random Sample" on p. 150.)

○ **Based on time or case range**. For time-series data with defined date variables (see Chapter 5), you can select a range of dates or times.

○ **Use filter variable**. You can select a numeric variable from the data file to use to filter or delete cases. Cases with any value other than 0 or missing for the filter variable are selected.

Unselected Cases. You can choose one of the following alternatives for the treatment of unselected cases:

○ **Filtered**. Unselected cases are not included in the analysis but remain in the data file. You can use the unselected cases later in the session if you turn filtering off. If you select a random sample or if you select cases based on a conditional expression, this generates a variable named *filter_$* with a value of 1 for selected cases and a value of 0 for unselected cases.

○ **Deleted**. Unselected cases are deleted from the data file. By reducing the number of cases in the open data file, you can save processing time. The cases can be recovered if you close the data file without saving any changes and then reopen it. The deletion of cases is permanent only if you save the changes to the data file.

Current Status. Status of filtering. There are two possible states:

Do not filter cases. Filtering is off. If All cases is selected or if unselected cases are deleted, filtering is off.

Filter cases by values of [variable name]. Filtering is on. The variable is either a user-specified variable or the system-generated variable *filter_$*. If filtering is on, the message Filter on appears on the status bar.

Selecting Cases Based on Conditional Expressions

To select cases based on a conditional expression, select If condition is satisfied and click on If... in the Select Cases dialog box. This opens the Select Cases If dialog box, as shown in Figure 6.20.

Figure 6.20   Select Cases If dialog box

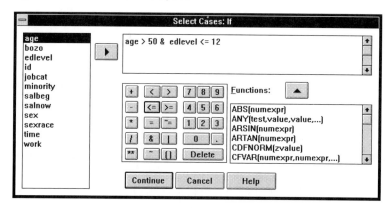

The conditional expression can use existing variable names, constants, arithmetic operators, logical operators, relational operators, and functions. You can type and edit the expression in the text box just like text in a syntax or output window (see Chapter 4). You can also use the calculator pad, variable list, and function list to paste elements into the expression. See Chapter 5 for more information on working with conditional expressions.

Selecting a Random Sample

To obtain a random sample, choose Random sample of cases in the Select Cases dialog box and click on Sample... This opens the Random Sample dialog box, as shown in Figure 6.21.

Figure 6.21   Random Sample dialog box

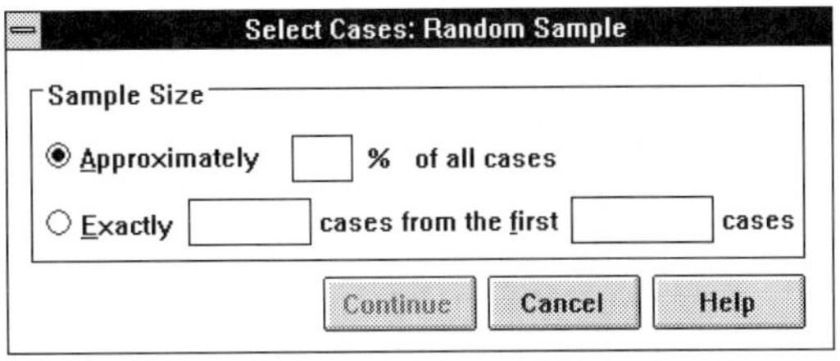

Sample Size. You can choose one of the following alternatives for sample size:

○ **Approximately.** A user-specified percentage. SPSS generates a random sample of approximately the specified percentage of cases.

○ **Exactly.** A user-specified number of cases. You must also specify the number of cases from which to generate the sample. This second number should be less than or equal to the total number of cases in the data file. If the number exceeds the total number of cases in the data file, the sample will contain proportionally fewer cases than the requested number.

Setting the Seed for Random Sampling

The SPSS pseudo-random number generator begins with a **seed**, a very large integer value. Within a session, SPSS uses a different seed each time you select a random sample, producing a different sample of cases. If you want to duplicate the same random sample, you can reset the seed value using the Random Number Seed dialog box. See Chapter 5 for more information.

Selecting a Range of Dates or Times

To select a range of dates and/or times (for time-series data in which each case represents a set of observations at a different time), select Based on time or case range and click on Range... in the Select Cases dialog box. This opens the Select Cases Range dialog box. If there are no defined date variables, the dialog box looks like Figure 6.22. If there are defined date variables, the dialog box provides a set of text entry boxes for each numeric date variable. For example, Figure 6.23 shows the Select Cases Range dialog box with date variables for year and month. To generate date variables for time-series data, use the Define Dates option on the Data menu. For more information on generating date variables, see Chapter 5.

Figure 6.22   Select Cases Range with no defined date variables

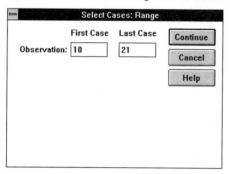

Figure 6.23   Select Cases Range with defined date variables

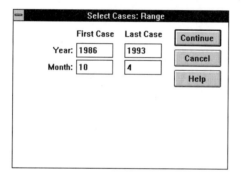

First Case. Enter the starting date and/or time values for the range. If no dates variables are defined, enter the starting observation number (row number in the Data Editor, unless Split File is on). If you don't specify a Last Case value, all cases from the starting date/time to the end of the time series are selected.

Last Case. Enter the ending date and/or time values for the range. If no date variables are defined, enter the ending observation number (row number in the Data Editor, unless Split File is on). If you don't specify a First Case value, all cases from the beginning of the time series up to the ending date/time are selected.

Case Selection Status

If you have selected a subset of cases but have not discarded unselected cases, unselected cases are marked in the Data Editor with a diagonal line through the row number, as shown in Figure 6.24.

Figure 6.24 Case selection status

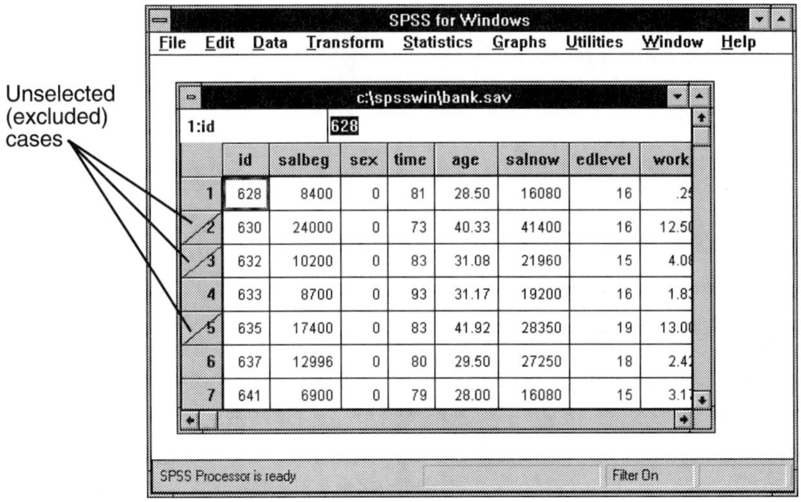

Weighting Cases

If each record in the data file represents more than one case, you can specify the replication factor with the Weight procedure. To apply weights to cases based on the value of a weighting variable, from the menus choose:

Data
  Weight Cases...

This opens the Weight Cases dialog box, as shown in Figure 6.25.

Figure 6.25   Weight Cases dialog box

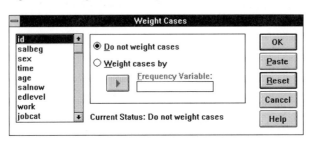

The numeric variables in the data file appear on the source variable list. Select Weight cases by and choose a single variable to use as a weight variable.

Turning Weights On and Off

Once you apply a weight variable, it remains in effect until you select another weight variable or turn weighting off. Cases with a negative value, 0, or a missing value for the weighting variable are excluded from all analyses. You can choose one of the following alternatives for the status of weighting:

○ **Do not weight cases**. Weighting is off. Any selected weight variable is ignored. This is the default.

○ **Weight cases by**. Weighting is on. Cases are weighted by the selected frequency variable.

The status bar at the bottom of the SPSS application window displays the message Weight on if weighting is in effect in the working data file.

Weights in Scatterplots and Histograms

Scatterplots and histograms have an option for turning case weights on and off, but this does not affect cases with a negative value, 0, or a missing value for the weight variable. These cases remain excluded from the chart even if you turn weighting off from within the chart.

7 Data Tabulation

Few people would dispute the effects of "rainy days and Mondays" on the body and spirit. It has long been known that more suicides occur on Mondays than other days of the week. An excess of cardiac deaths on Mondays has also been noted (Rabkin et al., 1980). In this chapter, using a study of coronary heart disease among male Western Electric employees (Paul et al., 1963), we will examine the day of death to see if an excess of deaths occurred on Mondays.

A Frequency Table

A first step in analyzing data about day of death might be to count the number of deaths occurring on each day of the week. Figure 7.1 contains this information.

Figure 7.1   Frequency of death by day of week

```
DAYOFWK    DAY OF DEATH
```

Value Label		Value	Frequency	Percent	Valid Percent	Cum Percent
SUNDAY		1	19	7.9	17.3	17.3
MONDAY		2	11	4.6	10.0	27.3
TUESDAY		3	19	7.9	17.3	44.5
WEDNESDAY		4	17	7.1	15.5	60.0
THURSDAY		5	15	6.3	13.6	73.6
FRIDAY		6	13	5.4	11.8	85.5
SATURDAY		7	16	6.7	14.5	100.0
MISSING		9	130	54.2	Missing	
		Total	240	100.0	100.0	

```
Valid cases    110    Missing cases    130
```

Each row of the frequency table describes a particular day of the week. The last row (labeled *MISSING*) represents cases for which the day of death is not known or death has not occurred. For the table in Figure 7.1, there are 110 cases for which day of death is known. The first column (*Value Label*) gives the name of the day, while the second column contains the **value**, which is the numeric or string value given to the computer to represent the day.

The number of people dying on each day (the **frequency**) appears in the third column. Monday is the least-frequent day of death, with 11 deaths. These 11 deaths represent 4.6% (11/240) of all cases. This **percentage** appears in the fourth column. However, of the 240 cases, 130 are **missing cases** (cases for which day of death is unknown or death has not occurred). The 11 deaths on Monday represent 10.0% of the total deaths for which day of death is known (11/110). This **valid percentage** appears in the fifth column.

The last column of the table contains the **cumulative percentage**. For a particular day, this percentage is the sum of the valid percentages of that day and of all other days that precede it in the table. For example, the cumulative percentage for Tuesday is 44.5, which is the sum of the percentage of deaths that occurred on Sunday, Monday, and Tuesday. It is calculated as

$$\frac{19}{110} + \frac{11}{110} + \frac{19}{110} = \frac{49}{110} = 44.5\% \hspace{3cm} \textbf{Equation 7.1}$$

Sometimes it is helpful to look at frequencies for a selected subset of cases. Figure 7.2 is a frequency table of day of death for a subset characterized by sudden cardiac death. This is a particularly interesting category, since it is thought that sudden death may be related to stressful events such as returning to the work environment. In Figure 7.2, deaths do not appear to cluster on any particular day. Twenty-two percent of deaths occurred on Sunday, while 8.3% occurred on Thursday. Since the number of sudden deaths in the table is small, the magnitude of the observed fluctuations is not very large.

Figure 7.2   Frequency of sudden cardiac death by day of week

DAYOFWK   DAY OF DEATH

Value Label	Value	Frequency	Percent	Valid Percent	Cum Percent
SUNDAY	1	8	22.2	22.2	22.2
MONDAY	2	4	11.1	11.1	33.3
TUESDAY	3	4	11.1	11.1	44.4
WEDNESDAY	4	7	19.4	19.4	63.9
THURSDAY	5	3	8.3	8.3	72.2
FRIDAY	6	6	16.7	16.7	88.9
SATURDAY	7	4	11.1	11.1	100.0
		-------	-------	-------	
	Total	36	100.0	100.0	

Valid cases   36   Missing cases   0

Visual Displays

While the numbers in the frequency table can be studied and compared, it is often useful to present results in a form that can be interpreted visually. Figure 7.3 is a pie chart of the data displayed in Figure 7.1. Each slice represents a day of the week. The size of the slice depends on the frequency of death for that day. Monday is represented by 10% of the pie chart, since 10.0% of the deaths for which the day is known occurred on Monday.

Figure 7.3   Pie chart of death by day of week

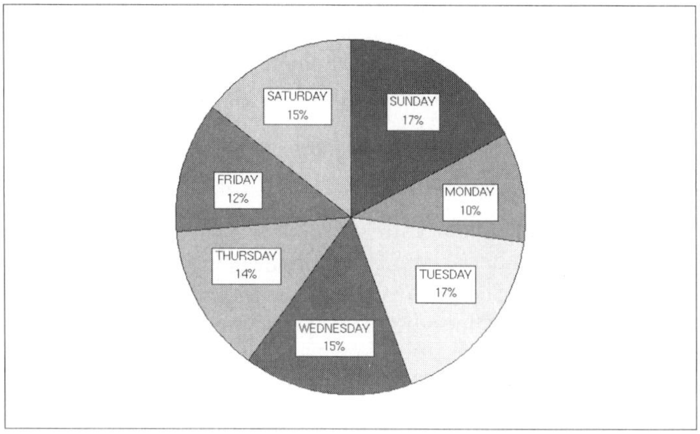

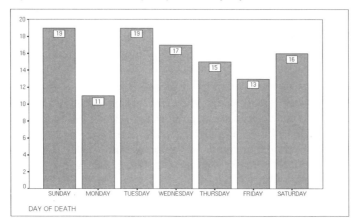

Another way to represent the data is with a bar chart, as shown in Figure 7.4. There is a bar for each day, and the height of the bar is proportional to the number of deaths observed on that day. The number of deaths, or frequency, is displayed at the top of each bar.

Figure 7.4   Bar chart of frequency of death by day of week

Only values that actually occur in the data are represented in the bar chart. For example, if no deaths occurred on Thursday, no space would be left for Thursday, and the bar for Wednesday would be followed by the bar for Friday. Likewise, if you charted the number of cars per family, the bar describing 6 cars might be next to the one for 25 cars if no family owned 7 to 24 cars. Therefore, you should pay attention to where categories with no cases may occur.

Although the basic information presented by frequency tables, pie charts, and bar charts is the same, the visual displays enliven the data. Differences among the days of the week are apparent at a glance, eliminating the need to pore over columns of numbers.

What Day?

Although the number of sudden cardiac deaths is small in this study, the data in Figure 7.2 indicate that the number of deaths on Mondays is not particularly large. In fact, the most deaths occurred on Sunday—slightly over 22%. A study of over 1000 sudden cardiac deaths in Rochester, Minnesota, also found a slightly increased incidence of death on weekends for men (Beard et al., 1982). The authors speculate that for men, this might mean that "the home environment is more stressful than the work environment." But you should be wary of explanations that are not directly supported by data. It is only too easy to find a clever explanation for any statistical finding.

Histograms

A frequency table or bar chart of all values for a variable is a convenient way of summarizing a variable that has a relatively small number of distinct values. Variables such as sex, country, and astrological sign are necessarily limited in the number of values they can have. For variables that can take on many different values, such as income to the penny or weight in ounces, a tally of the cases with each observed value may not be very informative. In the worst situation, when all cases have different values, a frequency table is little more than an ordered list of those values.

Variables that have many values can be summarized by grouping the values of the variables into intervals and counting the number of cases with values within each interval. For example, income can be grouped into $5,000 intervals such as 0–4999, 5000–9999, 10000–14999, and so forth, and the number of observations in each group can be tabulated. Such grouping should be done using SPSS during the actual analysis of the data. Whenever possible, the values for variables should be entered into the data file in their original, ungrouped form.

A histogram is a convenient way to display the distribution of such grouped values. Consider Figure 7.5, which is a histogram of body weight in pounds for the sample of 240 men from the Western Electric study. The numbers below the bars indicate the midpoint, or middle value, of each interval. Each bar represents the number of cases having values in the interval. Intervals that have no observations are included in the histogram, but no bars are printed. This differs from a bar chart, which does not leave space for the empty categories.

Figure 7.5   Histogram of body weight

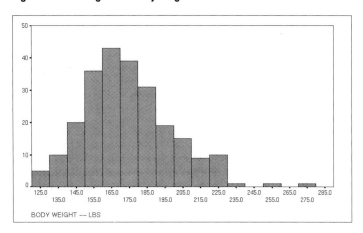

A histogram can be used whenever it is reasonable to group adjacent values. Histograms should not be used to display variables when there is no underlying order to the values. For example, if 100 different religions are arbitrarily assigned codes of 1 to 100, grouping values into intervals is meaningless. Either a bar chart or a histogram in which each interval corresponds to a single value should be used to display such data.

Percentiles

The information in a histogram can be further summarized by computing values above and below which a specified percentage of cases fall. Such values are called **percentiles**. For example, the 50th percentile, or median, is the value above and below which 50% (or half) of the cases fall. The 25th percentile is the value below which 25% and above which 75% of the cases fall.

Figure 7.6 contains values for the 25th, 50th, and 75th percentiles for the weight data shown in the histogram in Figure 7.5. You see that 25% of the men weigh less than 156 pounds, 50% weigh less than 171 pounds, and 75% weigh less than 187 pounds.

Figure 7.6   Percentiles for body weight

```
WT58       BODY WEIGHT -- LBS

Percentile    Value      Percentile    Value      Percentile    Value

  25.00      156.000       50.00      171.000       75.00      187.000

Valid cases     240     Missing cases      0
```

From these three percentiles, sometimes called **quartiles** (since they divide the distribution into four parts containing the same number of cases), you can tell that 50% of the men weigh between 156 and 187 pounds. (Remember that 25% of the men weigh less than 156 and 25% weigh more than 187. That leaves 50% of the men with weights between those two values.)

Screening Data

Frequency tables, bar charts, and histograms can serve purposes other than summarizing data. Unexpected codes in the tables may indicate errors in data entry or coding. Cases with day of death coded as 0 or 8 are in error if the numbers 1 through 7 represent the days of the week and 9 stands for unknown. Since errors in the data should be eliminated as soon as possible, it is a good idea to run frequency tables as the first step in analyzing data.

Frequency tables and visual displays can also help you identify cases with values that are unusual but possibly correct. For example, a tally of the number of cars in families may show a family with 25 cars. Although such a value is possible, especially if the survey did not specify cars in working condition, it raises suspicion and should be examined to ensure that it is really correct.

Incorrect data values distort the results of statistical analyses, and correct but unusual values may require special treatment. In either case, early identification is valuable.

How to Obtain Frequency Tables

The Frequencies procedure produces frequency tables, measures of central tendency and dispersion, histograms, and bar charts. You can sort frequency tables by value or by count, and you can display frequency tables in condensed format.

The minimum specification is one numeric or short string variable.

To get frequency tables, charts, and related statistics, from the menus choose:

Statistics
 Summarize ▶
  Frequencies...

This opens the Frequencies dialog box, as shown in Figure 7.7.

The numeric and short string variables are displayed on the source list. Select one or more variables for analysis. To get a standard frequency table showing counts, percentages, and valid and cumulative percentages, click on OK. The first 40 characters of any variable labels are shown in the output.

Figure 7.7   Frequencies dialog box

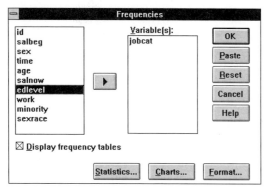

The following option is also available:

❏ **Display frequency tables**. By default, frequency tables are displayed. To suppress tables, deselect this item (for example, if you want to display only selected charts). If you suppress frequency tables without selecting any additional statistics or charts, only counts of cases with valid and missing values are shown.

Frequencies Statistics

To obtain optional descriptive and summary statistics for numeric variables, click on Statistics... in the Frequencies dialog box. This opens the Frequencies Statistics dialog box, as shown in Figure 7.8.

Figure 7.8   Frequencies Statistics dialog box

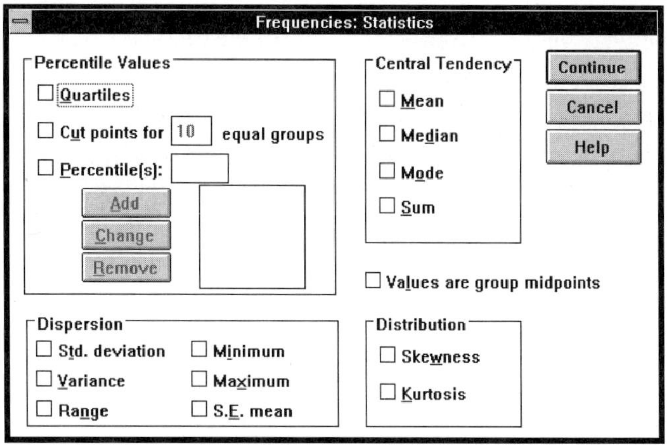

Percentile Values. You can choose one or more of the following:

❑ **Quartiles.** Displays the 25th, 50th, and 75th percentiles.

❑ **Cut points for n equal groups.** Displays percentile values that divide the sample into equal-size groups of cases. The default number of groups is 10. Optionally, you can request a different number of groups. Enter a positive integer between 2 and 100. For example, if you enter 4, quartiles are shown. The number of percentiles displayed is one fewer than the number of groups specified; you need only two values to divide a sample into three groups.

❑ **Percentile(s).** User-specified percentile values. Enter a percentile value between 0 and 100, and click on Add. Repeat this process for any other percentile values. Values appear in sorted order on the percentile list. To remove a percentile, highlight it on the list and click on Remove. To change a value, highlight it on the list, enter a new value, and click on Change.

If a requested percentile cannot be computed, SPSS displays a period (.) as the value associated with that percentile.

Dispersion. You can choose one or more of the following:

❑ **Std. deviation.** Standard deviation. A measure of how much observations vary from the mean, expressed in the same units as the data.

❑ **Variance.** A measure of how much observations vary from the mean, equal to the square of the standard deviation.

❑ **Range.** The difference between the largest (maximum) and smallest (minimum) values.

❑ **Minimum.** The smallest value.

❑ **Maximum.** The largest value.

❑ **S.E. mean.** Standard error of the mean. A measure of variability of the sample mean.

Central Tendency. You can choose one or more of the following:

❑ **Mean.** The arithmetic average.

❑ **Median.** The median is defined as the value below which half the cases fall. If there is an even number of cases, the median is the average of the two middle cases when the cases are sorted in ascending order. The median is not available if you request sorting by frequency counts (see "Frequencies Format" on p. 164).

❑ **Mode.** The most frequently occurring value. If several values are tied for the highest frequency, only the smallest value is displayed.

❑ **Sum.** The sum of all the values.

Distribution. You can choose one or more of the following:

❏ **Skewness.** An index of the degree to which a distribution is not symmetric. The standard error of the skewness statistic is also displayed.

❏ **Kurtosis.** A measure of the extent to which observations cluster around a central point. The standard error of the kurtosis statistic is also displayed.

For grouped or collapsed data, the following option is also available:

❏ **Values are group midpoints.** If the values represent midpoints of groups (for example, all people in their thirties are coded as 35), you can estimate percentiles for the original, ungrouped data, assuming that cases are uniformly distributed in each interval. Since this affects the values of the median and the percentiles for *all* variables, you should not select this option if any variable on the variable list contains ungrouped data.

Frequencies Charts

To get bar charts or histograms, click on Charts... in the Frequencies dialog box. This opens the Frequencies Charts dialog box, as shown in Figure 7.9.

Figure 7.9   Frequencies Charts dialog box

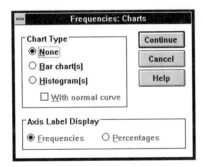

Chart Type. You can choose one of the following alternatives:

○ **None.** No charts. This is the default setting.

○ **Bar chart(s).** The scale is determined by the frequency count of the largest category plotted.

○ **Histogram(s).** Histograms are available for numeric variables only. The number of intervals plotted is 21 (or fewer if the range of values is less than 21).

   ❏ **With normal curve.** This option superimposes a normal curve over the histogram(s).

Axis Label Display. For bar charts, you can control labeling of the vertical axis. Choose one of the following alternatives:

○ **Frequencies.** The axis is labeled with frequencies. This is the default setting.

○ **Percentages.** The axis is labeled with percentages.

Frequencies Format

To modify the format of the frequency table output, select Display frequency tables in the Frequencies dialog box and click on Format... to open the Frequencies Format dialog box, as shown in Figure 7.10.

Figure 7.10   Frequencies Format dialog box

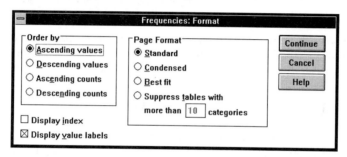

Order by. Order selection determines the order by which data values are sorted and displayed in a frequency table. You can choose one of the following alternatives:

○ **Ascending values.** Sorts categories by ascending order of values. This is the default setting.

○ **Descending values.** Sorts categories by descending order of values.

○ **Ascending counts.** Sorts categories by ascending order of frequency counts.

○ **Descending counts.** Sorts categories by descending order of frequency counts.

If you request a histogram or percentiles, categories of the frequency table are sorted by ascending order, regardless of your order selection.

Page Format. You can choose one of the following alternatives:

○ **Standard.** Displays as many frequency tables on a page as will fit. This is the default.

○ **Condensed.** Condensed format. This format displays frequency counts in three columns. It does not display value labels or percentages that include cases with missing values, and it rounds valid and cumulative percentages to integers.

○ **Best fit.** Conditional condensed format. If a table cannot fit on one page in default format, condensed format is used.

○ **Suppress tables with more than n categories.** Does not display tables for variables with more categories than specified. To override the default value of 10, enter an integer value greater than or equal to 1. This item is particularly useful if your variable list includes continuous variables for which summary statistics or histograms are requested, but for which a frequency table would be long and uninformative. For example, the frequency table that would accompany the histogram of weight in Figure 7.5 would have a separate entry for each one-pound weight increment.

The following additional format choices are also available:

❏ **Display index.** Displays a positional and alphabetic index of frequency tables. This is particularly useful if you have a large number of variables.

❏ **Display value labels.** The first 20 characters of the value labels are shown. This is the default setting. To suppress value labels, deselect this item. Value labels are automatically suppressed when condensed format is chosen.

Additional Features Available with Command Syntax

You can customize your frequencies if you paste your selections into a syntax window and edit the resulting FREQUENCIES command syntax (see Chapter 4). Additional features include:

- The ability to exclude ranges of data values from analysis (with the VARIABLES subcommand).
- Additional formatting options, such as the ability to begin each frequency table on a new page, double-space tables, or write tables to a file (with the FORMAT subcommand).
- For bar charts, user-specified lower and upper data bounds and maximum scale axis value (with the BARCHART subcommand).
- For histograms, user-specified lower and upper data bounds, maximum horizontal axis value, and interval width (with the HISTOGRAM subcommand).
- Additional options for processing of grouped data (with the GROUPED subcommand).

See Appendix A for command syntax rules. See the *SPSS Base System Syntax Reference Guide* for complete FREQUENCIES command syntax.

8

Descriptive Statistics

Survey data that rely on voluntary information are subject to many sources of error. People fail to recall events correctly, deliberately distort the truth, or refuse to participate. Refusals influence survey results by failing to provide information about certain types of people—those who refuse to answer surveys at all and those who avoid certain questions. For example, if college graduates tend to be unwilling to answer polls, results of surveys will be biased.

One possible way to examine the veracity of survey responses is to compare them to similar data recorded in official records. Systematic differences between actual data and self-reported responses jeopardize the usefulness of the survey. Unfortunately, in many sensitive areas—illicit drug use, abortion history, or even income—official records are usually unavailable.

Wyner (1980) examined the differences between the actual and self-reported numbers of arrests obtained from 79 former heroin addicts enrolled in the Vera Institute of Justice Supported Employment Experiment. As part of their regular quarterly interviews, participants were asked about their arrest histories in New York City. The self-reported value was compared to arrest-record data coded from New York City Police Department arrest sheets. The goal of the study was not only to quantify the extent of error but also to identify factors related to inaccurate responses.

Examining the Data

Figure 8.1 shows histograms for the following three variables—actual number of arrests, self-reported number of arrests, and the difference of the two. From a histogram, it is possible to see the shape of the distribution; that is, how likely the different values are, how much spread, or **variability**, there is among the values, and where typical values are concentrated. Such characteristics are important because of the direct insight they provide into the data and because many statistical procedures are based on assumptions about the underlying distributions of variables.

Figure 8.1   Self-reported and actual arrests

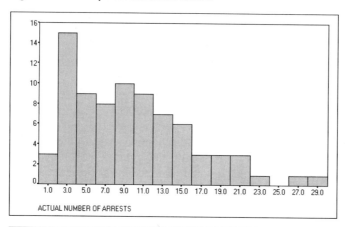

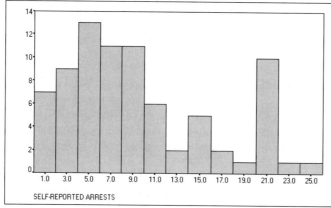

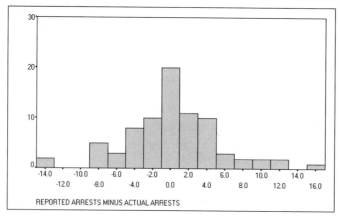

The distributions of the self-reported and actual number of arrests have a somewhat similar shape. Neither distribution has an obvious central value, although the self-reported values peak at 4 to 5 arrests, while the actual number of arrests peaks at 2 to 3 arrests. The distribution of self-reported arrests peaks again at 20 to 21 arrests. The peaks corresponding to intervals containing 5, 15, and 20 arrests arouse suspicion that people may be more likely to report their arrest records as round numbers. Examination of the actual number of arrests shows no corresponding peaks at multiples of five.

The distribution of the differences between reported and actual number of arrests is not as irregularly shaped as the two distributions from which it is derived. It has a peak at the interval with a midpoint of 0. Most cases cluster around the peak values, and cases far from these values are infrequent.

Summarizing the Data

Although frequency tables and bar charts are useful for summarizing and displaying data (see Chapter 7), further condensation and description is often desirable. A variety of summary measures that convey information about the data in single numbers can be computed. The choice of summary measure, or statistic, depends upon characteristics of both the data and the statistic. One important characteristic of the data that must be considered is the level of measurement of each variable being studied.

Levels of Measurement

Measurement is the assignment of numbers or codes to observations. **Levels of measurement** are distinguished by ordering and distance properties. A computer does not know what measurement underlies the values it is given. You must determine the level of measurement of your data and apply appropriate statistical techniques.

The traditional classification of levels of measurement into nominal, ordinal, interval, and ratio scales was developed by S. S. Stevens (1946). This remains the basic typology and is the one used throughout this manual. Variations exist, however, and issues concerning the statistical effect of ignoring levels of measurement have been debated (for example, see Borgatta & Bohrnstedt, 1980).

Nominal Measurement

The **nominal** level of measurement is the "lowest" in the typology because no assumptions are made about relations between values. Each value defines a distinct category and serves merely as a label or name (hence, *nominal* level) for the category. For example, the birthplace of an individual is a nominal variable. For most purposes, there is no inherent ordering among cities or towns. Although cities can be ordered according to size, density, or air pollution, as birthplaces they cannot be ordered or ranked against other cities. When numeric values are attached to nominal categories, they are merely identifiers. None of the properties of numbers, such as relative size, addition, or multiplication, can be applied to these numerically coded categories. Therefore, statistics that assume ordering or meaningful numerical distances between the values do not ordinarily give useful information about nominal variables.

Ordinal Measurement

When it is possible to rank or order all categories according to some criterion, the **ordinal** level of measurement is achieved. For example, classifying employees into clerical, supervisory, and managerial categories is an ordering according to responsibilities or skills. Each category has a position lower or higher than another category. Furthermore, knowing that supervisory is higher than clerical and that managerial is higher than supervisory automatically means that managerial is higher than clerical. However, nothing is known about how much higher; no distance is measured. Ordering is the sole mathematical property applicable to ordinal measurements, and the use of numeric values does not imply that any other property of numbers is applicable.

Interval Measurement

In addition to order, **interval** measurements have the property of meaningful distance between values. A thermometer, for example, measures temperature in degrees that are the same size at any point on the scale. The difference between 20°C and 21°C is the same as the difference between 5°C and 6°C. However, an interval scale does not have an inherently determined zero point. In the familiar Celsius and Fahrenheit systems, 0° is determined by an agreed-upon definition, not by the absence of heat. Consequently, interval-level measurement allows us to study differences between items but not their proportionate magnitudes. For example, it is incorrect to say that 80°F is twice as hot as 40°F.

Ratio Measurement

Ratio measurements have all the ordering and distance properties of an interval scale. In addition, a zero point can be meaningfully designated. In measuring physical distances between objects using feet or meters, a zero distance is naturally defined as the absence of any distance. The existence of a zero point means that ratio comparisons can be made. For example, it is quite meaningful to say that a 6-foot-tall adult is twice as tall as a 3-foot-tall child or that a 500-meter race is five times as long as a 100-meter race.

Because ratio measurements satisfy all the properties of the real number system, any mathematical manipulations appropriate for real numbers can be applied to ratio measures. However, the existence of a zero point is seldom critical for statistical analyses.

Summary Statistics

Figure 8.2 and Figure 8.3 contain a variety of summary statistics that are useful in describing the distributions of self-reported and actual numbers of arrests and their difference. The statistics can be grouped into three categories according to what they quantify: central tendency, dispersion, and shape.

Figure 8.2 was obtained with the Descriptives procedure; Figure 8.3, with the Frequencies procedure. If your computer has a math coprocessor, the Descriptives procedure is faster than the Frequencies procedure. However, the median and mode are not available with Descriptives.

Figure 8.2   Summary statistics from the Descriptives procedure

```
Variable  ACTUAL      ACTUAL NUMBER OF ARRESTS

Mean            9.253              S.E. Mean         .703
Std Dev         6.248              Variance        39.038
Kurtosis         .597              S.E. Kurt         .535
Skewness         .908              S.E. Skew         .271
Range         28.000              Minimum             1
Maximum           29              Sum           731.000

Valid observations -       79     Missing observations -        0

- - - - - - - - - - - - - - - - - - - - - - - - - - - - - - - - -

Variable  SELF        SELF-REPORTED ARRESTS

Mean            8.962              S.E. Mean         .727
Std Dev         6.458              Variance        41.704
Kurtosis        -.485              S.E. Kurt         .535
Skewness         .750              S.E. Skew         .271
Range         25.000              Minimum             0
Maximum           25              Sum           708.000

Valid observations -       79     Missing observations -        0

- - - - - - - - - - - - - - - - - - - - - - - - - - - - - - - - -

Variable  ERRORS      REPORTED ARRESTS MINUS ACTUAL ARRESTS

Mean           -.291              S.E. Mean         .587
Std Dev         5.216              Variance        27.209
Kurtosis        1.102              S.E. Kurt         .535
Skewness         .125              S.E. Skew         .271
Range         29.000              Minimum        -14.000
Maximum           15              Sum            -23.000

Valid observations -       79     Missing observations -        0
```

Figure 8.3   Summary statistics from the Frequencies procedure

```
ACTUAL     ACTUAL NUMBER OF ARRESTS


Mean          9.253    Std err        .703    Median       8.000
Mode          3.000    Std dev       6.248    Variance    39.038
Kurtosis       .597    S E Kurt       .535    Skewness      .908
S E Skew       .271    Range       28.000    Minimum      1.000
Maximum      29.000    Sum        731.000


Valid cases       79    Missing cases       0

- - - - - - - - - - - - - - - - - - - - - - - - - - - - - - -


SELF       SELF-REPORTED ARRESTS


Mean          8.962    Std err        .727    Median       7.000
Mode          5.000    Std dev       6.458    Variance    41.704
Kurtosis      -.485    S E Kurt       .535    Skewness      .750
S E Skew       .271    Range       25.000    Minimum       .000
Maximum      25.000    Sum        708.000


Valid cases       79    Missing cases       0

- - - - - - - - - - - - - - - - - - - - - - - - - - - - - - -

ERRORS     REPORTED ARRESTS MINUS ACTUAL ARRESTS


Mean         -.291    Std err        .587    Median        .000
Mode        -1.000    Std dev       5.216    Variance    27.209
Kurtosis     1.102    S E Kurt       .535    Skewness      .125
S E Skew       .271    Range       29.000    Minimum    -14.000
Maximum      15.000    Sum        -23.000

* Multiple modes exist.  The smallest value is shown.


Valid cases       79    Missing cases       0
```

Measures of Central Tendency

The mean, median, and mode are frequently used to describe the location of a distribution. The **mode** is the most frequently occurring value (or values). For the actual number of arrests, the mode is 3; for the self-reported values, it is 5. The distribution of the difference between the actual and self-reported values is multimodal. That is, it has more than one mode because the values −1 and 0 occur with equal frequency. SPSS, however, displays only one of the modes, the smaller value, as shown in Figure 8.3. The mode can be used for data measured at any level. It is not usually the preferred measure for interval and ordinal data, since it ignores much of the available information.

The **median** is the value above and below which one-half of the observations fall. For example, if there are 79 observations, the median is the 40th-largest observation. When there is an even number of observations, no unique center value exists, so the mean of the two middle observations is usually taken as the median value. For the arrest data, the median is 0 for the differences, 8 for the actual arrests, and 7 for the self-reported arrests. For ordinal data, the median is usually a good measure of central tendency, since it uses the ranking information. The median should not be used for nominal data, since ranking of the observations is not possible.

The **mean**, also called the arithmetic average, is the sum of the values of all observations divided by the number of observations. Thus,

$$\bar{X} = \sum_{i=1}^{N} \frac{X_i}{N}$$

Equation 8.1

where N is the number of cases and X_i is the value of the variable for the ith case. Since the mean utilizes the distance between observations, the measurements should be interval or ratio. Calculating the mean race, religion, and auto color provides no useful information. For dichotomous variables coded as 0 and 1, the mean has a special interpretation: it is the proportion of cases coded 1 in the data.

The three measures of central tendency need not be the same. For example, the mean number of actual arrests is 9.25, the median is 8, and the mode is 3. The arithmetic mean is greatly influenced by outlying observations, while the median is not. Adding a single case with 400 arrests would increase the mean from 9.25 to 14.1, but it would not affect the median. Therefore, if there are values far removed from the rest of the observations, the median may be a better measure of central tendency than the mean.

For symmetric distributions, the observed mean, median, and mode are usually close in value. For example, the mean of the differences between self-reported and actual arrest values is −0.291, the median is 0, and the modes are −1 and 0. All three measures give similar estimates of central tendency in this case.

Measures of Dispersion

Two distributions can have the same values for measures of central tendency and yet be very dissimilar in other respects. For example, if the actual number of arrests for five cases in two methadone clinics is 0, 1, 10, 14, and 20 for clinic A, and 8, 8, 9, 10, and 10 for clinic B, the mean number of arrests (9) is the same in both. However, even a cursory examination of the data indicates that the two clinics are different. In clinic B, all cases have fairly comparable arrest records, while in clinic A the records are quite disparate. A quick and useful index of dissimilarity, or dispersion, is the **range**. It is the difference between the maximum and minimum observed values. For clinic B, the range is 2, while for clinic A it is 20. Since the range is computed from only the minimum and maximum values, it is sensitive to extremes.

Although the range is a useful index of dispersion, especially for ordinal data, it does not take into account the distribution of observations between the maximum and minimum. A commonly used measure of variation that is based on all observations is the **variance**. For a sample, the variance is computed by summing the squared differences

from the mean for all observations and then dividing by one less than the number of observations. In mathematical notation, this is

$$S^2 = \sum_{i=1}^{N} \frac{(X_i - \bar{X})^2}{N-1}$$ **Equation 8.2**

If all observations are identical—that is, if there is no variation—the variance is 0. The
more spread out they are, the greater the variance. For the methadone clinic example
above, the sample variance for clinic A is 73, while for clinic B it's 1.

The square root of the variance is termed the **standard deviation**. While the variance
is expressed in squared units, the standard deviation is expressed in the same units of
measurement as the observations. This is an appealing property, since it is much clearer
to think of variability in terms of the number of arrests rather than the number of arrests
squared.

The Normal Distribution

For many variables, most observations are concentrated near the middle of the distribution. As distance from the central concentration increases, the frequency of observation
decreases. Such distributions are often described as "bell-shaped." An example is the
normal distribution (see Figure 8.4). A broad range of observed phenomena in nature
and in society is approximately normally distributed. For example, the distributions of
variables such as height, weight, and blood pressure are approximately normal. The normal distribution is by far the most important theoretical distribution in statistics and
serves as a reference point for describing the form of many distributions of sample data.

The normal distribution is symmetric: each half is a mirror image of the other. Three
measures of central tendency—the mean, median, and mode—coincide exactly. As
shown in Figure 8.4, 95% of all observations fall within two standard deviations (σ) of
the mean (μ), and 68% fall within one standard deviation. The exact theoretical propor-

tion of cases falling into various regions of the normal curve can be found in tables included in most introductory statistics textbooks.

Figure 8.4   Normal curve

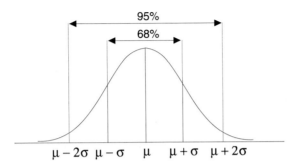

In SPSS, you can superimpose a normal distribution on a histogram. Consider Figure 8.5, a histogram of the differences in self-reported and actual arrests. The curved line indicates what the distribution of cases would be if the variable had a normal distribution with the same mean and variance. Tests for normality are available in the Explore procedure (see Chapter 9).

Figure 8.5   Histogram with normal curve superimposed

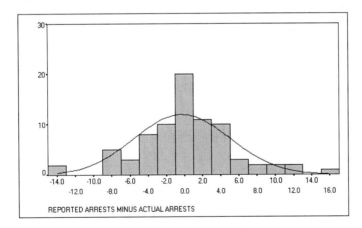

Measures of Shape

A distribution that is not symmetric but has more cases (more of a "tail") toward one end of the distribution than the other is said to be **skewed**. If the tail is toward larger values, the distribution is positively skewed, or skewed to the right. If the tail is toward smaller values, the distribution is negatively skewed, or skewed to the left.

Another characteristic of the form of a distribution is called **kurtosis**—the extent to which, for a given standard deviation, observations cluster around a central point. If cases within a distribution cluster more than those in the normal distribution (that is, the distribution is more peaked), the distribution is called **leptokurtic**. A leptokurtic distribution also tends to have more observations straggling into the extreme tails than does a normal distribution. If cases cluster less than in the normal distribution (that is, it is flatter), the distribution is termed **platykurtic**.

Although examination of a histogram provides some indication of possible skewness and kurtosis, it is often desirable to compute formal indexes that measure these properties. Values for skewness and kurtosis are 0 if the observed distribution is exactly normal. Positive values for skewness indicate a positive skew, while positive values for kurtosis indicate a distribution that is more peaked than normal. For samples from a normal distribution, measures of skewness and kurtosis typically will not be exactly 0 but will fluctuate around 0 because of sampling variation.

Standard Scores

It is often desirable to describe the relative position of an observation within a distribution. Knowing that a person achieved a score of 80 in a competitive examination conveys little information about performance. Judgment of performance would depend on whether 80 is the lowest, the median, or the highest score.

One way of describing the location of a case in a distribution is to calculate its **standard score**. This score, sometimes called the **Z score**, indicates how many standard deviations above or below the mean an observation falls. It is calculated by finding the difference between the value of a particular observation X_i and the mean of the distribution, and dividing this difference by the standard deviation:

$$Z_i = \frac{X_i - \bar{X}}{S}$$

Equation 8.3

The mean of Z scores is 0 and the standard deviation is 1. For example, a participant with five actual arrests would have a Z score of $(5 - 9.25)/6.25$, or -0.68. Since the score is negative, the case had fewer arrests than the average for the individuals studied. Figure 8.6 shows summary statistics for Z scores based on the difference between actual and self-reported arrests.

Figure 8.6   Summary statistics for Z scores

```
Variable  ZERRORS    Zscore:  REPORTED ARRESTS MINUS ACTUAL

Mean              .000         S.E. Mean        .113
Std Dev          1.000         Variance        1.000
Kurtosis         1.102         S.E. Kurt        .535
Skewness          .125         S.E. Skew        .271
Range            5.560         Minimum      -2.62812
Maximum       2.93146          Sum              .000
```

Standardization permits comparison of scores from different distributions. For example, an individual with Z scores of -0.68 for actual arrests and 1.01 for the difference between self-reported and actual arrests had fewer arrests than the average but exaggerated more than the average.

When the distribution of a variable is approximately normal and the mean and variance are known or are estimated from large samples, the Z score of an observation provides more specific information about its location. For example, if actual arrests and response error were normally distributed, 75% of cases would have more arrests than the example individual, but only 16% would have exaggerated as much as the example individual (75% of a standard normal curve lies above a Z score of -0.68, and 16% lies above a score of 1.01).

Who Lies?

The distribution of the difference between self-reported and actual arrests indicates that response error exists. Although observing a mean close to 0 is comforting, misrepresentation is obvious. What, then, are the characteristics that influence willingness to be truthful?

Wyner identifies three factors that are related to inaccuracies: the number of arrests before 1960, the number of multiple-charge arrests, and the perceived desirability of being arrested. The first factor is related to a frequently encountered difficulty—the more distant an event in time, the less likely it is to be correctly recalled. The second factor, underreporting of multiple-charge arrests, is probably caused by the general social undesirability of serious arrests. Finally, persons who view arrest records as laudatory are likely to inflate their accomplishments.

How to Obtain Descriptive Statistics

The Descriptives procedure computes univariate summary statistics and saves standardized variables. Although it computes statistics also available in the Frequencies procedure, Descriptives computes descriptive statistics for continuous variables more efficiently because it does not sort values into a frequencies table.

The minimum specification is one or more numeric variables.

To obtain descriptive statistics and Z scores, from the menus choose:

Statistics
  Summarize ▶
    Descriptives...

This opens the Descriptives dialog box, as shown in Figure 8.7.

Figure 8.7   Descriptives dialog box

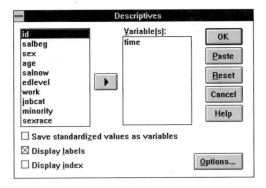

The numeric variables in your data file appear on the source list. Select one or more variables for which you want descriptive statistics. To obtain the default statistics (mean, standard deviation, minimum, and maximum) and display variable labels, click on OK.

You can also choose one or more of the following:

❑ **Save standardized values as variables.** Creates one Z-score variable for each variable. New variable names are created by prefixing the letter z to the first seven characters of original variable names. For example, *zsalnow* is the Z-score variable for *salnow*. If this naming convention would produce duplicate names, an alternate naming convention is used: first *zsc001* through *zsc099*, then *stdz01* through *stdz09*, then *zzzz01* through *zzzz09*, and then *zqzq01* through *zqzq09*.

Variable labels for Z-score variables are generated by prefixing *zscore* to the first 31 characters of the original variable label. If SPSS assigns a variable name that does not contain part of the original variable name, it prefixes *zscore(original variable name*) to the first 31 characters of the original variable's label. If the original variable has no label, it uses *zscore*(*original variable name*) for the label.

SPSS displays a table in the output showing the original variable name, the new variable name and its label, and the number of cases for which the Z score is computed.

❏ **Display labels.** Displays 40-character variable labels in the output. If requested statistics do not fit in the available page width, labels are truncated to 21 characters and then, if necessary, a serial output format is used. Labels are displayed by default.

❏ **Display index.** Displays a positional and alphabetical reference index showing the page location in the statistics output for each variable. The variables are listed by their position in the data file and alphabetically.

Descriptives Options

To obtain additional descriptive statistics or control the order by which variables appear in the output, click on Options... in the Descriptives dialog box. This opens the Descriptives Options dialog box, as shown in Figure 8.8.

Figure 8.8   Descriptives Options dialog box

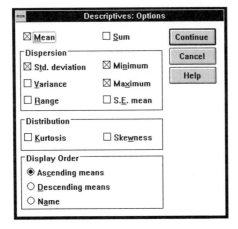

At least one statistic must be selected.

You can choose one or both of the following:

❏ **Mean.** The arithmetic average. Displayed by default.

❏ **Sum.** The sum of all the values.

Dispersion. You can choose one or more of the following dispersion statistics:

❏ **Std. deviation.** Standard deviation. Displayed by default. A measure of how much observations vary from the mean, expressed in the same units as the data.

❏ **Variance.** A measure of how much observations vary from the mean, equal to the square of the standard deviation.

❏ **Range.** The difference between the largest (maximum) and smallest (minimum) values.

❏ **Minimum.** The smallest value. Displayed by default.

❏ **Maximum.** The largest value. Displayed by default.

❏ **S. E. mean.** Standard error of the mean. A measure of variability of the sample mean.

Distribution. You can choose one or both of the following distribution statistics:

❏ **Kurtosis.** A measure of the extent to which observations cluster around a central point, given their standard deviation. The standard error of the kurtosis statistic is also displayed.

❏ **Skewness.** An index of the degree to which a distribution is not symmetric. The standard error of the skewness statistic is also displayed.

Display Order. You can choose one of the following:

○ **Ascending means.** Displays variables by order of ascending means. This is the default setting.

○ **Descending means.** Displays variables by order of descending means.

○ **Name.** Displays variables in alphabetical order by name.

Additional Features Available with Command Syntax

You can customize your descriptive statistics if you paste your selections into a syntax window and edit the resulting DESCRIPTIVES command syntax (see Chapter 4). Additional features include:

- Z scores for a subset of variables (with the VARIABLES subcommand).
- User-specified names for Z-score variables (with the VARIABLES subcommand).
- Exclusion from the analysis of cases with missing values for any variable (with the MISSING subcommand).
- Additional display order options such as sorting by variance (with the SORT subcommand).

See Appendix A for command syntax rules. See the *SPSS Base System Syntax Reference Guide* for complete DESCRIPTIVES command syntax.

9

Exploring Data

The first step of data analysis should always be a detailed examination of the data. Whether the problem you're solving is simple or complex, or whether you're planning to do a *t* test or a multivariate repeated measures analysis of variance, you should first take a careful look at the data. In this chapter, we'll consider a variety of descriptive statistics and displays useful as a preliminary step in data analysis. Using the SPSS Explore procedure, you can screen your data, visually examine the distributions of values for various groups, and test for normality and homogeneity of variance.

Reasons for Exploring Data

There are several important reasons for examining your data carefully before you begin your analysis. Let's start with the simplest.

Identifying Mistakes

Data must make a hazardous journey before finding final rest in a computer file. First, a measurement is made or a response elicited, sometimes with a faulty instrument or by a careless experimenter. The result is then recorded, often barely legibly, in a lab notebook, medical chart, or personnel record. Often this information is not actually coded and entered onto a data form until much later. From this form, the numbers must find their way into their designated slot in the computer file. Then they must be properly introduced to a computer program. Their correct location and missing values must be specified.

Errors can be introduced at any step. Some errors are easy to spot. For example, forgetting to declare a value as missing, using an invalid code, or entering the value 701 for age will be apparent from a frequency table. Other errors, such as entering an age of 54 instead of 45, may be difficult, if not impossible, to spot. Unless your first step is to carefully check your data for mistakes, errors may contaminate all of your analyses.

Exploring the Data

After completing data acquisition, entry, and checking, it's time to look at the data—not to search haphazardly for statistical significance, but to examine the data systematically using simple exploratory techniques. Why bother, you might ask? Why not just begin your analysis?

Data analysis has often been compared to detective work. Before the actual trial of a hypothesis, there is much evidence to be gathered and sifted. Based on the clues, the hypothesis itself may be altered, or the methods for testing it may have to be changed. For example, if the distribution of data values reveals a gap—that is, a range where no values occur—we must ask why. If some values are extreme (far removed from the other values), we must look for reasons. If the pattern of numbers is strange (for example, if all values are even), we must determine why. If we see unexpected variability in the data, we must look for possible explanations; perhaps there are additional variables that may explain it.

Preparing for Hypothesis Testing

Looking at the distribution of the values is also important for evaluating the appropriateness of the statistical techniques we are planning to use for hypothesis testing or model building. Perhaps the data must be transformed so that the distribution is approximately normal or so that the variances in the groups are similar; or perhaps a nonparametric technique is needed.

Ways of Displaying Data

Now that we've established why it's important to look at data, we'll consider some of the techniques available for exploring data. One technique is to create a graphical representation of the data. To illustrate, we'll use data from a study of coronary heart disease among male employees of Western Electric and salary data from a study of employees of a bank engaged in Equal Employment Opportunity litigation.

The Histogram

The **histogram** is commonly used to represent data graphically. The range of observed values is subdivided into equal intervals, and the number of cases in each interval is obtained. Each bar in a histogram represents the number of cases with values within the interval.

Figure 9.1 is a histogram of diastolic blood pressure for a sample of 239 men from the Western Electric study. The values on the vertical axis indicate the number of cases. The values on the horizontal axis are midpoints of value ranges. For example, the midpoint of the first bar is 65, and the midpoint of the second bar is 75, indicating that each bar covers a value range of 10. Thus, the first bar contains cases with diastolic blood pressures in the 60's. Cases with diastolic blood pressures in the 70's go into the next bar, and so on.

Figure 9.1   Histogram of diastolic blood pressure

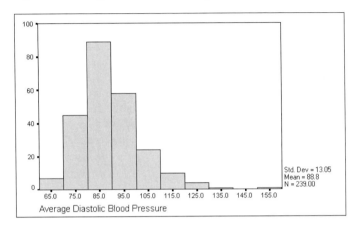

The Stem-and-Leaf Plot

A display closely related to the histogram is the stem-and-leaf plot. A **stem-and-leaf plot** provides more information about the actual values than does a histogram. Consider Figure 9.2, which is a stem-and-leaf plot of the diastolic blood pressures. As in a histogram, the length of each row corresponds to the number of cases that fall into a particular interval. However, a stem-and-leaf plot represents each case with a numeric value that corresponds to the actual observed value. This is done by dividing observed values into two components—the leading digit or digits, called the **stem**, and the trailing digit, called the **leaf**. For example, the value 75 has a stem of 7 and a leaf of 5.

Figure 9.2   Stem-and-leaf plot of diastolic blood pressure

```
Frequency     Stem &  Leaf

      .00      6 *
     7.00      6 .  5558889
    13.00      7 *  0000111223344
    32.00      7 .  55555555667777777777788888889999
    44.00      8 *  00000000000000000000001111122222333333334444
    45.00      8 .  5555555555666666677777777777777788888999999999
    31.00      9 *  0000000001111111122222222333334
    27.00      9 .  556666667777778888888888899999
    13.00     10 *  0000122233333
    11.00     10 .  55555577899
     5.00     11 *  00003
     5.00     11 .  55789
     2.00     12 *  01
     4.00 Extremes    (125), (133), (160)

Stem width:    10
Each leaf:     1 case(s)
```

In this example, each stem is divided into two rows. The first row of each pair has cases with leaves of 0 through 4, while the second row has cases with leaves of 5 through 9. Consider the two rows that correspond to the stem of 11. In the first row, we can see that there are four cases with diastolic blood pressure of 110 and one case with a reading of 113. In the second row, there are two cases with a value of 115 and one case each with a value of 117, 118, and 119.

The last row of the stem-and-leaf plot is for cases with extreme values (values far removed from the rest). In this row, the actual values are displayed in parentheses. In the frequency column, we see that there are four extreme cases. Their values are 125, 133, and 160. Only distinct values are listed.

To identify cases with extreme values, you can generate a table identifying cases with the largest and smallest values. Figure 9.3 shows the five cases with the largest and smallest values for diastolic blood pressure. Values of a case-labeling variable can be used to identify cases. Otherwise, the sequence of the case in the data file is reported.

Figure 9.3   Cases with extreme values

```
                        Extreme  Values
                        -------  ------

5     Highest     Case #              5    Lowest     Case #

      160         Case: 120           65             Case: 73
      133         Case: 56            65             Case: 156
      125         Case: 163           65             Case: 157
      125         Case: 42            68             Case: 153
      121         Case: 26            68             Case: 175
```

Other Stems

In Figure 9.2, each stem was divided into two parts—one for leaves of 0 through 4, and the other for leaves of 5 through 9. When there are few stems, it is sometimes useful to subdivide each stem even further. Consider Figure 9.4, a stem-and-leaf plot of cholesterol levels for the men in the Western Electric study. In this figure, stems 2 and 3 are divided into five parts, each representing two leaf values. The first row, designated by an asterisk, is for leaves of 0 and 1; the next, designated by *t*, is for leaves of 2's and 3's; the third, designated by *f*, is for leaves of 4's and 5's; the fourth, designated by *s*, is for leaves of 6's and 7's; and the fifth, designated by a period, is for leaves of 8's and 9's. Rows without cases are not represented in the plot. For example, in Figure 9.4, the first two rows for stem 1 (corresponding to 0–1 and 2–3) are omitted.

This stem-and-leaf plot differs from the previous one in another way. Since cholesterol values have a wide range—from 106 to 515 in this example—using the first two digits for the stem would result in an unnecessarily detailed plot. Therefore, we will use only the hundreds digit as the stem, rather than the first two digits. The stem setting of 100 appears in the column labeled *Stem width*. The leaf is then the tens digit. The last digit is ignored. Thus, from this stem-and-leaf plot, it is not possible to determine the exact cholesterol level for a case. Instead, each case is classified by only its first two digits.

Figure 9.4   Stem-and-leaf plot of cholesterol levels

```
Frequency    Stem & Leaf

    1.00 Extremes     (106)
    2.00      1 f   55
    6.00      1 s   677777
   12.00      1 .   888889999999
   23.00      2 *   00000000000001111111111
   36.00      2 t   222222222222222223333333333333333333
   35.00      2 f   44444444444444444445555555555555555
   42.00      2 s   666666666666666666667777777777777777777777
   28.00      2 .   8888888888888889999999999999
   18.00      3 *   000000011111111111
   17.00      3 t   22222222222233333
    9.00      3 f   444445555
    6.00      3 s   666777
    1.00      3 .   8
    3.00 Extremes     (393), (425), (515)

Stem width:   100
Each leaf:     1 case(s)
```

The Boxplot

Both the histogram and the stem-and-leaf plot provide useful information about the distribution of observed values. We can see how tightly cases cluster together. We can see if there is a single peak or several peaks. We can determine if there are extreme values.

A display that further summarizes information about the distribution of the values is the boxplot. Instead of plotting the actual values, a **boxplot** displays summary statistics for the distribution. It plots the median, the 25th percentile, the 75th percentile, and values that are far removed from the rest.

Figure 9.5 shows an annotated sketch of a boxplot. The lower boundary of the box is the 25th percentile and the upper boundary is the 75th percentile. (These percentiles, sometimes called Tukey's hinges, are calculated a little differently from ordinary percentiles.) The horizontal line inside the box represents the median. Fifty percent of the cases have values within the box. The length of the box corresponds to the interquartile range, which is the difference between the 75th and 25th percentiles.

The boxplot includes two categories of cases with outlying values. Cases with values that are more than 3 box-lengths from the upper or lower edge of the box are called **extreme values**. On the boxplot, these are designated with an asterisk (*). Cases with values that are between 1.5 and 3 box-lengths from the upper or lower edge of the box are called **outliers** and are designated with a circle. The largest and smallest observed values that aren't outliers are also shown. Lines are drawn from the ends of the box to these values. (These lines are sometimes called **whiskers** and the plot is called a **box-and-whiskers plot**.)

Figure 9.5   Annotated sketch of a boxplot

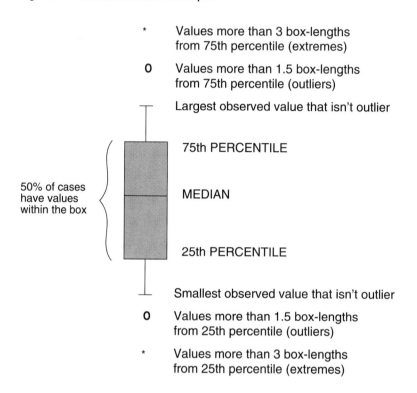

What can you tell about your data from a boxplot? From the median, you can determine the central tendency, or location. From the length of the box, you can determine the spread, or variability, of your observations. If the median is not in the center of the box, you know that the observed values are skewed. If the median is closer to the bottom of the box than to the top, the data are positively skewed. If the median is closer to the top of the box than to the bottom, the opposite is true: the distribution is negatively skewed. The length of the tail is shown by the whiskers and the outlying and extreme points.

Boxplots are particularly useful for comparing the distribution of values in several groups. For example, suppose you want to compare the distribution of beginning salaries for people employed in several different positions at a bank. Figure 9.6 contains boxplots of the bank salary data. From these plots, you can see that the first two job categories have similar distributions for salary, although the first category has several extreme values. The third job category has little variability; all 27 people in this category earn similar amounts of money. The last two groups have much higher median salaries than the other groups, and a larger spread as well.

Figure 9.6   Boxplots for bank salary data

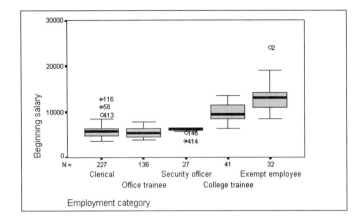

Evaluating Assumptions

Many statistical procedures, such as analysis of variance, require that all groups come from normal populations with the same variance. Therefore, before choosing a statistical hypothesis, we need to test the hypothesis that all the group variances are equal or that the samples come from normal populations. If it appears that the assumptions are violated, we may want to determine appropriate transformations.

The Levene Test

Numerous tests are available for evaluating the assumption that all groups come from populations with equal variances. Many of these tests, however, are heavily dependent on the data being from normal populations. Analysis-of-variance procedures, on the other hand, are reasonably robust to departures from normality. The **Levene test** is a homogeneity-of-variance test that is less dependent on the assumption of normality than most tests and thus is particularly useful with analysis of variance. It is obtained by computing, for each case, the absolute difference from its cell mean and performing a one-way analysis of variance on these differences.

From Figure 9.7, you can see that for the salary data, the null hypothesis that all group variances are equal is rejected. We should consider transforming the data if we plan to use a statistical procedure that requires equality of variance. Next we'll consider how to select a transformation.

Figure 9.7　The Levene test

```
Test of homogeneity of variance                   df1      df2      Significance
Levene Statistic                        28.9200     4       458         .0000
```

Spread-versus-Level Plots

Often there is a relationship between the average value, or level, of a variable and the variability, or spread, associated with it. For example, we can see in Figure 9.6 that as salaries increase, so does the variability.

One way of studying the relationship between spread and level is to plot the values of spread and level for each group. If there is no relationship, the points should cluster around a horizontal line. If this is not the case, we can use the observed relationship between the two variables to choose an appropriate transformation.

Determining the Transformation

A power transformation is frequently used to stabilize variances. A power transformation raises each data value to a specified power. For example, a power transformation of 2 squares all of the data values. A transformation of 1/2 calculates the square root of all the values. If the power is 0, the log of the numbers is used.

To determine an appropriate power for transforming the data, we can plot, for each group, the log of the median against the log of the interquartile range. Figure 9.8 shows such a plot for the salary data shown in Figure 9.6.

Figure 9.8　Spread-versus-level plot of bank data

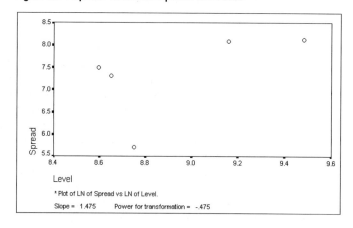

You see that there is a fairly strong linear relationship between spread and level. From the slope of the line, we can estimate the power value that will eliminate or lessen this relationship. The power is obtained by subtracting the slope from 1. That is,

Power = 1 − slope   **Equation 9.1**

Although this formula can result in all sorts of powers, for simplicity and clarity we usually choose the closest powers that are multiples of 1/2. Table 9.1 shows the most commonly used transformations.

Table 9.1   Commonly used transformations

Power	Transformation
3	Cube
2	Square
1	No change
1/2	Square root
0	Logarithm
−1/2	Reciprocal of the square root
−1	Reciprocal

As shown in Figure 9.8, the slope of the least-squares line for the bank data is 1.475, so the power for the transformation is −0.475. Rounding to the nearest multiple of a half, we will use the reciprocal of the square root.

After applying the power transformation, it is wise to obtain a spread-versus-level plot for the transformed data. From this plot, you can judge the success of the transformation.

Tests of Normality

Since the normal distribution is very important to statistical inference, we often want to examine the assumption that our data come from a normal distribution. One way to do this is with a normal probability plot. In a **normal probability plot**, each observed value is paired with its expected value from the normal distribution. (The expected value from the normal distribution is based on the number of cases in the sample and the rank order of the case in the sample.) If the sample is from a normal distribution, we expect that the points will fall more or less on a straight line.

The first plot in Figure 9.9 is a normal probability plot of a sample of 200 points from a normal distribution. Note how the points cluster around a straight line. You can also plot the actual deviations of the points from a straight line. This is called a **detrended normal plot** and is shown in the second plot in Figure 9.9. If the sample is from a normal population, the points should cluster around a horizontal line through 0, and there should be no pattern. A striking pattern suggests departure from normality.

Figure 9.9   Normal plots for a normal distribution

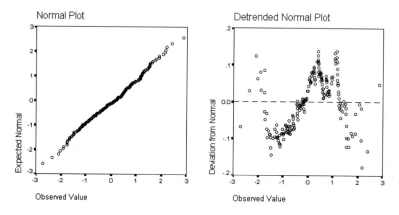

Figure 9.10 shows a normal probability plot and a detrended plot for data from a uniform distribution. The points do not cluster around a straight line, and the deviations from a straight line are not randomly distributed around 0.

Figure 9.10   Normal plots for a uniform distribution

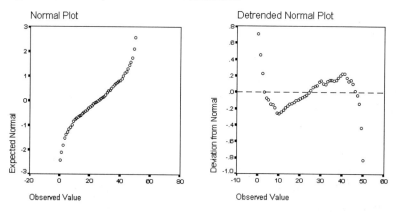

Although normal probability plots provide a visual basis for checking normality, it is often desirable to compute a statistical test of the hypothesis that the data are from a normal distribution. Two commonly used tests are the Shapiro-Wilks' test and the Lilliefors test. The **Lilliefors test,** based on a modification of the Kolmogorov-Smirnov test, is used when means and variances are not known but must be estimated from the data. The **Shapiro-Wilks' test** shows good power in many situations compared to other tests of normality (Conover, 1980).

Figure 9.11 contains normal probability plots and Figure 9.12 contains the Lilliefors test of normality for the diastolic blood pressure data. From the small observed significance levels, you see that the hypothesis of normality can be rejected. However, it is important to remember that whenever the sample size is large, almost any goodness-of-fit test will result in rejection of the null hypothesis. It is almost impossible to find data that are *exactly* normally distributed. For most statistical tests, it is sufficient that the data are approximately normally distributed. Thus, for large data sets, you should look not only at the observed significance level but also at the actual departure from normality.

Figure 9.11   Normal plots for diastolic blood pressure

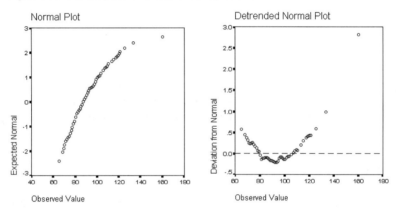

Figure 9.12   Normality test

	Statistic	df	Significance
K-S (Lilliefors)	.0974	239	.0000

Estimating Location with Robust Estimators

We often use the arithmetic mean to estimate central tendency, or location. We know, however, that the mean is heavily influenced by outliers. One very large or very small value can change the mean dramatically. The median, on the other hand, is insensitive to outliers; addition or removal of extreme values has little effect on it. The median is called a **resistant measure**, since its value depends on the main body of the data and not on outliers. The advantages of resistant measures are obvious: their values are not unduly influenced by a few observations, and they don't change much if small amounts of data are added or removed.

Although the median is an intuitive, simple measure of location, there are better estimators of location if we are willing to make some assumptions about the population from which our data originate. Estimators that depend on simple, fairly nonrestrictive assumptions about the underlying distribution and are not sensitive to these assumptions are called **robust estimators**. In the following sections, we will consider some robust estimators of central tendency that depend only on the assumption that the data are from a symmetric population.

The Trimmed Mean

A simple robust estimator of location can be obtained by "trimming" the data to exclude values that are far removed from the others. For example, a 20% trimmed mean disregards the smallest 20% and the largest 20% of all observations. The estimate is based on only the 60% of data values that are in the middle. What is the advantage of a trimmed mean? Like the median, it results in an estimate that is not influenced by extreme values. However, unlike the median, it is not based solely on a single value, or two values, that are in the middle. It is based on a much larger number of middle values. (The median can be considered a 50% trimmed mean, since half of the values above and below the median are ignored.) In general, a trimmed mean makes better use of the data than does the median.

M-Estimators

When calculating a trimmed mean, we divide our cases into two groups: those included and those excluded from the computation of the mean. We can consider the trimmed mean as a weighted mean in which cases have weights of 0 or 1, depending on whether they are included or excluded from the computations. A weighted mean is calculated by assigning a weight to each case and then using the formula $\overline{X} = (\Sigma w_i x_i) / (\Sigma w_i)$. In calculating the trimmed mean, we treat observations that are far from most of the others by excluding them altogether. A less extreme alternative is to include them but give them smaller weights than cases closer to the center, which we can do using the **M-estimator**, or generalized *m*aximum-likelihood estimator.

Since many different schemes can be used to assign weights to cases, there are many different M-estimators. (The usual mean can be viewed as an M-estimator with all cases having a weight of 1.) All commonly used M-estimators assign weights so that they decrease as distance from the center of the distribution increases. Figure 9.13 through Figure 9.16 show the weights used by four common M-estimators.

Common M-Estimators

Figure 9.13   Huber's (c = 1.339)

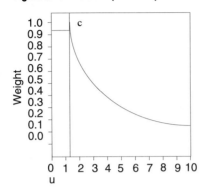

Figure 9.14   Tukey's biweight (c = 4.685)

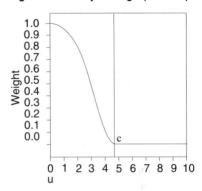

Figure 9.15   Hampel's (a = 1.7, b = 3.4, c = 8.5)

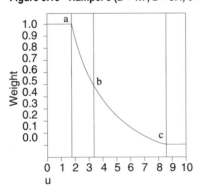

Figure 9.16   Andrew's (c = 1.339π)

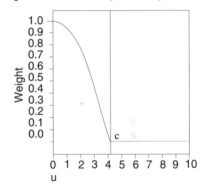

Consider Figure 9.13, which shows Huber's M-estimator. The value on the horizontal axis is a standardized distance from the estimate of location. It is computed using the following formula:

$$u_i = \frac{|\text{value for } i\text{th case} - \text{estimate of location}|}{\text{estimate of spread}}$$

Equation 9.2

The estimate of spread used is the median of the absolute deviations from the sample median, commonly known as MAD. It is calculated by first finding the median for the sample and then computing for each case the absolute value of the deviation from the median. The MAD is then the median of these absolute values. Since the weights for cases depend on the value of the estimate of central location, M-estimators must be computed iteratively.

From Figure 9.13, you can see that cases have weights of 1 up to a certain critical point, labeled c. After the critical point, the weights decrease as u, the standardized distance from the location estimate, increases. The SPSS values for these critical points are given in parentheses in Figure 9.13 through Figure 9.16.

The four M-estimators in Figure 9.13 through Figure 9.16 differ from each other in the way they assign weights. The Tukey biweight (Figure 9.14) does not have a point at which weights shift abruptly from 1. Instead, weights gradually decline to 0. Cases with values greater than c standardized units from the estimate are assigned weights of 0.

Hampel's three-part redescending M-estimator (Figure 9.15) has a more complicated weighting scheme than the Huber or the Tukey biweight. It uses four schemes for assigning weights. Cases with values less than a receive a weight of 1, cases with values between a and b receive a weight of a/u, and cases between b and c receive a weight of

$$\frac{a}{u} \times \frac{c - u}{c - b}$$

Equation 9.3

Cases with values greater than c receive a weight of 0. With Andrew's M-estimator (Figure 9.16), there is no abrupt change in the assignment of weights. A smooth function replaces the separate pieces.

Figure 9.17 contains basic descriptive statistics and values for the M-estimators for the diastolic blood pressure data. As expected, the estimates of location differ for the various methods. The mean produces the largest estimate: 88.79. That's because we have a positively skewed distribution and the mean is heavily influenced by the large values. Of the M-estimators, the Huber and Hampel estimates have the largest values. They too are influenced by the large data values. The remaining two M-estimates are fairly close in value.

Figure 9.17   M-estimates for blood pressure variable

```
DBP58        AVERAGE DIAST BLOOD PRESS

Valid cases:        239.0   Missing cases:       1.0   Percent missing:      .4


Mean        88.7908  Std Err       .8441  Min      65.0000  Skewness    1.2557
Median      87.0000  Variance  170.3006  Max     160.0000  S E Skew     .1575
5% Trim     88.0065  Std Dev    13.0499  Range    95.0000  Kurtosis    3.5958
                                          IQR      17.0000  S E Kurt     .3137

                              M-Estimators
                              ------------

Huber   (1.339)                87.1219   Tukey  (4.685)            86.4269
Hampel  (1.700,3.400,8.500)    87.1404   Andrew (1.340 * pi)       86.4105
```

In summary, M-estimators are good alternatives to the usual mean and median. The Huber M-estimator is good if the distribution is close to normal but is not recommended if there are extreme values. For further discussion of robust estimators, see Hogg (1979) and Hoaglin et al. (1983).

How to Explore Your Data

The Explore procedure provides a variety of descriptive plots and statistics, including stem-and-leaf plots, boxplots, normal probability plots, and spread-versus-level plots. Also available are the Levene test for homogeneity of variance, Shapiro-Wilks' and Lilliefors tests for normality, and several robust maximum-likelihood estimators of location. Cases can be subdivided into groups and statistics can be obtained for each group.

The minimum specification is one or more numeric dependent variables.

To obtain exploratory plots and statistics, from the menus choose:

Statistics
  Summarize ▶
    Explore...

This opens the Explore dialog box, as shown in Figure 9.18.

Figure 9.18   Explore dialog box

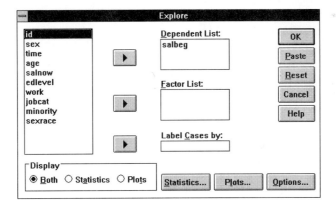

The variables in your data file appear on the source list. Select one or more numeric dependent variables and click on OK to get the default analysis, which includes boxplots, stem-and-leaf plots, and basic descriptive statistics for each variable. By default, cases with missing values for any dependent or factor variable are excluded from all summaries.

By default, output is produced for all cases. Optionally, you can obtain separate analyses for groups of cases based on their values for one or more numeric or short string **factor** variables. (For example, *jobcat* is the factor variable in Figure 9.6.) If you select more than one factor variable, separate summaries of each dependent variable are produced for each factor variable.

When output is produced showing individual cases (such as outliers), cases are identified by default by their sequence in the data file. Optionally, you can label cases with their values for a variable, such as a case ID variable. It can be a long string, short string, or numeric variable. For long string variables, the first 15 characters are used.

Display. You can also choose one of the following display options:

○ **Both.** Displays plots and statistics. This is the default.

○ **Statistics.** Displays statistics only (suppresses all plots).

○ **Plots.** Displays plots only (suppresses all statistics).

Explore Statistics

To obtain robust estimators or to display outliers, percentiles, or frequency tables, select Both or Statistics under Display and click on Statistics... in the Explore dialog box to open the Explore Statistics dialog box, as shown in Figure 9.19.

Figure 9.19   Explore Statistics dialog box

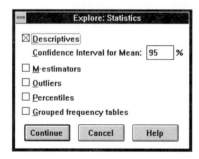

At least one statistic must be selected. You can choose one or more of the following statistics:

❑ **Descriptives.** Includes the mean and confidence intervals for the mean, median, 5% trimmed mean, standard error, variance, standard deviation, minimum, maximum, range, and interquartile range. Skewness and kurtosis and their standard errors are also shown. This is the default. Interquartile ranges are computed according to the HAVERAGE method.

Confidence intervals for mean. By default, the 95% confidence interval for the mean is displayed. You can specify any confidence interval between 1 and 99.99%.

❑ **M-estimators.** Robust maximum-likelihood estimators of location. Displays Huber's M-estimator ($c = 1.339$), Andrew's wave estimator ($c = 1.34\pi$), Hampel's redescending M-estimator ($a = 1.7$, $b = 3.4$, and $c = 8.5$), and Tukey's biweight estimator ($c = 4.685$). (See "M-Estimators" on p. 192.)

❑ **Outliers.** Displays cases with the five largest and five smallest values. These are labeled *Extreme Values* in the output (See Figure 9.3.)

❑ **Percentiles.** Displays the following percentiles: 5, 10, 25, 50, 75, 90, and 95. The weighted average at $X_{(W+1)p}$ (HAVERAGE) is used to calculate percentiles, where W is the sum of the weights for all cases with nonmissing values, p is the percentile divided by 100, i is the rank of the case when cases are sorted in ascending order, and X_i is the value for the ith case. The percentile value is the weighted average of X_i and X_{i+1} using the formula $(1-f)X_i + fX_{i+1}$, where $(W+1)p$ is decomposed into an integer part i and fractional part f. Also displays Tukey's hinges (25th, 50th, and 75th percentiles).

❑ **Grouped frequency tables.** Displays tables for the total sample and broken down by any factor variables. Starting value and increment are selected on the basis of observed data values.

Explore Plots

To obtain histograms, normality plots and tests, or spread-versus-level plots with Levene's statistic, select Both or Plots under Display and click on Plots... in the Explore dialog box to open the Explore Plots dialog box, as shown in Figure 9.20.

Figure 9.20   Explore Plots dialog box

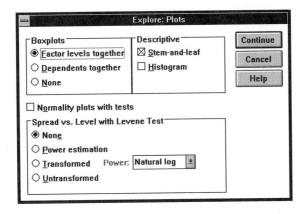

At least one plot must be selected.

Boxplots. You can choose one of the following boxplot display alternatives:

○ **Factor levels together.** For a given dependent variable, displays boxplots for each group side by side. This is the default. Select this display method when you want to compare groups for a variable. If no factor variable is selected, only a boxplot for the total sample is shown.

○ **Dependents together.** For a given group, displays boxplots for each dependent variable side by side. Select this display method when you want to compare variables for a particular group.

○ **None.** Suppresses boxplot.

Descriptive. You can choose one or both of the following descriptive plots:

❏ **Stem-and-leaf.** Displayed by default. Each observed value is divided into two components—the leading digits (stem) and trailing digits (leaf). To suppress stem-and-leaf plots, deselect this item.

❏ **Histogram.** The range of observed values is divided into equal intervals and the number of cases in each interval is displayed.

Spread vs. Level with Levene Test. For all spread-versus-level plots, the slope of the regression line and Levene's test for homogeneity of variance are displayed. Levene's test is based on the original data if no transformation is specified and on the transformed data if a transformation is specified. If no factor variable is selected, spread-versus-level plots are not produced.

You can choose one of the following alternatives:

○ **None.** Suppresses spread-versus-level plots and Levene's statistic. This is the default.

○ **Power estimation.** For each group, the natural log of the median is plotted against the log of the interquartile range. Estimated power is also displayed. Use this method to determine an appropriate transformation for your data.

○ **Transformed.** Data are transformed according to a user-specified power. The interquartile range and median of the transformed data are plotted. (See "Determining the Transformation" on p. 188.)

  ⬇ **Power.** To transform data, you must select a power for the transformation. You can choose one of the following alternatives:

  Natural log. Natural log transformation. This is the default.

  1/square root. For each data value, the reciprocal of the square root is calculated.

  Reciprocal. Reciprocal transformation.

  Square root. Square root transformation.

  Square. Data values are squared.

  Cube. Data values are cubed.

○ **Untransformed.** No transformation of the data is performed. *(Power value is 1.)*

The following option is available for normal probability and detrended probability plots:

❏ **Normality plots with tests.** Normal probability and detrended probability plots are produced, and the Shapiro-Wilks' statistic and the Kolmogorov-Smirnov statistic with a Lilliefors significance level for testing normality are calculated. The Shapiro-Wilks' statistic is not calculated if the sample size exceeds 50.

Explore Options

To modify the handling of missing values, click on Options... in the Explore dialog box. This opens the Explore Options dialog box, as shown in Figure 9.21.

Figure 9.21   **Explore Options dialog box**

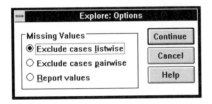

Missing Values. You can choose one of the following alternatives:

○ **Exclude cases listwise.** Cases with missing values for any dependent or factor variable are excluded from all analyses. This is the default.

○ **Exclude cases pairwise.** Cases with no missing values for variables in a cell are included in the analysis of that cell. The case may have missing values for variables used in other cells.

○ **Report values.** Missing values for factor variables are treated as a separate category. All output is produced for this additional category. Frequency tables include categories for missing values.

Additional Features Available with Command Syntax

You can customize your exploratory data analysis if you paste your selections into a syntax window and edit the resulting EXAMINE command syntax (see Chapter 4). Additional features include:

• Output for cells formed by *combinations* of factor variables (using the keyword BY).

• User-specified number of outliers displayed (with the STATISTICS subcommand).

- User-specified starting and increment values for frequency tables (with the FRE-QUENCIES subcommand).

- Alternative methods of percentile estimation and user-specified percentiles (with the PERCENTILES subcommand).

- Additional user-specified power values for spread-versus-level plot transformations (with the PLOT subcommand).

- User-specified critical points for M-estimators (with the MESTIMATORS subcommand).

See Appendix A for command syntax rules. See the *SPSS Base System Syntax Reference Guide* for complete EXAMINE command syntax.

10 Crosstabulation and Measures of Association

Newspapers headline murders in subway stations, robberies on crowded main streets, suicides cheered by onlookers. All are indications of the social irresponsibility and apathy said to characterize city residents. Since overcrowding, decreased sense of community, and other urban problems are usually blamed, you might ask whether small-town residents are more responsible and less apathetic than their urban counterparts.

Hansson and Slade (1977) used the "lost letter technique" to test the hypothesis that altruism is higher in small towns than in cities, unless the person needing assistance is a social deviant. In this technique, stamped and addressed letters are "lost," and the rate at which they are returned is examined. A total of 216 letters were lost in Hansson and Slade's experiment. Half were dropped within the city limits of Tulsa, Oklahoma, the others in 51 small towns within a 50-mile radius of Tulsa. The letters were addressed to three fictitious people at a post-office box in Tulsa: M. J. Davis; Dandee Davis, c/o Pink Panther Lounge; and M. J. Davis, c/o Friends of the Communist Party. The first person is considered a normal "control," the second, a person whose occupation is questionable, and the third, a subversive or political deviant.

Crosstabulation

To see whether the return rate is similar for the three addresses, the letters found and mailed and those not mailed must be tallied separately for each address. Figure 10.1 is a crosstabulation of address type and response. The number of cases (letters) for each combination of values of the two variables is displayed in a **cell** in the table, together with various percentages. These cell entries provide information about relationships between the variables.

Figure 10.1   Crosstabulation of status of letter by address

```
RETURNED  FOUND AND MAILED  by  ADDRESS  ADDRESS ON LETTER

                    ,ADDRESS                 Page 1 of 1
             Count
             Row Pct |CONTROL  DANDEE   COMMUNIS
             Col Pct |                   T
             Tot Pct |   1        2          3      Row
   RETURNED                                         Total
                  1  |   35       32        10       77
   YES               | 45.5     41.6      13.0      35.6
                     | 48.6     44.4      13.9
                     | 16.2     14.8       4.6
                     |
                  2  |   37       40        62      139
   NO                | 26.6     28.8      44.6      64.4
                     | 51.4     55.6      86.1
                     | 17.1     18.5      28.7

             Column     72       72        72      216
             Total    33.3     33.3      33.3     100.0

Number of Missing Observations:   0
```

In Figure 10.1, the address is called the **column variable**, since each address is displayed in a column of the table. Similarly, the status of the letter (whether it was returned or not) is called the **row variable**. With three categories of the column variable and two of the row, there are six cells in the table.

Cell Contents and Marginals

The first entry in the table is the number of cases, or **frequency**, in that cell. It is labeled as *Count* in the key displayed in the upper left corner of the table. For example, 35 letters addressed to the control were returned, and 62 letters addressed to the Communist were not returned. The second entry in the table is the **row percentage** (*Row Pct*). It is the percentage of all cases in a row that fall into a particular cell. Of the 77 letters returned, 45.5% were addressed to the control, 41.6% to Dandee, and 13.0% to the Communist.

The **column percentage** (*Col Pct*), the third item in each cell, is the percentage of all cases in a column that occur in a cell. For example, 48.6% of the letters addressed to the control were returned and 51.4% were not. The return rate for Dandee is similar (44.4%), while that for the Communist is markedly lower (13.9%).

The last entry in the table is the **table percentage** (*Tot Pct*). The number of cases in the cell is expressed as a percentage of the total number of cases in the table. For example, the 35 letters returned to the control represent 16.2% of the 216 letters in the experiment.

The numbers to the right and below the table are known as **marginals**. They are the counts and percentages for the row and column variables taken separately. In Figure 10.1, the row marginals show that 77 (35.6%) of the letters were returned, while 139 (64.4%) were not.

Choosing Percentages

Row, column, and table percentages convey different types of information, so it is important to choose carefully among them.

In this example, the row percentage indicates the distribution of address types for returned and "lost" letters. It conveys no direct information about the return rate. For example, if twice as many letters were addressed to the control, an identical return rate for all letters would give row percentages of 50%, 25%, and 25%. However, this does not indicate that the return rate is higher for the control. In addition, if each category had the same number of returned letters, the row percentages would have been 33.3%, 33.3%, and 33.3%, regardless of whether one or all letters were returned.

The column percentage is the percentage of letters returned and not returned for each address. By looking at column percentages across rows, you can compare return rates for the address types. Interpretation of this comparison is not affected if unequal numbers of letters are addressed to each category.

Since it is always possible to interchange the rows and columns of any table, general rules about when to use row and column percentages cannot be given. The percentages to use depend on the nature of the two variables. If one of the two variables is under experimental control, it is termed an **independent variable**. This variable is hypothesized to affect the response, or **dependent variable**. If variables can be classified as dependent and independent, the following guideline may be helpful: if the independent variable is the row variable, select row percentages; if the independent variable is the column variable, select column percentages. In this example, the dependent variable is the status of the letter, whether it was mailed or not. The type of address is the independent variable. Since the independent variable is the column variable in Figure 10.1, column percentages should be used for comparisons of return rates.

Adding a Control Variable

Since Figure 10.1 combines results from both the city and the towns, differences between the locations are obscured. Two separate tables, one for the city and one for the towns, are required. Figure 10.2 shows crosstabulations of response and address for each of the locations. SPSS produces a separate table for each value of the location (control) variable.

Figure 10.2   Crosstabulations of status of letter by address controlled for location

```
RETURNED  FOUND AND MAILED  by  ADDRESS  ADDRESS ON LETTER
Controlling for..
LOCATION  LOCATION LOST  Value = 1  CITY
```

	ADDRESS			Page 1 of 1
Count Col Pct	CONTROL	DANDEE	COMMUNIS T	
	1	2	3	Row Total
RETURNED				
YES 1	16 44.4	14 38.9	9 25.0	39 36.1
NO 2	20 55.6	22 61.1	27 75.0	69 63.9
Column Total	36 33.3	36 33.3	36 33.3	108 100.0

Chi-Square	Value	DF	Significance
Pearson	3.13043	2	.20904
Likelihood Ratio	3.21258	2	.20063
Mantel-Haenszel test for linear association	2.92252	1	.08735

Minimum Expected Frequency -   13.000

```
RETURNED  FOUND AND MAILED  by  ADDRESS  ADDRESS ON LETTER
Controlling for..
LOCATION  LOCATION LOST  Value = 2  TOWN
```

	ADDRESS			Page 1 of 1
Count Col Pct	CONTROL	DANDEE	COMMUNIS T	
	1	2	3	Row Total
RETURNED				
YES 1	19 52.8	18 50.0	1 2.8	38 35.2
NO 2	17 47.2	18 50.0	35 97.2	70 64.8
Column Total	36 33.3	36 33.3	36 33.3	108 100.0

Chi-Square	Value	DF	Significance
Pearson	24.92932	2	.00000
Likelihood Ratio	31.25344	2	.00000
Mantel-Haenszel test for linear association	19.54962	1	.00001

Minimum Expected Frequency -   12.667

Number of Missing Observations: 0

These tables show interesting differences between cities and towns. Although the over-all return rates are close, 36.1% for the city and 35.2% for the towns, there are striking differences between the addresses. Only 2.8% of the Communist letters were returned in towns, while 25.0% of them were returned in Tulsa. (At least two of the Communist letters were forwarded by small-town residents to the FBI for punitive action.) The return rates for both the control (52.8%) and Dandee (50.0%) are higher in towns.

The results support the hypothesis that suspected social deviance influences the response more in small towns than in big cities, although it is surprising that Dandee and the Pink Panther Lounge were deemed worthy of as much assistance as they received. If the Communist letter is excluded, inhabitants of small towns are somewhat more helpful than city residents, returning 51% of the other letters, in comparison to the city's 42%.

Graphical Representation of Crosstabulations

As with frequency tables, visual representation of a crosstabulation often simplifies the search for associations. Figure 10.3 is a **bar chart** of letters returned from the crosstabulations shown in Figure 10.2. In a bar chart, the height of each bar represents the frequencies or percentages for each category of a variable. In Figure 10.3, the percentages plotted are the column percentages shown in Figure 10.2 for the returned letters only. This chart clearly shows that the return rates for the control and Dandee are high compared to the return rate for the Communist. Also, it demonstrates more vividly than the crosstabulation that the town residents' return rates for the control and Dandee are higher than city residents' return rates, but that the reverse is true for the Communist.

Figure 10.3   Status of letter by address and by location

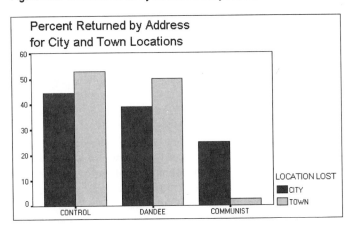

Using Crosstabulation for Data Screening

Errors and unusual values in data entry that cannot be spotted with frequency tables can sometimes be identified using crosstabulation. For example, a case coded as a male with a history of three pregnancies would not be identified as suspicious in frequency tables of sex and number of pregnancies. When considered separately, the code *male* is acceptable for sex and the value 3 is acceptable for number of pregnancies. The combination, however, is unexpected.

Whenever possible, crosstabulations of related variables should be obtained so that anomalies can be identified and corrected before further statistical analysis of the data.

Crosstabulation Statistics

Although examination of the various row and column percentages in a crosstabulation is a useful first step in studying the relationship between two variables, row and column percentages do not allow for quantification or testing of that relationship. For these purposes, it is useful to consider various indexes that measure the extent of association as well as statistical tests of the hypothesis that there is no association.

The Chi-Square Test of Independence

The hypothesis that two variables of a crosstabulation are independent of each other is often of interest to researchers. Two variables are by definition **independent** if the probability that a case falls into a given cell is simply the product of the marginal probabilities of the two categories defining the cell.

In Figure 10.1, for example, if returns of the letter and address type are independent, the probability of a letter being returned to a Communist is the product of the probability of a letter being returned and the probability of a letter being addressed to a Communist. From the table, 35.6% of the letters were returned and 33.3% of the letters were addressed to a friend of the Communist Party. Thus, if address type and status of the letter are independent, the probability of a letter being returned to the Communist is estimated to be

$$P(\text{return}) \, P(\text{Communist}) \;=\; 0.356 \times 0.333 \;=\; 0.119 \qquad\qquad \textbf{Equation 10.1}$$

The **expected** number of cases in that cell is 25.7, which is 11.9% of the 216 cases in the sample. From the table, the **observed** number of letters returned to the Communist is 10 (4.6%), nearly 16 fewer than expected if the two variables are independent.

To construct a statistical test of the independence hypothesis, you repeat the above calculations for each cell in the table. The probability under independence of an observation falling into cell (*ij*) is estimated by

$$P(\text{row} = i \text{ and column} = j) \;=\; \left(\frac{\text{count in row } i}{N}\right)\left(\frac{\text{count in column } j}{N}\right) \qquad \textbf{Equation 10.2}$$

To obtain the expected number of observations in cell (ij), the probability is multiplied by the total sample size:

$$E_{ij} = N\left(\left(\frac{\text{count in row } i}{N}\right)\left(\frac{\text{count in column } j}{N}\right)\right)$$

$$= \frac{(\text{count in row } i)(\text{count in column } j)}{N}$$

Equation 10.3

Figure 10.4 contains the observed and expected frequencies and the **residuals**, which are the observed minus the expected frequencies for the data in Figure 10.1.

Figure 10.4   Observed, expected, and residual values

```
RETURNED  FOUND AND MAILED  by  ADDRESS  ADDRESS ON LETTER

                      ADDRESS                 Page 1 of 1
            Count
            Exp Val  CONTROL  DANDEE   COMMUNIS
            Residual                   T          Row
                        1        2        3      Total
RETURNED
            1          35       32       10        77
YES                    25.7     25.7     25.7     35.6%
                       9.3      6.3      -15.7

            2          37       40       62       139
NO                     46.3     46.3     46.3     64.4%
                       -9.3     -6.3     15.7

            Column     72       72       72       216
            Total      33.3%    33.3%    33.3%    100.0%

          Chi-Square             Value         DF     Significance
    --------------------     -----------      ----    ------------

Pearson                        22.56265        2         .00001
Likelihood Ratio               24.68683        2         .00000
Mantel-Haenszel test for       18.83234        1         .00001
    linear association

Minimum Expected Frequency -    25.667


Number of Missing Observations:   0
```

A statistic often used to test the hypothesis that the row and column variables are independent is the **Pearson chi-square**. It is calculated by summing over all cells the squared residuals divided by the expected frequencies:

$$\chi^2 = \sum_i \sum_j \frac{(O_{ij} - E_{ij})^2}{E_{ij}}$$

Equation 10.4

The calculated chi-square is compared to the critical points of the theoretical chi-square distribution to produce an estimate of how likely (or unlikely) this calculated value is if the two variables are in fact independent. Since the value of the chi-square depends on the number of rows and columns in the table being examined, you must know the **degrees of freedom** for the table. The degrees of freedom can be viewed as the number of cells of a table that can be arbitrarily filled when the row and column totals (marginals) are fixed. For an $r \times c$ table, the degrees of freedom are $(r-1) \times (c-1)$, since once $(r-1)$ rows and $(c-1)$ columns are filled, frequencies in the remaining row and column cells must be chosen so that marginal totals are maintained.

In this example, there are two degrees of freedom (1×2) and the Pearson chi-square value is 22.56 (see Figure 10.4). If type of address and return rate are independent, the probability that a random sample would result in a chi-square value of at least that magnitude is 0.00001. This probability is also known as the **observed significance level** of the test. If the probability is small enough (usually less than 0.05 or 0.01), the hypothesis that the two variables are independent is rejected.

Since the observed significance level in Figure 10.1 is very small (based on the combined city and town data), the hypothesis that address type and return rate are independent is rejected. When the chi-square test is calculated for the city and town data separately (Figure 10.2), different results are obtained. The observed significance level of the city data is 0.209, so the independence hypothesis is not rejected. For the towns, the observed significance level is less than 0.000005, and the hypothesis that address and return rate are independent is rejected. These results support the theory that city and town residents respond differently.

An alternative to the commonly used Pearson chi-square is the **likelihood-ratio chi-square** (see Figure 10.4). This test is based on maximum-likelihood theory and is often used in the analysis of categorical data. For large samples, the Pearson and likelihood-ratio chi-square statistics give very similar results. (The Mantel-Haenszel test is discussed in "Ordinal Measures" on p. 215.)

The chi-square test is a test of independence; it provides little information about the strength or form of the association between two variables. The magnitude of the observed chi-square depends not only on the goodness of fit of the independence model but also on the sample size. If the sample size for a particular table increases n-fold, so does the chi-square value. Thus, large chi-square values can arise in applications where residuals are small relative to expected frequencies but where the sample size is large.

Certain conditions must be met for the chi-square distribution to be a good approximation of the distribution of the statistic in the equation given above. The data must be random samples from multinomial distributions and the expected values must not be too small. While it has been recommended that all expected frequencies be at least 5, studies indicate that this is probably too stringent and can be relaxed (Everitt, 1977). SPSS displays the number of cells with expected frequencies less than 5 and the minimum expected cell value.

To improve the approximation for a 2×2 table, **Yates' correction for continuity** is sometimes applied. Yates' correction for continuity involves subtracting 0.5 from positive differences between observed and expected frequencies (the residuals) and adding 0.5 to negative differences before squaring. For a discussion of the controversy over the merits of this correction, see Conover (1974) and Mantel (1974).

Fisher's exact test, based on the hypergeometric distribution, is an alternative test for the 2×2 table. It calculates exact probabilities of obtaining the observed results if the two variables are independent and the marginals are fixed. It is most useful when the total sample size and the expected values are small. SPSS calculates Fisher's exact test if any expected cell value in a 2×2 table is less than 5.

Measures of Association

In many research situations, the strength and nature of the dependence of variables is of central concern. Indexes that attempt to quantify the relationship between variables in a cross-classification are called **measures of association**. No single measure adequately summarizes all possible types of association. Measures vary in their interpretation and in the way they define perfect and intermediate association. These measures also differ in the way they are affected by various factors such as marginals. For example, many measures are "margin sensitive" in that they are influenced by the marginal distributions of the rows and columns. Such measures reflect information about the marginals along with information about association.

A particular measure may have a low value for a given table, not because the two variables are not related but because they are not related in the way to which the measure is sensitive. No single measure is best for all situations. The type of data, the hypothesis of interest, and the properties of the various measures must all be considered when selecting an index of association for a given table. It is not, however, reasonable to compute a large number of measures and then to report the most impressive as if it were the only one examined.

The measures of association available with crosstabulation in SPSS are computed only from bivariate tables. For example, if three dichotomous variables are specified in the table, two sets of measures are computed, one for each subtable produced by the values of the controlling variable. In general, if relationships among more than two variables are to be studied, examination of bivariate tables is only a first step. For an extensive discussion of more sophisticated multivariate procedures for the analysis of qualitative data, see Fienberg (1977), Everitt (1977), and Haberman (1978).

Nominal Measures

Consider measures that assume only that both variables in the table are nominally measured. As such, these measures can provide only some indication of the strength of association between variables; they cannot indicate direction or anything about the nature of the relationship. The measures provided are of two types: those based on the chi-square statistic and those that follow the logic of proportional reduction in error, denoted PRE.

Chi-Square-based Measures

As explained above, the chi-square statistic itself is not a good measure of the degree of association between two variables. But its widespread use in tests of independence has encouraged the use of measures of association based upon it. Each of these measures based on the chi-square attempts to modify the chi-square statistic to minimize the influence of sample size and degrees of freedom as well as to restrict the range of values of the measure to those between 0 and 1. Without such adjustments, comparison of chi-square values from tables with varying dimensions and sample sizes is meaningless.

The **phi coefficient** modifies the Pearson chi-square by dividing it by the sample size and taking the square root of the result:

$$\phi = \sqrt{\frac{\chi^2}{N}}$$

Equation 10.5

For a 2×2 table only, the phi coefficient is equal to the Pearson correlation coefficient, so the sign of phi matches that of the correlation coefficient. For tables in which one dimension is greater than 2, phi may not lie between 0 and 1, since the chi-square value can be greater than the sample size. To obtain a measure that must lie between 0 and 1, Pearson suggested the use of

$$C = \sqrt{\frac{\chi^2}{\chi^2 + N}}$$

Equation 10.6

which is called the **coefficient of contingency**. Although the value of this measure is always between 0 and 1, it cannot generally attain the upper limit of 1. The maximum value possible depends upon the number of rows and columns. For example, in a 4×4 table, the maximum value of C is 0.87.

Cramér introduced the following variant:

$$V = \sqrt{\frac{\chi^2}{N(k-1)}}$$

Equation 10.7

where k is the smaller of the number of rows and columns. This statistic, known as **Cramér's V**, can attain the maximum of 1 for tables of any dimension. If one of the table dimensions is 2, V and phi are identical.

Figure 10.5 shows the values of the chi-square-based measures for the letter data. The test of the null hypothesis that a measure is 0 is based on the Pearson chi-square probability.

Figure 10.5 Chi-square-based measures

```
RETURNED   FOUND AND MAILED   by   ADDRESS   ADDRESS ON LETTER

                      ADDRESS                    Page 1 of 1
            Count
                     CONTROL   DANDEE   COMMUNIS
                                              T      Row
                        1        2        3      Total
RETURNED   ───────────────────────────────────
               1      35       32       10        77
     YES                                         35.6

               2      37       40       62       139
      NO                                         64.4

           Column     72       72       72       216
           Total     33.3     33.3     33.3     100.0
```

```
                                                       Approximate
        Statistic              Value    ASE1   Val/ASE0  Significance
    --------------------       ------   ----   --------  ------------

Phi                            .32320                     .00001 *1
Cramer's V                     .32320                     .00001 *1
Contingency Coefficient        .30753                     .00001 *1

*1 Pearson chi-square probability

Number of Missing Observations:  0
```

The chi-square-based measures are hard to interpret. Although when properly standardized they can be used to compare strength of association in several tables, the strength of association being compared is not easily related to an intuitive concept of association.

Proportional Reduction in Error

Common alternatives to chi-square-based measurements are those based on the idea of **proportional reduction in error (PRE)**, introduced by Goodman and Kruskal (1954). With PRE measures, the meaning of association is clearer. These measures are all essentially ratios of a measure of error in predicting the values of one variable based on knowledge of that variable alone and the same measure of error applied to predictions based on knowledge of an additional variable.

For example, Figure 10.6 is a crosstabulation of depth of hypnosis and success in treatment of migraine headaches by suggestion (Cedercreutz, 1978). The best guess of the results of treatment when no other information is available is the outcome category with the largest proportion of observations (the modal category).

Figure 10.6   Depth of hypnosis and success of treatment

```
HYPNOSIS   DEPTH OF HYPNOSIS   by   MIGRAINE   OUTCOME

                        MIGRAINE              Page 1 of 1
              Count
              Col Pct  CURED    BETTER   NO
              Tot Pct                    CHANGE      Row
                        1.00     2.00     3.00   Total
    HYPNOSIS
              1.00       13        5                  18
    DEEP                56.5     15.6               18.0
                        13.0      5.0

              2.00       10       26       17         53
    MEDIUM              43.5     81.3     37.8       53.0
                        10.0     26.0     17.0

              3.00                 1       28         29
    LIGHT                         3.1     62.2       29.0
                                  1.0     28.0

              Column     23       32       45        100
              Total     23.0     32.0     45.0     100.0
```

```
                                                      Approximate
      Statistic                  Value     ASE1    Val/ASE0  Significance
-----------------------         -------   ------   -------- -------------


Lambda :
    symmetric                    .35294   .11335   2.75267
    with HYPNOSIS dependent      .29787   .14702   1.72276
    with MIGRAINE dependent      .40000   .10539   3.07580
Goodman & Kruskal Tau :
    with HYPNOSIS dependent      .29435   .06304            .00000 *2
    with MIGRAINE dependent      .34508   .04863            .00000 *2

*2 Based on chi-square approximation

Number of Missing Observations:   0
```

In Figure 10.6, *no change* is the largest outcome category, with 45% of the subjects. The estimate of the probability of incorrect classification is 1 minus the probability of the modal category:

$$P(1) \; = \; 1 - 0.45 \; = \; 0.55 \qquad\qquad \textbf{Equation 10.8}$$

Information about the depth of hypnosis can be used to improve the classification rule. For each hypnosis category, the outcome category that occurs most frequently for that hypnosis level is predicted. Thus, *no change* is predicted for participants achieving a light level of hypnosis, *better* for those achieving a medium level, and *cured* for those achieving a deep level. The probability of error when depth of hypnosis is used to predict outcome is the sum of the probabilities of all the cells that are not row modes:

$$P(2) = 0.05 + 0.10 + 0.17 + 0.01 = 0.33$$

Equation 10.9

Goodman and Kruskal's **lambda**, with outcome as the predicted (dependent) variable, is calculated as

$$\lambda_{outcome} = \frac{P(1) - P(2)}{P(1)} = \frac{0.55 - 0.33}{0.55} = 0.40$$

Equation 10.10

Thus, a 40% reduction in error is obtained when depth of hypnosis is used to predict outcome.

Lambda always ranges between 0 and 1. A value of 0 means the independent variable is of no help in predicting the dependent variable. A value of 1 means that the independent variable perfectly specifies the categories of the dependent variable (perfection can occur only when each row has at most one non-zero cell). When the two variables are independent, lambda is 0; but a lambda of 0 need not imply statistical independence. As with all measures of association, lambda is constructed to measure association in a very specific way. In particular, lambda reflects the reduction in error when values of one variable are used to predict values of the other. If this particular type of association is absent, lambda is 0. Other measures of association may find association of a different kind even when lambda is 0. A measure of association sensitive to every imaginable type of association does not exist.

For a particular table, two different lambdas can be computed, one using the row variable as the predictor and the other using the column variable. The two do not usually have identical values, so care should be taken to specify which is the dependent variable; that is, the variable whose prediction is of primary interest. In some applications, dependent and independent variables are not clearly distinguished. In those instances, a symmetric version of lambda, which predicts the row variable and column variable with equal frequency, can be computed. When the lambda statistic is requested, SPSS displays the symmetric lambda as well as the two asymmetric lambdas.

Goodman and Kruskal's Tau

When lambda is computed, the same prediction is made for all cases in a particular row or column. Another approach is to consider what happens if the prediction is randomly made in the same proportion as the marginal totals. For example, if you're trying to predict migraine outcome without any information about the depth of the hypnosis, you can use the marginal distributions in Figure 10.6 instead of the modal category to guess *cured* for 23% of the cases, *better* for 32% of the cases, and *no change* for 45% of the cases.

Using these marginals, you would expect to correctly classify 23% of the 23 cases in the *cured* category, 32% of the 32 cases in the *better* category, and 45% of the 45 cases in the *no change* category. This results in the correct classification of 35.78 out of 100 cases. When additional information about the depth of hypnosis is incorporated into the prediction rule, the prediction is based on the probability of the different outcomes for each depth of hypnosis. For example, for those who experienced deep hypnosis, you would predict *cure* 72% of the time (13/18) and *better* 28% of the time (5/18). Similarly, for those with light hypnosis, you would predict *better* 3% of the time and *no change* 97% of the time. This results in correct classification for about 58 of the cases.

Goodman and Kruskal's tau is computed by comparing the probability of error in the two situations. In this example, when predicting only from the column marginal totals, the probability of error is 0.64. When predicting from row information, the probability of error is 0.42. Thus,

$$\text{tau (migraine} \mid \text{hypnosis)} = (0.64 - 0.42)/0.64 = 0.34 \qquad \textbf{Equation 10.11}$$

By incorporating information about the depth of hypnosis, we have reduced our error of prediction by about 34%.

A test of the null hypothesis that tau is 0 can be based on the value of $(N-1)(c-1)$ tau (col | row), which has a chi-square distribution with $(c-1) \times (r-1)$ degrees of freedom. In this example, the observed significance level for tau is very small, and you can reject the null hypothesis that tau is 0. The asymptotic standard error for the statistic is shown in the column labeled *ASE1*. The asymptotic standard error can be used to construct confidence intervals.

Measuring Agreement

Measures of agreement allow you to compare the ratings of two observers for the same group of objects. For example, consider the data reported in Bishop et al. (1975), shown in Figure 10.7.

Figure 10.7 Student teachers rated by supervisors

```
SUPRVSR1  Supervisor 1  by  SUPRVSR2  Supervisor 2

                    SUPRVSR2                    Page 1 of 1
            Count
            Tot Pct  Authorit Democrat Permissi
                     arian    ic       ve        Row
                        1.00     2.00     3.00  Total
SUPRVSR1        ──────
           1.00       17        4        8        29
   Authoritarian     23.6      5.6     11.1      40.3

           2.00        5       12                 17
   Democratic         6.9     16.7              23.6

           3.00       10        3       13        26
   Permissive        13.9      4.2     18.1      36.1

           Column     32       19       21        72
           Total     44.4     26.4     29.2     100.0


                                                      Approximate
       Statistic              Value     ASE1  Val/ASE0 Significance
  --------------------        -----    ------  -------- ------------

  Kappa                      .36227   .09075   4.32902

  Number of Missing Observations:  0
```

Two supervisors rated the classroom style of 72 teachers. You are interested in measuring the agreement between the two raters. The simplest measure that comes to mind is just the proportion of cases for which the raters agree. In this case, it is 58.3%. The disadvantage of this measure is that no correction is made for the amount of agreement expected by chance. That is, you would expect the supervisors to agree sometimes even if they were assigning ratings by tossing dice.

To correct for chance agreement, you can compute the proportion of cases that you would expect to be in agreement if the ratings are independent. For example, supervisor 1 rated 40.3% of the teachers as authoritarian, while supervisor 2 rated 44.4% of the teachers as authoritarian. If their rankings are independent, you would expect that 17.9% (40.3% × 44.4%) of the teachers would be rated as authoritarian by both. Similarly, 6.2% (23.6% × 26.4%) would be rated as democratic and 10.5% (36.1% × 29.2%) as permissive. Thus, 34.6% of all the teachers would be classified the same merely by chance.

The difference between the observed proportion of cases in which the raters agree and that expected by chance is 0.237 (0.583 − 0.346). **Cohen's kappa** (Cohen, 1960) normalizes this difference by dividing it by the maximum difference possible for the marginal totals. In this example, the largest possible "non-chance" agreement is 1 − 0.346 (the chance level). Therefore,

$$\text{kappa} = 0.237 / (1 - 0.346) = 0.362 \qquad \text{\textbf{Equation 10.12}}$$

The test of the null hypothesis that kappa is 0 can be based on the ratio of the measure to its standard error, assuming that the null hypothesis is true. (See Benedetti and Brown, 1978, for further discussion of standard errors for measures of association.) This asymptotic error is not the one shown on the output. The asymptotic standard error on the output, *ASE1*, does not assume that the true value is 0.

Since the kappa statistic measures agreement between two raters, the two variables that contain the ratings must have the same range of values. If this is not true, SPSS will not compute kappa.

Ordinal Measures

Although relationships among ordinal variables can be examined using nominal measures, other measures reflect the additional information available from ranking. Consideration of the kind of relationships that may exist between two ordered variables leads to the notion of direction of relationship and to the concept of **correlation**. Variables are positively correlated if cases with low values for one variable also tend to have low values for the other, and cases with high values on one also tend to be high on the other. Negatively correlated variables show the opposite relationship: the higher the first variable, the lower the second tends to be.

The **Spearman correlation coefficient** is a commonly used measure of correlation between two ordinal variables. For all of the cases, the values of each of the variables are ranked from smallest to largest, and the Pearson correlation coefficient is computed on the ranks. The **Mantel-Haenszel chi-square** is another measure of linear association between the row and column variables in a crosstabulation. It is computed by multiplying the square of the Pearson correlation coefficient by the number of cases minus 1. The resulting statistic has one degree of freedom (Mantel & Haenszel, 1959). (Although the Mantel-Haenszel statistic is displayed whenever chi-square is requested, it should not be used for nominal data.)

Ordinal Measures Based on Pairs

For a table of two ordered variables, several measures of association based on a comparison of the values of both variables for all possible *pairs* of cases or observations are available. Cases are first compared to determine if they are concordant, discordant, or tied. A pair of cases is **concordant** if the values of both variables for one case are higher (or both are lower) than the corresponding values for the other case. The pair is **discordant** if the value of one variable for a case is larger than the corresponding value for the other case, and the direction is reversed for the second variable. When the two cases have identical values on one or on both variables, they are **tied**.

Thus, for any given pair of cases with measurements on variables X and Y, the pair may be concordant, discordant, or tied in one of three ways: they may be tied on X but not on Y, they may be tied on Y but not on X, or they may be tied on both variables. When data are arranged in crosstabulated form, the number of concordant, discordant, and tied pairs can be easily calculated since all possible pairs can be conveniently determined.

If the preponderance of pairs is concordant, the association is said to be positive: as ranks of variable X increase (or decrease), so do ranks of variable Y. If the majority of pairs is discordant, the association is negative: as ranks of one variable increase, those of the other tend to decrease. If concordant and discordant pairs are equally likely, no association is said to exist.

The ordinal measures presented here all have the same numerator: the number of concordant pairs (P) minus the number of discordant pairs (Q) calculated for all distinct pairs of observations. They differ primarily in the way in which $P - Q$ is normalized. The simplest measure involves subtracting Q from P and dividing by the total number of pairs. If there are no pairs with ties, this measure (**Kendall's tau-*a***) is in the range from -1 to $+1$. If there are ties, the range of possible values is narrower; the actual range depends on the number of ties. Since all observations within the same row are tied, so also are those in the same column, and the resulting tau-*a* measures are difficult to interpret.

A measure that attempts to normalize $P - Q$ by considering ties on each variable in a pair separately but not ties on both variables in a pair is **tau-*b***:

$$\tau_b = \frac{P - Q}{\sqrt{(P + Q + T_X)\ (P + Q + T_Y)}}$$ **Equation 10.13**

where T_X is the number of pairs tied on X but not on Y, and T_Y is the number of pairs tied on Y but not on X. If no marginal frequency is 0, tau-*b* can attain +1 or −1 only for a square table.

A measure that can attain, or nearly attain, +1 or −1 for any $r \times c$ table is **tau-*c***:

$$\tau_c = \frac{2m\,(P-Q)}{N^2\,(m-1)}$$

Equation 10.14

where m is the smaller of the number of rows and columns. The coefficients tau-*b* and tau-*c* do not differ much in value if each margin contains approximately equal frequencies.

Goodman and Kruskal's gamma is closely related to the tau statistics and is calculated as

$$G = \frac{P-Q}{P+Q}$$

Equation 10.15

Gamma can be thought of as the probability that a random pair of observations is concordant minus the probability that the pair is discordant, assuming the absence of ties. The absolute value of gamma is the proportional reduction in error between guessing the concordant and discordant ranking of each pair depending on which occurs more often and guessing the ranking according to the outcome of a fair toss of a coin. Gamma is 1 if all observations are concentrated in the upper left to lower right diagonal of the table. In the case of independence, gamma is 0. However, the converse (that a gamma of 0 necessarily implies independence) need not be true except in the 2×2 table.

In the computation of gamma, no distinction is made between the independent and dependent variables; the variables are treated symmetrically. Somers (1962) proposed an asymmetric extension of gamma that differs only in the inclusion of the number of pairs not tied on the independent variable (X) in the denominator. **Somers' *d*** is

$$d_Y = \frac{P-Q}{P+Q+T_Y}$$

Equation 10.16

The coefficient d_Y indicates the proportionate excess of concordant pairs over discordant pairs among pairs not tied on the independent variable. The symmetric variant of Somers' d uses for the denominator the average value of the denominators of the two asymmetric coefficients.

These ordinal measures for the migraine data are shown in Figure 10.8. All of the measures indicate that there is a fairly strong positive association between the two variables.

Figure 10.8 Ordinal measures

```
HYPNOSIS  DEPTH OF HYPNOSIS  by  MIGRAINE   OUTCOME

Number of valid observations = 100
```

Statistic	Value	ASE1	Val/ASE0	Approximate Significance
Kendall's Tau-b	.67901	.04445	11.96486	
Kendall's Tau-c	.63360	.05296	11.96486	
Gamma	.94034	.02720	11.96486	
Somers' D :				
symmetric	.67866	.04443	11.96486	
with HYPNOSIS dependent	.65774	.05440	11.96486	
with MIGRAINE dependent	.70096	.03996	11.96486	
Pearson's R	.71739	.04484	10.19392	.00000 *4
Spearman Correlation	.72442	.04317	10.40311	.00000 *4

```
*4 T-value and significance based on a normal approximation
```

Measures Involving Interval Data

If the two variables in the table are measured on an interval scale, various coefficients that make use of this additional information can be calculated. A useful symmetric coefficient that measures the strength of the *linear* relationship is the **Pearson correlation coefficient (r)**. It can take on values from −1 to +1, indicating negative or positive linear correlation.

The **eta coefficient** is appropriate for data in which the dependent variable is measured on an interval scale and the independent variable on a nominal or ordinal scale. When squared, eta can be interpreted as the proportion of the total variability in the dependent variable that can be accounted for by knowing the values of the independent variable. The measure is asymmetric and does not assume a linear relationship between the variables.

Estimating Risk in Cohort Studies

Often you want to identify variables that are related to the occurrence of a particular event. For example, you may want to determine if smoking is related to heart disease. A commonly used index that measures the strength of the association between presence of a factor and occurrence of an event is the **relative risk ratio**. It is estimated as the ratio of two incidence rates; for example, the incidence rate of heart disease in those who smoke and the incidence rate of heart disease in those who do not smoke.

For example, suppose you observe for five years 1000 smokers without a history of heart disease and 1000 nonsmokers without a history of heart disease, and you determine how many of each group develop heart disease during this time period. (Studies in which a group of disease-free people are studied to see who develops the disease are called **cohort** or **prospective studies**.) Figure 10.9 contains hypothetical results from such a cohort study.

Figure 10.9   Hypothetical cohorts

```
SMOKING  Smoking  by  HDISEASE  Heart Disease

                       HDISEASE       Page 1 of 1
              Count
                      Yes      No
                                           Row
                        1.00│   2.00│   Total
        SMOKING      ─────────────────
                        1.00│ 100 │ 900 │  1000
          Yes              │     │     │  50.0

                        2.00│  50 │ 950 │  1000
          No               │     │     │  50.0

                      Column  150   1850   2000
                      Total   7.5   92.5  100.0


        Statistic                  Value       95% Confidence Bounds
    ──────────────────              ────────   ──────────────────────
    Relative Risk Estimate (SMOKING 1.0 / SMOKING 2.0) :
        case control               2.11111      1.48544      3.00032
        cohort (HDISEASE 1.0 Risk) 2.00000      1.44078      2.77628
        cohort (HDISEASE 2.0 Risk)  .94737       .92390       .97143

    Number of Missing Observations:  0
```

The five-year incidence rate for smokers is 100/1000, while the incidence rate for non-smokers is 50/1000. The relative risk ratio is 2 (100/1000 divided by 50/1000). This indicates that, in the sample, smokers are twice as likely to develop heart disease as nonsmokers.

The estimated relative risk and its 95% confidence interval are in the row labeled *cohort (HDISEASE 1.0 Risk)* in Figure 10.9. In SPSS, the ratio is always computed by taking the incidence in the first row and dividing it by the incidence in the second row. Since either column can represent the event, separate estimates are displayed for each column. The 95% confidence interval does not include the value of 1, so you can reject the null hypothesis that the two incidence rates are the same.

Estimating Risk in Case-Control Studies

In the cohort study described above, we took a group of disease-free people (the cohort) and watched what happened to them. Another type of study that is commonly used is called a **retrospective**, or **case-control study**. In this type of study, we take a group of people with the disease of interest (the cases) and a comparable group of people without the disease (the controls) and see how they differ. For example, we could take 100 people with documented coronary heart disease and 100 controls without heart disease and establish how many in each group smoked. The hypothetical results are shown in Figure 10.10.

Figure 10.10 Hypothetical smoking control

```
GROUP   by   SMOKING

                       SMOKING        Page 1 of 1
             Count
             Row Pct |Yes      No
                     |                      Row
                     |    1.00      2.00|   Total
GROUP        --------|
             1.00    |    30        70  |   100
   Cases             |    30.0      70.0|   50.0

             2.00    |    10        90  |   100
   Control           |    10.0      90.0|   50.0

             Column       40        160     200
             Total        20.0      80.0    100.0
```

```
       Statistic                     Value         95% Confidence Bounds
-------------------------            --------       ----------------------
Relative Risk Estimate (GROUP 1.0 / GROUP 2.0) :
     case control                    3.85714         1.76660      8.42156
     cohort (SMOKING 1.0 Risk)       3.00000         1.55083      5.80335
     cohort (SMOKING 2.0 Risk)        .77778          .67348       .89823

Number of Missing Observations:  0
```

From a case-control study, we cannot estimate incidence rates. Thus, we cannot compute the relative risk ratio. Instead, we estimate relative risk using what is called an **odds ratio**. We compute the odds that a case smokes and divide it by the odds that a control smokes.

For example, from Figure 10.10, the odds that a case smokes are 30/70. The odds that a control smokes are 10/90. The odds ratio is then 30/70 divided by 10/90, or 3.85. The odds ratio and its confidence interval are in the row labeled *case control* in Figure 10.10. SPSS expects the cases to be in the first row and the controls in the second. Similarly, the event of interest must be in the first column. For further discussion of measures of risk, see Kleinbaum et al. (1982).

How to Obtain Crosstabulations

The Crosstabs procedure produces two-way to *n*-way crosstabulations and related statistics for numeric and short string variables. In addition to cell counts, you can obtain cell percentages, expected values, and residuals.

The minimum specifications are:

- One numeric or short string row variable.
- One numeric or short string column variable.

To obtain crosstabulations and related statistics as well as measures of association, from the menus choose:

Statistics
  Summarize ▶
    Crosstabs...

This opens the Crosstabs dialog box, as shown in Figure 10.11.

Figure 10.11 Crosstabs dialog box

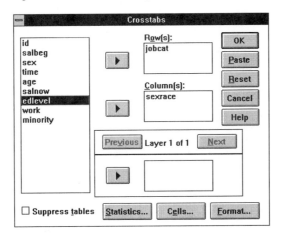

The numeric and short string variables in your data file are displayed on the source variable list. Select the variables you want to use as the row and column variables. A crosstabulation is produced for each combination of row and column variables. For example, if there are four variables on the Row(s) list and three variables on the Column(s) list, you will get 12 crosstabulations. To get a crosstabulation in default format (cell counts only and no measures of association), click on OK.

Optionally, you can select one or more layers of control variables. A separate crosstabulation is produced for each category of each control variable. For example, if you have one row variable, one column variable, and one control variable with two categories, you will get two crosstabulations, as in Figure 10.2.

You can add additional layers of control variables by clicking on Next. Each layer divides the crosstabulation into smaller subgroups. For example, if *jobcat* is the row variable, *sexrace* is the column variable, *edlevel* is the layer 1 control variable, and *age* is the layer 2 control variable, you will get separate crosstabulations of *jobcat* and *sexrace* for each category of *age* within each category of *edlevel*. If *age* and *edlevel* each have six categories, you will get 36 crosstabulations (probably not what you want).

You can add up to eight layers of control variables. Use Next and Previous to move between the control variables for the different layers.

The following option is also available:

❏ **Suppress tables.** If you are interested in crosstabulation statistical measures but don't want to display the actual tables, you can choose Suppress tables. However, if you haven't selected any statistics from the Crosstabs Statistics dialog box, no output will be generated.

Crosstabs Statistics

To obtain statistics and measures of association, click on Statistics... in the Crosstabs dialog box. This opens the Crosstabs Statistics dialog box, as shown in Figure 10.12.

Figure 10.12 Crosstabs Statistics dialog box

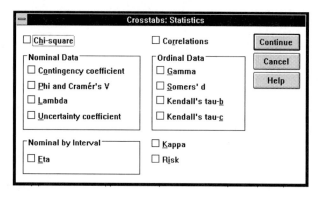

You can choose one or more of the following statistics:

❏ **Chi-square.** Pearson chi-square, likelihood-ratio chi-square, and Mantel-Haenszel linear association chi-square. For 2×2 tables, Fisher's exact test is computed when a table that does not result from missing rows or columns in a larger table has a cell with an expected frequency of less than 5. Yates' corrected chi-square is computed for all other 2×2 tables.

❑ **Correlations.** Pearson's r and Spearman's correlation coefficient. These are available for numeric data only.

❑ **Kappa.** Cohen's kappa. The kappa coefficient can only be computed for square tables in which the row and column values are identical (Kraemer, 1982).

❑ **Risk.** Relative risk ratio. This can only be calculated for 2×2 tables (Kleinbaum et al., 1982).

Nominal Data. Nominal measures assume that variables have values with no intrinsic order (such as *Catholic, Protestant, Jewish*). You can choose one or more of the following:

❑ **Contingency coefficient.**

❑ **Phi and Cramér's V.**

❑ **Lambda.** Symmetric and asymmetric lambda, and Goodman and Kruskal's tau.

❑ **Uncertainty coefficient.** Symmetric and asymmetric uncertainty coefficient.

Nominal by Interval. It is assumed that one variable is measured on a nominal scale, and the other is measured on an interval scale.

❑ **Eta.** Eta is not available for short string variables. The nominal variable must be coded numerically. Two eta values are computed: one treats the column variable as the nominal variable; the other treats the row variable as the nominal variable.

Ordinal Data. Ordinal measures assume that variables have values with some intrinsic order (such as *None, Some, A lot*). You can choose one or more of the following:

❑ **Gamma.** Zero-order gammas are displayed for 2-way tables, and conditional gammas are displayed for 3-way to 10-way tables.

❑ **Somers' d.** Symmetric and asymmetric Somers' *d*.

❑ **Kendall's tau-b.**

❑ **Kendall's tau-c.**

Crosstabs Cell Display

The default crosstabulation displays only the number of cases in each cell. You can also display row, column, and total percentages, expected values, and residuals. To change the cell display, click on Cells... in the Crosstabs dialog box. This opens the Crosstabs Cell Display dialog box, as shown in Figure 10.13.

Figure 10.13 Crosstabs Cell Display dialog box

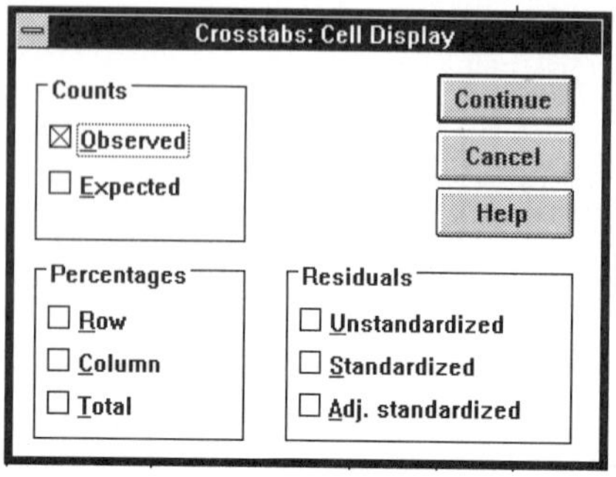

You can choose any combination of cell displays. For example, Figure 10.1 was produced by selecting row, column, and total percentages, in addition to the default observed count. At least one item must be selected.

Counts. You can choose one or more of the following:

❑ **Observed.** Observed frequencies. This is the default. To suppress observed frequencies, deselect this item.

❑ **Expected.** Expected frequencies. The number of cases expected in each cell if the two variables in the subtable are statistically independent.

Percentages. You can choose one or more of the following:

❑ **Row.** The number of cases in each cell expressed as a percentage of all cases in that row.

❑ **Column.** The number of cases in each cell expressed as a percentage of all cases in that column.

❑ **Total.** The number of cases in each cell expressed as a percentage of all cases in the subtable.

Residuals. You can choose one or more of the following:

❑ **Unstandardized.** The value of the observed cell count minus the expected value.

❑ **Standardized.** Standardized residuals (Haberman, 1978).

❑ **Adj. standardized.** Adjusted standardized residuals (Haberman, 1978).

Crosstabs Table Format

You can modify the table format by clicking on Format... in the Crosstabs dialog box. This opens the Crosstabs Table Format dialog box, as shown in Figure 10.14.

Figure 10.14 Crosstabs Table Format dialog box

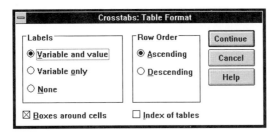

Labels. You can choose one of the following alternatives:

○ **Variable and value.** Displays both variable and value labels for each table. This is the default. Only the first 16 characters of the value labels are used. Value labels for the columns are displayed on two lines with eight characters per line.

○ **Variable only.** Displays variable labels but suppresses value labels.

○ **None.** Suppresses both variable and value labels.

Row Order. You can choose one of the following alternatives:

○ **Ascending.** Displays row variable values in ascending order from lowest to highest. This is the default.

○ **Descending.** Displays row variable values in descending order from highest to lowest.

The following format choices are also available:

❑ **Boxes around cells.** This is the default. To produce tables without boxes, deselect this item.

❑ **Index of tables.** The index lists all crosstabulations produced and the page number on which each table begins.

Additional Features Available with Command Syntax

You can customize your crosstabulation if you paste your selections to a syntax window and edit the resulting CROSSTABS command syntax (see Chapter 4). An additional feature is the option of using integer mode (with the VARIABLES subcommand). Integer mode, although not significantly faster, conserves memory when variables are coded as adjacent integers and allows you to display cells containing missing data. See Appendix A for command syntax rules. See the *SPSS Base System Syntax Reference Guide* for complete CROSSTABS command syntax.

11 Describing Subpopulation Differences

The 1964 Civil Rights Act prohibits discrimination in the workplace based on sex or race; employers who violate the act are liable to prosecution. Since passage of this legislation, women, blacks, and other groups have filed numerous lawsuits charging unfair hiring or advancement practices.

The courts have ruled that statistics can be used as *prima facie* evidence of discrimination, and many lawsuits depend heavily on complex statistical analyses to demonstrate that similarly qualified individuals are not treated equally. Identifying and measuring all variables that legitimately influence promotion and hiring is difficult, if not impossible, especially for nonroutine jobs. Years of schooling and prior work experience can be quantified, but what about the more intangible attributes, such as enthusiasm and creativity? How are they to be objectively measured so as not to become convenient smoke screens for concealing discrimination?

Searching for Discrimination

In this chapter, we analyze employee records for 474 individuals hired between 1969 and 1971 by a bank engaged in Equal Employment Opportunity litigation. Two types of unfair employment practices are of particular interest: shunting (placing some employees in lower job categories than other employees with similar qualifications) and salary and promotion inequities.

Although extensive and intricate statistical analyses are usually involved in studies of this kind (Roberts, 1980), the discussion here is necessarily limited. The SPSS Means procedure is used to calculate average salaries for groups of employees based on race and sex. Additional grouping variables are introduced to help "explain" some of the observed variability in salary.

Who Does What?

Figure 11.1 is a crosstabulation of job category at the time of hiring by sex and race characteristics. The first three job classifications contain 64% of white males (adding column percentages), 94% of both minority males and white females, and 100% of minority females. Among white males, 17% are in the college trainee program, compared with 4% of white females.

Figure 11.1   Crosstabulation of job category by sex–race

```
JOBCAT  EMPLOYMENT CATEGORY  by  SEXRACE  SEX & RACE CLASSIFICATION
```

		SEXRACE				Page 1 of 1
	Count Col Pct Tot Pct	WHITE MA LES 1	MINORITY MALES 2	WHITE FE MALES 3	MINORITY FEMALES 4	Row Total
JOBCAT						
CLERICAL	1	75 38.7 15.8	35 54.7 7.4	85 48.3 17.9	32 80.0 6.8	227 47.9
OFFICE TRAINEE	2	35 18.0 7.4	12 18.8 2.5	81 46.0 17.1	8 20.0 1.7	136 28.7
SECURITY OFFICER	3	14 7.2 3.0	13 20.3 2.7			27 5.7
COLLEGE TRAINEE	4	33 17.0 7.0	1 1.6 .2	7 4.0 1.5		41 8.6
EXEMPT EMPLOYEE	5	28 14.4 5.9	2 3.1 .4	2 1.1 .4		32 6.8
MBA TRAINEE	6	3 1.5 .6	1 1.6 .2	1 .6 .2		5 1.1
TECHNICAL	7	6 3.1 1.3				6 1.3
Column Total		194 40.9	64 13.5	176 37.1	40 8.4	474 100.0

```
Number of Missing Observations:   0
```

Although these observations are interesting, they do not imply discriminatory placement into beginning job categories because the qualifications of the various groups are not necessarily similar. If women and nonwhites are more qualified than white males in the same beginning job categories, discrimination may be suspected.

Level of Education

One easily measured employment qualification is years of education. Figure 11.2 shows the average years of education for the entire sample (labeled *For Entire Population*) and then for each of the two sexes (labeled *SEX*, *MALES* or *FEMALES*) and then for each of the two race categories within each sex category (labeled *MINORITY*, *WHITE* or *NONWHITE*).

Figure 11.2 Education by sex and race

```
                   - - Description of Subpopulations - -

Summaries of     EDLEVEL     EDUCATIONAL LEVEL
By levels of     SEX         SEX OF EMPLOYEE
                 MINORITY    MINORITY CLASSIFICATION


Variable       Value  Label              Mean     Std Dev    Cases

For Entire Population                   13.4916    2.8848      474

SEX              0    MALES             14.4302    2.9793      258
   MINORITY      0    WHITE             14.9227    2.8484      194
   MINORITY      1    NONWHITE          12.9375    2.8888       64

SEX              1    FEMALES           12.3704    2.3192      216
   MINORITY      0    WHITE             12.3409    2.4066      176
   MINORITY      1    NONWHITE          12.5000    1.9081       40

   Total Cases = 474
```

The entire sample has an average of 13.49 years of education. Males have more years of education than females—an average of 14.43 years compared with 12.37. White males have the highest level of education, almost 15 years, which is 2 years more than nonwhite males and approximately 2.5 years more than either group of females.

In Figure 11.3, the cases are further subdivided by their combined sex–race characteristics and by their initial job category. For each cell in the table, the average years of education, the standard deviation, and number of cases are displayed. White males have the highest average years of education in all job categories except MBA trainees, where the single minority male MBA trainee has 19 years of education. From this table, it does not appear that females and minorities are overeducated when compared to white males in similar job categories. However, it is important to note that group means provide information about a particular class of employees. While discrimination may not exist for a class as a whole, some individuals within that class may be victims (or beneficiaries) of discrimination.

Figure 11.3   Education by sex–race and job category

```
              - - Description of Subpopulations - -

Summaries of      EDLEVEL      EDUCATIONAL LEVEL
By levels of      JOBCAT       EMPLOYMENT CATEGORY
                  SEXRACE      SEX & RACE CLASSIFICATION


Variable         Value  Label                 Mean     Std Dev    Cases

For Entire Population                        13.4916    2.8848      474

JOBCAT             1    CLERICAL             12.7753    2.5621      227
  SEXRACE          1    WHITE MALES          13.8667    2.3035       75
  SEXRACE          2    MINORITY MALES       13.7714    2.3147       35
  SEXRACE          3    WHITE FEMALES        11.4588    2.4327       85
  SEXRACE          4    MINORITY FEMALES     12.6250    2.1213       32

JOBCAT             2    OFFICE TRAINEE       13.0221    1.8875      136
  SEXRACE          1    WHITE MALES          13.8857    1.4095       35
  SEXRACE          2    MINORITY MALES       12.5833    2.6097       12
  SEXRACE          3    WHITE FEMALES        12.8148    1.9307       81
  SEXRACE          4    MINORITY FEMALES     12.0000     .0000        8

JOBCAT             3    SECURITY OFFICER     10.1852    2.2194       27
  SEXRACE          1    WHITE MALES          10.2857    2.0542       14
  SEXRACE          2    MINORITY MALES       10.0769    2.4651       13

JOBCAT             4    COLLEGE TRAINEE      17.0000    1.2845       41
  SEXRACE          1    WHITE MALES          17.2121    1.3407       33
  SEXRACE          2    MINORITY MALES       17.0000      .           1
  SEXRACE          3    WHITE FEMALES        16.0000     .0000        7

JOBCAT             5    EXEMPT EMPLOYEE      17.2813    1.9713       32
  SEXRACE          1    WHITE MALES          17.6071    1.7709       28
  SEXRACE          2    MINORITY MALES       14.0000    2.8284        2
  SEXRACE          3    WHITE FEMALES        16.0000     .0000        2

JOBCAT             6    MBA TRAINEE          18.0000    1.4142        5
  SEXRACE          1    WHITE MALES          18.3333    1.1547        3
  SEXRACE          2    MINORITY MALES       19.0000      .           1
  SEXRACE          3    WHITE FEMALES        16.0000      .           1

JOBCAT             7    TECHNICAL            18.1667    1.4720        6
  SEXRACE          1    WHITE MALES          18.1667    1.4720        6

   Total Cases = 474
```

Beginning Salaries

The average beginning salary for the 474 persons hired between 1969 and 1971 is $6,806. The distribution by the four sex–race categories is shown in Figure 11.4.

Figure 11.4   Beginning salary by sex–race

```
              - - Description of Subpopulations - -

Summaries of      SALBEG       BEGINNING SALARY
By levels of      SEXRACE      SEX & RACE CLASSIFICATION


Variable         Value  Label                 Mean      Std Dev     Cases

For Entire Population                       6806.4346  3148.2553      474

SEXRACE            1    WHITE   MALES        8637.5258  3871.1017      194
SEXRACE            2    MINORITY MALES       6553.5000  2228.1436       64
SEXRACE            3    WHITE   FEMALES      5340.4886  1225.9605      176
SEXRACE            4    MINORITY FEMALES     4780.5000   771.4188       40

   Total Cases = 474
```

White males have the highest beginning salaries—an average of $8,638—followed by minority males. Because males are in higher job categories than females, this difference is not surprising.

Figure 11.5 shows beginning salaries subdivided by race, sex, and job category. For most of the job categories, white males have higher beginning salaries than the other groups. There is a $1,400 salary difference between white males and white females in the clerical jobs and a $1,000 difference in the general office trainee classification. In the college trainee program, white males averaged over $3,000 more than white females. However, Figure 11.3 shows that white females in the college trainee program had only an undergraduate degree, while white males had an average of 17.2 years of schooling.

Figure 11.5 Beginning salary by sex–race and job category

```
                     - - Description of Subpopulations - -

Summaries of      SALBEG      BEGINNING SALARY
By levels of      JOBCAT      EMPLOYMENT CATEGORY
                  SEXRACE     SEX & RACE CLASSIFICATION


Variable       Value  Label                        Mean

For Entire Population                           6806.4346

JOBCAT           1   CLERICAL                    5733.9471
  SEXRACE        1   WHITE MALES                 6553.4400
  SEXRACE        2   MINORITY MALES              6230.7429
  SEXRACE        3   WHITE FEMALES               5147.3176
  SEXRACE        4   MINORITY FEMALES            4828.1250

JOBCAT           2   OFFICE TRAINEE              5478.9706
  SEXRACE        1   WHITE MALES                 6262.2857
  SEXRACE        2   MINORITY MALES              5610.0000
  SEXRACE        3   WHITE FEMALES               5208.8889
  SEXRACE        4   MINORITY FEMALES            4590.0000

JOBCAT           3   SECURITY OFFICER            6031.1111
  SEXRACE        1   WHITE MALES                 6102.8571
  SEXRACE        2   MINORITY MALES              5953.8462

JOBCAT           4   COLLEGE TRAINEE             9956.4878
  SEXRACE        1   WHITE MALES                10467.6364
  SEXRACE        2   MINORITY MALES             11496.0000
  SEXRACE        3   WHITE FEMALES               7326.8571

JOBCAT           5   EXEMPT EMPLOYEE            13258.8750
  SEXRACE        1   WHITE MALES                13255.2857
  SEXRACE        2   MINORITY MALES             15570.0000
  SEXRACE        3   WHITE FEMALES              10998.0000

JOBCAT           6   MBA TRAINEE                12837.6000
  SEXRACE        1   WHITE MALES                14332.0000
  SEXRACE        2   MINORITY MALES             13992.0000
  SEXRACE        3   WHITE FEMALES               7200.0000

JOBCAT           7   TECHNICAL                  19996.0000
  SEXRACE        1   WHITE MALES                19996.0000

  Total Cases = 474
```

Introducing More Variables

The differences in mean beginning salaries between males and females are somewhat suspect. It is, however, unwise to conclude that salary discrimination exists, since several important variables, such as years of prior experience, have not been considered. It is necessary to **control** (or adjust statistically) for other relevant variables. **Cross-classifying** cases by the variables of interest and comparing salaries across the subgroups is one way of achieving control. However, as the number of variables increases, the number of cases in each cell rapidly diminishes, making statistically meaningful comparisons difficult. To circumvent these problems, you can use regression methods, which achieve control by specifying certain statistical relations that may describe what is happening. Regression methods are described in Chapter 18.

How to Obtain Subgroup Means

The Means procedure calculates subgroup means and related univariate statistics for dependent variables within categories of one or more independent variables. Optionally, you can also obtain one-way analysis of variance, eta, and a test of linearity.

The minimum specifications are:

- One numeric dependent variable.

- One numeric or short string independent variable.

To obtain subgroup means and related univariate statistics, from the menus choose:

Statistics
  Compare Means ▶
    Means...

This opens the Means dialog box, as shown in Figure 11.6.

Figure 11.6 Means dialog box

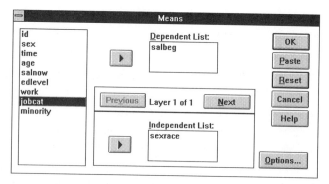

The numeric and short string variables in your data file appear on the source variable list. Select one or more numeric variables for the Dependent list, and select one or more numeric or short string variables for the Independent list. To obtain the default table of means and number of cases, click on OK. Subgroup means for each dependent variable are calculated for each category of each independent variable, as in Figure 11.4.

Optionally, you can specify additional **layers** of independent variables. Each layer further subdivides the sample. For example, Figure 11.2 was produced by using *edlevel* as the dependent variable, *sex* as the layer 1 independent variable, and *minority* as the layer 2 independent variable. Subgroup means of *edlevel* are calculated for each category of *minority* within each category of *sex*.

You can specify up to five layers of independent variables. Use Next and Previous to move between the independent variable lists for the different layers.

Means Options Dialog Box

To obtain additional univariate statistics, control the display of variable and value labels, or generate an analysis of variance for the first layer, click on Options... in the Means dialog box. This opens the Means Options dialog box, as shown in Figure 11.7.

Figure 11.7   Means Options dialog box

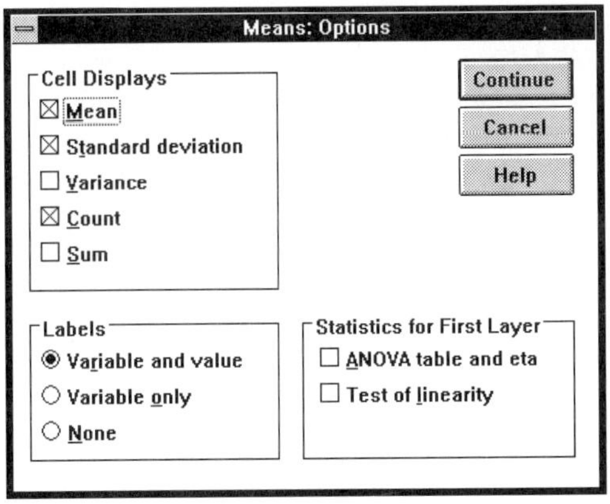

Cell Displays. You can choose one or more of the following subgroup statistics for the dependent variable(s) within each category (cell) of each independent variable:

❑ **Mean.** The arithmetic mean. Displayed by default.

❑ **Standard deviation.** A measure of how much observations vary from the mean, expressed in the same units as the data. Displayed by default.

❑ **Variance.** A measure of how much observations vary from the mean, equal to the square of the standard deviation. The units are the square of those of the variable itself.

❑ **Count.** The number of cases in each subgroup. Displayed by default.

❑ **Sum.** The sum of all the values in each subgroup.

Labels. You can choose one of the following alternatives:

○ **Variable and value.** Displays variable and value labels. This is the default.

○ **Variable only.** Displays variable labels but suppresses value labels.

○ **None.** Suppresses both variable and value labels.

Statistics for First Layer. For subgroups based on categories of the independent variables in the first layer only, you can choose one or more of the following additional statistics:

❑ **ANOVA table and eta.** Displays a one-way analysis-of-variance table and calculates eta and eta^2 for each independent variable in the first layer.

❑ **Test of linearity.** Calculates the sums of squares, degrees of freedom, and mean square associated with linear and nonlinear components, as well as the F ratio, R, and R^2. Linearity is not calculated if the independent variable is a short string.

Additional Features Available with Command Syntax

You can customize the Means procedure if you paste your selections into a syntax window and edit the resulting MEANS command syntax (see Chapter 4). An additional feature is the option to generate output in crosstabular format (with the CROSSBREAK subcommand). See Appendix A for command syntax rules. See the *SPSS Base System Syntax Reference Guide* for complete MEANS command syntax.

12 Multiple Response Analysis

Introduction to Multiple Response Data

The example in this section illustrates the use of multiple response items in a market research survey. The data in these tables are fictitious and should not be interpreted as real.

An airline might survey passengers flying a particular route to evaluate competing carriers. In this example, American Airlines wants to know about its passengers' use of other airlines on the Chicago–New York route and the relative importance of schedule and service in selecting an airline. The flight attendant hands each passenger a brief questionnaire upon boarding similar to the one shown in Figure 12.1. The first question is a multiple response question because the passenger can circle more than one response. However, this question cannot be coded directly because an SPSS variable can have only one value for each case. You must use several variables to map responses to the question. There are two ways to do this. One is to define a variable corresponding to each of the choices (for example, American, United, TWA, Eastern, and Other). If the passenger circles United, the variable *united* is assigned a code of 1—otherwise, 0. This is the **multiple dichotomy method** of mapping variables.

Figure 12.1   An in-flight questionnaire

```
Circle all airlines that you have flown at least one time
in the last six months on this route:


  American   United   TWA   Eastern   Other:_____


Which is more important in selecting a flight?
  Schedule              Service
(Circle only one.)


Thank you for your cooperation.
```

The other way to map the responses is the **multiple category method**, in which you estimate the maximum number of possible responses to the question and set up the same number of variables, with codes used to specify the airline flown. By perusing a sample of the questionnaires, you might discover that no user has flown more than 3 different airlines on this route in the last six months. Further, you find that due to the deregulation of airlines, 10 other airlines are named in the *Other* category. Using the multiple response method, you would define 3 variables, coded as 1 = *american*, 2 = *united*, 3 = *twa*, 4 = *eastern*, 5 = *republic*, 6 = *usair*, and so on. If a given passenger circles American and TWA, the first variable has a code of 1, the second has a code of 3, and the third has some missing-value code. Another passenger might have circled American and entered USAir. Thus, the first variable has a code of 1, the second a code of 6, and the third a missing-value code. If you use the multiple dichotomy method, on the other hand, you end up with 14 separate variables. Although either method of mapping is feasible for this survey, the method you choose depends on the distribution of responses.

Set Definition

Each SPSS variable created from the survey question is an elementary variable. To analyze a multiple response item, you must combine the variables into one of two types of multiple response sets: a multiple dichotomy set or a multiple category set. For example, if the airline survey asked about only three airlines (American, United, and TWA) and you used dichotomous variables to account for multiple responses, the separate frequency tables would resemble Table 12.1. When you define a **multiple dichotomy set**, each of the three variables in the set becomes a category of the group variable. The counted values represent the *Have flown* category of each elementary variable. Table 12.2 shows the frequencies for this multiple dichotomy set. The 75 people using American Airlines are the 75 cases with code 1 for the variable representing American Airlines in Table 12.1. Because some people circled more than one response, 120 responses are recorded for 100 respondents.

Table 12.1   Dichotomous variables tabulated separately

American

Category Label	Code	Frequency	Relative Frequency
Have flown	1	75	75.0
Have not flown	0	25	25.0
	Total	100	100.0

United

Category Label	Code	Frequency	Relative Frequency
Have flown	1	30	30.0
Have not flown	0	70	70.0
	Total	100	100.0

TWA

Category Label	Code	Frequency	Relative Frequency
Have flown	1	15	15.0
Have not flown	0	85	85.0
	Total	100	100.0

Table 12.2   Dichotomous variables tabulated as a group

Airlines

Variable	Frequency	Relative Frequency
American	75	62.5
United	30	25.0
TWA	15	12.5
Total	120	100.0

If you discover that no respondent mentioned more than two airlines, you could create two variables, each having three codes, one for each airline. The frequency tables for these elementary variables would resemble Table 12.3. When you define a **multiple category set**, the values are tabulated by adding the same codes in the elementary variables together. The resulting set of values is the same as those for each of the elementary variables. Table 12.4 shows the frequencies for this multiple category set. For example, the 30 responses for United are the sum of the 25 United responses for airline 1 and the five United responses for airline 2.

Table 12.3   Multiple response items tabulated separately

Airline 1

Category Label	Code	Frequency	Relative Frequency
American	1	75	75.0
United	2	25	25.0
	Total	100	100.0

Airline 2

Category Label	Code	Frequency	Relative Frequency
United	2	5	5.0
TWA	3	15	15.0
Missing	99	80	80.0
	Total	100	100.0

Table 12.4   Multiple response items tabulated as a group

Airlines

Category Label	Code	Frequency	Relative Frequency
American	1	75	62.5
United	2	30	25.0
TWA	3	15	12.5
	Total	120	100.0

Crosstabulations

Both multiple dichotomy and multiple category sets can be crosstabulated with other variables in the SPSS Multiple Response Crosstabs procedure. In the airline passenger survey, the airline choices can be crosstabulated with the question asking why people chose different airlines. If you have organized the first question into dichotomies as in Table 12.1, the three crosstabulations of the dichotomous variables with the schedule/service question would resemble Figure 12.2. If you had chosen the multiple category set method and created two variables, the two crosstabulations would resemble Figure 12.3 (cases with missing values are omitted from the table for airline 2). With either method, the crosstabulation of the elementary variable and the group variable would resemble Figure 12.4. Each row in Figure 12.4 represents the *Have flown* information for the three dichotomous variables. Like codes are added together for the multiple category set. For example, 21 respondents have flown United and think schedule is the most important consideration in selecting a flight. The 21 cases are a combination of 20 people who flew United as airline 1 and circled *Schedule* plus one person who flew United as airline 2 and circled *Schedule*.

Figure 12.2   Dichotomous variables crosstabulated separately

```
    AMERICAN
by  SELECT


                             SELECT

                Count   | Schedule Service
                        |                        Row
                        |                        Total
                        |    0         1
     AMERICAN   --------+----------------------
                   0    |   20         5          25
     Have not flown     |                        25.0

                   1    |   41        34          75
     Have flown         |                        75.0

                Column  |   61        39         100
                Total   | 61.0      39.0       100.0
```

```
    UNITED
by  SELECT


                             SELECT

                Count   | Schedule Service
                        |                        Row
                        |                        Total
                        |    0         1
     UNITED     --------+----------------------
                   0    |   40        30          70
     Have not flown     |                        70.0

                   1    |   21         9          30
     Have flown         |                        30.0

                Column  |   61        39         100
                Total   | 61.0      39.0       100.0
```

```
    TWA
by  SELECT


                             SELECT

                Count   | Schedule Service
                        |                        Row
                        |                        Total
                        |    0         1
     TWA        --------+----------------------
                   0    |   53        32          85
     Have not flown     |                        85.0

                   1    |    8         7          15
     Have flown         |                        15.0

                Column  |   61        39         100
                Total   | 61.0      39.0       100.0
```

Figure 12.3   Multiple response variables crosstabulated separately

```
    AIRLINE1
by SELECT
```

```
                              SELECT
                  Count  |Schedule Service
                         |                          Row
                         |                          Total
                         |     0         1
    AIRLINE1    ─────────┼──────────────────
                    1    |    41        34          75
      American           |                          75.0
                         |
                    2    |    20         5          25
      United             |                          25.0
                ─────────┴──────────────────
                Column        61        39         100
                Total         61.0      39.0       100.0
```

```
    AIRLINE2
by SELECT
```

```
                              SELECT
                  Count  |Schedule Service
                         |                          Row
                         |                          Total
                         |     0         1
    AIRLINE2    ─────────┼──────────────────
                    2    |     1         4           5
      United             |                          25.0
                         |
                    3    |     8         7          15
      TWA                |                          75.0
                ─────────┴──────────────────
                Column         9        11          20
                Total         45.0      55.0       100.0
```

Figure 12.4   A group crosstabulated

```
    AIRLINES (group)
by SELECT
```

```
                              SELECT
                  Count  |Schedule Service
                         |                          Row
                         |                          Total
                         |     0         1
    AIRLINES    ─────────┼──────────────────
                    1    |    41        34          75
      American           |                          62.5
                         |
                    2    |    21         9          30
      United             |                          25.0
                         |
                    3    |     8         7          15
      TWA                |                          12.5
                ─────────┴──────────────────
                Column        70        50         120
                Total         58.3      41.7       100.0
```

Analyzing Multiple Response Data

Two procedures are available for analyzing multiple dichotomy and multiple category sets (see "Introduction to Multiple Response Data" on p. 235). The Multiple Response Frequencies procedure displays frequency tables. The Multiple Response Crosstabs procedure displays two- and three-dimensional crosstabulations. Before using either procedure, you must first define your multiple response sets.

How to Define Multiple Response Sets

The Define Multiple Response Sets procedure groups elementary variables into multiple dichotomy and multiple category sets, for which you can obtain frequency tables and crosstabulations.

The minimum specifications are:

- Two or more numeric variables.
- Value(s) to be counted.
- A name for the multiple response set.

To define one or more multiple response sets, from the menus choose:

Statistics
  Multiple Response ▶
    Define Sets...

This opens the Define Multiple Response Sets dialog box, as shown in Figure 12.5.

Figure 12.5   Define Multiple Response Sets dialog box

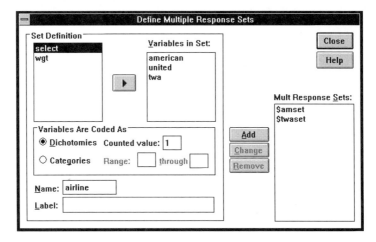

The numeric variables in your data file appear on the source list. To define a multiple response set, select two or more variables, indicate how variables are coded, and supply a set name; then click on Add to add the multiple response set to the list of defined sets. You can use the same variables in more than one set. After you define each set, all selected variables move back to the source variable list.

Variables Are Coded As. You can choose one of the following alternatives:

○ **Dichotomies.** Elementary variables having two categories. This is the default. Select this item to create a multiple dichotomy set. Enter an integer value for Counted value. Each variable having at least one occurrence of the counted value becomes a category of the multiple dichotomy set.

○ **Categories.** Elementary variables having more than two categories. Select this item to create a multiple category set having the same range of values as the component variables. Enter integer values for the minimum and maximum values of the range for categories of the multiple category set. SPSS totals each distinct integer value in the inclusive range across all component variables. Empty categories are not tabulated.

Name. The name for the multiple response set. Enter up to seven characters for the name. SPSS prefixes a dollar sign ($) to the name you assign. You cannot use the following reserved names: *casenum, sysmis, jdate, date, time, length*, and *width*. The name of the multiple response set exists only for use in multiple response procedures. You cannot refer to multiple response set names in other procedures.

Label. Enter an optional descriptive variable label for the multiple response set. The label can be up to 40 characters long.

You can define up to 20 multiple response sets. Each set must have a unique name. To remove a set, highlight it on the list of multiple response sets and click on Remove. To change a set, highlight it on the list, modify any set definition characteristics, and click on Change.

How to Obtain Multiple Response Frequencies

The Multiple Response Frequencies procedure produces frequency tables for multiple response sets.

The minimum specification is one or more defined multiple response sets.

To obtain multiple response frequencies for defined multiple response sets, you must first define one or more multiple response sets (see "How to Define Multiple Response Sets" on p. 241). Then, from the menus choose:

Statistics
  Multiple Response ▶
    Frequencies...

This opens the Multiple Response Frequencies dialog box, as shown in Figure 12.6.

Figure 12.6   Multiple Response Frequencies dialog box

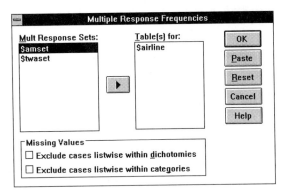

The currently defined multiple response sets appear on the source list. Select one or more sets for frequency tables. Click on OK to get the default frequency tables showing counts and percentages. Cases with missing values are excluded on a table-by-table basis.

For multiple dichotomy sets, category names shown in the output come from variable labels defined for elementary variables in the group. If variable labels are not defined, variable names are used as labels. For multiple category sets, category labels come from the value labels of the first variable in the group. If categories missing for the first variable are present for other variables in the group, define a value label for the missing categories.

Missing Values. You can choose one or both of the following:

❑ **Exclude cases listwise within dichotomies.** Excludes cases with missing values for any variable from the tabulation of the multiple dichotomy set. This applies only to multiple response sets defined as dichotomy sets. By default, a case is considered missing for a multiple dichotomy set if none of its component variables contains the counted value. Cases with missing values for some but not all variables are included in tabulations of the group if at least one variable contains the counted value.

❑ **Exclude cases listwise within categories.** Excludes cases with missing values for any variable from tabulation of the multiple category set. This applies only to multiple response sets defined as category sets. By default, a case is considered missing for a multiple category set only if none of its components has valid values within the defined range.

Additional Features Available with Command Syntax

You can customize your multiple response frequencies if you paste your selections into a syntax window and edit the resulting MULT RESPONSE command syntax. Additional features include output format options such as suppression of value labels (with the FORMAT subcommand).

See Appendix A for command syntax rules. See the *SPSS Base System Syntax Reference Guide* for complete MULT RESPONSE command syntax.

How to Crosstabulate Multiple Response Sets

The Multiple Response Crosstabs procedure crosstabulates defined multiple response sets, elementary variables, or a combination. You can also obtain cell percentages based on cases or responses, modify the handling of missing values, or get paired crosstabulations.

The minimum specifications are:

- One numeric variable or multiple response set for each dimension of the crosstabulation.
- Category ranges for any elementary variables.

To obtain crosstabulation tables for multiple response sets, you must first define one or more multiple response sets (see "How to Define Multiple Response Sets" on p. 241). Then, from the menus choose:

Statistics
  Multiple Response ▶
    Crosstabs...

This opens the Multiple Response Crosstabs dialog box, as shown in Figure 12.7.

Figure 12.7   Multiple Response Crosstabs dialog box

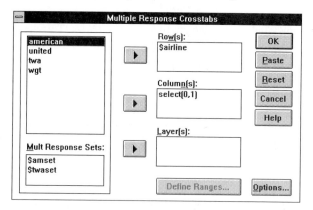

The numeric elementary variables in your data file appear on the source list. The currently defined multiple response sets appear on the list of multiple response sets. Select row and column items for the crosstabulation. A table is produced for each combination of row and column items.

After defining the value ranges of any elementary variables (see "Define Value Ranges," below), click on OK to get the default tables displaying cell counts. Cases with missing values are excluded on a table-by-table basis.

For multiple dichotomy sets, category names shown in the output come from variable labels defined for elementary variables in the group. If variable labels are not defined, variable names are used as labels. For multiple category sets, category labels come from the value labels of the first variable in the group. If categories missing for the first variable are present for other variables in the group, define a value label for the missing categories. SPSS displays category labels for columns on three lines, with up to eight characters per line. To avoid splitting words, you can reverse row and column items or redefine labels.

Optionally, you can obtain a two-way crosstabulation for each category of a control variable or multiple response set. Select one or more items for the Layer(s) list.

Define Value Ranges

Value ranges must be defined for any elementary variables in the crosstabulation. To define value ranges for an elementary variable, highlight the variable on the Row(s), Column(s), or Layer(s) list and click on Define Ranges... in the Multiple Response Crosstabs dialog box. This opens the Multiple Response Crosstabs Define Variable Ranges dialog box, as shown in Figure 12.8.

Figure 12.8   Multiple Response Crosstabs Define Variable Ranges dialog box

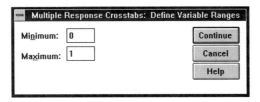

Enter integer minimum and maximum category values that you want to tabulate. Categories outside the range are excluded from analysis. Values within the inclusive range are assumed to be integers (non-integers are truncated).

Options

To obtain cell percentages, control the computation of percentages, modify the handling of missing values, or get a paired crosstabulation, click on Options... in the Multiple Response Crosstabs dialog box. This opens the Multiple Response Crosstabs Options dialog box, as shown in Figure 12.9.

Figure 12.9   Multiple Response Crosstabs Options dialog box

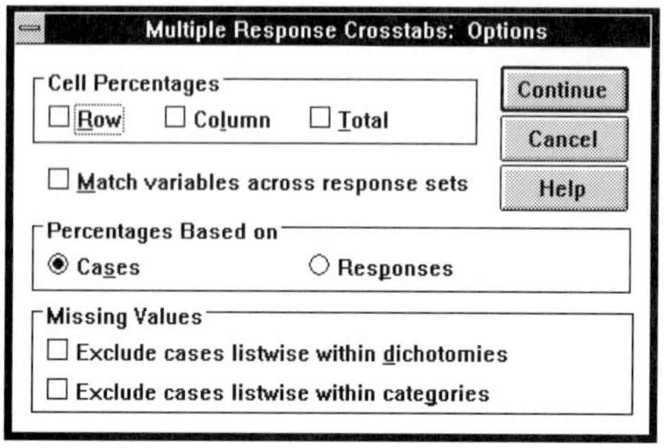

Cell Percentages. Cell counts are always displayed. You can also choose one or more of the following:

❑ **Row**. Displays row percentages.

❑ **Column**. Displays column percentages.

❑ **Total**. Displays two-way table total percentages.

Percentages Based on. You can choose one of the following alternatives:

○ **Cases**. Bases cell percentages on cases, or respondents. This is the default. This item is not available if you select matching of variables across multiple category sets.

○ **Responses**. Bases cell percentages on responses. For multiple dichotomy sets, the number of responses is equal to the number of counted values across cases. For multiple category sets, the number of responses is the number of values in the defined range (see "Define Value Ranges" on p. 245).

Missing Values. You can choose one or both of the following:

❑ **Exclude cases listwise within dichotomies**. Excludes cases with missing values for any variable from the tabulation of the multiple dichotomy set. This applies only to multiple response sets defined as dichotomy sets. By default, a case is considered missing for a multiple dichotomy set only if none of its elementary variables contains the counted value.

❑ **Exclude cases listwise within categories**. Excludes cases with missing values for any component variable from tabulation of the multiple category set. This applies only to multiple response sets defined as category sets. By default, a case is considered missing for a multiple category set only if none of its elementary variables has valid values falling within the defined range.

By default, when crosstabulating two multiple category sets, SPSS tabulates each variable in the first group with each variable in the second group and sums the counts for each cell. So, some responses can appear more than once in a table. You can choose the following option:

❏ **Match variables across response sets.** Pairs the first variable in the first group with the first variable in the second group, the second variable in the first group with the second variable in the second group, etc. If you select this option, SPSS bases cell percentages on responses rather than respondents. Pairing is not available for multiple dichotomy sets or elementary variables.

Additional Features Available with Command Syntax

You can customize your multiple response crosstabulation if you paste your selections into a syntax window and edit the resulting MULTIPLE RESPONSE command syntax. Additional features include:

• Crosstabulation tables with up to five dimensions (with the BY subcommand).

• Output formatting options, including suppression of value labels (with the FORMAT subcommand).

See Appendix A for command syntax rules. See the *SPSS Base System Syntax Reference Guide* for complete MULTIPLE RESPONSE command syntax.

13 Testing Hypotheses about Differences in Means

Would you buy a disposable raincoat, vegetables in pop-top cans, or investment counseling via closed-circuit television? These products and 17 others were described in questionnaires administered to 100 married couples (Davis & Ragsdale, 1983). Respondents were asked to rate on a scale of 1 (definitely want to buy) to 7 (definitely do not want to buy) their likelihood of buying the product. Of the 100 couples, 50 received questionnaires with pictures of the products and 50 received questionnaires without pictures. In this chapter, we will examine whether pictures affect consumer preferences and whether husbands' and wives' responses differ.

Testing Hypotheses

The first part of the table in Figure 13.1 contains basic descriptive statistics for the buying scores of couples receiving questionnaires with and without pictures. A couple's buying score is simply the sum of all ratings assigned to products by the husband and wife individually. Low scores indicate buyers, while high scores indicate reluctance to buy. The 50 couples who received questionnaires without pictures (group 1) had a mean score of 168, while the 48 couples who received forms with pictures had an average score of 159. (Two couples did not complete the questionnaire and are not included in the analysis.) The standard deviations show that scores for the second group were somewhat more variable than those for the first.

If you are willing to restrict the conclusions to the 98 couples included in the study, it is safe to say that couples who received forms with pictures indicated a greater willingness to purchase the products than couples who received forms without pictures. However, this statement is not very satisfying. What is needed is some type of statement about the effect of the two questionnaire types for all couples—or at least some larger group of couples—not just those actually studied.

Figure 13.1   Family buying scores by questionnaire type

Variable	Number of Cases	Mean	SD	SE of Mean
FAMSCORE FAMILY BUYING SCORE				
NO PICTURES	50	168.0000	21.787	3.081
PICTURES	48	159.0833	27.564	3.979

Mean Difference = 8.9167

Levene's Test for Equality of Variances: F= 1.382   P= .243

t-test for Equality of Means					95%	
Variances	t-value	df	2-Tail Sig	SE of Diff	CI for Diff	
Equal	1.78	96	.078	5.008	(-1.027, 18.860)	
Unequal	1.77	89.43	.080	5.032	(-1.084, 18.918)	

Samples and Populations

The totality of cases about which conclusions are desired is called the **population**, while the cases actually included in the study constitute the **sample**. The couples in this experiment can be considered a sample from the population of couples in the United States.

The field of statistics helps us draw inferences about populations based on observations obtained from **random samples**, or samples in which the characteristics and relationships of interest are independent of the probabilities of being included in the sample. The necessity of a good research design cannot be overemphasized. Unless precautions are taken to ensure that the sample is from the population of interest and that the cases are chosen and observed without bias, the results obtained from statistical analyses may be misleading. For example, if a sample contains only affluent suburban couples, conclusions about all couples may be unwarranted.

If measurements are obtained from an entire population, the population can be characterized by the various measures of central tendency, dispersion, and shape described in Chapter 8. The results describe the population exactly. If, however, you obtain information from a random sample—the usual case—the results serve as **estimates** of the unknown population values. Special notation is used to identify population values, termed **parameters**, and to distinguish them from sample values, termed **statistics**. The mean of a population is denoted by μ, and the variance by σ^2. The symbols $\bar{X}$ and S^2 are reserved for the mean and variance of samples.

Sampling Distributions

The observations actually included in a study are just one of many random samples that could have been selected from a population. For example, if the population consists of married couples in the United States, the number of different samples that could be chosen for inclusion in a study is mind-boggling. The estimated value of a population parameter depends on the particular sample chosen. Different samples usually produce different estimates.

Figure 13.2 is a histogram of 400 means produced by the SPSS Frequencies procedure. Each mean is calculated from a random sample of 25 observations from a population that has a normal distribution with a mean value of 0 and a standard deviation of 1. The estimated means are not all the same. Instead, they have a distribution. Most sample means are fairly close to 0, the population mean. The mean of the 400 means is 0, and the standard deviation of these means is 0.2. In fact, the distribution of the means appears approximately normal.

Figure 13.2   Means of 400 samples of size 25 from a normal distribution

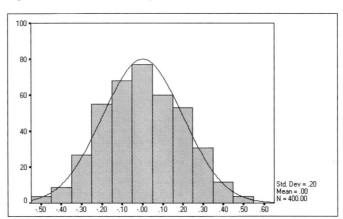

Although Figure 13.2 gives some idea of the appearance of the distribution of sample means of size 25 from a standard normal population, it is only an approximation since all possible samples of size 25 have not been taken. If the number of samples taken is increased to 1000, an even better picture of the distribution could be obtained. As the number of samples of a fixed size increases, the observed (or empirical) distribution of the means approaches the underlying or theoretical distribution.

The theoretical distribution of all possible values of a statistic obtained from a population is called the **sampling distribution** of the statistic. The mean of the sampling distribution is called the **expected value** of the statistic. The standard deviation is termed the **standard error**. The sampling distributions of most commonly used statistics calculated from random samples are tabulated and readily accessible. Knowing the sampling distribution of a statistic is very important for hypothesis testing, since from it you can calculate the probability of obtaining an observed sample value if a particular hypothesis is true. For example, from Figure 13.2, it appears quite unlikely that a sample mean based on a sample of size 25 from a standard normal distribution would be greater than 0.5 if the population mean were 0.

Sampling Distribution of the Mean

Since hypotheses about population means are often of interest, the sampling distribution of the mean is particularly important. If samples are taken from a normal population, the sampling distribution of the sample mean is also normal. As expected, the observed distribution of the 400 means in Figure 13.2 is approximately normal. The theoretical distribution of the sample mean, based on all possible samples of size 25, is exactly normal.

Even when samples are taken from a non-normal population, the distribution of the sample means will be approximately normal for sufficiently large samples. This is one reason for the importance of the normal distribution in statistical inference. Consider Figure 13.3, which shows a sample from a uniform distribution. In a uniform distribution, all values of a variable are equally likely; hence, the proportion of cases in each bin of the histogram is roughly the same.

Figure 13.3   Values from a uniform distribution

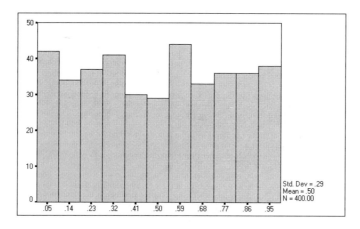

Figure 13.4 is a histogram of 400 means calculated from samples of size 25 from a uniform distribution. Note that the observed distribution is approximately normal even though the distribution from which the samples were taken is markedly non-normal.

Both the size of a sample and the shape of the distribution from which samples are taken affect the shape of the sampling distribution of the mean. If samples are small and come from distributions that are far from normal, the distribution of the means will not be even approximately normal. As the size of the sample increases, the sampling distribution of the mean will approach normality.

Figure 13.4   Distribution of 400 means from samples of size 25 from a uniform distribution

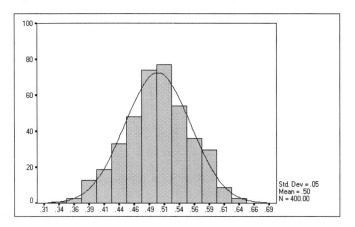

The mean of the theoretical sampling distribution of the means of samples of size N is μ, the population mean. The standard error, which is another name for the standard deviation of the sampling distribution of the mean, is

$$\sigma_{\bar{X}} = \frac{\sigma}{\sqrt{N}}$$

Equation 13.1

where σ is the standard deviation of the population and N is the sample size.

The standard deviation of the observed sampling distribution of means in Figure 13.2 is 0.20. This is the same as the value of the standard error for the theoretical distribution, which, from the previous formula, is $1/5$, or 0.20.

Usually, the value of the standard error is unknown and is estimated from a single sample using

$$S_{\bar{X}} = \frac{S}{\sqrt{N}}$$

Equation 13.2

where S is the *sample* standard deviation. The estimated standard error is displayed in the SPSS Frequencies procedure and is also part of the output shown in Figure 13.1. For example, for group 1 the estimated standard error of the mean is

$$\frac{21.787}{\sqrt{50}} = 3.081$$

Equation 13.3

This value is displayed in the column labeled *SE of Mean* in Figure 13.1.

The standard error of the mean depends on both the sample standard deviation and the sample size. For a fixed standard deviation, as the size of a sample increases, the standard error decreases. This is intuitively clear, since the more data are gathered, the more confident you can be that the sample mean is not too far from the population mean. Also, as the standard deviation of the observations decreases, the standard error decreases as well. Small standard deviations occur when observations are fairly homogeneous. In this case, means based on different samples should also not vary much.

The Two-Sample T Test

Consider again whether there is evidence that the type of form administered influences couples' buying decisions. The question is not whether the two sample means are equal, but whether the two population means are equal.

To test the hypothesis that, in the population, buying scores for the two questionnaire types are the same, the following statistic can be calculated:

$$t = \frac{\bar{X}_1 - \bar{X}_2}{\sqrt{\dfrac{S_1^2}{N_1} + \dfrac{S_2^2}{N_2}}}$$

Equation 13.4

where $\bar{X}_1$ is the sample mean of group 1, S_1^2 is the variance, and N_1 is the sample size.

Based on the sampling distribution of the above statistic, you can calculate the probability that a difference at least as large as the one observed would occur if the two population means (μ_1 and μ_2) are equal. This probability is called the **observed significance level**. If the observed significance level is small enough (usually less than 0.05, or 0.01), the hypothesis that the population means are equal is rejected.

The t value and its associated probability are given in Figure 13.1 in the row labeled *Unequal*. The t value is

$$t = \frac{168.0 - 159.08}{\sqrt{\dfrac{21.787^2}{50} + \dfrac{27.564^2}{48}}} = 1.77$$

Equation 13.5

If $\mu_1 = \mu_2$, the probability of observing a difference at least as large as the one in the sample is estimated to be about 0.08. Since this probability is greater than 0.05, the hypothesis that mean buying scores in the population are equal for the two types of forms is not rejected. The entry under *df* in Figure 13.1 is a function of the sample size in the two groups and is used together with the t value in establishing the observed significance level.

Another statistic based on the t distribution can be used to test the equality of means hypothesis. This statistic, known as the **pooled-variance t test**, is based on the assumption that the population variances in the two groups are equal and is obtained using a pooled estimate of that common variance. The test statistic is identical to the equation for t given previously except that the individual group variances are replaced by a pooled estimate, S_p^2. That is,

$$t = \frac{\bar{X}_1 - \bar{X}_2}{\sqrt{\dfrac{S_p^2}{N_1} + \dfrac{S_p^2}{N_2}}}$$

Equation 13.6

where S_p^2, the pooled variance, is a weighted average of the individual variances and is calculated as

$$S_p^2 = \frac{(N_1 - 1) S_1^2 + (N_2 - 1) S_2^2}{N_1 + N_2 - 2}$$

Equation 13.7

From the output in Figure 13.1, the pooled t test value for the study is 1.78. The degrees of freedom for the pooled t test are 96, the sum of the sample sizes in both groups minus 2. If the pooled-variance t test is used when the population variances are not equal, the probability level associated with the statistic may be in error. The amount of error depends on the inequality of the sample sizes and of the variances. However, using the separate-variance t value when the population variances are equal will usually result in an observed significance level somewhat larger than it should be. For large samples, the discrepancy between the two methods is small. In general, it is a good idea to use the separate-variance t test whenever you suspect that the variances are unequal.

Levene's test is used to test the hypothesis that the two population variances are equal. This test is less dependent on the assumption of normality than most tests of equality of variance. It is obtained by computing for each case the absolute difference from its group mean and then performing a one-way analysis of variance on these differences. In Figure 13.1, the value of the Levene statistic is 1.382. If the observed significance level for this test is small, the hypothesis that the population variances are equal is rejected and the separate-variance t test for means should be used. In this example, the significance level for the Levene statistic is large, and thus the pooled-variance t test is appropriate.

Significance Levels

The commonsense interpretation of a small observed significance level is straightforward: it appears unlikely that the two population means are equal. Of course, there is a possibility that the means are equal and the observed difference is due to chance. The observed significance level is the probability that a difference at least as large as the one observed would have arisen if the means were really equal.

When the observed significance level is too large to reject the equality hypothesis, the two population means may indeed be equal, or they may be unequal, but the difference cannot be detected. Failure to detect can be due to a true difference that is very small. For example, if a new cancer drug prolongs survival time by only one day when compared to the standard treatment, it is unlikely that such a difference will be detected, especially if survival times vary substantially and the additional day represents a small increment.

There are other reasons why true differences may not be found. If the sample sizes in the two groups are small or the variability large, even substantial differences may not be detected. Significant t values are obtained when the numerator of the t statistic is large compared to the denominator. The numerator is the difference between the sample means, and the denominator depends on the standard deviations and sample sizes of the two groups. For a given standard deviation, the larger the sample size, the smaller the denominator. Thus, a difference of a given magnitude may be significant if obtained with a sample size of 100 but not significant with a sample size of 25.

One-tailed versus Two-tailed Tests

A two-tailed test is used to detect a difference in means between two populations regardless of the direction of the difference. For example, in the study of buying scores presented in this chapter, we are interested in whether buying scores without pictures are larger *or* smaller than buying scores with pictures. In applications where you are interested in detecting a difference in one direction—such as whether a new drug is better than the current treatment—a so-called one-tailed test can be performed. The procedure is the same as for the two-tailed test, but the resulting probability value is divided by 2, adjusting for the fact that the equality hypothesis is rejected only when the difference between the two means is sufficiently large and in the direction of interest. In a two-tailed test, the equality hypothesis is rejected for large positive or negative values of the statistic.

What's the Difference?

It appears that the questionnaire type has no significant effect on couples' willingness to purchase products. Overall buying scores for the two conditions are similar. Pictures of the products do not appear to enhance their perceived desirability. In fact, the pictures actually appear to make several products somewhat less desirable. However, since the purpose of the questionnaires is to ascertain buying intent, including a picture of the actual product may help gauge true product response. Although the concept of disposable raincoats may be attractive, if they make the owner look like a walking trash bag, their appeal may diminish considerably.

Using Crosstabulation to Test Hypotheses

The SPSS Independent-Samples T Test procedure is used to test hypotheses about the equality of two means for variables measured on an interval or ratio scale. Crosstabulation and the Pearson chi-square statistic can be used to test hypotheses about a dichotomous variable, such as purchase of a particular product.

Figure 13.5 is an SPSS crosstabulation showing the number of husbands who would definitely want to buy vegetables in pop-top cans when shown a picture and when not shown a picture of the product (value 1 of variable *H2S*). The vegetables in pop-top cans were chosen by 6.0% of the husbands who were tempted with pictures and 16.0% of the husbands who were not shown pictures. The chi-square statistic provides a test of the hypothesis that the proportion of husbands selecting the vegetables in pop-top cans is the same for the picture and no-picture forms.

Figure 13.5 Preference of husbands for vegetables in pop-top cans

```
H2S  POP-TOP CANS HUSB SELF   by   VISUAL   PICTURE ACCOMPANIED QUESTION

                      VISUAL        Page 1 of 1
            Count
            Col Pct  NO PICTU PICTURES
                     RES
                         0       1     Row
                                       Total
       H2S
              1          8       3      11
        DEFINITELY      16.0     6.0    11.0

              2         42      47      89
        VERY LIKELY     84.0    94.0    89.0

           Column      50      50      100
           Total       50.0    50.0    100.0

         Chi-Square              Value      DF      Significance
  ---------------------       -----------   ----   ------------

  Pearson                       2.55363       1          .11004
  Continuity Correction         1.63432       1          .20111
  Likelihood Ratio              2.63933       1          .10425
  Mantel-Haenszel test for      2.52809       1          .11184
      linear association

  Minimum Expected Frequency -    5.500
```

The probability of 0.11 associated with the Pearson chi-square in Figure 13.5 is the probability that a difference at least as large as the one observed would occur in the sample if in the population there were no difference in the selection of the product between the two formats. Since the probability is large, the hypothesis of no difference between the two formats is not rejected.

Independent versus Paired Samples

Several factors contribute to the observed differences in response between two groups. Part of the observed difference in scores between the picture and no-picture formats may be attributable to form type. Another component is due to differences between individuals. Not all couples have the same buying desires, so even if the type of form does not affect buying, differences between the two groups will probably be observed due to differences between the couples within the two groups.

One method of minimizing the influence of individual variation is to choose the two groups so that the couples within them are comparable on characteristics that can influence buying behavior, such as income, education, family size, and so forth.

It is sometimes possible to obtain pairs of subjects, such as twins, and assign one member of each pair to each of the two treatments. Another frequently used experimental design is to expose the same individual to both types of conditions. (In this design, care must be taken to ensure that the sequential administration of treatments does not influence response by providing practice, decreasing attention span, or affecting the second treatment in other ways.) In both designs, subject-to-subject variability has substantially less effect. These designs are called **paired-samples designs**, since for each subject there is a corresponding pair in the other group. In the second design, a person is paired with himself or herself. In an **independent-samples design**, there is no pairing of cases; all observations are independent.

Analysis of Paired Data

Although the interpretation of the significance of results from paired experiments is the same as those from the two independent samples discussed previously, the actual computations are different. For each pair of cases, the difference in the responses is calculated. The statistic used to test the hypothesis that the mean difference in the population is 0 is

$$t = \frac{\bar{D}}{S_D / \sqrt{N}}$$

Equation 13.8

where $\bar{D}$ is the observed difference between the two means and S_D is the standard deviation of the differences of the paired observations. The sampling distribution of t, if the differences are normally distributed with a mean of 0, is Student's t with $N - 1$ degrees of freedom, where N is the number of pairs. If the pairing is effective, the standard error of the difference will be smaller than the standard error obtained if two independent samples with N subjects each were chosen. However, if the variables chosen for pairing do not affect the responses under study, pairing may result in a test that is less powerful since true differences can be detected less frequently.

For example, to test the hypothesis that there is no difference between husbands' and wives' buying scores, a paired *t* test should be calculated. A paired test is appropriate since husbands and wives constitute matched observations. Including both members of a couple helps control for nuisance effects such as socioeconomic status and age. The observed differences are more likely to be attributable to differences in sex.

Figure 13.6 contains output from the paired *t* test. The entry under *Number of pairs* is the number of pairs of observations. The mean difference is the difference between the mean scores for males and females. The *t* value is the mean difference divided by the standard error of the difference ($0.55 / 1.73 = 0.32$). The two-tailed probability for this test is 0.75, so there is insufficient evidence to reject the null hypothesis that married males and females have similar mean buying scores.

Figure 13.6   Husbands' versus wives' buying scores

```
         - - - t-tests for paired samples - - -

                  Number of        2-tail
Variable             pairs   Corr    Sig       Mean      SD     SE of Mean

HSSCALE  HUSBAND SELF SCALE                   82.0918   14.352    1.450
                      98      .367   .000
WSSCALE  WIFE SELF SCALE                      81.5408   15.942    1.610


           Paired Differences
  Mean       SD        SE of Mean  |   t-value    df   2-tail Sig

 .5510     17.095        1.727     |     .32      97      .750
95% CI  (-2.877, 3.979)           |
```

The correlation coefficient between husbands' and wives' scores is 0.367. A positive correlation indicates that pairing has been effective in decreasing the variability of the mean difference. The larger the correlation coefficient, the greater the benefit of pairing.

Hypothesis Testing: A Review

The purpose of hypothesis testing is to help draw conclusions about population parameters based on results observed in a random sample. The procedure remains virtually the same for tests of most hypotheses.

- A hypothesis of no difference (called a **null hypothesis**) and its alternative are formulated.

- A test statistic is chosen to evaluate the null hypothesis.

- For the sample, the test statistic is calculated.

- The probability, if the null hypothesis is true, of obtaining a test value at least as extreme as the one observed is determined.

- If the observed significance level is judged small enough, the null hypothesis is rejected.

The Importance of Assumptions

In order to perform a statistical test of any hypothesis, it is necessary to make certain assumptions about the data. The particular assumptions depend on the statistical test being used. Some procedures require stricter assumptions than others. For parametric tests, some knowledge about the distribution from which samples are selected is required.

The assumptions are necessary to define the sampling distribution of the test statistic. Unless the distribution is defined, correct significance levels cannot be calculated. For the equal-variance t test, the assumption is that the observations are random samples from normal distributions with the same variance.

For many procedures, not all assumptions are equally important. Moderate violation of some assumptions may not always be serious. Therefore, it is important to know for each procedure not only what assumptions are needed but also how severely their violation may influence results.

The responsibility for detecting violations of assumptions rests with the researcher. Unlike the chemist who ignores laboratory safety procedures, the investigator who does not comply with good statistical practice is not threatened by explosions. However, from a research viewpoint, the consequences can be just as severe.

Wherever possible, **tests of assumptions**—often called diagnostic checks of the model—should be incorporated as part of the hypothesis-testing procedures. Throughout SPSS, attempts have been made to provide facilities for examining assumptions. For example, in the Explore procedure, there are several tests for normality. Discussions of other such diagnostics are included with the individual procedures.

How to Obtain an Independent-Samples T Test

The Independent-Samples T Test procedure computes Student's t statistic for testing the significance of a difference in means for independent samples. Both equal- and unequal-variance t values are provided, as well as the Levene test for equality of variances.

The minimum specifications are:

- One or more numeric test variables.
- One numeric or short string grouping variable.
- Group values for the grouping variable.

To obtain an independent-samples t test, from the menus choose:

Statistics
 Compare Means ▶
  Independent-Samples T Test...

This opens the Independent-Samples T Test dialog box, as shown in Figure 13.7.

Figure 13.7 Independent-Samples T Test dialog box

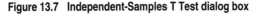
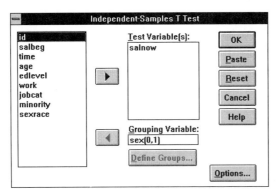

The numeric and short string variables in your data file appear on the source list. Select one or more numeric test variables. Each test variable produces one *t* test. Choose one numeric or short string grouping variable, which splits your file into two groups. After defining the categories of your grouping variable, you can click on OK to get the default independent-samples *t* test with two-tailed probabilities and a 95% confidence interval. (See Figure 13.1.) To obtain one-tailed probabilities, divide the *t* probabilities by 2.

Define Groups for Numeric Variables

You must define the two groups for the grouping variable. The procedure to follow for defining groups depends on whether your grouping variable is string or numeric. For both string and numeric variables, *t* tests are not performed if there are fewer than two non-empty groups.

To define groups, highlight the grouping variable and click on Define Groups... in the Independent-Samples T Test dialog box. For numeric variables, this opens the Define Groups dialog box, as shown in Figure 13.8.

Figure 13.8 Define Groups dialog box for numeric variables

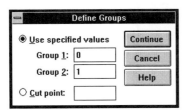

You can choose one of the following:

○ **Use specified values.** User-specified group values. This is the default. Enter a group 1 value and a group 2 value that correspond to the two categories of the grouping variable. Cases with other values are excluded from the analysis.

○ **Cut point.** User-specified cut point. All cases with values greater than or equal to the specified value are assigned to one group, and the remaining cases are assigned to the other group.

Define Groups for String Variables

The Define Groups dialog box for string variables is shown in Figure 13.9. Enter a group 1 value and a group 2 value that correspond to the two categories of the grouping variable. Cases with other values are excluded from the analysis.

Figure 13.9   Define Groups dialog box for string variables

Independent-Samples T Test Options

To change confidence interval bounds or control the handling of cases with missing values, click on Options... in the Independent-Samples T Test dialog box. This opens the Independent-Samples T Test Options dialog box, as shown in Figure 13.10.

Figure 13.10 Independent-Samples T Test Options dialog box

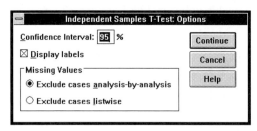

Confidence Interval. A 95% confidence interval for the difference in means is displayed by default. Optionally, you can request a different confidence level by entering a value between 1 and 99. For example, to obtain a 99% confidence interval, enter 99.

Missing Values. You can choose one of the following:

○ **Exclude cases analysis by analysis.** Cases with missing values on either the grouping variable or the test variable are excluded from the analysis of that variable. This is the default.

○ **Exclude cases listwise.** Cases with missing values on either the grouping variable or any test variable are excluded from all analyses.

You can also choose the following display option:

❑ **Display labels.** By default, any variable labels are displayed in the output. To suppress labels, deselect this setting.

How to Obtain a Paired-Samples T Test

The Paired-Samples T Test procedure computes Student's *t* statistic for testing the significance of a difference in means for paired samples.

The minimum specification is a pair of numeric variables.

To obtain a paired-samples *t* test, from the menus choose:

Statistics
  Compare Means ▶
    Paired-Samples T Test...

This opens the Paired-Samples T Test dialog box, as shown in Figure 13.11.

Figure 13.11 Paired-Samples T Test dialog box

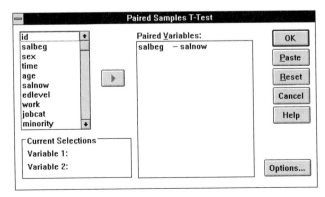

The numeric variables in your data file appear on the source list. Select one or more pairs of variables you want to use in the paired-samples tests. To select a pair:

1. Click on one of the variables. It appears as the first variable under Current Selections.

2. Click on another variable. It appears as the second variable. To remove a variable from Current Selections, click on it again.

3. Click on ▶ to move the pair to the Paired Variables list.

Repeat this process if you have more than one pair of variables.

To obtain the default test for paired samples with two-tailed probabilities and a 95% confidence interval for the mean difference, click on OK. To obtain one-tailed probabilities, divide the t probabilities by 2.

Paired-Samples T Test Options

To change confidence interval bounds or control the handling of cases with missing values, click on Options... in the Paired-Samples T Test dialog box. This opens the Paired-Samples T Test Options dialog box, as shown in Figure 13.12.

Figure 13.12 Paired-Samples T Test Options dialog box

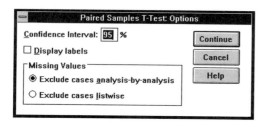

Confidence Interval. A 95% confidence interval for the mean difference is displayed by default. Optionally, you can request a different confidence level. Enter a value between 1 and 99. For example, to obtain a 99% confidence interval, enter 99.

Missing Values. You can choose one of the following:

○ **Exclude cases analysis by analysis.** Cases with missing values for either variable in a given pair are excluded from the analysis of that pair. This is the default.

○ **Exclude cases listwise.** Cases with missing values for any pair variable are excluded from all analyses.

You can also choose the following display option:

❏ **Display labels.** Displays any variable labels in output. This is the default setting.

Additional Features Available with Command Syntax

You can customize your paired-samples *t* tests if you paste your selections to a syntax window and edit the resulting T-TEST command syntax (see Chapter 4). An additional feature is the ability to test a variable against each variable on a list (with the PAIRS subcommand). See Appendix A for command syntax rules. See the *SPSS Base System Syntax Reference Guide* for complete T-TEST command syntax.

14 One-Way Analysis of Variance

Which of four brands of paper towels is the strongest? Do six models of intermediate-size cars get the same average gasoline mileage? Do graduates of the top ten business schools receive the same average starting salaries? There are many situations in which you want to compare the means of several independent samples and, based on them, draw conclusions about the populations from which they were selected. Consider, for example, the following problem.

You are a manufacturer of paper used for making grocery bags. You suspect that the tensile strength of the bags depends on the pulp hardwood concentration. You currently use 10% hardwood concentration in the pulp and produce paper with an average tensile strength of about 15 pounds per square inch (psi). You want to see what happens if you vary the concentration of the pulp.

In consultation with the process engineer, you decide on four concentrations: 5%, 10%, 15%, and 20%. You measure the tensile strength of six samples at each of the four concentrations. You want to test the null hypothesis that all four concentrations result in the same average tensile strength of the paper.

Examining the Data

As always, before you embark on any statistical analysis, you should look at the distribution of data values to make sure that there is nothing unusual. You can use the Explore procedure (see Chapter 9) to make a boxplot for each group.

From the plots in Figure 14.1, you see that the medians for the four groups differ. It appears that as the concentration increases, so does the tensile strength. The vertical length of the boxes, a measure of the spread or variability of the data values, also seems to differ for the concentrations, but not in any systematic fashion. There are no outlying or extreme values.

Figure 14.1   Boxplots for the four concentration groups

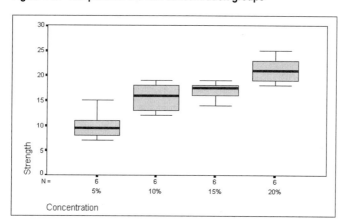

Sample Means and Confidence Intervals

The sample mean for a group provides the single best guess for the unknown population value μ_i. However, it is unlikely that the value of the sample mean is exactly equal to the population value. Instead, it is probably not too different. Based on the sample mean, you can calculate a range of values that, with a designated likelihood, includes the population value. Such a range is called a **confidence interval**. For example, as shown in Figure 14.2, the 95% confidence interval for the average tensile strength for a concentration of 10% is 12.72 to 18.61. This means that if you repeated the experiment under the same conditions and with the same sample sizes in each group, and each time calculated 95% confidence intervals, 95% of these intervals would contain the unknown population parameter value. Since the parameter value is not known, you don't know whether a particular interval contains the population value.

Figure 14.2 also shows descriptive statistics for the tensile strengths for the four concentrations. You see that as the concentration of hardwood increases, so does the mean strength. For a concentration of 5%, the average tensile strength is 10, while for a concentration of 20%, the average strength is 21.17. The group with a hardwood concentration of 15% has the smallest standard deviation. The others differ somewhat.

Figure 14.2   Sample means and confidence intervals for the four concentration groups

```
        Variable  STRENGTH
     By Variable  CONCENT

                           Standard   Standard
  Group   Count     Mean   Deviation     Error   Minimum   Maximum   95 Pct Conf Int for Mean

  5%          6  10.0000    2.8284     1.1547    7.0000   15.0000     7.0318  TO   12.9682
  10%         6  15.6667    2.8048     1.1450   12.0000   19.0000    12.7233  TO   18.6100
  15%         6  17.0000    1.7889      .7303   14.0000   19.0000    15.1227  TO   18.8773
  20%         6  21.1667    2.6394     1.0775   18.0000   25.0000    18.3968  TO   23.9366

  Total      24  15.9583    4.7226      .9640    7.0000   25.0000    13.9642  TO   17.9525
```

Testing the Null Hypothesis

The boxplots in Figure 14.1 and the means in Figure 14.2 suggest that the four concentrations result in different tensile strengths. Now you need to determine if the observed differences in the four sample means can be attributed to just the natural variability among sample means from the same population or whether it's reasonable to believe that the four concentrations come from populations that have different means. You must determine the probability of seeing results as remote as the ones you've observed when, in fact, all population means are equal.

The statistical technique you'll use to test the null hypothesis that several population means are equal is called **analysis of variance** (abbreviated ANOVA). This technique examines the variability of the observations within each group as well as the variability between the group means. Based on these two estimates of variability, you draw conclusions about the population means.

SPSS for Windows contains two different analysis-of-variance procedures: One-Way ANOVA and Simple Factorial ANOVA. This chapter discusses the One-Way ANOVA procedure. One-way analysis of variance is needed when only one variable is used to classify cases into the different groups. In the example on the tensile strength of paper, cases are assigned to groups based on their values for one variable: hardwood concentration. When two or more variables are used to form the groups, the Simple Factorial ANOVA procedure is required (see Chapter 15).

Note that you can use the One-Way ANOVA procedure only when your groups are independent. If you observe the same person under several conditions, you cannot use this procedure. You need a special class of procedures called *repeated measures analysis of variance*, available in the SPSS Advanced Statistics option.

Assumptions Needed for Analysis of Variance

Analysis-of-variance procedures require the following assumptions:

- Each of the groups is an independent random sample from a normal population.
- In the population, the variances of the groups are equal.

One way to check these assumptions is to use the Explore procedure to make stem-and-leaf plots or histograms for each group and calculate the variances. You can also use formal statistical tests to check the assumptions of normality and equal variances. See Chapter 9 for more information on stem-and-leaf plots and tests for normality.

The Levene Test

To test the null hypothesis that the groups come from populations with the same variance, you can use the **Levene test** (shown in Figure 14.3), which can be obtained with the One-Way ANOVA procedure. If the observed significance level is small, you can reject the null hypothesis that all variances are equal. In this example, since the observed significance level (0.583) is large, you can't reject the null hypothesis. This means you don't have sufficient evidence to suspect that the variances are unequal, confirming what you saw in the plot.

Figure 14.3   Levene test

```
Levene Test for Homogeneity of Variances

    Statistic    df1    df2    2-tail Sig.
       .6651      3     20         .583
```

Analyzing the Variability

Now you're ready to perform the analysis-of-variance test. In analysis of variance, the observed variability in the sample is divided, or partitioned, into two parts: variability of the observations within a group (that is, the variability of the observations around their group mean) and the variability among the group means.

If the null hypothesis is true, the population means for the four groups are equal and the observed data can be considered to be four samples from the same population. In this case, you should be able to estimate how much the four sample means should vary. If your observed sample means vary more than you expect, you have evidence to reject the null hypothesis. The analysis-of-variance table is shown in Figure 14.4.

Figure 14.4 One-way analysis-of-variance table

```
    Variable  STRENGTH
 By Variable  CONCENT

                             Analysis of Variance

                            Sum of        Mean         F      F
        Source      D.F.    Squares      Squares     Ratio   Prob.

Between Groups        3    382.7917     127.5972    19.6052  .0000
Within Groups        20    130.1667       6.5083
Total                23    512.9583
```

Between-Groups Variability

In Figure 14.4, the row labeled *Between Groups* contains an estimate of the variability of the observations based on the variability of the group means. To calculate the entry labeled *Sum of Squares,* start by subtracting the overall mean (the mean of all the observations) from each group mean (the overall and group means are listed in Figure 14.2). Then square each difference and multiply the square by the number of observations in its group. Finally, add the results together. For this example, the between-groups sum of squares is

$$6 \times (10 - 15.96)^2 + 6 \times (15.67 - 15.96)^2 + 6 \times (17 - 15.96)^2$$
$$+ 6 \times (21.17 - 15.96)^2 = 382.79$$

Equation 14.1

The column labeled *D.F.* contains the degrees of freedom. To calculate the degrees of freedom for the between-groups sum of squares, subtract 1 from the number of groups. In this example, there are four concentrations, so there are three degrees of freedom.

To calculate the between-groups mean square, divide the between-groups sum of squares by its degrees of freedom:

$$\frac{382.79}{3} = 127.60$$

Equation 14.2

Within-Groups Variability

The row labeled *Within Groups* contains an estimate of the variability of the observations based on how much the observations vary from their group means. The within-groups sum of squares is calculated by multiplying each of the group variances (the square of the standard deviation) by the number of cases in the group minus 1 and then adding up the results. In this example, the within-groups sum of squares is

$$5 \times 8.0000 + 5 \times 7.8667 + 5 \times 3.2000 + 5 \times 6.9667 = 130.17$$

Equation 14.3

To calculate the degrees of freedom for the within-groups sums of squares, take the number of cases in all groups combined and subtract the number of groups. In this example, there are 24 cases and 4 groups, so there are 20 degrees of freedom. The mean square is then calculated by dividing the sum of squares by the degrees of freedom:

$$\frac{130.17}{20} = 6.51$$

Equation 14.4

Calculating the F Ratio

You now have two estimates of the variability in the population: the within-groups mean square and the between-groups mean square. The within-groups mean square is based on how much the observations within each group vary. The between-groups mean square is based on how much the group means vary among themselves. If the null hypothesis is true, the two numbers should be close to each other. If you divide one by the other, the ratio should be close to 1.

The statistical test for the null hypothesis that all groups have the same mean in the population is based on this ratio, called an F statistic. You take the between-groups mean square and divide it by the within-groups mean square. For this example,

$$F = \frac{127.6}{6.51} = 19.6$$

Equation 14.5

This number appears in Figure 14.4 in the column labeled F *ratio*. It certainly doesn't appear to be close to 1. Now you need to obtain the observed significance level. You obtain the observed significance level by comparing the calculated F value to the **F distribution** (the distribution of the F statistic when the null hypothesis is true). The significance level is based on both the actual F value and the degrees of freedom for the two mean squares. In this example, the observed significance level is less than 0.00005, so you can reject the null hypothesis that the four concentrations of pulp result in paper with the same average tensile strength.

Multiple Comparison Procedures

A significant F value tells you only that the population means are probably not all equal. It doesn't tell you which pairs of groups appear to have different means. You reject the null hypothesis that all population means are equal if *any two* means are unequal. You need to use special tests called **multiple comparison procedures** to determine which means are significantly different from each other.

You might wonder why you can't just compare all possible pairs of means using a t test. The reason is that when you make many comparisons involving the same means, the probability that one comparison will turn out to be statistically significant increases. For example, if you have 5 groups and compare all pairs of means, you're making 10 comparisons. When the null hypothesis is true, the probability that at least one of the 10 observed significance levels will be less than 0.05 is about 0.29. The more comparisons you make, the more likely it is that you'll find one or more pairs to be statistically different, even if all population means are equal.

By adjusting for the number of comparisons you're making, multiple comparison procedures protect you from calling too many differences significant. The more comparisons you make, the larger the difference between pairs of means must be for a multiple comparison procedure to find it significant. When you use a multiple comparison procedure, you can be more confident that you are finding true differences.

Many multiple comparison procedures are available. They differ in how they adjust the observed significance level. One of the simplest is the **Bonferroni test**. It adjusts the observed significance level based on the number of comparisons you are making. For example, if you are making 5 comparisons, the observed significance level for the original comparison must be less than $0.05/5$, or 0.01, for the difference to be significant at the 0.05 significance level. For further discussion of multiple comparison techniques, see Winer et al. (1991).

Figure 14.5 shows a portion of the Bonferroni test results obtained with the One-Way ANOVA procedure. At the bottom, you see a table that orders the group means from smallest to largest in both the rows and columns. (In this example, the order happens to be the same as the order of the group code numbers.) An asterisk marks a pair of means that are different at the 0.05 level after the Bonferroni correction is made. Differences are marked only once, in the lower diagonal of the table. If the significance level is greater than 0.05, the space is left blank.

Figure 14.5   Bonferroni multiple comparisons

```
      Variable   STRENGTH
By Variable   CONCENT

Multiple Range Tests:  Modified LSD (Bonferroni) test with significance
                      level .05

The difference between two means is significant if
MEAN(J)-MEAN(I)  >= 1.8039 * RANGE * SQRT(1/N(I) + 1/N(J))
with the following value(s) for RANGE: 4.14

 (*) Indicates significant differences which are shown in the lower triangle

                                  1 1 2
                                  5 0 5 0
                                  % % % %
        Mean       CONCENT

        10.0000     5%
        15.6667    10%           *
        17.0000    15%           *
        21.1667    20%           * *
```

In this example, the asterisks in the first column indicate that the mean of the 5% hard-wood concentration group is significantly different from every other group. In the second column, the 10% group is different from the 20% group, but not from the 15% group. There are no asterisks in the third column. Thus, you see that all pairs of means are significantly different from each other except for the 10% and 15% groups.

The formula above the table indicates how large an observed difference must be for the multiple comparison procedure to call it significant. If no pairs are found to be significantly different, the table is omitted and a message is printed.

When the sample sizes in all of the groups are the same, you can also use the output of homogeneous subsets to identify subsets of means that are not different from each other. Figure 14.6 shows the homogeneous subsets output.

Figure 14.6   Homogeneous subsets

```
Subset 1

Group       5%

Mean       10.0000
- - - - - - - - - -

Subset 2

Group      10%            15%

Mean       15.6667       17.0000
- - - - - - - - - - - - - - - -

Subset 3

Group      15%            20%

Mean       17.0000       21.1667

- - - - - - - - - - - - - - - - -
```

Groups that appear in the same subset are not significantly different from each other. In this example, the 10% and 15% hardwood concentration groups are in the same subset, as are the 15% and 20% groups. The 5% group is in a subset of its own, since it is significantly different from all of the other means.

How to Obtain a One-Way Analysis of Variance

The One-Way ANOVA procedure produces a one-way analysis of variance for an interval-level dependent variable by a single factor (independent) variable. You can test for trends across categories, specify contrasts, and use a variety of range tests.

The minimum specifications are:

- One numeric dependent variable. The variable is assumed to be measured on an interval scale.
- One numeric factor variable. Factor variable values should be integers.
- A defined range for the factor variable.

To obtain a one-way analysis of variance, from the menus choose:

Statistics
  Compare Means ▶
    One-Way ANOVA...

This opens the One-Way ANOVA dialog box, as shown in Figure 14.7.

Figure 14.7   One-Way ANOVA dialog box

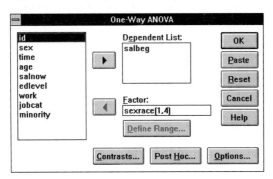

The numeric variables in your data file are displayed on the source variable list. Select your dependent variable(s) and a single factor (independent) variable. After defining a range for the factor variable (see "One-Way ANOVA Define Range," below), click on OK to obtain the default one-way analysis-of-variance table containing the F ratio, F probability, and sum of squares and mean squares for between groups and within groups. (See Figure 14.2.) A separate analysis-of-variance table is generated for each dependent variable.

One-Way ANOVA Define Range

A value range is required for the factor (independent) variable. To define the range, click on Define Range... in the One-Way ANOVA dialog box. This opens the One-Way ANOVA Define Range dialog box, as shown in Figure 14.8.

Figure 14.8   One-Way ANOVA Define Range dialog box

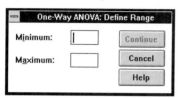

The minimum and maximum values must be integers. If any of the intervening values are non-integers, they are truncated in the analysis. Any empty categories are deleted from the analysis. If there are more than 50 categories of the factor variable, multiple comparison tests are not available.

One-Way ANOVA Contrasts

To partition the between-groups sum of squares into trend components or specify *a priori* contrasts, click on Contrasts... in the One-Way ANOVA dialog box. This opens the One-Way ANOVA Contrasts dialog box, as shown in Figure 14.9.

Figure 14.9   One-Way ANOVA Contrasts dialog box

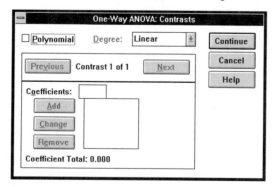

❏ **Polynomial.** Partitions the between-groups sum of squares into trend components. When you choose this option with balanced designs, SPSS computes the sum of squares for each order polynomial from weighted polynomial contrasts, using the group code as the metric. These contrasts are orthogonal; hence, the sum of squares for each order polynomial is statistically independent. If the design is unbalanced and there is equal spacing between groups, SPSS also computes sums of squares using the unweighted polynomial contrasts, which are not orthogonal. The deviation sums of squares are always calculated from the weighted sums of squares (Speed, 1976).

⬇ **Degree.** You can choose one of the following alternatives for the polynomial degree:

Linear. 1st-degree polynomial.

Quadratic. 2nd-degree polynomial.

Cubic. 3rd-degree polynomial.

4th. 4th-degree polynomial.

5th. 5th-degree polynomial.

Coefficients. User-specified *a priori* contrasts to be tested by the *t* statistic. Enter a coefficient value for each group (category) of the factor variable and click on Add after each entry. Each new value is added at the bottom of the coefficient list. To change a value on the list, highlight it, enter the new value in the text box, and click on Change. To remove a value, highlight it and click on Remove. To specify additional sets of contrasts, click on Next. You can specify up to 10 sets of contrasts and up to 50 coefficients for each set. Use Next and Previous to move between sets of contrasts.

The sequential order of the coefficients is important since it corresponds to the ascending order of the category values of the factor variable. The first coefficient on the list corresponds to the lowest group value of the factor variable, and the last coefficient corresponds to the highest value. For example, if there are six categories of the factor variable, the coefficient list $-1, -1, -1, -1, 2, 2$ contrasts the combination of the first four groups with the combination of the last two groups.

You can also specify fractional coefficients and exclude groups by assigning a coefficient of zero. For example, the coefficient list $-1, 0, 0, 0, 0.5, 0.5$ contrasts the first group with the combination of the fifth and sixth groups.

For most applications, the coefficients should sum to 0. Sets that do not sum to 0 can also be used, but a warning message is displayed.

Output for each contrast list includes the value of the contrast, the standard error of the contrast, the *t* statistic, the degrees of freedom for *t,* and the two-tailed probability of *t.* Both pooled- and separate-variance estimates are displayed.

One-Way ANOVA Post Hoc Multiple Comparisons

To produce post hoc multiple comparison tests, click on Post Hoc... in the One-Way ANOVA dialog box. This opens the One-Way ANOVA Post Hoc Multiple Comparisons dialog box, as shown in Figure 14.10.

Figure 14.10 One-Way ANOVA Post Hoc Multiple Comparisons dialog box

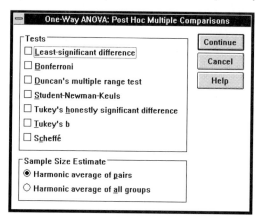

Tests. These tests always produce multiple comparisons between all groups. Non-empty group means are sorted by ascending order. Asterisks in the matrix indicate significantly different group means at an alpha level of 0.05. In addition to this output, homogeneous subsets are calculated for balanced designs if you also choose Harmonic average of all groups. You can choose one or more of the following tests:

❏ **Least-significant difference.** This is equivalent to doing multiple t tests between all pairs of groups. No "multiple comparisons" protection is provided.

❏ **Bonferroni.** The Bonferroni test is a modified least-significant-difference test.

❏ **Duncan's multiple range test.**

❏ **Student-Newman-Keuls.**

❏ **Tukey's honestly significant difference.**

❏ **Tukey's b.** Tukey's alternate procedure.

❏ **Scheffé.** This test is conservative for pairwise comparisons of means and requires larger differences between means for significance than the other multiple comparison tests.

Sample Size Estimate. You can choose one of the following alternatives:

○ **Harmonic average of pairs.** If the sample sizes are not equal in all groups, a separate harmonic mean is computed for each pair of groups being compared. This is the default.

○ **Harmonic average of all groups.** If the sample sizes are not equal in all groups, a single harmonic mean is computed for all groups. If you choose this alternative, homogeneous subsets are calculated for all multiple comparison tests.

One-Way ANOVA Options

To obtain additional statistics, change the treatment of missing values, or use value labels to identify groups in output, click on Options... in the One-Way ANOVA dialog box. This opens the One-Way ANOVA Options dialog box, as shown in Figure 14.11.

Figure 14.11 One-Way ANOVA Options dialog box

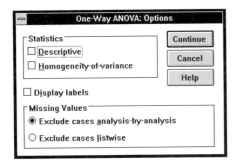

Statistics. You can choose one or more of the following:

❏ **Descriptive.** Calculates the number of cases, mean, standard deviation, standard error, minimum, maximum, and 95% confidence interval for each dependent variable for each group.

❏ **Homogeneity of variance.** Calculates the Levene statistic.

Missing Values. You can choose one of the following alternatives:

○ **Exclude cases analysis by analysis.** A case with a missing value for either the dependent variable or factor variable for a given analysis is not used in that analysis. Also, a case outside the range specified for the factor variable is not used. This is the default.

○ **Exclude cases listwise.** Cases with missing values for the factor variable or for *any* dependent variable included on the dependent list in the main dialog box are excluded from all analyses. If you have not specified multiple dependent variables, this has no effect.

The following labeling option is also available:

❏ **Display labels.** Uses the first eight characters from the value labels of the factor variable for group labels. By default, groups are labeled *GRP1*, *GRP2*, *GRP3*, etc., where the number indicates the value of the factor variable.

Additional Features Available with Command Syntax

You can customize your one-way analysis of variance if you paste your dialog box selections into a syntax window and edit the resulting ONEWAY command syntax (see Chapter 4). Additional features include:

- Fixed- and random-effects statistics. Standard deviation, standard error, and 95% confidence intervals for the fixed-effects model. Standard error, 95% confidence intervals, and estimate of between-component variance for the random-effects model (using STATISTICS=EFFECTS).

- User-specified alpha levels for the least-significant difference, Bonferroni, Duncan, and Scheffé multiple comparisons tests (with the RANGES subcommand).

- Matrix facility to write a matrix of means, standard deviations, and frequencies or to read a matrix of means, frequencies, pooled variances, and degrees of freedom for the pooled variances. These matrixes can be used in place of raw data to obtain a one-way analysis of variance (with the MATRIX subcommand).

See Appendix A for command syntax rules. See the *SPSS Base System Syntax Reference Guide* for complete ONEWAY command syntax.

15 Analysis of Variance

Despite constitutional guarantees, any mirror will testify that all citizens are not created equal. The consequences of this inequity are pervasive. Physically attractive individuals are generally perceived as more desirable social partners, more persuasive communicators, and more likeable and competent. Even cute children and attractive burglars are disciplined more leniently than their homely counterparts (Sigall & Ostrove, 1975).

Much research on physical attractiveness focuses on its impact on heterosexual relationships and evaluations. Its effect on same-sex evaluations has received less attention. Anderson and Nida (1978) examined the influence of attractiveness on the evaluation of writing samples by college students. In the study, 144 male and 144 female students were asked to appraise essays purportedly written by college freshmen. As supplemental information, a slide of the "author" was projected during the evaluation. Half of the slides were of authors of the same sex as the rater; the other half were of authors of the opposite sex. Each author had previously been determined to be of high, medium, or low attractiveness. Each rater evaluated one essay for creativity, ideas, and style. The three scales were combined to form a composite measure of performance.

Descriptive Statistics

Figure 15.1 contains average composite scores for the essays, subdivided by the three categories of physical attractiveness and the two categories of sex similarity. The table is similar to the summary table shown for the one-way analysis of variance in Chapter 14. The difference here is that there are two independent (or grouping) variables: attractiveness and sex similarity. The first mean displayed (25.11) is for the entire sample. The number of cases (288) is shown in parentheses. Then, for each of the independent variables, mean scores are displayed for each of the categories. The attractiveness categories are ordered from low (coded 1) to high (coded 3). Evaluations in which the rater and author are of the same sex are coded as 1, while opposite-sex evaluations are coded as 2. The possible combinations of the values of the two variables result in six cells. Finally, a table of means is displayed for cases classified by both grouping variables. Attractiveness is the row variable, and sex is the column variable. Each mean is based on the responses of 48 subjects.

Figure 15.1   Table of group means

```
                              * * *  C E L L   M E A N S  * * *

                     SCORE       COMPOSITE SCORE
                  BY ATTRACT    ATTRACTIVENESS LEVEL
                     SEX         SEX SIMILARITY

    TOTAL POPULATION

         25.11
    (    288)


    ATTRACT
          1              2            3

         22.98         25.78       26.59
    (     96)  (        96)  (      96)


    SEX
          1              2

         25.52         24.71
    (    144)  (       144)



             SEX
                  1              2
    ATTRACT
          1      22.79         23.17
             (      48)  (       48)

          2      28.63         22.92
             (      48)  (       48)

          3      25.13         28.04
             (      48)  (       48)
```

The overall average score is 25.11. Highly attractive individuals received the highest average score (26.59), while those rated low in physical appeal had the lowest score (22.98). There doesn't appear to be much difference between the average scores (across attractiveness levels) assigned by same-sex (25.52) and opposite-sex (24.71) evaluators. However, highly attractive individuals received an average rating of 25.13 when evaluated by people of the same sex and 28.04 when evaluated by people of the opposite sex.

Analysis of Variance

Three questions are of interest in the study: Does attractiveness relate to the composite scores? Does sex similarity relate to the scores? Is there an interaction between the effects of attractiveness and sex? The statistical technique used to evaluate these questions is an extension of the one-way analysis of variance outlined in Chapter 14. The same assumptions are needed for correct application; that is, the observations should be independently selected from normal populations with equal variances. Again, discussion here is limited to instances in which both grouping variables are considered **fixed**; that is, they constitute the populations of interest.

The total observed variation in the scores is subdivided into four components: the sums of squares due to attractiveness, sex, their interaction, and the residual. This can be expressed as

$$\text{Total SS} = \text{Attractiveness SS} + \text{Sex SS}$$
$$+ \text{Interaction SS} + \text{Residual SS}$$

Equation 15.1

Figure 15.2 is the analysis-of-variance table for this study. The first column lists the sources of variation. The sums of squares attributable to each of the components are given in the second column. The sums of squares for each independent variable alone are sometimes termed the **main effect** sums of squares. The **explained** sum of squares is the total sum of squares for the main effect and interaction terms in the model.

The degrees of freedom for sex and attractiveness, listed in the third column, are one fewer than the number of categories. For example, since there are three levels of attractiveness, there are two degrees of freedom. Similarly, sex has one degree of freedom. Two degrees of freedom are associated with the interaction term (the product of the degrees of freedom of each of the individual variables). The degrees of freedom for the residual are $N - 1 - k$, where k equals the degrees of freedom for the explained sum of squares.

Figure 15.2 Analysis-of-variance table

```
        * * *  A N A L Y S I S   O F   V A R I A N C E  * * *

        SCORE    COMPOSITE SCORE
     by ATTRACT  ATTRACTIVENESS LEVEL
        SEX      SEX SIMILARITY

                            Sum of              Mean          Sig
Source of Variation         Squares    DF       Square    F   of F

Main Effects                733.700     3      244.567  3.276  .022
    ATTRACT                 686.850     2      343.425  4.600  .011
    SEX                      46.850     1       46.850  0.628  .429

2-Way Interactions          942.350     2      471.175  6.311  .002
    ATTRACT  SEX            942.350     2      471.175  6.311  .002

Explained                  1676.050     5      355.210  4.490  .000

Residual                  21053.140   282       74.656

Total                     22729.190   287       79.196
```

The mean squares shown in the fourth column in Figure 15.2 are obtained by dividing each sum of squares by its degrees of freedom. Hypothesis tests are based on the ratios of the mean squares of each source of variation to the mean square for the residual. When the assumptions are met and the true means are in fact equal, the distribution of the ratio is an F with the degrees of freedom for the numerator and denominator terms.

Testing for Interaction

The F value associated with the attractiveness and sex interaction is 6.311, as shown in Figure 15.2. The observed significance level is approximately 0.002. Therefore, it appears that there is an interaction between the two variables. What does this mean?

Consider Figure 15.3, which is a plot of the cell, or group, means in Figure 15.1. Notice how the mean scores relate not only to the attractiveness of the individual and to the sex of the rater, but also to the particular combination of the values of the variables. Opposite-sex raters assign the highest scores to highly attractive individuals. Same-sex raters assign the highest scores to individuals of medium attractiveness. Thus, the ratings for each level of attractiveness depend on the sex variable. If there were no interaction between the two variables, a plot similar to the one shown in Figure 15.4 might result, in which the difference between the two types of raters is the same for the three levels of attractiveness.

Figure 15.3   Cell means

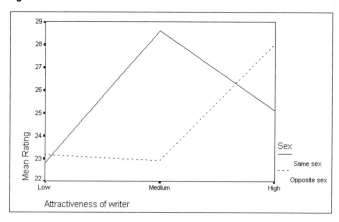

Figure 15.4   Cell means with no interaction

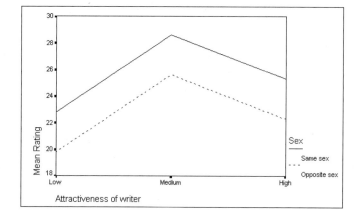

Tests for Sex and Attractiveness

Once the presence of interaction has been established, it is not particularly useful to continue hypothesis testing, since the two variables *jointly* affect the dependent variable. If there is no significant interaction, the grouping variables can be tested individually. The F value associated with attractiveness would provide a test of the hypothesis that attractiveness does not affect the rating. Similarly, the F value associated with sex would test the hypothesis that sex has no main effect on evaluation.

Note that the small F value associated with sex does not indicate that response is unaffected by sex, since sex is included in the significant interaction term. Instead, it shows that when response is averaged over attractiveness levels, the two sex-category means are not significantly different.

Explanations

Several explanations are consistent with the results of this study. Since people generally identify with individuals most like themselves, and since most people consider themselves moderately attractive, the highest degree of identification should be with same-sex individuals of moderate attractiveness. The higher empathy may result in the higher scores. An alternate theory is that moderately attractive individuals are generally perceived as more desirable same-sex friends; they have more favorable personality profiles and don't encourage unfavorable comparisons. Their writing scores may benefit from their perceived popularity.

Although we may not want friends who outshine us, attractive dates can reflect favorably on us and enhance our status. Physical beauty is generally advantageous for heterosexual relationships but may not be for same-sex friendships. This prejudice may affect all evaluations of highly attractive members of the opposite sex.

Extensions

Analysis-of-variance techniques can be used with any number of grouping variables. For example, the data in Figure 15.1 originated from a more complicated experiment than described here. There were four factors—essay quality, physical attractiveness, sex of writer, and sex of subject. The original data were analyzed with a $3 \times 3 \times 2 \times 2$ ANOVA table. (The numbers indicate how many categories each grouping variable has.) The conclusions from our simplified analysis are the same as those from the more elaborate analysis.

Each of the cells in our experiment had the same number of subjects. This greatly simplifies the analysis and its interpretation. When unequal sample sizes occur in the cells, the total sum of squares cannot be partitioned into nice components that sum to the total. Various techniques are available for calculating sums of squares in such **nonorthogonal designs**. The methods differ in the way they adjust the sums of squares to account for other effects in the model. Each method results in different sums of squares and tests different hypotheses. However, when all cell frequencies are equal, the methods yield the same results. For discussion of various procedures for analyzing designs with unequal cell frequencies, see Kleinbaum and Kupper (1978) and Overall and Klett (1972).

How to Obtain a Simple Factorial Analysis of Variance

The Simple Factorial ANOVA procedure tests the hypothesis that the group, or cell, means of the dependent variable are equal.

The minimum specifications are:

- One or more interval-level dependent variables.
- One or more categorical factor variables.
- Minimum and maximum group values for each factor variable.

To obtain a simple factorial ANOVA and optional statistics, from the menus choose:

Statistics
  ANOVA Models ▶
    Simple Factorial...

This opens the Simple Factorial ANOVA dialog box, as shown in Figure 15.5.

Figure 15.5   Simple Factorial ANOVA dialog box

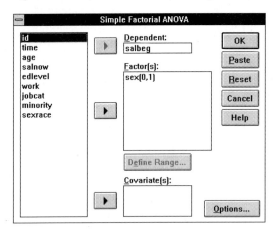

The numeric variables in your data file appear on the source list. Select an interval-level dependent variable. Choose one or more categorical variables, or factors, which split your file into two or more groups. After defining the range of the factor variable(s), click on OK to get the default analysis of variance using unique sums of squares. Cases with missing values for any variable are excluded from the analysis.

If there are five or fewer factors, the default model is **full factorial**, meaning that all factor-by-factor interaction terms are included. If you specify more than five factors, only interaction terms up to order five are included.

Optionally, you can select one or more continuous explanatory variables, or covariates, for the analysis.

Simple Factorial ANOVA Define Range

You must indicate the range of categories for each factor variable. To define categories, highlight a variable or group of variables on the Factor(s) list and click on Define Range... in the Simple Factorial ANOVA dialog box. This opens the Simple Factorial ANOVA Define Range dialog box, as shown in Figure 15.6.

Figure 15.6   Simple Factorial ANOVA Define Range dialog box

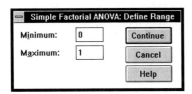

Enter values for minimum and maximum that correspond to the lowest and highest categories of the factor variable. Both values must be positive integers, and the minimum value you specify must be less than the maximum value. Cases with values outside the bounds are excluded. For example, if you specify a minimum value of 0 and a maximum value of 3, only the values 0, 1, 2, and 3 are used.

Repeat this process for each factor variable.

Simple Factorial ANOVA Options

To choose an alternate method for decomposing sums of squares, control the order of entry of covariates, obtain summary statistics, or suppress interaction terms, click on Options... in the Simple Factorial ANOVA dialog box. This opens the Simple Factorial ANOVA Options dialog box, as shown in Figure 15.7.

Figure 15.7 Simple Factorial ANOVA Options dialog box

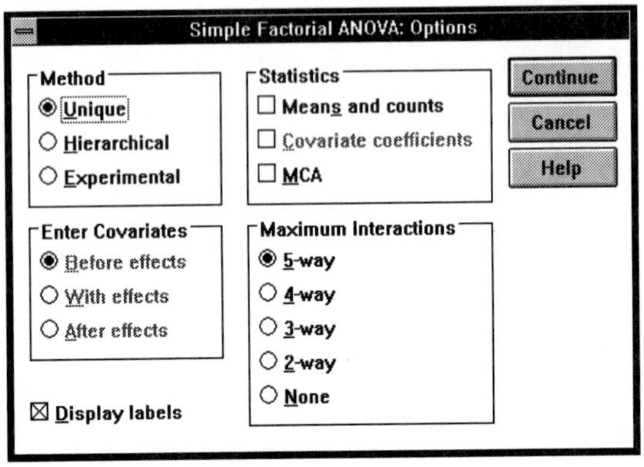

Method. Method selection controls how the effects are assessed. You can choose one of the following alternatives:

○ **Unique.** All effects are assessed simultaneously for their contribution. That is, each effect is adjusted for all other covariates, main effects, and interaction terms in the model. This is the default.

○ **Hierarchical.** Factor main effects and covariate effects are assessed hierarchically. If the default treatment of covariates is in effect, covariates are adjusted only for covariates that precede them on the Covariate(s) list. Main effects are adjusted for all covariates and for factors that precede them on the Factor(s) list. Interactions are not processed hierarchically; they are adjusted for all covariates, factors, and other interactions of the same and lower orders, just as in the experimental approach. Thus, the hierarchical method differs from the experimental method only in the treatment of covariates and main effects.

○ **Experimental.** If the default treatment of covariates (covariates entered before main effects) is in effect, effects are assessed in the following order: covariates, main effects, two-way interactions, three-way interactions, four-way interactions, and five-way interactions. This means that covariates are not adjusted for any other terms in the model except for other covariates; main effects are adjusted only for covariates and other main effects; and interactions are adjusted for all interactions of the same and lower order, as well as for all main effects and covariates. The effects within each type are adjusted for all other effects of that type and also for the effects of prior types. For example, all two-way interactions are adjusted for other two-way interactions and for all main effects and covariates.

Enter Covariates. Operation of the experimental and hierarchical methods depends on the order of entry of any covariates. If you want to select a covariate entry alternative, there must be at least one covariate on the Covariate(s) list. In addition, the experimental or hierarchical method must be specified (with the unique method, covariates are always entered concurrently with all other effects). You can choose one of the following alternatives:

○ **Before effects.** Processes covariates before main effects for factors. This is the default.

○ **With effects.** Processes covariates concurrently with main effects for factors.

○ **After effects.** Processes covariates after main effects for factors.

For example, if the experimental method is selected but you choose After effects, main effects are entered first and adjusted only for other main effects, and covariates are entered after the main effects and adjusted for other covariates and main effects. If, instead, you select the experimental method and With effects, covariates are entered together with main effects. This means that all covariates and main effects are adjusted for each other.

Statistics. You can choose one or more of the following:

❑ **Means and counts.** Requests means and counts for each dependent variable for groups defined for each factor and each combination of factors up to the fifth level. Means and counts are not available if you select unique sums of squares.

❑ **Covariate coefficients.** Unstandardized regression coefficients for the covariate(s). The coefficients are computed at the point where the covariates are entered into the model. Thus, their values depend on the method you specify. If you want covariate coefficients, there must be at least one covariate on the Covariate(s) list.

❑ **MCA.** Multiple classification analysis. In the MCA table, effects are expressed as deviations from the grand mean. The table includes a listing of unadjusted category effects for each factor, category effects adjusted for other factors, category effects adjusted for all factors and covariates, and eta and beta values. The MCA table is not available if you specify unique sums of squares.

Maximum Interactions. You can control the effects of various orders of interactions. Any interaction effects that are not computed are pooled into the residual sums of squares. You can choose one of the following alternatives:

○ **5-way.** Displays all interaction terms up to and including the fifth order. This is the default.

○ **4-way.** Displays all interaction effects up to and including the fourth order.

○ **3-way.** Displays all two- and three-way interaction effects.

○ **2-way.** Displays two-way interaction effects.

○ **None.** Deletes all interaction terms from the model. Only main effects and covariate effects appear in the ANOVA table.

You can also choose the following display option:

❑ **Display labels.** Displays any value and variable labels in the output. This is the default. To suppress labels, deselect this item.

Additional Features Available with Command Syntax

You can customize your analysis of variance if you paste your dialog box selections into a syntax window and edit the resulting ANOVA command syntax (see Chapter 4). An additional feature is the ability to specify more than one dependent variable. See Appendix A for command syntax rules. See the *SPSS Base System Syntax Reference Guide* for complete ANOVA command syntax.

16 Measuring Linear Association

Youthful lemonade-stand entrepreneurs as well as executives of billion-dollar corporations share a common concern—how to increase sales. Hand-lettered signs affixed to neighborhood trees, television campaigns, siblings and friends canvassing local playgrounds, and international sales forces are known to be effective marketing tactics. However, it can be difficult to measure the effectiveness of specific marketing techniques when they are part of an overall marketing strategy, so businesses routinely conduct market research to determine exactly what makes their products sell.

Churchill (1979) describes a study undertaken by the manufacturer of Click ballpoint pens to determine the effectiveness of the firm's marketing efforts. A random sample of 40 sales territories is selected, and sales, amount of advertising, and number of sales representatives are recorded. This chapter looks at the relationship between sales and these variables.

Examining Relationships

A scatterplot can reveal various types of associations between two variables. Some commonly encountered patterns are illustrated in Figure 16.1. In the first example, there appears to be no discernible relationship between the two variables. In the second example, the variables are related exponentially; that is, Y increases very rapidly for increasing values of X. In the third example, the relationship between the two variables is U-shaped. Small and large values of the X variable are associated with large values of the Y variable.

Figure 16.1 Scatterplots showing common relationships

Figure 16.2 is a scatterplot showing the amount of sales and the number of television spots in each of 40 territories from the study. From the figure, it appears that there is a positive association between sales and advertising. That is, as the amount of advertising increases, so does the number of sales. The relationship between sales and advertising may be termed **linear**, since the observed points cluster more or less around a straight line.

Figure 16.2   Scatterplot showing a linear relationship

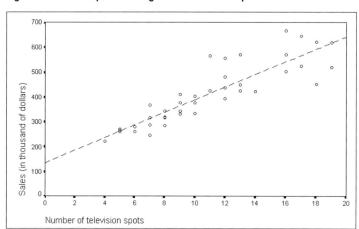

The Correlation Coefficient

Although a scatterplot is an essential first step in studying the association between two variables, it is often useful to quantify the strength of the association by calculating a summary index. One commonly used measure is the **Pearson correlation coefficient**, denoted by r. It is defined as

$$r = \frac{\sum_{i=1}^{N} (X_i - \bar{X})(Y_i - \bar{Y})}{(N-1)S_X S_Y}$$

Equation 16.1

where N is the number of cases and S_X and S_Y are the standard deviations of the two variables. The absolute value of r indicates the strength of the linear relationship. The largest possible absolute value is 1, which occurs when all points fall exactly on the line. When the line has a positive slope, the value of r is positive, and when the slope of the line is negative, the value of r is negative (see Figure 16.3).

Figure 16.3   Scatterplots with correlation coefficients of +1 and −1

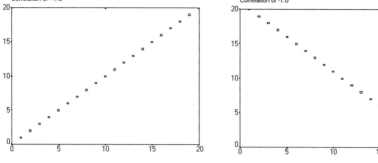

A value of 0 indicates no *linear* relationship. Two variables can have a strong associa-tion but a small correlation coefficient if the relationship is not linear. Figure 16.4 shows two plots with correlation coefficients of 0.

Figure 16.4   Scatterplots with correlation coefficients of 0

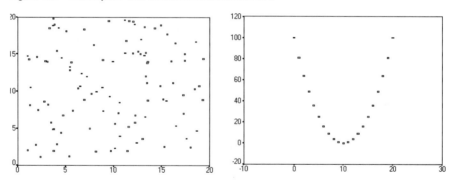

It is important to examine correlation coefficients together with scatterplots, since the same coefficient can result from very different underlying relationships. The variables plotted in Figure 16.5 have a correlation coefficient greater than 0.8, as do the variables plotted in Figure 16.2. But note how different the relationships are between the two sets of variables. In Figure 16.5, there is a strong positive linear association for only part of the graph. The relationship between the two variables is basically nonlinear. The scat-terplot in Figure 16.2 is very different. The points cluster more or less around a line. Thus, the correlation coefficient should be used only to summarize the strength of linear association.

Figure 16.5   Scatterplot showing nonlinear relationship

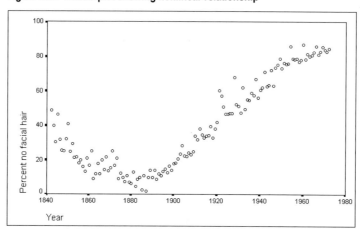

Some Properties of the Correlation Coefficient

A common mistake in interpreting the correlation coefficient is to assume that correlation implies causation. No such conclusion is automatic. While sales are highly correlated with advertising, they are also highly correlated with other variables, such as the number of sales representatives in a territory. Advertising alone does not necessarily result in increased sales. For example, territories with high sales may simply have more money to spend on TV spots, regardless of whether the spots are effective.

The correlation coefficient is a **symmetric measure**, since interchanging the two variables X and Y in the formula does not change the results. The correlation coefficient is not expressed in any units of measure, and it is not affected by linear transformations such as adding or subtracting constants or multiplying or dividing all values of a variable by a constant.

Calculating Correlation Coefficients

Figure 16.6 is a table of correlation coefficients for the number of television spots, number of sales representatives, and amount of sales. The entry in each cell is the correlation coefficient. For example, the correlation coefficient between advertising and sales is 0.8802. This value indicates that there is a fairly strong linear association between the two variables, as shown in Figure 16.2. The table is symmetric, since the correlation between X and Y is the same as the correlation between Y and X. The correlation values on the diagonal are all 1, since a variable is perfectly related to itself.

Figure 16.6 Correlation coefficients

```
    - -  Correlation Coefficients  - -

              ADVERTIS   REPS       SALES

ADVERTIS   1.0000      .7763**    .8802**
REPS        .7763**   1.0000       .8818**
SALES       .8802**    .8818**   1.0000

*  - Signif. LE .05      ** - Signif. LE .01     (2-tailed)

"  .  "  is printed if a coefficient cannot be computed
```

Hypothesis Tests about the Correlation Coefficient

Although the correlation coefficient is sometimes used only as a summary index to describe the observed strength of the association, in some situations description and summary are but a first step. The primary goal may be to test hypotheses about the unknown population correlation coefficient—denoted as ρ—based on its estimate, the sample correlation coefficient r. In order to test such hypotheses, certain assumptions must be made about the underlying joint distribution of the two variables. A common assumption is that independent random samples are taken from a distribution in which the two variables together are distributed normally. If this condition is satisfied, the test that the population coefficient is 0 can be based on the statistic

$$ t = r\sqrt{\frac{N-2}{1-r^2}} $$

Equation 16.2

which, if $\rho = 0$, has a Student's t distribution with $N - 2$ degrees of freedom. Either one- or two-tailed tests can be calculated. If nothing is known in advance, a two-tailed test is appropriate. That is, the hypothesis that the coefficient is 0 is rejected for both extreme positive and extreme negative values of t. If the direction of the association can be specified in advance, the hypothesis is rejected only for t values that are of sufficient magnitude and in the direction specified.

In SPSS, you can request that coefficients with two-tailed observed significance levels less than 0.05 be identified with a single asterisk and those with two-tailed significance levels less than 0.01 be identified with two asterisks. From Figure 16.6, the probability that a correlation coefficient of at least 0.88 in absolute value is obtained when there is no linear association in the population between sales and advertising is less than 0.01. Care should be exercised when examining the significance levels for large tables. Even if there is no association between the variables, if many coefficients are computed, some would be expected to be statistically significant by chance alone.

Special procedures must be employed to test more general hypotheses of the form $\rho = \rho_0$, where ρ_0 is a constant. If the assumptions of bivariate normality appear to be unreasonable, nonparametric measures such as Spearman's rho and Kendall's tau-*b* can be calculated. These coefficients make limited assumptions about the underlying distributions of the variables. (See "The Rank Correlation Coefficient" on p. 297.)

Correlation Matrices and Missing Data

For a variety of reasons, data files frequently contain incomplete observations. Respondents in surveys scrawl illegible responses or refuse to answer certain questions. Laboratory animals die before experiments are completed. Patients fail to keep scheduled clinic appointments.

Analysis of data with missing values is troublesome. Before even considering possible strategies, you should determine whether there is evidence that the missing-value pattern is not random. That is, are there reasons to believe that missing values for a variable are related to the values of that variable or other variables? For example, people with low incomes may be less willing to report their financial status than more affluent people. This may be even more pronounced for people who are poor but highly educated.

One simple method of exploring such possibilities is to subdivide the data into two groups—those observations with missing data for a variable and those with complete data—and examine the distributions of the other variables in the file across these two groups. The SPSS crosstabulation and independent-samples t test procedures are particularly useful for this. For a discussion of more sophisticated methods for detecting nonrandomness, see Frane (1976).

If it appears that the data are not missing randomly, use great caution in attempting to analyze the data. It may be that no satisfactory analysis is possible, especially if there are only a few cases.

If you are satisfied that the missing data are random, several strategies are available. First, if the same few variables are missing for most cases, exclude those variables from the analysis. Since this luxury is not usually available, alternately you can keep all variables but eliminate the cases with missing values. This is termed **listwise** missing-value treatment, since a case is eliminated if it has a missing value for any variable on the list. If many cases have missing data for some variables, listwise missing-value treatment can eliminate too many cases and leave you with a very small sample. One common technique is to calculate the correlation coefficient between a pair of variables based on all cases with complete information for the two variables, regardless of whether the cases have missing data for any other variable. For example, if a case has values for variables 1, 3, and 5 only, it is used in computations involving only variable pairs 1 and 3, 1 and 5, and 3 and 5. This is **pairwise** missing-value treatment.

Choosing Pairwise Missing-Value Treatment

Several problems can arise with pairwise matrices, one of which is inconsistency. There are some relationships between coefficients that are clearly impossible but may seem to occur when different cases are used to estimate different coefficients. For example, if age and weight and age and height have high positive correlations, it is impossible in the same sample for height and weight to have a high negative correlation. However, if the same cases are not used to estimate all three coefficients, such an anomaly can occur.

There is no single sample size that can be associated with a pairwise matrix, since each coefficient can be based on a different number of cases. Significance levels obtained from analyses based on pairwise matrices must be viewed with caution, since little is known about hypothesis testing in such situations.

It should be emphasized that missing-value problems should not be treated lightly. You should base your decision on careful examination of the data and not leave the choices up to system defaults.

The Rank Correlation Coefficient

The Pearson product-moment correlation is appropriate only for data that attain at least an interval level of measurement, such as the sales and advertising data used in this chapter. Normality is also assumed when testing hypotheses about this correlation coefficient. For ordinal data or interval data that do not satisfy the normality assumption, another measure of the linear relationship between two variables, **Spearman's rank correlation coefficient**, is available.

The rank correlation coefficient is the Pearson correlation coefficient based on the ranks of the data if there are no ties (adjustments are made if some of the data are tied). If the original data for each variable have no ties, the data for each variable are first ranked, and then the Pearson correlation coefficient between the ranks for the two variables is computed. Like the Pearson correlation coefficient, the rank correlation ranges between −1 and +1, where −1 and +1 indicate a perfect linear relationship between the ranks of the two variables. The interpretation is therefore the same except that the relationship between *ranks*, and not values, is examined.

Figure 16.7 shows the matrix of rank correlation coefficients for the sales and advertising data. SPSS displays a lower-triangular matrix in which redundant coefficients and the diagonal are omitted. As expected, these coefficients are similar in sign and magnitude to the Pearson coefficients shown in Figure 16.6.

Figure 16.7   Rank correlation coefficients

```
- - - S P E A R M A N   C O R R E L A T I O N   C O E F F I C I E N T S - - -


REPS            .7733
           N(    40)
           SIG .000


SALES           .9182       .8636
           N(    40)   N(    40)
           SIG .000    SIG .000


            ADVERTIS       REPS

" . " is printed if a coefficient cannot be computed.
```

How to Obtain Bivariate Correlations

The Bivariate Correlations procedure computes Pearson product-moment and two rank-order correlation coefficients, Spearman's rho and Kendall's tau-*b*, with their significance levels. Optionally, you can obtain univariate statistics, covariances, and cross-product deviations.

The minimum specification is two or more numeric variables.

To obtain bivariate correlations, from the menus choose:

Statistics
  Correlate ▶
    Bivariate...

This opens the Bivariate Correlations dialog box, as shown in Figure 16.8.

Figure 16.8   Bivariate Correlations dialog box

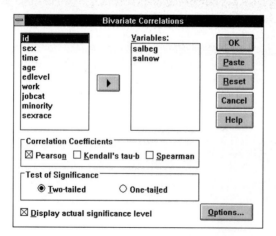

The numeric variables in your data file appear on the source list. Select two or more variables for analysis. To obtain the default Pearson correlations using two-tailed tests of significance, click on OK. If all cases have a missing value for one or both of a given pair of variables, or if they all have the same value for a variable, the coefficient cannot be computed and a period is displayed instead.

Correlation Coefficients. At least one type of correlation must be selected. You can choose one or more of the following:

❑ **Pearson.** This is the default setting. Displays a square correlation matrix. The correlation of a variable with itself is always 1.0000 and can be found on the diagonal of the matrix. Each variable appears twice in the matrix with identical coefficients, and the upper and lower triangles of the matrix are mirror images.

❑ **Kendall's tau-b.** A rank-order coefficient. Displays the correlations of each variable with every other variable in a lower-triangular matrix. The correlation of a variable with itself (the diagonal) and redundant coefficients are not displayed.

❑ **Spearman.** Spearman's rho. A rank-order coefficient. Displays a lower-triangular matrix.

Test of Significance. You can choose one of the following:

○ **Two-tailed.** This test is appropriate when the direction of the relationship cannot be determined in advance, as is often the case in exploratory data analysis. This is the default. See "Hypothesis Tests about the Correlation Coefficient" on p. 295.

○ **One-tailed.** This test is appropriate when the direction of the relationship between a pair of variables can be specified in advance of the analysis.

The following display option is also available:

❑ **Display actual significance level.** By default, actual significance levels are displayed. Deselect this item to indicate significance levels with asterisks. Correlation coefficients significant at the 0.05 level are identified with a single asterisk, and those significant at the 0.01 level are identified with two asterisks.

Bivariate Correlations Options

To obtain optional statistics for Pearson correlations or modify the treatment of cases with missing values, click on Options... in the Bivariate Correlations dialog box. This opens the Bivariate Correlations Options dialog box, as shown in Figure 16.9.

Figure 16.9   Bivariate Correlations Options dialog box

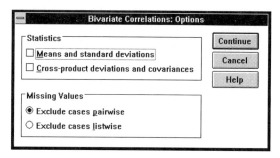

Statistics. For Pearson correlations, you can choose one or both of the following:

❏ **Means and standard deviations.** Displayed for each variable. The number of cases with nonmissing values is also shown. Missing values are handled on a variable-by-variable basis regardless of your missing values setting (see "Missing Values," below).

❏ **Cross-product deviations and covariances.** Displayed for each pair of variables. The cross-product deviation is equal to the sum of the products of mean-corrected variables. This is the numerator of the Pearson correlation coefficient, shown in Equation 16.1. The covariance is an unstandardized measure of the relationship between two variables, equal to the cross-product deviation divided by $N - 1$.

Missing Values. You can choose one of the following alternatives:

○ **Exclude cases pairwise.** Cases with missing values for one or both of a pair of variables for a correlation coefficient are excluded from the analysis. This is the default setting. Since each coefficient is based on all cases that have valid codes on that particular pair of variables, the maximum information available is used in every calculation. This can result in a set of coefficients based on a varying number of cases.

○ **Exclude cases listwise.** Cases with missing values for any variable are excluded from all analyses.

Additional Features Available with Command Syntax

You can customize your correlations if you paste your selections into a syntax window and edit the resulting CORRELATIONS (Pearson correlations) or NONPAR CORR (Spearman or Kendall correlations) command syntax (see Chapter 4). Additional features include:

- For Pearson correlations, a matrix facility to write a correlation matrix that can be used in place of raw data to obtain other analyses such as factor analysis (with the MATRIX subcommand).

- Correlations of each variable on a list with each variable on a second list (using the keyword WITH on the VARIABLES subcommand).

See Appendix A for command syntax rules. See the *SPSS Base System Syntax Reference Guide* for complete CORRELATIONS and NONPAR CORR command syntax.

17 Partial Correlation Analysis

Whenever you examine the relationship between two variables, you must be concerned with the effects of other variables on the relationship of interest. For example, if you are studying the relationship between education and income, you must worry about controlling for the effects of age and work experience. It may be that a small observed relationship between education and income is due to younger people being more highly educated but less experienced in the work force. If you control for job experience and age, the relationship between education and income may appear to be stronger.

The **partial correlation coefficient**, a technique closely related to multiple linear regression, provides us with a single measure of linear association between two variables while adjusting for the linear effects of one or more additional variables. Properly used, partial correlation is a useful technique for uncovering spurious relationships, identifying intervening variables, and detecting hidden relationships.

Computing a Partial Correlation Coefficient

Consider the steps involved in computing a partial correlation coefficient between salary and education, controlling for age. First, two regression equations must be estimated. The first equation predicts salary from age, and the second predicts education from age. For each of the regression equations, we compute the residuals for each case. The partial correlation coefficient between salary and education, controlling for age, is simply the usual Pearson correlation coefficient between the two sets of residuals.

In our example, the first regression equation removes the linear effects of age from salary. The residuals represent salary after the adjustment for age. The second regression equation removes the linear effects of age from education. The residuals represent education after the adjustment for age. The partial correlation coefficient estimates the linear association between the two variables after the effects of age are removed.

Because we used linear regression analysis to control for the age variable, we had to make the assumption that the relationships of interest are linear. If there is reason to suspect that the variables are related in a nonlinear way, the partial correlation coefficient is not an appropriate statistical technique to use.

The Order of the Coefficient

In the previous example, we controlled for the effect of only one variable, age. However, partial correlation analysis is not limited to a single control variable. The same procedure can be applied to several control variables.

The number of control variables determines the order of the partial correlation coefficient. If there is one control variable, the partial correlation coefficient is a **first-order partial**. If there are five control variables, it is a fifth-order partial. Sometimes the ordinary correlation coefficient is called a **zero-order correlation**, since there are no control variables.

(In fact, it is not necessary to keep computing regression equations, since partial correlation coefficients of a particular order can be computed recursively from coefficients of a lower order.)

Tests of Statistical Significance

The assumption of multivariate normality is required to test the null hypothesis that the population partial coefficient is 0. The test statistic is

$$t = r \sqrt{\frac{N - \theta - 2}{1 - r^2}}$$

Equation 17.1

where θ is the order of the coefficient and r is the partial correlation coefficient. The degrees of freedom for t are $N - \theta - 2$, where N is the number of cases.

Detecting Spurious Relationships

Partial correlation analysis can be used to detect spurious correlations between two variables. A **spurious correlation** is one in which the correlation between two variables results solely from the fact that one of the variables is correlated with a third variable that is the true predictor.

Consider the following example described by Kendall and Stuart (1973). Figure 17.1 is the correlation matrix between four variables measured in 16 large cities: crime rate, percentage of church membership, percentage of foreign-born males, and number of children under 5 per 1000 women between ages 15 and 44.

You can see that the correlation coefficient between crime rate (*CRIME*) and church membership (*CHURCH*) is negative (−0.14) . The simplest conclusion is that church membership is a deterrent to crime. Although such a conclusion is no doubt comforting to theologians, let's examine the observed relationship further.

Figure 17.1   Zero-order correlation matrix

```
Zero Order Partials

                CRIME      CHURCH     PCTFRNM     UNDER5

CRIME          1.0000      -.1400     -.3400      -.3100
              (    0)     (   14)    (   14)     (   14)
              P= .        P= .605    P= .198     P= .243

CHURCH         -.1400      1.0000      .3300       .8500
              (   14)     (    0)    (   14)     (   14)
              P= .605     P= .       P= .212     P= .000

PCTFRNM        -.3400       .3300     1.0000       .4400
              (   14)     (   14)    (    0)     (   14)
              P= .198     P= .212    P= .        P= .088

UNDER5         -.3100       .8500      .4400      1.0000
              (   14)     (   14)    (   14)     (    0)
              P= .243     P= .000    P= .088     P= .

(Coefficient / (D.F.) / 2-tailed Significance)

" . " is printed if a coefficient cannot be computed
```

From Figure 17.1, you see that the crime rate is negatively correlated with the percentage of foreign-born males (*PCTFRNM*) and with the number of children per woman (*UNDER5*). Both of these variables are positively correlated with church membership. That is, both foreigners and women with many children tend to be church members.

Let's see what happens to the relationship between crime and church membership when we control for the linear effects of being foreign born and having many children. Figure 17.2 shows the partial correlation coefficient between crime and church membership when the percentage of foreign-born males is held constant. Note that the correlation coefficient, −0.03, is now close to 0.

Figure 17.2   First-order partials, controlling for percentage of foreign-born males

```
Controlling for..    PCTFRNM

                CRIME      CHURCH

CRIME          1.0000      -.0313
              (    0)     (   13)
              P= .        P= .912

CHURCH         -.0313      1.0000
              (   13)     (    0)
              P= .912     P= .

(Coefficient / (D.F.) / 2-tailed Significance)

" . " is printed if a coefficient cannot be computed
```

Similarly, Figure 17.3 is the partial correlation coefficient between crime and church membership when the number of young children per woman is held constant. The partial correlation coefficient, 0.25, is now positive.

Figure 17.3   First-order partials, controlling for number of children

```
Controlling for..      UNDER5

               CRIME        CHURCH

CRIME         1.0000         .2466
             (     0)       (    13)
              P= .           P= .376

CHURCH         .2466        1.0000
             (    13)       (     0)
              P= .376        P= .

(Coefficient / (D.F.) / 2-tailed Significance)

" . " is printed if a coefficient cannot be computed
```

The second-order partial correlation coefficient controlling for both foreign-born males and number of children is shown in Figure 17.4. The relationship between church membership and crime, 0.23, is now positive.

Figure 17.4   Second-order partial correlations

```
Controlling for..      PCTFRNM    UNDER5

               CRIME        CHURCH

CRIME         1.0000         .2321
             (     0)       (    12)
              P= .           P= .425

CHURCH         .2321        1.0000
             (    12)       (     0)
              P= .425        P= .

(Coefficient / (D.F.) / 2-tailed Significance)

" . " is printed if a coefficient cannot be computed
```

From examination of the partial coefficients, it appears that the original negative relationship between church membership and crime may be due to the presence of law-abiding foreigners with large families. In 1935, when the study was done, foreigners were less likely to commit crimes and more likely to be church members than the general population. These relationships cause the overall coefficient between the two variables to be negative. However, when these two variables are controlled for, the relationship between church membership and crime changes drastically.

Detecting Hidden Relationships

Theory or intuition sometimes suggests that there should be a relationship between two variables even though the data indicate no correlation. In this situation, it is possible that one or more additional variables are suppressing the expected relationship. For example, it may be that A is not correlated with B because A is negatively related to C, which is positively related to B.

For example, assume that a marketing research company wants to examine the relationship between the need for transmission-rebuilding kits and the intent to purchase such a kit. Initial examination of the data reveals almost no correlation (0.01) between need for such a kit and intent to buy. However, the data show a *negative* relationship (-0.5) between income and need to buy and a *positive* relationship (0.6) between income and intent to buy. If we control for the effect of income using a partial correlation coefficient, the first-order partial between need and intent, controlling for income, is 0.45. Thus, income hid the relationship between need and intent to buy.

Interpreting the Results of Partial Correlation Analysis

Proper interpretation of partial correlation analysis requires knowledge about the way the variables may be related. You must know, for example, the nature of the relationship between need for a transmission and family income; that is, does income influence need, or does need influence income? If you assume that need for a transmission influences family income, then need is specified as the control variable. One way of codifying the requisite assumptions in using partials in multivariate analysis is known as **path analysis** (Wright, 1960; Duncan, 1966).

How to Obtain Partial Correlations

The Partial Correlations procedure computes partial correlation coefficients that describe the linear relationship between two variables while controlling for the effects of one or more additional variables. The procedure calculates a matrix of zero-order coefficients and bases the partial correlations on this matrix.

The minimum specifications are:

- Two or more numeric variables for which partial correlations are to be computed.
- One or more numeric control variables.

To obtain a partial correlation analysis, from the menus choose:

Statistics
  Correlate ▶
   Partial...

This opens the Partial Correlations dialog box, as shown in Figure 17.5.

Figure 17.5   Partial Correlations dialog box

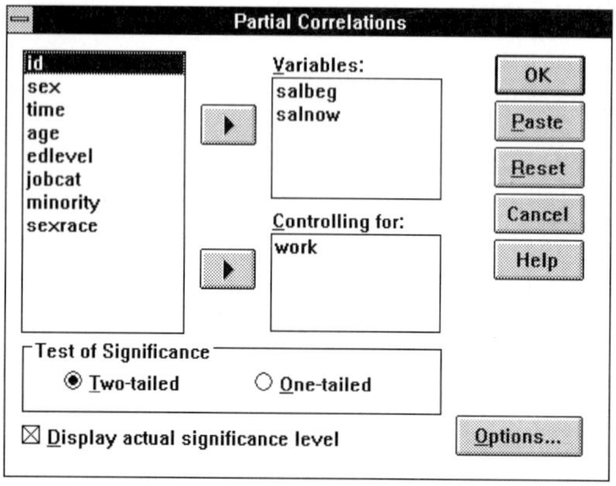

The numeric variables in your data file appear on the source list. Select two or more variables to be correlated and at least one control variable. To obtain the default partial correlation analysis with two-tailed probabilities, click on OK. SPSS produces a square matrix of the highest-order partial correlations. Cases with missing values for any of the variables are excluded from all analyses.

Test of Significance. You can choose one of the following alternatives:

○ **Two-tailed**. Two-tailed probabilities. This is the default.

○ **One-tailed**. One-tailed probabilities.

The following display option is also available:

❑ **Display actual significance level**. By default, the probability and degrees of freedom are shown for each coefficient. If you deselect this item, coefficients significant at the 0.05 level are identified with a single asterisk, coefficients significant at the 0.01 level are identified with a double asterisk, and degrees of freedom are suppressed. This setting affects both partial and zero-order correlation matrices.

Partial Correlations Options

To obtain optional univariate summary statistics or zero-order correlations, or to modify the handling of missing values, click on Options... in the Partial Correlations dialog box. This opens the Partial Correlations Options dialog box, as shown in Figure 17.6.

Figure 17.6 Partial Correlations Options dialog box

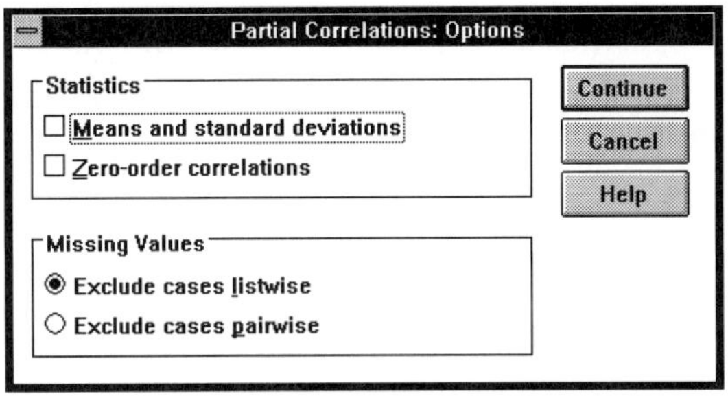

Statistics. You can choose one or both of the following:

❏ **Means and standard deviations.** Displayed for each variable. The number of cases with nonmissing values is also shown.

❏ **Zero-order correlations.** A matrix of simple correlations between all variables, including control variables, is displayed (see "The Order of the Coefficient" on p. 304).

Missing Values. You can choose one of the following alternatives:

○ **Exclude cases listwise.** Cases having missing values for any variable, including a control variable, are excluded from all computations. This is the default.

○ **Exclude cases pairwise.** For computation of the zero-order correlations on which the partial correlations are based, a case having missing values for one or both of a pair of variables is not used. Pairwise deletion uses as much of the data as possible. However, the number of cases may differ across coefficients. When pairwise deletion is in effect, the degrees of freedom for a particular partial coefficient are based on the smallest number of cases used in the calculation of any of the zero-order correlations.

Additional Features Available with Command Syntax

You can customize your partial correlations if you paste your selections into a syntax window and edit the resulting PARTIAL CORR command syntax (see Chapter 4). Additional features include:

- Matrix facility to read a zero-order correlation matrix or to write a partial correlation matrix (with the MATRIX subcommand).

- Partial correlations between two lists of variables (using the keyword WITH on the VARIABLES subcommand).

- Multiple analyses (with multiple VARIABLES subcommands).

- User-specified order values to request, for example, both first- and second-order partial correlations when you have two control variables (with the VARIABLES subcommand).
- The ability to suppress redundant coefficients (with the FORMAT subcommand).
- An option to display a matrix of simple correlations when some coefficients cannot be computed (with the STATISTICS subcommand).

See Appendix A for command syntax rules. See the *SPSS Base System Syntax Reference Guide* for complete PARTIAL CORR command syntax.

18 Multiple Linear Regression Analysis

The 1964 Civil Rights Act prohibits discrimination in the workplace based on sex or race; employers who violate the act are liable to prosecution. Since passage of the Civil Rights Act, women, blacks, and other groups have filed numerous lawsuits charging unfair hiring or advancement practices.

The courts have ruled that statistics can be used as *prima facie* evidence of discrimination. Many lawsuits depend heavily on complex statistical analyses to demonstrate that similarly qualified individuals are not treated equally (Roberts, 1980). In this chapter, employee records for 474 individuals hired between 1969 and 1971 by a bank engaged in Equal Employment Opportunity litigation are analyzed. A mathematical model is developed that relates beginning salary and salary progression to employee characteristics such as seniority, education, and previous work experience. One objective is to determine whether sex and race are important predictors of salary.

The technique used to build the model is linear regression analysis, one of the most versatile data analysis procedures. Regression can be used to summarize data as well as to study relations among variables.

Linear Regression

Before examining a model that relates beginning salary to several other variables, consider the relationship between beginning salary and current (as of March, 1977) salary. For employees hired during a similar time period, beginning salary should serve as a reasonably good predictor of salary at a later date. Although superstars and underachievers might progress differently from the group as a whole, salary progression should be similar for the others. The scatterplot of beginning salary and current salary shown in Figure 18.1 supports this hypothesis.

A scatterplot may suggest what type of mathematical functions would be appropriate for summarizing the data. Many functions, including parabolas, hyperbolas, polynomials, and trigonometric functions, are useful in fitting models to data. The scatterplot in Figure 18.1 shows current salaries tending to increase linearly with increases in beginning salary. If the plot indicates that a straight line is not a good summary measure of the relationship, you should consider other methods of analysis, including transforming the data to achieve linearity (see "Coaxing a Nonlinear Relationship to Linearity" on p. 334).

Figure 18.1   Scatterplot of beginning and current salaries

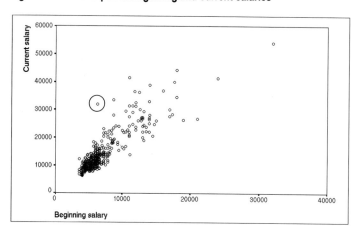

Outliers

A plot may also indicate the presence of points suspiciously different from the others. Examine such observations, termed **outliers**, carefully to see if they result from errors in gathering, coding, or entering data. The circled point in Figure 18.1 appears to be an outlier. Though neither the value of beginning salary ($6,300) nor the value of current salary ($32,000) is unique, jointly they are unusual.

The treatment of outliers can be difficult. If the point is incorrect due to coding or entry problems, you should correct it and rerun the analysis. If there is no apparent explanation for the outlier, consider interactions with other variables as a possible explanation. For example, the outlier may represent an employee who was hired as a low-paid clerical worker while pursuing an MBA degree. After graduation, the employee rose rapidly to a higher position; in this instance, the variable for education explains the unusual salary characteristics.

Choosing a Regression Line

Since current salary tends to increase linearly with beginning salary, a straight line can be used to summarize the relationship. The equation for the line is

predicted current salary $= B_0 + B_1$ (beginning salary)   **Equation 18.1**

The **slope** (B_1) is the change (in dollars) in the fitted current salary for a change in the beginning salary. The **intercept** (B_0) is the theoretical estimate of current salary for a beginning salary of 0.

However, the observed data points do not all fall on a straight line, they cluster around it. Many lines can be drawn through the data points; the problem is to select among the possible lines. The method of **least squares** results in a line that minimizes the sum of squared vertical distances from the observed data points to the line. Any other line has a larger sum. Figure 18.2 shows the least-squares line superimposed on the salary scatterplot. Some vertical distances from points to the line are also shown.

Figure 18.2   Regression line for beginning and current salaries

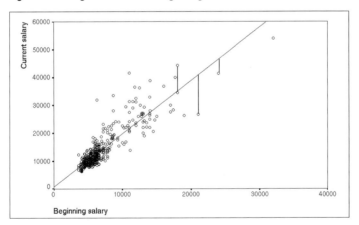

You can use SPSS to calculate the least-squares line. For the data in Figure 18.1, that line is

predicted current salary $= 771.28 + 1.91$ (beginning salary)   **Equation 18.2**

The slope and intercept values are shown in the column labeled *B* in the output shown in Figure 18.3.

Figure 18.3   Statistics for variables in the equation

```
----------------- Variables in the Equation -----------------

Variable              B        SE B       Beta        T   Sig T

SALBEG           1.909450     .047410    .880117   40.276  .0000
(Constant)     771.282303   355.471941             2.170  .0305
```

The Standardized Regression Coefficient

The **standardized regression coefficient**, labeled *Beta* in Figure 18.3, is defined as

$$\text{beta} = B_1 \frac{S_X}{S_Y}$$ **Equation 18.3**

Multiplying the regression coefficient (B_1) by the ratio of the standard deviation of the independent variable (S_X) to the standard deviation of the dependent variable (S_Y) results in a dimensionless coefficient. In fact, the beta coefficient is the slope of the least-squares line when both X and Y are expressed as Z scores. The beta coefficient is discussed further in "Beta Coefficients" on p. 342.

From Samples to Populations

Generally, more is sought in regression analysis than a description of observed data. You usually want to draw inferences about the relationship of the variables in the population from which the sample was taken. How are beginning and current salaries related for all employees, not just those included in the sample? Inferences about population values based on sample results are based on the following assumptions:

Normality and Equality of Variance. For any fixed value of the independent variable X, the distribution of the dependent variable Y is normal, with mean $\mu_{Y/X}$ (the mean of Y for a given X) and a constant variance of σ^2 (see Figure 18.4). This assumption specifies that not all employees with the same beginning salary have the same current salary. Instead, there is a normal distribution of current salaries for each beginning salary. Though the distributions have different means, they have the same variance: σ^2.

Figure 18.4   Regression assumptions

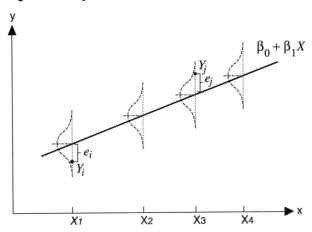

Independence. The Y's are statistically independent of each other; that is, observations are in no way influenced by other observations. For example, observations are *not* independent if they are based on repeated measurements from the same experimental unit. If three observations are taken from each of four families, the twelve observations are not independent.

Linearity. The mean values $\mu_{Y/X}$ all lie on a straight line, which is the population regression line. This is the line drawn in Figure 18.4. An alternative way of stating this assumption is that the linear model is correct.

When there is a single independent variable, the model can be summarized by

$$Y_i = \beta_0 + \beta_1 X_i + e_i \qquad \text{Equation 18.4}$$

The population parameters (values) for the slope and intercept are denoted by β_1 and β_0. The term e_i, usually called the **error**, is the difference between the observed value of Y_i and the subpopulation mean at the point X_i. The e_i are assumed to be normally distributed, independent, random variables with a mean of 0 and variance of σ^2 (see Figure 18.4).

Estimating Population Parameters

Since β_0 and β_1 are unknown population parameters, they must be estimated from the sample. The least-squares coefficients B_0 and B_1, discussed in "Choosing a Regression Line" on p. 313, are used to estimate the population parameters.

However, the slope and intercept estimated from a single sample typically differ from the population values and vary from sample to sample. To use these estimates for inference about the population values, the sampling distributions of the two statistics are needed. When the assumptions of linear regression are met, the sampling distributions of B_0 and B_1 are normal, with means of β_0 and β_1.

The standard error of B_0 is

$$\sigma_{B_0} = \sigma \sqrt{\frac{1}{N} + \frac{\bar{X}^2}{(N-1)\,S_X^2}}$$

Equation 18.5

where S_X^2 is the sample variance of the independent variable. The standard error of B_1 is

$$\sigma_{B_1} = \frac{\sigma}{\sqrt{(N-1)\,S_X^2}}$$

Equation 18.6

Since the population variance of the errors, σ^2, is not known, it must also be estimated. The usual estimate of σ^2 is

$$S^2 = \frac{\displaystyle\sum_{i=1}^{N} (Y_i - B_0 - B_1 X_i)^2}{N-2}$$

Equation 18.7

The positive square root of S^2 is termed the **standard error of the estimate**, or the standard deviation of the residuals. (The reason for this name is discussed in "Predicting a New Value" on p. 322.) The estimated standard errors of the slope and intercept are displayed in the third column (labeled *SE B*) in Figure 18.3.

Testing Hypotheses

A frequently tested hypothesis is that there is no linear relationship between X and Y—that the slope of the population regression line is 0. The statistic used to test this hypothesis is

$$t = \frac{B_1}{S_{B_1}}$$

Equation 18.8

The distribution of the statistic, when the assumptions are met and the hypothesis of no linear relationship is true, is Student's t distribution with $N-2$ degrees of freedom. The statistic for testing the hypothesis that the intercept is 0 is

$$t = \frac{B_0}{S_{B_0}}$$
                                                                        Equation 18.9

Its distribution is also Student's t with $N-2$ degrees of freedom.

These t statistics and their two-tailed observed significance levels are displayed in the last two columns of Figure 18.3. The small observed significance level (less than 0.00005) associated with the slope for the salary data supports the hypothesis that beginning salary and current salary have a linear association.

Confidence Intervals

A statistic calculated from a sample provides a point estimate of the unknown parameter. A point estimate can be thought of as the single best guess for the population value. While the estimated value from the sample is typically different from the value of the unknown population parameter, the hope is that it isn't too far away. Based on the sample estimate, it is possible to calculate a range of values that, within a designated likelihood, includes the population value. Such a range is called a **confidence interval**. For example, as shown in Figure 18.5, the 95% confidence interval for β_1, the population slope, is 1.816 to 2.003.

Figure 18.5   Confidence intervals

```
---- Variables in the Equation -----

Variable       95% Confdnce Intrvl B

SALBEG         1.816290    2.002610
(Constant)    72.778982  1469.785624
```

Ninety-five percent confidence means that if repeated samples are drawn from a population under the same conditions and 95% confidence intervals are calculated, 95% of the intervals will contain the unknown parameter β_1. Since the parameter value is unknown, it is not possible to determine whether a particular interval contains it.

Goodness of Fit

An important part of any statistical procedure that builds models from data is establishing how well the model actually fits, or its **goodness of fit**. This includes the detection of possible violations of the required assumptions in the data being analyzed.

The R-squared Coefficient

A commonly used measure of the goodness of fit of a linear model is R^2, or the **coefficient of determination**. It can be thought of in a variety of ways. Besides being the square of the correlation coefficient between variables X and Y, it is the square of the correlation coefficient between Y (the observed value of the dependent variable) and $\hat{Y}$ (the predicted value of Y from the fitted line). If you compute the predicted salary for each employee (based on the coefficients in the output in Figure 18.3) as follows

$$\text{predicted current salary} = 771.28 + 1.91\,(\text{beginning salary})$$ **Equation 18.10**

and then calculate the square of the Pearson correlation coefficient between predicted current salary and observed current salary, you will get R^2. If all the observations fall on the regression line, R^2 is 1. If there is no linear relationship between the dependent and independent variables, R^2 is 0.

Note that R^2 is a measure of the goodness of fit of a particular model and that an R^2 of 0 does not necessarily mean that there is no association between the variables. Instead, it indicates that there is no *linear* relationship.

In the output in Figure 18.6, R^2 is labeled *R Square* and its square root is labeled *Multiple R*. The sample R^2 tends to be an optimistic estimate of how well the model fits the population. The model usually does not fit the population as well as it fits the sample from which it is derived. The statistic adjusted R^2 attempts to correct R^2 to more closely reflect the goodness of fit of the model in the population. Adjusted R^2 is given by

$$R_a^2 = R^2 - \frac{p\,(1 - R^2)}{N - p - 1}$$ **Equation 18.11**

where p is the number of independent variables in the equation (1 in the salary example).

Figure 18.6   Summary statistics for the equation

```
Multiple R            .88012
R Square              .77461
Adjusted R Square     .77413
Standard Error    3246.14226
```

Analysis of Variance

To test the hypothesis that there is no linear relationship between X and Y, several equivalent statistics can be computed. When there is a single independent variable, the hypothesis that the population R^2 is 0 is identical to the hypothesis that the population slope is 0. The test for $R_{\text{pop}}^2 = 0$ is usually obtained from the analysis-of-variance table (see Figure 18.7).

Figure 18.7 Analysis-of-variance table

```
Analysis of Variance
                    DF      Sum of Squares        Mean Square
Regression           1   17092967800.01978   17092967800.0198
Residual           472    4973671469.79454     10537439.55465

F =    1622.11776      Signif F =   .0000
```

The total observed variability in the dependent variable is subdivided into two components—that which is attributable to the regression (labeled *Regression*) and that which is not (labeled *Residual*). Consider Figure 18.8. For a particular point, the distance from Y_i to $\bar{Y}$ (the mean of the Y's) can be subdivided into two parts:

$$Y_i - \bar{Y} = (Y_i - \hat{Y}_i) + (\hat{Y}_i - \bar{Y})$$ **Equation 18.12**

The distance from Y_i (the observed value) to $\hat{Y}_i$ (the value predicted by the regression line), or $Y_i - \hat{Y}_i$, is called the **residual from the regression**. It is zero if the regression line passes through the point. The second component $(\hat{Y}_i - \bar{Y})$ is the distance from the regression line to the mean of the Y's. This distance is "explained" by the regression in

Figure 18.8   Components of variability

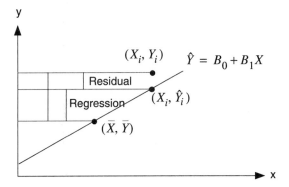

that it represents the improvement in the estimate of the dependent variable achieved by the regression. Without the regression, the mean of the dependent variable $\bar{Y}$ is used as the estimate. It can be shown that

$$\sum_{i=1}^{N} (Y_i - \bar{Y})^2 = \sum_{i=1}^{N} (Y_i - \hat{Y}_i)^2 + \sum_{i=1}^{N} (\hat{Y}_i - \bar{Y})^2$$ **Equation 18.13**

The first quantity following the equals sign is called the **residual sum of squares** and the second quantity is the **regression sum of squares**. The sum of these is called the **total sum of squares**.

The analysis-of-variance table in Figure 18.7 displays these two sums of squares under the heading *Sum of Squares*. The *Mean Square* for each entry is the sum of squares divided by the degrees of freedom (*DF*). If the regression assumptions are met, the ratio of the mean square regression to the mean square residual is distributed as an F statistic with p and $N - p - 1$ degrees of freedom. F serves to test how well the regression model fits the data. If the probability associated with the F statistic is small, the hypothesis that $R^2_{pop} = 0$ is rejected. For this example, the F statistic is

$$F = \frac{\text{mean square regression}}{\text{mean square residual}} = 1622 \qquad \text{Equation 18.14}$$

The observed significance level (*Signif F*) is less than 0.00005.

The square root of the F value (1622) is 40.28, which is the value of the t statistic for the slope in Figure 18.3. The square of a t value with k degrees of freedom is an F value with 1 and k degrees of freedom. Therefore, either t or F values can be computed to test that $\beta_i = 0$. Another useful summary statistic is the standard error of the estimate, S, which can also be calculated as the square root of the residual mean square (see "Predicting a New Value" on p. 322).

Another Interpretation of R-squared

Partitioning the sum of squares of the dependent variable allows another interpretation of R^2. It is the proportion of the variation in the dependent variable "explained" by the model:

$$R^2 = 1 - \frac{\text{residual sum of squares}}{\text{total sum of squares}} = 0.775 \qquad \text{Equation 18.15}$$

Similarly, adjusted R^2 is

$$R^2_a = 1 - \frac{\text{residual sum of squares} / (N - p - 1)}{\text{total sum of squares} / (N - 1)} \qquad \text{Equation 18.16}$$

where p is the number of independent variables in the equation (1 in the salary example).

Predicted Values and Their Standard Errors

By comparing the observed values of the dependent variable with the values predicted by the regression equation, you can learn a good deal about how well a model and the various assumptions fit the data (see the discussion of residuals beginning with "Searching for Violations of Assumptions" on p. 324). Predicted values are also of interest when the results are used to predict new data. You may wish to predict the mean Y for all cases with a given value of X (denoted X_0) or to predict the value of Y for a single case. For example, you can predict either the mean salary for all employees with a beginning salary of \$10,000 or the salary for a particular employee with a beginning salary of \$10,000. In both situations, the predicted value

$$\hat{Y}_0 = B_0 + B_1 X_0 = 771 + 1.91 \times 10,000 = 19,871$$ **Equation 18.17**

is the same. What differs is the standard error.

Predicting Mean Response

The estimated standard error for the predicted mean Y at X_0 is

$$S_{\hat{Y}} = S \sqrt{\frac{1}{N} + \frac{(X_0 - \bar{X})^2}{(N-1) S_X^2}}$$ **Equation 18.18**

The equation for the standard error shows that the smallest value occurs when X_0 is equal to $\bar{X}$, the mean of X. The larger the distance from the mean, the greater the standard error. Thus, the mean of Y for a given X is better estimated for central values of the observed X's than for outlying values. Figure 18.9 is a plot of the standard errors of predicted mean salaries for different values of beginning salary (obtained by saving the standard error as a new variable in the Linear Regression procedure and then using the Scatter option on the Graphs menu).

Figure 18.9   Standard errors for predicted mean responses

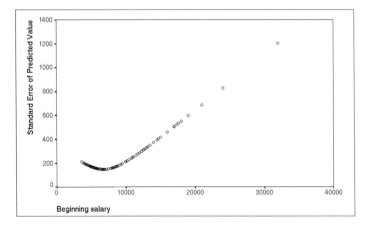

Prediction intervals for the mean predicted salary are calculated in the standard way. The 95% confidence interval at X_0 is

$$\hat{Y} \pm t_{(1-\frac{\alpha}{2}, N-2)} S_{\hat{Y}}$$ **Equation 18.19**

Figure 18.10 shows a typical 95% confidence band for predicted mean responses. It is narrowest at the mean of X and widens as the distance from the mean $(X_0 - \overline{X})$ increases.

Figure 18.10 95% confidence band for mean prediction

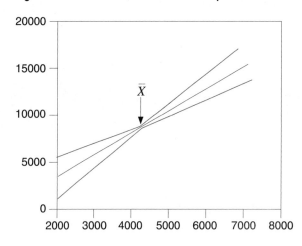

Predicting a New Value

Although the predicted value for a single new observation at X_0 is the same as the predicted value for the mean at X_0, the standard error is not. The two sources of error when predicting an individual observation are:

1. The individual value may differ from the population mean of Y for X_0.

2. The estimate of the population mean at X_0 may differ from the population mean.

The sources of error are illustrated in Figure 18.11.

Figure 18.11 Sources of error in predicting individual observations

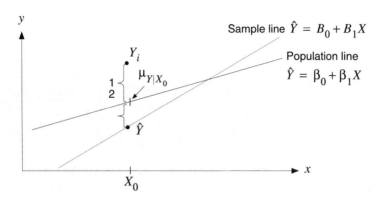

When estimating the mean response, only the second error component is considered. The variance of the individual prediction is the variance of the mean prediction plus the variance of Y_i for a given X. This can be written as

$$S^2_{\text{ind } \hat{Y}} = S^2_{\hat{Y}} + S^2 = S^2 \left(1 + \frac{1}{N} + \frac{(X_0 - \bar{X})^2}{(N-1) S^2_X} \right)$$

Equation 18.20

Prediction intervals for the new observation are obtained by substituting $S_{\text{ind } \hat{Y}}$ for $S_{\hat{Y}}$ in Equation 18.19. If the sample size is large, the terms $1/N$ and

$$\frac{(X_0 - \bar{X})^2}{(N-1) S^2_X}$$

Equation 18.21

are negligible. In that case, the standard error is simply S, which explains the name standard error of the estimate for S (see "Estimating Population Parameters" on p. 316). You can obtain plots of confidence intervals for predicted values using the Scatter option on the Graphs menu.

Reading the Casewise Plot

Figure 18.12 shows the output from the beginning and end of a plot of the salary data. The sequential number of the case is listed first, followed by the plot of standardized residuals, the observed (*SALNOW*), predicted (*PRED*), and residual (*RESID*) values. In SPSS, you can save predicted values and confidence intervals for the mean responses and for individual responses and use the List Cases procedure to display these values for all cases or for a subset of cases (see Chapter 21).

Figure 18.12 Casewise plot with predicted values

```
Casewise Plot of Standardized Residual

*: Selected   M: Missing

          -3.0             0.0             3.0
   Case #  O:..............:..............:O   SALNOW       *PRED       *RESID
      1    .              *.              .    16080    16810.6600    -730.6600
      2    .        *      .              .    41400    46598.0758   -5198.0758
      3    .              . *             .    21960    20247.6695    1712.3305
      4    .              . *             .    19200    17383.4949    1816.5051
      5    .        *      .              .    28350    33995.7076   -5645.7076
      6    .              . *             .    27250    25586.4910    1663.5090
      7    .              . *             .    16080    13946.4854    2133.5146
      8    .              .  *            .    14100    11082.3108    3017.6892
      9    .              . *             .    12420    10394.9089    2025.0911
     10    .             *.              .    12300    12800.8156     -500.8156
     11    .              . *             .    15720    12800.8156    2919.1844
     12    .          *   .               .     8880    12227.9807   -3347.9807
     ..
     ..
     ..
    470    .              *               .     9420     9592.9401     -172.9401
    471    .              .*              .     9780     9134.6721      645.3279
    472    .           *  .              .     7680     9249.2391    -1569.2391
    473    .           *  .              .     7380     8561.8372    -1181.8372
    474    .          *   .               .     8340    10738.6099    -2398.6099
   Case #  O:..............:..............:O   SALNOW       *PRED       *RESID
          -3.0             0.0             3.0
```

Searching for Violations of Assumptions

You usually don't know in advance whether a model such as linear regression is appropriate. Therefore, it is necessary to conduct a search focused on residuals to look for evidence that the necessary assumptions are violated.

Residuals

In model building, a **residual** is what is left after the model is fit. It is the difference between an observed value and the value predicted by the model:

$$E_i = Y_i - B_0 - B_1 X_i = Y_i - \hat{Y}_i \qquad \text{Equation 18.22}$$

In regression analysis, the true errors, e_i, are assumed to be independent normal values with a mean of 0 and a constant variance of σ^2. If the model is appropriate for the data, the observed residuals, E_i, which are estimates of the true errors, e_i, should have similar characteristics.

If the intercept term is included in the equation, the mean of the residuals is always 0, so the mean provides no information about the true mean of the errors. Since the sum of the residuals is constrained to be 0, the residuals are *not* strictly independent. However, if the number of residuals is large when compared to the number of independent variables, the dependency among the residuals can be ignored for practical purposes.

The relative magnitudes of residuals are easier to judge when they are divided by estimates of their standard deviations. The resulting **standardized residuals** are expressed in standard deviation units above or below the mean. For example, the fact that a particular residual is −5198.1 provides little information. If you know that its standardized form is −3.1, you know not only that the observed value is less than the predicted value but also that the residual is larger than most in absolute value.

Residuals are sometimes adjusted in one of two ways. The standardized residual for case i is the residual divided by the sample standard deviation of the residuals. Standardized residuals have a mean of 0 and a standard deviation of 1. The **Studentized residual** is the residual divided by an estimate of its standard deviation that varies from point to point, depending on the distance of X_i from the mean of X. Usually standardized and Studentized residuals are close in value, but not always. The Studentized residual reflects more precisely differences in the true error variances from point to point.

Linearity

For the bivariate situation, a scatterplot is a good means for judging how well a straight line fits the data. Another convenient method is to plot the residuals against the predicted values. If the assumptions of linearity and homogeneity of variance are met, there should be no relationship between the predicted and residual values. You should be suspicious of any observable pattern.

For example, fitting a least-squares line to the data in the plots shown in Figure 18.13 yields the residual plots shown in Figure 18.14. The two residual plots show patterns, since straight lines do not fit the data well. Systematic patterns between the predicted values and the residuals suggest possible violations of the assumption of linearity. If the assumption were met, the residuals would be randomly distributed in a band clustered around the horizontal line through 0, as shown in Figure 18.15.

Figure 18.13 Scatterplots of cubic and quadratic relationships

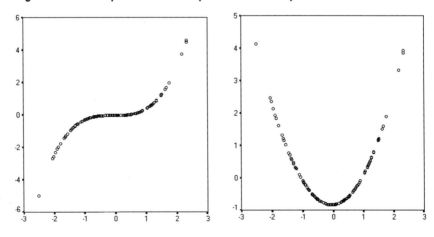

Figure 18.14 Standardized residuals scatterplots—cubic and quadratic relationships

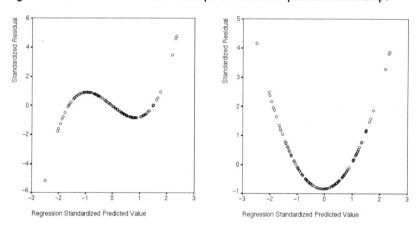

Figure 18.15 Randomly distributed residuals

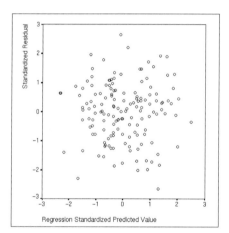

Residuals can also be plotted against individual independent variables by saving them in the Linear Regression procedure and then using the Scatter option on the Graphs menu. Again, if the assumptions are met, you should see a horizontal band of residuals. Consider as well plotting the residuals against independent variables not in the equation. If the residuals are not randomly distributed, you may want to include the variable in the equation for a multiple regression model (see "Multiple Regression Models" on p. 338).

Equality of Variance

You can also use the previously described plots to check for violations of the equality-of-variance assumption. If the spread of the residuals increases or decreases with values of the independent variables or with predicted values, you should question the assumption of constant variance of Y for all values of X.

Figure 18.16 is a plot of the Studentized residuals against the predicted values for the salary data. The spread of the residuals increases with the magnitude of the predicted values, suggesting that the variability of current salaries increases with salary level. Thus, the equality-of-variance assumption appears to be violated.

Figure 18.16 Unequal variance

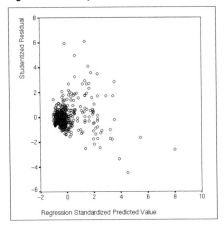

Independence of Error

Whenever the data are collected and recorded sequentially, you should plot residuals against the sequence variable. Even if time is not considered a variable in the model, it could influence the residuals. For example, suppose you are studying survival time after surgery as a function of complexity of surgery, amount of blood transfused, dosage of medication, and so forth. In addition to these variables, it is also possible that the surgeon's skill increased with each operation and that a patient's survival time is influenced by the number of prior patients treated. The plot of standardized residuals corresponding to the order in which patients received surgery shows a shorter survival time for earlier patients than for later patients (see Figure 18.17). If sequence and the residual are independent, you should not see a discernible pattern.

Figure 18.17 Serial plot

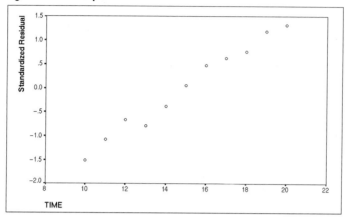

TIME

The **Durbin-Watson statistic**, a test for serial correlation of adjacent error terms, is defined as

$$d = \frac{\displaystyle\sum_{t=2}^{N} (E_t - E_{t-1})^2}{\displaystyle\sum_{t=1}^{N} E_t^2}$$

Equation 18.23

The possible values of the statistic range from 0 to 4. If the residuals are not correlated with each other, the value of d is close to 2. Values less than 2 mean that adjacent residuals are positively correlated. Values greater than 2 mean that adjacent residuals are negatively correlated. Consult tables of the d statistic for bounds upon which significance tests can be based.

Normality

The distribution of residuals may not appear to be normal for reasons other than actual non-normality: misspecification of the model, nonconstant variance, a small number of residuals actually available for analysis, etc. Therefore, you should pursue several lines of investigation. One of the simplest is to construct a histogram of the residuals, such as the one for the salary data shown in Figure 18.18.

Figure 18.18 Histogram of standardized residuals

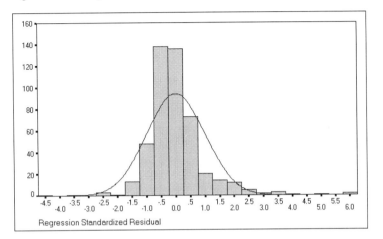

A normal distribution is superimposed on a histogram of observed frequencies (indicated by the bars). It is unreasonable to expect the observed residuals to be exactly normal—some deviation is expected because of sampling variation. Even if the errors are normally distributed in the population, sample residuals are only approximately normal.

In the histogram in Figure 18.18, the distribution does not seem normal, since there is an exaggerated clustering of residuals toward the center and a straggling tail toward large positive values. Thus, the normality assumption may be violated.

Another way to compare the observed distribution of residuals to the expected distribution under the assumption of normality is to plot the two cumulative distributions against each other for a series of points. If the two distributions are identical, a straight line results. By observing how points scatter about the expected straight line, you can compare the two distributions.

Figure 18.19 is a cumulative probability plot of the salary residuals. Initially, the observed residuals are above the "normal" line, since there is a smaller number of large negative residuals than expected. Once the greatest concentration of residuals is reached, the observed points are below the line, since the observed cumulative proportion exceeds the expected. Tests for normality are available using the Explore procedure (see Chapter 9).

Figure 18.19 Normal probability (P–P) plot

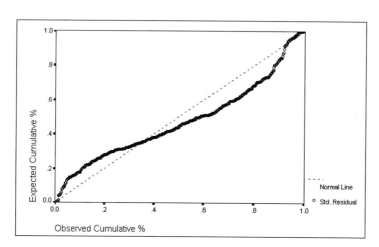

Locating Outliers

You can spot outliers readily on residual plots, since they are cases with very large positive or negative residuals. In general, standardized residual values greater than an absolute value of 3 are considered outliers. Since you usually want more information about outliers, you can use the casewise plotting facility to display identification numbers and a variety of other statistics for cases having residuals beyond a specified cutoff point.

Figure 18.20 displays information for the nine cases with standardized residuals greater than the absolute value of 3. Only two of these nine cases have current salaries less than those predicted by the model (cases 67 and 122). The others all have larger salaries, an average of $33,294, than the average for the sample, only $13,767. Thus, there is some evidence that the model may not fit well for the highly paid cases.

Figure 18.20 Casewise plot of residuals outliers

```
Casewise Plot of Standardized Residual

Outliers = 3.     *: Selected    M: Missing

          -6.     -3.  3.     6.
  Case #   O:.......:  :.......:O     SALNOW      *PRED        *RESID
     24    .         ..*        .      28000   17383.4949    10616.5051
     60    .         ..        *.      32000   12800.8156    19199.1844
     67    .        *..         .      26400   37043.1894  -10643.1894
    114    .         .. *       .      38800   27511.2163    11288.7837
    122    .    *    ..         .      26700   40869.7266  -14169.7266
    123    .         .. *       .      36250   24639.4039    11610.5961
    129    .         ..    *    .      33500   17383.4949    16116.5051
    149    .         ..       * .      41500   21782.8671    19717.1329
    177    .         ..   *     .      36500   23295.1513    13204.8487
```

Other Unusual Observations: Mahalanobis Distance

In the section "Outliers" on p. 312, one case was identified as an outlier because the combination of values for beginning and current salaries was atypical. This case (case 60) also appears in Figure 18.20, since it has a large value for the standardized residual. Another unusual case (case 56) has a beginning salary of $31,992. Since the average beginning salary for the entire sample is only $6,806 and the standard deviation is 3148, the case is eight standard deviations above the mean. But since the standardized residual is not large, this case does not appear in Figure 18.20.

However, cases that have unusual values for the independent variables can have a substantial impact on the results of analysis and should be identified. One measure of the distance of cases from average values of the independent variables is **Mahalanobis distance**. In the case of a regression equation with a single independent variable, it is the square of the standardized value of X:

$$D_i = \left(\frac{X_i - \bar{X}}{S_X} \right)^2$$

Equation 18.24

When there is more than one independent variable—where Mahalanobis distance is most valuable—the computations are more complex.

You can save Mahalanobis distances with SPSS and display cases with the five highest and lowest values using the Explore procedure (see Chapter 9). As shown in Figure 18.21, the Mahalanobis distance for case 56 is 64 (8^2) .

Figure 18.21 Mahalanobis distances

```
                        Extreme Values
                        ------- ------

5    Highest    Case #            5   Lowest     Case #

     63.99758   Case: 56              .00011     Case: 78
     29.82579   Case: 2               .00075     Case: 448
     20.32559   Case: 122             .00088     Case: 302
     14.99121   Case: 67              .00088     Case: 192
     12.64145   Case: 55              .00088     Case: 203
```

Influential Cases: Deleted Residuals and Cook's Distance

Certain observations in a set of data can have a large influence on estimates of the parameters. Figure 18.22 shows such a point. The regression line obtained for the data is quite different if the point is omitted. However, the residual for the circled point is not particularly large when the case (case 8) is included in the computations and does not therefore arouse suspicion (see the column labeled RES_1 in Figure 18.23).

Figure 18.22 Influential observation

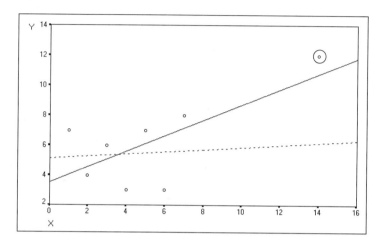

One way to identify an influential case is to compare the residuals for a case when the suspected case is included in the equation and when it is not. The **adjusted predicted value** for case *i* when it is not included in the computation of the regression line is

$$\hat{Y}_i^{(i)} = B_0^{(i)} + B_1^{(i)} X_i$$

Equation 18.25

where the superscript *(i)* indicates that the *i*th case is excluded. The change in the predicted value when the *i*th case is deleted is

$$\hat{Y}_i - \hat{Y}_i^{(i)}$$

Equation 18.26

The residual calculated for a case when it is not included is called the **deleted residual**, computed as

$$Y_i - \hat{Y}_i^{(i)}$$

Equation 18.27

The deleted residual can be divided by its standard error to produce the **Studentized deleted residual**.

Although the difference between the deleted residual and ordinary residual for a case is useful as an index of the influence of that case, this measure does not reflect changes in residuals of other observations when the ith case is deleted. **Cook's distance** does consider changes in all residuals when case i is omitted (Cook, 1977). It is defined as

$$C_i = \frac{\sum\limits_{j=1}^{N} (\hat{Y}_j^{(i)} - \hat{Y}_j)^2}{(p+1)\,S^2}$$

Equation 18.28

With SPSS you can save influence measures and display them with the List Cases procedure (see Chapter 21). Influence measures for the data in Figure 18.22 are shown in Figure 18.23. The measures for case 8 (the circled point) are given in the last row. The case has neither a very large Studentized residual (*SRE_1*), nor a very large Studentized deleted residual (*SDR_1*). However, the deleted residual (*DRE_1*), 5.86, is somewhat larger than the ordinary residual *(RES_1)*. The large Mahalanobis distance (*MAH_1*) identifies the case as having an X value far from the mean, while the large Cook's D (*COO_1*) identifies the case as an influential point.

Figure 18.23 Influence measures

CASEID	Y	RES_1	SRE_1	SDR_1	ADJ_1	DRE_1	MAH_1	COO_1
1.00	7	2.93939	1.48192	1.69900	2.90963	4.09037	1.09471	.42996
2.00	4	-.57580	-.27801	-.25543	4.73486	-.73486	.64013	.01067
3.00	6	.90910	.42617	.39506	4.90624	1.09376	.30683	.01845
4.00	3	-2.60609	-1.20001	-1.25657	6.02516	-3.02516	.09469	.11578
5.00	7	.87881	.40164	.37168	5.99502	1.00498	.00379	.01158
6.00	3	-3.63638	-1.66607	-2.07474	7.17913	-4.17913	.03410	.20715
7.00	8	.84852	.39369	.36412	6.99996	1.00004	.18559	.01384
8.00	12	1.24246	1.15294	1.19289	6.14264	5.85736	4.64016	2.46867

The regression coefficients with and without case 8 are shown in Figure 18.24 and Figure 18.25. Both $B_0^{(8)}$ and $B_1^{(8)}$ are far removed from B_0 and B_1, since case 8 is an influential point.

Figure 18.24 Regression coefficients from all cases

```
---------------------------- Variables in the Equation ----------------------------
--
```

Variable	B	SE B	95% Confdnce Intrvl B		Beta	T	Sig T
X	.515145	.217717	-.017587	1.047877	.694761	2.366	.0558
(Constant)	3.545466	1.410980	.092941	6.997990		2.513	.0457

Figure 18.25 Regression coefficients without case 8

```
---------------------------- Variables in the Equation ----------------------------
```

Variable	B	SE B	95% Confdnce Intrvl B		Beta	T	Sig T
X	.071407	.427380	-1.027192	1.170005	.074513	.167	.8739
(Constant)	5.142941	1.911317	.229818	10.056065		2.691	.0433

You can examine the change in the regression coefficients when a case is deleted from the analysis by saving the change in intercept and X values. For case 8 in Figure 18.26, you see that the change in the intercept (*DFB0_1*) is -1.5975 and the change in slope (*DFB1_1*) is 0.4437.

Figure 18.26 Diagnostic statistics for influential observations

```
CASEID   Y     DFB0_1      DFB1_1

 1.00    7    1.30149     -.15051
 2.00    4     -.20042     .02068
 3.00    6      .24859    -.02131
 4.00    3     -.55002     .03274
 5.00    7      .13704    -.00218
 6.00    3     -.37991    -.02714
 7.00    8      .04546     .01515
 8.00   12    -1.59748     .44374
```

When Assumptions Appear to Be Violated

When there is evidence of a violation of assumptions, you can pursue one of two strategies. You can formulate an alternative model, such as weighted least squares, or you can transform the variables so that the current model will be more adequate. For example, taking logs, square roots, or reciprocals can stabilize the variance, achieve normality, or linearize a relationship.

Coaxing a Nonlinear Relationship to Linearity

To try to achieve linearity, you can transform either the dependent or independent variables, or both. If you alter the scale of independent variables, linearity can be achieved without any effect on the distribution of the dependent variable. Thus, if the dependent variable is normally distributed with constant variance for each value of X, it remains normally distributed.

When you transform the dependent variable, its distribution is changed. This new distribution must then satisfy the assumptions of the analysis. For example, if logs of the values of the dependent variable are taken, log Y—not the original Y—must be normally distributed with constant variance.

The choice of transformation depends on several considerations. If the form of the true model governing the relationship is known, it should dictate the choice. For instance, if it is known that $\hat{Y} = AC^X$ is an adequate model, taking logs of both sides of the equation results in

$$\log \hat{Y}_i = (\log A) + (\log C) X_i$$
$$\quad\quad\quad [B_0] \quad\quad\quad [B_1]$$

Equation 18.29

Thus, log Y is linearly related to X.

If the true model is not known, you should choose the transformation by examining the plotted data. Frequently, a relationship appears nearly linear for part of the data but is curved for the rest (for example, Figure 18.27). Taking the log of the dependent variable results in an improved linear fit (see Figure 18.28).

Figure 18.27 Nonlinear relationship

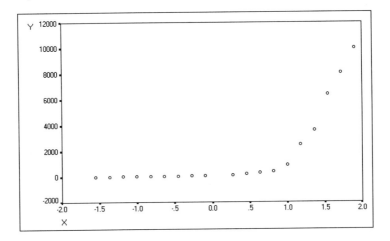

Figure 18.28 Transformed relationship

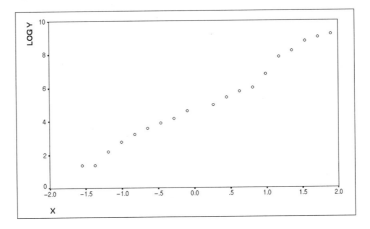

Other transformations that may diminish curvature are $-1/Y$ and the square root of Y. The choice depends, to a certain extent, on the severity of the problem.

Coping with Skewness

When the distribution of residuals is positively skewed, the log transformation of the dependent variable is often helpful. For negatively skewed distributions, the square transformation is common. It should be noted that the F tests used in regression hypothesis testing are usually quite insensitive to moderate departures from normality.

Stabilizing the Variance

If the variance of the residuals is not constant, you can try a variety of remedial measures:

- When the variance is proportional to the mean of Y for a given X, use the square root of Y if all Y_i are positive.
- When the standard deviation is proportional to the mean, try the logarithmic transformation.
- When the standard deviation is proportional to the square of the mean, use the reciprocal of Y.
- When Y is a proportion or rate, the arc sine transformation may stabilize the variance.

Transforming the Salary Data

The assumptions of constant variance and normality appear to be violated with the salary data (see Figure 18.16 and Figure 18.18). A regression equation using logs of beginning salary and current salary was developed to obtain a better fit to the assumptions. Figure 18.29 is a scatterplot of Studentized residuals against predicted values when logs of both variables are used in the regression equation.

Figure 18.29 Scatterplot of transformed salary data

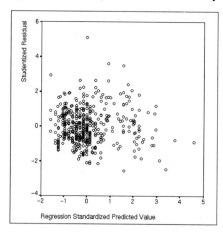

Compare Figure 18.16 and Figure 18.29, and note the improvement in the behavior of the residuals shown in Figure 18.29. The spread no longer increases with increasing salary level. Also compare Figure 18.18 and Figure 18.30, and note that the distribution in Figure 18.30 is nearly normal.

Figure 18.30 Histogram of transformed salary data

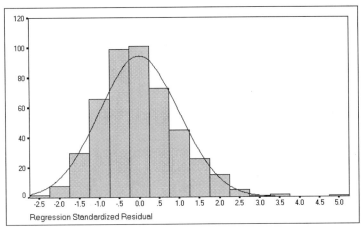

Regression Standardized Residual

For the transformed data, the multiple R increases slightly to 0.8864, and the outlier plot contains only four cases (compare with Figure 18.6 and Figure 18.20). Thus, the transformation appears to have resulted in a better model. (For more information on transformations, see Chapter 5.)

A Final Comment on Assumptions

Rarely are assumptions not violated one way or another in regression analysis and other statistical procedures. However, this is not a justification for ignoring the assumptions. Cranking out regressions without considering possible violations of the necessary assumptions can lead to results that are difficult to interpret and apply. Significance levels, confidence intervals, and other results are sensitive to certain types of violations and cannot be interpreted in the usual fashion if serious violations exist.

By carefully examining residuals and, if need be, using transformations or other methods of analysis, you are in a much better position to pursue analyses that solve the problems you are investigating. Even if everything isn't perfect, you can at least knowledgeably gauge the potential for difficulties.

Multiple Regression Models

Beginning salary seems to be a good predictor of current salary, given the evidence shown above. Nearly 80% ($R^2 = 0.77$ from Figure 18.6) of the observed variability in current salaries can be explained by beginning salary levels. But how do variables such as education level, years of experience, race, and sex affect the salary level at which one enters the company?

Predictors of Beginning Salary

Multiple linear regression extends bivariate regression by incorporating multiple independent variables. The model can be expressed as

$$Y_i = \beta_0 + \beta_1 X_{1i} + \beta_2 X_{2i} + \ldots + \beta_p X_{pi} + e_i$$

Equation 18.30

The notation X_{pi} indicates the value of the pth independent variable for case i. Again, the β terms are unknown parameters and the e_i terms are independent random variables that are normally distributed with mean 0 and constant variance σ^2. The model assumes that there is a normal distribution of the dependent variable for every combination of the values of the independent variables in the model. For example, if child's height is the dependent variable and age and maternal height are the independent variables, it is assumed that for every combination of age and maternal height there is a normal distribution of children's heights and, though the means of these distributions may differ, all have the same variance.

The Correlation Matrix

One of the first steps in calculating an equation with several independent variables is to calculate a correlation matrix for all variables, as shown in Figure 18.31. The variables are the log of beginning salary, years of education, sex, years of work experience, minority status (race), and age in years. Variables *sex* and *minority* are represented by **indicator variables**, that is, variables coded as 0 or 1. *Sex* is coded 1 for female and 0 for male, and *minority* is coded 1 for nonwhite and 0 for white.

Figure 18.31 The correlation matrix

```
Correlation:

               LOGBEG    EDLEVEL       SEX      WORK    MINORITY       AGE

LOGBEG          1.000       .686     -.548      .040       -.173      -.048
EDLEVEL          .686      1.000     -.356     -.252       -.133      -.281
SEX             -.548      -.356     1.000     -.165       -.076       .052
WORK             .040      -.252     -.165     1.000        .145       .804
MINORITY        -.173      -.133     -.076      .145       1.000       .111
AGE             -.048      -.281      .052      .804        .111      1.000
```

The matrix shows the correlations between the dependent variable (*logbeg*) and each independent variable, as well as the correlations between the independent variables. Note particularly any large intercorrelations between the independent variables, since such correlations can substantially affect the results of multiple regression analysis.

Correlation Matrices and Missing Data

For a variety of reasons, data files frequently contain incomplete observations. Respondents in surveys scrawl illegible responses or refuse to answer certain questions. Laboratory animals die before experiments are completed. Patients fail to keep scheduled clinic appointments. Thus, before computing the correlation matrix, you must usually decide what to do with cases that have missing values for some of the variables.

Before even considering possible strategies, you should determine whether there is evidence that the missing-value pattern is not random. That is, are there reasons to believe that missing values for a variable are related to the values of that variable or other variables? For example, people with low incomes may be less willing to report their financial status than more affluent people. This may be even more pronounced for people who are poor but highly educated.

One simple method of exploring such possibilities is to subdivide the data into two groups—those with missing values for a variable and those with complete information—and examine the distributions of the other variables in the file across these two groups. SPSS crosstabulation and independent-samples *t* tests are particularly useful for this. For a discussion of other methods for detecting nonrandomness, see Frane (1976).

If it appears that the data are not missing randomly, use great caution in attempting an analysis. It may be that no satisfactory analysis is possible, especially if there are only a few cases.

If you are satisfied that the missing data are random, several strategies are available. If, for most cases, values are missing for the same few variables, consider excluding those variables from the analysis. Since this luxury is not usually available, you can alternatively keep all variables but eliminate the cases with missing values for any of them. This is termed **listwise** missing-value treatment, since a case is eliminated if it has a missing value for any variable on the list.

If many cases have missing data for some variables, listwise missing-value treatment may eliminate too many cases and leave you with a very small sample. One common technique is to calculate the correlation coefficient between a pair of variables based on all cases with complete information for the two variables, regardless of whether the cases have missing data for any other variable. For example, if a case has values only for variables 1, 3, and 5, it is used only in computations involving variable pairs 1 and 3, 1 and 5, and 3 and 5. This is **pairwise** missing-value treatment.

Several problems can arise with pairwise matrices, one of which is inconsistency. There are some relationships between coefficients that are impossible but may occur when different cases are used to estimate different coefficients. For example, if age and weight, and age and height, have a high positive correlation, it is impossible in the same sample for height and weight to have a high negative correlation. However, if the same cases are not used to estimate all three coefficients, such an anomaly can occur.

Another problem with pairwise matrices is that no single sample size can be obtained, since each coefficient may be based on a different number of cases. In addition, signif- icance levels obtained from analyses based on pairwise matrices must be viewed with caution, since little is known about hypothesis testing in such situations.

Missing-value problems should not be treated lightly. You should always select a missing-value treatment based on careful examination of the data and not leave the choices up to system defaults. In this example, complete information is available for all cases, so missing values are not a problem.

Partial Regression Coefficients

The summary output when all independent variables are included in the multiple regres- sion equation is shown in Figure 18.32. The F test associated with the analysis-of-vari- ance table is a test of the null hypothesis that

$$\beta_1 = \beta_2 = \beta_3 = \beta_4 = \beta_5 = 0 \qquad\qquad \text{Equation 18.31}$$

In other words, it is a test of whether there is a linear relationship between the dependent variable and the entire set of independent variables.

Figure 18.32 Statistics for the equation and analysis-of-variance table

```
Multiple R              .78420
R Square                .61498
Adjusted R Square       .61086
Standard Error          .09559

Analysis of Variance
                    DF     Sum of Squares    Mean Square
Regression           5           6.83039        1.36608
Residual           468           4.27638         .00914

F =     149.50125      Signif F =   .0000
```

The statistics for the independent variables in Figure 18.33 are parallel to those obtained in regression with a single independent variable (see Figure 18.3). In multiple regres-

Figure 18.33 Statistics for variables in the equation

```
------------------ Variables in the Equation ------------------

Variable              B         SE B        Beta        T    Sig T

AGE              .001015  6.6132E-04     .078106    1.535   .1254
SEX             -.103576     .010318    -.336987  -10.038   .0000
MINORITY        -.052366     .010837    -.141573   -4.832   .0000
EDLEVEL          .031443     .001748     .591951   17.988   .0000
WORK             .001608  9.2407E-04     .091428    1.740   .0826
(Constant)      3.385300     .033233              101.866   .0000
```

sion, the coefficients labeled B are called **partial regression coefficients**, since the coefficient for a particular variable is adjusted for other independent variables in the equation. The equation that relates the predicted log of beginning salary to the independent variables is

$$\text{logbeg} = 3.3853 + 0.00102(\text{age}) - 0.10358(\text{sex})$$
$$- 0.05237(\text{minority}) + 0.03144(\text{edlevel}) \qquad \textbf{Equation 18.32}$$
$$+ 0.00161(\text{work})$$

Since the dependent variable is in log units, the coefficients can be approximately interpreted in percentage terms. For example, the coefficient of -0.104 for *sex* when females are coded as 1 indicates that female salaries are estimated to be about 10% less than male salaries after statistical adjustment for age, education, work history, and minority status.

Determining Important Variables

In multiple regression, you sometimes want to assign relative importance to each independent variable. For example, you might want to know whether education is more important in predicting beginning salary than previous work experience. There are two possible approaches, depending on which of the following questions is asked:

- How important are education and work experience when each one is used alone to predict beginning salary?
- How important are education and work experience when they are used to predict beginning salary along with other independent variables in the regression equation?

The first question is answered by looking at the correlation coefficients between salary and the independent variables. The larger the absolute value of the correlation coefficient, the stronger the linear association. Figure 18.31 shows that education correlates more highly with the log of salary than does previous work experience (0.686 and 0.040, respectively). Thus, you would assign more importance to education as a predictor of salary.

The answer to the second question is considerably more complicated. When the independent variables are correlated among themselves, the unique contribution of each is difficult to assess. Any statement about an independent variable is contingent upon the other variables in the equation. For example, the regression coefficient (B) for work experience is 0.0007 when it is the sole independent variable in the equation, compared to 0.00161 when the other four independent variables are also in the equation. The second coefficient is more than twice the size of the first.

Beta Coefficients

It is also inappropriate to interpret the B's as indicators of the relative importance of variables. The actual magnitude of the coefficients depends on the units in which the variables are measured. Only if all independent variables are measured in the same units—years, for example—are their coefficients directly comparable. When variables differ substantially in units of measurement, the sheer magnitude of their coefficients does not reveal anything about relative importance.

One way to make regression coefficients somewhat more comparable is to calculate beta weights, which are the coefficients of the independent variables when all variables are expressed in standardized (Z score) form (see Figure 18.33). The **beta coefficients** can be calculated directly from the regression coefficients using

$$\text{beta}_k = B_k \left(\frac{S_k}{S_Y} \right) \qquad \qquad \text{Equation 18.33}$$

where S_k is the standard deviation of the kth independent variable.

However, the values of the beta coefficients, like the B's, are contingent on the other independent variables in the equation. They are also affected by the correlations of the independent variables and do not in any absolute sense reflect the importance of the various independent variables.

Part and Partial Coefficients

Another way of assessing the relative importance of independent variables is to consider the increase in R^2 when a variable is entered into an equation that already contains the other independent variables. This increase is

$$R^2_{\text{change}} = R^2 - R^2_{(i)} \qquad \qquad \text{Equation 18.34}$$

where $R^2_{(i)}$ is the square of the multiple correlation coefficient when all independent variables except the ith are in the equation. A large change in R^2 indicates that a variable provides unique information about the dependent variable that is not available from the other independent variables in the equation. The signed square root of the increase is called the **part correlation coefficient**. It is the correlation between Y and X_i when the linear effects of the other independent variables have been removed from X_i. If all independent variables are uncorrelated, the change in R^2 when a variable is entered into the equation is simply the square of the correlation coefficient between that variable and the dependent variable.

The value of $RsqCh$ in Figure 18.34 shows that the addition of years of education to an equation that contains the other four independent variables results in a change in R^2 of 0.266. This value tells only how much R^2 increases when a variable is added to the regression equation. It does not indicate what proportion of the unexplained variation this increase constitutes. If most of the variation had been explained by the other variables, a small change in R^2 is all that is possible for the remaining variable.

Figure 18.34 Change in R-squared

```
Block Number 5. Method: Enter EDLEVEL

Step  MultR   Rsq   AdjRsq  F(Eqn)  SigF  RsqCh   FCh     SigCh     Variable  BetaIn  Correl
  5   .7842  .6150  .6109  149.501  .000  .2662  323.554  .000  In:  EDLEVEL   .5920   .6857
```

A coefficient that measures the proportional reduction in variation is

$$Pr_i^2 = \frac{R^2 - R^2_{(i)}}{1 - R^2_{(i)}}$$

Equation 18.35

The numerator is the square of the part coefficient; the denominator is the proportion of unexplained variation when all but the ith variable are in the equation. The signed square root of Pr_i^2 is the **partial correlation coefficient**. It can be interpreted as the correlation between the ith independent variable and the dependent variable when the linear effects of the other independent variables have been removed from both X_i and Y. Since the denominator of Pr_i^2 is always less than or equal to 1, the part correlation coefficient is never larger in absolute value than the partial correlation coefficient.

Plots of the residuals of Y and X_i, when the linear effects of the other independent variables have been removed, are a useful diagnostic aid. They are discussed in "Checking for Violations of Assumptions" on p. 351.

Building a Model

Our selection of the five variables to predict beginning salary has been arbitrary to some extent. It is unlikely that all relevant variables have been identified and measured. Instead, some relevant variables have no doubt been excluded, while others that were included may not be very important determinants of salary level. This is not unusual; you must try to build a model from available data, as voluminous or scanty as the data may be. Before considering several formal procedures for model building, we will examine some of the consequences of adding and deleting variables from regression equations. The regression statistics for variables not in the equation are also described.

Adding and Deleting Variables

The first step in Figure 18.35 shows the summary statistics when years of education is the sole independent variable and log of beginning salary is the dependent variable. Consider the second step in the same figure, when another variable, *sex*, is added. The value displayed as *RsqCh* in the second step is the change in R^2 when *sex* is added. R^2 for *edlevel* alone is 0.4702, so R^2_{change} is $0.5760 - 0.4702$, or 0.1058.

Figure 18.35 Adding a variable to the equation

```
Equation Number 1    Dependent Variable..   LOGBEG

Block Number  1.  Method:  Enter       EDLEVEL

Step   MultR    Rsq  AdjRsq   F(Eqn)  SigF   RsqCh       FCh SigCh
  1    .6857   .4702   .4691  418.920  .000   .4702   418.920  .000

End Block Number   1   All requested variables entered.

Block Number  2.  Method:  Enter       SEX

Step   MultR    Rsq  AdjRsq   F(Eqn)  SigF   RsqCh       FCh SigCh
  2    .7589   .5760   .5742  319.896  .000   .1058   117.486  .000

End Block Number   2   All requested variables entered.
```

The null hypothesis that the true population value for the change in R^2 is 0 can be tested using

$$F_{change} = \frac{R^2_{change}\,(N-p-1)}{q\,(1-R^2)} = \frac{(0.1058)\,(474-2-1)}{1\,(1-0.5760)} = 117.49 \qquad \textbf{Equation 18.36}$$

where N is the number of cases in the equation, p is the total number of independent variables in the equation, and q is the number of variables entered at this step. This is also referred to as a **partial F test**. Under the hypothesis that the true change is 0, the significance of the value labeled *FCh* can be obtained from the F distribution with q and $N-p-1$ degrees of freedom.

The hypothesis that the real change in R^2 is 0 can also be formulated in terms of the β parameters. When only the ith variable is added in a step, the hypothesis that the change in R^2 is 0 is equivalent to the hypothesis that β_i is 0. The F value displayed for the change in R^2 is the square of the t value for the test of the coefficient.

When q independent variables are entered in a single step, the test that R^2 is 0 is equivalent to the simultaneous test that the coefficients of all q variables are 0. For example, if sex and age were added in the same step to the regression equation that contains education, the F test for R^2 change would be the same as the F test which tests the hypothesis that $\beta_{sex} = \beta_{age} = 0$.

Entering sex into the equation with education has effects in addition to changing R^2. For example, the magnitude of the regression coefficient for education from step 1 to step 2 decreases from 0.0364 to 0.0298. This is attributable to the correlation between sex and level of education.

When highly intercorrelated independent variables are included in a regression equation, results may appear anomalous. The overall regression may be significant, while none of the individual coefficients are significant. The signs of the regression coefficients may be counterintuitive. High correlations between independent variables inflate the variances of the estimates, making individual coefficients quite unreliable without adding much to the overall fit of the model. The problem of linear relationships between independent variables is discussed further in "Measures of Collinearity" on p. 355.

Statistics for Variables Not in the Equation

When you have independent variables that have not been entered into the equation, you can examine what would happen if they were entered at the next step. Statistics describing these variables are shown in Figure 18.36. The column labeled *Beta In* is the standardized regression coefficient that would result if the variable were entered into the equation at the next step. The t test and level of significance are for the hypothesis that the coefficient is 0. (Remember that the t test and the partial F test for the hypothesis that a coefficient is 0 are equivalent.) The partial correlation coefficient with the dependent variable adjusts for the variables already in the equation.

Figure 18.36 Coefficients for variables not in the equation

```
------------- Variables not in the Equation -------------

Variable      Beta In  Partial  Min Toler       T  Sig T

WORK          .144245  .205668    .773818   4.556  .0000
MINORITY     -.129022 -.194642    .847583  -4.302  .0000
AGE           .139419  .205193    .804253   4.545  .0000
```

From statistics calculated for variables not in the equation, you can decide what variable should be entered next. This process is detailed in "Procedures for Selecting Variables" on p. 346.

The "Optimal" Number of Independent Variables

Having seen what happens when sex is added to the equation containing education (Figure 18.35), consider now what happens when the remaining three independent variables are entered one at a time in no particular order. Summary output is shown in Figure 18.37. Step 5 shows the statistics for the equation with all independent variables entered. Step 3 describes the model with education, sex, and work experience as the independent variables.

Figure 18.37 All independent variables in the equation

Step	MultR	Rsq	AdjRsq	F(Eqn)	SigF	RsqCh	FCh	SigCh	In:	Variable
1	.6857	.4702	.4691	418.920	.000	.4702	418.920	.000	In:	EDLEVEL
2	.7589	.5760	.5742	319.896	.000	.1058	117.486	.000	In:	SEX
3	.7707	.5939	.5913	229.130	.000	.0179	20.759	.000	In:	WORK
4	.7719	.5958	.5923	172.805	.000	.0019	2.149	.143	In:	AGE
5	.7842	.6150	.6109	149.501	.000	.0192	23.349	.000	In:	MINORITY

Examination of Figure 18.37 shows that R^2 never decreases as independent variables are added. This is always true in regression analysis. However, this does not necessarily mean that the equation with more variables better fits the population. As the number of parameters estimated from the sample increases, so does the goodness of fit to the sample as measured by R^2. For example, if a sample contains six cases, a regression equation with six parameters fits the sample exactly, even though there may be no true statistical relationship at all between the dependent variable and the independent variables.

As indicated in "The R-squared Coefficient" on p. 318, the sample R^2 in general tends to overestimate the population value of R^2. Adjusted R^2 attempts to correct the optimistic bias of the sample R^2. Adjusted R^2 does not necessarily increase as additional variables are added to an equation and is the preferred measure of goodness of fit because it is not subject to the inflationary bias of unadjusted R^2. This statistic is shown in the column labeled *AdjRsq* in the output.

Although adding independent variables increases R^2, it does not necessarily decrease the standard error of the estimate. Each time a variable is added to the equation, a degree of freedom is lost from the residual sum of squares and one is gained for the regression sum of squares. The standard error may increase when the decrease in the residual sum of squares is very slight and not sufficient to make up for the loss of a degree of freedom for the residual sum of squares. The F value for the test of the overall regression decreases when the regression sum of squares does not increase as fast as the degrees of freedom for the regression.

Including a large number of independent variables in a regression model is never a good strategy, unless there are strong, previous reasons to suggest that they all should be included. The observed increase in R^2 does not necessarily reflect a better fit of the model in the population. Including irrelevant variables increases the standard errors of all estimates without improving prediction. A model with many variables is often difficult to interpret.

On the other hand, it is important not to exclude potentially relevant independent variables. The following sections describe various procedures for selecting variables to be included in a regression model. The goal is to build a concise model that makes good prediction possible.

Procedures for Selecting Variables

You can construct a variety of regression models from the same set of variables. For instance, you can build seven different equations from three independent variables: three with only one independent variable, three with two independent variables, and one with all three. As the number of variables increases, so does the number of potential models (ten independent variables yield 1,023 models).

Although there are procedures for computing all possible regression equations, several other methods do not require as much computation and are more frequently used. Among these procedures are forward selection, backward elimination, and stepwise selection. None of these variable selection procedures are "best" in any absolute sense; they merely identify subsets of variables that, for the sample, are good predictors of the dependent variable.

Forward Selection

In **forward selection**, the first variable considered for entry into the equation is the one with the largest positive or negative correlation with the dependent variable. The F test for the hypothesis that the coefficient of the entered variable is 0 is then calculated. To determine whether this variable (and each succeeding variable) is entered, the F value is compared to an established criterion. You can specify one of two criteria in SPSS. One criterion is the minimum value of the F statistic that a variable must achieve in order to enter, called **F-to-enter (FIN)**, with a default value of 3.84. The other criterion you can specify is the probability associated with the F statistic, called **probability of F-to-enter (PIN)**, with a default of 0.05. In this case, a variable enters into the equation only if the probability associated with the F test is less than or equal to the default 0.05 or the value you specify. By default, PIN is the criterion used. (In the output, SPSS generally displays t values and their probabilities. These t probabilities are equivalent to those associated with F. You can obtain F values by squaring t values, since $t^2 = F$.)

The PIN and FIN criteria are not necessarily equivalent. As variables are added to the equation, the degrees of freedom associated with the residual sum of squares decrease while the regression degrees of freedom increase. Thus, a fixed F value has different significance levels depending on the number of variables currently in the equation. For large samples, the differences are negligible.

The actual significance level associated with the F-to-enter statistic is not the one usually obtained from the F distribution, since many variables are being examined and the largest F value is selected. Unfortunately, the true significance level is difficult to compute, since it depends not only on the number of cases and variables but also on the correlations between independent variables.

If the first variable selected for entry meets the criterion for inclusion, forward selection continues. Otherwise, the procedure terminates with no variables in the equation. Once one variable is entered, the statistics for variables not in the equation are used to select the next one. The partial correlations between the dependent variable and each of the independent variables not in the equation, adjusted for the independent variables in the equation, are examined. The variable with the largest partial correlation is the next candidate. Choosing the variable with the largest partial correlation in absolute value is equivalent to selecting the variable with the largest F value.

If the criterion is met, the variable is entered into the equation and the procedure is repeated. The procedure stops when there are no other variables that meet the entry criterion.

Figure 18.38 shows output generated from a forward-selection procedure using the salary data. The default entry criterion is PIN = 0.05. In the first step, education (variable *edlevel*) is entered, since it has the highest correlation with beginning salary. The significance level associated with education is less than 0.0005, so it certainly meets the criterion for entry.

Figure 18.38 Summary statistics for forward selection

Step	MultR	Rsq	F(Eqn)	SigF		Variable	BetaIn
1	.6857	.4702	418.920	.000	In:	EDLEVEL	.6857
2	.7589	.5760	319.896	.000	In:	SEX	-.3480
3	.7707	.5939	229.130	.000	In:	WORK	.1442
4	.7830	.6130	185.750	.000	In:	MINORITY	-.1412

To see how the next variable, *sex*, was selected, look at the statistics shown in Figure 18.39 for variables not in the equation when only *edlevel* is in the equation. The variable with the largest partial correlation is *sex*. If entered at the next step, it would have a t value of −10.839. Since the probability associated with the t value is less than 0.05, variable *sex* is entered in the second step.

Figure 18.39 Status of the variables at the first step

```
------------------ Variables in the Equation ------------------
```

Variable	B	SE B	Beta	T	Sig T
EDLEVEL	.036424	.001780	.685719	20.468	.0000
(Constant)	3.310013	.024551		134.821	.0000

```
------------ Variables not in the Equation ------------
```

Variable	Beta In	Partial	Min Toler	T	Sig T
SEX	-.348017	-.446811	.873274	-10.839	.0000
WORK	.227473	.302405	.936316	6.885	.0000
MINORITY	-.083181	-.113267	.982341	-2.474	.0137
AGE	.157180	.207256	.921128	4.598	.0000

Once variable *sex* enters at step 2, the statistics for variables not in the equation must be examined (see Figure 18.36). The variable with the largest absolute value for the partial correlation coefficient is now years of work experience. Its t value is 4.556 with a probability less than 0.05, so variable *work* is entered in the next step. The same process takes place with variable *minority*, leaving *age* as the only variable out of the equation. However, as shown in Figure 18.40, the significance level associated with the *age* coefficient t value is 0.1254, which is too large for entry. Thus, forward selection yields the summary table for the four steps shown in Figure 18.38.

Figure 18.40 Forward selection at the last step

```
------------ Variables not in the Equation ------------
```

Variable	Beta In	Partial	Min Toler	T	Sig T
AGE	.078106	.070796	.297843	1.535	.1254

Backward Elimination

While forward selection starts with no independent variables in the equation and sequentially enters them, **backward elimination** starts with all variables in the equation and sequentially removes them. Instead of entry criteria, removal criteria are used.

Two removal criteria are available in SPSS. The first is the minimum F value that a variable must have in order to remain in the equation. Variables with F values less than this **F-to-remove (FOUT)** are eligible for removal. The second criterion available is the maximum **probability of F-to-remove (POUT)** that a variable can have. The default FOUT value is 2.71 and the default POUT value is 0.10. The default criterion is probability of F-to-remove.

Look at the salary example again, this time constructing the model with backward elimination. The output in Figure 18.41 is from the first step, in which all variables are entered into the equation. The variable with the smallest partial correlation coefficient, *age*, is examined first. Since the probability of its t (0.1254) is greater than the default POUT criterion value of 0.10, variable *age* is removed. (Recall that the t test and the partial F test for the hypothesis that a coefficient is 0 are equivalent.)

Figure 18.41 Backward elimination at the first step

```
----------------- Variables in the Equation -----------------

Variable            B        SE B       Beta          T   Sig T

AGE            .001015  6.6132E-04    .078106      1.535   .1254
SEX           -.103576     .010318   -.336987    -10.038   .0000
MINORITY      -.052366     .010837   -.141573     -4.832   .0000
EDLEVEL        .031443     .001748    .591951     17.988   .0000
WORK           .001608  9.2407E-04    .091428      1.740   .0826
(Constant)    3.385300     .033233               101.866   .0000
```

The equation is then recalculated without *age*, producing the statistics shown in Figure 18.42. The variable with the smallest partial correlation is *minority*. However, its significance is less than the 0.10 criterion, so backward elimination stops. The equation resulting from backward elimination is the same as the one from forward selection. This is not always the case, however. Forward-selection and backward-elimination procedures can give different results, even with comparable entry and removal criteria.

Figure 18.42 Backward elimination at the last step

```
----------------- Variables in the Equation -----------------

Variable            B        SE B       Beta          T   Sig T

SEX           -.099042     .009901   -.322234    -10.003   .0000
MINORITY      -.052245     .010853   -.141248     -4.814   .0000
EDLEVEL        .031433     .001751    .591755     17.956   .0000
WORK           .002753  5.4582E-04    .156592      5.044   .0000
(Constant)    3.411953     .028380               120.225   .0000


------------- Variables not in the Equation -------------

Variable   Beta In  Partial  Min Toler      T   Sig T

AGE        .078106  .070796   .297843    1.535   .1254
```

Stepwise Selection

Stepwise selection of independent variables is really a combination of backward and forward procedures and is probably the most commonly used method. The first variable is selected in the same manner as in forward selection. If the variable fails to meet entry requirements (either FIN or PIN), the procedure terminates with no independent variables in the equation. If it passes the criterion, the second variable is selected based on the highest partial correlation. If it passes entry criteria, it also enters the equation.

After the first variable is entered, stepwise selection differs from forward selection: the first variable is examined to see whether it should be removed according to the removal criterion (FOUT or POUT) as in backward elimination. In the next step, variables not in the equation are examined for entry. After each step, variables already in the equation are examined for removal. Variables are removed until none remain that meet the removal criterion. To prevent the same variable from being repeatedly entered and removed, the PIN must be less than the POUT (or FIN greater than FOUT). Variable selection terminates when no more variables meet entry and removal criteria.

In the salary example, stepwise selection with the default criteria results in the same equation produced by both forward selection and backward elimination (see Figure 18.43).

Figure 18.43 Stepwise output at the last step

```
Multiple R             .78297
R Square               .61304
Adjusted R Square      .60974
Standard Error         .09573

F =        185.74958        Signif F =   .0000


----------------- Variables in the Equation -----------------

Variable           B          SE B        Beta           T    Sig T

EDLEVEL        .031433      .001751      .591755     17.956    .0000
SEX           -.099042      .009901     -.322234    -10.003    .0000
WORK           .002753    5.4582E-04     .156592      5.044    .0000
MINORITY      -.052245      .010853     -.141248     -4.814    .0000
(Constant)    3.411953      .028380                 120.225    .0000


Equation Number 1     Dependent Variable..    LOGBEG

------------- Variables not in the Equation -------------

Variable     Beta In   Partial   Min Toler        T    Sig T

AGE          .078106    .070796    .297843     1.535    .1254
```

The three procedures do not always result in the same equation, though you should be encouraged when they do. The model selected by any method should be carefully studied for violations of the assumptions. It is often a good idea to develop several acceptable models and then choose among them based on interpretability, ease of variable acquisition, parsimony, and so forth.

Checking for Violations of Assumptions

The procedures for checking for violations of assumptions in bivariate regression (see "Searching for Violations of Assumptions" on p. 324) apply in multiple regression as well. Residuals should be plotted against predicted values as well as against each independent variable. The distribution of residuals should be examined for normality.

Several additional residual plots may be useful for multiple regression models. One of these is the **partial regression plot**. For the *j*th independent variable, it is obtained by calculating the residuals for the dependent variable when it is predicted from all the independent variables excluding the *j*th and by calculating the residuals for the *j*th independent variable when it is predicted from all of the other independent variables. This removes the linear effect of the other independent variables from both variables. For each case, these two residuals are plotted against each other.

A partial regression plot for educational level for the regression equation that contains work experience, minority, sex, and educational level as the independent variables is shown in Figure 18.44. (Summary statistics for the regression equation with all independent variables are displayed in the last step of Figure 18.43.) The partial regression plot (created by saving residuals in the Linear Regression procedure and then using the Scatter option on the Graphs menu) shows residuals for *logbeg* on the *y* axis and residual values for *edlevel* on the *x* axis.

Figure 18.44 Partial regression plot

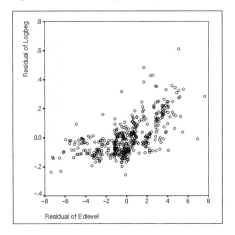

Several characteristics of the partial regression plot make it a particularly valuable diagnostic tool. The slope of the regression line for the two residual variables (0.03143) is equal to the coefficient for the *edlevel* variable in the multiple regression equation after the last step (step 4 in Figure 18.43). Thus, by examining the bivariate plot, you can conveniently identify points that are influential in the determination of the particular regression coefficient. The correlation coefficient between the two residuals, 0.638, is the partial correlation coefficient discussed in "Part and Partial Coefficients" on p. 342. The residuals from the least-squares line in Figure 18.44 are equal to the residuals from the final multiple regression equation, which includes all the independent variables.

The partial regression plot also helps you assess the inadequacies of the selected model and violations of the underlying assumptions. For example, the partial regression plot of educational level does not appear to be linear, suggesting that an additional term, such as years of education squared, might also be included in the model. This violation is much easier to spot using the partial regression plot than the plot of the independent variable against the residual from the equation with all independent variables. Figure 18.45 shows the residual scatterplot created with the Graph procedure and Figure 18.46 shows the partial regression plot produced by the Regression procedure. Note that the nonlinearity is much more apparent in the partial regression plot.

Figure 18.45 Residual plot

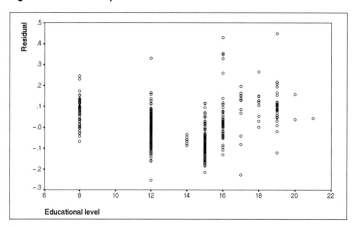

Figure 18.46 Partial regression plot

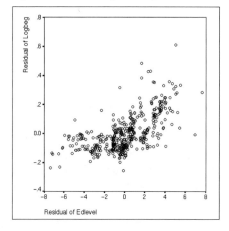

Figure 18.47 contains the summary statistics generated when the number of years of education squared is included in the multiple regression equation. The multiple R^2 increases from 0.61 (step 4 in Figure 18.43) to 0.71, a significant improvement.

Figure 18.47 Regression equation with education squared

```
Multiple R            .84302
R Square              .71068
Adjusted R Square     .70759
Standard Error        .08286

Analysis of Variance
                      DF      Sum of Squares      Mean Square
Regression             5             7.89331          1.57866
Residual             468             3.21345           .00687

F =      229.91286        Signif F =  .0000
```

Looking for Influential Points

As discussed earlier, when building a regression model it is important to identify cases that are influential, or that have a disproportionately large effect on the estimated model. (See "Locating Outliers" on p. 330.) We can look for cases that change the values of the regression coefficients and of predicted values, cases that increase the variances of the coefficients, and cases that are poorly fitted by the model.

Among the important influence measures is the **leverage** of a case. The predicted values of the dependent variable can be expressed as

$$\hat{Y} = HY \hspace{6cm} \text{Equation 18.37}$$

The diagonal elements of the H matrix (commonly called the hat matrix) are called **leverages**. The leverage for a case describes the impact of the observed value of the dependent variable on the prediction of the fitted value. Leverages are important in their own right and as fundamental building blocks for other diagnostic measures. For example, the Mahalanobis distance for a point is obtained by multiplying the leverage value by $N-1$.

SPSS computes centered leverages. They range from 0 to $(N-1)/N$, where N is the number of observations. The mean value for the centered leverage is p/N, where p is the number of independent variables in the equation. A leverage of 0 identifies a point with no influence on the fit, while a point with a leverage of $(N-1)/N$ indicates that a degree of freedom has been devoted to fitting the data point. Ideally, you would like each observation to exert a roughly equal influence. That is, you want all of the leverages to be near p/N. It is a good idea to examine points with leverage values that exceed $2p/N$.

To see the effect of a case on the estimation of the regression coefficients, you can look at the change in each of the regression coefficients when the case is removed from the analysis. SPSS can display or save the actual change in each of the coefficients, including the intercept and the standardized change.

Figure 18.48 is a plot of standardized change values for the *minority* variable on the vertical axis against a case ID number on the horizontal axis. Note that as expected, most of the points cluster in a horizontal band around 0. However, there are a few points far removed from the rest. Belsley et al. (1980) recommend examining standardized change values that are larger than $(2/\sqrt{N})$.

Figure 18.48 Plot of standardized change values for minority status

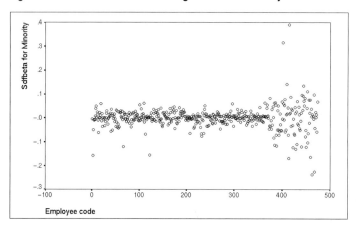

In addition to looking at the change in the regression coefficients when a case is deleted from an analysis, we can look at the change in the predicted value or at the standardized change. Cases with large values far removed from the rest should be examined. As a rule of thumb, you may want to look at standardized values larger than $2/\sqrt{p/N}$.

Another type of influential observation is one that influences the variance of the estimated regression coefficients. A measure of the impact of an observation on the variance-covariance matrix of the parameter estimates is called the **covariance ratio**. It is computed as the ratio of the determinant of the variance-covariance matrix computed without the case to the determinant of the variance-covariance matrix computed with all cases. If this ratio is close to 1, the case leaves the variance-covariance matrix relatively unchanged. Belsley et al. (1980) recommend examining points for which the absolute value of the ratio minus 1 is greater than $3p/N$.

You can save covariance ratios with the Linear Regression procedure and plot them using the Scatter option on the Graphs menu. Figure 18.49 is a plot of covariance ratios for the salary example. Note the circled point, which has a covariance ratio substantially smaller than the rest.

Figure 18.49 Plot of the covariance ratio

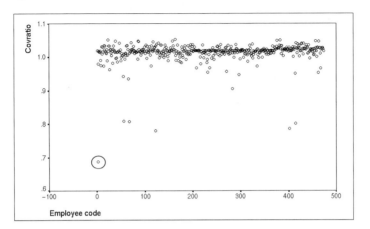

Measures of Collinearity

Collinearity refers to the situation in which there is a high multiple correlation when one of the independent variables is regressed on the others (that is, when there is a high correlation between independent variables). The problem with collinear variables is that they provide very similar information, and it is difficult to separate out the effects of the individual variables. Diagnostics are available which allow you to detect the presence of collinear data and to assess the extent to which the collinearity has degraded the estimated parameters.

The **tolerance** of a variable is a commonly used measure of collinearity. The tolerance of variable i is defined as $1 - R_i^2$, where R_i is the multiple correlation coefficient when the ith independent variable is predicted from the other independent variables. If the tolerance of a variable is small, it is almost a linear combination of the other independent variables.

The **variance inflation factor** (**VIF**) is closely related to the tolerance. In fact, it is defined as the reciprocal of the tolerance. That is, for the ith variable,

$$\text{VIF}_i = \frac{1}{(1 - R_i^2)}$$

Equation 18.38

This quantity is called the variance inflation factor, since the term is involved in the calculation of the variance of the ith regression coefficient. As the variance inflation factor increases, so does the variance of the regression coefficient.

Figure 18.50 shows the tolerances and VIF's for the variables in the final model. Note the low tolerances and high VIF's for *edlevel* and *ed2* (the square of *edlevel*). This is to be expected, since there is a relationship between these two variables.

Figure 18.50 Measures of collinearity—tolerance and VIF

```
--------------------------- Variables in the Equation ---------------------------

Variable              B        SE B       Beta   Tolerance        VIF         T   Sig T

WORK            .001794  4.7859E-04    .102038    .834367      1.199     3.749   .0002
MINORITY       -.038225     .009460   -.103342    .945107      1.058    -4.041   .0001
SEX            -.082503     .008671   -.268426    .776799      1.287    -9.515   .0000
EDLEVEL        -.089624     .009751  -1.687260    .018345     54.511    -9.191   .0000
ED2             .004562  3.6303E-04   2.312237    .018263     54.756    12.567   .0000
(Constant)     4.173910     .065417                                     63.804   .0000
```

Two useful tools for examining the collinearity of a data matrix are the eigenvalues of the scaled, uncentered cross-products matrix and the decomposition of regression variance corresponding to the eigenvalues.

Eigenvalues and Condition Indexes

We can compare the eigenvalues of the scaled, uncentered cross-products matrix to see if some are much larger than others. If this is the case, the data matrix is said to be **ill-conditioned**. If a matrix is ill-conditioned, small changes in the values of the independent or dependent variables may lead to large changes in the solution. The condition index is defined as

$$\text{condition index} = \sqrt{\frac{\text{eigenvalue}_{max}}{\text{eigenvalue}_i}} \qquad \text{Equation 18.39}$$

There are as many near-dependencies among the variables as there are large condition indexes.

Figure 18.51 shows the eigenvalues and condition indexes for the salary example. You can see that the last two eigenvalues are much smaller than the rest. Their condition indexes are 10.29 and 88.22.

Figure 18.51 Measures of collinearity—eigenvalues and condition indexes

```
Collinearity Diagnostics

Number  Eigenval    Cond  Variance Proportions
                    Index  Constant      SEX MINORITY   EDLEVEL      ED2     WORK
     1   4.08812   1.000    .00019   .01223   .01375    .00004   .00013   .01466
     2    .79928   2.262    .08212   .08212   .65350    .00002   .00009   .04351
     3    .59282   2.626    .00001   .37219   .22139    .00003   .00022   .17437
     4    .48061   2.917    .00005   .14964   .05421    .00012   .00091   .51370
     5    .03864  10.286    .05223   .37811   .04876    .00004   .02337   .20721
     6    .00053  88.221    .94746   .00571   .00839    .99975   .97527   .04655
```

Variance Proportions

The variances of each of the regression coefficients, including the constant, can be decomposed into a sum of components associated with each of the eigenvalues. If a high proportion of the variance of two or more coefficients is associated with the same eigenvalue, there is evidence for a near-dependency.

Consider Figure 18.51 again. Each of the columns following the condition index tells you the proportion of the variance of each of the coefficients associated with each of the eigenvalues. Consider the column for the *sex* coefficient. You see that 1.22% of the variance of the coefficient is attributable to the first eigenvalue, 8.2% to the second, and 0.57% to the sixth (the proportions in each column sum to 1).

In this table you're looking for variables with high proportions for the same eigenvalue. For example, looking at the last eigenvalue, you see that it accounts for 95% of the variance of the constant, almost 100% of the variance of *edlevel*, and 98% of the variance of *ed2*. This tells you that these three variables are highly dependent. Since the other independent variables have small variance proportions for the sixth eigenvalue, it does not appear that the observed dependencies are affecting their coefficients. (See Belsley et al., 1980, for an extensive discussion of these diagnostics.)

Interpreting the Equation

The multiple regression equation estimated above suggests several findings. Education appears to be the best predictor of beginning salary, at least among the variables included in this study (Figure 18.41). The sex of the employee also appears to be important. Women are paid less than men, since the sign of the regression coefficient is negative (men are coded 0 and women are coded 1). Years of prior work experience and race are also related to salary, but when education and sex are included in the equation, the effect of experience and race is less striking.

Do these results indicate that there is sex discrimination at the bank? Not necessarily. It is well recognized that all education is not equally profitable. Master's degrees in business administration and in political science are viewed quite differently in the marketplace. Thus, a possible explanation of the observed results is that women enter areas that just don't pay very well. Although this may suggest inequities in societal evaluation of skills, it does not necessarily imply discrimination at the bank. Further, many other potential job-related skills or qualifications are not included in the model. As well, some of the existing variables, such as age, may make nonlinear as well as linear contributions to the fit. Such contributions can often be approximated by including new variables that are simple functions of the existing one. For example, the age values squared may improve the fit.

How to Obtain a Linear Regression Analysis

The Linear Regression procedure provides five equation-building methods: forward selection, backward elimination, stepwise selection, forced entry, and forced removal. It can produce residual analyses to help detect influential data points, outliers, and violations of regression model assumptions. You can also save predicted values, residuals, and related measures.

The minimum specifications are:

- One numeric dependent variable.
- One or more numeric independent variables.

To obtain a linear regression analysis, from the menus choose:

Statistics
  Regression ▶
    Linear...

This opens the Linear Regression dialog box, as shown in Figure 18.52.

Figure 18.52 Linear Regression dialog box

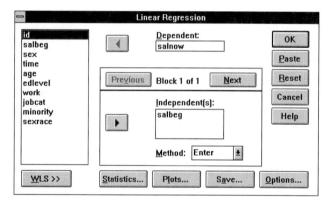

The numeric variables in your data file appear on the source list. Select a dependent variable and a block of one or more independent variables and click on OK to get the default analysis using the forced-entry method. By default, cases with missing values for any variable are excluded from the analysis.

⬇ **Method.** Method selection determines the method used in developing the regression model. You can choose one of the following alternatives:

Enter. Forced entry. This is the default method. Variables in the block are entered in a single step.

Stepwise. Stepwise variable entry and removal. Variables in the block are examined at each step for entry or removal.

Remove. Forced removal. Variables in the block are removed in a single step.

Backward. Backward variable elimination. Variables in the block are entered one at a time and then removed one at a time based on removal criteria.

Forward. Forward variable selection. Variables in the block are entered one at a time based on entry criteria.

All variables must pass the tolerance criterion to be entered in the equation, regardless of the entry method specified. The default tolerance level is 0.0001. A variable also is not entered if it would cause the tolerance of another variable already in the model to drop below the tolerance criterion.

For the stepwise method, the maximum number of steps is twice the number of independent variables. For the forward and backward methods, the maximum number of steps equals the number of variables meeting entry and removal criteria. The maximum number of steps for the total model equals the sum of the maximum number of steps for each method in the model.

All independent variables selected are added to a single regression model. However, you can specify different entry methods for different subsets of variables. For example, you can enter one block of variables into the regression model using forward selection and a second block of variables using stepwise selection. To add a second block of variables to the regression model, click on Next. Select an alternate selection method if you do not want the default (forced entry). To move back and forth between blocks of independent variables, use Previous and Next. You can specify up to nine different blocks.

Optionally, you can obtain a weighted least-squares model. Click on WLS and select a variable containing the weights. An independent or dependent variable cannot be used as a weighting variable. If the value of the weighting variable is zero, negative, or missing, the case is excluded from the analysis.

Linear Regression Statistics

To control the display of statistical output, click on Statistics... in the Linear Regression dialog box. This opens the Linear Regression Statistics dialog box, as shown in Figure 18.53.

Figure 18.53 Linear Regression Statistics dialog box

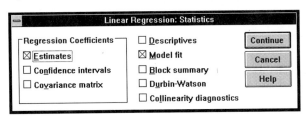

Regression Coefficients. You can choose one or more of the following:

❑ **Estimates.** Displays regression coefficients and related measures. These statistics are displayed by default. For variables in the equation, statistics displayed are regression coefficient B, standard error of B, standardized coefficient beta, t value for B, and two-tailed significance level of t.

For independent variables not in the equation, statistics displayed are beta if the variable was entered, t value for beta, t probability, partial correlation with the dependent variable controlling for variables in the equation, and minimum tolerance.

❑ **Confidence intervals.** Displays the 95% confidence interval for each unstandardized regression coefficient.

❑ **Covariance matrix.** Variance-covariance matrix of unstandardized regression coefficients. Displays a matrix with covariances below the diagonal, correlations above the diagonal, and variances on the diagonal.

You can also choose one or more of the following statistics:

❑ **Descriptives.** Variable means, standard deviations, and a correlation matrix with one-tailed probabilities.

❑ **Model fit.** R, R^2, adjusted R^2, and the standard error. Also, an ANOVA table displays degrees of freedom, sums of squares, mean squares, F value, and the observed probability of F. Model fit statistics are shown by default.

❑ **Block summary.** Summary statistics for each step (backward, forward, or stepwise method) or block (forced entry or removal method).

❑ **Durbin-Watson.** Durbin-Watson test statistic. Also displays summary statistics for standardized and unstandardized residuals and predicted values.

❑ **Collinearity diagnostics.** Variance inflation factor (VIF), eigenvalues of the scaled and uncentered cross-products matrix, condition indices, and variance-decomposition proportions (Belsley et al., 1980). Also displays tolerance for variables in the equation; for variables not in the equation, displays the tolerance a variable would have if it were the only variable entered next.

Linear Regression Plots

To obtain scatterplots for variables in the equation, click on Plots... in the Linear Regression dialog box. This opens the Linear Regression Plots dialog box, as shown in Figure 18.54.

Figure 18.54 Linear Regression Plots dialog box

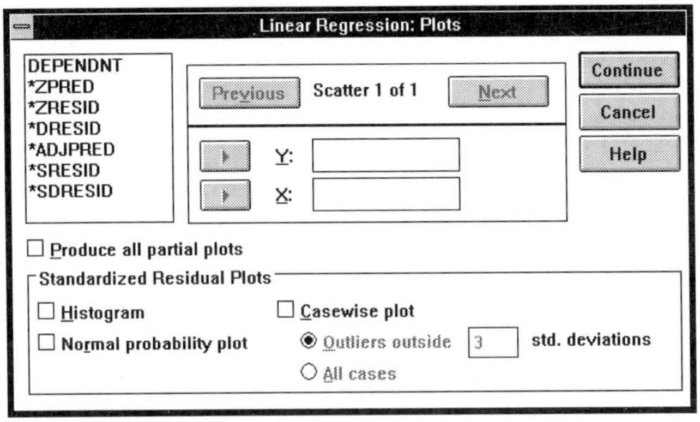

Your dependent variable and the following predicted and residual variables appear on the source list:

- *ZPRED*. Standardized predicted values.
- *ZRESID*. Standardized residuals.
- *DRESID*. Deleted residuals.
- *ADJPRED*. Adjusted predicted values.
- *SRESID*. Studentized residuals.
- *SDRESID*. Studentized deleted residuals.

Select one variable for the vertical (*y*) axis and one variable for the horizontal (*x*) axis. To request additional plots, click on Next and repeat this process. You can specify up to nine scatterplots. All plots are standardized.

Standardized Residual Plots. You can choose one or more of the following:

❑ **Histogram.** Histogram of standardized residuals. A normal curve is superimposed.

❑ **Normal probability plot.** Normal probability $(P - P)$ plot of standardized residuals.

❑ **Casewise plot.** Casewise plot of standardized residuals accompanied by a listing of the values of the dependent and unstandardized predicted (*PRED*) and residual (*RESID*) values. For casewise plots, you can choose one of the following:

    ○ **Outliers outside n std. deviations.** Limits casewise plot to cases with an absolute standardized residual value greater than a specified value. The default value is 3. To override this value, enter a positive standard deviation value. For example, to display cases with residual values of more than 2 standard deviations above or below the mean, enter 2. A plot is not displayed if no case has an absolute standardized residual value greater than the specified value.

○ **All cases.** Includes all cases in the casewise plot.

If any plots are requested, summary statistics are displayed for unstandardized predicted and residual values (*PRED* and *RESID*, respectively) and for standardized predicted and residual values (*ZPRED* and *ZRESID*).

The following option is also available:

❑ **Produce all partial plots.** A partial residual plot is a scatterplot of residuals of the dependent variable and an independent variable when both variables are regressed separately on the rest of the independent variables. Plots are displayed for each independent variable in the equation in descending order of standard errors of regression coefficients. All plots are standardized. At least two independent variables must be in the equation for a partial plot to be produced.

Linear Regression Save New Variables

To save residuals, predicted values, or related measures as new variables, click on Save... in the Linear Regression dialog box. This opens the Linear Regression Save New Variables dialog box, as shown in Figure 18.55.

Figure 18.55 Linear Regression Save New Variables dialog box

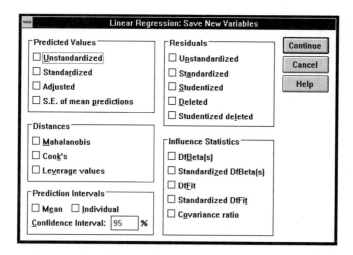

SPSS automatically assigns new variable names for any measures you save as new variables. A table in the output shows the name of each new variable and its contents.

Predicted Values. You can choose one or more of the following:

❏ **Unstandardized.** Unstandardized predicted values.

❏ **Standardized.** Standardized predicted values.

❏ **Adjusted.** Adjusted predicted values.

❏ **S. E. of mean predictions.** Standard errors of the predicted values.

Distances. You can choose one or more of the following:

❏ **Mahalanobis.** Mahalanobis distance.

❏ **Cook's.** Cook's distance.

❏ **Leverage values.** Centered leverage values. (See Velleman & Welsch, 1981.)

Prediction Intervals. You can choose one or both of the following:

❏ **Mean.** Lower and upper bounds for the prediction interval of the mean predicted response. (See Dillon & Goldstein, 1984.)

❏ **Individual.** Lower and upper bounds for the prediction interval for a single observation. (See Dillon & Goldstein, 1984.)

Confidence Interval. For mean and individual confidence intervals, the default is 95%. To override this value, enter a value greater than 0 and less than 100. For example, if you want 99% confidence intervals, enter 99.

Residuals. You can choose one or more of the following:

❏ **Unstandardized.** Unstandardized residuals.

❏ **Standardized.** Standardized residuals.

❏ **Studentized.** Studentized residuals.

❏ **Deleted.** Deleted residuals.

❏ **Studentized deleted.** Studentized deleted residuals. (See Hoaglin & Welsch, 1978.)

Influence Statistics. You can choose one or more of the following:

❏ **DfBeta(s).** The change in the regression coefficient that results from the exclusion of a particular case. A value is computed for each term in the model, including the constant.

❏ **Standardized DfBeta(s).** Standardized DfBeta values. A value is computed for each term in the model, including the constant.

❏ **DfFit.** The change in the predicted value when a particular case is excluded.

❏ **Standardized DfFit.** Standardized DfFit value.

❏ **Covariance ratio.** The ratio of the determinant of the covariance matrix with a particular case excluded to the determinant of the covariance matrix with all cases included.

If you request one or more new variables, summary statistics are displayed for the following measures:

- **ZPRED*. Standardized predicted values.
- **PRED*. Unstandardized predicted values.
- **SEPRED*. Standard errors of the mean predicted values.
- **ADJPRED*. Adjusted predicted values.
- **ZRESID*. Standardized residuals.
- **RESID*. Unstandardized residuals.
- **SRESID*. Studentized residuals.
- **DRESID*. Deleted residuals.
- **SDRESID*. Studentized deleted residuals.
- **MAHAL*. Mahalanobis distances.
- **COOK D*. Cook's distances.
- **LEVER*. Leverages.

Linear Regression Options

To control the criteria by which variables are chosen for entry or removal from the regression model, to suppress the constant term, or to control the handling of cases with missing values, click on Options... in the Linear Regression dialog box. This opens the Linear Regression Options dialog box, as shown in Figure 18.56.

Figure 18.56 Linear Regression Options dialog box

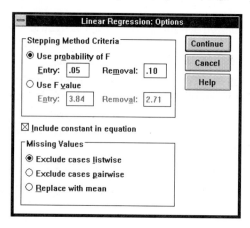

Stepping Method Criteria. The stepping method criteria apply to the forward, backward, and stepwise methods. You can choose one of the following:

○ **Use probability of F.** Use probability of *F*-to-enter (PIN) and probability of *F*-to-remove (POUT) as entry and removal criteria. This is the default. The default entry value is 0.05. The default removal value is 0.10. To override these settings, enter new values. Both values must be greater than 0 and less than or equal to 1, and the entry value must be less than the removal value.

○ **Use F value.** Use *F* values as entry and removal criteria. The default entry value (FIN) is 3.84. The default removal value (FOUT) is 2.71. To override these settings, enter new values. Both values must be greater than 0, and the entry value must be greater than the removal value.

Missing Values. You can choose one of the following:

○ **Exclude cases listwise.** Only cases with valid values for all variables are included in the analyses. This is the default.

○ **Exclude cases pairwise.** Cases with complete data for the pair of variables being correlated are used to compute the correlation coefficient on which the regression analysis is based. Degrees of freedom are based on the minimum pairwise *N*.

○ **Replace with mean.** Replace missing values with the variable mean. All cases are used for computations, with the mean of a variable substituted for missing observations.

The following option is also available:

❑ **Include constant in equation.** Regression model contains a constant term. This is the default. To suppress this term and obtain regression through the origin, deselect this item.

Additional Features Available with Command Syntax

You can customize your regression analysis if you paste your selections to a syntax window and edit the resulting REGRESSION command syntax (see Chapter 4). Additional features include:

- Matrix facility for writing a correlation matrix or for reading a matrix in place of raw data to obtain your regression analysis (with the MATRIX subcommand).
- User-specified tolerance levels (with the CRITERIA subcommand).
- Multiple models for the same or different dependent variables (with the METHOD and DEPENDENT subcommands).
- Additional statistics (with the DESCRIPTIVES and STATISTICS subcommands).

See Appendix A for command syntax rules. See the *SPSS Base System Syntax Reference Guide* for complete REGRESSION command syntax.

19 Curve Estimation

In many situations when you have two related variables, you want to be able to predict the values of one variable from the other. There are many statistical techniques that allow you to model the relationship between the two variables. They range from the very simple—drawing a straight line—to intricate time-series models. In this chapter, you'll see how the Curve Estimation procedure can be used to fit a variety of simple two-variable models. If you are modeling time-series data, you can specify *time* as the independent variable.

Selecting a Model

Whenever you want to summarize the relationship between two variables, the first step should be to plot them. If the plot resembles a mathematical function that you recognize, you can fit it to the data. For example, if your data points cluster around a straight line, a simple linear regression model may be all that is needed. When the data points don't cluster around a straight line, you can try to apply a transformation, such as taking logs of the independent variable, to try to coax the data to linearity. If this doesn't work, you may have to fit a more complicated model.

The Curve Estimation procedure has 11 regression models that you can fit to your data. The equations for these models, as well as the transformed linear models actually used by the procedure, are given in Table 19.1 on p. 374.

If you aren't sure which of these models fits your data best, you can fit several potential models and then select among them. Consider an example.

The Health Care Composite Index

Figure 19.1 is a plot of the values of Standard and Poor's Health Care Composite Index from January 1987 to January 1993. The Health Care Composite Index tracks the values of 26 stocks. From the plot, you see that, overall, the values of the index increased with time, but the points do not cluster around a straight line. Instead, they seem to follow some type of curve. Although the linear model may not be a particularly good choice, we'll fit linear, quadratic, and cubic models to these data to see how the models compare.

Figure 19.1   Plot of Health Care Composite Index over time

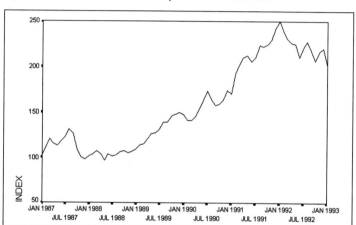

Figure 19.2 contains summary statistics for the three models. The column labeled *Rsq* contains the R^2 for each model. The models are identified in the column labeled *Mth* (for method). The residual degrees of freedom are in the column labeled *d.f.* Since each model estimates a different number of coefficients, the residual degrees of freedom are different for each. The *F* statistic for testing the null hypothesis that all the coefficients in the model are 0 is displayed next, together with its observed significance level (*Sigf*). The coefficients for the models are in the columns labeled *b0, b1, b2*, and *b3*.

Figure 19.2   Summary statistics for curve estimation models

```
Independent:  Time
```

Dependent	Mth	Rsq	d.f.	F	Sigf	b0	b1	b2	b3
INDEX	LIN	.847	71	392.02	.000	80.1320	2.0972		
INDEX	QUA	.875	70	245.27	.000	99.0087	.5870	.0204	
INDEX	CUB	.948	69	418.33	.000	136.221	-5.2498	.2163	-.0018

More detailed output for the cubic model is shown in Figure 19.3. Here you see both the coefficients and their standard errors, as well as observed significance levels and a complete analysis of variance table. See Chapter 18 for further discussion of this output.

Figure 19.3   Detailed statistics and ANOVA table

```
Dependent variable.. INDEX              Method.. CUBIC

Listwise Deletion of Missing Data

Multiple R            .97359
R Square              .94788
Adjusted R Square     .94562
Standard Error      11.27687

             Analysis of Variance:

             DF    SUM OF SQUARES      MEAN SQUARE

REGRESSION    3        159592.64         53197.546
RESIDUALS    69          8774.59          127.168

F =    418.32527     Signif F =   .0000

------------------ Variables in the Equation ------------------

Variable               B        SE B      Beta        T   Sig T

Time            -5.249826    .646586  -2.303398   -8.119  .0000
Time**2           .216262    .020229   7.245640   10.691  .0000
Time**3          -.001764    .000180  -4.137587   -9.815  .0000
(Constant)     136.221223   5.562684              24.488  .0000
```

The linear model has the smallest R^2. This will always be the case when you compare a linear model to the quadratic and cubic models, since the only difference between them is the additional coefficients. The more coefficients you estimate, the better your model will fit the sample data. However, as mentioned in Chapter 18, you don't want a model with unnecessary coefficients. You want to select the cubic model only if it offers significant advantages over the linear or quadratic models. In this example, there is a reasonable increase in R^2 when the cubic term is added to the quadratic model and the cubic coefficient is significantly different from 0, so the cubic model may be the model of choice.

Predicted Values and Residuals

The Curve Estimation procedure allows you to save four new variables for each model you fit. For each case, these variables contain the predicted value, the residual, and the upper and lower 95% confidence limits for the predicted value.

Figure 19.4 shows the new variables created for this example. You see that *fit_1* is the predicted value for the first model, the linear model; *fit_2* is the predicted value for the quadratic model; and *fit_3* is the predicted value for the cubic model. Figure 19.5 is a plot of the observed values and the three fitted models.

Figure 19.4   New variables created for values of fitted models

```
The following new variables are being created:

   Name          Label

   FIT_1         Fit for INDEX from CURVEFIT, MOD_1 LINEAR
   ERR_1         Error for INDEX from CURVEFIT, MOD_1 LINEAR
   LCL_1         95% LCL for INDEX from CURVEFIT, MOD_1 LINEAR
   UCL_1         95% UCL for INDEX from CURVEFIT, MOD_1 LINEAR
   FIT_2         Fit for INDEX from CURVEFIT, MOD_1 QUADRATIC
   ERR_2         Error for INDEX from CURVEFIT, MOD_1 QUADRATIC
   LCL_2         95% LCL for INDEX from CURVEFIT, MOD_1 QUADRATIC
   UCL_2         95% UCL for INDEX from CURVEFIT, MOD_1 QUADRATIC
   FIT_3         Fit for INDEX from CURVEFIT, MOD_1 CUBIC
   ERR_3         Error for INDEX from CURVEFIT, MOD_1 CUBIC
   LCL_3         95% LCL for INDEX from CURVEFIT, MOD_1 CUBIC
   UCL_3         95% UCL for INDEX from CURVEFIT, MOD_1 CUBIC
```

Figure 19.5   Plot of observed values and three fitted models

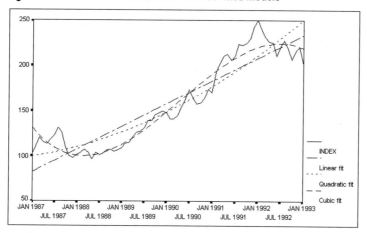

The magnitude of R^2 is only one criterion that is used to see how well a model fits the data. (In fact, you shouldn't use R^2 to compare models if the dependent variable is not in the same units for all of the models.) Examination of the residuals provides very important information about the adequacy of the model.

Consider Figure 19.6, which is a plot of the residuals for the cubic model against time, the independent variable. You see that the residuals do not appear to be randomly distributed about the 0 line. Instead, you see "clumps" of positive and negative residuals. The autocorrelations of the errors are shown in Figure 19.7. You see that the first-order autocorrelation is quite large. This indicates that the cubic model does not fit the data well, since for certain time intervals it always underestimates, while for other intervals it consistently overestimates. In a good model, the residuals don't show any pattern.

Figure 19.6 Residuals for cubic model

Figure 19.7 Autocorrelations for cubic model residuals

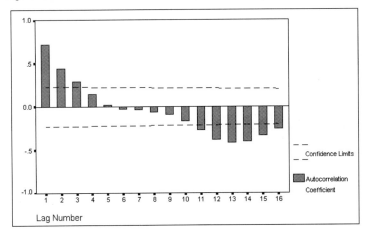

Testing for Normality

You also want to examine the residuals to see if their distribution is normal. You can perform a visual check using the normal probability plot shown in Figure 19.8. If the errors are normally distributed, the values should fall more or less on a straight line. In this example, you see a slight curvature in the plot, suggesting that the distribution is not quite normal.

Figure 19.8 Normal probability plot of cubic residuals

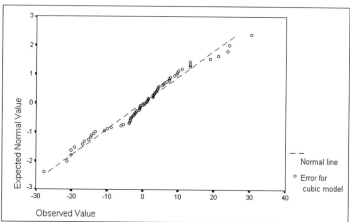

Note that the residuals computed by the Curve Estimation procedure are always in the same units as the original dependent variable. If you fit one of the models in Table 19.1 on p. 374 that transforms the dependent variable, you must examine the residuals for the transformed model, since they must satisfy the regression assumptions. For the Compound, Power, S, Growth, and Exponential models, you can obtain the residuals in the transformed metric by taking the natural log of the observed value minus the natural log of the predicted value. For the Logistic model, calculate the difference between the natural log of the reciprocal of the observed value and the natural log of the reciprocal of the predicted value.

How to Obtain Curve Estimation

The Curve Estimation procedure produces curve estimation regression statistics and related plots for 11 different curve estimation regression models. You can also save predicted values, residuals, and prediction intervals as new variables.

The minimum specifications are:

- One or more dependent variables
- An independent variable that can be either a variable in the working data file or *time*.

To obtain curve estimation regression analysis and related plots, from the menus choose:

Statistics
  Regression ▶
    Curve Estimation...

This opens the Curve Estimation dialog box, as shown in Figure 19.9.

Figure 19.9 Curve Estimation dialog box

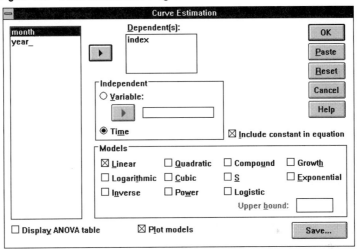

The numeric variables in the working data file are displayed on the source variable list. Select one or more dependent variables and an independent variable and click on OK to obtain the default analysis for the linear model.

If you select Time instead of a variable from the working data file as the independent variable, the dependent variable should be a **time-series** measure. Time-series analysis requires a data file structure in which each case (row) represents a set of observations at a different time and the length of time between cases is uniform.

Models. You can choose one or more curve estimation regression models. At least one model must be selected. The available models and corresponding equations are listed in Table 19.1.

Upper bound. For the Logistic model, you can specify the upper boundary value to use in the regression equation. The value must be a positive number, greater than the largest dependent variable value. If you leave the text box blank, infinity is used as the upper boundary, so that $1/u = 0$ and is dropped from the equation. This is the default.

Table 19.1 Curve Estimation regression models

Model	Equation	Linear Equation
Linear	$Y = b_0 + b_1 t$	
Logarithmic	$Y = b_0 + b_1 ln(t)$	
Inverse	$Y = b_0 + (b_1/t)$	
Quadratic	$Y = b_0 + b_1 t + b_2 t^2$	
Cubic	$Y = b_0 + b_1 t + b_2 t^2 + b_3 t^3$	
Compound	$Y = b_0 (b_1)^t$	$ln(Y) = ln(b_0) + [ln(b_1)]t$
Power	$Y = b_0 (t^{b_1})$	$ln(Y) = ln(b_0) + b_1 ln(t)$
S	$Y = e^{(b_0 + b_1/t)}$	$ln(Y) = b_0 + b_1/t$
Growth	$Y = e^{(b_0 + b_1 t)}$	$ln(Y) = b_0 + b_1 t$
Exponential	$Y = b_0 (e^{b_1 t})$	$ln(Y) = ln(b_0) + b_1 t$
Logistic	$Y = 1/(1/u + b_0 (b_1^t))$	$ln(1/Y - 1/u) = ln(b_0) + [ln(b_1)]t$

where

b_0 = a constant
b_n = regression coefficient
t= a time value or the value of an independent variable
ln= natural log (base e)
e= the natural log base
u= upperbound value for the logistic model

The following options are also available:

❏ **Include constant in equation.** Estimates a constant term in the regression equation. The constant is included by default. Deselect this item to remove the constant term.

❏ **Display ANOVA table.** Displays a summary analysis-of-variance table for each selected model.

❑ **Plot models**. Plots the values of the dependent variable and each selected model against the independent variable. A separate chart is produced for each dependent variable. Selected by default. Deselect this item to suppress the charts.

Saving Predicted Values and Residuals

To save predicted values, residuals, and prediction intervals as new variables, click on Save... in the Curve Estimation dialog box. This opens the Curve Estimation Save dialog box, similar to the one shown in Figure 19.10.

Figure 19.10 Curve Estimation Save dialog box

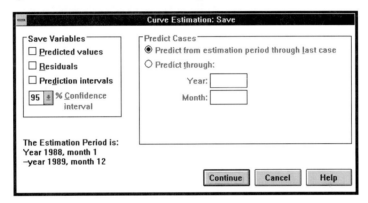

Save Variables. You can choose one or more of the following:

❑ **Predicted values**. Saves the predicted values for each selected model.

❑ **Residuals**. Saves the residuals (actual value of the dependent variable minus the model predicted value) for each selected model.

❑ **Prediction intervals**. Saves the upper and lower bounds (two variables) for the prediction interval of each case for each selected model.

⬇ **Confidence interval**. Confidence interval for the prediction intervals. You can select 90, 95, or 99% from the drop-down list. The default is 95%.

The new variable names and descriptive labels are displayed in a table in the output window.

Predict Cases. If you select Time instead of a variable in the working data file as the independent variable, you can specify a forecast period beyond the end of the time series. You can choose one of the following alternatives:

○ **Predict from estimation period through last case.** Predicts values for all cases in the file, based on the cases in the estimation period. The estimation period, displayed at the bottom of the dialog box, is defined with the Range subdialog box of the Select Cases option on the Data menu (see Chapter 5). If no estimation period has been defined, all cases are used to predict values. This is the default.

○ **Predict through.** Predicts values through the specified date, time, or observation number, based on the cases in the estimation period. This can be used to forecast values beyond the last case in the time series. The available text boxes for specifying the end of the prediction period are dependent on the currently defined date variables. If there are no defined date variables, you can specify the ending observation (case) number.

Use the Define Dates option on the Data menu to create date variables. See Chapter 5 for more information, including valid ranges for each date variable.

20 Distribution-Free or Nonparametric Tests

Broccoli and Brussels sprouts have recently joined coffee, carrots, red meat, oat bran, saccharin, tobacco, and alcohol on the ever-expanding list of substances thought to contribute to the development or prevention of cancer. This list is necessarily tentative and complicated. The two major sources of evidence—experiments on animals and examination of the histories of people with cancer—are problematic. It is difficult to predict, based on the results of giving large doses of suspect substances to small animals, the consequences for humans of consuming small amounts over a long time span.

In studies of people, lifestyle components are difficult to isolate, and it is challenging—if not impossible—to unravel the contribution of a single factor. For example, what conclusions may be drawn about the role of caffeine, based on a sample of overweight, sedentary, coffee- and alcohol-drinking, cigarette-smoking urban dwellers?

In addition to certain lifestyle factors, dietary fat is thought to play an important role in the development and progression of cancer. Wynder (1976) showed that the per capita consumption of dietary fats is positively correlated with the incidence of breast and colon cancer in humans. In another study, King et al. (1979) examined the relationship between diet and tumor growth in rats. Three groups of animals of the same age, species, and physical condition were injected with tumor cells. The rats were divided into three groups and fed diets of either low, saturated, or unsaturated fat.

One hypothesis of interest is whether the length of time it takes for tumors to develop differs in two of the groups—rats fed saturated fats and rats fed unsaturated fats. If we assume a normal distribution of the tumor-free time, the independent-samples t test (described in Chapter 13) can be used to test the hypothesis that the population means are equal. However, if the distribution of times does not appear to be normal, and especially if the sample sizes are small, we should consider statistical procedures that do not require assumptions about the shape of the underlying distribution.

The Mann-Whitney Test

The **Mann-Whitney test,** also known as the Wilcoxon test, does not require assumptions about the shape of the underlying distributions. It tests the hypothesis that two independent samples come from populations having the same distribution. The form of

377

the distribution need not be specified. The test does not require that the variable be measured on an interval scale; an ordinal scale is sufficient.

Ranking the Data

To compute the test, the observations from both samples are first combined and ranked from smallest to largest value. Consider Table 20.1, which shows a sample of the King data reported by Lee (1992). Case 4 has the shortest elapsed time to development of a tumor: 68 days. It is assigned a rank of 1. Case 3 has the next shortest time (81), so it is assigned a rank of 2. Cases 5 and 6 both exhibited tumors after 112 days. They are both assigned a rank of 3.5, the average of the ranks (3 and 4) for which they are tied. Case 2, with the next longest elapsed time (126 days), is given a rank of 5, and case 1, with the longest elapsed time (199 days), is given a rank of 6.

Table 20.1 Ranking the data

Saturated			Unsaturated		
Case	Time	Rank	Case	Time	Rank
1	199	6	4	68	1
2	126	5	5	112	3.5
3	81	2	6	112	3.5

Calculating the Test

The statistic for testing the hypothesis that the two distributions are equal is the sum of the ranks for each of the two groups. If the groups have the same distribution, their sample distributions of ranks should be similar. If one of the groups has more than its share of small or large ranks, there is reason to suspect that the two underlying distributions are different.

Figure 20.1 shows the output from the Mann-Whitney test for the complete King data. For each group, the mean rank and number of cases is given. (The mean rank is the sum of the ranks divided by the number of cases.) Note that the saturated-fats group has only 29 cases, since one rat died of causes unrelated to the experiment. The number (963) displayed under W is the sum of the ranks for the group with the smaller number of observations. If both groups have the same number of observations, W is the rank sum for the group named first in the Two-Independent-Samples Define Groups dialog box (see Figure 20.23). In this example, the value of W is 963, the sum of the ranks for the saturated-fats group.

Figure 20.1 Mann-Whitney output

```
- - - - - Mann-Whitney U - Wilcoxon Rank Sum W Test

       TUMOR
  by DIET

    Mean Rank    Cases
       26.90        30  DIET = 0  UNSATURATED
       33.21        29  DIET = 1  SATURATED
                    --
                    59  Total

                                   Corrected for ties
         U              W            Z      2-Tailed P
       342.0          963.0      -1.4112       .1582
```

The number (342) identified in the output as U represents the number of times a value in the unsaturated-fats group precedes a value in the saturated-fats group. To understand what this means, consider again the data in Table 20.1. All three cases in the unsaturated-fats group have smaller ranks than the first case in the saturated-fats group, so they all precede case 1 in the rankings. Similarly, all three cases in the unsaturated-fats group precede case 2. Only one unsaturated-fats case (case 4) is smaller in value than case 3. Thus, the number of times the value for an unsaturated-fats case precedes the value for a saturated-fats case is $3 + 3 + 1 = 7$. The number of times the value of a saturated-fats case precedes the value of an unsaturated-fats case is 2, since case 3 has a smaller rank than both cases 5 and 6. The smaller of these two numbers is displayed in the output as U. If the two distributions are equal, values from one group should not consistently precede values in the other.

The significance levels associated with U and W are the same. They can be obtained by transforming the score to a standard normal deviate (Z). If the total sample size is less than 30, an exact probability level based on the distribution of the score is also displayed. From Figure 20.1, the observed significance level for this example is 0.158. Since the significance level is large, the hypothesis that tumor-free time has the same distribution for the two diet groups is not rejected.

Which Diet?

You should not conclude from these findings that it doesn't matter—as far as tumors are concerned—what kind of fat you (or rats) eat. King et al. found that rats fed the unsaturated diet had a total of 96 tumors at the end of the experiment, while rats fed the saturated diet had only 55 tumors. They also found that large tumors were more common in the unsaturated-diet group than in the saturated-diet group. Thus, unsaturated fats may be more hazardous than saturated fats.

Assumptions

The Mann-Whitney test requires only that the sample be random and that values can be ordered. These assumptions—especially randomness—should not be made lightly, but they are less restrictive than those for the two-sample t test for means. The t test requires further that the observations be selected from approximately normally distributed populations with equal variances.

Since the Mann-Whitney test can always be calculated instead of the t test, what determines which should be used? If the assumptions needed for the t test are met, the t test is more powerful than the Mann-Whitney test. That is, the t test will detect true differences between the two populations more often than the Mann-Whitney test, since the t test uses more information from the data. Substituting ranks for the actual values eliminates potentially useful information. On the other hand, using the t test when its assumptions are substantially violated may result in an erroneous observed significance level.

In general, if the assumptions of the t test appear to be reasonable, it should be used. When the data are ordinal—or interval but from a markedly non-normal distribution—the Mann-Whitney test is the procedure of choice.

Nonparametric Tests

Like the Mann-Whitney test, many statistical procedures require limited distributional assumptions about the data. Collectively, these procedures are termed **distribution-free tests** or **nonparametric tests**. Like the Mann-Whitney test, distribution-free tests are generally less powerful than their parametric counterparts. They are most useful in situations where parametric procedures are not appropriate—for example, when the data are nominal or ordinal, or when interval data are from markedly non-normal distributions. Significance levels for certain nonparametric tests can be determined regardless of the shape of the population distribution, since they are based on ranks.

In the following sections, various nonparametric tests will be used to analyze some of the data described in previous chapters. Since the data were chosen to illustrate parametric procedures, they satisfy assumptions that are more restrictive than those required for nonparametric procedures. However, using the same data provides an opportunity to learn new procedures easily and to compare results obtained from different types of analyses.

One-Sample Tests

Various one-sample nonparametric procedures are available for testing hypotheses about the parameters of a population. These include procedures for examining differences in paired samples.

The Sign Test

In Chapter 16, the paired *t* test for means is used to test the hypothesis that mean buying scores for husbands and wives are equal. Remember that this test requires the assumption that differences are normally distributed.

The **sign test** is a nonparametric procedure used with two related samples to test the hypothesis that the distributions of two variables are the same. This test makes no assumptions about the shape of these distributions.

To compute the sign test, the difference between the buying scores of husbands and wives is calculated for each case. Next, the numbers of positive and negative differences are obtained. If the distributions of the two variables are the same, the numbers of positive and negative differences should be similar.

The output in Figure 20.2 shows that the number of negative differences is 56, while the number of positive differences is 39. The total number of cases is 98, including three with no differences. The observed significance level is 0.1007. Since this value is large, the hypothesis that the distributions are the same is not rejected.

Figure 20.2   Sign test

```
- - - - - Sign Test

      HSSCALE    HUSBAND SELF SCALE
with  WSSCALE    WIFE SELF SCALE


          Cases

          56   - Diffs (WSSCALE LT HSSCALE)              Z =    1.6416
          39   + Diffs (WSSCALE GT HSSCALE)
           3     Ties                        2-Tailed P =     .1007
         ---
          98     Total
```

The Wilcoxon Signed-Rank Test

The sign test uses only the direction of the differences between the pairs and ignores the magnitude. A discrepancy of 15 between husbands' and wives' buying scores is treated in the same way as a discrepancy of 1. The **Wilcoxon signed-rank test** incorporates information about the magnitude of the differences and is therefore more powerful than the sign test.

To compute the Wilcoxon signed-rank test, the differences are ranked without considering the signs. In the case of ties, average ranks are assigned. The sums of the ranks for positive and negative differences are then calculated.

As shown in Figure 20.3, the average rank of the 56 negative differences is 45.25. The average positive rank is 51.95. In the row labeled *Ties*, there are three cases with the same value for both variables. The observed significance level associated with the test is large (0.3458), and once again the hypothesis of no difference is not rejected.

Figure 20.3   Wilcoxon signed-rank test

```
- - - - - Wilcoxon Matched-Pairs Signed-Ranks Test

        HSSCALE    HUSBAND SELF SCALE
with WSSCALE    WIFE SELF SCALE


    Mean Rank    Cases
        45.25       56   - Ranks (WSSCALE LT HSSCALE)
        51.95       39   + Ranks (WSSCALE GT HSSCALE)
                     3    Ties  (WSSCALE EQ HSSCALE)
                   ---
                    98    Total

      Z =    -.9428              2-Tailed P =  .3458
```

The Wald-Wolfowitz Runs Test

The runs test is a test of randomness. That is, given a sequence of observations, the runs test examines whether the value of one observation influences the values for later observations. If there is no influence (the observations are independent), the sequence is considered random.

A **run** is any sequence of like observations. For example, if a coin is tossed 15 times and the outcomes recorded, the following sequence might result:

HHHTHHHHTTTTTTT

There are four runs in this sequence: HHH, T, HHHH, and TTTTTTT. The total number of runs is a measure of randomness, since too many runs, or too few, suggest dependence between observations. The **Wald-Wolfowitz runs test** converts the total number of runs into a Z statistic having approximately a normal distribution. The only requirement for this test is that the variable tested be dichotomous (have only two possible values).

Suppose, for example, that a weather forecaster records whether it snows for 20 days in February and obtains the following sequence (1=snow, 0=no snow):

01111111010111111100

To test the hypothesis that the occurrence or nonoccurrence of snow on one day has no effect on whether it snows on later days, the runs test is performed, resulting in the output shown in Figure 20.4.

Figure 20.4   Runs test

```
- - - - - Runs Test

     SNOW

         Runs:      7           Test Value = 1

         Cases:     5    Lt 1
                   15    Ge 1              Z =   -.6243
                   --
                   20    Total 2-tailed P =    .5324
```

Since the observed significance level is quite large (0.5324), the hypothesis of random-ness is not rejected. It does not appear, from these data, that snowy (or nonsnowy) days affect the later occurrence of snow.

The Binomial Test

With data that are binomially distributed, the hypothesis that the probability p of a par-ticular outcome is equal to some number is often of interest. For example, you might want to find out if a tossed coin was unbiased. To check this, you could test to see wheth-er the probability of heads was equal to 1/2. The **binomial test** compares the observed frequencies in each category of a binomial distribution to the frequencies expected un-der a binomial distribution with the probability parameter p.

For example, a nickel is tossed 20 times, with the following results (1=heads, 0=tails):

10011111101111011011

The output in Figure 20.5 shows a binomial test of the hypothesis that the probability of heads equals 1/2 for these data.

Figure 20.5   Binomial test

```
- - - - - Binomial Test

     HEADS

     Cases
                               Test Prop. =    .5000
            5    = 0           Obs. Prop. =    .2500
           15    = 1
           --                 Exact Binomial
           20    Total        2-tailed P =    .0414
```

The test proportion of cases for the first value (0) is 0.5000 and the observed proportion is 0.2500; that is, 1/4 of the actual tosses were tails. The small (0.0414) observed significance level indicates that it is not likely that p equals 1/2 and it appears that the coin is biased.

The Kolmogorov-Smirnov One-Sample Test

The **Kolmogorov-Smirnov test** is used to determine how well a random sample of data fits a particular distribution (uniform, normal, or Poisson). It is based on comparison of the sample cumulative distribution function to the hypothetical cumulative distribution function.

Suppose we are analyzing the data from an evaluation of 35 beers. The beers were rated on overall quality and a variety of other attributes, such as price, calories, sodium, and alcohol content. We can use the Kolmogorov-Smirnov one-sample test to see whether it is reasonable to assume that the *alcohol* variable is normally distributed. The Kolmogorov-Smirnov output in Figure 20.6 shows an observed significance level of 0.05, small enough to cast doubt on the assumption of normality.

Figure 20.6   Kolmogorov-Smirnov test

```
- - - - - Kolmogorov - Smirnov Goodness of Fit Test

    ALCOHOL    ALCOHOL BY VOLUME (IN %)


    Test Distribution  -  Normal                Mean:  4.577
                                   Standard Deviation:   .603

          Cases:  35

            Most Extreme Differences
      Absolute        Positive        Negative         K-S Z      2-tailed P
      0.22940         0.15585         -0.22940         1.357         0.050
```

The One-Sample Chi-Square Test

In Chapter 7, frequencies of deaths for the days of the week are examined. The output suggests that all days of the week are equally hazardous in regard to death. To test this conclusion, the one-sample chi-square test can be used. This nonparametric test requires only that the data be a random sample.

To calculate the one-sample chi-square statistic, the data are first classified into mutually exclusive categories of interest—days of the week in this example—and then expected frequencies for these categories are computed. Expected frequencies are the frequencies that would be expected if the null hypothesis is true. For the death data, the hypothesis to be tested is that the probability of death is the same for each day of the week. The day of death is known for 110 subjects. The hypothesis implies that the expected frequency of deaths for each weekday is $110/7$, or 15.71. Once the expected frequencies are obtained, the chi-square statistic is computed as

$$\chi^2 = \sum_{i=1}^{k} \frac{(O_i - E_i)^2}{E_i}$$

Equation 20.1

where O_i is the observed frequency for the ith category, E_i is the expected frequency for the ith category, and k is the number of categories.

If the null hypothesis is true, the chi-square statistic has approximately a chi-square distribution with $k - 1$ degrees of freedom. This statistic will be large if the observed and expected frequencies are substantially different. Figure 20.7 shows the output from the one-sample chi-square test for the death data. The observed chi-square value is 3.4, and the associated significance level is 0.757. Since the observed significance level is large, the hypothesis that deaths are evenly distributed over days of the week is not rejected.

Figure 20.7   One-sample chi-square test

```
- - - - - Chi-square Test

    DAYOFWK    DAY OF DEATH

                                Cases
                     Category  Observed  Expected  Residual

        SUNDAY          1         19      15.71      3.29
        MONDAY          2         11      15.71     -4.71
        TUESDAY         3         19      15.71      3.29
        WEDNESDAY       4         17      15.71      1.29
        THURSDAY        5         15      15.71      -.71
        FRIDAY          6         13      15.71     -2.71
        SATURDAY        7         16      15.71       .29
                                 ---
                     Total       110

        Chi-Square            D.F.           Significance
          3.400                 6                .757
```

The Friedman Test

The **Friedman test** is used to compare two or more related samples. (This is an extension of the tests for paired data.) The k variables to be compared are ranked from 1 to k for each case, and the mean ranks for the variables are calculated and compared, resulting in a test statistic with approximately a chi-square distribution.

The Friedman test can be used to analyze data from a psychology experiment concerned with memory. In this experiment, subjects were asked to memorize first a two-digit number, then a three-digit number, and finally a four-digit number. After each number was memorized, they were shown a single digit and asked if that digit was present in the number memorized. The times taken to reach a decision for the two-, three-, and four-digit numbers are the three related variables of interest.

Figure 20.8 shows the results of the Friedman test, examining the hypothesis that the number of digits memorized has no effect on the time taken to reach a decision. The observed significance level is extremely small, so it appears that the number of digits does affect decision time.

Figure 20.8   Friedman test

```
- - - - - Friedman Two-way ANOVA


    Mean Rank    Variable

        1.21     P2DIGIT
        2.13     P3DIGIT
        2.67     P4DIGIT

        Cases        Chi-Square        D.F.   Significance
         24           26.0833            2         .0000
```

Tests for Two or More Independent Samples

A variety of nonparametric tests involve comparisons between two or more independent samples. (The Mann-Whitney test is one such test.) In this respect, these tests resemble the *t* tests and one-way analyses of variance described in Chapter 13 and Chapter 14.

The Two-Sample Median Test

The **two-sample median test** is used to determine whether two populations have the same median. The two samples are combined and the median for the total distribution is calculated. The number of observations above this median, as well as the number of observations less than or equal to this median, is counted for each sample. The test statistic is based on these counts.

This test can be used to determine whether median sodium levels are the same for the highest-rated and lowest-rated beers in the beer data described earlier. The output in Figure 20.9 shows the largest possible *p* value, 1. Therefore, there is no reason to suspect different medians.

Figure 20.9   Median test of sodium by rating

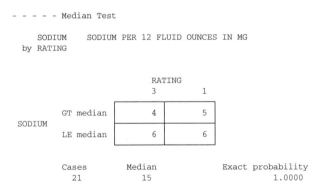

```
- - - - - Median Test

      SODIUM    SODIUM PER 12 FLUID OUNCES IN MG
   by RATING


                              RATING
                              3         1

                GT median     4         5
      SODIUM
                LE median     6         6


        Cases         Median            Exact probability
         21             15                    1.0000
```

The Two-Sample Wald-Wolfowitz Runs Test

A runs test can be used to test the hypothesis that two samples come from populations with the same distributions. To perform this test, the two samples are combined and the values are sorted. A run in this combined and sorted sample consists of a sequence of values belonging to the first sample or a sequence of values belonging to the second sample. If there are too few runs, it suggests that the two populations have different distributions.

The Wald-Wolfowitz test can be used with the beer data to compare calories for the highest-ranked and lowest-ranked beers. The output in Figure 20.10 shows an observed significance level of 0.0119. Since this is small, the distribution of calories for the highest-ranked beers appears to differ from the distribution of calories for the lowest-ranked beers.

Figure 20.10 Wald-Wolfowitz runs test

```
- - - - - Wald-Wolfowitz Runs Test

      CALORIES   CALORIES PER 12 FLUID OUNCES
   by RATING


         Cases

            10  RATING = 3  FAIR
            11  RATING = 1  VERY GOOD
            --
            21  Total
                                          Exact
                        Runs        Z   1-tailed P
      Minimum Possible:    6    -2.2335     .0119
      Maximum Possible:    6    -2.2335     .0119

      WARNING -- There are   1 Inter-group Ties involving    5 cases.
```

The Two-Sample Kolmogorov-Smirnov Test

The Kolmogorov-Smirnov test for two samples provides another method for testing whether two samples come from populations with the same distributions. It is based on a comparison of the distribution functions for the two samples.

This test can be used with the beer data to compare the alcohol content of the highest-ranked and lowest-ranked beers. Since the observed significance level in Figure 20.11 is small, the alcohol distributions do not appear to be the same. The approximation used to obtain the observed significance level may be inadequate in this case, however, because of the small sample size.

Figure 20.11 Kolmogorov-Smirnov two-sample test

```
- - - - - Kolmogorov - Smirnov 2-Sample Test

    ALCOHOL    ALCOHOL BY VOLUME (IN %)
  by RATING


      Cases

      10  RATING = 3  FAIR
      11  RATING = 1  VERY GOOD
      --
      21  Total

WARNING - Due to small sample size, probability tables should be consulted.

           Most Extreme Differences
     Absolute        Positive        Negative        K-S Z      2-tailed P
     0.60000         0.0            -0.60000         1.373         0.046
```

The K-Sample Median Test

An extension of the two-sample median test, the **k-sample median test** compares the medians of three or more independent samples. Figure 20.12 shows a *k*-sample median test comparing median prices for the highest-, middle-, and lowest-quality beers. The observed significance level is fairly large (0.091), indicating no real difference in the median price of the three types of beer.

Figure 20.12 K-sample median test

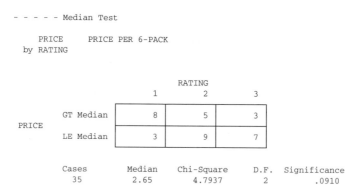

```
- - - - - Median Test

    PRICE     PRICE PER 6-PACK
  by RATING
```

		RATING		
		1	2	3
PRICE	GT Median	8	5	3
	LE Median	3	9	7

```
      Cases       Median     Chi-Square    D.F.   Significance
       35          2.65        4.7937        2         .0910
```

The Kruskal-Wallis Test

The experiment described at the beginning of this chapter investigates the effects of three diets on tumor development. The Mann-Whitney test was calculated to examine possible differences between saturated and unsaturated diets. To test for differences among all three diets, an extension of the Mann-Whitney test can be used. This test is known as the **Kruskal-Wallis one-way analysis of variance**.

The procedure for computing the Kruskal-Wallis test is similar to the procedure used in the Mann-Whitney test. All cases from the three groups are combined and ranked. Average ranks are assigned in the case of ties. For each group, the ranks are summed, and the Kruskal-Wallis H statistic is computed from these sums. The H statistic has approximately a chi-square distribution under the hypothesis that the three groups have the same distribution.

The output in Figure 20.13 shows that the third group, the low-fat-diet group, has the largest average rank. The value of the Kruskal-Wallis statistic is 11.1257. When the statistic is adjusted for the presence of ties, the value changes to 11.2608. The small observed significance level suggests that the time interval until development of a tumor is not the same for all three groups.

Figure 20.13 Kruskal-Wallis one-way analysis of variance output

```
- - - - - Kruskal-Wallis 1-way ANOVA

        TUMOR
    by DIET


    Mean Rank    Cases

        34.12        30     DIET = 0     UNSATURATED
        43.50        29     DIET = 1     SATURATED
        56.24        29     DIET = 2     LOW-FAT
                     --
                     88     Total

                                              Corrected for Ties
        CASES    Chi-Square  Significance    Chi-Square  Significance
         88        11.1257        0.0038       11.2608        0.0036
```

How to Obtain the Chi-Square Test

The Chi-Square Test procedure tabulates a variable into categories and computes a chi-square statistic based on the differences between observed and expected frequencies.

The minimum specification is one or more numeric variables.

To obtain the chi-square test, from the menus choose:

Statistics
  Nonparametric Tests ▶
    Chi-Square...

This opens the Chi-Square Test dialog box, as shown in Figure 20.14.

Figure 20.14 Chi-Square Test dialog box

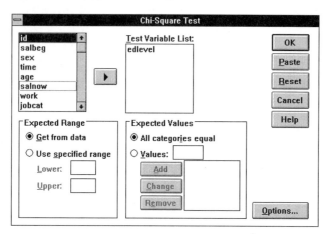

The numeric variables in your data file appear on the source variable list. Select one or more test variables, and click on OK to obtain the default chi-square test using equal expected frequencies for each observed category of your variable(s). (See Figure 20.7.) Each variable produces a separate test. To obtain chi-square tests of the relationship between two or more variables, use the Crosstabs procedure (see Chapter 10).

Expected Range. You can choose one of the following alternatives:

○ **Get from data.** Each distinct value encountered is defined as a category. This is the default.

○ **Use specified range.** Enter integer values for lower and upper bounds. Categories are established for each value within the inclusive range, and cases with values outside the bounds are excluded. For example, if you specify a lowerbound value of 1 and an upperbound value of 4, only the integer values of 1 through 4 are used for the chi-square test. The lowerbound value must be less than the upperbound value, and both values must be specified.

Expected Values. You can choose one of the following alternatives:

○ **All categories equal.** All categories have equal expected values. This is the default.

○ **Values.** Categories have user-specified expected proportions. Enter a value greater than 0 for each category of the test variable, and click on Add. Each time you add a value, it appears at the bottom of the value list. The sequential order of the values is important, since it corresponds to the ascending order of the category values of the test variable. The first value on the list corresponds to the lowest group value of the test variable, and the last value corresponds to the highest value. Elements of the value list are summed, and then each value is divided by this sum to calculate the proportion of cases expected in the corresponding category. For example, a value list of 3, 4, 5, 4 specifies expected proportions of $3/16$, $4/16$, $5/16$, and $4/16$ for categories 1, 2, 3, and 4, respectively. To remove a value, highlight it on the list and click on Remove. To change a value, highlight it, enter a new value, and click on Change.

Chi-Square Test Options

To obtain optional summary statistics or to modify the treatment of cases with missing values, click on Options... in the Chi-Square Test dialog box. This opens the Chi-Square Test Options dialog box, as shown in Figure 20.15.

Figure 20.15 Chi-Square Test Options dialog box

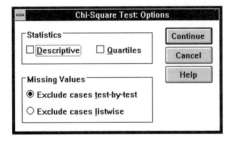

Statistics. You can choose one or both of the following summary statistics:

❑ **Descriptive.** Displays the mean, minimum, maximum, standard deviation, and the number of nonmissing cases.

❑ **Quartiles.** Displays values corresponding to the 25th, 50th, and 75th percentiles.

Missing Values. You can choose one of the following alternatives:

○ **Exclude cases test-by-test.** When several tests are specified, each test is evaluated separately for missing values. This is the default.

○ **Exclude cases listwise.** Cases with missing values for any variable are excluded from all analyses.

Additional Features Available with Command Syntax

You can customize your one-sample chi-square test if you paste your selections into a syntax window and edit the resulting NPAR TESTS command syntax (see Chapter 4). Additional features include:

- Specification of different minimum and maximum values or expected frequencies for different variables (with the CHISQUARE subcommand).
- Tests of the same variable against different expected frequencies or using different ranges (with the EXPECTED subcommand).

See Appendix A for command syntax rules. See the *SPSS Base System Syntax Reference Guide* for complete NPAR TESTS command syntax.

How to Obtain the Binomial Test

The Binomial Test procedure compares the observed frequency in each category of a dichotomous variable with expected frequencies from the binomial distribution.

The minimum specification is one or more numeric variables.

To obtain the binomial test, from the menus choose:

Statistics
  Nonparametric Tests ▶
    Binomial...

This opens the Binomial Test dialog box, as shown in Figure 20.16.

Figure 20.16 Binomial Test dialog box

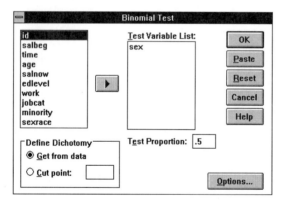

The numeric variables in your data file appear on the source variable list. Select one or more test variables to use in the binomial test. If your variables are dichotomous, you can click on OK to obtain the default binomial test using equal probabilities for each group. Otherwise, you must specify a cut point.

Define Dichotomy. You can choose one of the following alternatives:

○ **Get from data.** Assigns cases with the lower category of a dichotomous variable to one group and cases with the higher category to the other group. This is the default.

○ **Cut point.** User-specified cut point. Assigns cases with values less than the cut point to one group and cases with values equal to or greater than the cut point to the other group.

Test Proportion. The default null hypothesis is that the data are from a binomial distribution with a probability of 0.5 for both groups. To change the probabilities, enter a test proportion for the first group. For example, specifying .25 tests the null hypothesis that the data are from a binomial distribution with a probability of 0.25 for the first value and 0.75 for the second value. The value you specify must be between .001 and .999 and cannot include leading zeros.

Binomial Test Options

To get optional summary statistics or to modify the treatment of cases with missing values, click on Options... in the Binomial Test dialog box. This opens the Binomial Test Options dialog box, as shown in Figure 20.17.

Figure 20.17 Binomial Test Options dialog box

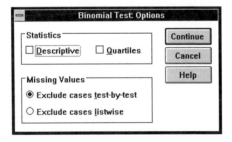

Statistics. You can choose one or both of the following summary statistics:

❏ **Descriptive.** Displays the mean, minimum, maximum, standard deviation, and the number of nonmissing cases.

❏ **Quartiles.** Displays values corresponding to the 25th, 50th, and 75th percentiles.

Missing Values. You can choose one of the following alternatives:

○ **Exclude cases test-by-test.** When several tests are specified, each test is evaluated separately for missing values. This is the default.

○ **Exclude cases listwise.** Cases with missing values for any variable are excluded from all analyses.

Additional Features Available with Command Syntax

You can customize your binomial test if you paste your selections into a syntax window and edit the resulting NPAR TESTS command syntax (see Chapter 4). Additional features include:

- Selection of specific groups (and exclusion of others) when a variable has more than two categories (with the BINOMIAL subcommand).
- Different cut points or probabilities for different variables (with the BINOMIAL subcommand).
- Tests of the same variable against different cut points or probabilities (with the EXPECTED subcommand).

See Appendix A for command syntax rules. See the *SPSS Base System Syntax Reference Guide* for complete NPAR TESTS command syntax.

How to Obtain the Runs Test

The Runs Test procedure tests whether the order of occurrence of two values of a variable is random. A **run** is defined as a sequence of one of the values that is preceded and followed by the other data value (or the end of the series). For example, the sequence

1 1 | 0 0 0 | 1 | 0 0 0 0 | 1 1 | 0 | 1|

contains seven runs (vertical bars separate the runs). For a sample of a given size, very many or very few runs suggest that the sample is not random. The Z statistic, which has an approximately normal distribution, is computed.

The minimum specification is one or more numeric variables.

To obtain the runs test, from the menus choose:

Statistics
  Nonparametric Tests ▶
    Runs...

This opens the Runs Test dialog box, as shown in Figure 20.18.

Figure 20.18 Runs Test dialog box

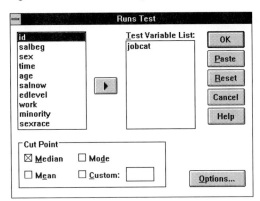

The numeric variables in your data file appear on the source variable list. Select one or more test variables, and click on OK to obtain the default runs test using the median to dichotomize your variable(s).

Cut Point. Assigns cases with values less than the cut point to one group and cases with values equal to or greater than the cut point to the other group. You must select at least one cut point, and one test is performed for each cut point chosen.

You can choose one or more of the following:

❏ **Median.** The observed median is the cut point. This is the default.

❏ **Mean.** The observed mean is the cut point.

❏ **Mode.** The observed mode is the cut point.

❏ **Custom.** User-specified cut point. For example, if the variable has values of 0 and 1, enter 1 as the cut point.

Runs Test Options

To get optional summary statistics or to modify the treatment of cases with missing values, click on Options... in the Runs Test dialog box. This opens the Runs Test Options dialog box, as shown in Figure 20.19.

Figure 20.19 Runs Test Options dialog box

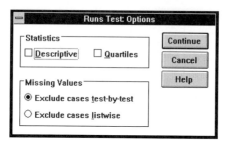

Statistics. You can choose one or both of the following summary statistics:

❑ **Descriptive.** Displays the mean, minimum, maximum, standard deviation, and the number of nonmissing cases.

❑ **Quartiles.** Displays values corresponding to the 25th, 50th, and 75th percentiles.

Missing Values. You can choose one of the following alternatives:

○ **Exclude cases test-by-test.** When several tests are specified, each test is evaluated separately for missing values. This is the default.

○ **Exclude cases listwise.** Cases with missing values for any variable are excluded from all analyses.

Additional Features Available with Command Syntax

You can customize your runs test if you paste your selections into a syntax window and edit the resulting NPAR TESTS command syntax (see Chapter 4). Additional features include:

• Different cut points for different variables (with the RUNS subcommand).

• Tests of the same variable against different custom cut points (with the RUNS subcommand).

See Appendix A for command syntax rules. See the *SPSS Base System Syntax Reference Guide* for complete NPAR TESTS command syntax.

How to Obtain the One-Sample Kolmogorov-Smirnov Test

The One-Sample Kolmogorov-Smirnov Test procedure compares the observed cumulative distribution function for a variable with a specified theoretical distribution, which may be normal, uniform, or Poisson. The Kolmogorov-Smirnov Z is computed from the largest difference (in absolute value) between the observed and theoretical distribution functions.

The minimum specification is one or more numeric variables.

To obtain the one-sample Kolmogorov-Smirnov test, from the menus choose:

Statistics
  Nonparametric Tests ▶
    1-Sample K-S...

This opens the One-Sample Kolmogorov-Smirnov Test dialog box, as shown in Figure 20.20.

Figure 20.20 One-Sample Kolmogorov-Smirnov Test dialog box

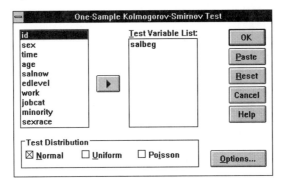

The numeric variables in your data file appear on the source variable list. Select at least one test variable, and click on OK to obtain the default (Kolmogorov-Smirnov) test using the normal distribution. Each variable produces a separate test.

Test Distribution. At least one test distribution must be selected. You can choose one or more of the following:

❏ **Normal.** The observed mean and standard deviation are the parameters. This is the default.

❏ **Uniform.** The observed minimum and maximum values define the range of the distribution.

❏ **Poisson.** The observed mean is the parameter.

Tests produced by Kolmogorov-Smirnov assume that the parameters of the test distribution are specified *in advance*. When the parameters of the test distribution are estimated from the sample, the distribution of the test statistic changes. Tests for normality that make this correction are available using the Explore procedure (see Chapter 9). See also "Additional Features Available with Command Syntax," below.

One-Sample Kolmogorov-Smirnov Options

To obtain optional summary statistics or to modify the treatment of cases with missing values, click on Options... in the One-Sample Kolmogorov-Smirnov Test dialog box. This opens the One-Sample K-S Options dialog box, as shown in Figure 20.21.

Figure 20.21 One-Sample K-S Options dialog box

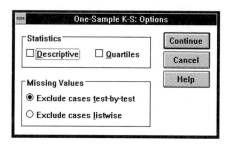

Statistics. You can choose one or both of the following summary statistics:

❑ **Descriptive.** Displays the mean, minimum, maximum, standard deviation, and the number of nonmissing cases.

❑ **Quartiles.** Displays values corresponding to the 25th, 50th, and 75th percentiles.

Missing Values. You can choose one of the following alternatives:

○ **Exclude cases test-by-test.** When several tests are specified, each test is evaluated separately for missing values. This is the default.

○ **Exclude cases listwise.** Cases with missing values for any variable are excluded from all analyses.

Additional Features Available with Command Syntax

You can customize your Kolmogorov-Smirnov test if you paste your selections into a syntax window and edit the resulting NPAR TESTS command syntax (see Chapter 4). As an additional feature, you can specify the parameters of the test distribution (with the K-S subcommand). See Appendix A for command syntax rules. See the *SPSS Base System Syntax Reference Guide* for complete NPAR TESTS command syntax.

How to Obtain Two-Independent-Samples Tests

The Two-Independent-Samples Tests procedure compares two groups of cases on one variable (see "The Mann-Whitney Test" on p. 377).

The minimum specifications are:

- One or more numeric test variables.
- One numeric grouping variable.
- Group values for the grouping variable.

To obtain two-independent-samples tests, from the menus choose:

Statistics
  Nonparametric Tests ▶
    2 Independent Samples...

This opens the Two-Independent-Samples Tests dialog box, as shown in Figure 20.22.

Figure 20.22 Two-Independent-Samples Tests dialog box

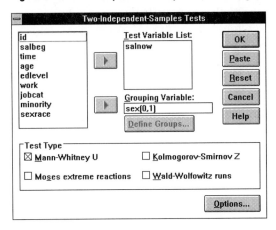

The numeric variables in your data file appear on the source variable list. Select one or more test variables and a grouping variable that splits the file into two groups or samples. After defining values of the grouping variable, click on OK to obtain the default (Mann-Whitney U) two-independent-samples test.

Test Type. At least one test type must be selected. You can choose one or more of the following:

❏ **Mann-Whitney U.** All cases are ranked in order of increasing size, and U (the number of times a score from group 1 precedes a score from group 2) is computed. This is the default test. If the samples are from the same population, the distribution of scores from the two groups on the ranked list should be similar; an extreme value of U indicates a nonrandom pattern. For samples with fewer than 30 cases, the exact significance level for U is computed using the Dineen and Blakesly (1973) algorithm. For larger samples, U is transformed into a normally distributed Z statistic.

❏ **Moses extreme reactions.** Arranges the scores from the groups in a single ascending sequence. The span of the control group is computed as the number of cases in the sequence containing the lowest and highest control score. The exact significance level can be computed for the span. The control group is defined by the group 1 value in the Two-Independent-Samples Define Groups dialog box (see Figure 20.23). Because chance outliers can easily distort the range of the span, 5% of the cases are trimmed automatically from each end. No adjustments are made for tied observations.

❏ **Kolmogorov-Smirnov Z.** Computes the observed cumulative distributions for both groups and the maximum positive, negative, and absolute differences. The Kolmogorov-Smirnov Z is then computed along with the two-tailed probability level based on the Smirnov (1948) formula.

❏ **Wald-Wolfowitz runs.** Combines observations from both groups and ranks them from lowest to highest. If the samples are from the same population, the two groups should be randomly scattered throughout the ranking. A runs test is performed using group membership as the criterion. If there are ties involving observations from both groups, both the minimum and maximum number of runs possible are calculated. If the total sample size is 30 or fewer cases, the exact one-tailed significance level is calculated. Otherwise, the normal approximation is used.

Two-Independent-Samples Define Groups

To define groups based on the values of the grouping variable, highlight the grouping variable and click on Define Groups... to open the Two-Independent-Samples Define Groups dialog box, as shown in Figure 20.23.

Figure 20.23 Two-Independent-Samples Define Groups dialog box

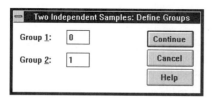

Enter integer values for group 1 and group 2. Cases with other values are excluded.

Two-Independent-Samples Options

To obtain optional summary statistics or to modify the treatment of cases with missing values, click on Options... in the Two-Independent-Samples Tests dialog box. This opens the Two-Independent-Samples Options dialog box, as shown in Figure 20.24.

Figure 20.24 Two-Independent-Samples Options dialog box

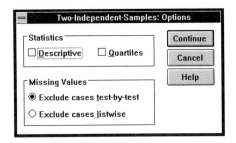

Statistics. You can choose one or both of the following summary statistics:

❑ **Descriptive.** Displays the mean, minimum, maximum, standard deviation, and the number of nonmissing cases.

❑ **Quartiles.** Displays values corresponding to the 25th, 50th, and 75th percentiles.

Missing Values. You can choose one of the following alternatives:

○ **Exclude cases test-by-test.** When several tests are specified, each test is evaluated separately for missing values. This is the default.

○ **Exclude cases listwise.** Cases with missing values for any variable are excluded from all analyses.

Additional Features Available with Command Syntax

You can customize your two-independent-samples tests if you paste your selections into a syntax window and edit the resulting NPAR TESTS command syntax (see Chapter 4). As an additional feature, you can specify the number of cases to be trimmed for the Moses test (with the MOSES subcommand). See Appendix A for command syntax rules. See the *SPSS Base System Syntax Reference Guide* for complete NPAR TESTS command syntax.

How to Obtain Tests for Several Independent Samples

The Tests for Several Independent Samples procedure compares two or more groups of cases on one variable.

The minimum specifications are:

- One or more numeric test variables.
- One numeric grouping variable.
- Minimum and maximum values for the grouping variable.

To obtain tests for several independent samples, from the menus choose:

Statistics
  Nonparametric Tests ▶
    K Independent Samples...

This opens the Tests for Several Independent Samples dialog box, as shown in Figure 20.25.

Figure 20.25 Tests for Several Independent Samples dialog box

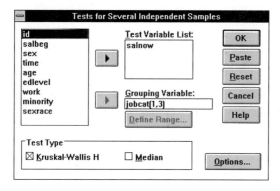

The numeric variables in your data file appear on the source variable list. Select one or more test variables and a grouping variable that splits the file into two or more groups. After defining the range of the grouping variable, click on OK to obtain the default (Kruskal-Wallis *H*) test.

Test Type. At least one test type must be selected. You can choose one or both of the following:

- ❏ **Kruskal-Wallis H.** Ranks all cases from the specified range in a single series, computes the rank sum for each group, and computes the Kruskal-Wallis *H* statistic, which has approximately a chi-square distribution. This is the default.

❑ **Median.** Produces a contingency table that indicates, for each group, the number of cases with values greater than the observed median and less than or equal to the median. A chi-square statistic for the table is computed.

Several Independent Samples Define Range

To define ranges based on the values of the grouping variable, highlight the grouping variable and click on Define Range... in the Tests for Several Independent Samples dialog box to open the Several Independent Samples Define Range dialog box, as shown in Figure 20.26.

Figure 20.26 Several Independent Samples Define Range dialog box

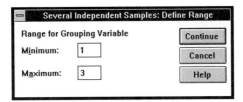

Enter values for minimum and maximum that correspond to the lowest and highest categories of the grouping variable. Both values must be integers, and cases with values outside the bounds are excluded. For example, if you specify a minimum value of 1 and a maximum value of 4, only the integer values of 1 through 4 are used. The minimum value must be less than the maximum value, and both values must be specified.

Several Independent Samples Options

To obtain optional summary statistics or to modify the treatment of cases with missing values, click on Options... in the Tests for Several Independent Samples dialog box. This opens the Several Independent Samples Options dialog box, as shown in Figure 20.27.

Figure 20.27 Several Independent Samples Options dialog box

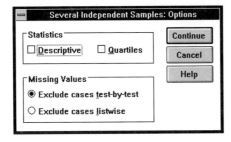

Statistics. You can choose one or both of the following summary statistics:

❑ **Descriptive.** Displays the mean, minimum, maximum, standard deviation, and the number of nonmissing cases.

❑ **Quartiles.** Displays values corresponding to the 25th, 50th, and 75th percentiles.

Missing Values. You can choose one of the following alternatives:

○ **Exclude cases test-by-test.** When several tests are specified, each test is evaluated separately for cases with missing values. This is the default.

○ **Exclude cases listwise.** Cases with missing values for any variable are excluded from all analyses.

Additional Features Available with Command Syntax

You can customize your test for several independent samples if you paste your selections into a syntax window and edit the resulting NPAR TESTS command syntax (see Chapter 4). As an additional feature, you can specify a value other than the observed median for the median test (with the MEDIAN subcommand). See Appendix A for command syntax rules. See the *SPSS Base System Syntax Reference Guide* for complete NPAR TESTS command syntax.

How to Obtain Two-Related-Samples Tests

The Two-Related-Samples Tests procedure compares the distributions of two variables (see "The Sign Test" on p. 381).

The minimum specification is one or more pairs of numeric variables.

To obtain two-related-samples tests, from the menus choose:

Statistics
  Nonparametric Tests ▶
    2 Related Samples...

This opens the Two-Related-Samples Tests dialog box, as shown in Figure 20.28.

Figure 20.28 Two-Related-Samples Tests dialog box

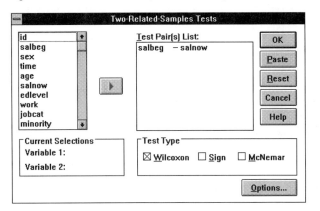

The numeric variables in your data file appear on the source list. Select one or more pairs of variables to use in the two-related-samples tests. To select a pair:

1. Click on one of the variables. It appears as the first variable under Current Selections.

2. Click on another variable. It appears as the second variable. To remove a variable from Current Selections, click on it again.

3. Click on ▶ to move the pair to the Test Pair(s) list.

Repeat this process if you have more than one pair of variables. To obtain the default (Wilcoxon signed-rank) test for two related samples, click on OK.

Test Type. At least one test type must be selected. You can choose one or more of the following:

❑ **Wilcoxon.** Computes differences between pairs of variables, ranks the absolute differences, sums ranks for the positive and negative differences, and computes the test statistic Z from the positive and negative rank sums. This is the default. Under the null hypothesis, the distribution for Z is approximately normal, with a mean of 0 and a variance of 1 for large sample sizes.

❑ **Sign.** Analyzes the signs of the differences between two paired values. Counts the positive and negative differences between each pair of variables and ignores 0 differences. Under the null hypothesis for large sample sizes, the distribution for the test statistic Z is approximately normal, with a mean of 0 and a variance of 1. The binomial distribution is used to compute an exact significance level if 25 or fewer differences are observed.

❑ **McNemar.** Examines the cases with different values for two dichotomous variables. Tests the hypothesis that both combinations of different values are equally likely.

McNemar produces a 2×2 table for each pair of variables. Pairs of variables being tested must be coded with the same two values. If your variables are not dichotomous, or if they have different values, recode them (see Chapter 5). A chi-square statistic is computed for cases with different values for the two variables. If fewer than 25 cases have different values for the two variables, the binomial distribution is used to compute the significance level.

Two-Related-Samples Options

To get optional summary statistics or to modify the treatment of cases with missing values, click on Options... in the Two-Related-Samples Tests dialog box. This opens the Two-Related-Samples Options dialog box, as shown in Figure 20.29.

Figure 20.29 Two-Related-Samples Options dialog box

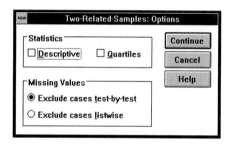

Statistics. You can choose one or both of the following summary statistics:

❑ **Descriptive.** Displays the mean, minimum, maximum, standard deviation, and the number of nonmissing cases.

❑ **Quartiles.** Displays values corresponding to the 25th, 50th, and 75th percentiles.

Missing Values. You can choose one of the following alternatives:

○ **Exclude cases test-by-test.** When several tests are specified, each test is evaluated separately for missing values. This is the default.

○ **Exclude cases listwise.** Cases with missing values for any variable are excluded from all analyses.

Additional Features Available with Command Syntax

You can customize your two-related-samples test if you paste your selections into a syntax window and edit the resulting NPAR TESTS command syntax (see Chapter 4). As an additional feature, you can test a variable with each variable on a list. See Appendix A for command syntax rules. See the *SPSS Base System Syntax Reference Guide* for complete NPAR TESTS command syntax.

How to Obtain Tests for Several Related Samples

The Tests for Several Related Samples procedure compares the distributions of two or more variables.

The minimum specification is two or more numeric variables.

To obtain tests for several related samples, from the menus choose:

Statistics
  Nonparametric Tests ▶
    K Related Samples...

This opens the Tests for Several Related Samples dialog box, as shown in Figure 20.30.

Figure 20.30 Tests for Several Related Samples dialog box

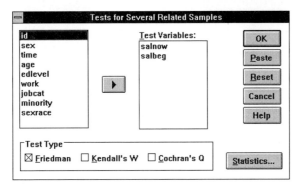

The numeric variables in your data file appear on the source variable list. Select two or more test variables, and click on OK to obtain the default (Friedman) test for several related samples. Cases with missing values for any of the variables are excluded.

Test Type. At least one test type must be selected. You can choose one or more of the following:

❑ **Friedman.** Ranks each variable from 1 to k for each case (where k is the number of variables), calculates the mean rank for each variable over all cases, and then calculates a test statistic with approximately a chi-square distribution. This is the default.

❑ **Kendall's W.** Ranks k variables from 1 to k for each case, calculates the mean rank for each variable over all cases, and then calculates Kendall's W and a corresponding chi-square statistic, correcting for ties. W ranges between 0 and 1, with 0 signifying no agreement and 1 signifying complete agreement. This test assumes that each case is a judge or rater. If you want to perform this test with variables as judges and cases as entities, you must first transpose your data matrix (see Chapter 6).

❏ **Cochran's Q.** Tests the null hypothesis that the proportion of cases in a particular category is the same for several dichotomous variables. Produces a $k \times 2$ contingency table (variable versus category) and computes the proportions for each variable. If your variables are not dichotomous or if they have different values, recode them (see Chapter 5). Cochran's Q statistic has approximately a chi-square distribution.

Several Related Samples Statistics

To obtain optional summary statistics, click on Statistics... in the Tests for Several Related Samples dialog box. This opens the Several Related Samples Statistics dialog box, as shown in Figure 20.31.

Figure 20.31 Several Related Samples Statistics dialog box

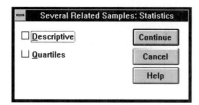

You can choose one or both of the following summary statistics:

❏ **Descriptive.** Displays the mean, maximum, minimum, standard deviation, and the number of nonmissing cases.

❏ **Quartiles.** Displays values corresponding to the 25th, 50th, and 75th percentiles.

21 Listing Cases

It is sometimes necessary or useful to review the actual contents of your data file. You may want to make sure data created in another application are being read correctly by SPSS, or you may want to verify the results of transformations or examine cases you suspect contain coding errors. You can review and print the contents of the data file using the Data Editor (see Chapter 3) or the List Cases procedure.

How to Obtain Case Listings

The List Cases procedure produces case listings of selected variables for all cases or a subset of cases.

The minimum specification is one variable.

To obtain case listings with the List Cases procedure, from the menus choose:

Statistics
  Summarize ▶
    List Cases...

This opens the List Cases dialog box, as shown in Figure 21.1.

Figure 21.1   List Cases dialog box

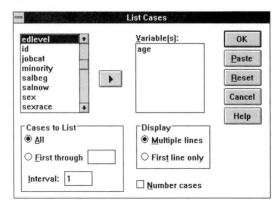

The variables in your data file are displayed on the source list. Select one or more variables for which you want case listings. To obtain the default listing of all cases in the file, click on OK.

Cases to List. You can choose one of the following:

○ **All**. Lists all cases in the data file. This is the default.

○ **First through n**. Lists cases from the first case to the specified number. The number represents the sequential number in the current file order, regardless of the value of any case ID variable that may exist in the file.

The following option is also available for cases to list:

Interval. Increment used to choose cases for listing. For example, if you want to see only every fifth case, enter a value of 5. The default value is 1.

Display. You can choose one of the following:

○ **Multiple lines**. This is the default. SPSS automatically determines the format of the case listing. If all the variables can fit on one line, the variable names are used as column heads (see Figure 21.2). If it can display all variables on one line by displaying some variable names vertically, it does so (see Figure 21.3). If there is not enough room on one line to display all the requested variables, multiple lines are used for each case. SPSS generates a table indicating which variables appear on each line, and the name of the first variable on each line is displayed in the case listings (see Figure 21.4).

○ **First line only**. If there is not enough room for all the variables on a single line, the listing is truncated to include only those variables that fit on a single line per case. Since the multiple line format can be difficult to read, you may want to use this alternative.

The following display option is also available:

❏ **Number cases**. Displays the sequential case number in the current file order. This is the value of the system variable $casenum$, which reflects the current order of cases in the file.

Figure 21.2   Single-line case listing with variable names displayed horizontally

NAME	ID	SALBEG	SEX	TIME	AGE	SALNOW	EDLEVEL	WORK	JOBCAT
Delbert McManus	926	3600	0	91	53.50	12300	12	26.17	3
Karen Nigida	921	3600	1	97	60.67	6780	12	10.33	1
Kendall Newton	1010	3600	1	97	51.58	8460	15	14.25	1
Christine Martin	1096	3600	1	96	60.50	7680	15	1.92	1
Dakota Becking	741	3900	1	98	27.25	8760	12	.00	1
Kay Lewis	754	3900	1	92	55.50	6480	8	.00	1
Donna Paul	945	3900	1	86	52.00	8760	12	13.00	1
Harriet Smith	995	3900	1	86	62.00	7260	12	6.00	1
Laurie Stolarz	1107	3900	1	88	62.50	6660	8	34.33	1
Lowell George	1077	3900	0	94	29.17	9000	8	3.00	2

Figure 21.3   Single-line case listing with some variable names displayed vertically

```
                        S                    S            J
                        A                    A            O
                        L      T             L            B
                        B  S   I             N            C
                        E  E   M             O            A
NAME             ID     G  X   E    AGE      W EDLEVEL  WORK T

Delbert McManus  926   3600 0  91  53.50 12300     12   26.17 3
Karen Nigida     921   3600 1  97  60.67  6780     12   10.33 1
Kendall Newton  1010   3600 1  97  51.58  8460     15   14.25 1
Christine Martin 1096  3600 1  96  60.50  7680     15    1.92 1
Dakota Becking   741   3900 1  98  27.25  8760     12    .00 1
Kay Lewis        754   3900 1  92  55.50  6480      8    .00 1
Donna Paul       945   3900 1  86  52.00  8760     12   13.00 1
Harriet Smith    995   3900 1  86  62.00  7260     12    6.00 1
Laurie Stolarz  1107   3900 1  88  62.50  6660      8   34.33 1
Lowell George   1077   3900 0  94  29.17  9000      8    3.00 2
```

Figure 21.4   Case listing with multiple lines

```
THE VARIABLES ARE LISTED IN THE FOLLOWING ORDER:

LINE   1: NAME ID SALBEG SEX TIME AGE SALNOW EDLEVEL WORK

LINE   2: JOBCAT MINORITY SEXRACE

    NAME: Delbert McManus     926     3600 0 91  53.50     12300 12      26
  JOBCAT:          3 1      2.00

    NAME: Karen Nigida        921     3600 1 97  60.67      6780 12      10
  JOBCAT:          1 1      4.00

    NAME: Kendall Newton     1010     3600 1 97  51.58      8460 15      14
  JOBCAT:          1 1      4.00

    NAME: Christine Martin   1096     3600 1 96  60.50      7680 15       2
  JOBCAT:          1 1      4.00

    NAME: Dakota Becking      741     3900 1 98  27.25      8760 12       0
  JOBCAT:          1 0      3.00

    NAME: Kay Lewis           754     3900 1 92  55.50      6480  8       0
  JOBCAT:          1 0      3.00

    NAME: Donna Paul          945     3900 1 86  52.00      8760 12      13
  JOBCAT:          1 0      3.00

    NAME: Harriet Smith       995     3900 1 86  62.00      7260 12       6
  JOBCAT:          1 0      3.00

    NAME: Laurie Stolarz     1107     3900 1 88  62.50      6660  8      34
  JOBCAT:          1 0      3.00

    NAME: Lowell George      1077     3900 0 94  29.17      9000  8       3
  JOBCAT:          2 1      2.00
```

Additional Features Available with Command Syntax

You can customize your descriptive statistics if you paste your selections to a syntax window and edit the resulting LIST command syntax (see Chapter 4). An additional feature is the ability to list cases beginning with any case you specify. See Appendix A for command syntax rules. See the *SPSS Base System Syntax Reference Guide* for complete LIST command syntax.

22 Reporting Results

Case listings and descriptive statistics are basic tools for studying and presenting data. You can obtain case listings with the Data Editor or the List Cases procedure, frequency counts and descriptive statistics with the Frequencies procedure, and subpopulation statistics with the Means procedure. Each of these uses a format designed to make information clear. If you want to display the information in a different format, the Report procedure gives you the control you need over data presentation.

Basic Report Concepts

Reports can contain summary statistics for groups of cases, listings of individual cases, or a combination of both statistics and listings. The number of columns in a report is determined by the number of report variables and break variables. Each report variable selected is displayed in a separate column. If the summaries are in columns, you can select a variable more than once.

Report variables are the variables for which you want case listings or summary statistics. These are displayed in **data columns**. Optional **break variables** divide the data into groups. These are displayed in **break columns**, which appear on the left side of the report.

Summary Reports

Summary reports display summary statistics but do not display case listings. The summary information consists of the statistics you request for the report variables. You can report summary statistics in rows or in columns. Using break variables, you can report summary statistics for various subgroups of cases. Figure 22.1 is an example of a summary report with summary statistics reported in rows, while Figure 22.2 is an example of a report with summary statistics in columns.

Figure 22.1   Summary report (summaries in rows)

Report variables in
data columns

Break variable in
break column

Subgroup
summary statistics
in rows

```
                              Tenure    Tenure
                                in        in
          Division    Age    Company    Grade   Salary--Annual

          Carpeting
          Mean        30.75    4.04      3.31      $11,754
          Minimum     22.00    2.67      2.17       $9,200
          Maximum     44.00    6.00      5.33      $19,500

          Appliances
          Mean        31.11    3.81      3.54      $12,508
          Minimum     21.00    2.67      2.08       $7,500
          Maximum     42.00    6.50      6.50      $28,300

          Furniture
          Mean        36.87    4.79      4.08      $13,255
          Minimum     25.00    3.17      3.17       $8,975
          Maximum     43.00    6.83      6.25      $17,050
```

In the summary report shown in Figure 22.1:

- Age, tenure in company, tenure in grade, and salary are the report variables presented in data columns.

- Division is the break variable presented in the break column.

- Mean, minimum value, and maximum value are the summary statistics reported on summary lines for each division.

Figure 22.2   Summary report (summaries in columns)

Summaries of variables
in data columns

Break variable in
break column

```
                               Mean     Minimum   Maximum
                              Annual    Annual    Annual
          Division  Mean Age  Salary    Salary    Salary


          Carpeting   30.75   $11,754   $9,200    $19,500

          Appliances  31.11   $12,508   $7,500    $28,300

          Furniture   36.87   $13,255   $8,975    $17,050

          Hardware    36.20   $17,580   $7,450    $22,500
```

In the summary report shown in Figure 22.2:

- Age and salary are the report variables. Salary is presented in several columns, each column having a different summary statistic.
- Division is the break variable presented in the break column.
- The age column shows the mean age for each division.
- The salary columns show the mean salary, minimum salary, and maximum salary for each division.

Listing Reports

Listing reports list individual cases. The case listings can display the actual data values or the defined value labels recorded for each of the report variables. As with summary reports, you divide a listing report into subgroups using break variables, as in Figure 22.3. Listing reports are available only for summaries in rows.

Figure 22.3   Listing report (summaries in rows)

Division	Age	Tenure in Company	Tenure in Grade	Salary--Annual
Carpeting	27.00	3.67	2.17	$9,200
	22.00	3.92	3.08	$10,900
	23.00	3.92	3.08	$10,900
	24.00	4.00	3.25	$10,000
	30.00	4.08	3.08	$10,000
	27.00	4.33	3.17	$10,000
	33.00	2.67	2.67	$9,335
	33.00	3.75	3.25	$10,000
	44.00	4.83	4.33	$15,690
	36.00	3.83	3.25	$10,000
	35.00	3.50	3.00	$15,520
	35.00	6.00	5.33	$19,500
Appliances	21.00	2.67	2.67	$8,700
	26.00	2.92	2.08	$8,000
	32.00	2.92	2.92	$8,900
	33.00	3.42	2.92	$8,900
	34.00	5.08	4.50	$15,300
	24.00	3.17	3.17	$8,975
	42.00	6.50	6.50	$18,000
	30.00	2.67	2.67	$7,500
	38.00	5.00	4.42	$28,300

Combined Reports

You can combine individual case listings and summary statistics in a single report (only for summaries in rows), as in Figure 22.4. Combined case listing and summary reports are available only with summaries in rows.

Figure 22.4   Combined report with case listings and summary statistics (summaries in rows)

Division	Age	Tenure in Company	Tenure in Grade	Salary--Annual
Carpeting	27.00	3.67	2.17	$9,200
	22.00	3.92	3.08	$10,900
	23.00	3.92	3.08	$10,900
	24.00	4.00	3.25	$10,000
	30.00	4.08	3.08	$10,000
	27.00	4.33	3.17	$10,000
	33.00	2.67	2.67	$9,335
	33.00	3.75	3.25	$10,000
	44.00	4.83	4.33	$15,690
	36.00	3.83	3.25	$10,000
	35.00	3.50	3.00	$15,520
	35.00	6.00	5.33	$19,500
Mean	30.75	4.04	3.31	$11,754
Appliances	21.00	2.67	2.67	$8,700
	26.00	2.92	2.08	$8,000
	32.00	2.92	2.92	$8,900
	33.00	3.42	2.92	$8,900
	34.00	5.08	4.50	$15,300
	24.00	3.17	3.17	$8,975
	42.00	6.50	6.50	$18,000
	30.00	2.67	2.67	$7,500
	38.00	5.00	4.42	$28,300
Mean	31.11	3.81	3.54	$12,508

Multiple Break Variables

You can use more than one break variable to divide your report into groups, and you can display different summary statistics for each break variable division. In Figure 22.5, for example, each division is further divided by store location. For each store location, the minimum and maximum values are displayed and for each division, the mean and standard deviation are presented.

Figure 22.5   Multiple break variables in a summary report (summaries in rows)

	Division	Branch Store	Age	Tenure in Company	Tenure in Grade	Salary--Annual
	Carpeting	Suburban				
		Minimum	22.00	3.67	2.17	$9,200
		Maximum	35.00	6.00	5.33	$19,500
		Downtown				
		Minimum	24.00	2.67	2.67	$9,335
Statistics for first		Maximum	44.00	4.83	4.33	$15,690
break variable	Mean		30.75	4.04	3.31	$11,754
	StdDev		6.47	.80	.81	$3,288
	Appliances	Suburban				
		Minimum	21.00	2.67	2.08	$8,000
Statistics for second		Maximum	42.00	6.50	6.50	$28,300
break variable		Downtown				
		Minimum	30.00	2.67	2.67	$7,500
		Maximum	34.00	5.08	4.50	$15,300
	Mean		31.11	3.81	3.54	$12,508
	StdDev		6.70	1.37	1.37	$6,944

Summary Columns

When the report shows summaries in columns, you can combine two or more data columns in an additional column called a **total column**. In Figure 22.6, the next-to-last column presents the ratio of the two previous columns. The total column can be positioned next to any other data column. The summary function specified for the total column can be a sum, mean, minimum, maximum, difference, ratio, percentage, or product of other data columns.

Figure 22.6   A report with a column that summarizes other columns (summaries in columns)

Total column using the ratio summary function

Division	Branch Store	Average Tenure in Job	Average Tenure in Company	Ratio of Tenure in Job to Tenure in Company	Average Salary
Carpeting	Suburban	3.42	4.38	.78	$12,625
	Downtown	3.25	3.88	.84	$11,318
Appliances	Suburban	3.77	4.05	.93	$14,395
	Downtown	3.25	3.52	.92	$10,150
Furniture	Suburban	4.32	4.71	.92	$12,975
	Downtown	3.86	4.86	.79	$13,500
Hardware	Suburban	4.33	4.33	1.00	$22,500
	Downtown	4.63	4.67	.99	$16,350

Grand Total Summary Statistics

In addition to reporting summary statistics for subgroups based on break variables, you can also include summary statistics for all cases in the report, as in Figure 22.7 and Figure 22.8. Overall report summary statistics are referred to as **grand totals**.

Figure 22.7   Summary report with grand totals (summaries in rows)

Division	Branch Store	Age	Tenure in Company	Tenure in Grade	Salary--Annual
Furniture	Suburban				
	Minimum	25.00	3.17	3.17	$8,975
	Maximum	42.00	6.25	6.25	$17,050
	Downtown				
	Minimum	32.00	4.42	3.50	$12,000
	Maximum	43.00	6.83	5.33	$14,400
Mean		36.87	4.79	4.08	$13,255
StdDev		5.71	.89	.89	$2,126
Hardware	Suburban				
	Minimum	32.00	4.33	4.33	$22,500
	Maximum	32.00	4.33	4.33	$22,500
	Downtown				
	Minimum	26.00	2.67	2.50	$7,450
	Maximum	44.00	6.00	6.00	$22,000
Mean		36.20	4.60	4.57	$17,580
StdDev		7.16	1.28	1.35	$6,103
Grand Total					
Mean		33.73	4.34	3.79	$13,179
N		41	41	41	41
StdDev		6.76	1.08	1.10	$4,589

Grand total rows ——

Figure 22.8   Summary report with grand totals (summaries in columns)

Division	Branch Store	Average Age	Average Tenure in Job	Average Tenure in Company	Average Annual Salary
Carpeting	Suburban	26.75	3.42	4.38	$12,625
	Downtown	32.75	3.25	3.88	$11,318
Appliances	Suburban	30.20	3.77	4.05	$14,395
	Downtown	32.25	3.25	3.52	$10,150
Furniture	Suburban	35.29	4.32	4.71	$12,975
	Downtown	38.25	3.86	4.86	$13,500
Hardware	Suburban	32.00	4.33	4.33	$22,500
	Downtown	37.25	4.63	4.67	$16,350
All divisions		33.73	3.79	4.34	$13,179

Grand total row —

Formatting Reports

The Report procedure offers a great deal of control over the appearance of your report. You can add titles and footnotes, change the column headings, adjust column width and alignment, and control the display of values or value labels.

Titles and Footnotes

You can add titles and footnotes to reports. You can also include the values of variables in titles and footnotes, including special variables for page number and current date, as shown in Figure 22.9.

Figure 22.9 Titles and footnotes

```
Special variable       07 Apr 92   Monthly Summary Report --  Carpeting Division       Value label for current
for current date                                                                       value of break variable
                                              Tenure      Tenure
                                   Branch        in          in
                       Division    Store    Age  Company    Grade    Salary--Annual
                       _____   _____  ___  _____    _____    _____

                       Carpeting   Suburban
                                   Minimum  22.00   3.67     2.17         $9,200
                                   Maximum  35.00   6.00     5.33        $19,500

                                   Downtown
                                   Minimum  24.00   2.67     2.67         $9,335
                                   Maximum  44.00   4.83     4.33        $15,690
                       Mean                 30.75   4.04     3.31        $11,754
                       StdDev                6.47    .80      .81         $3,288



                                   1        Special variable for
                                            page number
```

Column Headings

Each column in a report has a heading. By default, the variable label is used for the heading if summaries are in rows. For summaries in columns, the statistic plus the variable label is used. In either type of report, if there is no label, the variable name is used. You can also create headings of your own and control their alignment, as shown in Figure 22.10.

Figure 22.10 User-specified column headings

```
07 Apr 92  Monthly Summary Report --  Appliances Division

           Store       Employee   Company    Job       Annual
Division   Location    Age        Tenure     Tenure    Salary
_____   _____    _____   _____    _____   _____


Appliances Suburban
           Minimum     21.00      2.67       2.08      $8,000
           Maximum     42.00      6.50       6.50      $28,300

           Downtown
           Minimum     30.00      2.67       2.67      $7,500
           Maximum     34.00      5.08       4.50      $15,300

Mean                   31.11      3.81       3.54      $12,508
StdDev                 6.70       1.37       1.37      $6,944
```

Displaying Value Labels

For break variables, value labels are displayed by default. For report variables in listing reports, data values are displayed by default. You can display actual data values for break variables and/or value labels for report variables in listing reports. For example, if you want to produce a personnel report that includes employee's gender, you might want to display the value labels *Male* and *Female* instead of the numeric values 1 and 2, as in Figure 22.11.

Figure 22.11 Displaying value labels in a listing report

```
                         Annual
Last Name    Gender      Salary    Job Grade            Shift
_____    _____      _____   _____            _____

Ford         Female      $9,200    Support Staff        First
Cochran      Female      $10,900   Sales Staff          First
Hoawinski    Female      $10,900   Sales Staff          First
Tygielski    Male        $19,500   Supervisory Staff    Weekend
Gates        Female      $10,000   Sales Staff          Second
Mulvihill    Male        $10,000   Sales Staff          First
Lavelle      Female      $10,000   Sales Staff          Weekend
Mahr         Female      $9,335    Sales Staff          First
Katz         Male        $10,000   Sales Staff          Weekend
Jones        Female      $15,690   Sales Staff          First
Dan          Male        $10,000   Sales Staff          Weekend
McAndrews    Female      $15,520   Supervisory Staff    First
Powell       Female      $8,700    Support Staff        Weekend
Martin       Female      $8,000    Sales Staff          First
Parris       Female      $8,975    Sales Staff          First
Johnson      Female      $18,000   Sales Staff          Second
Sanders      Male        $28,300   Managerial Staff     First
Shavilje     Male        $8,900    Sales Staff          First
Provenza     Female      $8,900    Sales Staff          First
Snolik       Male        $15,300   Sales Staff          First
Sedowski     Male        $7,500    Sales Staff          Weekend
```

How to Obtain Listing Reports and Reports with Summaries in Rows

The minimum specifications for a listing report or a report with summaries in rows are:

- One or more report variables on the Data Columns list.
- One or more summary statistics or selection of the Display cases check box.

To obtain and modify row summary reports and case listing reports, from the menus choose:

Statistics
  Summarize ▶
    Report Summaries in Rows...

This opens the Report Summaries in Rows dialog box, as shown in Figure 22.12.

Figure 22.12 Report Summaries in Rows dialog box

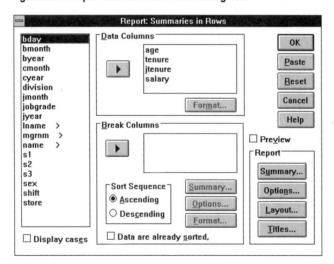

Data Columns. The report variables for which you want case listings or summary statistics. You must select at least one variable for the Data Columns list.

Break Columns. Optional break variables that divide the report into groups. Each successive break variable divides the report into subgroups within groups of the previous break variable. For example, if you select *division* and then *store* as break variables, there will be a separate group for each category of store within each category of division, as shown in Figure 22.5.

    Sort Sequence. Sort order for categories of the break variables. Sort order is based on data values, not value labels. String variables are sorted alphabetically, and uppercase letters precede lowercase letters in sort order. For each break variable, you can choose one of the following alternatives for sort sequence:

○ **Ascending**. Sorts break variable values by ascending order from low to high. This is the default.

○ **Descending**. Sorts break variable values by descending order from high to low.

The following option saves processing time.

❏ **Data are already sorted**. Data are already sorted by values of the break variables. The Report procedure creates a new break category each time the value of a break variable changes in the data file. Therefore, meaningful summary reports require that the data file be sorted by values of the break variables. By default, the file is automatically sorted before the report is generated. If the data file is already sorted in the proper order, you can save processing time by selecting this option. This option is particularly useful once you have run a report and want to refine the format.

Report. The items in the Report group control the display of grand total summary statistics, treatment of missing values, page layout and numbering, and report titles and footers.

The following display options are also available:

❏ **Preview.** Displays only the first page of the report. This option is useful for previewing the format of your report without processing the whole report.

❏ **Display cases**. Displays individual case listings. Select this option to produce listing reports, as shown in Figure 22.3.

Data Column Format

To modify data column headings, column width, and alignment of headings and data, and to control the display of value labels, select a report variable on the Data Columns list and click on Format... in the Report Summaries in Rows dialog box. This opens the Report Data Column Format dialog box, as shown in Figure 22.13.

Figure 22.13 Report Data Column Format dialog box

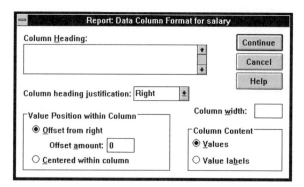

Column Heading. The heading that appears at the top of the column for the selected report variable. If you don't specify a heading, the variable label is used by default. If there is no variable label, the variable name is used. Default column headings are automatically wrapped onto multiple lines to fit in the column width. User-specified column headings are wrapped unless you specify line breaks in the heading. To specify line breaks, press ⏎Enter at the end of each line.

⬇ **Column heading justification**. Alignment of the column heading. Alignment of the column heading does not affect alignment of the data displayed in the column. You can choose one of the following alternatives:

Left. Column headings are left-justified. This is the default for string variables.

Center. Column headings are centered based on column width.

Right. Column headings are right-justified. This is the default for numeric variables.

Value Position within Column. Alignment of data values or value labels within the column. Alignment of values or labels does not affect alignment of column headings. You can choose one of the following alternatives:

○ **Offset from right/Offset from left**. Enter a number of characters for the offset amount. The default is zero. If numeric values are displayed, the offset is from the right side of the column. If alphanumeric values are displayed, the offset is from the left side of the column. The offset value cannot exceed the defined column width.

○ **Centered within column**. Data values or value labels are centered in the column.

Column width. Column width expressed as a number of characters. If you don't specify a value, a default column width is determined based on the largest of the following:

• If you specify a column heading, the length of the longest word in the heading. You can string more than one word together by joining them with underscores. The underscores are displayed as spaces in the output.

• If you don't specify a column heading, the length of the longest word in the variable label.

• If value labels are displayed, the length of the longest value label for the variable.

• If values are displayed, the variable format width.

If you specify a value for column width that is shorter than the display format of the variable, numeric values that don't fit in the specified width are converted to scientific notation. If the specified width is less than six characters, asterisks are displayed for numeric values that don't fit. String values and value labels are wrapped onto multiple lines to fit in the column width.

Column Content. You can choose one of the following alternatives:

○ **Values**. Data values are displayed. This is the default for data column variables.

○ **Value labels**. Value labels are displayed. This is the default for break column variables. If a value doesn't have a defined label, the data value is displayed.

Break Category Summary Statistics

To specify summary statistics for data column variables within categories of a break variable, select a break variable on the Break Columns list and click on Summary... in the Report Summaries in Rows dialog box. This opens the Report Summary Lines dialog box, as shown in Figure 22.14.

Figure 22.14 Report Summary Lines dialog box (summaries in rows)

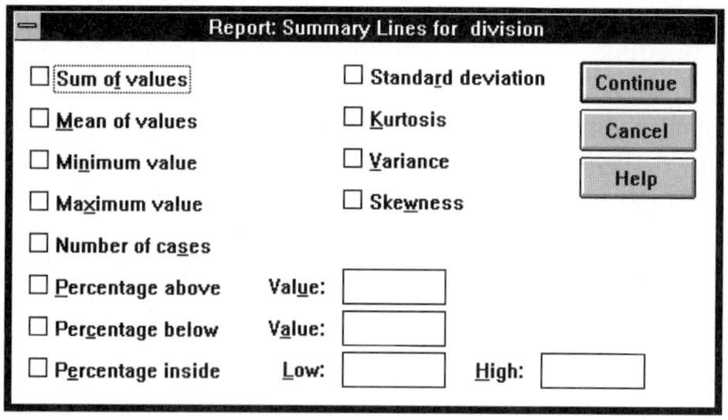

Each summary statistic selected is calculated for all data column variables within each category of the break variable. If you choose more than one summary statistic, each statistic is displayed on a separate row in the report. You can select different summary statistics for each break variable. You can choose one or more of the following summary statistics:

❑ **Sum of values**. The sum of data values in the break category.

❑ **Mean of values**. The arithmetic average of data values in the break category.

❑ **Minimum value**. The smallest data value in the break category.

❑ **Maximum value**. The largest data value in the break category.

❑ **Number of cases**. Number of cases in the break category.

❑ **Percentage above**. Percentage of cases in the break category above a user-specified value. If you select this item, you must enter a value in the text box before you can continue.

❑ **Percentage below**. Percentage of cases in the break category below a user-specified value. If you select this item, you must enter a value in the text box before you can continue.

❏ **Percentage inside**. Percentage of cases in the break category inside a user-specified range. If you select this item, you must enter a Low and High value before you can continue.

❏ **Standard deviation**. A measure of how much observations vary from the mean of values in the break category, expressed in the same units as the data.

❏ **Kurtosis**. A measure of the extent to which data values in the break category cluster around a central point, given their standard deviation.

❏ **Variance**. A measure of how much values vary from the mean of values in the break category, equal to the square of the standard deviation. The units are the square of those of the variable itself.

❏ **Skewness**. An index of the degree to which the distribution of data values in the break category is not symmetric.

Break Spacing and Page Options for Summaries in Rows

To change the line spacing between break categories or between break headings and summary statistics, or to display each break category on a separate page, select a break variable on the Break Columns list and click on Options... in the Report Summaries in Rows dialog box. This opens the Report Break Options dialog box, as shown in Figure 22.15.

Figure 22.15 Report Break Options dialog box (summaries in rows)

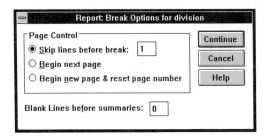

Page Control. You can select one of the following alternatives for spacing between break categories:

○ **Skip lines before break**. The number of blank lines between break categories. The default is 1. You can specify 0 to 20 blank lines between break categories.

○ **Begin next page**. Starts each break category on a new page.

○ **Begin new page & reset page number**. Starts each break category on a separate page and numbers pages for each break category separately.

Blank lines before summaries. The number of blank lines between the break category heading and the summary statistics. The default is 0. You can specify up to 20 blank lines between the break category heading and the rows of summary statistics.

Break Column Format

To modify break column headings, column width, and alignment of headings and data, and to control the display of value labels, select a break variable on the Break Columns list and click on Format... in the Report Summaries in Rows dialog box. This opens the Report Break Column Format dialog box, which offers selections identical to those in the Report Data Column Format dialog box, shown in Figure 22.13. See "Data Column Format" on p. 422 for information on the selections available in this dialog box and defaults.

Report Total Summary Statistics

To specify grand total summary statistics for the entire report, click on Summary... in the Report group of selections in the main dialog box. This opens the Report Final Summary Lines dialog box, which offers selections identical to those in the Report Summary Lines dialog box shown in Figure 22.14. For more information on the available summary statistics, see "Break Category Summary Statistics" on p. 424.

Report Options for Summaries in Rows

To change the treatment and display of missing values, save processing time for pre-sorted data, and control the report page numbering, click on Options... in the Report group of selections in the Report Summaries in Rows dialog box. This opens the Report Options dialog box, as shown in Figure 22.16.

Figure 22.16 Report Options dialog box (summaries in rows)

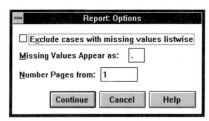

The following options are available:

❏ **Exclude cases with missing values listwise.** Excludes cases that have missing data for any variable in the report. By default, cases with missing data are included in the report if they have valid values for any report variable.

Missing Values Appear as. The character used to indicate both system- and user-missing data. By default, a period (.) is used. You can use any single character.

Number Pages from. The starting page number of the report. By default, pages are numbered from 1. The starting page number can be any integer from 0 to 99999.

Report Layout for Summaries in Rows

To change the width and length of each report page, control the placement of the report on the page, and control the insertion of blank lines and labels, click on Layout... in the Report Summaries in Rows dialog box. This opens the Report Layout dialog box, as shown in Figure 22.17.

Figure 22.17 Report Layout dialog box (summaries in rows)

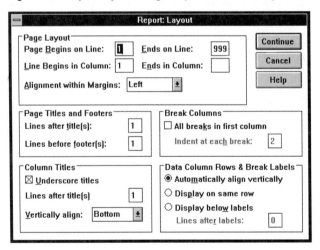

Page Layout. The following options control the placement of the report on the page:

Page begins on line/Ends on line. By default, each report page begins on the first line of the page and ends on the last line of the page as defined by the page length in the Preferences dialog box (see Chapter 36). The number of the beginning line must be less than the number of the ending line.

If you specify beginning and ending line values that do not provide the minimum number of lines per page required for the report, the ending line value will be overridden, and a message at the end of the report will indicate this.

Line begins in column/Ends in column. The left and right margins of the report are expressed as the number of characters (columns) across the page. By default, the report begins in column 1 and ends in the column that corresponds to the page width value defined in the Preferences dialog box (see Chapter 36). You can specify a value up to 255.

If you specify beginning and ending column values that do not provide a wide enough space for the report, the report will not be generated. If you don't specify an ending column value, the Report procedure will override the default if necessary to display reports that are too wide for the default width. The maximum width of a report is 255 characters.

- **Alignment within margins.** The report can be left-aligned, centered, or right-aligned within the left and right page margins. The default is left alignment. If you don't specify beginning and ending column positions for the left and right margins, center and right alignment have no effect.

Page Titles and Footers. The following options control the number of blank lines near the top and bottom of a page:

Lines after title(s)/Lines before footer(s). Indicates the number of blank lines between the report title(s) and the first line of the report, and the number of lines between the bottom of the report and any footers; by default, there is one blank line between the title and the report and one blank line between the bottom of the report and any footers.

Break Columns. If multiple break variables are specified, they can be in separate columns or in the first column. The default is a separate column for each break variable.

- ❏ **All breaks in first column.** Selecting this item causes the values of all break variables to be listed in the first column.

  Indent at each break. If all break categories are in the first column, each break level is indented by the number of spaces specified. The default indentation is two spaces.

Column Titles. The following options apply to columns titles.

- ❏ **Underscore titles.** Displays a horizontal line underneath each column title. This item is selected by default.

Lines after titles. Indicates the number of blank lines between the column titles and the first line of values.

Vertically align: Indicates whether the tops or bottoms of column titles will be aligned. Bottom alignment of column titles is the default.

Data Column Rows & Break Labels. The following options are for reports with summaries in rows only.

○ **Automatically align vertically.** In a summary report, places the first summary on the next line after the break value. In a listing report, places the first case listing on the same line as the break value.

○ **Display on same row.** In a summary report, places the first summary statistic on the same line as the break value and suppresses the first summary title. In a listing report, places the first case listing on the same line as the break value.

○ **Display below labels.** Places the number of blank lines specified between a break value and the next summary row or case listing.

Lines after labels. Specifies the number of lines to display below labels.

Titles and Footers

To add titles and footers to a report, click on Titles... in the Report Summaries in Rows or the Report Summaries in Columns dialog box. This opens the Report Titles dialog box, as shown in Figure 22.18.

Figure 22.18 Report Titles dialog box

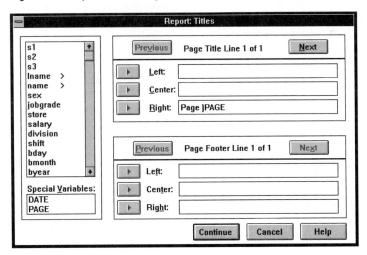

Page Titles. Titles and other text that appears above the report on each page. You can specify any combination of left, center, and right titles. To specify multiple-line titles, click on Next after each title line to specify the next line. You can have up to 10 title lines. By default, the current page number is used as the right title.

Page Footers. Text, such as footnotes, that appears below the report on each page. You can specify any combination of left, center, and right footers. To specify multiple-line footers, click on Next after each footer to specify the next footer line. You can have up to 10 footer lines.

If the combined width of the left, center, and right titles or footers exceeds the defined width of the page, the titles or footers are truncated in the report. Left and right titles and footers are truncated before center ones.

Positioning Titles and Footers

The position of titles and footers is based on the report width unless you explicitly specify left and right report margins (see "Report Layout for Summaries in Rows" on p. 427). If you specify report margins, the position of titles and footers is based on alignment within those margins. For example, if you specify a right margin of 90 but the report is only 70 characters wide, center titles will not be aligned over the center of the report. You can adjust the position of titles and footers by changing the left and right margins.

Using Variables in Titles and Footers

To use a variable in a title or footer, position the cursor in the line where you want the variable to appear and click on the corresponding ▶ pushbutton. The variable name appears in the line, preceded by a right parenthesis. Two special variables, *DATE* and *PAGE*, are also available to display the current date and page number.

In titles, the value label corresponding to the value of the variable at the beginning of the page is displayed (see Figure 22.9). In footers, the value label corresponding to the value of the variable at the end of the page is displayed. If there is no value label, the actual value is displayed.

How to Obtain a Report with Summaries in Columns

The minimum specification for a report with summaries in columns is one or more report variables on the Data Columns list.

To obtain and modify column summary reports, from the menus choose:

Statistics
  Summarize ▶
    Report Summaries in Columns...

This opens the Report Summaries in Columns dialog box, as shown in Figure 22.19.

Figure 22.19 Report Summaries in Columns dialog box

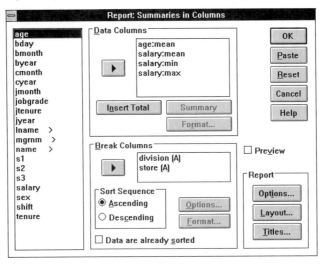

Data Columns. The report variables for which you want summary statistics. You can select a variable more than once and then specify a different summary statistic for each instance of the variable. You must select at least one variable for the Data Columns list.

The default summary statistic for each variable is sum. To specify a different summary statistic for a variable, select the variable and click on Summary.

> **Insert Total.** Inserts a column that summarizes other columns, after the currently selected column. You must click on Summary and then specify which other columns are summarized and the type of summary.

Break Columns. Optional break variables that divide the report into groups. Each successive break variable divides the report into subgroups within groups of the previous break variable. For example, if you select *division* and then *store* as break variables, there will be a separate group for each category of *store* within each category of *division*, as shown in Figure 22.6.

> **Sort Sequence.** Sort order for categories of the break variables. Sort order is based on data values, not value labels. String variables are sorted alphabetically, and uppercase letters precede lowercase letters in sort order. For each break variable, you can choose one of the following alternatives for sort sequence:
>
> ○ **Ascending.** Sorts break variable values by ascending order from low to high. This is the default.

○ **Descending**. Sorts break variable values by descending order from high to low.

The following option saves processing time.

❏ **Data are already sorted**. Data are already sorted by values of the break variables. The Report procedure creates a new break category each time the value of a break variable changes in the data file. Therefore, meaningful summary reports require that the data file be sorted by values of the break variables. By default, the file is automatically sorted before the report is generated. If the data file is already sorted in the proper order, you can save processing time by selecting this option. This option is particularly useful once you have run a report and want to refine the format.

Report. The items in the Report group control the display of grand total summary statistics, treatment of missing values, page layout and numbering, and report titles and footers.

The following display option is also available:

❏ **Preview**. Displays only the first page of the report. This option is useful for previewing the format of your report.

Data Column Summary Statistic for a Variable

To specify a statistic for a data column variable, select a variable on the Data Columns list and click on Summary... in the Report Summaries in Columns dialog box. This opens the Report Summary Lines dialog box, as shown in Figure 22.20.

Figure 22.20 Report Summary Lines dialog box (summaries in columns)

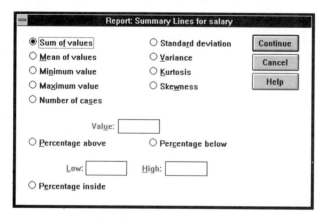

You can select only one summary statistic for a variable column. To add another column with a different summary of the same variable, move the variable again to the Data Columns list in the Report Summaries in Columns dialog box. You can choose one of the following summary statistics for each variable column:

○ **Sum of values**. The sum of data values in the break category.

○ **Mean of values**. The arithmetic average of data values in the break category.

○ **Minimum value**. The smallest data value in the break category.

○ **Maximum value**. The largest data value in the break category.

○ **Number of cases**. Number of cases in the break category.

○ **Percentage above**. Percentage of cases in the break category above a user-specified value. If you select this item, you must enter a value in the text box before you can continue.

○ **Percentage below**. Percentage of cases in the break category below a user-specified value. If you select this item, you must enter a value in the text box before you can continue.

○ **Percentage inside**. Percentage of cases in the break category inside a user-specified range. If you select this item, you must enter a Low value and a High value before you can continue.

○ **Standard deviation**. A measure of how much observations vary from the mean of values in the break category, expressed in the same units as the data.

○ **Variance**. A measure of how much values vary from the mean of values in the break category, equal to the square of the standard deviation. The units are the square of those of the variable itself.

○ **Kurtosis**. A measure of the extent to which data values in the break category cluster around a central point, given their standard deviation.

○ **Skewness**. An index of the degree to which the distribution of data values in the break category is not symmetric.

Composite Summary (Total) Columns

To specify a composite summary for an inserted Total column, select the Total column on the Data Columns list and click on Summary... in the Report Summaries in Columns dialog box. This opens the Report Summary Column dialog box, as shown in Figure 22.21.

Figure 22.21 Report Summary Column dialog box

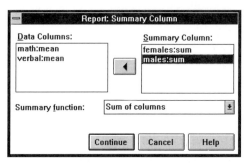

Move the variables you want in the composite summary from the Data Columns list to the Summary Column list. Then, select the function from the Summary function drop-down list.

⬇ **Summary function.** You can choose one of the following functions for the summary function:

Sum of columns. Add the values in the columns on the Summary Column list.

Mean of columns. Display the mean of the values in the columns on the Summary Column list.

Minimum of columns. Display the minimum value in the columns on the Summary Column list.

Maximum of columns. Display the maximum value in the columns on the Summary Column list.

1st column - 2nd column. Subtract the value in the second column from the value in the first column and display the difference. Only two columns are allowed on the Summary Column list.

1st column / 2nd column. Divide the value in the first column by the value in the second column and display the quotient. Only two columns are allowed on the Summary Column list.

% 1st column / 2nd column. Divide the value in the first column by the value in the second column, multiply by 100, and display the result. Only two columns are allowed on the Summary Column list.

Product of columns. Multiply the values in the columns on the Summary Column list.

Data Column Format

To modify data column headings, column width, and alignment of headings and data, and to control the display of value labels, select a report variable or a Total column on the Data Columns list and click on Format... in the Report Summaries in Columns dialog box. This opens the Report Data Column Format dialog box, as shown in Figure 22.13. For information on this dialog box, see "Data Column Format" on p. 422.

Break Options for Summaries in Columns

To change the line spacing between break categories or between break headings and summary statistics, or to display each break category on a separate page, select a break variable on the Break Columns list and click on Options... in the Report Summaries in Columns dialog box. This opens the Report Break Options dialog box, as shown in Figure 22.22.

Figure 22.22 Report Break Options dialog box (summaries in columns)

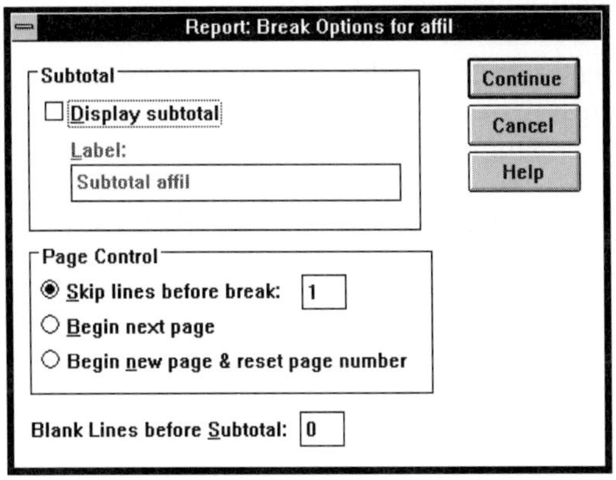

Break options are ignored for the last variable on the Break Columns list.

Subtotal. You can control whether or not to display subtotals.

❑ **Display subtotal.** Displays a subtotal for each break group category.

Label. You can edit the default label for the break group subtotal. This label is available only if Display subtotal is selected.

Page Control. You can select one of the following alternatives for spacing between break categories:

○ **Skip lines before break**. The number of blank lines between break categories. The default is 1. You can specify 0 to 20 blank lines between break categories.

○ **Begin next page**. Starts each break category on a new page.

○ **Begin new page & reset page number**. Starts each break category on a separate page and numbers pages for each break category separately.

Blank Lines before Subtotal. The number of blank lines before the subtotal. The default is 0. You can specify up to 20 blank lines between the break category heading and the break column subtotal.

Break Column Format

To modify break column headings, column width, and alignment of headings and data, and to control the display of value labels, select a break variable on the Break Columns list and click on Format... in the Report Summaries in Columns dialog box. This opens the Report Break Column Format dialog box, which offers selections identical to those in the Report Data Column Format dialog box, shown in Figure 22.13. See "Data Column Format" on p. 422 for information on the selections available in this dialog box.

Report Options for Summaries in Columns

To display a grand total summary statistic for each column, change the treatment and display of missing values, and control the report page numbering, click on Options... in the Report group of selections in the Report Summaries in Columns dialog box. This opens the Report Options dialog box, as shown in Figure 22.23.

Figure 22.23 Report Options dialog box (summaries in columns)

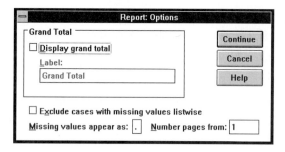

Grand Total. You can display a summary statistic at the bottom of each column and specify a label for the row.

❏ **Display grand total.** Displays at the bottom of each column a statistic summarizing all cases. The statistic is the one specified previously for the column.

Label. Text appearing in the break column that identifies the grand total summary row. The default label is *Grand Total*.

❏ **Exclude cases with missing values listwise.** Excludes cases that have missing data for any variable in the report. By default, cases with missing data are excluded in the report summaries but included in case listings.

Missing values appear as. The character used to indicate both system- and user-missing data. By default, a period (.) is used. You can use any single character.

Number pages from. The starting page number of the report. By default, pages are numbered from 1. The starting page number can be any integer from 0 to 99999.

Report Layout for Summaries in Columns

To change the width and length of each report page, or control the placement of the report on the page, extra blank lines, alignment of break columns, and layout of column titles, click on Layout... in the Report Summaries in Rows dialog box. This opens the Report Layout dialog box, as shown in Figure 22.24.

Figure 22.24 Report Layout dialog box (summaries in columns)

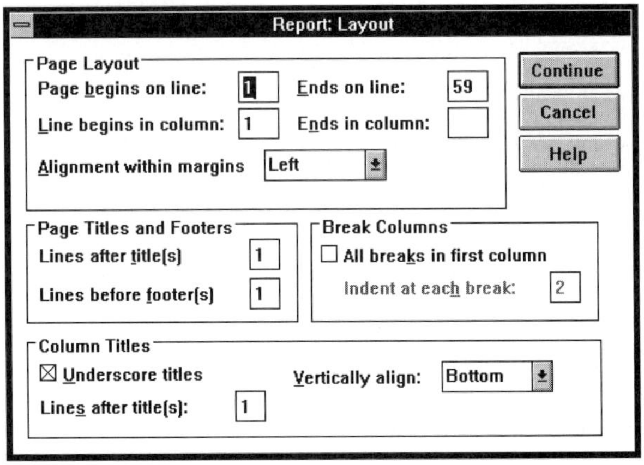

Except for the Data Column Rows & Break Labels group, which is not available here, this dialog box offers selections identical to those in the Report Layout dialog box for Summaries in Rows, shown in Figure 22.17. See "Report Layout for Summaries in Rows" on p. 427 for information on the selections available in this dialog box.

Titles and Footers

To add titles and footers to a report, click on Titles... in the Report Summaries in Columns dialog box. This opens the Report Titles dialog box, as shown in Figure 22.18. For information on this dialog box, see "Titles and Footers" on p. 429.

Additional Features Available with Command Syntax

You can customize your report if you paste your selections into a syntax window and edit the resulting REPORT command syntax (see Chapter 4). Additional features include:

- Control of spacing between cases in listing reports (with the FORMAT subcommand).
- Stacking of multiple report variables in a single column in listing reports (with the VARIABLES subcommand).
- Summary statistics calculated for specific data column variables instead of all data column variables (with the SUMMARY subcommand).
- Control of descriptive headings for summary statistics (with the SUMMARY subcommand).

See Appendix A for command syntax rules. See the *SPSS Base System Syntax Reference Guide* for complete REPORT command syntax.

23 Overview of the SPSS Chart Facility

High-resolution charts and plots are created by the procedures on the Graphs menu and by many of the procedures on the Statistics menu. Chapter 23 through Chapter 32 offer a systematic discussion of the various aspects of creating and enhancing charts:

- **Overview of the SPSS Chart Facility** (Chapter 23)
- **Bar, Line, Area, and Pie Charts** (Chapter 24)
- **High-Low Charts** (Chapter 25)
- **Boxplots and Error Bar Charts** (Chapter 26)
- **Scatterplots and Histograms** (Chapter 27)
- **Pareto and Control Charts** (Chapter 28)
- **Normal Probability Plots** (Chapter 29)
- **Sequence Charts** (Chapter 30)
- **Autocorrelation and Cross-Correlation** (Chapter 31)
- **Modifying Charts** (Chapter 32)

This chapter provides an overview of the SPSS chart facility and includes the following information:

- **Tutorial.** Detailed steps showing how to create and modify a simple chart.
- **Chart Carousel.** Discussion of the SPSS window that holds and displays charts as they are created. You can view, save, copy, and print charts from this window.
- **Chart definition global options.** Definition options that apply to all charts, including titles and subtitles, footnotes, missing data values, and templates.

How to Create and Modify a Chart

Suppose that you have recorded the temperature in your office in the early morning and late afternoon every day for a week and you want a chart that emphasizes how much the temperature varies, such as the one in Figure 23.1.

Figure 23.1   Temperature chart

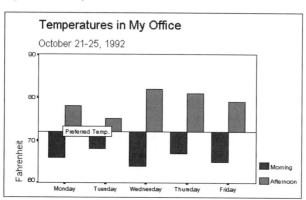

You must first enter the data, then create a chart, and, finally, modify the chart to make the message clear.

Entering the Data

For the purposes of this tutorial, the data are entered directly from the keyboard. Keyboard entry is appropriate if the amount of data is small. Once the data have been entered, the basic steps for creating a chart are the same, regardless of how the data were entered or the size of the data file.

1 If the Data Editor window is not active, from the Window menu choose the Data Editor window, which bears the name Newdata or the name of the data file you have already opened.

2 If an empty Newdata file is displayed, go on to step 3. If you have a data file already open, from the menus choose:

File
  New ▶
    Data...

This opens a Data Editor window containing the Newdata file.

3 In the Newdata file, enter the morning temperatures in the first column and the afternoon temperatures in the second column, as shown in Figure 23.2. After entering the last value, press ⏎Enter or move to another cell.

Figure 23.2   Data entered in Data Editor

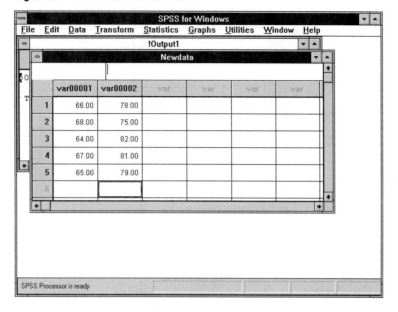

You have now created two variables: *var00001* and *var00002*. Later, you may want to give them more descriptive names, such as *amtemp* and *pmtemp*. After creating a chart, you will find out how to revise the labeling within the chart.

To avoid the chore of entering the temperature data again when you want to repeat some part of this tutorial, you should save this data file now.

Creating the Chart

Now that you have entered your data, you can get on with creating a chart.

① From the menus choose:

Graphs
  Bar...

This opens the Bar Charts dialog box, as shown in Figure 23.3.

Figure 23.3   Bar Charts dialog box

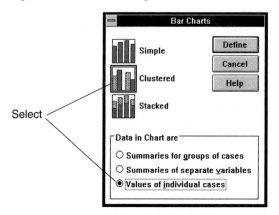

2. Select the picture button Clustered.

3. Select Values of individual cases.

4. Click on Define. This opens the Define Clustered Bar Values of Individual Cases dialog box, as shown in Figure 23.4.

Figure 23.4   Define Clustered Bar Values of Individual Cases dialog box

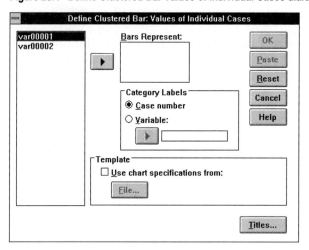

5. Move *var00001* and *var00002* from the variable source list to the Bars Represent list by highlighting them and clicking on ▶.

6. Click on OK. The chart appears in the Chart Carousel, as shown in Figure 23.5.

Figure 23.5   Original chart in Chart Carousel

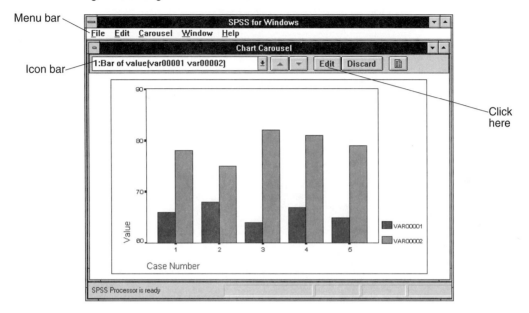

The Chart Carousel is a holding area for newly entered charts. The Chart Carousel menu bar replaces the main menu bar, and a corresponding icon bar appears above the chart. The chart as it stands contains an interpretable graphic representation of the data. You could save and print this chart from the Chart Carousel and use it in a report. There are several modifications, however, that will enhance the chart so that it will deliver a clearer message.

Modifying the Chart

The first step in chart modification is to transfer the chart from the Chart Carousel to a chart window.

1. Click on Edit on the icon bar. This places the chart in a chart window, as shown in Figure 23.6.

Figure 23.6   Original chart in chart window

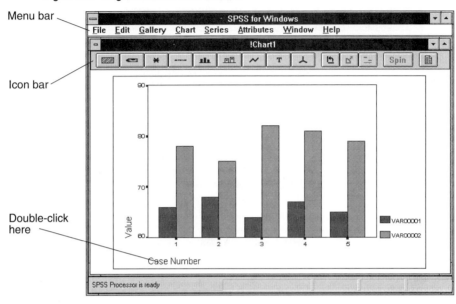

Menu bar

Icon bar

Double-click
here

Notice that the Chart Editor menu bar and icon bar replace those of the Chart Carousel.

② To edit the category axis at the base of the chart, double-click anywhere within the words *Case Number*. This opens the Category Axis dialog box, as shown in Figure 23.7. (If a different dialog box opens, click on Cancel in that dialog box and try again; you probably double-clicked too far from the category axis.)

Figure 23.7   Category Axis dialog box

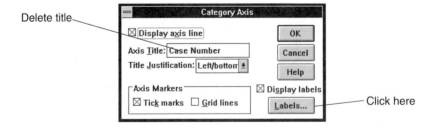

Delete title

Click here

③ Delete the axis title from the text box. It will not be meaningful when the labels are changed.

④ Click on Labels.... This opens the Category Axis Labels dialog box, as shown in Figure 23.8. The first label, the numeral *1*, is highlighted on the Label Text list and also appears in the Label text box.

Figure 23.8   Category Axis Labels dialog box

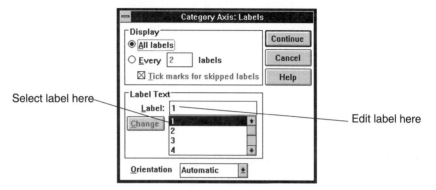

⑤ To edit the first label, delete the *1* in the text box, enter *Monday*, and click on Change.

⑥ In the same manner, click on the second label, *2*, and change it to *Tuesday*.

⑦ Click on the next label, *3*. The labels now appear, as shown in Figure 23.9.

Figure 23.9   Category labels changed

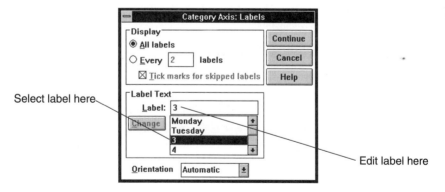

⑧ Change *3, 4*, and *5* to *Wednesday, Thursday*, and *Friday*, respectively, and click on Continue, which returns you to the Category Axis dialog box.

⑨ To return to the chart, click on OK. The results are shown in Figure 23.10.

Figure 23.10 Labeled chart

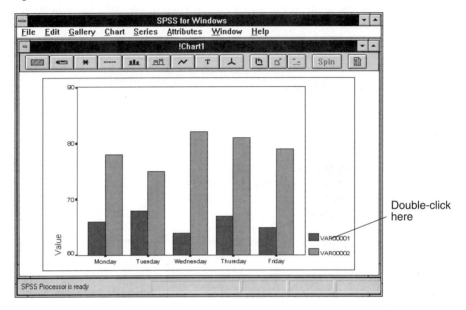

⑩ To edit the legend, double-click on the legend labels. This opens the Legend dialog box, as shown in Figure 23.11.

Figure 23.11 Legend dialog box

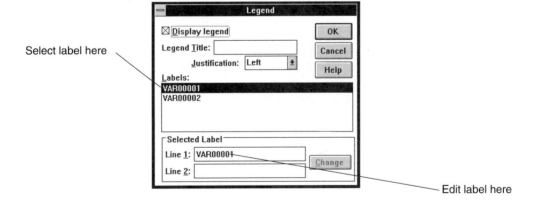

⑪ On the Labels list, *var00001* is highlighted. In the text box for Line 1, delete *var00001* and type *Morning*; then click on Change.

⑫ Select *var00002* on the list of labels.

⑬ In the Line 1 text box, delete *var00002* and type *Afternoon*; then click on Change.

⑭ Click on OK to return to the chart (Figure 23.12).

Figure 23.12 Chart with edited legend

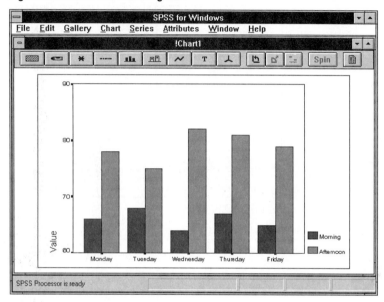

Further Enhancements

Now that the categories and subgroups are identified, you can enhance the chart for presentation.

① From the menus choose:

Chart
  Title...

This opens the Titles dialog box, as shown in Figure 23.13.

② Type a title in the Title 1 text box and a subtitle in the Subtitle text box as shown, and click on OK. The revised chart is shown in Figure 23.14.

Figure 23.13 Titles dialog box

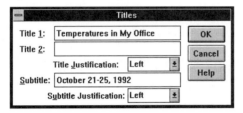

Figure 23.14 Revised chart with title and subtitle

Double-click here

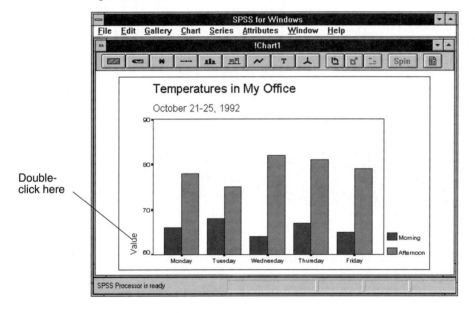

③ On the left side of the chart, double-click on the word *Value*. This opens the Scale Axis dialog box, as shown in Figure 23.15.

④ In the Axis Title text box, delete *Value* and enter *Fahrenheit*.

⑤ Select Bar origin line and change the value to 72.

Figure 23.15 Scale Axis dialog box

Edit text

Click here

Edit number

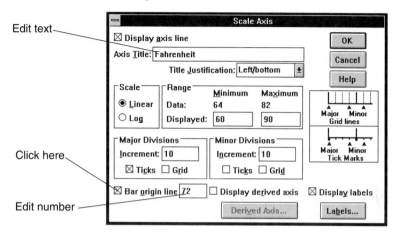

6 Click on OK. The revised chart now has hanging bars and a new axis title, as shown in Figure 23.16.

Figure 23.16 Revised chart with hanging bars and new axis title

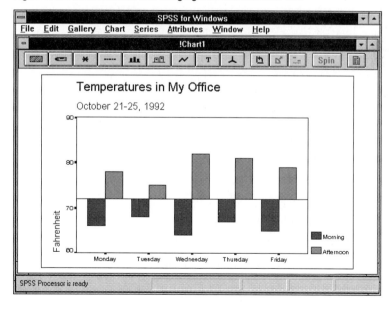

⑦ To further enhance the chart, from the menus choose:

Chart
  Annotation...

This opens the Annotation dialog box, as shown in Figure 23.17.

⑧ Enter *Preferred Temp.* in the text box, select Display frame around text, and change the Scale axis position to 72.

Figure 23.17 Annotation dialog box

Enter text

Click here

Edit scale
axis position

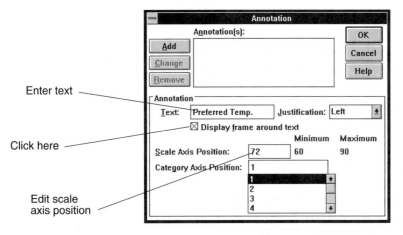

⑨ Click on Add and then OK. This displays the completed chart, as shown in Figure 23.18.

Figure 23.18 Final chart

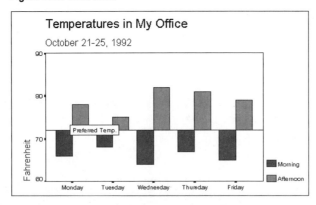

To print the chart or copy it into a document, see Chapter 33.

Chart Carousel

The tutorial showed the complete process of creating a chart. This section and the remainder of the chapter describe in detail features that apply to all or most chart types. High-resolution charts and plots are initially drawn in the Chart Carousel, as shown in Figure 23.19. This is a holding area from which you can save the chart, discard it, print it, copy it to the Clipboard, or transfer it to a chart window for editing.

Figure 23.19 Chart Carousel

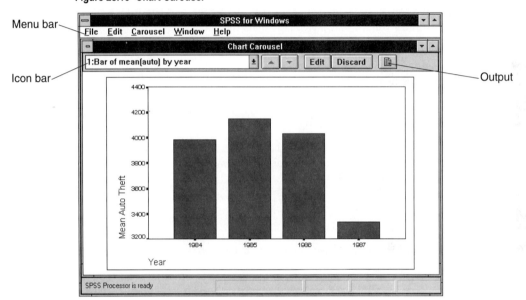

Chart Carousel Menus

When the Chart Carousel is the active window, its menu bar replaces the main menu bar. The Chart Carousel menu bar contains five menus:

File. Use the File menu to create a new SPSS file, open an existing file, save the current chart, or print the current chart.

Save As opens the Save As dialog box, which lets you select a name and a directory for the current chart. Charts are saved in SPSS chart format. You can also save all the charts in the Carousel in one step, either when you close the Carousel or when you exit from SPSS. For more information, see "Saving Charts in the Chart Carousel" on p. 452.

Print opens the Print Chart Carousel dialog box. See Chapter 33 for more information.

Edit. Use the Edit menu to change your Graphics preferences (see Chapter 36) or to copy the chart to the Clipboard.

Carousel. Use the Carousel menu to move the current chart to a chart window for editing or to move from chart to chart within the Carousel. You can redraw the current chart by selecting Refresh. You can also accomplish these tasks by clicking on pushbuttons on the icon bar, described in the section below.

Window. Use the Window menu to select, arrange, and control the attributes of the various SPSS windows, just as on the main menu bar.

Help. Use the Help menu to open a standard Microsoft Help window containing information on how to use the many features of SPSS. Context-sensitive help is also available through the dialog boxes.

Chart Carousel Pushbuttons

Several pushbuttons appear on the icon bar. For the most part, they duplicate functions that can be accessed from the Carousel menu. The pushbuttons behave as follows:

⬇ **Select**. Opens a drop-down list, from which you can choose one of the charts. The selected chart becomes the current chart.

▼ **Next**. Selects the next chart in the Carousel as the current chart.

▲ **Previous**. Selects the previous chart in the Carousel as the current chart.

Edit. Removes the current chart from the Carousel and places it in its own chart window for editing. From the chart window, you can modify most chart attributes, including colors, fonts, orientation, and type of chart displayed (see Chapter 32).

Discard. Removes the current chart from the Carousel and discards it.

Output icon. Switches to the output window, placing the cursor at the line where the currently displayed chart is listed. You can switch back by clicking on the chart icon in the output window.

Saving Charts in the Chart Carousel

To save only the current chart in the Chart Carousel, from the menus choose

File
  Save As...

This opens the *.CHT Save SPSS Chart As dialog box, which is similar to the Save As Chart Carousel dialog box discussed below. It does not have the Next Chart, Save All, or Discard All pushbutton.

To leave the Chart Carousel and save one or more of the charts, from the menus choose

File
  Close

This opens the Save As Chart Carousel dialog box, as shown in Figure 23.20. You can access this dialog box either when you close the Carousel or when you exit from SPSS.

Figure 23.20 Save As Chart Carousel dialog boxes

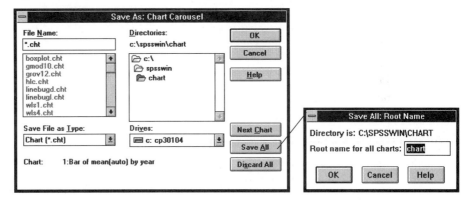

To save one chart at a time, type in a name for the current chart and click on OK. The current chart is saved and the name of the next chart is displayed. You can either save or discard each chart in turn. You can cycle through the charts without saving each one by clicking on Next Chart.

If you want to save all of the charts, click on Save All. This opens the Save All Root Name dialog box, as shown in Figure 23.20. Type a root name of one to five characters. SPSS will append a unique number for each chart and the extension *.cht*. For example, suppose you are working with food data and you type *food* as the root name. The filenames for the charts will be *food1.cht*, *food2.cht*, etc. After the charts are saved, you can edit them by opening each one from the File menu.

Chart Definition Global Options

When you are defining a chart, the specific chart definition dialog box usually contains the pushbuttons Titles... and Options..., and a Template group, as shown in Figure 23.21. These global options are available for most charts, regardless of type. They are not available for normal P-P plots, normal Q-Q plots, sequence charts, or time series charts.

Figure 23.21 A chart definition dialog box

Template
group

Titles

Options
(missing values)

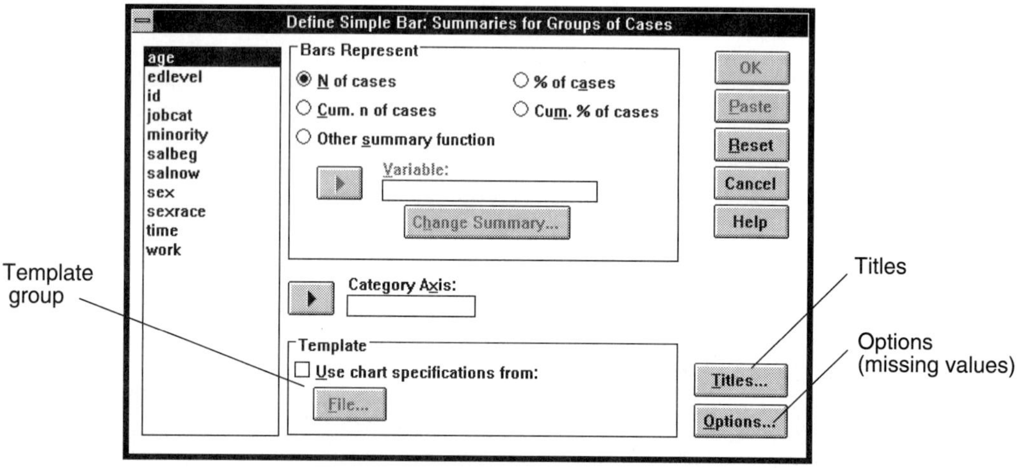

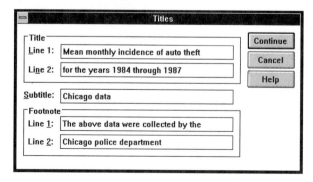

The Titles dialog box allows you to specify titles, subtitles, and footnotes. Clicking on Options... allows you to control the treatment of missing values. You can apply a template of previously selected attributes either when you are defining the chart or after the chart has been created. The next few sections describe how to define these characteristics at the time you define the chart.

Titles, Subtitles, and Footnotes

In any chart, you can define two title lines, one subtitle line, and two footnote lines as part of your original chart definition. To specify titles while defining a chart, click on Titles... in the chart definition dialog box, as shown in Figure 23.21. This opens the Titles dialog box, as shown in Figure 23.22.

Figure 23.22 Titles dialog box

Each line can be up to 72 characters long. The number of characters that will actually fit in the chart depends upon the font and size. Most titles are left justified by default and, if too long, are cropped on the right. Pie chart titles, by default, are center justified and, if too long, are cropped at both ends. Figure 23.23 shows the title, subtitle, and footnote in their default font, size, and justification.

Figure 23.23 Chart with title, subtitle, and footnote in default settings

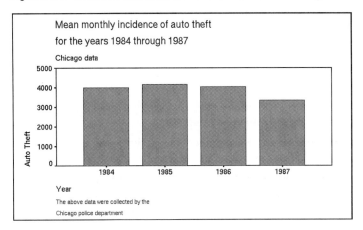

You can also add, delete, or revise text lines, as well as change their font, size, and justification, within the Chart Editor (see Chapter 32).

Missing Values

If there are missing values in the data, SPSS takes account of choices you make about treatment of missing values when it summarizes the data. To access the missing-value options available for your chart, click on Options... in the chart definition dialog box, as shown in Figure 23.21. This opens the Options dialog box, as shown in Figure 23.24. The specific options available depend on your previous choices.

Missing-value options are not available for charts using values of individual cases or for histograms.

Figure 23.24 Options dialog box

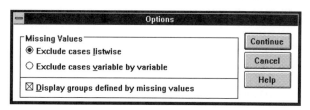

Missing Values. If you selected summaries of separate variables for a categorical chart or if you are creating a scatterplot, you can choose one of the following alternatives for exclusion of cases having missing values:

○ **Exclude cases listwise.** If any of the variables in the chart has a missing value for a given case, the whole case is excluded from the chart.

○ **Exclude cases variable by variable.** If a selected variable has any missing values, the cases having those missing values are excluded when the variable is analyzed.

The following option is also available for missing values:

❑ **Display groups defined by missing values.** If there are missing values in the data for variables used to define categories or subgroups, user-missing values (values identified as missing by the user) and system-missing values are included together in a category labeled *Missing*. The "missing" category is displayed on the category axis or in the legend, adding, for example, an extra bar, a slice to a pie chart, or an extra box to a boxplot. In a scatterplot, missing values add a "missing" category to the set of markers. If there are no missing values, the "missing" category is not displayed.

This option is selected by default. If you want to suppress display after the chart is drawn, select Displayed... from the Series menu and move the categories you want suppressed to the Omit group. (See sections "Bar, Line, and Area Chart Displayed Data" on p. 675 through "Histogram Displayed Data" on p. 685 in Chapter 32.)

This option is not available for an overlay scatterplot or for single-series charts in which the data are summarized by separate variables.

To see the difference between listwise and variable-by-variable exclusion of missing values, consider Figure 23.25, which shows a bar chart for each of the two options. The charts were created from a version of the data file *bank.sav* that was edited to have some system-missing (blank) values in the variables for current salary and job category. In some other cases of the job category variable, the value 9 was entered and defined as missing. For both charts, the option Display groups defined by missing values is selected, which adds the category *Missing* to the other job categories displayed. In each chart, the values of the summary function, *Number of cases*, are displayed in the bar labels.

Figure 23.25 Examples of missing-data treatment in charts

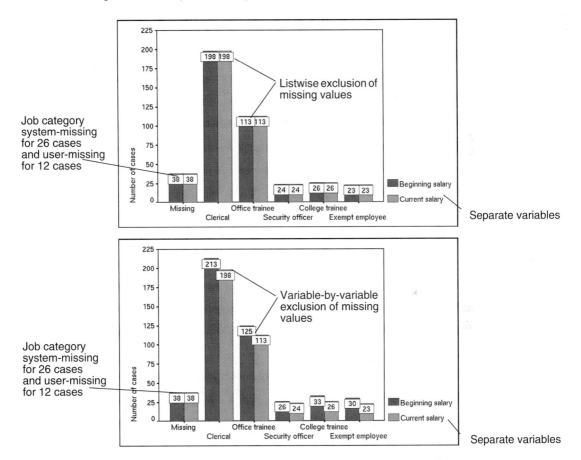

In both charts, 26 cases have a system-missing value for the job category and 12 cases have the user-missing value (9). In the listwise chart, the number of cases is the same for both variables in each bar cluster because whenever a value was missing, the case was excluded for all variables. In the variable-by-variable chart, the number of nonmissing cases for each variable in a category is plotted without regard to missing values in other variables.

Display of Missing Values in a Line Chart

If you create a line chart using data that have a missing value for a category and deselect Break Line at Missing on the Attributes menu, a line connects markers across the missing category. It is then easy to overlook the fact that there is no value there. Figure 23.26 shows two line charts, each drawn from the same data. The markers in the line chart were displayed by selecting Display Markers and Straight in the Line Interpolation dialog box (see Chapter 32).

Figure 23.26 Line charts with missing values

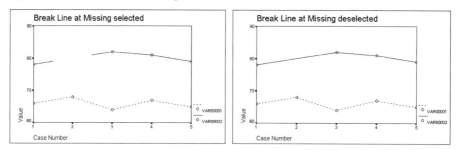

The first chart has Break Line at Missing selected. The second has no break for the missing value.

Chart Templates

You can apply many of the attributes and text elements from one chart to another. This allows you to modify one chart, save that chart, and then use it as a template to create a number of other, similar charts.

To use a template when creating a chart, select Use chart specifications from (in the Template group in the chart definition dialog box shown in Figure 23.21), and click on File.... This opens the Use Template from File dialog box, as shown in Figure 23.27.

Figure 23.27 Use Template from File dialog box

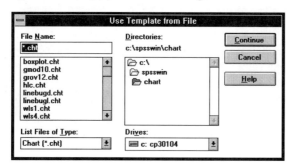

To apply a template to a chart already in a chart window, from the menus choose:

File
  Apply Chart Template...

This opens the Apply Chart Template dialog box, as shown in Figure 23.28.

Figure 23.28 Apply Chart Template dialog box

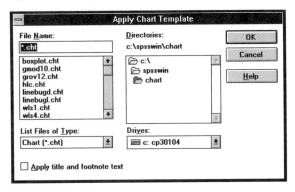

The two dialog boxes are similar. The chart files in the current directory are listed under the File Name box. The subdirectories in the current directory are listed on the Directories list and the drives on the computer are on the Drives drop-down list. Select a file to use as a template and click on Continue (for a new chart) or OK (in the Chart Editor). If you are creating a new chart, the filename you select is displayed in Template group when you return to the chart definition dialog box.

A template is used to borrow the format from one chart and apply it to the new chart you are generating. In general, any formatting information from the old chart that can apply to the new chart will automatically apply. For example, if the old chart is a clustered bar chart with bar colors modified to yellow and green and the new chart is a multiple line chart, the lines will be yellow and green. If the old chart is a simple bar chart with drop shadows and the new chart is a simple line chart, the lines will not have drop shadows because drop shadows don't apply to line charts. If there are titles in the template chart but not in the new chart, you will get the titles from the template chart. If there are titles defined in the new chart, they will override the titles in the old chart.

❏ **Apply title and footnote text.** Applies the text of the title and footnotes of the template to the current chart, overriding any text defined in the Titles dialog box in the current chart. The attributes of the title and footnotes (font, size, and color) are applied whether or not this item is selected. This check box appears only if you are applying the template in a chart window, not when creating a new chart.

Rotated Vertical Chart Text

Axis, category, and scale labels displayed in vertical format are rotated for TrueType fonts and stacked for bitmap fonts. To switch from stacked to rotated text (or vice versa) you must change the type of font used. Figure 23.29 shows both rotated TrueType and stacked bitmap fonts displayed in a chart.

Figure 23.29

Stacked vertical bitmap font

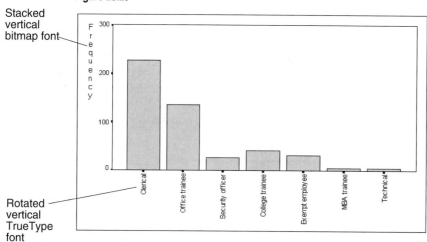

Rotated vertical TrueType font

24 Bar, Line, Area, and Pie Charts

Are American cities more violent today than they were several years ago? At what time of the year do major crimes occur? Do different types of crime show similar or different patterns of increase or decrease? These are the kinds of questions that are important to police departments across the United States. And these are the kinds of questions that are often most effectively answered in categorical charts, such as bar, line, area, and pie charts.

Chicago Uniform Crime Reports Data

The Uniform Crime Reports required by the FBI show reported incidents of murder, rape, aggravated assault, armed robbery, burglary, theft, and auto theft on a month-by-month basis. The crimes for which reports are required are called **index crimes**. Each crime is recorded as a separate variable. Each case indicates the number of crimes that occurred that month. A case is identified by two variables, *month* and *year*. Two other variables, *violent* and *property*, record the total number of violent crimes (murder, rape, aggravated assault, and armed robbery) and the total number of property crimes (burglary, theft, and auto theft), respectively. Figure 24.1 shows the first seven cases of the data collected by the Chicago Police Department from 1972 to 1987.

Figure 24.1 Chicago Uniform Crime Reports data

	year	month	murder	rape	assault	robbery	burglary	theft	auto	violent	property
1	`72	Jan	53	174	2061	740	2994	5972	2404	3028	11370
2	`72	Feb	54	110	1671	709	2650	5791	2097	2544	10538
3	`72	Mar	57	78	1541	753	2718	6435	1912	2429	11065
4	`72	Apr	56	139	1728	1018	3069	7010	2578	2941	12657
5	`72	May	51	138	1971	1118	3041	8233	2812	3278	14086
6	`72	Jun	55	122	1770	1051	2935	9030	3083	2998	15048
7	`72	Jul	73	117	2218	1200	3410	9814	3085	3608	16309

c:\spss\data\index.sav — 1:theft 5972

Simple Charts

In a bar chart showing the mean monthly incidence of armed robbery each year, it is immediately apparent that the number of robberies stayed fairly constant over the eleven-year period between 1972 and 1982 and then sharply increased.

Figure 24.2   Simple bar chart

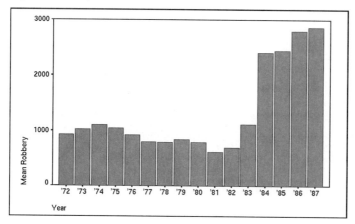

Figure 24.2 is a simple bar chart in which each bar represents the mean monthly incidence of robberies for one year. Often, a long series such as this is best displayed as a simple line chart. Though the data are the same, the chart in Figure 24.3 emphasizes the continuity from one element to the next.

Figure 24.3   Simple line chart

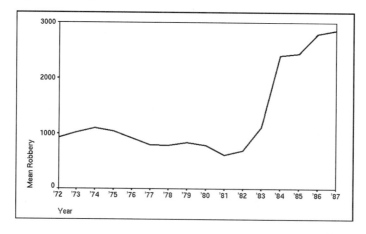

To emphasize the change, the same data might be displayed as a simple area chart, as shown in Figure 24.4. Notice that an area chart is just a line chart with the space underneath the line filled in.

Figure 24.4 Simple area chart

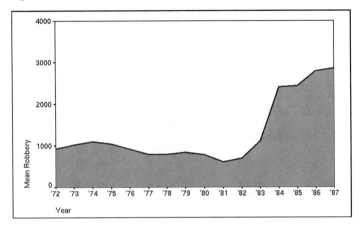

Robbery is only one crime. How does the armed robbery rate compare with that of other crimes? From a chart that shows the mean value of each crime variable as a separate bar, it can be seen that robbery is more common than murder or rape but less common than the other reported crimes (see Figure 24.5).

Figure 24.5 Simple bar chart

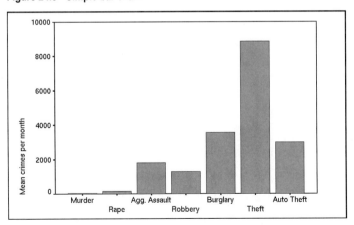

Figure 24.5 clearly shows which is the least and which is the most common index crime. If, however, the intent is to show what proportion of the total index crimes each constitutes, a pie chart is more appropriate, as shown in Figure 24.6. While Figure 24.5 shows the average for one month in each category, Figure 24.6 shows the totals for the entire 16-year period.

Figure 24.6   Simple pie chart

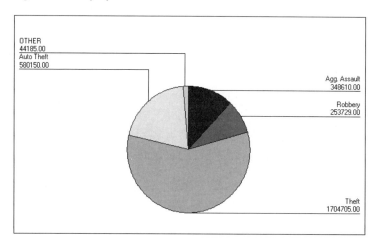

Clustered Bar and Multiple Line Charts

Theft, burglary, and auto theft are collectively known as "property crimes." In a clustered bar chart, as shown in Figure 24.7, we can show the mean monthly incidence of each property crime for each year.

Figure 24.7   Clustered bar chart

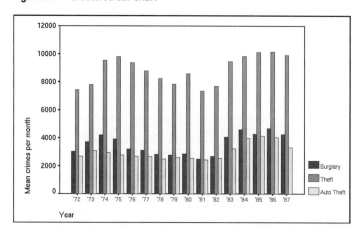

While a bar chart looks good and is fairly clear, we really want to explore patterns. Figure 24.8 shows the data series in Figure 24.7 as a multiple line chart. Here you can see that the three property crimes follow a similar pattern.

Figure 24.8   Multiple line chart

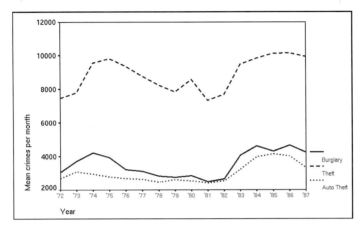

Drop-Line Charts

Sometimes the relationship between two or more changing values is more important than the values themselves. The drop-line chart in Figure 24.9 compares violent crimes in Chicago with violent crimes in Dallas.

Figure 24.9   Drop-line chart

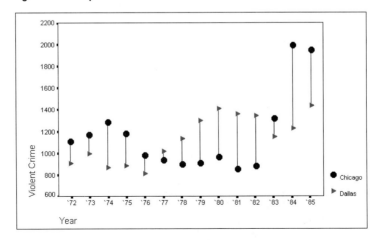

If there are only two values to be compared as in the example above, a difference line chart can also be used. For more information about difference line charts, see Chapter 25.

Stacked Bar and Area Charts

There are three property crimes tracked in the Chicago data. Each crime rate can be thought of as a part of a whole, which is the total recorded number of property crimes. To emphasize that these data are parts of a whole, we can display them in a stacked bar chart, as shown in Figure 24.10. The height of each bar shows the total number of property crimes committed during each year. The colored or patterned segments show the contribution of each individual property crime to that total.

Figure 24.10 Stacked bar chart

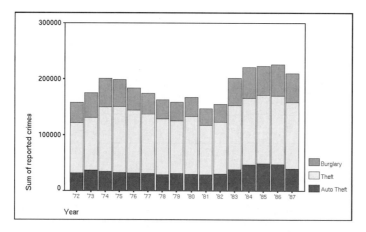

While Figure 24.10 is clear, it returns us to bars, which fail to emphasize the sequential nature of the data. In Figure 24.11, the same data are shown as a stacked area chart.

Figure 24.11 Stacked area chart

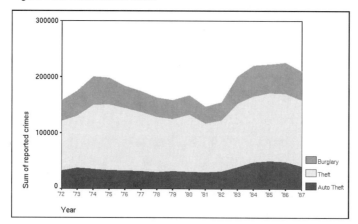

Variations in Bar, Line, and Area Charts

The following chart types require some level of modification from the basic chart types described previously. For a discussion of how to obtain these chart types with the Chart Editor, see Chapter 32.

100% Stacked Bar and Area Charts

Stacked bar and area charts show how property crimes as a whole fluctuate and at the same time show how the contribution of each individual crime type changes. In some circumstances, you might just want to show how the percentage contribution of each individual crime type changes, ignoring how property crimes as a whole change. This type of chart is called a 100% stacked chart. A 100% stacked area chart and a 100% stacked bar chart are shown in Figure 24.12.

Figure 24.12 100% stacked area chart and 100% stacked bar chart

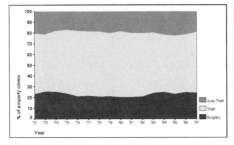 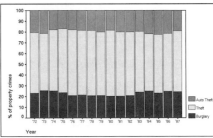

Hanging Bar Charts

A hanging bar chart is often used to show how values fluctuate around a fixed value (the **origin**), as shown in Figure 24.13.

Figure 24.13 Hanging bar chart

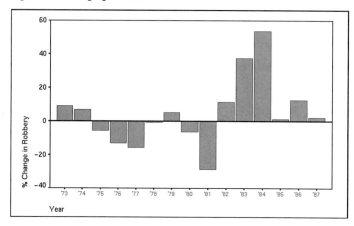

Mixed Charts

A mixed chart overlays one chart type on top of another. This is sometimes a useful way to differentiate between data that are related but somehow qualitatively different. The mixed line and bar chart in Figure 24.14 shows national crime data as a line superimposed over Chicago crime data as bars.

Figure 24.14 Mixed line and bar chart

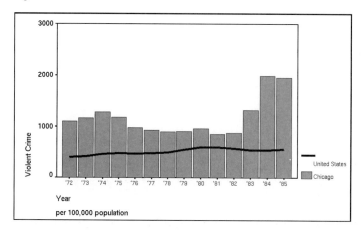

How to Obtain Bar, Line, Area, and Pie Charts

To obtain bar, line, area, or pie charts, choose the appropriate chart type from the Graphs menu, as shown in Figure 24.15.

Figure 24.15 Graphs Menu

This opens a chart dialog box for the selected chart type, as shown in Figure 24.16 (chart dialog boxes for line, area, and pie charts are shown in Figure 24.28, Figure 24.40, and Figure 24.49, respectively).

Figure 24.16 Bar Charts dialog box

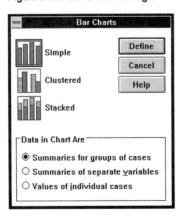

From the chart dialog box, choose the type of chart you want. Your choices depend upon the type of chart you selected on the Graphs menu. For bar charts, the choices are: simple, clustered, or stacked.

Data in Chart Are. Select the choice that describes the structure of your data organization.

○ **Summaries for groups of cases.** Cases are counted, or one variable is summarized, in subgroups. The subgroups are determined by one variable for simple charts or by two variables for complex charts.

○ **Summaries of separate variables.** More than one variable is summarized. Simple charts summarize each variable over all cases in the file. Complex charts summarize each variable within categories determined by another variable.

○ **Values of individual cases.** Individual values of one variable are plotted in simple charts. Values of more than one variable are plotted in complex charts.

Examples of these choices, shown with data organization structures and the charts they produce, are presented in the tables at the beginning of each section.

Bar Charts

To obtain a bar chart, from the menus choose:

Graphs
  Bar...

This opens the Bar Charts dialog box, as shown in Figure 24.16 (chart dialog boxes for line, area, and pie charts are shown in Figure 24.28, Figure 24.40, and Figure 24.49).

Select the type of bar chart you want, and select the choice that describes the structure of your data organization. Click on Define to open a dialog box specific to your selections. Examples of these choices, shown with data structures and the charts they produce, are presented in Table 24.1.

Table 24.1   Types of bar charts

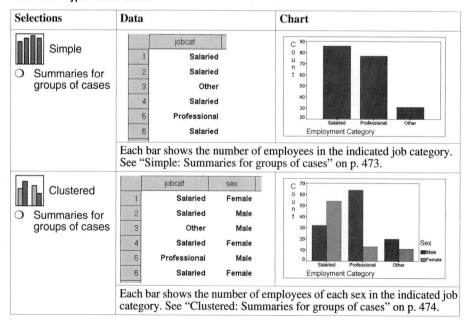

Selections	Data	Chart
Simple ○ Summaries for groups of cases	jobcat: 1 Salaried, 2 Salaried, 3 Other, 4 Salaried, 5 Professional, 6 Salaried	(bar chart: Count by Employment Category)
	Each bar shows the number of employees in the indicated job category. See "Simple: Summaries for groups of cases" on p. 473.	
Clustered ○ Summaries for groups of cases	jobcat / sex: 1 Salaried Female, 2 Salaried Male, 3 Other Male, 4 Salaried Female, 5 Professional Male, 6 Salaried Female	(clustered bar chart: Count by Employment Category, Sex)
	Each bar shows the number of employees of each sex in the indicated job category. See "Clustered: Summaries for groups of cases" on p. 474.	

Table 24.1   Types of bar charts (Continued)

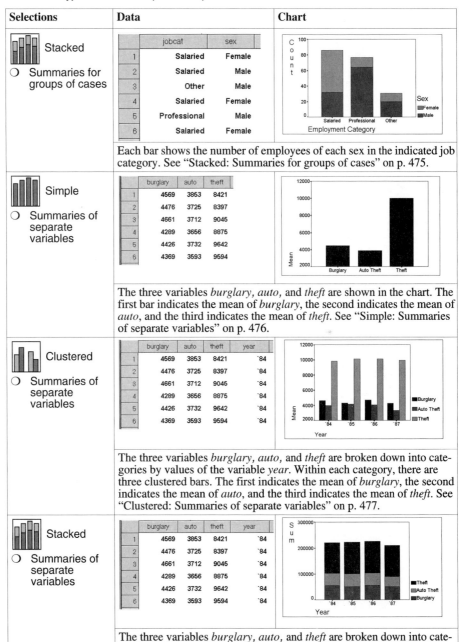

Selections	Data	Chart
Stacked — Summaries for groups of cases		

Each bar shows the number of employees of each sex in the indicated job category. See "Stacked: Summaries for groups of cases" on p. 475.

| Simple — Summaries of separate variables | | |

The three variables *burglary, auto,* and *theft* are shown in the chart. The first bar indicates the mean of *burglary,* the second indicates the mean of *auto,* and the third indicates the mean of *theft.* See "Simple: Summaries of separate variables" on p. 476.

| Clustered — Summaries of separate variables | | |

The three variables *burglary, auto,* and *theft* are broken down into categories by values of the variable *year.* Within each category, there are three clustered bars. The first indicates the mean of *burglary,* the second indicates the mean of *auto,* and the third indicates the mean of *theft.* See "Clustered: Summaries of separate variables" on p. 477.

| Stacked — Summaries of separate variables | | |

The three variables *burglary, auto,* and *theft* are broken down into categories by values of the variable *year.* Within each category, there are three bars stacked one on top of the other. The first indicates the sum of *burglary,* the second indicates the sum of *auto,* and the third indicates the sum of *theft.* See "Stacked: Summaries of separate variables" on p. 478.

Table 24.1   Types of bar charts (Continued)

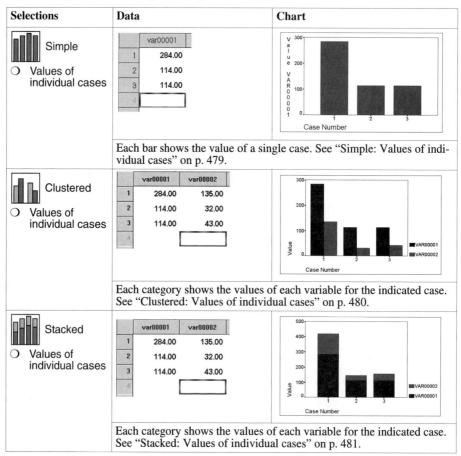

Selections	Data	Chart
Simple ○ Values of individual cases		
Each bar shows the value of a single case. See "Simple: Values of individual cases" on p. 479.		
Clustered ○ Values of individual cases		
Each category shows the values of each variable for the indicated case. See "Clustered: Values of individual cases" on p. 480.		
Stacked ○ Values of individual cases		
Each category shows the values of each variable for the indicated case. See "Stacked: Values of individual cases" on p. 481.		

Defining Bar Charts

Each combination of chart type and data organization structure produces a different definition box. Each is discussed briefly below. The icon and section title indicate the choices that have to be made in the chart dialog box to open that chart definition dialog box. The discussion for each chart type always describes the selections required to enable the OK pushbutton. Optional selections are discussed only with the first chart using each data structure. For a detailed description of optional statistics, see "Summary Functions" on p. 506.

All chart definition dialog boxes have a Titles pushbutton and Template group. These are discussed in "Titles, Subtitles, and Footnotes" on p. 454 and "Chart Templates" on p. 458, both in Chapter 23. Chart definition dialog boxes for summaries for groups of cases and for summaries of separate variables also have an Options... pushbutton. The Options... pushbutton brings up a dialog box that controls missing-value options, discussed in "Missing Values" on p. 455 in Chapter 23.

Simple:
Summaries for groups of cases

Figure 24.17 shows a chart definition dialog box and the resulting simple bar chart with summaries for groups of cases.

Figure 24.17 Simple bar chart with summaries for groups of cases

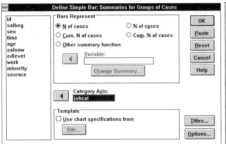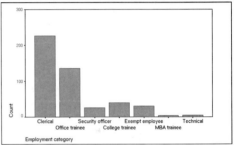

The minimum specification is a category axis variable.

The numeric, short string, and long string variables in your data file are displayed on the source variable list. Select a variable to define the category axis. To get a simple chart showing number of cases for groups of cases in default format, click on OK.

Optionally, you can select a different summary statistic, use a template to control the format of the chart, or add a title, subtitle, or footnote. Optional summary statistics are discussed in "Summary Functions" on p. 506. The other options are discussed in detail in Chapter 23.

Category Axis. Select a variable to define the categories shown in the chart. There is one bar for each value of the variable.

If you select Other summary function in the Define Simple Bar Summaries for Groups of Cases dialog box, you must also select a variable to be summarized. Figure 24.18 shows the chart definition dialog box with a variable to be summarized and the resulting simple bar chart with a summarized variable.

Figure 24.18   Simple bar chart with summary of a variable

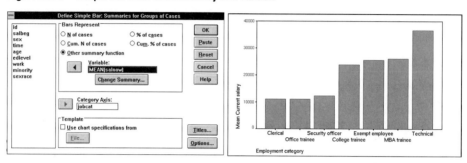

The default chart shows the mean of the selected variable within each category (determined by the category axis variable).

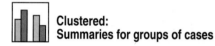

Clustered:
Summaries for groups of cases

Figure 24.19 shows a chart definition dialog box and the resulting clustered bar chart with summaries for groups of cases.

Figure 24.19   Clustered bar chart with summaries for groups of cases

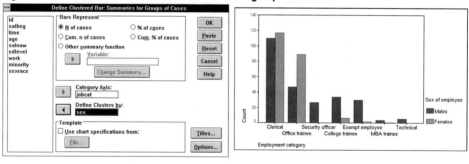

The minimum specifications are:

• A category axis variable.
• A cluster member definition variable.

Category Axis. Select a variable to define the categories shown in the chart. There is one cluster of bars for each value of the variable.

Define Clusters by. Select a variable to define the bars within each cluster. There is one set of differently colored or patterned bars for each value of the variable.

Stacked:
Summaries for groups of cases

Figure 24.20 shows a chart definition dialog box and the resulting stacked bar chart with summaries for groups of cases.

Figure 24.20   Stacked bar chart with summaries for groups of cases

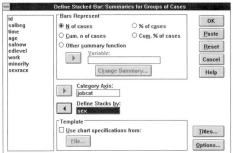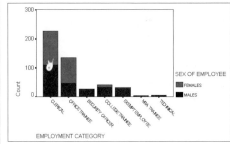

The minimum specifications are:

- A category axis variable.
- A bar segment definition variable.

Category Axis. Select a variable to define the categories shown on the chart. There is one stack of bars for each value of the variable.

Define Stacks by. Select a variable to define the bar segments within each stack. There is one bar segment within each stack for each value of the variable.

Simple:
Summaries of separate variables

Figure 24.21 shows a chart definition dialog box and the resulting simple bar chart with summaries of separate variables.

Figure 24.21   Simple bar chart with summaries of separate variables

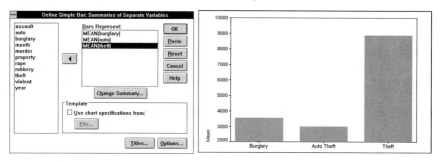

The minimum specifications are two or more bar variables.

The numeric variables in your data file are displayed on the source variable list. Select the variables you want to define the bars. To get a simple bar chart showing the mean value of each variable in default format, click on OK.

Optionally, you can select a different summary statistic, use a template to control the format of the chart, or add a title, subtitle, or footnote. Summary statistics are discussed in "Summary Functions" on p. 506. The other options are discussed in detail in Chapter 23.

Bars Represent. Select two or more variables to define the categories shown in the chart. There is one bar for each variable. By default, the bar shows the mean of the selected variables.

Clustered:
Summaries of separate variables

Figure 24.22 shows a chart definition dialog box and the resulting clustered bar chart with summaries of separate variables.

Figure 24.22   Clustered bar chart with summaries of separate variables

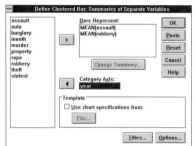 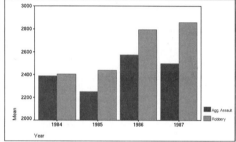

The minimum specifications are:

- Two or more bar variables.
- A category axis variable.

Bars Represent. Select two or more variables. There is one bar within each group for each variable. By default, the bars show the mean of the selected variables.

Category Axis. Select a variable to define the categories shown in the chart. There is one cluster of bars for each value of the variable.

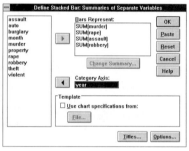

Stacked:
Summaries of separate variables

Figure 24.23 shows a chart definition dialog box and the resulting stacked bar chart with summaries of separate variables.

Figure 24.23   Stacked bar chart with summaries of separate variables

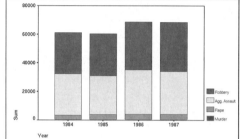

The minimum specifications are:

- Two or more segment variables.
- A category axis variable.

Bars Represent. Select two or more variables. There is one bar within each stack for each variable. By default, the bars show the sum of the selected variables.

Category Axis. Select a variable to define the categories shown in the chart. There is one stack of bars for each value of the variable.

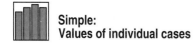

Simple:
Values of individual cases

Figure 24.24 shows a chart definition dialog box and the resulting simple bar chart with values of individual cases.

Figure 24.24   Simple bar chart with values of individual cases

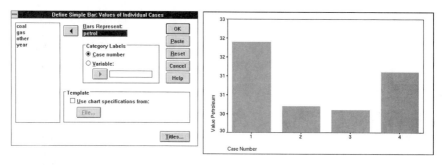

The minimum specification is a bar variable.

The numeric, short string, and long string variables in your data file are displayed on the source variable list. Select the numeric variable you want to define the bars. To get a simple bar chart showing the value of each case in default format, click on OK.

Optionally, you can change the value labels shown in the chart, use a template to control the format of the chart, or add a title, subtitle, or footnote. These options are discussed in detail in Chapter 23.

Bars Represent. Select a numeric variable to define the bars. Each case is represented by a separate bar.

Category Labels. Determines how the bars are labeled. You can choose one of the following category label sources:

○ **Case number.** Each category is labeled with the case number. This is the default.

○ **Variable.** Each category is labeled with the current value label of the selected variable.

Figure 24.25 shows a chart definition dialog box with a label variable selected and the resulting bar chart.

Figure 24.25   Bar chart with category labels from the variable year

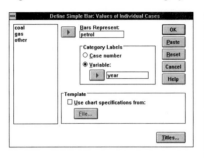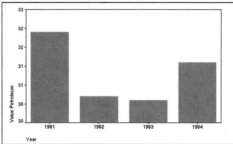

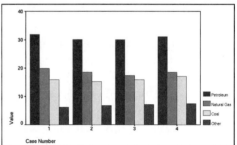

Clustered:
Values of individual cases

Figure 24.26 shows a chart definition dialog box and the resulting clustered bar chart with values of individual cases.

Figure 24.26   Clustered bar chart with bars as values of individual cases

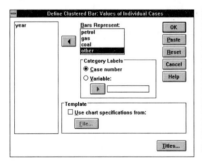

The minimum specification is two or more bar variables.

Bars Represent. Select two or more numeric variables. There is one separately colored or patterned set of bars for each variable. Each case is represented by a separate cluster of bars. The height of each bar represents the value of the variable.

Stacked:
Values of individual cases

Figure 24.27 shows a chart definition dialog box and the resulting stacked bar chart with values of individual cases.

Figure 24.27   Stacked bar chart with values of individual cases

 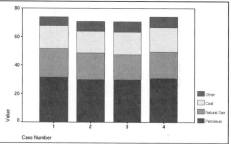

The minimum specifications are two or more segment variables.

Bars Represent. Select two or more numeric variables. Each case is represented by a separate stack. Each variable is represented by a separate bar within each stack.

Line Charts

To obtain a line chart, from the menus choose:

Graphs
  Line...

This opens the Line Charts dialog box, as shown in Figure 24.28.

Figure 24.28 Line Charts dialog box

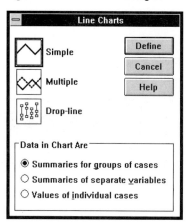

Select the type of line chart you want, and select the choice that describes the structure of your data organization. Click on Define to open a dialog box specific to your selections. Examples of these choices, shown with data structures and the charts they produce, are presented in Table 24.2.

Table 24.2 Types of line chart

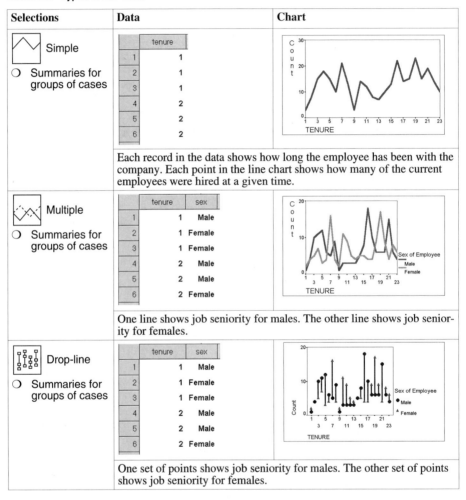

Selections	Data	Chart
Simple — Summaries for groups of cases	tenure: 1→1, 2→1, 3→1, 4→2, 5→2, 6→2	
Each record in the data shows how long the employee has been with the company. Each point in the line chart shows how many of the current employees were hired at a given time.		
Multiple — Summaries for groups of cases	tenure/sex: 1→1 Male, 2→1 Female, 3→1 Female, 4→2 Male, 5→2 Male, 6→2 Female	
One line shows job seniority for males. The other line shows job seniority for females.		
Drop-line — Summaries for groups of cases	tenure/sex: 1→1 Male, 2→1 Female, 3→1 Female, 4→2 Male, 5→2 Male, 6→2 Female	
One set of points shows job seniority for males. The other set of points shows job seniority for females.		

Table 24.2 Types of line chart (Continued)

Selections	Data	Chart

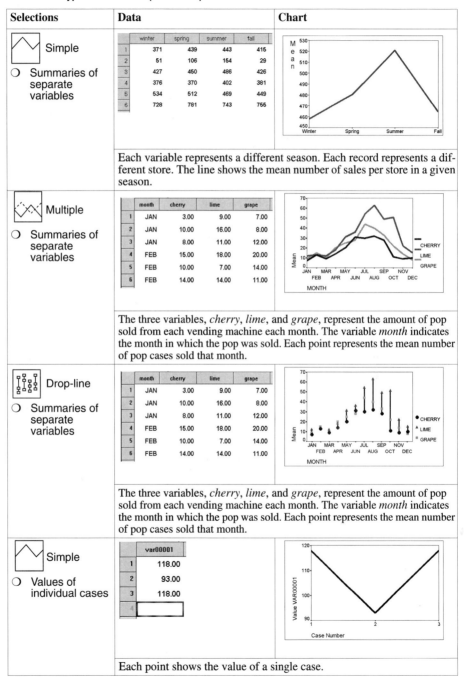

Simple

○ Summaries of separate variables

	winter	spring	summer	fall
1	371	439	443	415
2	51	106	154	29
3	427	450	486	426
4	376	370	402	381
5	534	512	469	449
6	728	781	743	755

Each variable represents a different season. Each record represents a different store. The line shows the mean number of sales per store in a given season.

Multiple

○ Summaries of separate variables

	month	cherry	lime	grape
1	JAN	3.00	9.00	7.00
2	JAN	10.00	16.00	8.00
3	JAN	8.00	11.00	12.00
4	FEB	15.00	18.00	20.00
5	FEB	10.00	7.00	14.00
6	FEB	14.00	14.00	11.00

The three variables, *cherry*, *lime*, and *grape*, represent the amount of pop sold from each vending machine each month. The variable *month* indicates the month in which the pop was sold. Each point represents the mean number of pop cases sold that month.

Drop-line

○ Summaries of separate variables

	month	cherry	lime	grape
1	JAN	3.00	9.00	7.00
2	JAN	10.00	16.00	8.00
3	JAN	8.00	11.00	12.00
4	FEB	15.00	18.00	20.00
5	FEB	10.00	7.00	14.00
6	FEB	14.00	14.00	11.00

The three variables, *cherry*, *lime*, and *grape*, represent the amount of pop sold from each vending machine each month. The variable *month* indicates the month in which the pop was sold. Each point represents the mean number of pop cases sold that month.

Simple

○ Values of individual cases

	var00001
1	118.00
2	93.00
3	118.00
4	

Each point shows the value of a single case.

Table 24.2   Types of line chart (Continued)

Selections	Data	Chart
Multiple ○ Values of individual cases	var00001 / var00002 1 118.00 195.00 2 93.00 80.00 3 118.00 43.00	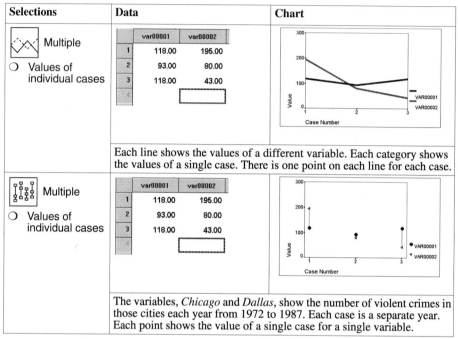

Each line shows the values of a different variable. Each category shows the values of a single case. There is one point on each line for each case.

| Multiple
○ Values of individual cases | var00001 / var00002
1 118.00 195.00
2 93.00 80.00
3 118.00 43.00 | |

The variables, *Chicago* and *Dallas*, show the number of violent crimes in those cities each year from 1972 to 1987. Each case is a separate year. Each point shows the value of a single case for a single variable.

Simple:
Summaries for groups of cases

Figure 24.29 shows a chart definition dialog box and the resulting simple line chart with summaries for groups of cases.

Figure 24.29   Simple line chart with summaries for groups of cases

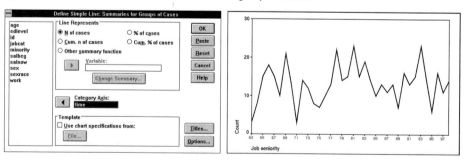

The minimum specification is a category axis variable.

The numeric, short string, and long string variables in your data file are displayed on the source variable list. Select a variable to define the category axis. To get a simple line chart showing the number of cases in each category, click on OK.

Optionally, you can select a different summary statistic, use a template to control the format of the chart, or add a title, subtitle, or footnote. Summary statistics are discussed in "Summary Functions" on p. 506. The other options are discussed in detail in Chapter 23.

Category Axis. Select a variable to define the categories shown in the chart. There is one point for each value of the variable.

If you select Other summary function in the Define Simple Line Summaries for Groups of Cases dialog box, you must also select a variable to be summarized. Figure 24.30 shows the chart definition dialog box with a variable to be summarized and the resulting chart.

Figure 24.30   Simple line chart with summary of a variable

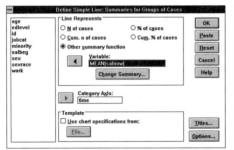 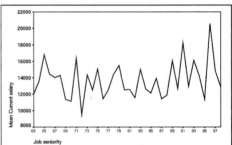

The chart generated by default shows the mean of the selected variable within each category (determined by the category axis variable).

Multiple:
Summaries for groups of cases

Figure 24.31 shows a chart definition dialog box and the resulting multiple line chart with summaries for groups of cases.

Figure 24.31   Multiple line chart with summaries for groups of cases

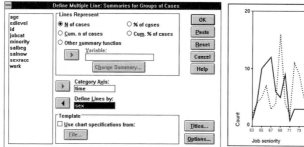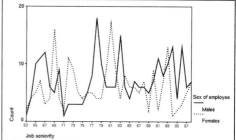

The minimum specifications are:

- A category axis variable.
- A line definition variable.

Category Axis. Select a variable to define the categories shown in the chart. There is one point on each line for each value of the variable.

Define Lines by. Select a variable to define the lines. There is one line for each value of the variable.

Drop-line:
Summaries for groups of cases

Figure 24.32 shows a chart definition dialog box and the resulting drop-line chart with summaries for groups of cases.

Figure 24.32   Drop-line chart with summaries for groups of cases

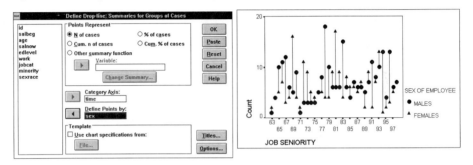

The minimum specifications are:

- A category axis variable.
- A point definition variable.

Category Axis. Select a variable to define the categories shown in the chart. There is one vertical line for each value of the variable.

Define Points by. Select a variable to define the points. There is one sequence of differently colored, patterned, or shaped points for each value of the variable.

Simple:
Summaries of separate variables

Figure 24.33 shows a chart definition dialog box and the resulting simple line chart with summaries of separate variables.

Figure 24.33   Simple line chart with summaries of separate variables

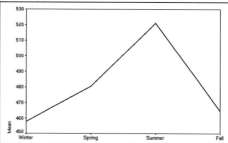

The minimum specifications are two or more point variables.

The numeric variables in your data file are displayed on the source variable list. Select the variables you want the line to represent. To get a simple line chart showing the mean value of each variable in default format, click on OK.

Optionally, you can select a different summary statistic, use a template to control the format of the chart, or add a title, subtitle, or footnote. Summary statistics are discussed in "Summary Functions" on p. 506. The other options are discussed in detail in Chapter 23.

Line Represents. Select two or more variables to define the categories shown in the chart. There is one point on the line for each variable. By default, the points show the mean of the selected variables.

Multiple:
Summaries of separate variables

Figure 24.34 shows a chart definition dialog box and the resulting multiple line chart with summaries of separate variables.

Figure 24.34   Multiple line chart with summaries of separate variables

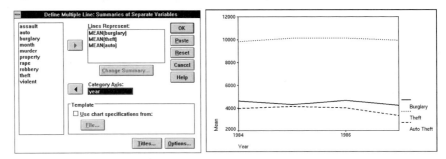

The minimum specifications are:

- Two or more line variables.
- A category axis variable.

Lines Represent. Select two or more variables to define the lines. There is one line for each variable. By default, the lines show the mean of the selected variables.

Category Axis. Select a variable to define the categories shown in the chart. There is one point on each line for each value of the variable.

Drop-line:
Summaries of separate variables

Figure 24.35 shows a chart definition dialog box and the resulting drop-line chart with summaries of separate variables.

Figure 24.35 Drop-line chart with summaries of separate variables

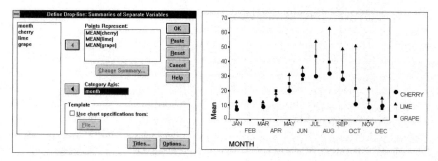

The minimum specifications are:

- Two or more point variables.
- A category axis variable.

Points Represent. Select two or more variables to define the points. There is one sequence of differently colored, patterned, or shaped points for each variable. By default, the points show the mean of the selected variables.

Category Axis. Select a variable to define the categories shown in the chart. There is one vertical line for each value of the variable.

Simple:
Values of individual cases

Figure 24.36 shows a chart definition dialog box and the resulting simple line chart with values of individual cases.

Figure 24.36 Simple line chart with values of individual cases

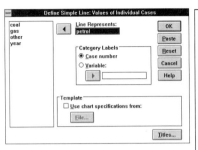 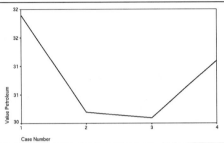

The minimum specification is a line variable.

The numeric, short string, and long string variables in your data file are displayed on the source variable list. Select the numeric variable you want to define the line. To get a simple line chart showing the value of each case in default format, click on OK.

Optionally, you can change the value labels shown in the chart, use a template to control the format of the chart, or add a title, subtitle, or footnote. These options are discussed in detail in Chapter 23.

Line Represents. Select a numeric variable to define the line. Each case will be displayed as a point.

Category Labels. Determines how the categories are labeled. You can choose one of the following category label sources:

O **Case number.** Each category is labeled with the case number. This is the default.

O **Variable.** Each category is labeled with the current value label of the selected variable.

Figure 24.37 shows a chart definition dialog box with a label variable selected and the resulting simple line chart with category labels.

Figure 24.37   Line chart with category labels from the variable year

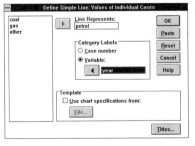 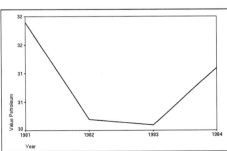

Multiple:
Values of individual cases

Figure 24.38 shows a chart definition dialog box and the resulting multiple line chart with values of individual cases.

Figure 24.38   Multiple line chart with values of individual cases

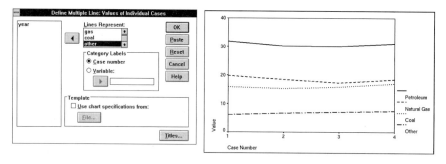

The minimum specification is two or more line variables.

Lines Represent. Select two or more numeric variables to define the lines. There is one line for each variable. There is one point on each line for each case.

Drop-line:
Values of individual cases

Figure 24.39 shows a chart definition dialog box and the resulting drop-line chart with values of individual cases.

Figure 24.39 Drop-line chart with values of individual cases

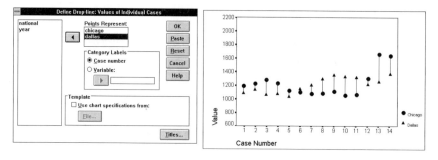

The minimum specification is two or more point variables.

Points Represent. Select two or more numeric variables to define the points. There is one sequence of differently colored, patterned, or shaped points for each variable. There is one vertical line for each case.

Area Charts

To obtain an area chart, from the menus choose:

Graphs
 Area...

This opens the Area Charts dialog box, as shown in Figure 24.40.

Figure 24.40   Area Charts dialog box

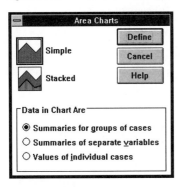

Select the type of area chart you want, and select the choice that describes the structure of your data organization. Click on Define to open a dialog box specific to your selections. Examples of these choices, shown with data structures and the charts they produce, are presented in Table 24.3.

Table 24.3 Types of area chart

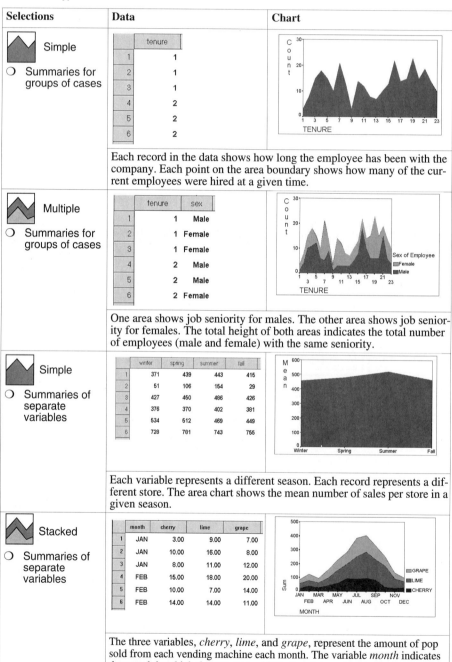

Selections	Data	Chart
Simple ○ Summaries for groups of cases	*(tenure)* 1:1, 2:1, 3:1, 4:2, 5:2, 6:2	Count vs TENURE area chart

Each record in the data shows how long the employee has been with the company. Each point on the area boundary shows how many of the current employees were hired at a given time.

| **Multiple** ○ Summaries for groups of cases | *(tenure, sex)* 1:1 Male, 2:1 Female, 3:1 Female, 4:2 Male, 5:2 Male, 6:2 Female | Count vs TENURE area chart, Sex of Employee (Female, Male) |

One area shows job seniority for males. The other area shows job seniority for females. The total height of both areas indicates the total number of employees (male and female) with the same seniority.

| **Simple** ○ Summaries of separate variables | *(winter, spring, summer, fall)* 1: 371, 439, 443, 415; 2: 51, 106, 154, 29; 3: 427, 450, 486, 426; 4: 376, 370, 402, 381; 5: 534, 512, 469, 449; 6: 728, 781, 743, 755 | Mean vs Winter/Spring/Summer/Fall area chart |

Each variable represents a different season. Each record represents a different store. The area chart shows the mean number of sales per store in a given season.

| **Stacked** ○ Summaries of separate variables | *(month, cherry, lime, grape)* 1: JAN 3.00 9.00 7.00; 2: JAN 10.00 16.00 8.00; 3: JAN 8.00 11.00 12.00; 4: FEB 15.00 18.00 20.00; 5: FEB 10.00 7.00 14.00; 6: FEB 14.00 14.00 11.00 | Sum vs MONTH stacked area chart (GRAPE, LIME, CHERRY) |

The three variables, *cherry*, *lime*, and *grape*, represent the amount of pop sold from each vending machine each month. The variable *month* indicates the month in which the pop was sold. Each point represents the total number of pop cases sold that month.

Table 24.3   Types of area chart (Continued)

Selections	Data	Chart
Simple ○ Values of individual cases	var00001 1 284.00 2 114.00 3 114.00	
	Each point on the boundary of the area shows the value of a single case.	
Stacked ○ Values of individual cases	var00001 var00002 1 118.00 195.00 2 93.00 80.00 3 118.00 43.00 4	
	Each area shows the values of a different variable. Each category shows the values of a single case. There is one point on each area for each case.	

Simple:
Summaries for groups of cases

Figure 24.41 shows a chart definition dialog box and the resulting simple area chart with summaries for groups of cases.

Figure 24.41   Simple area chart with summaries for groups of cases

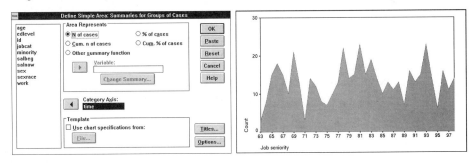

The minimum specification is a category axis variable.

The numeric, short string, and long string variables in your data file are displayed on the source variable list. Select the variable you want to define the category axis. To get a simple area chart showing the number of cases in each category, click on OK.

Optionally, you can select a different summary statistic, use a template to control the format of the chart, or add a title, subtitle, or footnote. Summary statistics are discussed in "Summary Functions" on p. 506. The other options are discussed in detail in Chapter 23.

Category Axis. Select a variable to define the categories shown in the chart. There is one point on the boundary of the area for each value of the variable.

If you select Other summary function in the chart definition dialog box, you must also select a variable to be summarized. Figure 24.42 shows the dialog box with a variable to be summarized and the resulting chart.

Figure 24.42   Summary of a variable in a simple area chart

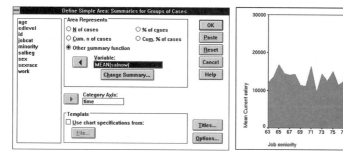

The chart generated by default shows the mean of the selected variable within each category (determined by the category axis variable). For a detailed description of optional statistics, see "Summary Functions" on p. 506.

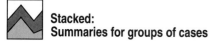

Stacked:
Summaries for groups of cases

Figure 24.43 shows a chart definition dialog box and the resulting stacked area chart with summaries for groups of cases.

Figure 24.43   Stacked area chart with summaries for groups of cases

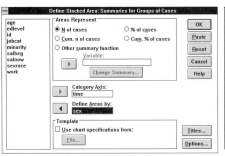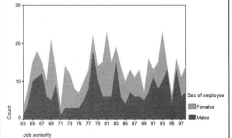

The minimum specifications are:

- A category axis variable.
- An area definition variable.

Category Axis. Select a variable to define the categories shown in the chart. There is one point on the boundary of each area for each value of the variable.

Define Areas by. Select a variable to define the areas. There is one differently colored or patterned area for each value of the variable.

Simple:
Summaries of separate variables

Figure 24.44 shows a chart definition dialog box and the resulting simple area chart with summaries of separate variables.

Figure 24.44   Simple area chart with summaries of separate variables

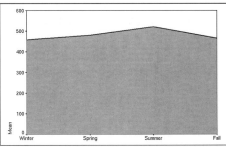

The minimum specifications are two or more point variables.

The numeric variables in your data file are displayed on the source variable list. Select the variables you want to define points on the boundary of the area. To get a simple area chart showing the mean value of each variable in default format, click on OK.

Optionally, you can select a different summary statistic, use a template to control the format of the chart, or add a title, subtitle, or footnote. Summary statistics are discussed in "Summary Functions" on p. 506. The other options are discussed in detail in Chapter 23.

Area Represents. Select two or more variables to define the categories shown in the chart. There is one point on the boundary of the area for each variable. By default, the points show the mean of the selected variables.

Stacked:
Summaries of separate variables

Figure 24.45 shows a chart definition dialog box and the resulting stacked area chart with summaries of separate variables.

Figure 24.45   Stacked area chart with summaries of separate variables

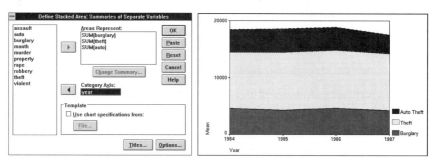

The minimum specifications are:

• Two or more area variables.

• A category axis variable.

Areas Represent. Select two or more variables to define the areas. There is one area for each variable. By default, the value axis shows the sum of the selected variables.

Category Axis. Select a variable to define the categories shown in the chart. There is one point on the boundary of each area for each value of the variable.

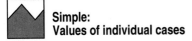

Simple:
Values of individual cases

Figure 24.46 shows a chart definition dialog box and the resulting simple area chart with values of individual cases.

Figure 24.46   Simple area chart with values of individual cases

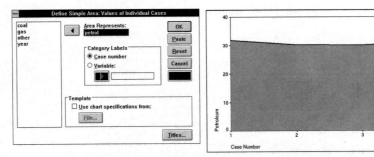

The minimum specification is an area variable.

The numeric, short string, and long string variables in your data file are displayed on the source variable list. Select the numeric variable you want to define the area. To get a simple area chart showing the value of each case in default format, click on OK.

Optionally, you can change the value labels shown in the chart, use a template to control the format of the chart, or add a title, subtitle, or footnote. These options are discussed in detail in Chapter 23.

Area Represents. Select a numeric variable to define the area. Each case will be displayed as a category.

Category Labels. Determines how the categories are labeled. You can choose one of the following category label sources:

○ **Case number.** Each category is labeled with the case number. This is the default.

○ **Variable.** Each category is labeled with the current value label of the selected variable.

Figure 24.47 shows the chart definition dialog box with a label variable selected and the resulting area chart.

Figure 24.47   Area chart with category labels from the variable year

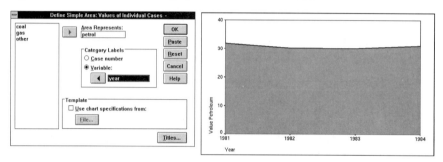

Stacked:
Values of individual cases

Figure 24.48 shows the chart definition dialog box and the resulting stacked area chart with values of individual cases.

Figure 24.48   Stacked area chart with values of individual cases

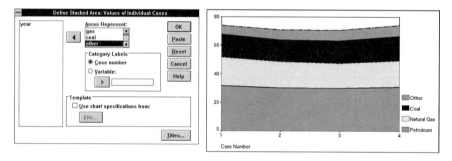

The minimum specifications are two stacked area variables.

Areas Represent. Select two or more numeric variables. There is one area for each variable. There is one point on the boundary of each area for each case.

Pie Charts

To obtain a pie chart, from the menus choose:

Graphs
  Pie...

This open the Pie Charts dialog box, as shown in Figure 24.49.

Figure 24.49   Pie Charts dialog box

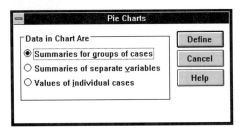

Select the choice that describes the structure of your data organization, and click on Define to open a dialog box specific to your selection (see Table 24.4).

Table 24.4   Types of pie charts

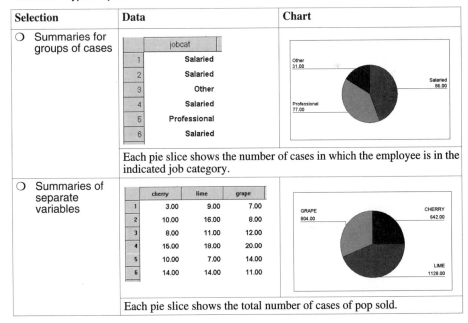

Table 24.4   Types of pie charts (Continued)

Selection	Data	Chart
○ Values of individual cases	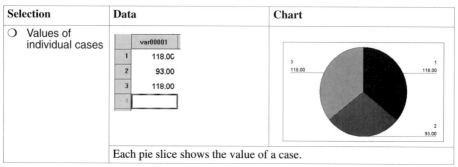	
	Each pie slice shows the value of a case.	

Summaries for Groups of Cases

Figure 24.50 shows a chart definition dialog box and the resulting simple pie chart with summaries for groups of cases.

Figure 24.50   Pie chart with summaries for groups of cases

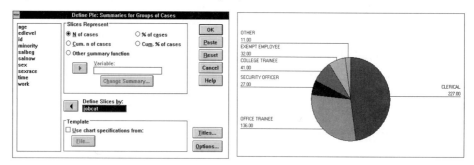

The minimum specification is a slice definition variable.

The numeric, short string, and long string variables in your data file are displayed on the source variable list. Select the variable you want to define the categories or slices. To get a simple pie chart showing the number of cases in each category, click on OK.

Optionally, you can select a different summary statistic, use a template to control the format of the chart, or add a title, subtitle, or footnote. Summary statistics are discussed in "Summary Functions" on p. 506. The other options are discussed in detail in Chapter 23.

Define Slices by. Select a variable to define the pie slices shown in the chart. There is one slice for each value of the variable. A slice definition variable must be selected to enable the OK pushbutton.

If you select Other summary function in the Define Pie Summaries for Groups of Cases dialog box, you must also select a variable to be summarized. Figure 24.51 shows the chart definition dialog box with a variable to be summarized and the resulting simple pie chart.

Figure 24.51   Simple pie chart with summary of a variable

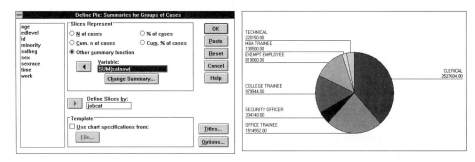

The chart generated by default shows the sum of the selected variable within each category (determined by the slice variable).

Summaries of Separate Variables

Figure 24.52 shows a chart definition dialog box and the resulting simple pie chart with summaries of separate variables.

Figure 24.52   Pie chart with summaries of separate variables

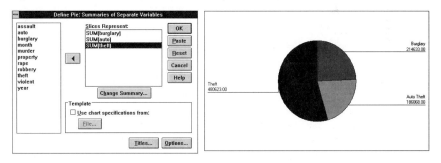

The minimum specifications are two or more slice variables.

The numeric variables in your data file are displayed on the source variable list. Select the variables you want to define the pie slices. To get a simple pie chart showing the sum of each variable in default format, click on OK.

Optionally, you can select a different summary statistic, use a template to control the format of the chart, or add a title, subtitle, or footnote. Summary statistics are discussed in "Summary Functions" on p. 506. The other options are discussed in detail in Chapter 23.

Slices Represent. Select two or more variables to define the slices shown in the chart. There is one slice for each variable. By default, the slices show the sum of the selected variables. Two or more slice variables must be selected to enable the OK pushbutton.

Values of Individual Cases

Figure 24.53 shows a chart definition dialog box and the resulting simple pie chart with values of individual cases.

Figure 24.53   Pie chart with values of individual cases

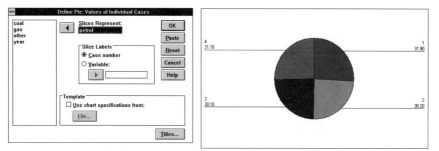

The minimum specification is a slice variable.

The numeric, short string, and long string variables in your data file are displayed on the source variable list. Select the numeric variable you want slices to represent. To get a simple pie chart showing the value of each case in default format, click on OK.

Optionally, you can change the value labels shown in the chart, use a template to control the format of the chart, or add a title, subtitle, or footnote. These options are discussed in detail in Chapter 23.

Slices Represent. Select a numeric variable to define the slices. Each case will be displayed as a separate pie slice. A variable must be selected to enable the OK pushbutton.

Slice Labels. Determines how the slices are labeled. You can choose one of the following sector label sources:

○ **Case number.** Each slice is labeled with the case number. This is the default.

○ **Variable.** Each slice is labeled with the current value label of the selected variable.

Figure 24.54 shows the chart definition dialog box with a label variable selected and the resulting pie chart.

Figure 24.54   Pie chart with category labels from the variable petrol

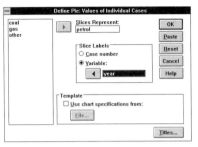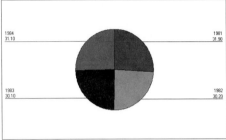

Transposed Charts

Sometimes, especially with inventory or accounting time-series data, the categories you want are defined as separate cases or values while each date is a separate variable. For example, the inventory data in Figure 24.55 are defined this way.

Figure 24.55   Inventory data

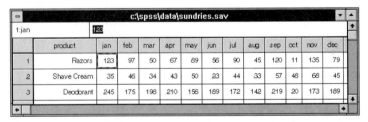

If you draw a line chart of these data, you get the chart in Figure 24.56.

To flip this chart so that each line is a separate product and each month is a separate category, edit the chart. From the menu of the chart window select:

Series
  Transpose Data

This produces the chart shown in Figure 24.57.

Figure 24.56   Chart of inventory data

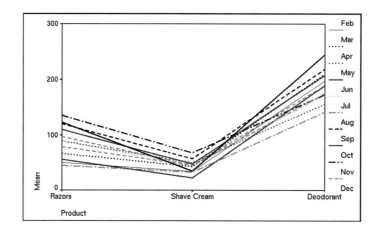

Figure 24.57   Transposed chart

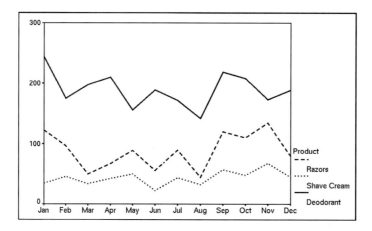

You can transpose other multiple-series categorical charts, such as clustered bar charts (see "Transposing Data" on p. 686 in Chapter 32).

Summary Functions

Data can be summarized by counting the number of cases in each category or subcategory, or by calculating a statistic summarizing the values in each category or subcategory.

Count Functions

For simple summaries of groups of cases, the dialog box in Figure 24.58 shows the general layout of the chart definition dialog boxes for bar, line, area, and pie charts. For complex summaries of groups of cases, the summaries in the dialog box are similar, as shown in Figure 24.59.

Figure 24.58   Define simple summaries for groups of cases dialog box

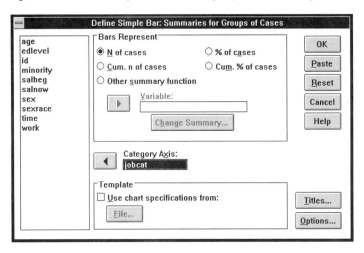

Figure 24.59   Define multi-series summaries for groups of cases dialog box

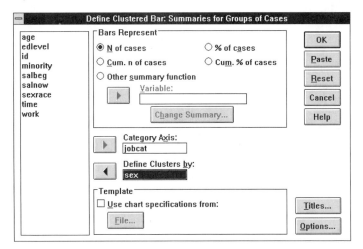

Bars/Lines/Areas/Slices Represent. Determines the summary statistic used to generate the data series illustrated by the chart. You can choose one of the following alternatives:

○ **N of cases.** Each bar, point on a line, point on the boundary of an area, or pie slice represents the number of cases in a category. This is the default.

○ **% of cases.** Each bar, point on a line, point on the boundary of an area, or pie slice represents the percentage of cases in a category.

○ **Cum. n of cases.** Cumulative number of cases. Each bar, point on a line, point on the boundary of an area, or pie slice represents the number of cases in the current category plus all cases in previous categories. This function is not appropriate for some charts; see "Cumulative Functions" on p. 510.

○ **Cum. % of cases.** Cumulative percentage of cases. Each bar, point on a line, or point on the boundary of an area represents the cumulative number of cases as a percentage of the total number of cases. This function is not appropriate for some charts; see "Cumulative Functions" on p. 510.

○ **Other summary function.** The values in a series are calculated from a summary measure of a variable. In most cases, the mean of the variable is the default. For stacked bar, stacked area, and pie charts, the sum of the variable is the default.

Other Summary Functions

You can request statistical summary functions for any chart where values are summarized. When values are summarized for *groups of cases*, select Other summary function; then select a variable to summarize and click on ▶. The Variable box indicates the default summary function (mean or sum). If you want a summary function other than the default, click on Change Summary.... This opens the Summary Function dialog box, as shown in Figure 24.60.

When values are summarized for *separate variables*, first move the variables to the box for bars, lines, areas, or slices, as shown in Figure 24.21 and Figure 24.52. The default measure (mean or sum) is indicated for each variable on the list. If you want a summary function other than the default, select a variable on the list and click on Change Summary.... This opens the Summary Function dialog box, as shown in Figure 24.60. If you want the same summary function to apply to more than one variable, you can select several variables by dragging over them and then clicking on Change Summary....

Figure 24.60   Summary Function dialog box

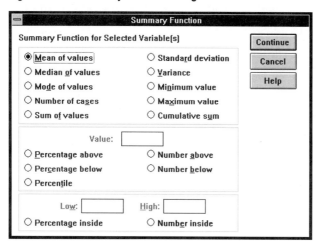

You can choose one of the following summary functions:

○ **Mean of values.** The arithmetic average within the category. This is the default in most cases.

○ **Median of values.** The value below which half the cases fall.

○ **Mode of values.** The most frequently occurring value.

○ **Number of cases.** The number of cases having a nonmissing value of the selected variable. If there are no missing values, this is the same as N of cases in the previous dialog box.

○ **Sum of values.** The default for stacked bar charts, stacked area charts, or pie charts.

○ **Standard deviation.** A measure of how much observations vary from the mean, expressed in the same units as the data.

○ **Variance.** A measure of how much observations vary from the mean, expressed in squared units.

○ **Minimum value.** The smallest value.

○ **Maximum value.** The largest value.

○ **Cumulative sum.** The sum of all values in the current category plus all values in previous categories. This function is not appropriate for some charts; see "Cumulative functions," below.

○ **Percentage above.** The percentage of cases above the indicated value.

○ **Percentage below.** The percentage of cases below the indicated value.

○ **Percentile.** The data value below which the specified percentage of values fall.

○ **Number above.** The number of cases above the specified value.

○ **Number below.** The number of cases below the specified value.

○ **Percentage inside.** The percentage of cases with values between the specified high and low value, including the high and low values. Select this item and then type in the high and low values.

○ **Number inside.** The number of cases with values between the specified high and low values, including the high and low values. Select this item and then type in the high and low values.

Cumulative Functions

Cum. N of cases, *Cum. % of cases*, and *Cumulative sum* are inappropriate in pie charts. These functions are also inappropriate in stacked bar charts and area charts that have been transposed so that the cumulative function is along the scale axis. Because the Chart Editor does not recalculate summary functions, many Displayed Data operations (from the Series menu) will invalidate cumulative functions, particularly if scaled to 100%.

25 High-Low Charts

Stocks, commodities, currencies, and other market data fluctuate considerably from hour to hour, day to day, or week to week. To graph the long-term changes and still convey a sense of the short-term changes, each category in a chart must show a range of values. High-low charts are designed to graph these kinds of data.

Simple High-Low Charts

Typically, market data have three important values: the highest value during a period of time, the lowest value during the same period, and the closing value, or value at the end of the period. These kinds of data are displayed in a high-low-close chart, as shown in Figure 25.1.

Figure 25.1 Simple high-low-close chart

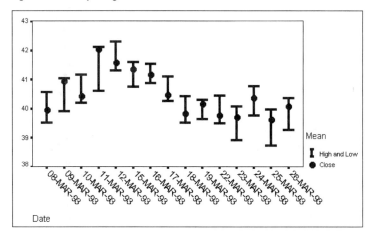

The chart shows the mean stock values for eight medical companies on the New York Stock Exchange. A bar shows the mean high and low value for each day, and a point on the bar shows the mean closing value for the day.

Often, you have data with high and low values but you don't want to show closing values. You can display the data either as a high-low-close chart without close points or as a range bar chart. The range bar chart shown in Figure 25.2 shows the daily mean high and low for the eight medical stocks.

Figure 25.2   Simple range bar chart

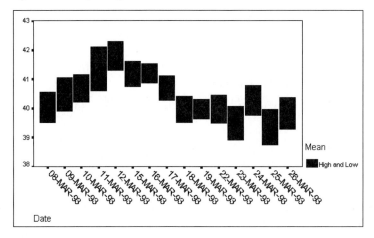

Clustered High-Low Charts

Medical companies can be divided into two groups: those that are exclusively pharmaceutical companies and those that are not. To show the mean high, low, and close values for the two groups, use a clustered high-low-close chart, as shown in Figure 25.3.

Figure 25.3   Clustered high-low-close chart

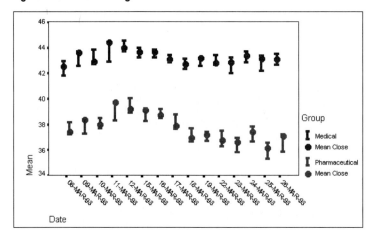

To show just the high and low values, use either a high-low-close chart without close points or a range bar chart, as shown in Figure 25.4.

Figure 25.4   Clustered range bar chart

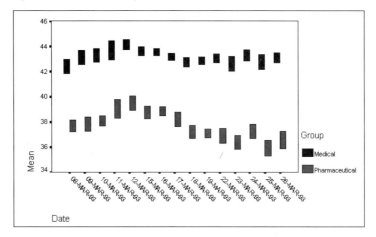

Difference Line Charts

High-low-close charts and range bar charts are useful for showing high and low data where one value is consistently high and the other value is consistently low. What about data where sometimes one value is high and sometimes the other value is high? To show the changing relationship between two such values, use a difference line chart. For example, Figure 25.5 compares the daily closing value of a medical company's stocks with similarly valued stocks from a petroleum company.

Figure 25.5   Difference line chart

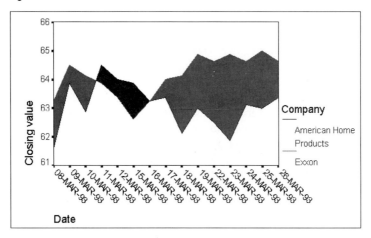

The two types of shaded areas between the lines show where the values of both the medical and petroleum companies' stocks are high. If you want to compare more than two changing values at the same time, use a drop-line chart, as described in Chapter 24.

How to Obtain High-Low Charts

To obtain a high-low chart, from the menus choose:

Graphs
  High-Low...

This opens the High-Low Charts dialog box, as shown in Figure 25.6.

Figure 25.6   High-Low Charts dialog box

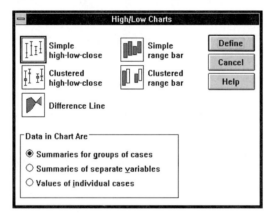

From the High-Low Charts dialog box, choose one of the chart types, and then select the choice that describes the structure of your data organization.

Data in Chart Are. Select the choice that describes the structure of your data organization.

○ **Summaries for groups of cases.** There is one bar, point on a line, or cluster of bars for each category of the category axis variable. In simple charts (simple high-low-close, simple range bar, and difference line), a variable with two values defines the high and low points for each category. In a simple high-low-close chart, a variable with three values may be used instead to define high, low, and closing values. In clustered charts, two variables determine the high and low values, and a third variable defines the bars within each cluster. In a clustered high-low-close chart, another variable may also be used to determine a closing value for each bar.

○ **Summaries of separate variables.** More than one variable is summarized. Simple high-low charts summarize each variable over all cases in the file. Clustered high-low charts summarize each variable within categories determined by another variable.

○ **Values of individual cases.** Each case in the data is a separate category in the chart.

Examples of these choices, shown with data structures and the charts they produce, are presented in Table 25.1.

Table 25.1   Types of high-low charts

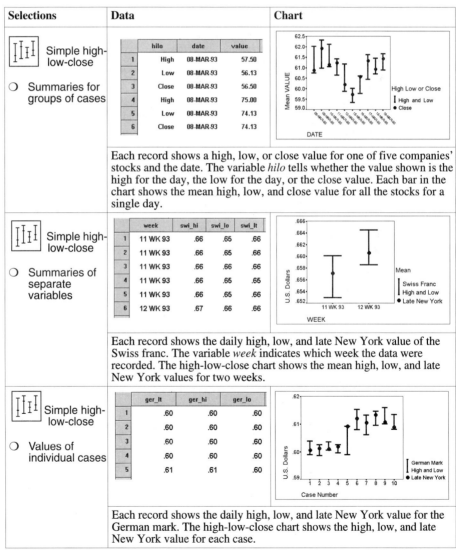

Selections	Data	Chart
Simple high-low-close ○ Summaries for groups of cases		

Each record shows a high, low, or close value for one of five companies' stocks and the date. The variable *hilo* tells whether the value shown is the high for the day, the low for the day, or the close value. Each bar in the chart shows the mean high, low, and close value for all the stocks for a single day.

Each record shows the daily high, low, and late New York value of the Swiss franc. The variable *week* indicates which week the data were recorded. The high-low-close chart shows the mean high, low, and late New York values for two weeks.

Each record shows the daily high, low, and late New York value for the German mark. The high-low-close chart shows the high, low, and late New York value for each case.

Table 25.1   Types of high-low charts (Continued)

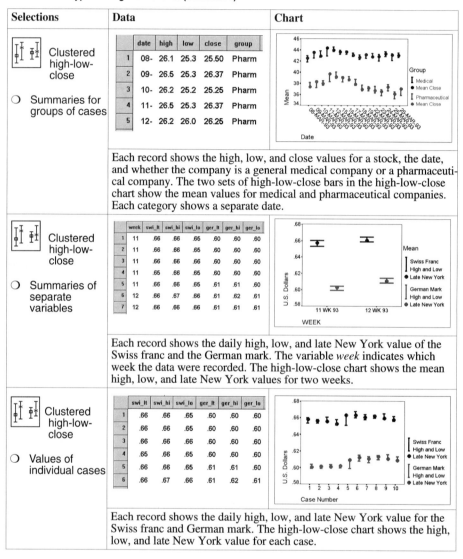

Selections	Data	Chart
Clustered high-low-close ⃝ Summaries for groups of cases	*(see data table)*	*(see chart)*

Each record shows the high, low, and close values for a stock, the date, and whether the company is a general medical company or a pharmaceutical company. The two sets of high-low-close bars in the high-low-close chart show the mean values for medical and pharmaceutical companies. Each category shows a separate date.

Each record shows the daily high, low, and late New York value of the Swiss franc and the German mark. The variable *week* indicates which week the data were recorded. The high-low-close chart shows the mean high, low, and late New York values for two weeks.

Each record shows the daily high, low, and late New York value for the Swiss franc and German mark. The high-low-close chart shows the high, low, and late New York value for each case.

Table 25.1   Types of high-low charts (Continued)

Selections	Data	Chart

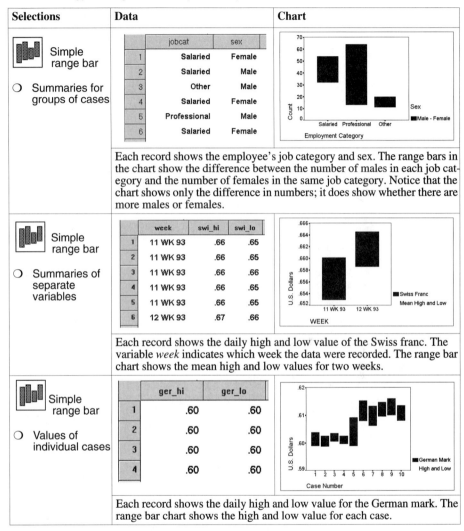

Simple range bar

○ Summaries for groups of cases

	jobcat	sex
1	Salaried	Female
2	Salaried	Male
3	Other	Male
4	Salaried	Female
5	Professional	Male
6	Salaried	Female

Each record shows the employee's job category and sex. The range bars in the chart show the difference between the number of males in each job category and the number of females in the same job category. Notice that the chart shows only the difference in numbers; it does show whether there are more males or females.

Simple range bar

○ Summaries of separate variables

	week	swi_hi	swi_lo
1	11 WK 93	.66	.65
2	11 WK 93	.66	.65
3	11 WK 93	.66	.66
4	11 WK 93	.66	.65
5	11 WK 93	.66	.65
6	12 WK 93	.67	.66

Each record shows the daily high and low value of the Swiss franc. The variable *week* indicates which week the data were recorded. The range bar chart shows the mean high and low values for two weeks.

Simple range bar

○ Values of individual cases

	ger_hi	ger_lo
1	.60	.60
2	.60	.60
3	.60	.60
4	.60	.60

Each record shows the daily high and low value for the German mark. The range bar chart shows the high and low value for each case.

Table 25.1   Types of high-low charts (Continued)

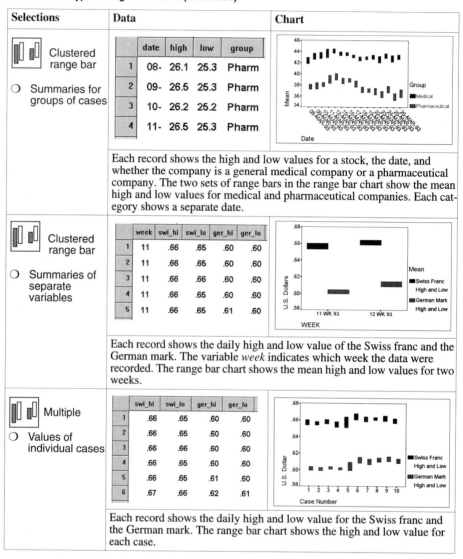

Selections	Data	Chart

Clustered range bar

○ Summaries for groups of cases

	date	high	low	group
1	08-	26.1	25.3	Pharm
2	09-	26.5	25.3	Pharm
3	10-	26.2	25.2	Pharm
4	11-	26.5	25.3	Pharm

Each record shows the high and low values for a stock, the date, and whether the company is a general medical company or a pharmaceutical company. The two sets of range bars in the range bar chart show the mean high and low values for medical and pharmaceutical companies. Each category shows a separate date.

Clustered range bar

○ Summaries of separate variables

	week	swi_hi	swi_lo	ger_hi	ger_lo
1	11	.66	.65	.60	.60
2	11	.66	.65	.60	.60
3	11	.66	.66	.60	.60
4	11	.66	.65	.60	.60
5	11	.66	.65	.61	.60

Each record shows the daily high and low value of the Swiss franc and the German mark. The variable *week* indicates which week the data were recorded. The range bar chart shows the mean high and low values for two weeks.

Multiple

○ Values of individual cases

	swi_hi	swi_lo	ger_hi	ger_lo
1	.66	.65	.60	.60
2	.66	.65	.60	.60
3	.66	.66	.60	.60
4	.66	.65	.60	.60
5	.66	.65	.61	.60
6	.67	.66	.62	.61

Each record shows the daily high and low value for the Swiss franc and the German mark. The range bar chart shows the high and low value for each case.

Table 25.1   Types of high-low charts (Continued)

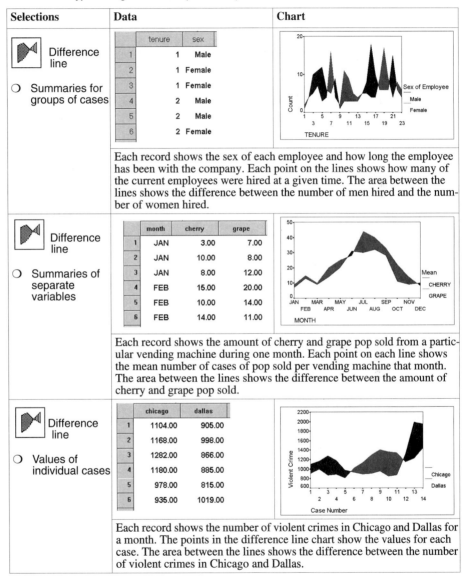

Selections	Data	Chart

Difference line — Summaries for groups of cases

Each record shows the sex of each employee and how long the employee has been with the company. Each point on the lines shows how many of the current employees were hired at a given time. The area between the lines shows the difference between the number of men hired and the number of women hired.

Difference line — Summaries of separate variables

Each record shows the amount of cherry and grape pop sold from a particular vending machine during one month. Each point on each line shows the mean number of cases of pop sold per vending machine that month. The area between the lines shows the difference between the amount of cherry and grape pop sold.

Difference line — Values of individual cases

Each record shows the number of violent crimes in Chicago and Dallas for a month. The points in the difference line chart show the values for each case. The area between the lines shows the difference between the number of violent crimes in Chicago and Dallas.

Each combination of chart type and data organization structure produces a different definition box. Each is discussed briefly below. The icon and section title indicate the choices that have to be made in the chart dialog box to open that chart definition dialog box. The discussion for each chart type always describes the selections required to enable the OK pushbutton. Optional selections are discussed only with the first chart using each data structure. For a detailed description of optional statistics, see "Summary Functions" on p. 506 in Chapter 24.

Simple high-low-close:
Summaries for groups of cases

Figure 25.7 shows a chart definition dialog box and the resulting simple high-low-close chart with summaries for groups of cases.

Figure 25.7   Simple high-low-close chart with summaries for groups of cases

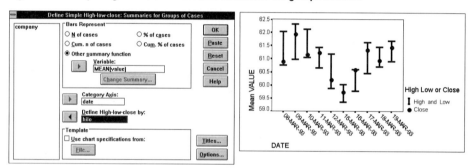

The minimum specifications are:

- A category axis variable.
- A high-low-close variable. This variable must have two or three values.
- If Other summary function is selected, you must specify a variable.

The numeric, short string, and long string variables in your data file are displayed on the source variable list. Select the variable you want to define the category axis and select the variable you want to define the high-low-close bars. The high-low-close variable must have either two or three values. To get a simple high-low-close chart showing high-low-close bars for each category, click on OK.

Optionally, you can select a different summary statistic, use a template to control the format of the chart, or add a title, subtitle, or footnote. Summary statistics are discussed in "Summary Functions" on p. 506 in Chapter 24. The other options are discussed in detail in Chapter 23.

Bars Represent. If Other summary function in the chart definition dialog box is selected, you must select a variable to be summarized. The chart generated by default shows the mean of the selected variable within each category (determined by the category axis variable). For a detailed description of optional statistics, see "Summary Functions" on p. 506 in Chapter 24.

Category Axis. Select a variable to define the categories shown in the chart. There is one high-low-close bar for each value of the variable.

Define High-Low-Close by. Select a variable with two or three values. If there are two values, they are shown as high-low-close bars without close points. If there are three values, the first and second define the high and low ends of the bars and the third value determines the position of the close points. If your data are coded in the wrong order and all the close points appear above or below the high-low bars, you can edit the displayed series in the chart so that the close points appear between the high and low points. See Chapter 32 for more information on editing the displayed series. Figure 25.8 shows a high-low-close chart for a variable with two categories.

Figure 25.8   Simple high-low-close chart without close points

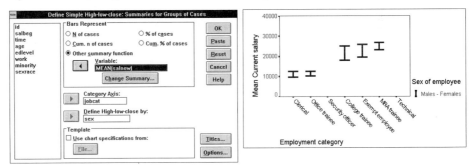

If Other summary function is not selected, you do not need to specify a variable. Figure 25.9 shows a high-low-close chart that shows number of cases.

Figure 25.9   High-low-close chart with number of cases

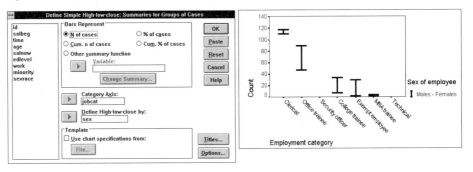

Simple range bar:
Summaries for groups of cases

Figure 25.10 shows a chart definition dialog box and the resulting simple range bar chart with summaries for groups of cases.

Figure 25.10 Simple range bar chart with summaries for groups of cases

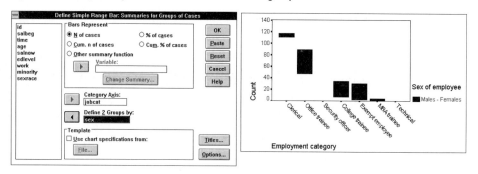

The minimum specifications are:

- A category axis variable.
- A variable that defines two groups (has two values).

Category Axis. Select a variable to define the categories shown in the chart. There is one range bar for each value of the variable.

Define 2 Groups by. Select a variable with two values. The top of each range bar is determined by cases with one value; the bottom of each range bar is determined by cases with the other value.

Difference line:
Summaries for groups of cases

Figure 25.11 shows a chart definition dialog box and the resulting difference line chart with summaries for groups of cases.

Figure 25.11 Difference line chart with summaries for groups of cases

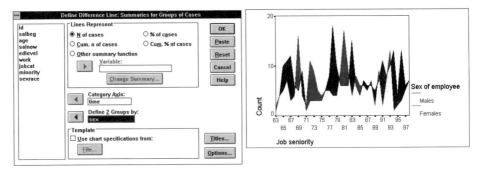

The minimum specifications are:

- A category axis variable.
- A line definition variable. The line definition variable must have exactly two values.

Category Axis. Select a variable to define the categories shown in the chart. There is one point on each line for each value of the variable.

Define 2 Groups by. Select a variable to define the lines. The variable must have two values. There are two differently colored or patterned lines in the chart, one for each value of this variable.

Clustered high-low-close:
Summaries for groups of cases

Figure 25.12 shows a chart definition dialog box and the resulting clustered high-low-close chart with summaries for groups of cases.

Figure 25.12 Clustered high-low-close chart with summaries for groups of cases

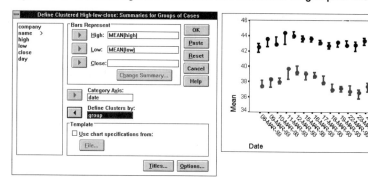

The minimum specifications are:

- A high variable.
- A low variable.
- A category axis variable.
- A cluster definition variable.

High. Select a variable to determine one end of each high-low-close bar. By default, the bars show the mean of the selected value.

Low. Select a variable to determine the other end of each high-low-close bar. By default, the bars show the mean of the selected value.

Close. You may optionally select a variable to determine the position of close points. By default, the close points show the mean of the selected value. Close points are connected by a line.

Category Axis. Select a variable to define the categories shown in the chart. There is one cluster of high-low-close bars for each value of the category axis variable.

Define Clusters by. Select a variable to define the bars within each cluster. There is a differently colored or patterned series of high-low-close bars for each value of the cluster variable.

Clustered range bar:
Summaries for groups of cases

Figure 25.13 shows a chart definition dialog box and the resulting clustered range bar chart with summaries for groups of cases.

Figure 25.13 Clustered range bar chart with summaries for groups of cases

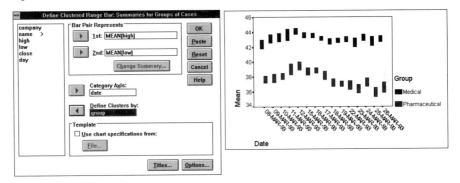

The minimum specifications are:

- A 1st variable.
- A 2nd variable.
- A category axis variable.
- A cluster definition variable.

1st. Select a variable to determine one end of each range bar. By default, each bar shows the mean of the selected value.

2nd. Select a variable to determine the other end of each range bar. By default, each bar shows the mean of the selected value.

Category Axis. Select a variable to define the categories shown in the chart. There is one cluster of range bars for each value of the category axis variable.

Define Clusters by. Select a variable to define the bars within each cluster. There is a differently colored or patterned series of range bars for each value of the cluster variable.

Simple high-low-close:
Summaries of separate variables

Figure 25.14 shows a chart definition dialog box and the resulting simple high-low-close chart with summaries for groups of cases.

Figure 25.14 Simple high-low-close chart with summaries of separate variables

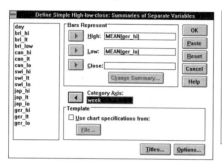
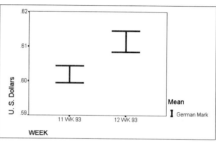

The minimum specifications are:

- A high variable.
- A low variable.
- A category variable.

The numeric, short string, and long string variables in your data file are displayed on the source variable list. Select the variable you want to define the high end of each bar, the variable you want to define the low end of each bar, and a category axis variable. The high and low variables must be numeric. To get a simple high-low-close chart showing means for each category, click on OK.

Optionally, you can add close points, select a different summary statistic, use a template to control the format of the chart, or add a title, subtitle, or footnote. Summary statistics are discussed in "Summary Functions" on p. 506 in Chapter 24. The other options are discussed in detail in Chapter 23.

High. Select a variable to determine one end of each high-low-close bar. By default, the bars show the mean of the selected variable.

Low. Select a variable to determine the other end of each high-low-close bar. By default, the bars show the mean of the selected variable.

Close. You may optionally select a variable to determine the position of close points. By default, the close points show the mean of the selected variable. Figure 25.15 shows a high-low-close chart with close points.

Figure 25.15 Simple high-low-close chart with close points

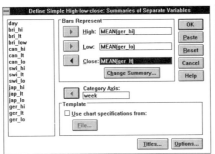
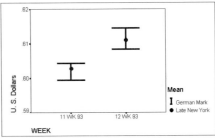

Category Axis. Select a variable to define the categories shown in the chart. There is one high-low-close bar for each value of the variable.

Simple range bar:
Summaries of separate variables

Figure 25.16 shows a chart definition dialog box and the resulting simple range bar chart with summaries of separate variables.

Figure 25.16 Simple range bar chart with summaries of separate variables

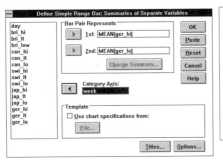
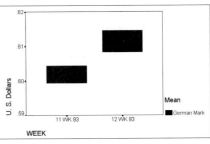

The minimum specifications are:

- Two bar variables.
- A category axis variable.

1st. Select a variable to determine one end of each range bar. By default, each bar shows the mean of the selected variable.

2nd. Select a variable to determine the other end of each range bar. By default, each bar shows the mean of the selected variable.

Category Axis. Select a variable to define the categories shown in the chart. There is one range bar for each value of the variable.

Difference line:
Summaries of separate variables

Figure 25.17 shows a chart definition dialog box and the resulting difference line chart with summaries of separate variables.

Figure 25.17 Difference line chart with summaries of separate variables

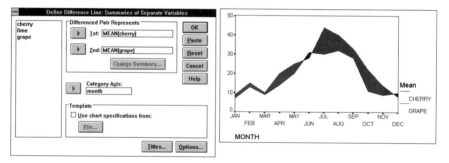

The minimum specifications are:
- Two 1st variables.
- Two 2nd variables.
- A category axis variable.

1st. Select a variable to determine one line in the set. By default, the line shows the mean of the selected value.

2nd. Select a variable to determine the other line in the set. By default, the line shows the mean of the selected value.

Category Axis. Select a variable to define the categories shown in the chart. There is one point on each line for each value of the category axis variable.

Clustered high-low-close: Summaries of separate variables

Figure 25.18 shows a chart definition dialog box and the resulting clustered high-low-close chart with summaries of separate variables.

Figure 25.18 Clustered high-low-close chart with summaries of separate variables

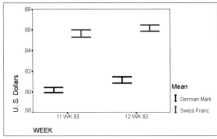

The minimum specifications are:

- Two high variables.
- Two low variables.
- A category axis variable.

High. Select a variable to determine one end of each high-low-close bar in the set. By default, the bars show the mean of the selected variable. To edit a different set of high, low, and close values, press Previous or Next.

Low. Select a variable to determine the other end of each high-low-close bar in the set. By default, the bars show the mean of the selected variable. To edit a different set of high, low, and close values, press Previous or Next.

Close. You may optionally select a variable to determine the position of close points in the set. By default, the close points show the mean of the selected variable. To edit a different set of high, low, and close values, press Previous or Next.

Category Axis. Select a variable to define the categories shown in the chart. There is one cluster of high-low-close bars for each value of the category axis variable.

Clustered range bar:
Summaries of separate variables

Figure 25.19 shows a chart definition dialog box and the resulting clustered range bar chart with summaries of separate variables.

Figure 25.19 Clustered range bar chart with summaries of separate variables

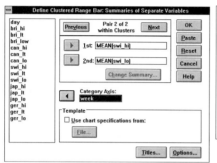 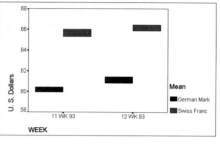

The minimum specifications are:

- Two 1st variables.
- Two 2nd variables.
- A category axis variable.

1st. Select a variable to determine one end of each range bar in the set. By default, the bars show the mean of the selected variable. To edit a different set of 1st and 2nd values, press Previous or Next.

2nd. Select a variable to determine the other end of each range bar in the set. By default, the bars show the mean of the selected variable. To edit a different set of 1st and 2nd values, press Previous or Next.

Category Axis. Select a variable to define the categories shown in the chart. There is one cluster of high-low-close bars for each value of the category axis variable.

Simple high-low-close:
Values of individual cases

Figure 25.20 shows a chart definition dialog box and the resulting simple high-low-close chart with values of individual cases.

Figure 25.20 Simple high-low-close chart with values of individual cases

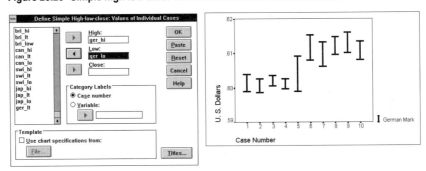

The minimum specifications are:

- A high variable.
- A low variable.

The numeric, short string, and long string variables in your data file are displayed on the source variable list. Select the numeric variable you want to define the high end of each bar and the numeric variable you want to define the low end of each bar. To get a simple high-low-close chart showing the value for each case, click on OK.

Optionally, you can add close points, add category labels, use a template to control the format of the chart, or add a title, subtitle, or footnote. Summary statistics are discussed in "Summary Functions" on p. 506 in Chapter 24. The other options are discussed in detail in Chapter 23.

High. Select a variable to determine one end of each high-low-close bar. Each case is represented by a separate bar.

Low. Select a variable to determine the other end of each high-low-close bar. Each case is represented by a separate bar.

Close. You may optionally select a variable to determine the position of close points. Figure 25.21 shows a high-low-close chart with close points.

Figure 25.21 Simple high-low-close chart with close points

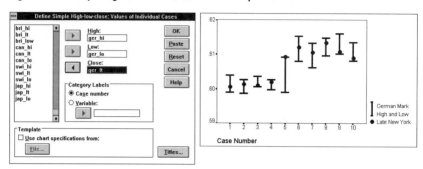

Category Labels. Determines how the bars are labeled. You can choose one of the following category label sources:

○ **Case number.** Each category is labeled with the case number.

○ **Variable.** Each category is labeled with the current value label of the selected variable.

Figure 25.22 shows a chart definition dialog box with a label variable selected and the resulting high-low-close chart.

Figure 25.22 High-low-close chart with category labels from variable day

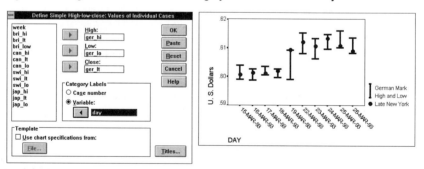

Simple range bar:
Values of individual cases

Figure 25.23 shows a chart definition dialog box and the resulting simple range bar chart with values of individual cases.

Figure 25.23 Simple range bar chart with values of individual cases

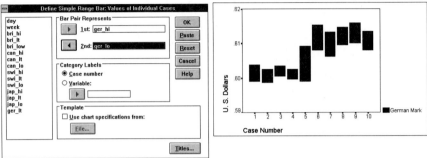

The minimum specifications are:

• Two bar variables.

1st. Select a variable to determine one end of each range bar. Each case is represented by a separate bar.

2nd. Select a variable to determine the other end of each range bar. Each case is represented by a separate bar.

Difference line:
Values of individual cases

Figure 25.24 shows a chart definition dialog box and the resulting difference line chart with values of individual cases.

Figure 25.24 Difference line chart with values of individual cases

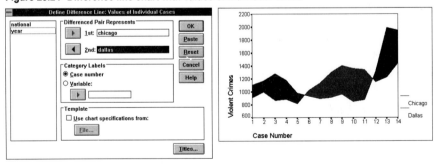

The minimum specifications are:

- A 1st variable.
- A 2nd variable.

1st. Select a variable to determine one line in the set. Each case is represented by a separate point on the line.

2nd. Select a variable to determine the other line in the set. Each case is represented by a separate point on the line.

Clustered high-low-close:
Values of individual cases

Figure 25.25 shows a chart definition dialog box and the resulting clustered high-low-close chart with values of individual cases.

Figure 25.25 Clustered high-low-close chart with values of individual cases

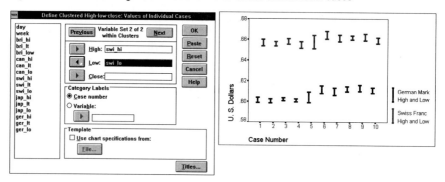

The minimum specifications are:

- Two high variables.
- Two low variables.

High. Select a variable to determine one end of each high-low-close bar in the set. Each case is represented by a separate bar. To edit a different set of high, low, and close values, press Previous or Next.

Low. Select a variable to determine the other end of each high-low-close bar in the set. Each case is represented by a separate bar. To edit a different set of high, low, and close values, press Previous or Next.

Close. You may optionally select a variable to determine the position of close points in the set. Each case is represented by a separate close point. Close points are connected by a line. To edit a different set of high, low, and close values, press Previous or Next.

Clustered range bar:
Values of individual cases

Figure 25.26 shows a chart definition dialog box and the resulting clustered range bar chart with values of individual cases.

Figure 25.26 Clustered range bar chart with values of individual cases

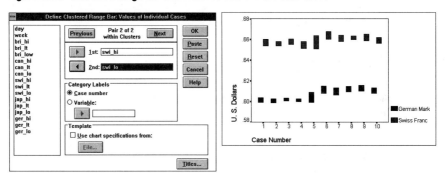

The minimum specifications are:

- Two 1st variables.
- Two 2nd variables.

1st. Select a variable to determine one end of each range bar in the set. Each case is represented by a separate bar. To edit a different set of 1st and 2nd values, press Previous or Next.

2nd. Select a variable to determine the other end of each range bar in the set. Each case is represented by a separate bar. To edit a different set of 1st and 2nd values, press Previous or Next.

26 Boxplots and Error Bar Charts

Boxplots and error bar charts help you visualize distributions and dispersion. Boxplots show the actual distribution of the data. Error bar charts show confidence intervals, standard deviations, or standard errors of the mean. You can get simple boxplots from the Explore statistical procedure or the Boxplot graphics procedure. More complex boxplots can be obtained only from the Boxplot procedure. Error bar charts can be obtained from the Error Bar graphics procedure. This chapter describes the Boxplot and Error Bar graphics procedures. For a description of the components of a boxplot, see Chapter 9, which also describes other methods of exploratory analysis.

Boxplots

In Chapter 9, there is an example of a simple boxplot, which is used to compare the distribution of beginning salaries for people employed in several different positions at a bank. If we break the data down further by sex, we can see the distribution of male and female salaries in different positions throughout the company. Figure 26.1 shows a clustered boxplot of beginning salary.

Figure 26.1 Clustered boxplot of beginning salary by job category and sex

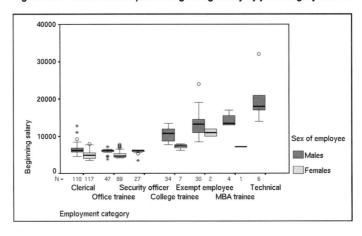

Each cluster shows both sexes. Each category shows the job category of the employees. You can see that women's starting salaries were lower in all job categories, especially the categories with higher pay. You can also see that the men's salaries in the four high-er-paid categories have similar distributions, while all the other salaries have much less variability. Also, notice how few women are in the higher-paid categories. In the college trainee, exempt employee, MBA trainee, and technical categories, there are seven, two, one, and zero, respectively.

Both this example and the chart in Chapter 9 show data summarized by groups of cas-es. Often, we are interested in comparing the distribution of two or more different vari-ables. For example, the starting and current salaries of bank employees are recorded as two separate variables. The simple boxplot of starting salary and current salary is shown in Figure 26.2. Here you can see that starting salary is lower and has a little less variabil-ity than current salary.

Figure 26.2   Boxplot of starting and current salaries

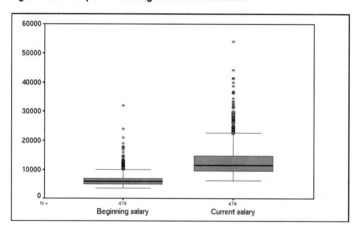

If you want to see beginning salary and current salary by job category, use a clustered boxplot, as shown in Figure 26.3. Here you can see that the spread of current salaries for employees in the technical, exempt, and college trainee categories are larger than for the other categories. Also, as expected, the higher categories generally show a greater dif-ference between starting salary and current salary.

Figure 26.3   Boxplot of starting and current salary by job category

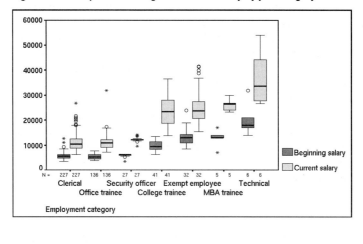

Error Bar Charts

While boxplots show the distribution of your data, error bar charts show the estimated dispersion of the population from which the data were drawn. Like boxplots, error bar charts can be simple or clustered and can show summaries for groups of cases or summaries of separate variables. Unlike boxplots, error bar charts can show one of three different statistics: confidence intervals, standard errors, or standard deviations.

Assume that the bank data are a random sample of bank employees and that the number of employees in the study is the sample size. The sample is used to represent all the employees in the bank, or the population of the study.

Error bars can be used to show confidence intervals for the mean. Figure 26.4 shows the 95% confidence intervals for mean salary by job category.

Figure 26.4   Simple error bar chart showing a 95% confidence interval

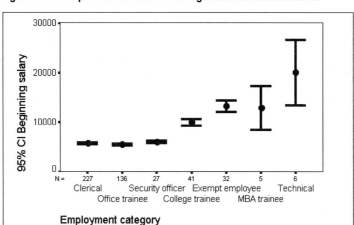

Confidence intervals are one way to specify the estimated dispersion. A 95% confidence interval reaches approximately two standard deviations on either side of the mean. Instead of a confidence interval, you can specify a number of standard deviations, as in Figure 26.5.

Figure 26.5   Simple error bar chart showing three standard deviations

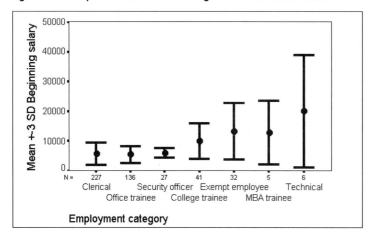

This chart shows the mean values with bars that stretch three standard deviations on either side of the mean.

The mean of a sample will, in general, differ from the mean of another sample. The standard error of the mean is an estimate of how much different samples of the same size vary. An error bar chart can show a specified number of standard errors on either side of the mean, as in Figure 26.6.

Figure 26.6   Simple error bar chart showing two standard errors of the mean

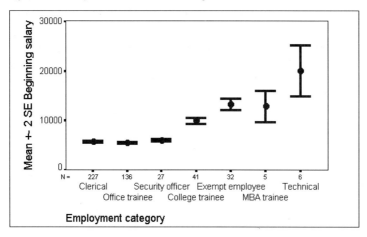

This chart shows the mean salary within each job category with bars that stretch two standard errors on either side of the mean.

How to Obtain a Boxplot

To obtain a boxplot, from the menus choose:

Graphs
  Boxplot...

This opens the Boxplot dialog box, as shown in Figure 26.7.

Figure 26.7   Boxplot dialog box

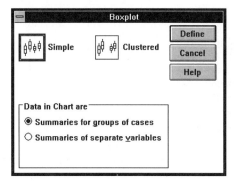

From the Boxplot dialog box, choose either simple or clustered boxplots, and then select the choice that describes the structure of your data organization.

Data in Chart Are. Select the choice that describes the structure of your data organization.

○ **Summaries for groups of cases.** One variable is summarized in subgroups. The subgroups are determined by one variable for simple boxplots or two variables for clustered boxplots.

○ **Summaries of separate variables.** More than one variable is summarized. Simple boxplots summarize each variable over all cases in the file. Clustered boxplots summarize each variable within categories determined by another variable.

Examples of these choices, shown with data structures and the charts they produce, are presented in Table 26.1.

Table 26.1   Boxplot types and data organization

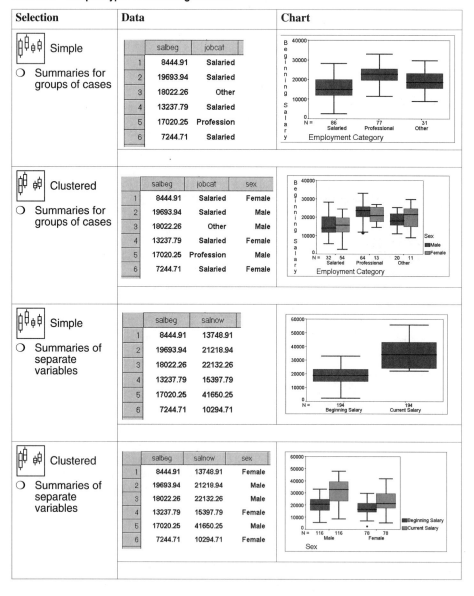

Defining Boxplots

Each combination of boxplot type and data structure produces a different definition dialog box. Each is briefly discussed below. The icon and section title indicate the choices that have to be made in the Boxplot dialog box to open that chart definition dialog box. The discussion for each boxplot type always describes the selection required to enable the OK pushbutton. Optional selections are discussed only with the first chart using each data structure.

Simple:
Summaries for groups of cases

Figure 26.8 shows a simple boxplot with summaries for groups of cases. The specifications are on the left and the resulting chart is on the right.

Figure 26.8   Simple boxplot of groups of cases

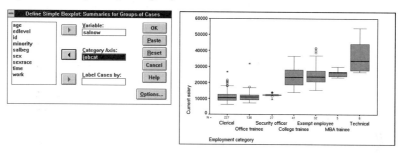

The minimum specifications are:

- A variable to be summarized.
- A category axis variable.

The numeric, short string, and long string variables in your data file are displayed on the source variable list. Select the numeric variable you want summarized and the variable you want to use to define the categories. To get a simple boxplot showing the distribution of cases in each category, click on OK.

Variable. Select a numeric variable to be summarized.

Category Axis. Select a variable to define the categories shown in the boxplot. There is one boxplot for each value of the variable.

Label Cases by. Select a variable whose value labels are to be used to label outliers and extremes. For instance, if the boxplot variable is *salnow* and cases are labeled by *sex* and the third case is an outlier, the boxplot will indicate the sex of the person with that outlier salary. If this field is left blank, case numbers are used to label outliers and extremes. If two outliers or extremes have the same value, but different case labels, no label is displayed. In the Chart Editor, you can turn off labels altogether, as was done in Figure 26.8.

Clustered:
Summaries for groups of cases

Figure 26.9 shows a clustered boxplot with summaries for groups of cases. The specifications are on the left and the resulting boxplot is on the right.

Figure 26.9 Clustered boxplot of groups of cases

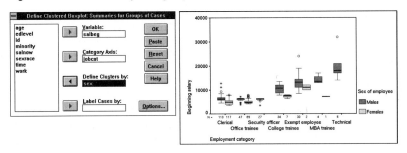

The minimum specifications are:

- A variable to be summarized.
- A category axis variable.
- A cluster variable.

Variable. Select a numeric variable to be summarized.

Category Axis. Select a variable to define the categories shown in the boxplot. There is one boxplot for each value of the variable.

Define Clusters by. Select a variable to define the boxplots within each cluster. In each cluster, there is one boxplot for each value of the variable. A cluster variable must be selected to enable the OK pushbutton.

Simple:
Summaries of separate variables

Figure 26.10 shows a simple boxplot with summaries of separate variables. The specifications are on the left and the resulting boxplot is on the right.

Figure 26.10 Simple boxplot of separate variables

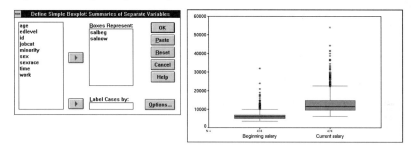

The minimum specification is one or more box variables.

The numeric, short string, and long string variables in your data file are displayed on the source variable list. Select the numeric variables you want to define the boxplots. To get a simple boxplot showing the distribution of each variable in default format, click on OK.

Boxes Represent. Select one or more variables to define the boxplots shown in the chart. There is one boxplot for each variable.

Clustered:
Summaries of separate variables

Figure 26.11 shows a clustered boxplot of separate variables. The specifications are on the left and the resulting boxplot is on the right.

Figure 26.11 Clustered boxplot of separate variables

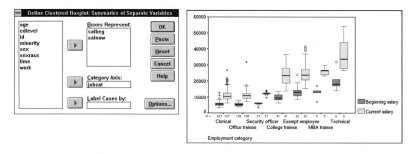

The minimum specification are:

- Two or more box variables.
- A category axis variable.

Boxes Represent. Select two or more variables to define the boxplots shown in the chart. There is one boxplot for each variable. Two or more box variables must be selected to enable the OK pushbutton.

Category Axis. Select a variable to define the categories shown in the boxplot. There is one cluster of boxplots for each value of the variable. A category axis variable must be selected to enable the OK pushbutton.

How to Obtain an Error Bar Chart

To obtain an error bar chart, from the menus choose:

Graphs
  Error Bar...

This opens the Error Bar dialog box, as shown in Figure 26.12.

Figure 26.12 Error Bar dialog box

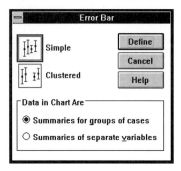

From the Error Bar dialog box, choose either simple or clustered error bars, and then select the choice that describes the structure of your data organization.

Data in Chart Are. Select the choice that describes the structure of your data organization.

- ○ **Summaries for groups of cases.** One variable is summarized in subgroups. The subgroups are determined by one variable for simple error bars or two variables for clustered error bars.

○ **Summaries of separate variables.** More than one variable is summarized. Simple error bars summarize each variable over all cases in the file. Clustered error bars summarize each variable within categories determined by another variable.

Examples of these choices, shown with data structures and the charts they produce, are presented in Table 26.2.

Table 26.2 Error bar types and data organization

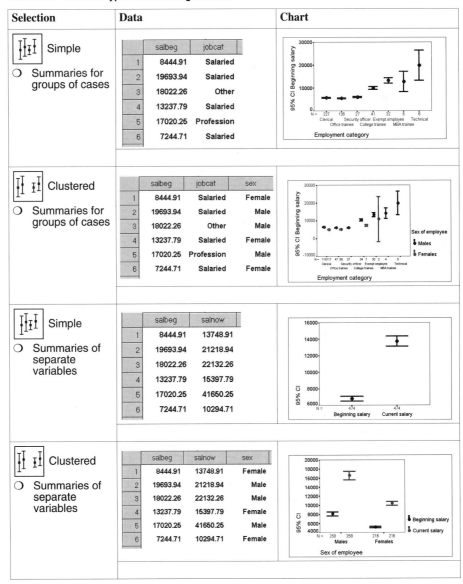

Defining Error Bar Charts

Each combination of error bar type and data structure produces a different definition dialog box. Each is briefly discussed below. The icon and section title indicate the choices that have to be made in the Error Bar dialog box to open that chart definition dialog box. The discussion for each error bar type always describes the selection required to enable the OK pushbutton. Optional selections are discussed only with the first chart using each data structure.

Simple:
Summaries for groups of cases

Figure 26.13 shows a simple error bar chart with summaries for groups of cases. The specifications are on the left and the resulting chart is on the right.

Figure 26.13 Simple error bar chart of groups of cases

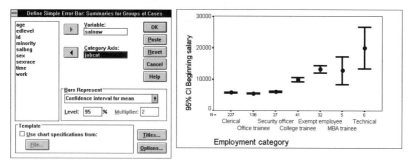

The minimum specifications are:

- A numeric variable to be summarized.
- A category axis variable.

The numeric, short string, and long string variables in your data file are displayed on the source variable list. Select the numeric variable you want summarized and the variable you want to use to define the categories. To get a simple error bar chart showing the 95% confidence interval in each category, click on OK.

Variable. Select a numeric variable to be summarized.

Category Axis. Select a variable to define the categories shown in the error bar chart. There is one error bar for each value of the variable.

Bars Represent. Select the statistic used to determine the length of the error bars.

⬇ **Confidence interval for mean.** Bars represent confidence intervals. Enter the confidence level.

Standard error of mean. The multiplier indicates the number of standard errors each bar represents.

Standard deviation. The multiplier indicates the number of standard deviations each bar represents.

Clustered:
Summaries for groups of cases

Figure 26.14 shows a clustered error bar chart with summaries for groups of cases. The specifications are on the left and the resulting error bar chart is on the right.

Figure 26.14 Clustered error bar chart of groups of cases

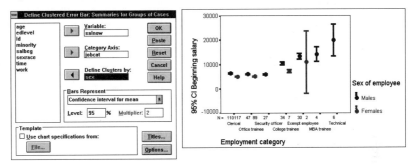

The minimum specifications are:

- A numeric variable to be summarized.
- A category axis variable.
- A cluster variable.

Variable. Select a numeric variable to be summarized.

Category Axis. Select a variable to define the categories shown in the error bar chart. There is one error bar for each value of the variable.

Define Clusters by. Select a variable to define the error bars within each cluster. In each cluster, there is one error bar for each value of the variable. A cluster variable must be selected to enable the OK pushbutton.

Simple:
Summaries of separate variables

Figure 26.15 shows a simple error bar chart with summaries of separate variables. The specifications are on the left and the resulting error bar chart is on the right.

Figure 26.15 Simple error bar chart of separate variables

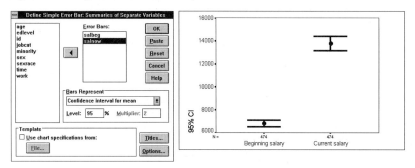

The minimum specification is one or more error bar variables.

The numeric, short string, and long string variables in your data file are displayed on the source variable list. Select the numeric variables you want to define the error bars. To get a simple error bar chart showing the confidence interval of each variable in default format, click on OK.

Error Bars. Select one or more numeric variables to define the error bars shown in the chart. There is one error bar for each variable.

Clustered:
Summaries of separate variables

Figure 26.16 shows a clustered error bar chart of separate variables. The specifications are on the left and the resulting error bar chart is on the right.

Figure 26.16 Clustered error bar of separate variables

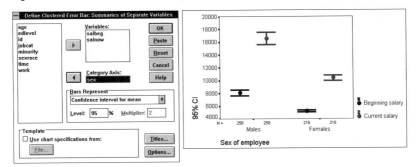

The minimum specifications are:

- Two or more numeric error bar variables.
- A category axis variable.

Variables. Select two or more variables to define the error bars shown in the chart. There is one error bar in each category for each variable. Two or more variables must be selected to enable the OK pushbutton.

Category Axis. Select a variable to define the categories shown in the error bar chart. There is one cluster of error bars for each value of the variable. A category axis variable must be selected to enable the OK pushbutton.

27 Scatterplots and Histograms

Summaries that describe data are useful, but nothing beats taking a look at the actual values. You wouldn't consider buying a house based solely on an appraiser's report. You know there's much more to a house than square footage and number of rooms. Similarly, you shouldn't draw conclusions about data based only on summary statistics, such as the mean and the correlation coefficient. Your data have a story that only a picture can tell.

In Chapter 7 and Chapter 9 you saw how histograms and stem-and-leaf plots (from the Frequencies and Explore procedures) are used to examine the distribution of the values of single variables. In this chapter you'll see how plotting two or more variables together helps you untangle and identify possible relationships.

Further discussion of how to obtain histograms from the Graphs menu is also included.

A Simple Scatterplot

As American corporations come under increasing scrutiny, the compensation paid to CEO's is often described as excessive and unrelated to corporate performance. Let's look at the relationship between 1989 total yearly compensation (in thousands) and profits (in millions). The data are a sample from those published in *Forbes* (1990).

Figure 27.1 is a scatterplot of total compensation (on the vertical axis) and profits (on the horizontal axis). Total compensation does not appear to be strongly related to profits, though there does appear to be a weak positive relationship.

Figure 27.1 Scatterplot of compensation with profits

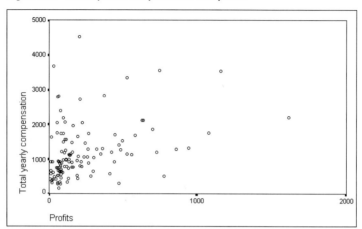

The plot is somewhat difficult to read, since many points overlap in the bottom left corner. Traditionally, in a plotting system which had limited resolution, such overlapping points were represented by a numeral which indicated how many cases each point represented. Such numerals, however, don't easily translate to a visual representation of density. You still tend to "see" only one case at each point on the plot.

Cleveland and McGill (1984) proposed that overlapping or nearly overlapping points be represented by **sunflowers**. The idea is fairly simple. You divide the entire plotting grid into equal-sized regions (cells) and count the number of points that fall into each region, just as for a low-resolution plot. Instead of a numeral, you then use the sunflower symbol to display this count. If a cell contains only one point, it is represented by a small circle. If a cell has more than one point, each point is represented by a short line (a "petal") originating from the circle. Optionally, you can specify an integer larger than 1 for the number of cases represented by each petal. (For more details, see Chapter 32.)

The sunflower plot for the CEO compensation data is shown in Figure 27.2.

Figure 27.2   Sunflower scatterplot of compensation with profits

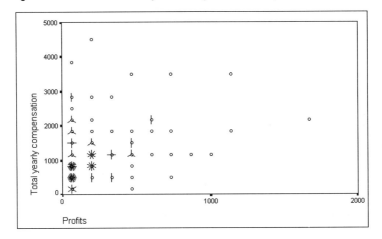

You can see that the overlapping points are now represented by sunflowers. It's easy to see where the cases cluster. The more petals on a sunflower, the more cases there are. But although it's easier to read the plot now, the relationship between CEO compensation and company profits doesn't appear to be straightforward.

Profits, Growth, and Compensation

Profits are, of course, only one indication of the success of a business, albeit an important one. Variables like corporate growth are also indicators of a CEO who performs well. Let's look at the relationship between growth, profits, and CEO compensation. Instead of considering the actual values, we'll look at the ranks assigned to the total compensation, profits, and growth for the selected companies. (*Forbes* ranked approximately 800 companies on these variables. A rank of 1 was assigned to the best performer.)

Figure 27.3 is a scatterplot of the ranks of profit and growth for the selected companies.

Figure 27.3   Scatterplot with summary curve

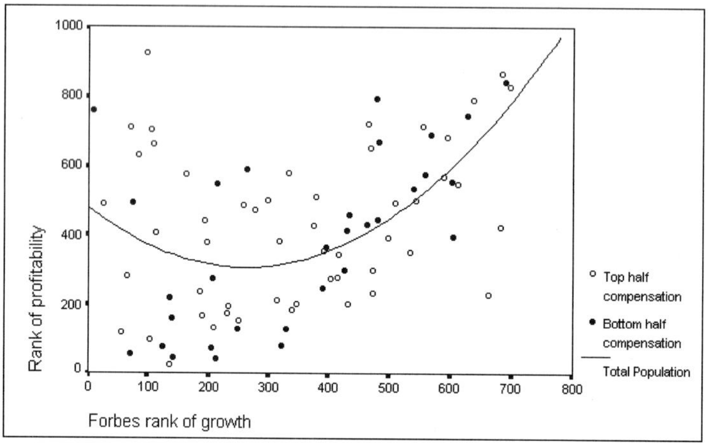

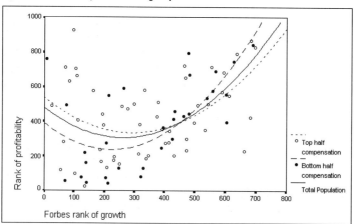

In this plot, different markers are used to identify the points in different categories. The squares are for companies with CEO's in the top half of the compensation ratings. The crosses are for companies whose CEO's are in the bottom half of compensation. There is also a summary curve drawn on the plot—a quadratic regression. From Figure 27.3 you see that the relationship between growth and profits is somewhat U-shaped. Once again there's not a clear relationship between compensation and the other two variables.

If you think that the relationship between growth and profit ranks may be different for the two types of CEO's (high pay and "low" pay), you can draw separate summary curves for the two categories and for the total sample. These are shown in Figure 27.4.

Figure 27.4   Scatterplot with subgroup curves

The relationship between ranks of growth and profits appears to be similar for each of the two categories of CEO's.

Scatterplot Matrices

When you want to examine the relationships between several pairs of variables, instead of plotting all pairs separately, you can select a **scatterplot matrix**. Consider Figure 27.5, which is a scatterplot matrix of the ranks of compensation, profits, and growth.

Figure 27.5 Scatterplot matrix with lowess fit lines

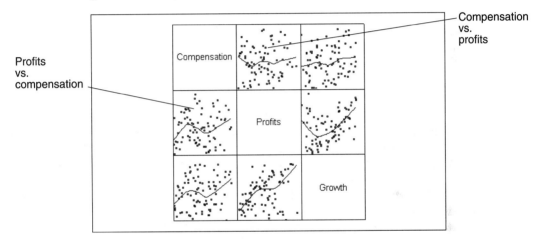

A scatterplot matrix has the same number of rows and columns as there are variables. In this example, the scatterplot matrix contains three rows and three columns. Each cell of the matrix is a plot of a pair of variables. The diagonal cells identify the variables plotted in the other cells. The first diagonal cell contains the label *Compensation*. That tells you that, for all plots in the first row, the rank of total compensation is plotted on the *y* axis (vertical). For all plots in the first column, the rank of compensation is plotted on the *x* axis (horizontal). Similarly, the label *Profits* is in the second diagonal cell, indicating that the rank of profits is plotted on the vertical axis for all plots in the second row and on the horizontal axis for all plots in the second column.

Look at the first plot in the first row. It is the plot of compensation (*y* axis) against profits (*x* axis). The second plot in the first row is the plot of compensation (*y* axis) against growth (*x* axis). The easiest way to read a scatterplot matrix is to scan across an entire row or column. For example, if you read across the first row you see how total compensation relates first to profit and then to growth. The third row tells you how growth relates to compensation and then how growth relates to profitability.

Similarly, the easiest way to identify an individual plot in a scatterplot matrix is to scan up or down to find which variable is on the horizontal axis, and scan right or left to find out which variable is on the vertical axis.

In a scatterplot matrix, all possible pairs of plots are displayed. The plots above the diagonal are the same as the plots below the diagonal. The only difference is that the variables are "flipped." That is, the horizontal and vertical variables are switched. For example, above the diagonal you see a plot of compensation and profits where compensation is on the vertical axis and profits are on the horizontal axis. Below the diagonal you see a plot of profits on the vertical axis and compensation on the horizontal axis.

The scatterplot matrix in Figure 27.5 reinforces our previous conclusions about compensation, profits, and growth. There appears to be little relationship between compensation and either profits or growth. However, there does appear to be a relationship between profits and growth.

Smoothing the Data

The curves added to the plots in the scatterplot matrix help you see possible trends in the data. There are many different lines and curves which can be superimposed on plots. If you know that a linear, quadratic, or cubic regression model fits your data (see Chapter 18), you can plot the appropriate model by choosing Options... from the Chart menu (see the section "Fit Options" on p. 517 in Chapter 32). If you don't know what kind of model fits your data, you can request lowess smoothing (Chambers et al., 1983).

Lowess smoothing doesn't require you to specify a particular model. Instead, for each value of the independent variable, it computes a predicted value using cases that have similar values for the independent variable. Points that are close to the one being predicted are assigned more importance in the computations. Lowess smoothing is robust, meaning that it isn't affected much by extreme values. That's a desirable property. Lowess smoothing requires many computations, especially for large data sets, so it may take a while for your plots to be drawn.

Plotting in Three Dimensions

So far, all of the plots you have seen in this chapter have been two-dimensional. That is, points are plotted only on two axes. You can also create scatterplots in three dimensions. Consider Figure 27.6, which is a three-dimensional plot of the ranks of compensation, growth, and profits.

Figure 27.6   3-D plot

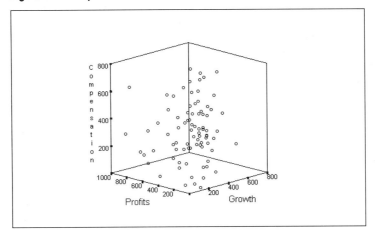

The position of each point is based on its values for all three variables. Unfortunately, since there isn't a strong relationship among the three variables, the plot is not particularly informative.

To see a more interesting three-dimensional plot, consider a hypothetical compensation strategy in which the rank of compensation is simply the average of the ranks of growth and profits. The plot of the hypothetical compensation rank is shown in Figure 27.7 for a sample including approximately a quarter of the cases. The smaller number of cases makes it easier to interpret the plot.

Figure 27.7   3-D plot with hypothetical relationship

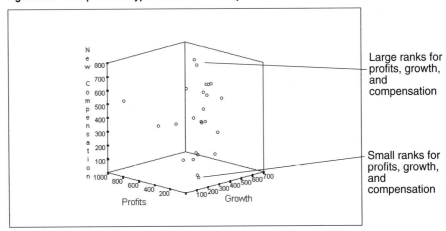

If you examine the plot carefully, you'll see the relationship between the three variables. Cases with low ranks for profits and growth have a low rank for compensation. Similarly, cases with large ranks for profits and growth have large ranks for compensation. Other cases have intermediate values.

It's easier to see the relationship between the three variables if you spin the plot until you notice a pattern. For example, if you spin Figure 27.7, you can obtain Figure 27.8. (See "Using Spin Mode" on p. 702 in Chapter 32.)

Figure 27.8   Previous 3-D plot with spin applied

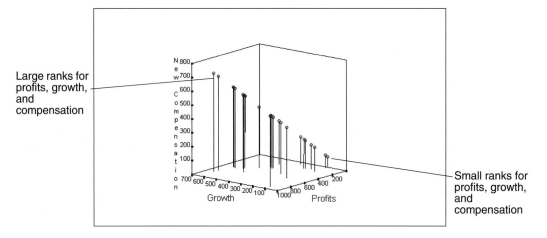

This figure has been further enhanced with **spikes** connecting each point to the floor (the bottom plane of the plot). For information on obtaining spikes, see "3-D Scatterplot Options" on p. 650 in Chapter 32. By looking at the base of a spike, you can see which point on the floor each plotted point is directly above. This strengthens the three-dimensional impression. From this figure, it's easy to see what the relationship is between compensation and the other two variables. Spinning a three-dimensional plot is useful for examining the relationships among the variables, as well as for identifying points which are far removed from the rest.

How to Obtain a Scatterplot

Scatterplots and histograms are graphical ways of looking at the actual values in a data set. In the examples in the remainder of this chapter, a survey of colleges will be used to illustrate most of the scatterplots and histograms you can obtain. Each record in this data set represents a different college. The data show SAT scores of admitted students, tuition, number of students, number of faculty, and other similar statistics. Examples that don't use the colleges data use the bank data.

To obtain a scatterplot, from the menus choose:

Graph
  Scatter...

This opens the Scatterplot dialog box, as shown in Figure 27.9.

Figure 27.9   Scatterplot dialog box

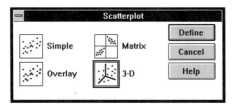

You can choose one of the following scatterplot types:

Simple. Each point represents the values of two variables for each case.

Matrix. Defines a square matrix of simple scatterplots, two for each combination of variables specified.

Overlay. Plots multiple scatterplots in the same frame.

3-D. Each point represents the value of three variables for each case. The points are plotted in a 3-D coordinate system which can be rotated.

Defining Simple Scatterplots

To obtain a simple scatterplot, select the Simple picture button in the Scatterplot dialog box and click on Define. This opens the Simple Scatterplot dialog box, as shown in Figure 27.10. The specifications are on the left and the resulting scatterplot is on the right.

Figure 27.10   Simple Scatterplot dialog box and chart

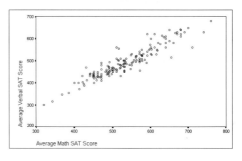

The minimum specifications are:

- An *x* axis variable.
- A *y* axis variable.

The numeric, short string, and long string variables in your data file are displayed on the source variable list. Select the numeric variables you want to define the *x* and *y* axis. To get a simple scatterplot in default format, click on OK.

Optionally, you can divide the scatterplot points into groups, label each point, use a template to control the format of the scatterplot, add a title, subtitle, or footnote, or change the missing value options.

Y Axis. Select the variable that will determine the vertical position of each point.

X Axis. Select the variable that will determine the horizontal position of each point.

Set Markers by. Select a variable to determine the categories that will be shown on the chart. Each value of the variable is a different color or marker symbol on the scatterplot.

Label Cases by. Select a variable to provide labels for each marker. The value label of each case is placed above the point on the scatterplot. If there is no value label, the actual value will be placed above the point. The value label displayed is truncated after the 20th character.

Template. You can use another file to define the format of your charts (see "Chart Templates" on p. 458 in Chapter 23).

Titles. You can add titles, subtitles, and footnotes to your charts (see "Titles, Subtitles, and Footnotes" on p. 454 in Chapter 23).

Options. You can exclude cases with missing values listwise or by variable. You can also display groups defined by missing values. For more details, see "Missing Values" on p. 455 in Chapter 23.

Defining Scatterplot Matrices

To obtain a scatterplot matrix, select Matrix in the Scatterplot dialog box and click on Define. This opens the Scatterplot Matrix dialog box, as shown in Figure 27.11. The specifications are on the left and the resulting scatterplot is on the right.

Figure 27.11   Scatterplot Matrix dialog box and chart

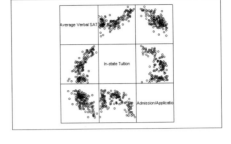

The minimum specification is two or more matrix variables.

The numeric, short string, and long string variables in your data file are displayed on the source variable list. Select two or more numeric variables to define the cells of the matrix. To get a scatterplot matrix in the default format, click on OK.

Optionally, you can show different markers for different categories, use a template to control the format of the scatterplot, or add a title, subtitle, or footnote.

Matrix Variables. Select two or more variables to define the cells of the matrix. There is one row and one column for each variable. Each cell contains a simple scatterplot of the row variable and the column variable.

Set Markers by. Select a variable to determine the categories that will be shown on the chart. Each value of the variable is a different marker symbol on the scatterplot matrix.

Label Cases by. Select a variable to provide labels for each marker. The value label of each case is placed above the point on the scatterplot. If there is no value label, the actual value will be placed above the point. The value label displayed is truncated after the 20th character.

Template. You can use another file to define the format of your charts (see "Chart Templates" on p. 458 in Chapter 23).

Titles. You can add titles, subtitles, and footnotes to your charts (see "Titles, Subtitles, and Footnotes" on p. 454 in Chapter 23).

Options. You can exclude cases with missing values listwise or by variable. You can also display groups defined by missing values. For more details, see "Missing Values" on p. 455 in Chapter 23.

Defining Overlay Scatterplots

To obtain an overlay scatterplot, select Overlay in the Scatterplot dialog box and click on Define. This opens the Overlay Scatterplot dialog box, as shown in Figure 27.12. The specifications are on the left and the resulting overlay scatterplot is on the right.

Figure 27.12   Overlay Scatterplot dialog box and chart

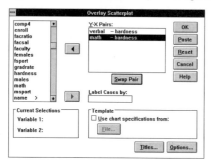 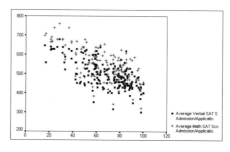

The minimum specification is two or more *y-x* pairs.

The numeric, short string, and long string variables in your data file are displayed on the source variable list. Select two or more numeric *y-x* variable pairs. To get an overlay scatterplot in default format, click on OK.

Optionally, you can label the scatterplot points, use a template to control the format of the scatterplot, or add a title, subtitle, or footnote.

Y-X Pairs. Select two or more variable pairs. Each pair of variables is plotted on the same scatterplot with a separate marker symbol. To select a variable pair, highlight two variables on the source variable list by clicking on each one. The selected variables are indicated on the Current Selections list. Click on the ▶ pushbutton. This copies the variables from the Current Selection list to the *y-x* pairs list. The same variable may be selected in multiple variable pairs. To swap the *y* and *x* variables in a *y-x* pair, highlight the pair and click on Swap Pair.

Label Cases by. Select a variable to provide labels for each marker. The value label of each case is placed beside the point on the scatterplot. If there is no value label, the actual value will be placed beside the point. The value label displayed is truncated after the 20th character.

Template. You can use another file to define the format of your charts (see "Chart Templates" on p. 458 in Chapter 23).

Titles. You can add titles, subtitles, and footnotes to your charts (see "Titles, Subtitles, and Footnotes" on p. 454 in Chapter 23).

Options. You can exclude cases with missing values listwise or by variable. You can also display groups defined by missing values. For more details, see "Missing Values" on p. 455 in Chapter 23.

Defining 3-D Scatterplots

To obtain a 3-D scatterplot, select 3-D in the Scatterplot dialog box and click on Define. This opens the 3-D Scatterplot dialog box, as shown in Figure 27.13. The specifications are on the left and the resulting 3-D scatterplot is on the right.

Figure 27.13   3-D Scatterplot dialog box and chart

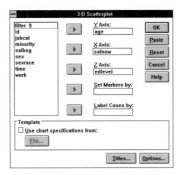
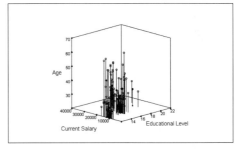

The minimum specifications are:

- A *y* axis variable.
- An *x* axis variable.
- A *z* axis variable.

The numeric, short string, and long string variables in your data file are displayed on the source variable list. Select the numeric variables you want to define the *z*, *y*, and *x* axes. To get a 3-D scatterplot in default format, click on OK.

Optionally, you can show different markers for different categories, label each point, use a template to control the format of the scatterplot, and add a title, subtitle, and footnote.

Y Axis. Select the variable that will determine the height of each point.

X Axis. Select the variable that will determine the horizontal position of each point.

Z Axis. Select the variable that will determine the depth of each point.

Set Markers by. Select a variable to determine the categories that will be shown on the chart. Each value of the variable is a different marker symbol on the scatterplot.

Label Cases by. Select a variable to provide labels for each marker. The value label of each case is placed beside the point on the scatterplot. If there is no value label, the actual value will be placed beside the point. The value label displayed is truncated after the 20th character.

Template. You can use another file to define the format of your charts (see "Chart Templates" on p. 458 in Chapter 23).

Titles. You can add titles, subtitles, and footnotes to your charts (see "Titles, Subtitles, and Footnotes" on p. 454 in Chapter 23).

Options. You can exclude cases with missing values listwise or by variable. You can also display groups defined by missing values. For more details, see "Missing Values" on p. 455 in Chapter 23.

How to Obtain a Histogram

For a discussion of how to interpret histograms, see Chapter 7. To obtain a histogram, from the menus choose:

Graphs
  Histogram...

This opens the Histogram dialog box, as shown in Figure 27.14.

Figure 27.14   Histogram dialog box and chart

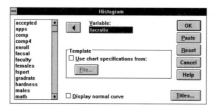 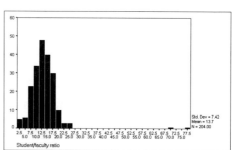

The minimum specification is a variable.

The numeric variables in your data file are displayed on the source variable list. Select the variable for which you want a histogram. To get a histogram in the default format, as shown above, click on OK.

Optionally, you can use a template to control the format of the histogram, add a title, subtitle, or footnote, or superimpose a normal curve on the histogram.

Variable. Select the variable for which you want a histogram. By default, you get bars showing the data divided into several evenly spaced intervals. The height of each bar shows the number of cases in each interval. The data series used to create the bar chart contains the individual values of each case. This means you can alter the intervals shown on the bar chart from the chart editor.

Template. You can use another file to define the format of your charts (see "Chart Templates" on p. 458 in Chapter 23).

Display normal curve. Select this to superimpose over the histogram a normal curve with the same mean and variance as your data.

Titles. You can add titles, subtitles, and footnotes to your charts (see "Titles, Subtitles, and Footnotes" on p. 454 in Chapter 23).

28 Pareto and Control Charts

Pareto and control charts are tools used to analyze and improve the quality of an ongoing process. Pareto charts focus attention on the most important category out of a wide variety of possibilities. Control charts help differentiate between random variations in a process and variations that are meaningful. Pareto and control charts can be used in manufacturing processes, where the things being measured are physical and are usually produced on an assembly line. Or, these charts can be used in service processes, where the things being measured, such as opinions, budgetary flows, or the effect of a medical treatment, are more abstract.

Pareto Charts

A **Pareto chart** is a bar chart, sorted in descending order; a line may be added to show the cumulative frequency across categories.

Often managers or researchers are confronted with a wide variety of categories and need a quick, visual way to gauge the relative importance of each. For example, pneumonia can be caused by a wide variety of flora. In most cases, only normal upper respiratory flora can be found with a sputum gram stain test. To see which of the remaining flora are found in the majority of pneumonia patients at a hospital, a Pareto chart can be generated. Figure 28.1 shows a simple Pareto chart based on results of a sputum gram stain test.

Figure 28.1 Simple Pareto chart

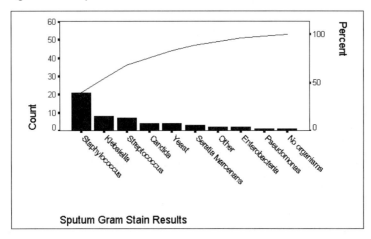

In this chart, you can quickly see that staphylococcus is found in one third of the patients with abnormal flora.

Control Charts

Any process naturally has random variations. A control chart helps differentiate between random variations and variations with an assignable cause. The kind of control chart used depends upon the data. Figure 28.2 shows an example of an X-Bar chart.

Figure 28.2   X-Bar chart

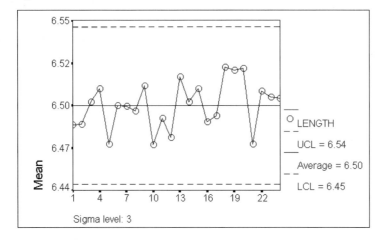

Each point on the fluctuating line represents the mean of a measured value within each subgroup. The center line is the mean of the subgroups and the dotted lines are the upper and lower control limits.

In any control chart, each **subgroup** usually represents a time interval. This can be either an abstract measurement, such as a batch number, or an actual measure of time, such as an hour or a day. The subgroups are sorted in ascending order, so hour 2 is shown to the right of hour 1, and so on. If your subgroups are time intervals, they should be recorded as numeric variables or date variables so that they will be sorted in the expected order. Usually, each subgroup contains multiple units. A **unit** is the thing being measured.

The types of control charts available are:

- **X-Bar and s.** Shows the mean of a measured value within each subgroup in the X-Bar chart and the standard deviation of the value within each subgroup in the s chart. Use this rather than the X-Bar and R charts when the number of values in each subgroup is large (more than 10).

- **X-Bar and R.** Shows the mean of a measured value within each subgroup in the X-Bar chart and the range of values within each subgroup.

- **Individuals and moving range.** Shows each measured value in the individuals chart. The individual values appear in the chart in the same order as the data. The moving range chart shows the range of values within the selected span. That is, if the span is 3, the moving range shows the range of values between the current case, the previous case, and the case before that.

- **p.** Shows the number of nonconforming units as a fraction of the total number of units in each subgroup. Use this rather than an np chart when the number of units varies between subgroups.

- **np.** Shows the number of nonconforming units in each subgroup.

- **u.** Shows the number of nonconformities as a fraction of the total number of units in each subgroup. Use this rather than a p chart when each unit can have multiple nonconformities.

- **c.** Shows the number of nonconformities in each subgroup. Use this rather than an np chart when each unit can have multiple nonconformities.

Table 28.1 shows which chart types to use depending upon the type of data available.

Table 28.1 Choosing the appropriate control chart

The data contain variable measured values, such as length, tensile strength, or age.	The number of units per subgroup is large (greater than 10).		X-Bar and s
	The number of units per subgroup is small.		X-Bar and R
	There is one unit per subgroup.		individual and moving range
The data contain attributes such as the number of nonconformities or the number of nonconforming units.	The data contain the number of nonconforming units.	The number of units per subgroup is constant.	p or np
		The number of units per subgroup varies.	p
	The data contain the number of nonconformities, and each unit can have multiple nonconformities.	The number of units per subgroup is constant.	c or u
		The number of units per subgroup varies.	u

Using the Same Data in Pareto and Control Charts

Pareto charts, p, np, c, and u charts all show attribute data. However, data structured for display in a Pareto chart often need to be modified before they can be displayed in a control chart. Figure 28.3 shows a Pareto chart of types of defects found on circuit boards.

Figure 28.3 Defects on circuit boards

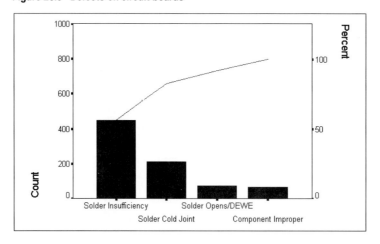

Each record in the data shows defects for a batch of 500 parts. Each type of defect is recorded as a separate variable that counts the number of boards with that type of defect. The variables are: *cmpimp*, which counts the number of boards with improper components, *sldropen*, which counts the number of boards with open solder joints, *sldrcold*, which counts the number of boards with cold solder joints, and *sldrins*, which counts the number of boards with insufficient solder.

To generate a p chart from this data, a new variable showing the total number of defective parts needs to be computed. To open the Compute Variable dialog box, select Compute on the Transform menu. For Target Variable, enter the name of the new variable—in this case, *totdef*. For Numeric Expression, enter the names of the existing defect variables separated by plus signs. For the circuit board defects, you would enter

```
cmpimp + sldropen + sldrcold + sldrins
```

When you click on OK, the new variable, *cmpimp*, is generated. Figure 28.4 shows a p chart of defective circuit boards.

Figure 28.4   p chart for circuit boards

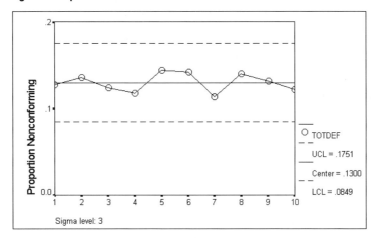

How to Obtain a Pareto Chart

To obtain a Pareto chart, from the menus choose:

Graphs
  Pareto...

This opens the Pareto Charts dialog box, as shown in Figure 28.5.

Figure 28.5   Pareto Charts dialog box

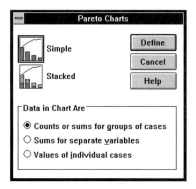

From the Pareto Charts dialog box, choose one of the chart types, and then select the choice that describes the structure of your data organization.

Data in Chart Are. Select the choice that describes the organization of your data.

○ **Counts or sums for groups of cases.** One variable is counted or summed in subgroups. The subgroups are determined by one variable for simple Pareto charts or two variables for stacked Pareto charts.

○ **Sums of separate variables.** More than one variable is summed. Simple Pareto charts sum each variable over all cases in the file. Stacked Pareto charts sum each variable within categories determined by another variable.

○ **Values of individual cases.** Each case in the data is a separate category in the chart.

Examples of these choices, along with data structures and the charts they produce, are shown in Table 28.2.

Table 28.2   Types of Pareto charts

Selections	Data	Chart
Simple ○ Counts or sums for groups of cases With counts selected in the chart definition dialog box	**sputres** 1 Staphylococcus 2 Staphylococcus 3 Normal up Resp Flora 4 Normal up Resp Flora 5 Staphylococcus	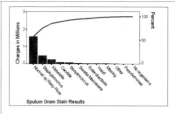
	Each case shows the sputum gram stain results for a different patient. The results indicate the type of flora present. The chart shows a bar for each type of flora. The bars are sorted in descending order, so the one on the left is highest. A line shows the cumulative sum across types of flora.	
Simple ○ Counts or sums for groups of cases With sums selected in the chart definition dialog box	**totalchg sputres** 1 $2,973 Staphyloc 2 $1,925 Staphyloc 3 $4,081 Normal u 4 $7,823 Normal u	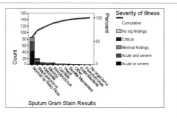
	Each case shows the sputum gram stain results for a different patient and the cost of treatment. The results indicate the type of flora present. The chart shows a bar for each type of flora. The bars are sorted in descending order, so the one on the left is highest. A line shows the cumulative sum across types of flora.	
Stacked ○ Counts or sums for groups of cases With counts selected in the chart definition dialog box	**severity sputres** 1 No sig findings Staphyloco 2 No sig findings Staphyloco 3 Minimal findings Normal up 4 Minimal findings Normal up 5 Minimal findings Staphyloco	[chart: Severity of Illness, Cumulative, No sig findings, Critical, Minimal findings, Acute and severe, Acute or severe]
	Each case shows the severity and the sputum gram stain results for a different patient. The chart shows a bar for each type of flora. Each bar is broken down into segments by the severity of the illness.	
Stacked ○ Counts or sums for groups of cases With sums selected in the chart definition dialog box	**asg totalchg sputres** 1 No sig findi $2,973 Staphy 2 No sig findi $1,925 Staphy 3 Minimal fin $4,081 Normal 4 Minimal fin $7,823 Normal 5 Minimal fin $7,454 Staphy	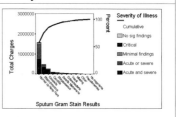
	Each case shows the severity, cost of treatment, and the sputum gram stain results for a different patient. The chart shows a bar for each type of flora. Each bar is broken down into segments by the severity of the illness.	

Table 28.2   Types of Pareto charts (Continued)

Selections	Data	Chart

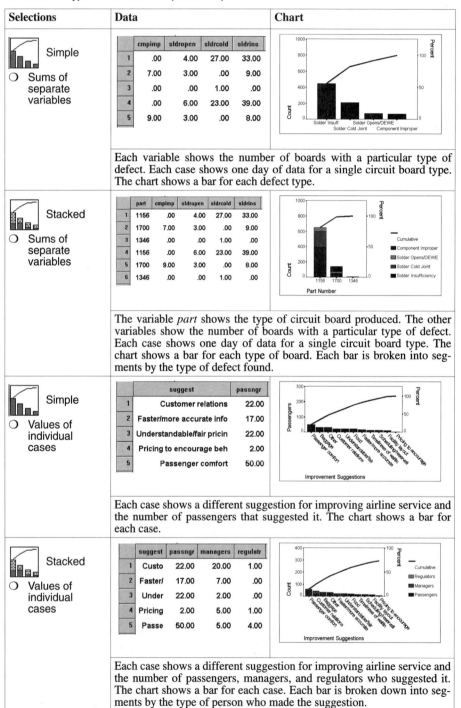

Simple

○ Sums of separate variables

	cmpimp	sldropen	sldrcold	sldrins
1	.00	4.00	27.00	33.00
2	7.00	3.00	.00	9.00
3	.00	.00	1.00	.00
4	.00	6.00	23.00	39.00
5	9.00	3.00	.00	8.00

Each variable shows the number of boards with a particular type of defect. Each case shows one day of data for a single circuit board type. The chart shows a bar for each defect type.

Stacked

○ Sums of separate variables

	part	cmpimp	sldropen	sldrcold	sldrins
1	1156	.00	4.00	27.00	33.00
2	1700	7.00	3.00	.00	9.00
3	1346	.00	.00	1.00	.00
4	1156	.00	6.00	23.00	39.00
5	1700	9.00	3.00	.00	8.00
6	1346	.00	.00	1.00	.00

The variable *part* shows the type of circuit board produced. The other variables show the number of boards with a particular type of defect. Each case shows one day of data for a single circuit board type. The chart shows a bar for each type of board. Each bar is broken into segments by the type of defect found.

Simple

○ Values of individual cases

	suggest	passngr
1	Customer relations	22.00
2	Faster/more accurate info	17.00
3	Understandable/fair pricin	22.00
4	Pricing to encourage beh	2.00
5	Passenger comfort	50.00

Each case shows a different suggestion for improving airline service and the number of passengers that suggested it. The chart shows a bar for each case.

Stacked

○ Values of individual cases

	suggest	passngr	managers	regulatr
1	Custo	22.00	20.00	1.00
2	Faster/	17.00	7.00	.00
3	Under	22.00	2.00	.00
4	Pricing	2.00	5.00	1.00
5	Passe	50.00	5.00	4.00

Each case shows a different suggestion for improving airline service and the number of passengers, managers, and regulators who suggested it. The chart shows a bar for each case. Each bar is broken down into segments by the type of person who made the suggestion.

Each combination of chart type and data organization structure produces a different definition box. Each is discussed briefly below. The icon and section title indicate the choices that have to be made in the chart dialog box to open that chart definition dialog box. The discussion for each chart type always describes the selections required to enable the OK pushbutton. Optional selections are discussed only with the first chart using each data structure.

Simple:
Counts or sums for groups of cases

Figure 28.6 shows a chart definition dialog box and the resulting simple Pareto chart with counts for groups of cases.

Figure 28.6   Simple Pareto chart with counts for groups of cases

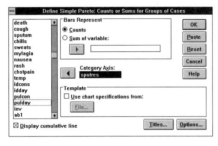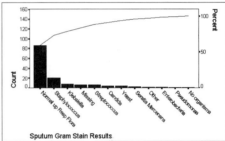

The minimum specification is a category axis variable.

The numeric, short string, and long string variables in your data file are displayed on the source variable list. Select a variable to define the category axis. To get a simple chart showing number of cases for groups of cases in default format, click on OK.

Optionally, you can select sums of a variable rather than counts, use a template to control the format of the chart, turn off the cumulative line, or add a title, subtitle, or footnote. Templates, titles, subtitles, and footnotes are discussed in detail in Chapter 23.

Bars Represent. Determines what the scale axis of the Pareto chart represents. Choose one of the following:

○ **Counts.** The number of cases in each category determines the height of each bar.

○ **Sum of variable.** The height of each bar is calculated from the sum of the specified variable. If you select Sum of variable, you must specify a numeric variable to be summed. Figure 28.7 shows the chart definition dialog box with a variable to be summed and the resulting simple Pareto chart.

Category Axis. Select a variable to define the categories shown in the chart. There is one bar for each value of the variable. The bars are sorted in descending order.

Display cumulative line. By default, a line will be drawn in the Pareto chart. This line indicates the cumulative sum of the values shown by the bars. Deselect this option to get a Pareto chart without the line.

Figure 28.7   Simple Pareto chart with sums of a variable

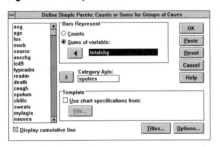 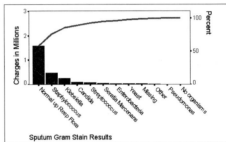

Stacked:
Counts or sums for groups of cases

Figure 28.8 shows a chart definition dialog box and the resulting clustered bar chart with summaries for groups of cases.

Figure 28.8   Stacked Pareto chart with counts for groups of cases

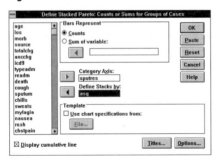 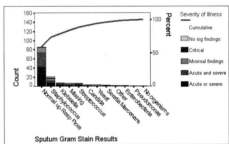

The minimum specifications are:

- A category axis variable.
- A variable that defines segments in each bar.

Category Axis. Select a variable to define the categories shown in the chart. There is one stack of bars for each value of the variable.

Define Stacks by. Select a variable to define the bar segments within each stack. There is one bar segment within each stack for each value of the variable.

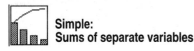

Simple:
Sums of separate variables

Figure 28.9 shows a chart definition dialog box and the resulting simple bar chart with sums of separate variables.

Figure 28.9   Simple Pareto chart with sums of separate variables

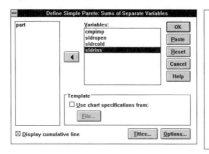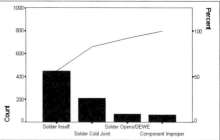

The minimum specification is two or more variables.

The numeric variables in your data file are displayed on the source variable list. Select the variables you want to define the bars. To get a simple Pareto chart showing the sum of each variable in default format, click on OK.

Optionally, use a template to control the format of the chart, or add a title, subtitle, or footnote. These options are discussed in detail in Chapter 23.

Variables. Select two or more variables to define the categories shown in the chart. There is one bar for each variable. The bars show the sum of each variable and are sorted in descending order.

Stacked:
Sums of separate variables

Figure 28.10 shows a chart definition dialog box and the resulting stacked Pareto chart with sums of separate variables.

Figure 28.10 Stacked Pareto chart with summaries of separate variables

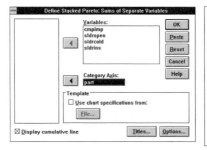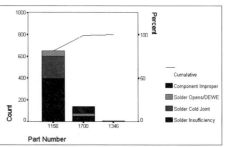

The minimum specifications are:

- Two or more numeric variables which define the segments within each bar.
- A category axis variable.

Variables. Select two or more variables. There is one bar within each stack for each variable. The bars show the sum of the selected variables.

Category Axis. Select a variable to define the categories shown in the chart. There is one stack of bars for each value of the variable.

Simple:
Values of individual cases

Figure 28.11 shows a chart definition dialog box and the resulting simple Pareto chart with values of individual cases.

Figure 28.11 Simple Pareto chart with values of individual cases

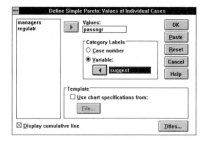 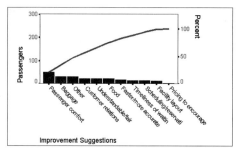

The minimum specifications are:

- A numeric values variable.
- If Variable is selected for Category Labels, a category label variable.

The numeric, short string, and long string variables in your data file are displayed on the source variable list. Select the numeric variable you want to define the bars. To get a simple Pareto chart showing the value of each case in default format, click on OK.

Optionally, you can change the value labels shown in the chart, use a template to control the format of the chart, disable the cumulative line, or add a title, subtitle, or footnote. Templates, titles, subtitles, and footnotes are discussed in detail in Chapter 23.

Values. Select a numeric variable to define the bars. Each case will be displayed as a separate bar.

Category Labels. Determines how the bars are labeled. You can choose one of the following category label sources:

○ **Case number.** Each category is labeled with the case number.

○ **Variable.** Each category is labeled with the current value of the selected variable.

Stacked:
Values of individual cases

Figure 28.12 shows a chart definition dialog box and the resulting stacked Pareto chart with values of individual cases.

Figure 28.12 Stacked Pareto chart with values of individual cases

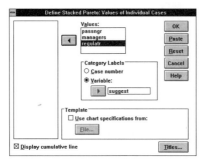 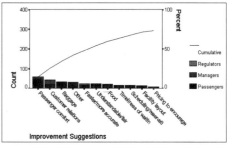

The minimum specifications are:

- Two or more numeric variables that define bar segments.
- A category label variable, if Variable is selected under Category Labels.

Values. Select two or more numeric variables. There is one bar within each stack for each variable. The bars show the value of each case. If there is a cumulative line, there is one point on the line for each case.

How to Obtain a Control Chart

To obtain a control chart, from the menus choose:

Graphs
  Control...

This opens the Control Charts dialog box, as shown in Figure 28.13.

Figure 28.13 Control Charts dialog box

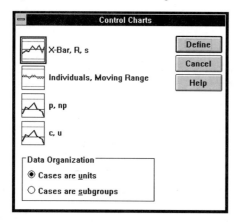

From the Control Charts dialog box, choose one of the chart types, and then select the choice that describes the structure of your data organization.

Data Organization. Select the choice that describes the organization of your data.

○ **Cases are units.** Each unit is a separate case (row of data). One variable identifies the subgroup to which the unit belongs. Another variable records the value being measured. Each point in the control chart shows a different subgroup. The number of units can vary from subgroup to subgroup.

○ **Cases are subgroups.** All units within a subgroup are recorded in a single case. Each unit is a separate variable. Like the previous organization, each point in the control chart shows a different subgroup. The number of samples per subgroup should be the same.

Examples of these choices, along with data structures and the charts they produce, are shown in Table 28.3.

Table 28.3   Types of control charts

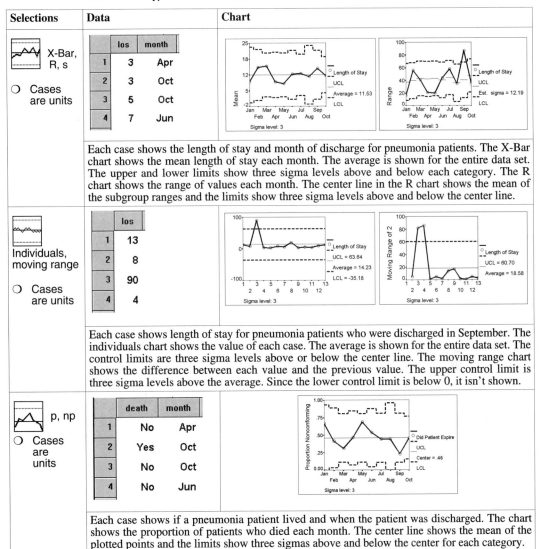

Selections	Data	Chart

X-Bar, R, s

○ Cases are units

	los	month
1	3	Apr
2	3	Oct
3	5	Oct
4	7	Jun

Each case shows the length of stay and month of discharge for pneumonia patients. The X-Bar chart shows the mean length of stay each month. The average is shown for the entire data set. The upper and lower limits show three sigma levels above and below each category. The R chart shows the range of values each month. The center line in the R chart shows the mean of the subgroup ranges and the limits show three sigma levels above and below the center line.

Individuals, moving range

○ Cases are units

	los
1	13
2	8
3	90
4	4

Each case shows length of stay for pneumonia patients who were discharged in September. The individuals chart shows the value of each case. The average is shown for the entire data set. The control limits are three sigma levels above or below the center line. The moving range chart shows the difference between each value and the previous value. The upper control limit is three sigma levels above the average. Since the lower control limit is below 0, it isn't shown.

p, np

○ Cases are units

	death	month
1	No	Apr
2	Yes	Oct
3	No	Oct
4	No	Jun

Each case shows if a pneumonia patient lived and when the patient was discharged. The chart shows the proportion of patients who died each month. The center line shows the mean of the plotted points and the limits show three sigmas above and below the center for each category.

Table 28.3   Types of control charts (Continued)

Selections	Data	Chart

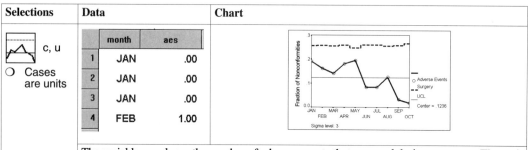

The variable *aes* shows the number of adverse events that occurred during a surgery. The variable *month* shows the month in which the surgery occurred. The chart shows the number of adverse events per surgery for each month. The center line shows the mean of the plotted points. The upper limit shows three sigma levels above the center line. The lower limit is not shown because it is below 0.

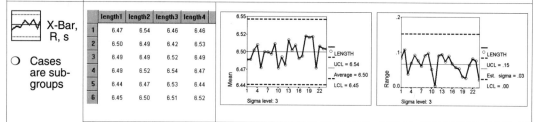

Each variable shows the length of a part manufactured on a separate machine. Each case shows the data for all four machines taken at one-hour intervals. The X-Bar chart on the left shows the mean length for each hour. The R chart on the right shows the range of values for each hour. The center line is the mean of the plotted points. The upper and lower limits are three sigma levels above and below the center line.

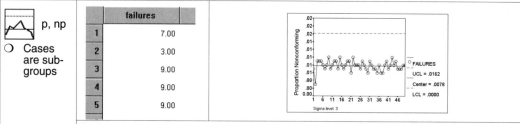

Each case shows the number of failed parts found in a batch of 100. The chart shows the proportion of nonconforming parts in each batch. The center line shows the mean of the plotted points. The upper limit shows three sigma levels above the center line. The lower limit is not shown because it is below 0.

Each case shows the number of errors found in a batch of 100 parts. The chart shows the number of errors per part in each batch. The center line shows the mean of the plotted points. The control limits show three sigma levels above and below the center line.

Each combination of chart type and data organization structure produces a different definition box. Each is discussed briefly below. The icon and section title indicate the choices that have to be made in the chart dialog box to open that chart definition dialog box.

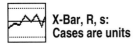

X-Bar, R, s:
Cases are units

Figure 28.14 shows a chart definition dialog box and the resulting X-bar and R charts with cases as units. To plot this type of chart, your data file must contain one variable (column) that measures the process in question and one variable that breaks the process into subgroups. A subgroup can contain one or more rows from the data file. Each subgroup is plotted as a single point.

Figure 28.14 X-Bar and R charts with cases as units

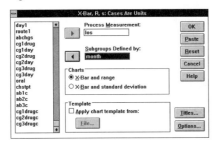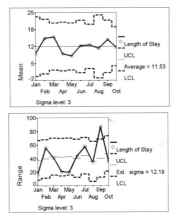

The minimum specifications are:

- A numeric process measurement variable.
- A subgroups variable.

All variables are shown on the source variable list. Select a variable that measures the process of interest and select a variable that breaks the process into subgroups. To get a chart that shows the mean value for each subgroup and a chart that shows the range within each subgroup, click on OK.

Optionally, you can select standard deviation rather than range, change the number of sigmas used for control limits, specify an upper or a lower limit, alter the minimum subgroup sample size, display subgroups defined by missing values, use a template to control the format of the chart, or add a title, subtitle, or footnote. Templates, titles, subtitles, and footnotes are discussed in detail in Chapter 23. The number of sigmas in the calculated control limits, specified control limits, minimum subgroup sample size, and missing values are described in "Control Chart Options" on p. 598.

If you don't have a subgroup variable but know that cases are sorted by subgroup within the file, it is easy to compute a subgroup variable. For Target Variable in the Compute Variable dialog box (select Compute on the Transform menu), type the name of your new subgroup variable. For the Numeric Expression, enter

```
trunc(($CASENUM-1)/n)+1
```

where n is the number of cases in each subgroup.

Process Measurement. Select a numeric variable that measures the process of interest. The charts show the mean and range or standard deviation of this variable within each subgroup. (See Figure 28.15.)

Subgroups Defined by. Select a variable that divides the process into subgroups. There is one point on the process line for each value of this variable. Usually the variable represents a unit of time.

Charts. Two charts are produced. The first is an X-Bar chart. The second can be either a range chart (an R chart) or a standard deviation chart (an s chart).

An X-Bar chart shows the mean of the process for each subgroup. The center line is the mean of the process over the entire data set and the control limits are a number of standard deviations above and below the center line for each category. The number of standard deviations is shown as the sigma level.

○ **X-Bar and range.** A range chart shows the range of the process within each subgroup. The center line shows the mean of the subgroup ranges (which is different for subgroups of different size). The upper and lower limits show three sigma levels above and below the center line for each category.

○ **X-Bar and standard deviation.** A standard deviation chart shows the standard deviation of the process within each subgroup. The center line shows the mean of the subgroup standard deviations. The upper and lower limits show three sigma levels above and below the center line for each category.

Figure 28.15 X-Bar and s charts with cases as units

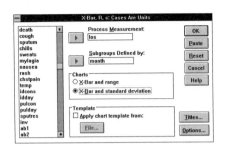

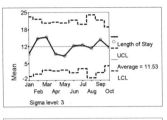

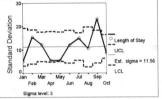

Individuals, moving range:
Cases are units

Figure 28.16 shows a chart definition dialog box and the resulting control charts for individuals with cases as units. To plot this type of chart, your data file must contain a variable (column) that measures the process in question; each row in the data file is plotted as a single point.

Figure 28.16 Control charts for individuals with cases as units

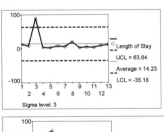

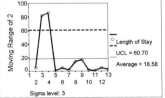

The minimum specification is a numeric process measurement variable.

All variables are shown on the source variable list. Select a numeric variable that measures the process of interest. To obtain control charts that show the value of each case and the moving range in default format, click on OK.

Optionally, you can select a subgroup label variable, suppress the moving range chart, select a different span, change the number of sigmas used for control limits, specify an upper or a lower limit, use a template to control the format of the chart, or add a title, subtitle, or footnote. Templates, titles, subtitles, and footnotes are discussed in detail in Chapter 23. The number of sigmas in the calculated control limits and specified control limits are described in "Control Chart Options" on p. 598.

Process Measurement. Select a numeric variable that measures the process of interest. The charts show the value of the variable for each case and the moving range.

Subgroups Labeled by. When a subgroup label variable is used, each category is labeled with the current value label of the selected variable. Figure 28.17 shows a control chart for individuals with a subgroup labels variable.

Figure 28.17 Control chart for individuals with category labels from variable ab1

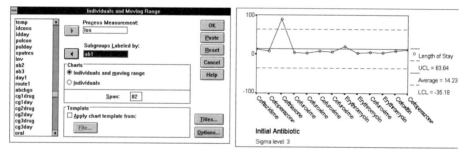

Charts. Determines the types of charts generated. You can choose from the following options:

○ **Individuals and moving range.** Both an individuals and a moving range chart are generated.

○ **Individuals.** Only an individuals chart is generated.

Span. Indicate the number of cases used for calculating the control limits in both charts and for calculating the moving range. For example, if the span is 3, the current case and the previous two cases are used in the calculations.

p, np:
Cases are units

Figure 28.18 shows a chart definition dialog box and the resulting p chart with cases as units. To plot this type of chart, your data file must contain a variable (column) that indicates the presence of a nonconforming characteristic and a variable that divides the data into subgroups. A subgroup can contain one or more rows from the data file. Each subgroup is plotted as a single point.

Figure 28.18 p chart with cases as units

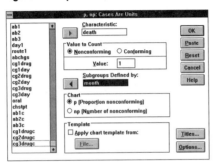
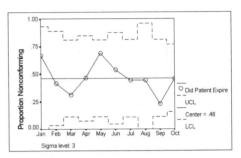

The minimum specifications are:

- A characteristic variable.
- A subgroup variable.

All variables are shown on the source variable list. Select a variable that indicates the presence of the characteristic of interest and a variable that divides the data into subgroups. Then, enter the value to count. To obtain a control chart that shows the proportion of nonconforming cases in default format, click on OK.

Optionally, you can change the value to be counted, get an np chart rather than a p chart, change the number of sigmas used for control limits, display subgroups defined by missing values, use a template to control the format of the chart, or add a title, subtitle, or footnote. Templates, titles, subtitles, and footnotes are discussed in detail in Chapter 23. The number of sigmas in the calculated control limits and missing values are described in "Control Chart Options" on p. 598.

Characteristic. Select a variable that indicates the presence of the characteristic to be measured.

Value to Count. Either nonconforming or conforming cases can be counted. In both instances, the chart shows the proportion or number of nonconforming cases.

○ **Nonconforming.** The indicated value is a nonconforming value. The chart shows the proportion or number of cases with this value.

○ **Conforming.** The indicated value is a conforming value. The chart shows the proportion or number of cases that do not have this value.

Value. Indicate the value to be counted. The value must be of the same type as the characteristic variable. (For example, if the characteristic variable is numeric, the value must be a number.)

Subgroups Defined by. Select a variable that divides the process into subgroups. There is one point on the process line for each value of this variable. Usually the variable represents a unit of time.

Chart. Determines the type of chart generated. You can choose one of the following chart types:

○ **p (Proportion nonconforming).** The chart shows the proportion of nonconformities within each subgroup. Use this chart type if the number of cases varies between subgroups.

○ **np (Number of nonconforming).** The chart show the number of nonconformities within each subgroup. Use this chart type if all subgroups have the same number of cases. Figure 28.19 shows a chart definition dialog box and the resulting np chart.

Figure 28.19 np chart with cases as units

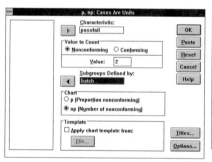 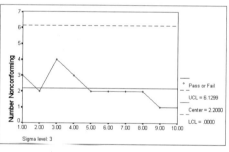

c, u:
Cases are units

Figure 28.20 shows a chart definition dialog box and the resulting u chart with cases as units. To plot this type of chart, your data file must contain one variable (column) that counts the number of nonconformities and one variable that divides the data into subgroups. A subgroup can contain one or more rows from the data file. Each subgroup is plotted as a single point.

Figure 28.20 u chart with cases as units

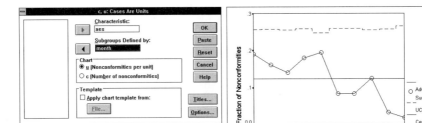

The minimum specifications are:

- A numeric characteristic variable.
- A subgroups variable.

All variables are shown on the source variable list. Select a numeric variable that counts the characteristic of interest and select a variable that divides the data into subgroups. To get a control chart that shows the number of nonconformities per unit for each subgroup in default format, click on OK.

Optionally, you can get a c chart rather than a u chart, change the number of sigmas used for control limits, display subgroups defined by missing values, use a template to control the format of the chart, or add a title, subtitle, or footnote. Templates, titles, subtitles, and footnotes are discussed in detail in Chapter 23. The number of sigmas in the calculated control limits and missing values are described in "Control Chart Options" on p. 598.

Characteristic. Select a numeric variable that indicates the number of times the characteristic to be measured is found.

Subgroups Defined by. Select a variable that divides the process into subgroups. There is one point on the process line for each value of this variable. Usually the variable represents a unit of time.

Chart. Determines the type of chart generated. You can choose one of the following chart types:

○ **u (Nonconformities per unit).** The chart shows the proportion of nonconformities per case within each subgroup. Use this chart type if each subgroup does not have the same number of items.

○ **c (Number of nonconformities).** The chart shows the total number of nonconformities per subgroup. Use this chart type if each subgroup has the same number of items. Figure 28.21 shows a chart definition dialog box and the resulting c chart.

Figure 28.21 c chart with cases as units

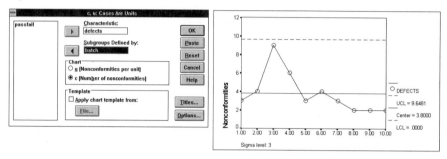

 X-Bar, R, s:
Cases are subgroups

Figure 28.22 shows a chart definition dialog box and the resulting X-bar and R charts with cases as subgroups. To plot this type of chart, your data file must contain two or more variables (columns) that measure the process in question; each row in the data file is plotted as a single point.

Figure 28.22 X-Bar and R charts with cases as subgroups

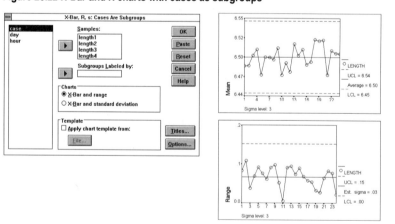

The minimum specification is two or more numeric sample variables.

All variables are shown on the source variable list. Select two or more numeric sample variables. To get a chart that shows the mean value for each subgroup and a chart that shows the range within each subgroup, click on OK.

Optionally, you can show standard deviation rather than the range, specify a variable to be used for subgroup labels, change the number of sigmas used for control limits, specify an upper or a lower limit, alter the minimum subgroup sample size, display subgroups defined by missing values, use a template to control the format of the chart, or add a title, subtitle, or footnote. Templates, titles, subtitles, and footnotes are discussed in detail in Chapter 23. The number of sigmas in the calculated control limits, specified control limits, minimum subgroup sample size, and missing values are described in "Control Chart Options" on p. 598.

Samples. Select two or more numeric variables. A single value from each selected variable is incorporated into each point. The charts show the mean and range or standard deviation for each row of data.

Subgroups Labeled by. Select a variable to use for labels. Each subgroup is labeled with the value label from the selected variable. If there is no value label, the actual value is used. Figure 28.23 shows an X-Bar chart using the variable *day* for labels.

Figure 28.23 X-Bar chart using variable day for labels

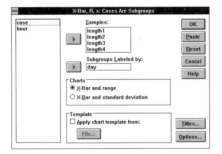 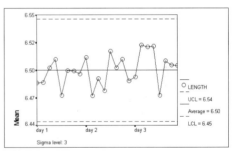

Charts. Two charts are produced. The first is an X-Bar chart. The second can be either a range chart (an R chart) or a standard deviation chart (an s chart).

An X-Bar chart shows the mean of the process for each subgroup. A subgroup contains all the values of the sample variables from a single row of data. The center line is the mean of the process and the control limits are a number of standard deviations above and below the center line for each category. The number of standard deviations is shown as the sigma level.

○ **X-Bar and range.** A range chart shows the range of the process within each subgroup. The center line shows the mean of the subgroup ranges. The upper and lower limits show three sigma levels above and below the center line for each category.

○ **X-Bar and standard deviation.** A standard deviation chart shows the standard deviation of the process for each subgroup. The center line shows the mean of the subgroup standard deviations. The upper and lower limits show three sigma levels above and below the center line for each category. Figure 28.24 shows X-Bar and s charts with cases as subgroups.

Figure 28.24 X-Bar and s charts with cases as subgroups

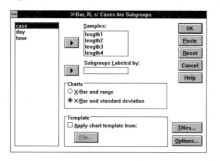
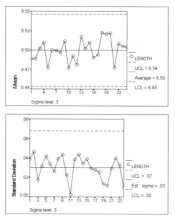

 p, np:
Cases are subgroups

Figure 28.25 shows a chart definition dialog box and the resulting p chart with cases as subgroups. To plot this type of chart, your data file must contain a variable (column) that counts the number of nonconformities; each row in the data file is plotted as a single point.

Figure 28.25 p chart with cases as subgroups

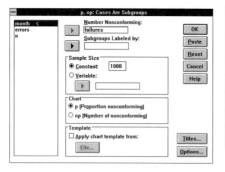
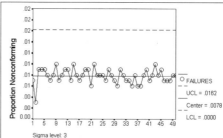

The minimum specifications are:

- A numeric variable containing the number of nonconforming cases.
- A constant or variable defining the sample size.

All variables in your data file are displayed on the source variable list. Select a numeric variable that indicates the number of nonconforming cases in each sample and enter the sample size. To see a control chart that shows the proportion of nonconforming cases in default format, click on OK.

Optionally, you can specify a variable sample size, specify the name of a variable to be used for labels, generate an np chart rather than a p chart, change the number of sigmas used for control limits, display subgroups defined by missing values, use a template to control the format of the chart, or add a title, subtitle, or footnote. Templates, titles, subtitles, and footnotes are discussed in detail in Chapter 23. The number of sigmas in the calculated control limits and missing values are described in "Control Chart Options" on p. 598.

Number Nonconforming. Select a numeric variable indicating the number of nonconforming units in each sample. The chart shows the number or proportion of nonconforming units for each sample.

Subgroups Labeled by. Select a variable to use for labels. Each subgroup is labeled with the value label from the selected variable (if the variable has not been labeled, the value of the variable will be displayed). Figure 28.26 shows a p chart using the variable *month* for labels.

Figure 28.26 p chart using variable month for labels and sample size

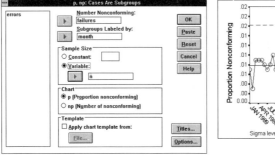 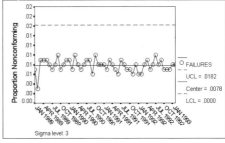

Sample Size. The number of units per sample can be constant or variable.

- ○ **Constant.** Enter the number of units per sample.
- ○ **Variable.** Select a variable that indicates the number of units in each sample.

Chart. Determines the type of chart generated. You can choose one of the following chart types:

○ **p (Proportion nonconforming).** The chart shows the proportion of nonconformities out of the total sample. Use this chart type if the sample size varies between cases.

○ **np (Number of nonconforming).** The chart shows the total number of nonconformities for each subgroup. Use this chart type if the sample size is constant. Figure 28.27 shows a chart definition dialog box and the resulting np chart.

Figure 28.27 np chart with cases as subgroups

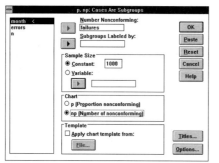
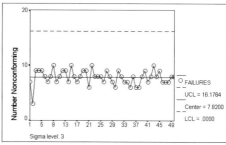

c, u:
Cases are subgroups

Figure 28.28 shows a chart definition dialog box and the resulting u chart with cases as subgroups. To plot this type of chart, your data file must contain a variable (column) that counts the number of nonconformities; each row in the data file is plotted as a single point.

Figure 28.28 u chart with cases as subgroups

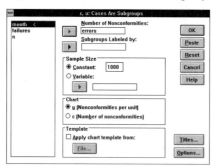
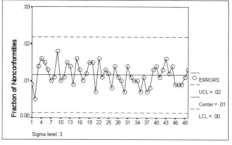

The minimum specifications are:

- A numeric variable specifying the number of nonconformities.
- A constant value or variable defining the sample size.

All variables in the working data file are displayed on the source variable list. Select a numeric variable that specifies the number of nonconformities for each case and enter the sample size. To generate a control chart that shows the number of nonconformities per unit for each subgroup in default format, click on OK.

Optionally, you can specify a variable sample size, specify a variable to use for labels, generate a c chart rather than a u chart, change the number of sigmas used for control limits, display subgroups defined by missing values, use a template to control the format of the chart, or add a title, subtitle, or footnote. Templates, titles, subtitles, and footnotes are discussed in detail in Chapter 23. The number of sigmas in the calculated control limits and missing values are described in "Control Chart Options" on p. 598.

Number of Nonconformities. Select a variable indicating the number of nonconformities in each sample. The chart shows the number or proportion of nonconformities for each row of data.

Subgroups Labeled by. Select a variable to use for labels. Each subgroup is labeled with the value label from the selected variable. If there is no value label, the value of the variable will be displayed. Figure 28.29 shows a u chart using the variable *month* for labels.

Figure 28.29 u chart using variable month for labels and sample size

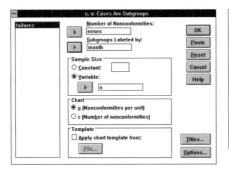 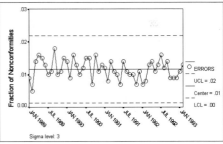

Sample Size. The number of units per sample can be constant or variable.

- **Constant.** Enter the number of units per sample.
- **Variable.** Select a variable that indicates the number of units in each sample.

Chart. Determines the type of chart generated. You can choose one of the following chart types:

○ **u (Nonconformities per unit).** The chart shows the proportion of nonconformities per unit within each subgroup. Use this chart type if the sample size differs between cases.

○ **c (Number of nonconformities).** The chart shows the total number of nonconformities per subgroup. Use this chart type if the sample size does not vary between cases. Figure 28.30 shows a c chart with cases as subgroups.

Figure 28.30 c chart with cases as subgroups

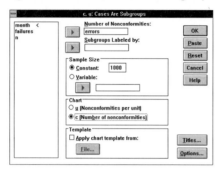
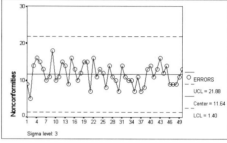

Control Chart Options

Figure 28.31 shows the Options dialog box for X-Bar, R, and s charts, which includes all of the options found in other control chart Options dialog boxes.

Figure 28.31 Options dialog box for X-Bar, R, and s charts

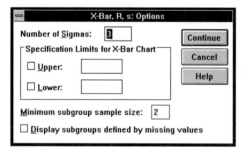

Number of Sigmas. Determines the number of standard deviations above and below the center line for the calculated upper and lower control limits.

Specification Limits for X-Bar Chart. You may specify upper and lower control limits in addition to the calculated limits for X-Bar and individuals charts. This is useful if you want to see if the process falls within predetermined tolerances.

❏ **Upper.** Displays the specified upper control limit.

❏ **Lower.** Displays the specified lower control limit.

Minimum subgroup sample size. In X-Bar, R, and s charts, you can change the minimum subgroup sample size. Subgroups with fewer units than the specified size are not shown in the chart.

❏ **Display subgroups defined by missing values.** In all control charts except individuals and moving range charts, you can display subgroups defined by missing values.

29 Normal Probability Plots

The normal distribution plays an important role in many statistical analyses. That's why you often want to check whether your data appear to be a sample from a normal distribution. Similarly, after you have fit a statistical model to the data, you want to examine the distribution of the residuals, or errors, to see if it is approximately normal. Both visual displays and formal statistical tests, such as the Shapiro Wilks' test (see Chapter 9), can be used for assessing normality.

Histograms and stem-and-leaf plots are useful displays for visually assessing the distributions of data values. However, it can sometimes be difficult to mentally superimpose a normal distribution on the data values. The normal probability plot is a special type of display for checking for normality. In a normal probability plot, the data points cluster around a straight line if your sample is from a normal distribution.

Consider Figure 29.1, which shows a normal probability plot of 100 values from a normal distribution, with a mean of 0 and a variance of 1. You see that the points fall almost exactly on a straight line. In Figure 29.1, the observed values are plotted against expected values from a normal distribution. That is, each observed value is paired with an "expected" value from the normal distribution. The expected values are based on the rank of the observed value and the number of cases in the sample. Figure 29.1 is called a **Q-Q normal probability plot**.

Figure 29.1   Q-Q normal probability plot of a normally distributed variable

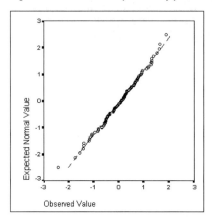

Another type of normal probability plot, the **P-P plot**, is based on the cumulative probability distributions of the observed data and the normal distribution. For a series of points, you plot the observed cumulative proportion against the cumulative proportion that would be expected if the data were a sample from a normal distribution. Again, if the sample is from a normal distribution, the points should cluster around a straight line. Figure 29.2 is the corresponding P-P plot for the data shown in Figure 29.1.

Figure 29.2   P-P normal probability plot

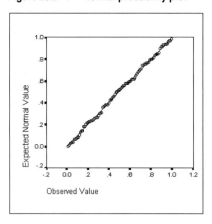

How to Obtain Normal Probability Plots

To obtain P-P or Q-Q normal probability plots and detrended normal probability plots, from the menus choose:

Graphs
  Normal P-P...

or

Graphs
  Normal Q-Q...

The Normal P-P Plots and Normal Q-Q Plots dialog boxes are identical. The Normal P-P Plots dialog box is shown in Figure 29.3.

Figure 29.3   Normal P-P Plots dialog box

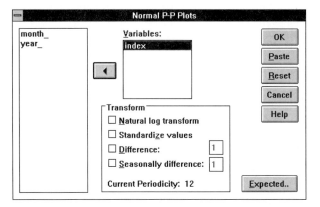

The numeric variables in the working data file are displayed on the source variable list. The minimum specification is one or more variables. A normal probability plot and a detrended normal probability chart are produced for each variable.

Transform. You can produce normal probability plots for transformed values using any combination of the following transformation options:

❏ **Natural log transform.** Transforms the variable using the natural logarithm (base e) of the variable. This is useful for removing varying amplitude over time in time series data. If a variable contains any values that are less than or equal to 0, the normal probability plot for that variable will not be produced because non-positive values cannot be log transformed.

❏ **Standardize values.** Transforms the variable into a sample with a mean of 0 and a standard deviation of 1.

❑ **Difference**. Transforms the variable by calculating the difference between successive values of the variable. Enter a positive integer to specify the degree of differencing (the number of previous values used to calculate the difference). The number of values used in the calculations decreases by 1 for each degree of differencing. Differencing a time series converts a nonstationary series to a stationary one with a constant mean and variance.

❑ **Seasonally difference**. Transforms time series data by calculating the difference between series values a constant span apart. The span is based on the currently defined periodicity. Enter a positive integer to specify the degree of differencing (the number of previous seasonal periods used to calculate the difference). To compute seasonal differences, you must have defined date variables that include a periodic component (such as months of the year).

Current Periodicity. Indicates the currently defined period used to calculate seasonal differences for time series data. If the current periodicity is None, seasonal differencing is not available. To create a date variable with a periodic component used to define periodicity, select the Define Dates option on the Data menu (see Chapter 5).

These transformations affect only the normal probability plot and do not alter the values of the variables. For time series data, you can create new time series variables based on transformed values of existing time series with the Create Time Series option on the Transform menu (see Chapter 5).

Method Used to Calculate Expected Normal Distribution

To change the method used to calculate the expected normal distribution, click on Expected.. in the Normal P-P Plots or Normal Q-Q Plots dialog box. The Normal P-P Plots Expected dialog box is shown in Figure 29.4.

Figure 29.4   Normal P-P Plots Expected dialog box

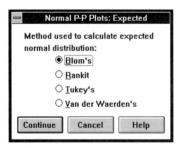

Method used to calculate expected normal distribution. Choose one of the following alternatives:

○ **Blom's.** Uses Blom's transformation, defined by the formula

$$(r - (3/8)) / (n + (1/4))$$

where n is the number of observations and r is the rank, ranging from 1 to n (Blom, 1958). This is the default.

○ **Rankit.** Uses the formula

$$(r - (1/2)) / n$$

where n is the number of observations and r is the rank, ranging from 1 to n (Chambers et al., 1983).

○ **Tukey's.** Uses Tukey's transformation, defined by the formula

$$(r - (1/3)) / (n + (1/3))$$

where n is the number of observations and r is the rank, ranging from 1 to n (Tukey, 1962).

○ **Van der Waerden's.** Uses Van der Waerden's transformation, defined by the formula

$$r / (n + 1)$$

where n is the number of observations and r is the rank, ranging from 1 to n (Lehmann, 1975)

Weighted Data

The Normal P-P Plots and Normal Q-Q Plots procedures do not use case weights. If weighting is in effect, case weights are ignored for these plots. To obtain normal Q-Q plots for weighted data, use the Explore procedure (Statistics menu, Summarize submenu) and select Normality plots with tests from the Explore Plots dialog box. See Chapter 9 for more information on the Explore procedure.

30 Sequence Charts

For most of the statistical analyses described in this book, the sequence in which you obtain your data values is not important. In fact, for hypothesis tests, you assume that the observations are independent and that the order in which you observe your data values has no effect.

Data for which time, or the sequence in which the values occur, is an essential component are known as **time series** data. In a time series, the values of a variable are recorded at regular intervals over a period of time. Examples of time series are daily stock prices, the annual GNP, the quarterly unemployment rate, and monthly sales data. This chapter contains examples of how time series can be displayed using sequence charts.

Plotting Health Care Stock

As an illustration of time series data, consider Standard and Poor's Health Care Composite Index, which is based on the values of stocks of 26 businesses in the health care industry. The index is a composite measure of how well these stocks perform in the stock market and is used as an indicator of how the health care industry is performing.

Figure 30.1 is a plot of the values of the Health Care Composite Index from January, 1987, to December, 1992. The horizontal axis displays the time points—in this example, the months. The vertical axis displays the values of the index. Looking at the plot, you see that although there have been substantial fluctuations in the index during the five years, the overall impression is that the value of the index is rapidly rising. That is, there is an upward trend.

Figure 30.1   Sequence chart of Health Care Composite Index

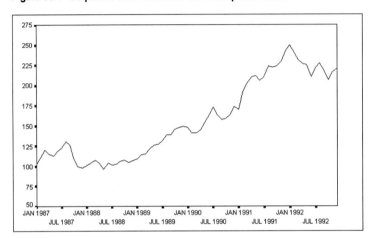

Seasonal Trends

When you examine plots of time series data, you should always check to see if there is any type of repeating, or seasonal, pattern to the values. In the health care index data there doesn't seem to be a particular month or season associated with increases or decreases. The peaks and troughs do not occur at regular intervals. However, in many types of time series data, there is a strong seasonal pattern. For example, consider the plot of college textbook sales shown in Figure 30.2.

Figure 30.2   Sequence chart of college textbook sales

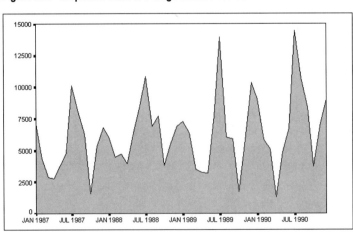

You see that there are spikes associated with certain months. The largest volume of academic book sales is in July, when bookstores place orders for the fall term. There are smaller spikes for each January, when orders for the second semester are placed. The January spike is smaller because the same books are often used throughout the year, and bookstores often have stock remaining from the first semester. When a seasonal pattern exists in time series data, as shown in Figure 30.2, the data are said to show a **seasonal trend**, or component.

Forecasting

Many decisions are dependent on predicting future values of time series data, and there are countless statistical techniques devoted to modeling time series data. If there is a strong relationship between successive values of a time series, you can use moving averages to predict the next value in a series. You can use the prior moving average function in the Create Time Series facility (see Chapter 5) to predict each time point as the average of the values of a specified number of preceding time points. Figure 30.3 is a plot of the Health Care Composite Index and predicted values based on a prior moving average of five points. From the plot, you see that, overall, the predicted values based on the moving average do reasonably well. However, whenever there is a sharp change in the series, the prediction is poor, since the only information the prediction uses are the preceding points.

Figure 30.3   Sequence chart with prior moving average prediction

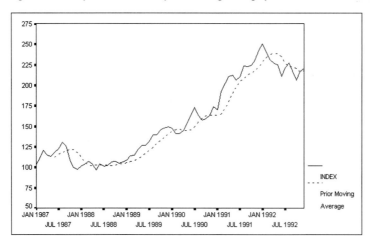

Examining the Errors

Whenever you obtain predictions, you should look at the residuals—that is, the differences between the observed and predicted values. The residuals provide you with much useful information about how well the model fits. Figure 30.4 is a plot of the residuals from the prior moving average model. You see that the errors have a definite pattern. There are clusters of positive and negative values. This is an indication that your prediction model has undesirable properties.

Figure 30.4   Residuals (errors) from prior moving average prediction

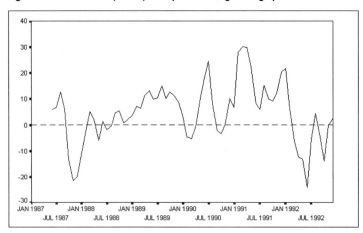

How to Obtain Sequence Charts

To obtain sequence charts, from the menus choose:

Graphs
  Sequence...

This opens the Sequence Charts dialog box, as shown in Figure 30.5.

Figure 30.5   Sequence Charts dialog box

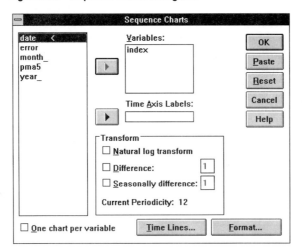

The numeric variables in the working data file are displayed on the source variable list. The minimum specification is one or more numeric sequence or time series variables. Sequence charts require a data file structure in which cases (rows) are sorted in a sequential order or represent observations at regular time intervals.

Time Axis Labels. You can use a numeric or string variable to label the time (sequence) axis of the chart. By default, the time axis is simply labeled 1 to *n*, or it is labeled with the values of the string variable *date_* if you have defined date variables (see Chapter 5).

Transform. You can plot transformed data values using any combination of the following transformation options:

❑ **Natural log transform**. Transforms data values using the natural logarithm (base *e*) of the values. This is useful for removing varying amplitude over time. If a variable contains values that are less than or equal to 0, no chart will be created for the variable because non-positive values cannot be log transformed.

❑ **Difference**. Transforms the data values by calculating the difference between successive values of the variable. Enter a positive integer to specify the degree of differencing (the number of previous values used to calculate the difference). The number of values used in the calculations decreases by one for each degree of differencing. Differencing a time series converts a nonstationary series to a stationary one with a constant mean and variance.

❏ **Seasonally difference**. Transforms the data values by calculating the difference between values a constant span apart. The span is based on the currently defined periodicity. Enter a positive integer to specify the degree of differencing (the number of
previous seasonal periods used to calculate the difference). To compute seasonal differences, you must have defined date variables that include a periodic component
(such as months of the year).

> **Current Periodicity**. Indicates the currently defined period used to calculate season-
> al differences. If the current periodicity is None, seasonal differencing is not avail-
> able. To create a date variable with a periodic component used to define
> periodicity, use the Define Dates option on the Data menu (see Chapter 5).

These transformations affect only the plotted values in the sequence chart and do not alter the values of the actual variables. To create new time series variables based on transformed values of existing time series, use the Create Time Series option on the
Transform menu (see Chapter 5).

The following option is also available:

❏ **One chart per variable**. Creates a separate sequence chart for each selected variable. By
default, all selected variables are plotted in a single chart.

Time Axis Reference Lines

To display reference lines on the time (sequence) axis at each change in a reference variable or at a specific date or time, click on Time Lines... in the Sequence Charts dialog
box. This opens the Time Axis Reference Lines dialog box, similar to the one shown in
Figure 30.6.

Figure 30.6   Time Axis Reference Lines dialog box

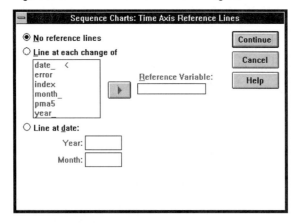

You can choose one of the following alternatives:

○ **No reference lines**. This is the default.

○ **Line at each change of**. Displays a reference line each time the value of the selected reference variable changes. For example, you could use the date variable *year_* to display a reference line at the beginning of each year. (Do *not* use the date variable *date_*, since that would display a reference line at each case.)

○ **Line at date**. You can display a single reference line at the value of a specific date, time or observation number. The available text boxes for specifying the date and/or time are dependent on the currently defined date variables. If there are no defined date variables, you can specify an observation (case) number.

If you enter a value for a lower-order date variable, you must also enter a value for all higher-order date variables above it. For example, in Figure 30.6, you cannot specify a Month value without a Year value. If you enter a value for a higher-order date variable without entering any values for lower-order date variables, the reference line will be drawn at the first occurrence of the value.

Use the Define Dates option on the Data menu to create date variables. See Chapter 5 for more information, including valid ranges for each date variable.

Formatting Options

To change formatting options, such as switching the axis used as the time (sequence) axis or displaying area charts instead of line charts, click on Format... in the Sequence Charts dialog box. This opens the Sequence Charts Format dialog box, as shown in Figure 30.7.

Figure 30.7   Sequence Charts Format dialog box

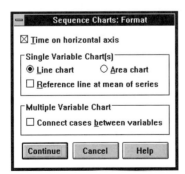

The following formatting options are available:

❏ **Time on horizontal axis**. Uses the horizontal axis as the time (sequence) axis. This is the default. Deselect this item to use the vertical axis as the time axis.

Single Variable Chart(s). If only a single variable is plotted in each chart, you can choose one of the following alternatives:

○ **Line chart**. Displays a line chart for each variable. This is the default.

○ **Area chart**. Displays an area chart for each variable, with the area between the line and the time (sequence) axis filled in with a color or pattern.

The following option is also available for single variable charts:

❏ **Reference line at mean of series**. Displays a reference line on the scale axis at the mean value of the variable.

Multiple Variable Chart. If more than one variable is plotted in a chart, the following formatting option is available:

❏ **Connect cases between variables**. Draws a line at each case between values of the plotted variables.

31 Autocorrelation and Cross-Correlation

In time series, adjacent data values are often highly correlated. **Autocorrelation** coefficients are used to examine the strength of the relationship among the values at different lags. Identifying the pattern of autocorrelation is especially important for selecting parameters for certain types of statistical models used for time series and for evaluating the residuals from a model. In this chapter, you'll see examples of how autocorrelation, partial autocorrelation, and cross-correlation functions can be used to explore time series data.

The Autocorrelation Function

Consider again the Health Care Composite Index, described in Chapter 30. From the time sequence plot of the data values, you saw that successive monthly values are closely related to each other. Another way of demonstrating this is to plot each value of the series with the value that precedes it. (Note that there won't be a value for the first time point, since there is no value that precedes it.) Figure 31.1 is a plot of the series values against the values that precede them, the values lagged by one. You see that there is an almost perfect linear relationship between the two values. The R^2 value (labeled Rsq in the chart) is 0.976. The square root of that value, 0.988, is the simple correlation coefficient. This is called the **first-order autocorrelation coefficient**, since it is the correlation coefficient of values within the same series when the values are lagged by one.

Figure 31.1   Scatterplot of first-order autocorrelation

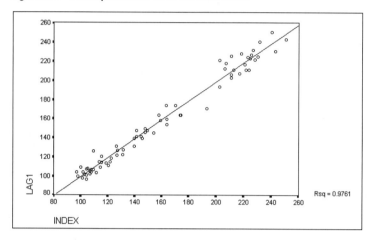

Similarly, if you plotted each value with the value two time points before, the lag 2 values, you would obtain the plot shown in Figure 31.2. Again, you note that there is a strong linear relationship. The correlation coefficient is called the **second-order autocorrelation coefficient**. You can create such plots and compute autocorrelation coefficients for any number of lags.

Figure 31.2   Scatterplot of second-order autocorrelation

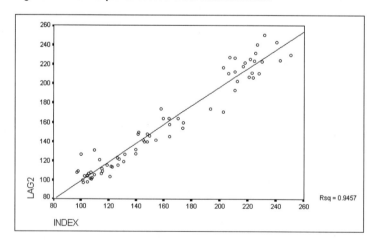

The autocorrelation coefficients at various lags can be displayed in an autocorrelation plot, as shown in Figure 31.3. Each bar corresponds to a particular lag. The 95% confidence limits of the autocorrelations around 0 are also displayed in the chart. If your observed autocorrelation falls within the confidence limits around 0, you don't have enough evidence to reject the null hypothesis that the true value is 0. In this example, all of the observed autocorrelations fall outside the confidence limits.

The autocorrelation coefficients produced by the Autocorrelations procedure will not be identical to simple correlation coefficients produced with the Correlations procedure. That's because the autocorrelation coefficients and simple correlation coefficients are calculated slightly differently. Autocorrelation computations utilize as much of the available information as possible, while the simple correlation coefficient computations exclude cases that have missing values due to lagging.

Figure 31.3   Autocorrelation coefficients

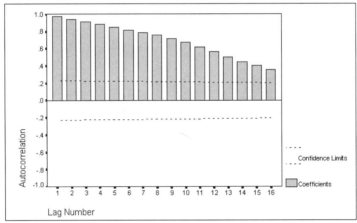

If you are using autocorrelation plots to evaluate residuals from a time series model, your autocorrelation plot should not show anything of interest. The autocorrelations should be small and there should be no patterns or spikes. The **Box-Ljung statistic**, which is displayed in the output window, can be used to test the hypothesis that the series appears to be white noise.

The Partial Autocorrelation Function

From the large value of the autocorrelation coefficient at the first lag, you know that there is a very strong relationship between the values at adjacent time points, the lag 1 values. The large value of the lag 2 autocorrelation tells you that values two time points away are also closely related. The interesting question is whether the autocorrelations of order greater than one are really important or whether they are large only because of the presence of lag 1 autocorrelations. If you were to build a regression model that predicts a current value from previous ones, how many preceding values would you have to include?

You can examine the **partial autocorrelation** function shown in Figure 31.4 to answer this question. In this chart, each correlation coefficient has the effects of lower-order correlation coefficients removed. That is, each coefficient can be thought of as the coefficient for that lag when lower-order lags are already in a regression model. From Figure 31.4, you see that only lag 1 autocorrelation appears to be important. All other partial autocorrelation coefficients fall within the confidence limits of plus and minus two standard errors.

Figure 31.4   Partial autocorrelation coefficients

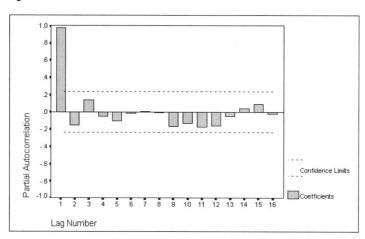

The Cross-Correlation Function

Autocorrelation and partial autocorrelation plots show the relationships between lagged values in the same series. If you want to examine the relationship between two time series, you can compute **cross-correlation** functions. Cross-correlation functions are useful for determining whether one series can be predicted from another and what orders of lags may be most useful. When current values of one series are used to predict future values of a second series, the first series is known as a **leading indicator**. For example, current dollars spent on marketing may be a leading indicator for future sales. Cross-correlation plots are also useful as diagnostics for evaluating the relationships between residuals and other variables in time series models.

Whenever you want to look at the relationship between two series using the cross-correlation function, you must make sure that the two series are **stationary**—that is, that the mean and the variance of each of the series stay about the same during the series. The reason for this is that if you take series which are increasing or decreasing over time, you can always line them up so that they appear to be highly correlated even though the two series are not related. One way to make a series stationary is to **difference** it. When you difference a series, you replace each value of the original series by the differences between adjacent values in the original series. As an example of cross-correlation functions, let's consider the relationship between Standard and Poor's weekly index for computer software and services (variable *softserv*) and the weekly index for computer systems (variable *systems*) during the last 45 weeks of 1992. Both of these series are not stationary, so the cross-correlations are computed not from the original series but from the differenced series.

Figure 31.5   Cross-correlation coefficients

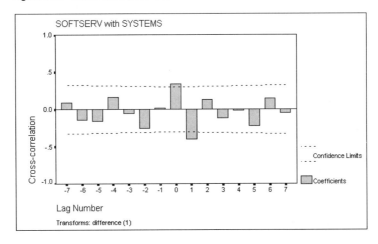

Figure 31.5 is the cross-correlation plot for the differenced computer software and services index and the computer systems index. Notice that both positive and negative lags are shown in the plot. A negative lag indicates that the second series, computer systems in this example, is the leading indicator. That is, it is used as the predictor of system sales. For example, when the lag is –3, the correlation is between the software and service index and the computer system index three weeks prior. A positive lag indicates that the first series, software and services, is the leading indicator, or predictor, of computer systems. A zero lag indicates that the correlation is for the two differenced series when neither one is lagged. Based on the cross-correlation plot, it appears that for the short time period under consideration, the computer systems index is not a good leading indicator for the software and services index. However, the software and services index may be a leading indicator for computer systems.

How to Obtain Autocorrelation and Partial Autocorrelation Charts

To obtain autocorrelation charts, partial autocorrelation charts, and related statistics for time series data, from the menus choose:

Graphs
  Time Series ▶
    Autocorrelations...

This opens the Autocorrelations dialog box, as shown in Figure 31.6.

Figure 31.6   Autocorrelations dialog box

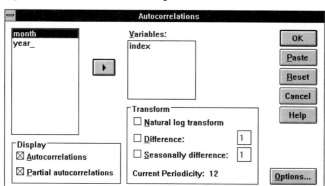

The numeric variables in the working data file are displayed on the source variable list. The minimum specification is one or more time series variables. Time Series analysis requires a data file structure in which each case (row) represents a set of observations at a different time, and the length of time between cases is uniform.

Display. You can choose one or both of the following display options:

❏ **Autocorrelations.** Displays a chart of autocorrelation coefficients and confidence intervals (two standard errors). Autocorrelation coefficient values, standard errors, the Box-Ljung statistic, and probabilities for each lag are displayed in the output window.

❏ **Partial autocorrelations.** Displays a chart of partial autocorrelation coefficients and confidence intervals (two standard errors). Partial autocorrelation coefficient values and standard errors for each lag are displayed in the output window.

Transform. You can calculate autocorrelations for transformed time series values using any combination of the following transformation options:

❑ **Natural log transform**. Transforms the time series using the natural logarithm (base e) of the series. This is useful for removing varying amplitude over time. If a series contains values that are less than or equal to 0, autocorrelations will not be calculated for that series because non-positive values cannot be log transformed.

❑ **Difference**. Transforms the time series by calculating the difference between successive values in the series. Enter a positive integer to specify the degree of differencing (the number of previous values used to calculate the difference). The number of values used in the calculations decreases by one for each degree of differencing. Differencing the series converts a nonstationary series to a stationary one with a constant mean and variance.

❑ **Seasonally difference**. Transforms the time series by calculating the difference between series values a constant span apart. The span is based on the currently defined periodicity. Enter a positive integer to specify the degree of differencing (the number of previous seasonal periods used to calculate the difference). To compute seasonal differences, you must have defined date variables that include a periodic component (such as months of the year).

Current Periodicity. Indicates the currently defined period used to calculate seasonal differences. If the current periodicity is None, seasonal differencing is not available. To create a date variable with a periodic component used to define periodicity, use the Define Dates option on the Data menu (see Chapter 5).

These transformations affect only the calculation of the autocorrelations and do not alter the values of the time series variables. To create new time series variables based on transformed values of existing time series, use the Create Time Series option on the Transform menu (see Chapter 5).

Options

To change the maximum number of lags plotted, or change the method used to calculate the standard error, or display autocorrelations of periodic lags, click on Options... in the Autocorrelations dialog box. This opens the Autocorrelations Options dialog box, as shown in Figure 31.7.

Figure 31.7 Autocorrelations Options dialog box

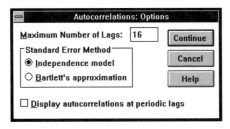

Maximum number of lags. Controls the maximum number of lags plotted. The default is 16.

Standard Error Method. For autocorrelations, you can change the method used to calculate the standard error. (This option is not available for partial autocorrelations.) You can choose one of the following methods:

○ **Independence model**. Assumes the underlying process is white noise. This is the default.

○ **Bartlett's approximation**. Standard errors grow at increased lags. Appropriate where the order of the moving average process is *k*-1.

The following option is also available for time series data with defined periodicity:

❑ **Display autocorrelations at periodic lags**. Displays autocorrelations *only* for periodic intervals, based on the currently defined periodicity.

How to Obtain Cross-Correlation Charts

To obtain cross-correlation charts and related statistics, from the menus choose:

Graphs
  Time Series ▶
    Cross-Correlations...

This opens the Cross-Correlations dialog box, as shown in Figure 31.8.

Figure 31.8   Cross-Correlations dialog box

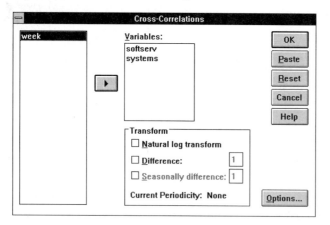

The numeric variables in the working data file are displayed on the source variable list. The minimum specification is two or more time series variables. A separate cross-correlation chart is created for each possible pair of variables. Time Series analysis requires a data file structure in which each case (row) represents a set of observations at a different time, and the length of time between cases is uniform.

Transform. You can calculate cross-correlations for transformed time series values using any combination of the following transformation options:

❏ **Natural log transform**. Transforms the time series using the natural logarithm (base e) of the series. This is useful for removing varying amplitude over time. If any values in a pair of series are less than or equal to 0, cross-correlations will not be calculated for that pair because non-positive values cannot be log transformed.

❏ **Difference**. Transforms the time series by calculating the difference between successive values in the series. Enter a positive integer to specify the degree of differencing (the number of previous values used to calculate the difference). The number of values used in the calculations decreases by 1 for each degree of differencing. Differencing the series converts a nonstationary series to a stationary one with a constant mean and variance.

❏ **Seasonally difference**. Transforms the time series by calculating the difference between series values a constant span apart. The span is based on the currently defined periodicity. Enter a positive integer to specify the degree of differencing (the number of previous seasonal periods used to calculate the difference). To compute seasonal differences, you must have defined date variables that include a periodic component (such as months of the year).

> **Current Periodicity**. Indicates the currently defined period used to calculate seasonal differences. If the current periodicity is None, seasonal differencing is not available. To create a date variable with a periodic component used to define periodicity, use the Define Dates option on the Data menu (see Chapter 5).

These transformations affect only the calculation of the cross-correlations and do not alter the values of the time series variables. To create new time series variables based on transformed values of existing time series, use the Create Time Series option on the Transform menu (see Chapter 5).

Options

To change the maximum number of lags plotted or display cross-correlations of periodic lags, click on Options... in the Cross-Correlations dialog box. This opens the Cross-Correlations Options dialog box, as shown in Figure 31.9.

Figure 31.9   Cross-Correlations Options dialog box

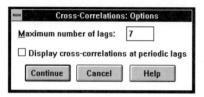

Maximum number of lags. Controls the maximum number of lags plotted. The default is 7.

The following option is also available for time series data with defined periodicity:

❑ **Display cross-correlations at periodic lags**. Displays cross-correlations *only* for periodic intervals, based on the currently defined periodicity.

32 Modifying Charts

After creating a chart and viewing it in the Chart Carousel, you may wish to modify it, either to obtain more information about the data or to enhance the chart for presentation. The chart modification capabilities of SPSS allow you to select data, change chart types, add information, and alter chart appearance to accomplish both of those goals.

Two brief examples are given in this chapter. The first example illustrates a process for exploring data relationships graphically; the second, enhancing a bar chart for presentation. Another example, the tutorial in Chapter 23, describes explicit steps for creating and enhancing a bar chart.

Following the two examples in this chapter, detailed explanations of the chart editing menus and dialog boxes are presented. A table summarizing the chapter is provided on p. 703 to help you locate information on specific chart modification facilities.

Exploring Data with the Chart Editor

Figure 32.1 shows a preliminary scatterplot matrix of graduation rate, verbal SAT score, and student-faculty ratio in 250 colleges and universities.

Figure 32.1 Scatterplot matrix of gradrate, verbal, and facratio

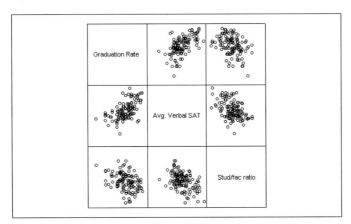

Two of the available options for scatterplots, adding axis labels and linear regression lines, help make relationships more apparent. In Figure 32.2, labels and regression lines have been added.

Figure 32.2   Scatterplot matrix with labels and regression lines

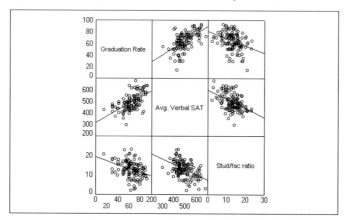

For a closer look at the relationship between schools' graduation rates and the average SAT verbal test scores of their students, we can turn to the Gallery menu and select a bivariate (simple) scatterplot of those variables. In the bivariate scatterplot, we can see more detail (see Figure 32.3).

Figure 32.3   Scatterplot of gradrate and verbal

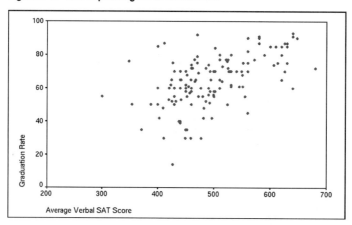

We might want to look more closely at the univariate distribution of the two variables, which we can do by returning to the Gallery menu and selecting histogram (see Figure 32.4).

Figure 32.4   Histograms of verbal and gradrate

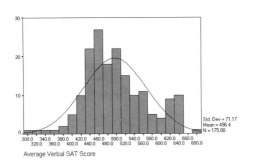
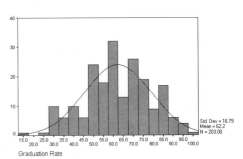

Enhancing Charts for Presentation

Although charts as originally generated by SPSS contain the requested information in a logical format, they may require some changes to make the presentation clearer or more dramatic. Figure 32.5 is the unedited clustered bar chart of *verbal* and *math* (the average verbal and math SAT scores for each university) by *comp* (level of competitiveness).

Figure 32.5   Default bar chart of verbal and math by comp

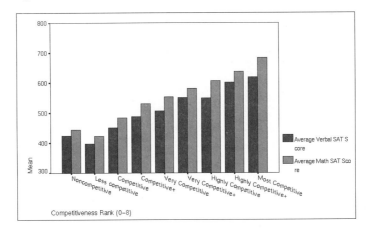

While the information is clear, at least some changes are desirable to prepare the chart for presentation. The following modifications create the chart shown in Figure 32.6:

- A title and subtitle are added.
- 3-D effect is selected for the bars.

- The cluster spacing is widened.
- Both axis titles are removed, since the information they contain appears elsewhere in the chart. This allows more room for the chart itself and the chart enlarges itself automatically.
- The noncompetitive category is removed.
- Several labels are removed from the category axis and the orientation of the remaining labels is changed. This makes the labels easier to read, yet still conveys the essential information.
- The legend labels are edited to remove unnecessary information.
- The range of the scale axis is enlarged to start at 200, the lowest possible SAT score, in order to give a better representation of the relative differences between schools in each competitiveness level.
- Annotations are added to indicate the overall averages for the two SAT tests. (These averages are easily obtained by leaving the chart window for a moment to run descriptive statistics from the Statistics menu.)

Figure 32.6   Enhanced bar chart

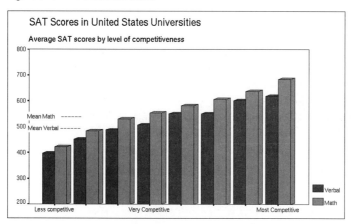

Figure 32.7 shows further bar chart variations.
- The axes, tick marks, and inner frame have been removed.
- Grid lines have been added.
- The sides and tops of the bars have been shaded a different color to enhance the 3-D effect.
- Inter-cluster spacing has been increased.
- The annotation indicating overall averages has been refined.

Figure 32.7   Another bar chart variation

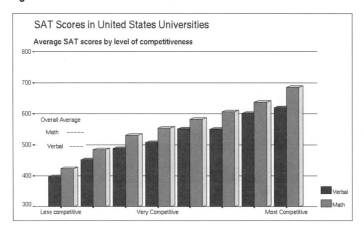

Editing in a Chart Window

All modifications to charts are done in a chart window. You open a chart window by selecting Edit from the Chart Carousel or by opening a previously saved chart from the File menu. Closing a chart window closes the chart.

Several chart windows can be open at the same time, each containing a single chart. The exact number depends on your system and on how many other windows are open at the time. If you see a message telling you that there are not enough system resources, you can close some windows to free resources.

Chart Menus

When a chart window is active, the Chart Editor menu bar, shown in Figure 32.8, replaces the main menu bar.

Figure 32.8   Chart Editor menu bar

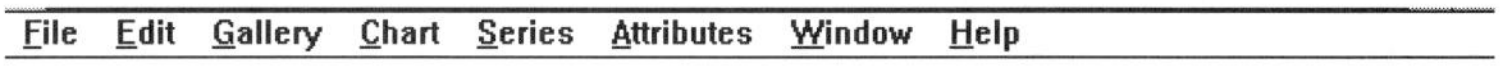

File   Edit   Gallery   Chart   Series   Attributes   Window   Help

The Chart Editor menu bar contains eight menus:

File. From the File menu, you can save the chart, print it, or apply specifications from an existing chart template.

If you choose Save and get an I/O error, check (without exiting from SPSS) to see if you ran out of disk space. If so, delete some files you don't need and try to save the chart again.

Edit. From the Edit menu, you can copy the chart to the Clipboard. On the Clipboard, you can use the Display menu to select either Picture (Windows metafile) or Bitmap format.

You can also choose Preferences to open the Preferences dialog box (see Chapter 36). Graphics preferences include global chart characteristics such as preferred type font, use of color versus pattern in lines and areas, and use of grid lines. If you select an aspect ratio, it applies immediately to all charts currently in chart windows or in the Chart Carousel. The other preferences are applied as each chart is initially drawn; they also apply to all charts currently in the Chart Carousel. They do not apply to a chart that is already in a chart window for editing or to saved charts.

The Edit menu does not include items for modifying charts; the following four menus contain those items.

Gallery. From the Gallery menu, you can select another compatible chart type to display the data in your chart. After selecting a new chart type, you can click on Replace to replace the current chart or click on New to create another chart in a new window. See "Changing Chart Types (Gallery Menu)" on p. 632 for more information.

Chart. From the Chart menu, you can modify many of the layout and labeling characteristics of your chart, such as the scaling and labeling of axes, all titles and labels, inner and outer frames, and whether the chart should expand to fill areas where titles are not assigned. See "Modifying Chart Elements (Chart Menu)" on p. 635 for more information.

Series. From the Series menu, you can select data series and categories to display or omit. Only data elements present in the original chart can be included. For bar, line, and area charts, you can select whether each series should be displayed as a line, an area, or a set of bars. See "Selecting and Arranging Data (Series Menu)" on p. 674 for more information.

Attributes. From the Attributes menu, you can open a set of palettes from which you can select fill patterns, colors, line style, bar style, bar label style (for displaying values within bars), interpolation type, and text fonts and sizes. To use these, you must have a mouse, with which you click on the element whose attributes you want to change. Then you can make a selection from any appropriate palette. You can also swap axes of plots, explode one or more slices of a pie chart, change the treatment of missing values in lines, and rotate 3-D scatterplots. The Attributes menu choices are duplicated on the chart window icon bar so you can select them quickly with the mouse. See "Modifying Attributes (Attributes Menu)" on p. 687 for more information.

Window. From the Window menu, you can select and arrange windows as you can throughout the system.

Help. The Help menu provides the same access to help as it does throughout the system.

Selecting Objects to Modify

The objects that make up a chart fall into two general categories:

- **Series objects** are the bars, lines, and markers that represent the data. They are always selected and manipulated as a series.

- **Chart objects** are the layout and labeling components of the chart—everything other than the series objects.

To modify one of these objects, double-click on it in the chart. If you double-click on a series object, the Displayed Data dialog box for the current chart type is opened (see "Selecting and Arranging Data (Series Menu)" on p. 674). If you double-click on a chart object, one of the dialog boxes from the Chart menu is opened: Axis if you have selected an axis, Title if you have selected a title, and so on (see "Modifying Chart Elements (Chart Menu)" on p. 635). If you double-click on an object for which a specific dialog box does not exist, or if you double-click away from any object, the Options dialog box for the current chart type is opened.

Instead of double-clicking on objects, you can open the series dialog boxes from the Series and Chart menus. A few items on those menus can be accessed only from the menus, not by double-clicking on an object or clicking on an icon.

The following items are available only from the Chart menu:

- Bar Spacing
- Title, Footnote, and Annotation (when none appear in the chart)
- Toggles for the Inner Frame and Outer Frame

The following item is available only from the Series menu:

- Transpose Data

Both series and chart objects have **attributes** such as color and pattern. To modify the attributes of an object, select the object with a single mouse click. There is no keyboard mechanism for selecting objects. If the object is within the chart itself, **handles** (small, solid-black rectangles) indicate which object is selected. For objects outside the chart axes, such as titles or labels, a **selection rectangle** indicates that an object is selected. Selection of an inner or outer frame is indicated by handles.

Applying Attributes

After an object is selected, select a palette from the Attributes menu or from the icon bar. Figure 32.9 shows handles and the Colors palette. Select the quality (color, pattern, style, etc.) you want to apply to the selected object, and click on Apply. You can apply attributes from as many palettes as you choose; the object stays selected until you select another or click somewhere away from any object. Palettes remain open until you close them. You can leave a palette open while you select and modify different objects. See "Modifying Attributes (Attributes Menu)" on p. 687 for more details.

Figure 32.9   Bar chart showing selection handles and Colors palette

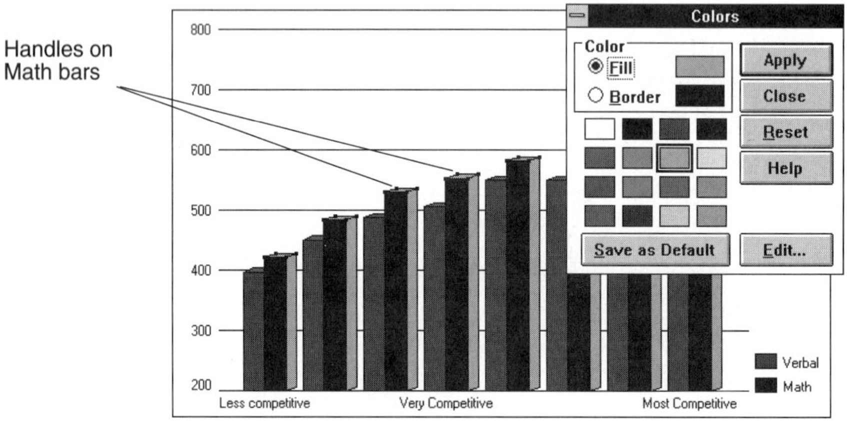

Changing Chart Types (Gallery Menu)

The Gallery menu allows you to change from one chart type to another. The choices are primarily the same as those available from the Graph menu, with a few additions. (See Chapter 24 to Chapter 31 for detailed descriptions of chart types.)

Additional Chart Types

Some types of charts are available only after you have created a chart. These include mixed charts, drop-line charts, and exploded pie charts.

Mixed Charts. Mixed charts are available on the Gallery menu. You can have bars, lines, and areas, all in the same chart, after defining a bar, line, or area multiple series chart. Figure 32.10 is an example of a mixed chart with both bars and lines.

Figure 32.10 Mixed chart

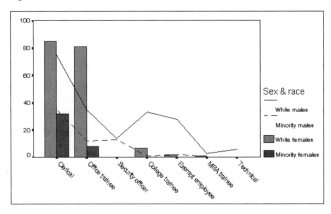

You can also define a mixed chart by choosing:

Series
  Displayed...

from the menus. For more information on mixed charts, see "Selecting and Arranging Data (Series Menu)" on p. 674.

Exploded Pie Chart. Exploded pie charts can be generated from the Pie Charts dialog box. To explode all slices of a pie chart at once, from the menus choose:

Gallery
  Pie...

This opens the Pie Charts dialog box. Click on Exploded and then click on Replace or New. Each slice of the pie is moved outward from the center, along a radius, as shown in Figure 32.11.

Figure 32.11 Exploded pie chart

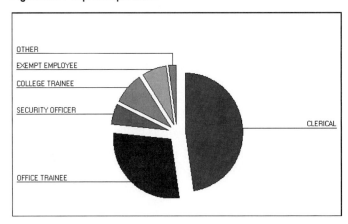

Changing Types

You can change freely among chart types, with the following restrictions:

- You must have enough data to draw the selected chart. Thus, you cannot change from a simple bar chart to a clustered bar chart if you have only one data series defined. However, if your original chart had more than one series, and you omitted all but one of those series to obtain the simple bar, you can change to a chart that requires multiple series. See "Selecting and Arranging Data (Series Menu)" on p. 674 for information on selecting series.
- You cannot change in either direction between categorical charts (bar, line, area, pie, and high-low charts) and plots based on casewise data (scatterplots and histograms).
- You cannot change from or into a boxplot. Thus, boxplot is not on the Gallery menu.
- You cannot change into an error bar chart, but you can change from an error bar chart into another categorical chart if there are enough data series for the type of chart selected.

If there is an obvious transition between the display of series in the current chart and the display of series in the selected chart, the new chart is drawn automatically. If not, the Displayed Data dialog box for the new chart opens for you to indicate how to display the series. For example:

- Changing from a single series chart such as a simple bar, simple line, or pie, to another single series chart is automatic.
- Changing from a clustered bar chart to a simple bar chart opens the Displayed Data dialog box for you to indicate which series to plot.
- Changing from a clustered or stacked bar chart to a multiple line chart is automatic. All series in the bar chart are plotted as lines.
- Changing from a simple bar chart to a multiple line chart opens the Displayed Data dialog box if you have series from your original chart not displayed in the simple bar chart. See "Selecting and Arranging Data (Series Menu)" on p. 674 for more information on omitting and restoring series.
- Changing from a clustered bar chart to a clustered range bar chart opens the Displayed Data dialog box for you to select which series are to be paired.
- Changing from a range bar chart to a difference line chart opens the Displayed Data dialog box for you to select which two series are to be displayed.
- Changing from a 3-D scatterplot to a scatterplot matrix is automatic. Changing from a scatterplot matrix to a simple scatterplot opens the Displayed Data dialog box.
- Changing into a mixed chart type always opens the Bar/Line/Area Displayed Data dialog box for you to indicate which series are to be displayed as bars, areas, or lines.
- Changing into a high-low chart always opens the Displayed Data dialog box.

You can change among bar, line, and area charts and create mixed charts within the Bar/Line/Area Displayed Data dialog box without using the Gallery menu (see "Bar,

Line, and Area Chart Displayed Data" on p. 675). You can create simple bar, line, or area charts from multiple versions of the charts by omitting all but one series. You can also change between stacked bars and clustered bars in the Bar/Line/Areas Options dialog box (see "Bar/Line/Area Options" on p. 637). To change to a pie chart, however, you must use the Gallery menu.

You cannot change among scatterplot types by adding or deleting series; you must use the Gallery menu. For example, if you omit all but two series in a matrix scatterplot, you are left with a 2×2 matrix. To make a simple scatterplot from the same data, from the menus choose:

Gallery
  Scatter...
    Simple

Each type of scatterplot has its own Displayed Data dialog box. See "Bar, Line, and Area Chart Displayed Data" on p. 675 through "Histogram Displayed Data" on p. 685 for more information.

Inheritance of Attributes and Other Chart Elements

When you change from one chart type to another, if an attribute in the current chart is applicable to the new chart, it is preserved. For example, if you change from clustered bars to multiple lines, the series represented by red bars is now represented by a red line and the green bars translate to a green line.

If a change in displayed data or in chart type makes a current chart specification invalid, that specification is set to the default. For example, suppose you are changing a clustered bar chart to a stacked bar chart. The range and increment on the scale axis are no longer valid and the stacked bar defaults are used.

Modifying Chart Elements (Chart Menu)

This section explains how to modify the layout and annotation of your chart by accessing dialog boxes available from the Chart menu (see Figure 32.12). For changes to data elements (removing and restoring series and/or categories), see "Selecting and Arranging Data (Series Menu)" on p. 674; for changes you can make to the color and style of objects, see "Modifying Attributes (Attributes Menu)" on p. 687.

From the Chart menu, you can:

- Alter the arrangement of the display or connect data points.
- Fit a variety of curves.
- Alter the scale, range, appearance, and labels of either axis, if appropriate.
- Adjust spacing between bars and between clusters of bars.

- Move the origin line in a bar chart to show how data values fall above and below the new origin line.
- Outside the chart itself, add or remove a one- or two-line title, a subtitle, and footnotes, any of which can be left- or right-justified or centered.
- Suppress or edit the legend.
- Add annotation text, at any position in the plot area, framed or unframed.
- Add horizontal and vertical reference lines.
- Add or remove the inner frame or outer frame.

Figure 32.12 Chart menu

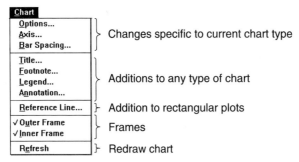

The three menu choices at the top of the Chart menu help you to modify the objects in the chart itself. For example, if you choose Options... when a line chart is displayed, the Bar/Line/Area Options dialog box opens, but if you choose Options... when a scatterplot is displayed, the Scatterplot Options dialog box opens.

The next four menu choices—Title, Footnote, Legend, and Annotation—are used to add information to many types of charts. Reference Line (the next choice) can be added to most rectangular charts.

The next two choices control the display of frames, and the last choice allows you to redraw the current chart.

Accessing Chart Options

The Options dialog box appropriate to the type of chart is determined by the system. You can access options in one of two ways:

- From the menus choose:

  Chart
    Options...

or

- Double-click in an area of the chart away from the chart objects.

Bar/Line/Area Options

To change options for a bar, line, or area chart, double-click away from the chart objects, or from the menus choose:

Chart
 Options...

This opens the Bar/Line/Area Options dialog box, as shown in Figure 32.13.

Figure 32.13 Bar/Line/Area Options dialog box (bar chart active)

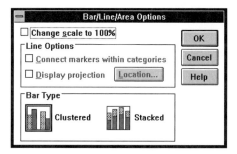

For bar or area charts, you can change the scale axis to percentage representation.

❑ **Change scale to 100%.** In a bar chart, this option automatically stacks the bars and changes each resulting bar to the same total length, representing 100% for the category (see Figure 32.14). In an area chart, the total distance from the axis, representing 100%, is the same for each category. This feature is useful for comparing the relative percentages of different categories.

Figure 32.14 Stacked and 100% bar charts

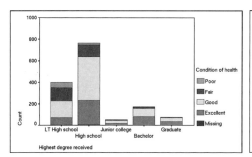 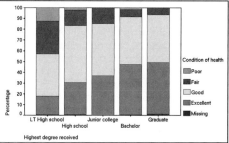

Line Options. Line options are available for line charts. You can choose one or both of the following options:

❑ **Connect markers within categories.** Applies to charts with more than one line. If this option is selected, vertical lines are drawn connecting the data points in the same category on different lines (different series). This option does not affect the current state of interpolation or line markers.

❑ **Display projection.** Select this option to differentiate visually between values to the left and values to the right in a line chart. To specify the category at which the projection begins, click on Location... in the Bar/Line/Area Options dialog box. This opens the Projection dialog box, as shown in Figure 32.15.

Figure 32.15 Bar/Line/Area Options Projection dialog box

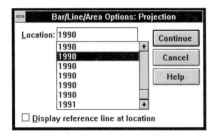

Choose the category where you want the projection line to start. The projection line will be displayed with a weight or style different from the original line. To make the projection stand out, you can select each part of the line individually and change its attributes. For example, the left part of the data line could be red and heavy while the right part of the data line, representing the projection, could be blue, thin, and dotted. An example is shown in Figure 32.16

❑ **Display reference line at location.** Displays a line perpendicular to the category axis at the selected location.

Figure 32.16 Projection line chart

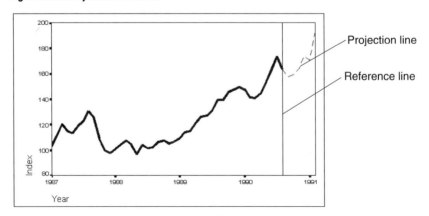

Bar Type. If two or more series are displayed on a bar chart, two bar types are available. You can choose one of the following options:

 Clustered. Bars are grouped in clusters by category. Each series has a different color or pattern, identified in the legend.

 Stacked. Bar segments, representing the series, are stacked one on top of the other for each category.

Pie Options

To change options for a pie chart, double-click away from the chart objects, or from the menus choose:

Chart
  Options...

This opens the Pie Options dialog box, as shown in Figure 32.17.

Figure 32.17 Pie Options dialog box

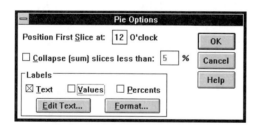 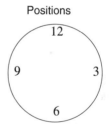

Position First Slice at n O'clock. Enter an integer from 1 to 12 to determine the position of the first sector or "slice" of the pie. The integers represent the positions of the hours on a clock face. The default position is 12.

To combine the smallest slices into one slice labeled *Other*, select the following option:

❏ **Collapse (sum) slices less than n%.** Adds the values of the summary functions of the smallest slices and displays the sum as one slice labeled *Other*. This formatting option does not recalculate any statistics and is appropriate only for functions that have a meaningful sum—that is, if you defined the summary function as N of cases, % of cases, Number of cases, Sum of values, Number above, Number below, or Number within.

If you select this option, each category for which the summary function has a value less than the specified percentage of the whole pie becomes part of the slice labeled

Other. You can enter an integer from 0 to 100. If you create another chart type from the Gallery menu, all of the original categories are available.

Labels. You can choose one or more of the following label options. You can also control the format of labels. See "Label Format," below.

❏   **Text.** Displays a text label for each slice. To edit the labels, see "Edit Text Labels," below.

❏   **Values.** Displays the value of the summary function for each slice.

❏   **Percents.** Displays the percentage of the whole pie that each slice represents.

Edit Text Labels

To edit text labels, click on Edit Text... in the Pie Options dialog box. This opens the Edit Text Labels dialog box, as shown in Figure 32.18.

Figure 32.18 Edit Text Labels dialog box

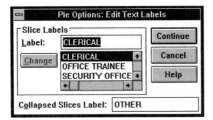

Slice Labels. To change the text of a slice label, select the label from the scroll list, edit it in the Label text box, and click on Change. Text labels can be up to 20 characters long.

Collapsed Slices Label. To change the text of collapsed slices label, edit it directly. (This label is available only if Collapse (sum) slices less than n% is selected in the Pie Options dialog box.)

When you have finished editing, click on Continue.

Label Format

To control the format of labels, click on Format... in the Pie Options dialog box. This opens the Label Format dialog box, as shown in Figure 32.19. (You can also select the labels in the chart and change the color, font, and size attributes.)

Figure 32.19 Label Format dialog box

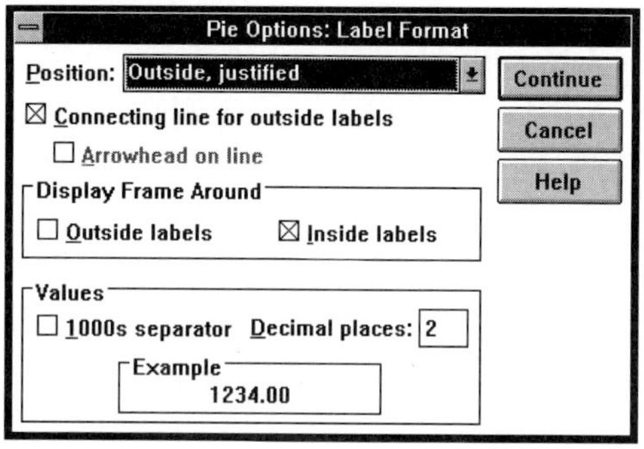

▿ **Position.** Places labels in relation to the pie. You can choose one of the following alternatives:

Outside, justified. Labels are placed outside the pie slices. Labels to the left of the pie are left-justified; labels to the right of the pie are right-justified.

Outside. Labels are placed outside the pie slices.

Inside. Labels are placed inside the pie slices.

Best fit. Labels are placed in the space available.

Numbers inside, text outside. Values and percentages are placed inside of the slices; their labels are placed outside of the slices.

Display Frame Around. Both inside and outside labels can have frames around them. You can select one or both sets of frames.

❑ **Outside labels.** Displays a frame around each label outside the pie.

❑ **Inside labels.** Displays a frame around each label within the pie.

Values. This group controls the format of displayed numbers. Your selections are displayed in the Example box.

❑ **1000s separator.** Displays values greater than 1000 with the separator (period or comma) currently in effect.

Decimal places. You can specify any number of decimal places from 0 to 19 for values. However, the number of decimal places will be truncated to fit within the 20-character limit for values. If you specify 0, percentages, if selected, will also have no decimal places. If you specify an integer from 1 to 19, percentages will be shown with one decimal place.

You can also choose the following option:

❑ **Connecting line for outside labels.** Displays a line connecting each outside label with the slice of the pie to which it applies.

  ❑ **Arrowhead on line.** Places arrowheads on connecting lines pointing to the slices. Arrowheads are not available if the position selected is Outside, justified.

Boxplot Options

To change options for a boxplot, double-click away from the chart objects, double-click on one of the *n* values on the category axis, or from the menus choose:

Chart
  Options...

This opens the Boxplot Options dialog box, as shown in Figure 32.20.

Figure 32.20 Boxplot Options dialog box

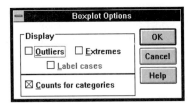

Display. Options in this group control whether outliers and extremes are shown in the chart. The height of the box is the interquartile range (IQR) computed from Tukey's hinges. You can choose one or more of the following alternatives:

❑ **Outliers.** Displays values that are more than 1.5 IQR's, but less than 3 IQR's, from the end of a box.

❑ **Extremes.** Displays values that are more than 3 IQR's from the end of a box.

  ❑ **Label cases.** Labels the outliers or extremes with case numbers or a labeling variable. Available if outliers or extremes are displayed. If two outliers or extremes have the same value but different case labels, no label is displayed.

You can also choose the following option:

❑ **Counts for categories.** Displays the number of cases under each category.

Error Bar Options

To change options for an error bar chart, double-click away from the chart objects, double-click on one of the *n* values on the category axis, or from the menus choose:

Chart
  Options...

This opens the Error Bar Options dialog box, as shown in Figure 32.21.

Figure 32.21 Error Bar Options dialog box

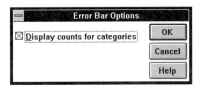

You can choose the following option:

❏ **Display counts for categories.** Displays the number of cases under each category. This option is selected by default.

Scatterplot Options: Simple and Matrix

The options for a scatterplot vary according to the type of scatterplot—simple and matrix, overlay, or 3-D. To change options for a simple or matrix scatterplot, double-click away from the chart objects, or from the menus choose:

Chart
  Options...

This opens the Scatterplot Options dialog box for simple and matrix scatterplots, as shown in Figure 32.22.

Figure 32.22 Scatterplot Options dialog box for simple and matrix scatterplots

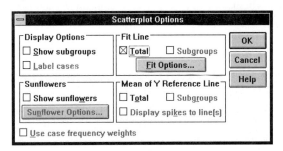

Display Options. Selected display options control how the groups and cases are differentiated. You can choose one or both of the following alternatives:

❏ **Show subgroups.** If a control variable was defined using Set markers by, this option is selected and markers of different colors or styles are used to differentiate the groups defined by the control variable. This option must be selected for subgroup options in other dialog boxes to be enabled.

❏ **Label cases.** If a label variable was defined, this option is selected and labels are attached to individual data points in the chart. This option is useful for data that are organized into a relatively small number of cases. This option is not available for a matrix scatterplot.

Fit Line. Fit Line options add one or more lines or curves to the chart, showing the best fit according to the method you select for Fit Options (see "Fit Options" on p. 645). You can choose one or both of the following alternatives:

❏ **Total.** Fits the total set of data points.

❏ **Subgroups.** Fits the selected type of curve to each subgroup. This option is enabled only if subgroups are defined and shown.

Sunflowers. The Sunflowers option allows you to group the data points into two-dimensional cells in the chart, with a **sunflower** in each cell. The process is similar to grouping the values for one variable into bars on a histogram. The number of cases in a cell is represented by the number of petals on the sunflower. You can also customize the display of sunflowers. See "Sunflower Options" on p. 647.

❏ **Show sunflowers.** To represent the data as sunflowers, select this option.

Mean of Y Reference Line. You can draw a reference line through the y axis at the mean of all the y values and reference lines at the means of defined subgroups. If you have a scatterplot matrix, any items apply to each part of the matrix. You can choose one or more of the following alternatives:

❏ **Total.** Produces one line at the mean y value for all the data points.

❏ **Subgroups.** Controls whether a line is shown for the mean of each subgroup. This option is available only if you specified a control variable to define subgroups and if Show subgroups is selected for Display Options.

❏ **Display spikes to line(s).** Produces a spike from each point to the appropriate mean reference line. If both Total and Subgroups are selected, spikes are drawn to the subgroup lines.

If you have defined a weight variable by selecting Weight Cases... from the Data menu, the weights are automatically applied to a simple or overlay plot.

❏ **Use case frequency weights.** Selected by default if a weight variable was previously defined. (The SPSS status bar indicates Weight On.) When weight is on, a message appears in a footnote below the chart. Weighted values are used to compute fit lines, mean of y reference lines, confidence limits, intercept, R^2, and sunflowers. Deselecting this option does not restore cases that were excluded from the chart because of missing or non-positive weights.

Fit Options

To select a method for fitting the points to a line, click on Fit Options... in the Scatterplot Options dialog box. This opens the Fit Line dialog box, as shown in Figure 32.23.

Figure 32.23 Fit Line dialog box

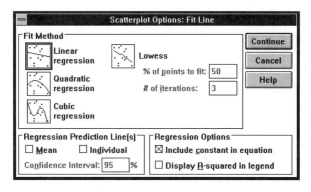

Fit Method. The picture buttons illustrate three regression types and another method for fitting the data points in a scatterplot. Examples of curves drawn by the fit methods are shown in Figure 32.24. You can choose one of the following options:

 Linear regression. Produces a linear regression line that best fits the data points on a scatterplot according to the least-squares principle. This is the default fit method.

 Quadratic regression. Produces a quadratic regression curve that best fits the data points on a scatterplot according to the least-squares principle.

 Cubic regression. Produces a cubic regression curve that best fits the data points on a scatterplot according to the least-squares principle.

 Lowess. Produces the locally weighted regression scatterplot smoothing method (Cleveland, 1979; Chambers et al., 1983). Lowess uses an iterative weighted least-squares method to fit a line to a set of points. At least 13 data points are needed. This method fits a specified percentage of the data points. The default is 50%. It also uses a specified number of iterations. The default is 3.

Regression Prediction Line(s). Produces lines illustrating the confidence level that you specify. The default confidence level is 95%. These prediction lines are available only if one of the regression types is selected. You can choose one or both of the following alternatives:

❏ **Mean.** Plots the prediction intervals of the mean predicted responses.

❏ **Individual.** Plots the prediction intervals for single observations.

Confidence Interval. Specify a confidence level between 10.0 and 99.9. The default value is 95.

Regression Options. Available only if one of the regression types is selected. You can choose one or both of the following alternatives:

❏ **Include constant in equation.** Displays a regression line passing through the y intercept. If this option is deselected, the regression line passes through the origin.

❏ **Display R-squared in legend.** Displays the value of R^2 for each regression line in the legend, if it is displayed. This option is not available on matrix scatterplots. To display the legend, from the menus choose:

Chart
  Legend...

and select Display legend.

Figure 32.24 Examples of fit methods

Linear regression

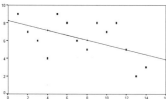

Cubic regression

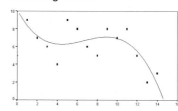

Quadratic regression

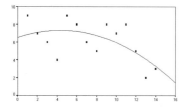

Lowess

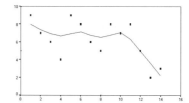

To access other methods of connecting the points in a scatterplot, from the menus choose:

Attributes
 Interpolation...

See "Line Interpolation" on p. 695 for more information.

Sunflower Options

To customize the display of sunflowers, click on Sunflower Options... in the Scatterplot Options dialog box. This opens the Sunflowers dialog box, as shown in Figure 32.25.

Figure 32.25 Sunflowers dialog box

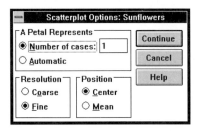

A Petal Represents. The petal number is equal to the number of cases in the cell (weighted or not) divided by the number of cases specified per petal. If the petal number is between 0 and 1.5, the center of the sunflower is displayed in the cell. If the petal number is 1.5 or greater, it is rounded, and the rounded number of petals is displayed. For example, in a nonweighted situation where each petal represents one case, a cell containing one case has only a sunflower center. A cell containing two cases has a sunflower with two petals, a cell with three cases has three petals, and so on.

You can choose one of the following alternatives:

○ **Number of cases.** Enter the number of cases per petal.

○ **Automatic.** The system determines the number of cases per petal automatically.

Resolution. Controls the size of the cells. You can choose one of the following alternatives:

○ **Coarse.** Plots cases from a large area on one sunflower. Each dimension of a sunflower cell is 1/8 of the appropriate range.

○ **Fine.** Plots cases from a small area on one sunflower. Each dimension of a sunflower cell is 1/15 of the appropriate range.

Position. Controls the placement of the sunflower within the cell. You can choose one of the following alternatives:

○ **Center.** Positions each sunflower in the center of its cell.

○ **Mean.** Positions each sunflower at the intersection of the means for the points in the cell.

Figure 32.26 contains examples of data plotted as a simple scatterplot and the same data displayed with sunflowers.

Figure 32.26 Sunflowers

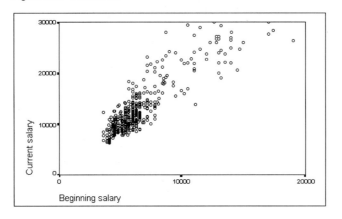

No sunflowers

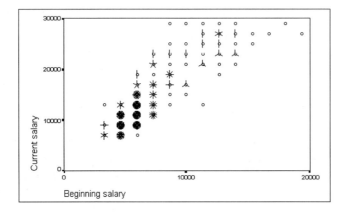

Sunflowers
(fine, center)

Overlay Scatterplot Options

To change options for an overlay scatterplot, double-click away from the chart objects, or from the menus choose:

Chart
 Options...

This opens the Overlay Scatterplot Options dialog box, as shown in Figure 32.27.

Figure 32.27 Overlay Scatterplot Options dialog box

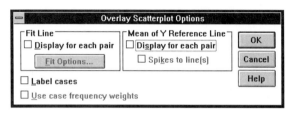

Fit Line. You can add lines or curves to the chart, showing the best fit.

❑ **Display for each pair**. If this item is selected, a line or curve is fitted for each pair of variables. To choose the type of line or curve, click on Fit Options... to open the Fit Line dialog box, shown in Figure 32.23. Available options are described in "Fit Options" on p. 645.

Mean of Y Reference Line. You can request a line drawn at the mean of the y values.

❑ **Display for each pair**. Draws a separate reference line for each pair of variables.

   ❑ **Spikes to line(s).** Produces a spike from each point to the appropriate mean reference line. Spikes are available only if the reference lines are displayed for each pair.

You can also choose one or both of the following case options for overlay scatterplots:

❑ **Label cases.** If a label variable was defined in the Overlay Scatterplot dialog box, its value for each case is displayed in the chart next to the corresponding point.

❑ **Use case frequency weights**. Selected by default if a weight variable was previously defined by selecting Weight Cases... from the Data menu. (The status bar indicates Weight On.) When weighting is on, a message appears in a footnote below the chart. Weighted values are used to compute fit lines, mean of y reference lines, confidence limits, and intercepts. Deselecting this option does not restore cases that were excluded from the chart because of missing or non-positive weights.

3-D Scatterplot Options

To change options for a 3-D scatterplot, double-click away from the chart objects, or from the menus choose:

Chart
  Options...

This opens the 3-D Scatterplot Options dialog box, as shown in Figure 32.28.

Figure 32.28 3-D Scatterplot Options dialog box

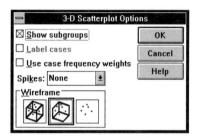

You can choose one or more of the following alternatives:

❑ **Show subgroups**. If a control variable was defined using Set markers by in the 3-D Scatterplot dialog box, markers of different colors or styles are used to differentiate the subgroups defined by the control variable.

❑ **Label cases.** If this item is selected and a variable was selected for Label cases by when the chart was defined, the selected variable is used to label each case.

❑ **Use case frequency weights.** Selected by default if a weight variable was previously defined by selecting Weight Cases... from the Data menu. (The status bar indicates Weight On.) When weighting is turned on, a message appears in a footnote below the chart. Weighted values are used to calculate the centroid. Deselecting this option does not restore cases that were excluded from the chart because of missing or nonpositive weights.

⬇ **Spikes.** Displays a line from each data point to the location that you specify. Spikes are especially useful when printing a 3-D scatterplot. You can choose one of the following alternatives:

None. No spikes are displayed.

Floor. Spikes are dropped to the plane of the x and z axes of a 3-D scatterplot.

Origin. Spikes end at the origin (0,0,0). The origin may be outside of the display.

Centroid. Spikes are displayed from each point to the centroid of all the points. The coordinates of the centroid are the weighted means of the three variables. A missing value in any one of the three variables excludes the case from the calculation. Changing the scale does not affect the calculation of the centroid.

Wireframe. The wireframe option draws a frame around the 3-D scatterplot to help you interpret it. You can choose one of the following alternatives:

 The full frame shows all of the edges of a cube surrounding the data points.

 The half frame shows the orientation of the three axes and their planes. This is the default wireframe.

 The cloud button allows you to suppress the wireframe entirely. You may want to use this view when rotating the cloud of points while looking for a pattern.

If you selected Spikes, the spikes are shown with or without a wireframe.

Histogram Options

To change options for a histogram, double-click away from the chart objects, or from the menus choose:

Chart
  Options...

This opens the Histogram Options dialog box, as shown in Figure 32.29.

Figure 32.29 Histogram Options dialog box

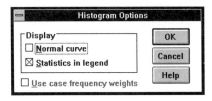

Display. You can choose one or both of the following display options:

❑ **Normal curve.** Superimposes a normal curve centered on the mean. The default histogram does not have a normal curve.

❑ **Statistics in legend.** Displays in the legend the standard deviation, the mean, and the number of cases. This item is selected by default. If you deselect the legend (see "Legends" on p. 668), the statistics display is also turned off.

The following option is also available:

❏ **Use case frequency weights.** Selected by default if a weight variable was previously defined by selecting Weight Cases... from the Data menu. (The SPSS status bar indicates Weight On.) When weighting is on, a message appears in a footnote below the chart. Weighting affects the height of the bars and the computation of statistics. Deselecting this option does not restore cases that were excluded from the chart because of missing or non-positive weights. If the histogram was generated from the Frequencies procedure, the case weights cannot be turned off.

Axis Characteristics

You can modify, create, and change the orientation of axes in a chart. Axis dialog boxes can be opened in one of the following ways:

• Double-click near the axis.

or

• Select an axis or axis label and from the menus choose:

Chart
　Axis...

to open the appropriate (scale, category, or interval) axis dialog box.

or

• Without an axis selected, from the menus choose:

Chart
　Axis...

to open an Axis Selection dialog box, similar to the one shown in Figure 32.30. The types of axes represented in the current chart are listed in the dialog box. Select the type of axis you want to modify and click on OK.

Figure 32.30 Axis Selection dialog box showing scale and category axes

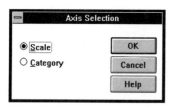

Scale Axis

If you select a scale axis, the Scale Axis dialog box appears, as shown in Figure 32.31.

Figure 32.31 Scale Axis dialog box

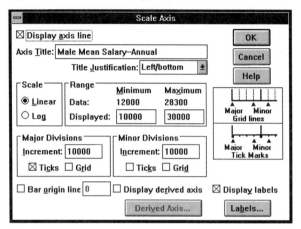

To display the axis line, select the following item:

❏ **Display axis line.** Controls the display of the axis line. Since it coincides with the inner frame, if you want no line displayed, you must also turn off the inner frame (see "Inner Frame" on p. 673). This item is not available for 3-D scatterplots.

Axis Title. You can type up to 72 characters for the axis title. To delete the title, delete all of the characters.

↧ **Title Justification.** Controls the position of the title relative to the axis. You can select one of the following alternatives:

Left/bottom. Axis title aligns to the left for horizontal axes and at the bottom for vertical axes.

Center. Axis title is centered (applies to both horizontal and vertical axes).

Right/top. Axis title aligns to the right for horizontal axes and at the top for vertical axes.

↧ **Title Orientation.** Available for 3-D scatterplots only. Controls the orientation of the title. You can select one of the following alternatives:

Horizontal. A horizontal title has one end near the center of the axis.

Parallel. A parallel title is parallel to the axis.

Scale. Controls whether the scale is linear or logarithmic. You can choose one of the following alternatives:

○ **Linear.** Displays a linear scale. This is the default.

○ **Log.** Displays a base 10 logarithmic scale. If you select this item, you can type new values for the range or you can click on OK and then click on Yes when the program asks if you want the default range. Logarithmic is not available for boxplots.

Range. Controls the displayed range of values. The minimum and maximum actual data values are listed for your information. If you change the range, you may also want to change the increments in Major Divisions and Minor Divisions.

If the scale is logarithmic, the range values are specified in the same units as the data values. The minimum must be greater than 0 and both values must be even logarithmic values (base 10)—that is, each must be an integer from 1 to 9 times a power of 10. For example, the range might be 9000 to 30000. If you enter unacceptable values, when you click on OK, the system asks if you want them adjusted.

Major Divisions/Minor Divisions. Allows you to control the marked increments along the axis. The number you enter for the increment must be positive and the range must be a multiple of the increment. The major increment must be a multiple of the minor increment. If the scale is logarithmic, you cannot change the increment.

❑ **Ticks.** If you do not want tick marks displayed, deselect this item.

❑ **Grid.** If you want grid lines displayed perpendicular to the axis, select this item.

The following option is available for bar charts:

❑ **Bar origin line.** Allows you to specify a location for the origin line from which bars will hang (vertical bars) or extend (horizontal bars). The specified value must fall within the current range. For example, two versions of a bar chart are shown in Figure 32.32, one with the origin line at 0 and the other with the origin line at 12,000. The second version emphasizes the differences in current salary for employees who have 16 or more years of education.

Figure 32.32 Bar origin lines

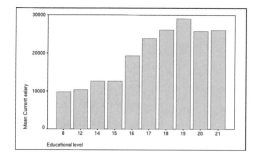 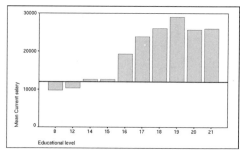

The following option allows you to display another scale opposite the original scale axis. It is selected by default in Pareto charts.

❏ **Display derived axis.** Allows you to specify an axis on the opposite side of the chart that has a different scale. In a Pareto chart, this axis commonly shows percentages. To specify the scale, title, increments, and labels, click on Derived Axis.... This option is not available for histograms or scatterplots.

The following option is also available for most charts:

❏ **Display labels.** Allows you to suppress or display the labels on the original scale axis. To modify the labels, click on Labels....

Derived Scale Axis

The derived axis is opposite the original scale axis. To specify or change the details of the derived axis, click on Derived Axis... in the Scale Axis dialog box. This opens the Scale Axis Derived Axis dialog box, as shown in Figure 32.33.

Figure 32.33 Scale Axis Derived Axis dialog box

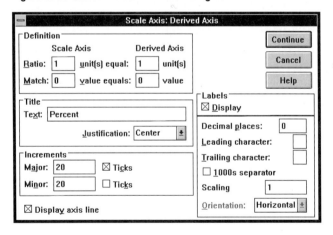

Definition. This group defines the derived axis in relation to the scale axis. The scale axis is not affected by these specifications.

Ratio: n unit(s) equal: n unit(s). The size of a unit on the derived axis is defined by its ratio to the size of a unit on the scale axis. In Figure 32.33, 100 units on the derived axis are the same size as 41 units on the scale axis. The numbers specified must be positive. When you have specified a ratio here, be sure to consider the size of increments near the bottom of this dialog box.

Match: n value equals: n value. Relates a specific position on the scale axis to a specific position on the derived axis. In Figure 32.33, the position of 0 on the scale axis matches the position of 0 on the derived axis. The match points do not have to be visible in the chart.

Title. The title is arranged so that it reads from top to bottom.

Text. The text of the title can be up to 72 characters. To delete the title, delete all of the characters.

⬇ **Justification.** Controls the position of the title relative to the axis: top, center, or bottom. You can select one of the following alternatives:

Top. The derived axis title is aligned with the top of the axis. This is the default for a Pareto chart.

Center. The title is centered with respect to the axis.

Bottom. The end of the title is at the bottom of the axis.

Increments. Controls the definition and marking of increments along the derived axis. Increments should be considered in conjunction with the range displayed on this axis, which is determined by the definition of the ratio.

Major. These increments have labels if Display is selected in the Labels group in this dialog box. Major tick marks are emphasized when selected.

Minor. These increments do not have labels. If minor ticks are selected, the minor increment must divide evenly into the major increment.

The following option is available for the derived axis:

❑ **Display axis line.** Controls whether or not the axis line is displayed for the derived axis. If you want no line at this position, you must deselect the inner frame on the Chart menu.

Labels. The following options control the labels of the derived axis:

❑ **Display.** Controls the display of labels at major increments.

Decimal Places. Enter the number of digits you want displayed to the right of the decimal point. The number of decimal places is also applied to bar labels, if present.

Leading Character. Adds the specified character at the beginning of each axis label automatically. The most commonly used leading character is a currency symbol, such as the dollar sign ($).

Trailing Character. Adds the specified character to the end of each axis label automatically. The most commonly used trailing character is the percent sign (%).

To insert a thousands-digit separator in numeric axis labels, select the following option:

❏ **1000s separator.** Displays values greater than 1000 with the separator (period or comma) currently in effect.

Scaling Factor. Computes each label on the derived axis by dividing the original value by the scaling factor. For example, the labels 1,000,000, 2,000,000, etc., can be scaled to 1, 2, etc., and the word *millions* added to the axis title. The default value is 1. Bar labels, if present, are not affected.

Scale Axis Labels

To modify axis labels, click on Labels... in the Scale Axis dialog box. This opens the Scale Axis Labels dialog box, as shown in Figure 32.34. Any changes you make are reflected in the Example box.

Figure 32.34 Scale Axis Labels dialog box

Decimal Places. Enter the number of digits you want displayed to the right of the decimal point. The number of decimal places is also applied to bar labels, if present.

Leading Character. Adds the specified character at the beginning of each axis label automatically. The most commonly used leading character is a currency symbol, such as the dollar sign ($).

Trailing Character. Adds the specified character to the end of each axis label automatically. The most commonly used trailing character is the percent sign (%).

To insert a thousands-digit separator in numeric axis labels, select the following option:

❏ **1000s separator.** Displays values greater than 1000 with the separator (period or comma) currently in effect.

Scaling Factor. Computes each label on the scale axis by dividing the original value by the scaling factor. For example, the labels 1,000,000, 2,000,000, etc., can be scaled to 1, 2, etc., and the word *millions* added to the axis title. The default value is 1. Bar labels, if present, are not affected.

Scatterplot Matrix Scale Axes

The dialog box for scatterplot matrix scale axes is shown in Figure 32.35. You can open the dialog box in one of the following ways:

- From the menus, choose:

  Chart
    Axis...

or

- Double-click on an axis.

or

- Double-click on one of the titles on the diagonal.

Figure 32.35 Scatterplot Matrix Scale Axes dialog box

The options at the left in the dialog box apply to all of the plots in the matrix.

To display diagonal and axis titles, choose one or both of the following alternatives:

- ❏ **Display diagonal titles.** Displays titles on the diagonal of the matrix. Displayed by default.
- ❏ **Display axis titles.** Displays titles on the outer rim of the matrix.

Horizontal Display/Vertical Display. Items apply globally to all plots. Axis lines are displayed by default.

Individual Axes. Select one variable at a time and click on Edit... to edit the selected axis. (See "Edit Selected Axis," below.)

Edit Selected Axis

To edit individual Scatterplot Matrix axes, click on Edit... in the Scale Axes dialog box. This opens the Edit Selected Axis dialog box, as shown in Figure 32.36.

Figure 32.36 Edit Selected Axis dialog box

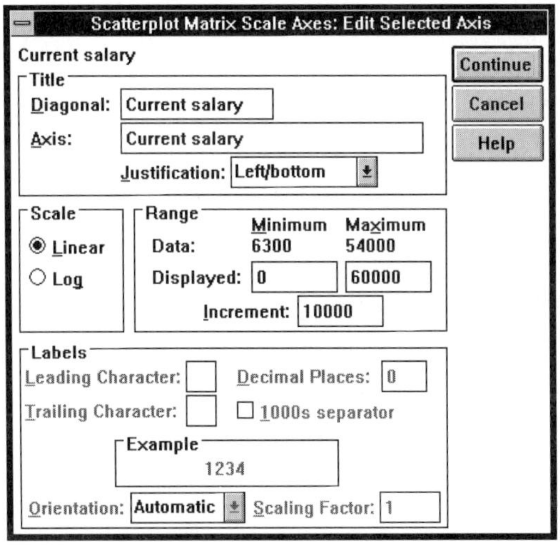

Title. Changes made to titles will be displayed only if you select the title display options in the Scale Axes dialog box. To fit titles into the space available, you can edit the text in the dialog box or select the text in the chart and change the size (see "Text" on p. 698).

Diagonal. Allows you to edit the title that appears on the matrix diagonal.

Axis. Allows you to edit the text of the axis title. With several plots in the matrix, the title for the axis often needs shortening.

Justification. Controls the position of the title relative to the axis. You can select one of the following alternatives: Left/bottom, Center, or Right/top. Top and bottom apply to vertical axes. Left and right apply to horizontal axes. See "Axis Title" under "Scale Axis" on p. 653 for more information.

Scale. You can change the type of scale used for the axis.

○ **Linear.** Displays a linear scale. This is the default.

○ **Log.** Displays a logarithmic scale (base 10).

Range. Controls the displayed range of values.

Data. The minimum and maximum actual data values are displayed for your information.

Displayed. You can change the displayed range by typing the new minimum and maximum. The range must be an even multiple of the increment. If the scale is logarithmic, the range values are specified in the same units as the data values. The minimum must be greater than 0 and both values must be even logarithmic values (base 10)—that is, the values of minimum and maximum must each be an integer from 1 to 9 times a power of 10. For example, a range could be 9000 to 30000. If you enter an unacceptable value, when you click on OK, the system asks if you want the values adjusted.

Increment. The value of the increment must divide evenly into the range.

Labels. The Labels group is available only if you selected Axis labels in either Horizontal Display or Vertical Display in the Scale Axes dialog box. Any changes you make are illustrated in the Example box.

Leading Character. Adds the specified character at the start of each axis label automatically. The most common leading character is a currency symbol, such as the dollar sign ($).

Trailing Character. Adds the specified character to the end of each axis label automatically. The most commonly used trailing character is the percent sign (%).

Decimal Places. Enter the number of digits you want displayed to the right of the decimal point.

❑ **1000s separator.** Displays values greater than 1000 with the separator (period or comma) currently in effect.

⬇ **Orientation.** Controls the orientation of axis labels. Available only for a horizontal axis. You can select one of the following alternatives: Automatic, Horizontal, Vertical, Staggered, or Diagonal.

Scaling Factor. You can enter up to 20 characters in the box. The system divides each label by the factor. For example, the labels 1,000,000, 2,000,000, etc., can be scaled to 1, 2, etc., and the word *millions* added to the axis title. The default value is 1.

Category Axis

Selecting a category axis opens the Category Axis dialog box, as shown in Figure 32.37.

Figure 32.37 Category Axis dialog box

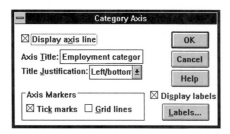

To display the category axis, select this option:

❑ **Display axis line.** Controls display of the axis line. Since it coincides with the inner frame, if you want no line displayed, you must also turn off the inner frame (see "Inner Frame" on p. 673).

Axis Title. You can type up to 72 characters for the axis title. To omit the title, delete all of the characters.

⬇ **Title Justification.** Controls the position of the title relative to the axis. You can select one of the following alternatives: Left/bottom, Center, or Right/top. Top and bottom apply to vertical axes. Left and right apply to horizontal axes. See "Axis Title" under "Scale Axis" on p. 653 for more information.

Axis Markers. Controls whether tick marks and grid lines are turned on or off.

❑ **Tick marks.** Controls the display of the tick marks for all categories.

❑ **Grid lines.** Controls the display of grid lines.

The following option is also available:

❑ **Display labels.** To display axis labels, select this item.

Category Axis Labels

To modify axis labels, click on Labels... in the Category Axis dialog box. This opens the Category Axis Labels dialog box, as shown in Figure 32.38.

Figure 32.38 Category Axis Labels dialog box

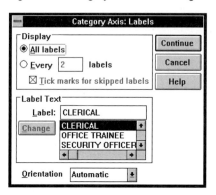

Display. Controls the display of axis labels. You can choose one of the following alternatives:

○ **All labels.** Displays a label for every category included in the display. To omit entire categories from the display, see "Bar, Line, and Area Chart Displayed Data" on p. 675.

○ **Every n labels.** Allows you to specify an increment governing the number of categories not labeled between displayed labels. Enter an integer that is 1 greater than the number of labels to be skipped. For example, if you want to label the first category, skip the next two, and label the fourth, enter 3.

❏ **Tick marks for skipped labels.** To turn off tick marks, deselect this item.

Label Text. Allows you to edit the text of labels. First select a label from the scroll list. It appears in the Label text box. Edit the text and click on Change.

⬇ **Orientation.** Controls the orientation of axis labels. Available only for a horizontal category axis. You can select one of the following alternatives: Automatic, Horizontal, Vertical, Staggered, or Diagonal. See "Orientation" under "Scale Axis Labels" on p. 657 for more information.

Interval Axis

The bars of a histogram extend from an interval axis. The Interval Axis dialog box is shown in Figure 32.39.

Figure 32.39 Interval Axis dialog box

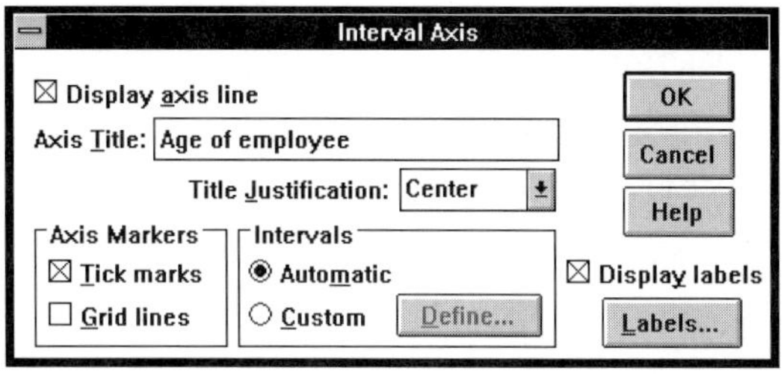

To display an axis line, select the following option:

❏ **Display axis line.** Turns the axis line off or on. If you want *no line* at this position, you must also turn off display of the inner frame (see "Inner Frame" on p. 673).

Axis Title. You can type up to 72 characters for the axis title. To omit the title, delete all the characters.

⬇ **Title Justification.** Controls the position of the title relative to the axis. You can select one of the following alternatives: Left/bottom, Center, or Right/top. Top and bottom apply to vertical axes. Left and right apply to horizontal axes. Justification is with respect to the ends of the displayed axis. See "Axis Title" under "Scale Axis" on p. 653 for more information.

Axis Markers. Controls whether tick marks and grid lines are turned on or off. You can choose one or both of the following alternatives:

❏ **Tick marks.** Controls the display of the tick marks for all categories. Tick marks are at the centers of the intervals.

❏ **Grid lines.** Controls the display of grid lines. Grid lines are at the bounds of intervals.

Intervals. Allows you to define the size of the intervals represented by the bars in the histogram. You can choose one of the following alternatives:

○ **Automatic.** The number and size of intervals are determined automatically, based on your data. This is the default.

○ **Custom.** Allows you to define the size of equal intervals. Click on Define... to change the number of intervals, the width of each interval, or the range of data displayed. See "Defining Custom Intervals," below.

The following display option is also available:

❏ **Display labels.** To display axis labels, select this item.

Defining Custom Intervals

To modify the number or width of intervals in a histogram, select Custom in the Interval Axis dialog box and click on Define... to open the Define Custom Intervals dialog box, as shown in Figure 32.40.

Figure 32.40 Interval Axis Define Custom Intervals dialog box

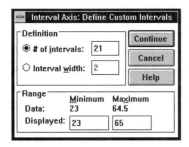

Definition. Two methods of specifying custom intervals are available. You can choose one of the following alternatives:

○ **# of intervals.** You can specify the number of intervals by entering an integer greater than 1. The system calculates the width of each interval, based on the range.

○ **Interval width.** You can enter a width for each interval, starting at the minimum listed under Range. The system calculates the number of intervals, based on the range.

Range. Allows you to adjust the range of data displayed. The minimum and maximum data values are listed for your information. You can adjust the range when you change the number of intervals or the interval width. For example, if you specify 10 intervals and a range of 20 to 70, the intervals start at 20 and are 5 units wide. (See Figure 32.41.) You can get the same result by specifying 5 as the interval width, along with the range of 20 to 70.

Figure 32.41 Histogram with custom intervals

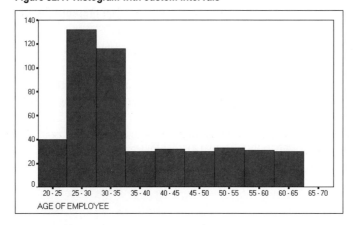

Modifying Interval Labels

Labels on an interval axis can be suppressed or modified. To modify the labels on the interval axis, click on Labels... in the Interval Axis dialog box. This opens the Interval Axis Labels dialog box, as shown in Figure 32.42. Any changes you make are illustrated in the Example box.

Figure 32.42 Interval Axis Labels dialog box

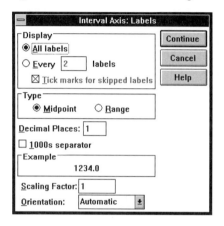

Display. Controls the display of axis labels.

○ **All labels.** Displays a label for every interval included in the display.

○ **Every n labels.** Allows you to specify an increment governing the number of intervals not labeled between displayed labels. Enter an integer that is 1 greater than the number of labels to be skipped. For example, if you want to label the first interval, skip the next two, and label the fourth, enter 3.

❑ **Tick marks for skipped labels.** To turn off tick marks, deselect this item.

Type. Allows you to select whether each label will denote the midpoint or the range of the interval.

○ **Midpoint.** Displays the midpoint of each interval as the label.

○ **Range.** Displays the lower and upper bounds of each interval as the label.

Decimal Places. You can specify the number of decimal places. Enter a value from 0 to 19.

To insert a thousands-digit separator in numeric axis labels, select the following option:

❑ **1000s separator.** Displays values greater than 1000 with the separator (period or comma) currently in effect.

Scaling Factor. You can enter up to 20 characters. The system divides each label by the factor. For example, the labels 1,000,000, 2,000,000, etc., can be scaled to 1, 2, etc., and the word *millions* added to the axis title. This factor does not affect the scale axis or bar labels.

☟ **Orientation.** Controls the orientation of axis labels. Available only for a horizontal axis. You can select one of the following alternatives: Automatic, Horizontal, Vertical, Diagonal, or Staggered.

Bar Spacing

To adjust the spacing of the bars in a bar chart, error bar chart, high-low-close chart, range bar chart, or histogram, from the menus choose:

Chart
  Bar Spacing...

The Bar Spacing dialog box for a bar chart is shown in Figure 32.43.

In a bar chart, you can change the margin spacing at both ends of the series of bars, the inter-bar spacing, and the inter-cluster spacing. The system adjusts the size of the bars to meet the new specifications.

For a histogram, the Bar Spacing dialog box contains only the bar margin specification.

Figure 32.43 Bar Spacing dialog box (bar chart)

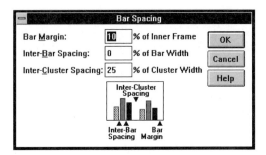

Bar Margin. The percentage (0 to 99) of the inner frame left blank on both sides of the series of bars. This percentage is split equally between the two sides. The default is 10% for bar charts and 0% for histograms.

Inter-Bar Spacing. The distance between bars within a cluster or the distance between bars in a simple bar chart. Enter the percentage of the bar width (0 to 100) that you want left blank between bars. The default is 0% for a clustered bar chart or 20% for a simple bar chart.

Inter-Cluster Spacing. The distance between clusters. Enter the percentage of the cluster width (0 to 100). The default is 25%.

Adding or Changing Explanatory Text

Explanatory text can be added to charts in the form of titles, footnotes, a legend, and text annotation.

Titles

To add a title to the top of a chart, from the menus choose:

Chart
  Title...

This opens the Titles dialog box, as shown in Figure 32.44. If you already have a title for the chart, you can double-click on it to open the dialog box.

Figure 32.44 Titles dialog box

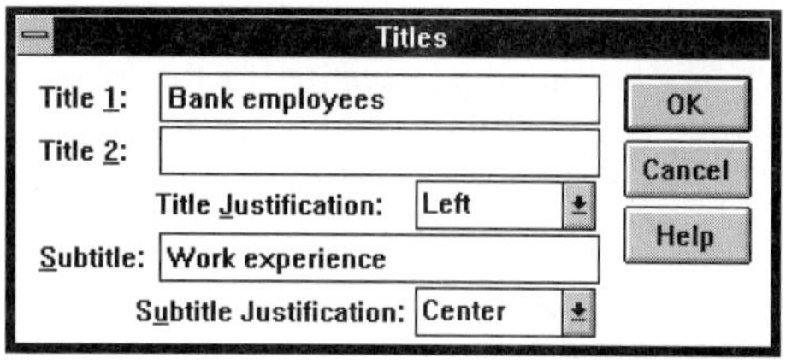

Title 1/Title 2. You can enter up to 72 characters for each title. The amount of the title that is displayed depends on the length of the title and the size of the type font selected.

- **Title Justification.** Both titles are justified together. You can choose one of the following alternatives: Left, Center, or Right. Left aligns the first character with the axis on the left; right aligns the last character with the right side of the inner frame.

Subtitle. You can enter up to 72 characters for the subtitle.

- **Subtitle Justification.** A subtitle can be left- or right-justified or centered, independent of titles 1 and 2. The default font size for the subtitle is smaller than the font size for titles 1 and 2. You can choose one of the following alternatives: Left, Center, or Right.

To delete any title, delete all of the characters in its text.

Footnotes

To add up to two footnotes to a chart, from the menus choose:

Chart
  Footnote...

This opens the Footnotes dialog box, as shown in Figure 32.45. If you already have a footnote, you can double-click on it to open the dialog box.

Figure 32.45 Footnotes dialog box

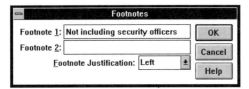

Footnote 1/Footnote 2. You can enter up to 72 characters for each footnote. The portion of a footnote that is displayed depends on the length of the footnote and the size of the type font selected.

⬇ **Footnote Justification.** Footnotes are justified relative to the inner frame. You can choose one of the following alternatives: Left, Center, or Right. Left aligns the first character with the axis on the left; right aligns the last character with the right side of the inner frame. See "Axis Title" under "Scale Axis" on p. 653 for more information.

To delete a footnote, delete all of the characters in its text.

Legends

If you have more than one series in a chart, the system provides a legend to distinguish between the series. A legend is also displayed automatically if you have statistics displayed for a histogram or R^2 for a regression line in a scatterplot. To make changes to the legend, double-click on the legend or from the menus choose:

Chart
  Legend...

This opens the Legend dialog box, as shown in Figure 32.46. The legend resulting from the specifications is shown in Figure 32.47.

Figure 32.46 Legend dialog box

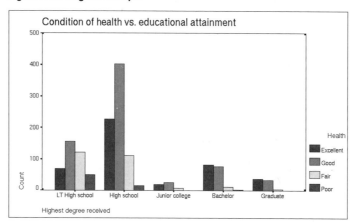

Figure 32.47 Legend example

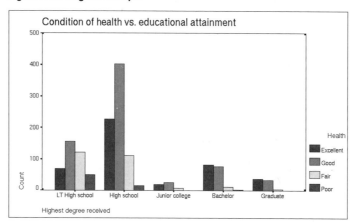

To display a legend for your chart, select the following option:

❑ **Display legend.** Controls whether the legend is displayed.

Legend Title. You can edit the legend title or add one if none exists. The legend title can be up to 20 characters long.

📤 **Justification.** Aligns the legend title within the area occupied by the legend. You can choose one of the following alternatives: Left, Center, or Right.

Labels. The labels in the legend are listed. When you select one of the labels from the list, it appears starting in Line 1 of the Selected Label group. You can edit the text and add a second line if it is not already there. Each line can be up to 20 characters long. When you have finished editing the label, click on Change.

Annotation

Annotation places text within the chart area, anchored to a specific point within the chart. To add annotation to the chart or edit existing annotation, from the menus choose:

Chart
  Annotation...

This opens the Annotation dialog box, as shown in Figure 32.48. The annotations resulting from these specifications are shown in Figure 32.49.

Figure 32.48 Annotation dialog box

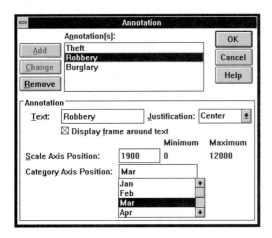

Figure 32.49 Annotation example

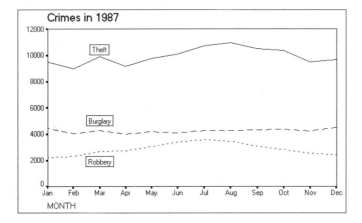

If you already have an annotation in the chart, you can edit it or add others by double-clicking on it. Since you position annotations at axis coordinates, the form of the Annotation dialog box depends on the kind of axes in your chart. Figure 32.48 shows an annotation dialog box for a chart containing a scale axis and a category axis.

For a new annotation, when the text and coordinates have been specified, click on Add and then OK. To make changes to an existing annotation, select the annotation on the Annotation(s) list, edit the text or position, and click on Change.

Annotation. The default position for annotation is the intersection of the displayed axes (the lower left corner).

Text. Type up to 20 characters in the Text box.

⬇ **Justification.** The choices available on the drop-down list are Left, Center, or Right. The default is left, indicating that the leftmost character of the annotation will be positioned at the selected coordinates. In Figure 32.49, the annotations are *centered* above the tick mark for Mar.

❑ **Display frame around text.** Adds a frame around the annotation text.

Scale Axis Position. The scale axis position is a number between the minimum and maximum values.

Category Axis Position. If you have a category axis, the annotation will be positioned at the category you select from the scroll list. In Figure 32.49, all annotations are positioned at the category Mar, which makes them appear directly above one another.

Adding Reference Lines

To add one or more horizontal and vertical reference lines, from the menus choose:

Chart
 Reference Line...

This opens an Axis Selection dialog box appropriate for your chart. Dialog boxes for Category Axis Reference Lines and Scale Axis Reference Lines are shown in Figure 32.50 and Figure 32.51. The dialog box for Interval Axis Reference Lines is similar to the dialog box for Scale Axis Reference Lines.

Figure 32.50 Category Axis Reference Lines dialog box

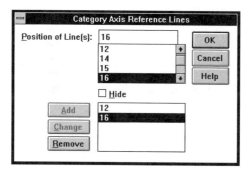

Figure 32.51 Scale Axis Reference Lines dialog box

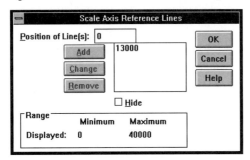

If you already have a reference line in the chart, you can open the dialog box to edit it or add other parallel reference lines by double-clicking on the line.

Position of Line(s). For a category axis, to add a new reference line, select one of the available categories and click on Add. The category is added to the list.

For a scale axis or interval axis, to add a new reference line, type a value and click on Add. The value is added to the list. If you type a value outside the displayed range, a warning message is displayed.

To remove a reference line, highlight it on the list and click on Remove. To change the position of a line, highlight it on the list, select a category or type a new value, and click on Change.

❏ **Hide.** Select this option to hide the reference line that is currently highlighted on the list. Then click on Add or Change. To display a previously hidden reference line, highlight it on the list, deselect Hide, and click on Change.

Figure 32.52 shows a chart that has one reference line perpendicular to the scale axis and two reference lines perpendicular to the category axis, as specified in the dialog boxes in Figure 32.50 and Figure 32.51.

Figure 32.52 Reference lines

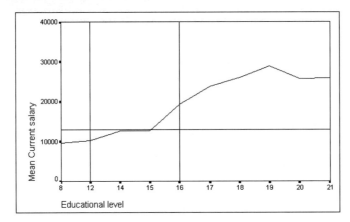

Inner and Outer Frames

A chart has an inner frame and an outer frame. You can select either one by clicking on it and you can change its attributes. If you want a fill color within a selected frame, be sure that the selection in the Fill Pattern dialog box is a pattern other than empty. Both frames are displayed in Figure 32.53. To set the default display for either frame, from the menus choose:

Edit
 Preferences...

and click on Graphics.

Figure 32.53 Inner and outer frames

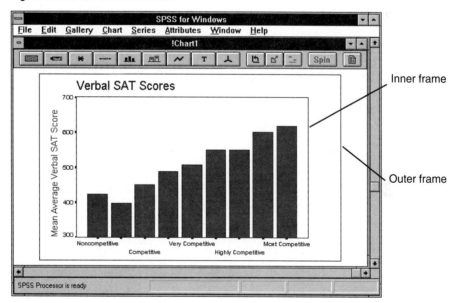

Inner Frame

The inner frame completes a rectangle, two sides of which coincide with the two axes. For most charts, the inner frame is displayed by default. To suppress or display the inner frame, from the menus choose:

Chart
 Inner Frame

When it is displayed, a check mark appears to the left of Inner Frame on the Chart menu.

Outer Frame

The outer frame encloses the titles, footnotes, and legend, as well as the chart. To display or suppress the outer frame, from the menus choose:

Chart
  Outer Frame

When it is displayed, a check mark appears to the left of Outer Frame on the Chart menu.

Refreshing the Screen

If your chart does not redraw correctly after you change the size of its window, from the menus choose:

Chart
  Refresh

The chart will be redrawn with the correct proportions. This is almost never necessary if you are using TrueType fonts in Windows 3.1.

Selecting and Arranging Data (Series Menu)

The Series menu allows you to modify your chart by selecting data and reassigning data elements within the chart. All of the data must exist within the original chart; you cannot add new data in the Chart Editor. You also cannot change values within the data. The options available vary by chart type:

- For bar, line, and area charts, you can omit data series and categories as long as enough data remain to generate the chart, and change the order of series and categories. You can specify for each series individually whether it is to be displayed as a bar, line, or area chart. You can also transpose the data so that series become categories and categories become series.

- For pie charts, you can omit categories (slices). If the original chart defined more than one data series, you can select the series to be displayed.

- For boxplots, series operations are not available.

- For scatterplots, you can reassign series to axes, omitting those not needed in the plot. You cannot omit individual values within a series. Since the assignment of series to axes differs for each type of scatterplot, there are different Displayed Data dialog boxes for each type of scatterplot.

- For histograms, if the original chart was a scatterplot with more than one series, you can select which one of the series is to be displayed.

All of these options, except transposing data, are specified in Displayed Data dialog boxes, which are specific to the chart type and are discussed in the following sections.

When you choose:

Series
  Transpose

data transposition takes place without further query.

Cumulative Distributions in Charts

Data distributions are never recalculated in the chart editor. Thus, removing categories from a cumulative distribution, for example, will not change the values of the remaining categories. Cumulative distributions in pie charts, or in the scale dimension of stacked bar and area charts, will yield charts whose interpretation is unclear.

Bar, Line, and Area Chart Displayed Data

To arrange the data in a bar, line, area, or mixed chart, from the menus choose:

Series
  Displayed...

This opens a Displayed Data dialog box. Figure 32.54 shows the Displayed Data dialog box for the bar chart in Figure 32.6.

Figure 32.54 Bar/Line/Area Displayed Data dialog box

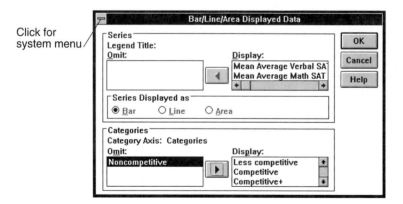

The controls in the Bar/Line/Area Displayed Data dialog box fall into two groups: those having to do with series and those having to do with categories.

Series. The legend title, if any, is listed for your information. (To change it, see "Legends" on p. 668). Since multiple series are identified in the legend, this title may help to clarify what the series represent. The series are displayed in two list boxes: those omitted from the chart and those displayed in the chart. To move a series from one list box to the other, select it and click on  or ◄ . You must have at least one series displayed for the OK pushbutton to be enabled.

The order of series on the Display list controls the order of bars within clusters, the order of segments within stacked bars, the order of stacked areas, and the order of legend items for all bar, area, and line charts. You can reorder the Display list by selecting a variable and using the system menu to move your selection up or down (see Chapter 34). In mixed charts, lines appear in the legend above areas and areas above bars.

Series Displayed as. On the list of series, each series name is followed by a colon and the word *Bar*, *Line*, or *Area* to indicate how it will be displayed when the chart is next drawn. To change the display for a series, select the series and then select one of the Series Displayed as alternatives. The chart in Figure 32.55 was derived from the chart in Figure 32.10 by changing the lines to areas and stacking the bars.

Categories. You can select categories to omit or display in the same way you select series. Displayed categories form the category axis in the order listed. You can reorder the Display list by selecting a category and using the system menu (see Chapter 34).

Figure 32.55 Mixed chart with bars and areas

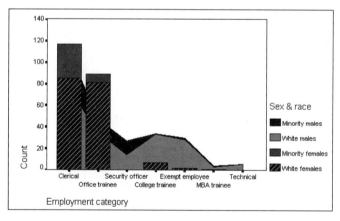

Pie Chart Displayed Data

To adjust the display of series and categories in a pie chart, from the menus choose:

Series
  Displayed...

This opens the Pie Displayed Data dialog box, as shown in Figure 32.56.

Figure 32.56 Pie Displayed Data dialog box

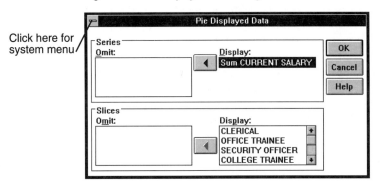

Click here for
system menu

Series. If you created the chart as a pie chart, there is only one series listed. If you selected Pie from the Gallery menu with a multiple series chart, there are several series in the Omit group and one under Display. If you don't want the selected series, first move the series to the Omit group. Then select the series you want.

Slices. You can reorder the Display list by selecting a category and using the system menu to move your selection up or down (see Chapter 34). You can delete categories from the display by moving them to the Omit list in the Slices group. If you omit any categories, the size of each slice is recalculated, using only the categories to be displayed.

High-Low-Close Displayed Data

To adjust the display of data series in a high-low-close chart, from the menus choose:

Series
  Displayed...

This opens the High-Low-Close Displayed Data dialog box, as shown in Figure 32.57.

Figure 32.57 High-Low-Close Displayed Data dialog box

Click here for
system menu

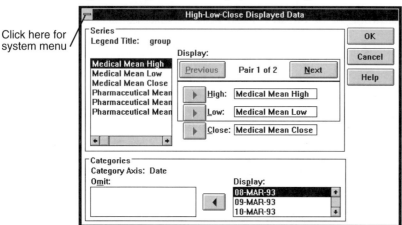

Series. The legend title, if any, is listed for your information. (To change it, see "Legends" on p. 668). Since multiple series are identified in the legend, this title may help to clarify what the series represent. The series available are displayed in the list box on the left. The series displayed in the chart are grouped in sets of a pair of high and low series along with an optional close series. To move a series between a high, low, or close box and the list of available series, select it and click on ▶ or ◀. You must have at least one pair of High and Low specifications for the OK pushbutton to be enabled. A Close specification is optional.

To view additional high-low pairs or to specify a new set, click on Next or Previous. Duplicate sets of high-low-close specifications are not allowed. You can, however, use a series in more than one set, although you should be careful to select meaningful pairs.

Categories. The category axis title is listed for your information. You can select categories to omit or display. To move a category from one list box to the other, select it and click on ▶ or ◀. Displayed categories form the category axis in the order listed. You can reorder the Display list by selecting a category and using the system menu (see Chapter 34).

Range Bar Displayed Data

To adjust the display of data series in a range bar chart, from the menus choose:

Series
  Displayed...

This opens the Range Bar Displayed Data dialog box, as shown in Figure 32.58.

Figure 32.58 Range Bar Displayed Data dialog box

Click here for
system menu

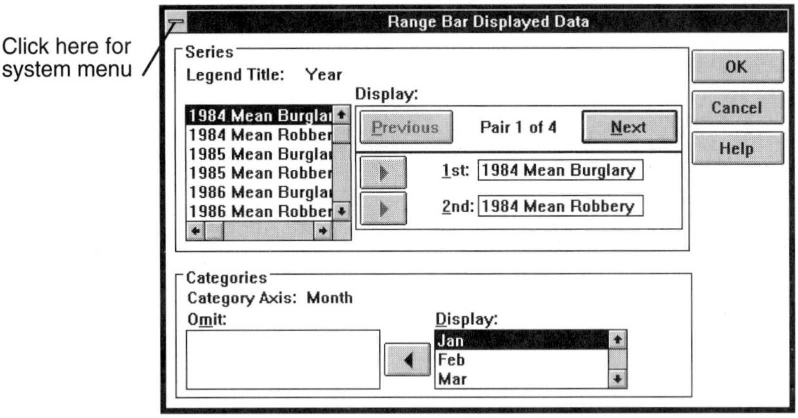

Series. The legend title, if any, is listed for your information. (To change the legend title, see "Legends" on p. 668). Since multiple series are identified in the legend, this title may help to clarify what the series represent. The series available are displayed in the list box on the left. The series displayed in the chart are grouped in pairs of series. To copy a series between a pair box and the list of available series, select it and click on ► or ◄. You must have at least one pair of specifications for the OK pushbutton to be enabled.

To view additional pairs or to specify a new pair, click on Next or Previous. Duplicate sets of pair specifications are not allowed. You can, however, use a series in more than one pair, although you should be careful to select meaningful pairs.

Categories. The category axis title is listed for your information. You can select categories to omit or display. To move a category from one list box to the other, select it and click on ► or ◄. Displayed categories form the category axis in the order listed. You can reorder the Display list by selecting a category and using the system menu (see Chapter 34).

Difference Line Displayed Data

To adjust the display of data series in a difference line chart, from the menus choose:

Series
 Displayed...

This opens the Difference Line Displayed Data dialog box, as shown in Figure 32.59.

Figure 32.59 Difference Line Displayed Data dialog box

Click here for
system menu

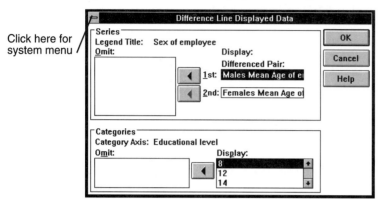

Series. The legend title, if any, is listed for your information. (To change it, see "Legends" on p. 668). Since multiple series are identified in the legend, this title may help to clarify what the series represent. The series are displayed in two boxes: those omitted from the chart and those displayed in the chart. To move a series between the Omit list box and one of the Differenced Pair boxes, select it and click on ▶ or ◀. You must have two series displayed for the OK pushbutton to be enabled.

Categories. You can select categories to omit or display in the same way you select series. Displayed categories form the category axis in the order listed. You can reorder the Display list by selecting a category and using the system menu (see Chapter 34).

Error Bar Displayed Data

To adjust the display of data series in an error bar chart, from the menus choose:

Series
 Displayed...

This opens the Error Bar Displayed Data dialog box, as shown in Figure 32.60.

Figure 32.60 Error Bar Displayed Data dialog box

Click here for
system menu

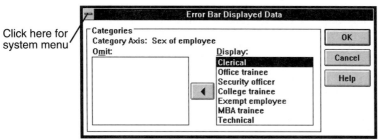

Categories. The category axis title is listed for your information. You can select categories to omit or display. To move a category from one list box to the other, select it and click on ▶ or ◀. Displayed categories form the category axis in the order listed. You can reorder the Display list by selecting a category and using the system menu (see Chapter 34).

Simple Scatterplot Displayed Data

To adjust the display of data series on a simple scatterplot, from the menus choose:

Series
  Displayed...

This opens the Simple Scatterplot Displayed Data dialog box, which controls the assignment of data series to the axes. You can use it to swap axes in a simple scatterplot. In changing to a simple scatterplot from a chart that includes more than two series, you can select the series you want to display on each axis. For example, suppose you have produced the overlay scatterplot shown in Figure 32.61, and you want to plot the verbal score against the math score.

Figure 32.61 Overlay scatterplot of SAT scores

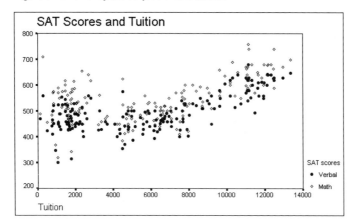

From the menus choose:

Gallery
  Scatter...

Then click on Simple and New. The Simple Scatterplot Displayed Data dialog box appears, as shown in Figure 32.62.

Figure 32.62 Simple Scatterplot Displayed Data dialog box

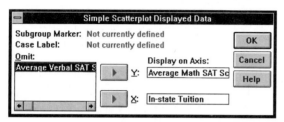

The variable that determines subgroup markers and the variable that supplies case labels (if either is assigned) are listed for your information. (Display of subgroup markers and case labels is controlled in Scatterplot Options. See "Overlay Scatterplot Options" on p. 649.)

To create a simple scatterplot where average verbal SAT is on the *x* axis and average math SAT is on the *y* axis, first select In-state Tuition in Display on Axis for X and click on ◀ to move it to the Omit list box. Then select Average Verbal SAT and click on ▶ to move it to Display on Axis for Y. Both Y and X must be specified for the OK pushbutton to be enabled.

If the current chart data is limited to two variables, you can use this dialog box to swap the *x* and *y* axes by first moving the variables to the Omit box and then back to the appropriate Y and X boxes. When you have finished specifying variables, click on OK to display the new chart.

Overlay Scatterplot Displayed Data

To manipulate the display of series in an overlay scatterplot, from the menus choose:

Series
  Displayed...

This opens a dialog box similar to the one in Figure 32.63.

Figure 32.63 Overlay Scatterplot Displayed Data dialog box

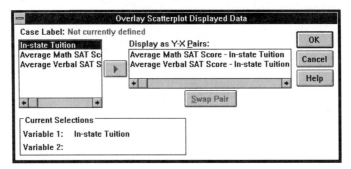

The case label variable, if any, is listed for your information. Underneath it is a box containing a list of the variables available for the chart. You cannot add any other variables. In the box labeled Display as Y-X Pairs are the pairs of variables plotted in the current chart. To remove a pair, select it and click on ◄ .

You can add pairs selected from the available variables. When you select one variable, it appears in the Current Selections group in the first position. The next variable you select appears in the second position. To deselect a variable, click on it again. When a pair of variables is in the Current Selections group and you click on ► , the pair appears in the Display box. For example, you might add the pair Average Math SAT-Average Verbal SAT. However, if you want the plots overlaid, you should consider the range on each axis. In the example just considered, the first two pairs listed have Tuition, which ranges into the thousands. SAT scores are in the hundreds, and the plot will look like a narrow line on the scale of thousands.

Clicking on Swap Pair reverses the axis assignments of a selected pair.

Scatterplot Matrix Displayed Data

If your chart is a scatterplot matrix, to change which series and categories are displayed, from the menus choose:

Series
 Displayed...

This opens a dialog box similar to the one shown in Figure 32.64.

Figure 32.64 Scatterplot Matrix Displayed Data dialog box

Click here for
system menu

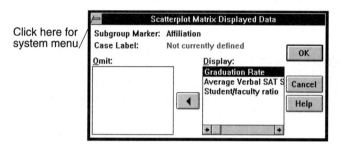

The subgroup marker and case label variable, if any, are listed for your information. The Display list box shows a list of available variables. To remove a variable from this list, select it and click on ◀ so that it moves to the Omit box. There must be at least two variables in the Display list box for the OK button to be enabled.

You can reorder the Display list by selecting a variable and using the system menu to move your selection up or down (see Chapter 34).

3-D Scatterplot Displayed Data

To change the series displayed on a 3-D scatterplot, from the menus choose:

Series
 Displayed...

This opens the dialog box shown in Figure 32.65. This box is also displayed if you change to a 3-D scatterplot from the Gallery menu.

Figure 32.65 3-D Scatterplot Displayed Data dialog box

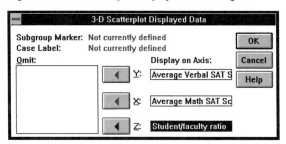

The subgroup marker and case label are listed for your information. The variable for each axis is listed under Display on Axis. To move a variable to the Omit list box, select it and click on ◀. You can swap the axes by moving the variables to the Omit list box and then moving them back to the axes you want. In the default position, the *y* axis is vertical and perpendicular to the plane formed by the *x* and *z* axes.

Histogram Displayed Data

If a scatterplot is displayed (as in Figure 32.1), to obtain a histogram of one of the variables, from the menus choose:

Gallery
  Histogram...

This opens the Histogram Displayed Data dialog box, as shown in Figure 32.66. It can also be opened when a histogram is displayed by choosing:

Series
  Displayed...

Figure 32.66 Histogram Displayed Data dialog box

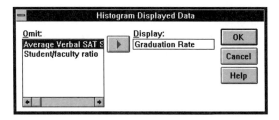

If you want to change the variable selected for display in the histogram, first select the variable in the Display box and move it to the Omit list box. Then select another variable in the Omit list box and move it to the Display box.

Transposing Data

In a multiple bar, line, or area chart, you can transpose series and categories. You can also transpose data in a high-low-close, range bar, or difference line chart. For example, in a clustered bar chart, the categories (designated on the category axis) become series (designated in the legend) and the series become categories. To do this, from the menus choose:

Series
  Transpose Data

The system redraws the chart if possible. If there is too much data or assignment is ambiguous, the appropriate Displayed Data dialog box is displayed.

An example is shown in Figure 32.67. The difference between transposing data and swapping axes is illustrated in "Swapping Axes in Two-dimensional Charts" on p. 701. Data transposition is not available for boxplots, scatterplots, or histograms.

Figure 32.67 Example of transposing data

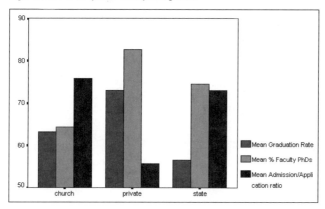

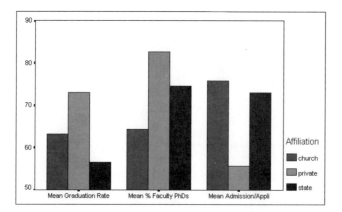

Modifying Attributes (Attributes Menu)

The objects that make up a chart have attributes that can be modified:

- Almost all objects have color.
- Lines, including data lines, axes, and the borders surrounding areas, have style and weight.
- Areas have fill pattern.
- Markers have style (shape) and size.
- Bars have bar style (normal, drop-shadows, or 3-D effect) and labels that indicate the exact values they represent along the scale axis.
- Data lines have interpolation style.
- Text items have font and size.
- Pie slices have position (normal or exploded).
- Axes have orientation that can be swapped (for two-dimensional charts) or rotated (for three-dimensional charts).
- Data lines can be discontinuous ("broken") at missing values.

Modifying these attributes requires a mouse. With the mouse, you select an object to modify and then make selections from palettes (see "Selecting Objects to Modify" on p. 631). The quickest way to select a palette or perform an Attributes menu action is to click on the appropriate button on the chart window icon bar. The attributes and their corresponding icon buttons are shown in Figure 32.68.

Figure 32.68 Attributes menu and chart window icon bar

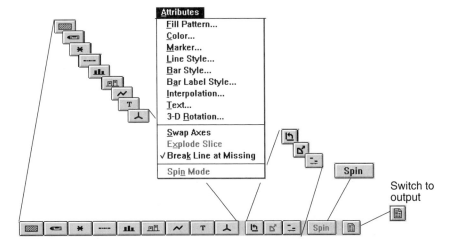

Palettes

When you select an item from the Attributes menu or click on the corresponding button on the icon bar, a palette or dialog box opens. It contains picture buttons illustrating the patterns or styles and several action buttons.

- If you click on Apply, the selected picture button is applied to the currently selected series or object.
- If you click on Apply All, the selected picture button is applied to all series in the chart.
- If you click on Close, the palette is closed without applying the selection.
- If you click on Help, the SPSS Help window for the palette opens.

The pattern or style of the selected chart object is highlighted by a box drawn around a picture button. If you select a different object in the chart while the palette is open, the attribute of the new selection is highlighted in the palette.

You can drag the palette anywhere on the screen, and you can have more than one palette open at a time.

Fill Patterns

To fill in enclosed areas such as bars, areas under lines, and background area, from the menus choose:

Attributes
  Fill Pattern...

or click on ▨ . This opens the Fill Patterns palette, as shown in Figure 32.69.

Figure 32.69 Fill Patterns palette

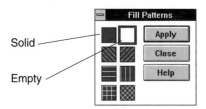

You can use a fill pattern to make distinctions between the areas, especially if the chart is to be presented in black and white or a limited number of colors. In the palette itself, patterns appear in only one color, but your pattern selection is applied to whatever color is in the selected area.

The white picture button represents an empty area. If this fill pattern is selected, the selected object will appear white or have the same color as the background, no matter what color is selected in the Colors palette.

If the bar style is drop-shadow or 3-D effect, you can select any surface of a series of bars and change the fill pattern. For example, you can select the top surface of the 3-D bars for one pattern and the right side for another pattern.

Colors

You can change the color of chart objects, including areas, lines, markers, and text. To change a color, select the object you want to change and from the menus choose:

Attributes
  Color...

or click on |⬚| . This opens the Colors palette, as shown in Figure 32.70.

Figure 32.70 Colors palette

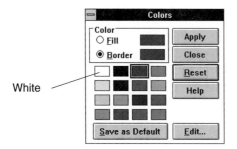

The color of a chart object is associated with a position in the palette and takes on whatever color is currently in that position.

Color. You can change the fill color or the border color (if the object has a border).

○ **Fill.** Specifies the color inside the element if it is an area, or the color of other elements such as lines or text. To change the fill color, select an object in the chart, choose Fill, and then click on the color you want. When you click on Apply, the selected element changes to the color at the position you clicked on. Be sure that a *non-empty fill pattern* was previously selected and applied.

○ **Border.** Specifies the color of the border of an enclosed area. To change the border color, select an area in the chart, choose Border, and then click on a color from the palette. When you click on Apply, the color of the border of the selected area changes.

Reset. If you have edited the color palette but have not saved it, clicking on Reset restores the colors in the default palette. It also changes the colors of elements in the chart to match the ones in the default palette.

Save as Default. If you change the colors in the palette, you can save the palette as the default palette. Then whenever you click on Reset, the saved default palette will appear and colors of chart objects change to match their associated positions in the palette.

Edit. If you want to change a color in the palette, select the color you want to replace in the Colors palette shown in Figure 32.70 and click on Edit..., which opens the Colors Edit Color dialog box, shown in Figure 32.71. (You cannot edit the colors white or black.)

Figure 32.71 Colors Edit Color dialog box

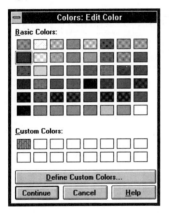

The color you selected in the palette is highlighted. Click on either a basic color or a custom color and then click on OK. The selected color appears in the palette, in the position you selected before editing. Any chart objects associated with that position also take on the new color.

To define a new custom color, click on Define Custom Colors, which expands the Colors Edit Color dialog box, as shown in Figure 32.72.

Figure 32.72 Colors Edit Color dialog box, expanded

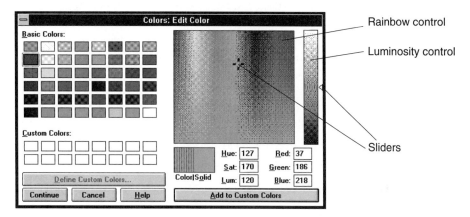

Select one of the rectangles under Custom Colors and use *one* of the following methods to specify the custom color:

- **Rainbow control.** Move the sliders in the rainbow control and the luminosity control until the color in the left half of the Color|Solid box is the one you want. Click on Add to Custom Colors.

- **HSL.** A color can be specified by typing numbers for hue, saturation, and luminosity. Hue corresponds to moving the rainbow control slider horizontally, Sat to moving it vertically, and Lum to moving the luminosity slider. Hue can have any integer value from 0 to 239 and Sat and Lum can have values from 0 to 240. Specifications for common colors are under HSL in Table 32.1. After typing the numbers, click on Add to Custom Colors.

- **RGB.** A color can be specified by typing numbers between 0 and 255 for Red, Green, and Blue. Specifications for common colors are under RGB in Table 32.1. This type of specification is commonly used to specify a color to be used in a light-emitting device, such as a video display. After typing the numbers, click on Add to Custom Colors.

Table 32.1   Common color specifications

Color	HSL			RGB		
	Hue	Sat	Lum	Red	Green	Blue
Black	0	0	0	0	0	0
White	0	0	240	255	255	255
Red	0	240	120	255	0	0
Yellow	40	240	120	255	255	0
Green	80	240	120	0	255	0
Cyan	120	240	120	0	255	255
Blue	160	240	120	0	0	255
Magenta	200	240	120	255	0	255

Markers

Markers are used to indicate the location of data points in a line chart, area chart, or scatterplot, and the data points for the close series on a high-low-close chart. To change the size or style of markers in a chart, from the menus choose:

Attributes
  Marker...

or click on [✳] . This opens the Markers palette, as shown in Figure 32.73.

Figure 32.73 Markers palette

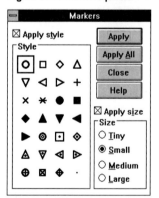

You can change the marker style and size for a single series (click on Apply) or for all the series at once (click on Apply All). To change only the style, select Apply style and deselect Apply size. To change only the size, select Apply size and deselect Apply style.

By default, each series appears in a different color or with a different marker style, according to how your graphic preferences are set.

The speed of drawing scatterplots on the screen may vary with the type of marker. Squares and triangles tend to be faster than circles on a computer with a graphics accelerator. Hollow markers tend to be faster than filled ones.

If you have a line chart in which the markers are not displayed, open the Line Interpolation palette (see "Line Interpolation" on p. 695) and select Straight (or another interpolation style) and Display Markers.

Line Styles

The lines in a chart, including the data lines and the axes, can have different weights and different styles. To change the weight or style of a line, select it and from the menus choose:

Attributes
  Line Style...

or click on ![---]. This opens the Line Styles palette, as shown in Figure 32.74.

Figure 32.74   Line Styles palette

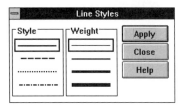

Style. Controls the pattern of the line. The default is solid.

Weight. Controls the thickness of the line. The default is thin.

Bar Styles

To add a drop shadow or a 3-D effect to a bar chart or a range bar chart, from the menus choose:

Attributes
  Bar Style...

or click on ![bar icon]. This opens the Bar Styles palette, as shown in Figure 32.75. Bars for every series in a chart have the same bar style.

Figure 32.75 Bar Styles palette

Normal. No shadows or 3-D effect. This is the default.

Drop shadow. Displays a shadow behind each bar. You can specify the depth of the shadow as a positive or negative percentage of the width of each original bar. The default is 20%. Positive depth places the shadow to the right of the bar, negative to the left.

3-D effect. Displays each bar as a rectangular solid. You can specify depth as a percentage of the width of each original bar. The default is 20%. Switching from positive to negative depth changes the perspective of the viewer. With a positive value you see the tops and right sides of the bars. With a negative value, you see the left sides.

If you have already changed the color or pattern of the original bars, the new block surfaces are displayed in the *default color and pattern*, while the front surface retains the attributes you selected previously. Once the shadows or 3-D bars are displayed, you can change the color and pattern of each type of individual surface, including the shadows or the side and top surfaces for each series.

Bar Label Styles

To label with its numerical value, each bar in a bar chart, range bar chart, or histogram, from the menus choose:

Attributes
  Bar Label Style...

or click on [⊞] . This opens the Bar Label Styles palette, as shown in Figure 32.76.

Figure 32.76 Bar Label Styles palette

The bar label style applies to all of the bars in the chart. In a bar chart, the number of decimal places in the bar labels is the same as the number of decimal places in the scale axis labels.

None. No values appear on the bars. This is the default.

Standard. Displays a value at the top of each bar. It may or may not be easy to read, depending on the color and pattern of the bar. You can change the color, font, or size of the value text.

Framed. Displays the values in white frames at the tops of the bars. You can change the color, font, or size of the value text and the color of the frames.

Line Interpolation

In a line chart, scatterplot, difference line chart, mean series in an error bar chart, or the close series in a high-low-close chart, several styles are available for connecting data points. To select a method used to connect the data points, from the menus choose:

Attributes
 Interpolation...

or click on ![line icon]. This opens the Line Interpolation palette, as shown in Figure 32.77. The Step, Jump, and Spline picture buttons each have a drop-down list. Examples of various types of interpolation are shown in Figure 32.78.

Figure 32.77 Line Interpolation palette

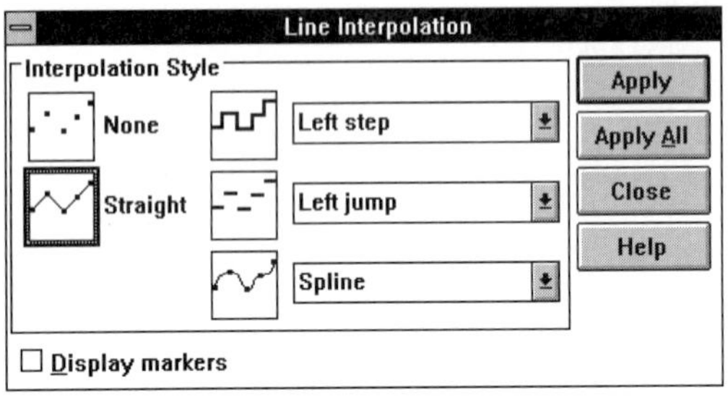

None. No lines connect the points.

Straight. The data points are connected in succession by straight lines. This is the default for line charts.

☀ **Step.** Each data point has a horizontal line drawn through it, with vertical risers joining the steps. Selecting left, center, or right from the drop-down list specifies the location of the data point on the horizontal line.

☀ **Jump**. Each data point has a horizontal line drawn through it, with no risers. Selecting left, center, or right from the drop-down list specifies the location of the data point on the horizontal line.

☀ **Spline.** The data points are connected by a cubic spline. Lines are always drawn from left to right. For scatterplots, the parametric cubic form is used, and lines are drawn in order of data entry. On the Spline drop-down list are two more types of interpolation:

3rd-order Lagrange. Produces third-order Lagrange interpolations in which the third-order polynomial is fitted through the closest four points. The parametric cubic form is used with scatterplots.

5th-order Lagrange. Produces fifth-order Lagrange interpolations in which the fifth-order polynomial is fitted through the closest six points. The parametric form is used with scatterplots.

The following option is also available:

❏ **Display markers**. Displays markers at the data points. To change the style and size of the markers, see "Markers" on p. 692.

For scatterplots, to obtain more interpolation types, from the menus choose:

Chart
 Options...

Then select Total or Subgroups and click on Fit Options.

Figure 32.78 Examples of line interpolation with markers displayed

None

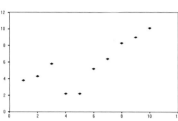

Straight

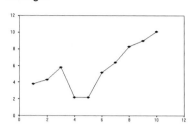

Center step

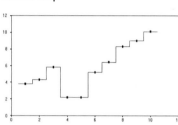

Left step

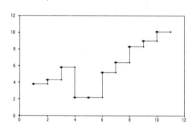

Left jump

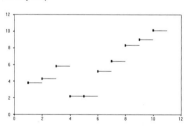

Spline

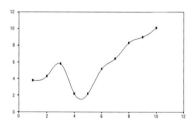

3rd-order Lagrange

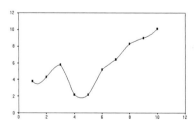

5th-order Lagrange

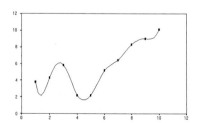

Text

To change the font or size of a text element of the chart, such as an axis label, select the text and from the menus choose:

Attributes
  Text...

or click on 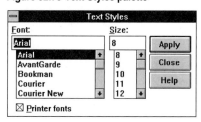. This opens the Text Styles palette, as shown in Figure 32.79.

Figure 32.79 Text Styles palette

Font. The scroll list contains a list of fonts installed on your system. To change the font, select it from the list.

Size. To change the font size, select the size from the list or type it.

The following option is also available:

❑ **Printer fonts.** Controls whether the list displays printer fonts or screen fonts. If you're planning to print the chart, use printer fonts.

Exploding Pie Chart Slices

You can **explode** (separate) one or more slices from a pie chart for emphasis (see Figure 32.80).

Figure 32.80 Pie chart with exploded slice selected

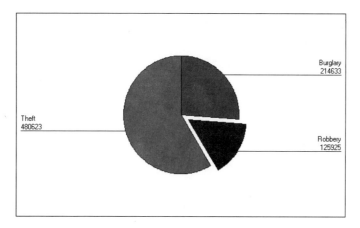

To explode a slice, select it and from the menus choose:

Attributes
  Explode Slice

or click on 🔲 . To reverse the explosion, select the slice and click on the icon or menu choice again. A check mark on the menu indicates that the currently selected slice is exploded. You can explode two or more slices, one at a time.

To explode the whole pie, from the menus choose:

Gallery
  Pie...

and then click on Exploded.

Handling Missing Data in a Line Chart

You can choose how to display a line chart that has some data missing. By default, the line has a break where the missing values should be. This is indicated by a check mark to the left of Break Line at Missing on the Attributes menu. To connect all existing points, even though data is missing in between, from the menus choose:

Attributes
  Break Line at Missing

or click on 🔲 . To break a line connected at missing values, click on 🔲 .

In Figure 32.81, the top chart has no missing data. The other two charts each have a missing temperature value for Day 3. When Break Line at Missing is selected, the missing data point is not connected within the chart line. This is the default for a line chart. When Break Line at Missing is deselected, the surrounding points are connected, and it is easy to overlook the fact that there is no value there.

Figure 32.81 Missing data in a line chart

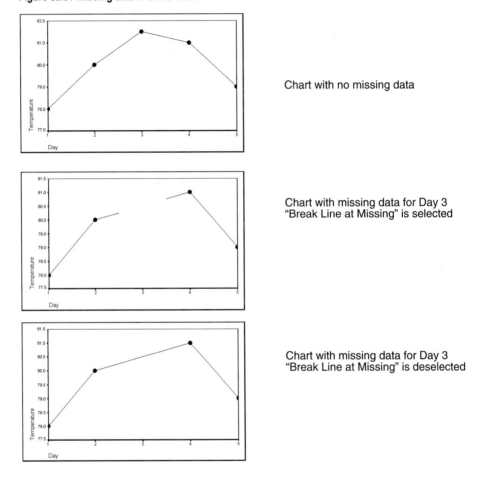

Chart with no missing data

Chart with missing data for Day 3 "Break Line at Missing" is selected

Chart with missing data for Day 3 "Break Line at Missing" is deselected

Changing or Rotating the Axes

You can change the perspective of a chart by swapping axes or rotating the chart.

Swapping Axes in Two-dimensional Charts

Category Charts and Histograms. In a 2-D bar chart, line chart, area chart, mixed chart, boxplot, or high-low chart with one scale axis, you can swap the axes. Swapping axes changes the orientation between vertical and horizontal. The bars, lines, or areas still represent the same values.

This is different from transposing, where the categories change places with the series named in the legend (see "Transposing Data" on p. 686). The difference between swapping axes and transposing data is illustrated in Figure 32.82.

Figure 32.82 Swapping axes and transposing data

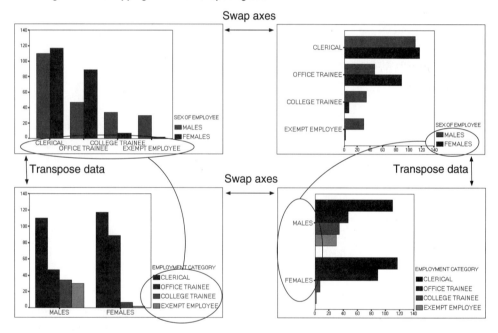

To swap axes, from the menus choose:

Attributes
  Swap Axes

or click on [⬚]. You can also use this procedure for boxplots and histograms.

Scatterplots. To swap the axes on a scatterplot, from the menus choose:

Series
  Displayed...

and assign the variables to different axes, as described in "Simple Scatterplot Displayed Data" on p. 681.

Rotating a 3-D Chart

If the current chart is a 3-D scatterplot, you can rotate in six directions. To rotate a 3-D scatterplot, from the menus choose:

Attributes
  3-D Rotation...

or click on ⬛. This opens the 3-D Rotation dialog box, as shown in Figure 32.83.

Figure 32.83 3-D Rotation dialog box

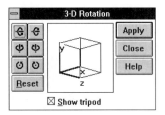

The direction of rotation is indicated on each button. Rotation is about one of three lines: a horizontal line in the plane of the screen, a vertical line in the plane of the screen, or a line perpendicular to the plane of the screen. You can click on a rotation button and release it, or you can click and hold the mouse button until you get as much rotation as you want. The rotation is illustrated in the center of the dialog box. When you have reached the orientation you want, click on Apply and then click on Close. Clicking on the Reset pushbutton returns the chart to the default orientation.

❏ **Show tripod.** Displays a tripod composed of lines parallel to the x, y, and z axes, with their intersection at the center of the wireframe.

Using Spin Mode

For another way to rotate 3-D charts, from the menus choose:

Attributes
  Spin Mode

or click on ⬛ Spin. This displays the chart with a new icon bar having the same rotation buttons as the 3-D Rotation dialog box. However, in this mode, the chart is stripped down for the duration of spinning. Only the tripod is shown and solid markers are hollow.

Spin mode allows you to watch the pattern of the points change while you spin the chart. As in the other rotation mode, you can click on a rotation button and release it, or you can hold it down while the chart spins. When you are satisfied with the chart orientation, click on End Spin. The rotated chart is returned to the full version in the new position with its other attributes and options restored. The Reset button returns the chart to its default orientation.

To increase the speed of spinning, you can reduce the screen area to be updated by changing the size of the window.

Finding Information in This Chapter

The following table summarizes the chapter contents by menu selection, section reference, and function to help you locate specific chart modification facilities.

Table 32.2   Finding information in this chapter

Menu Selection	Reference	Function
	"Editing in a Chart Window" on p. 629	Summary of menu functions
	"Selecting Objects to Modify" on p. 631	How to select various chart objects
Gallery	"Changing Chart Types (Gallery Menu)" on p. 632	Standard plus additional chart types (mixed, drop-line, and exploded pie)
Gallery/Bar, Line, Area, Mixed, Pie		Change type among bar, line, area, mixed, pie, and high-low charts
Gallery/Scatter, Histogram		Change between types of scatterplots and histograms
Chart/Options	"Bar/Line/Area Options" on p. 637	100% scale, connect markers, projection line, clustered/stacked bars
	"Pie Options" on p. 639	Position slices, collapse slices, labels
	"Boxplot Options" on p. 642	Outliers, extremes, labels, counts
	"Error Bar Options" on p. 643	Counts
	"Scatterplot Options: Simple and Matrix" on p. 643 "Overlay Scatterplot Options" on p. 649 "3-D Scatterplot Options" on p. 650	Subgroups, fit line, sunflowers, mean reference line, label cases, case frequency weights, spikes, prediction lines, intercept, R^2, wireframe (3-D)
	"Histogram Options" on p. 651	Normal curve, statistics, weights
Chart/Axis	"Scale Axis" on p. 653	Axis title, scale, range, divisions, labels, tick marks, grid lines, hanging bars
	"Scatterplot Matrix Scale Axes" on p. 658	Axis title, diagonal title, labels, tick marks, grid lines
	"Category Axis" on p. 661	Axis title, markers, labels
	"Interval Axis" on p. 662	Axis title, markers, intervals, labels
Chart/Bar Spacing	"Bar Spacing" on p. 666	Spacing of bars and bar clusters
Chart/Titles	"Titles" on p. 667	Adding or editing chart titles
Chart/Footnotes	"Footnotes" on p. 668	Adding or editing chart footnotes
Chart/Legend	"Legends" on p. 668	Adding or editing chart legend
Chart/Annotation	"Annotation" on p. 670	Adding or editing text within the chart area
Chart/Reference Line	"Adding Reference Lines" on p. 671	Adding or deleting horizontal and vertical reference lines

Table 32.2   Finding information in this chapter (Continued)

Menu Selection	Reference	Function
Chart/Inner Frame	"Inner Frame" on p. 673	Frame coincident with axes
Chart/Outer Frame	"Outer Frame" on p. 674	Frame outside titles and footnotes
Chart/Refresh	"Refreshing the Screen" on p. 674	Redrawing a chart
Series/Displayed Data	"Bar, Line, and Area Chart Displayed Data" on p. 675 "Pie Chart Displayed Data" on p. 677 "High-Low-Close Displayed Data" on p. 677 "Range Bar Displayed Data" on p. 678 "Difference Line Displayed Data" on p. 679 "Error Bar Displayed Data" on p. 680 "Simple Scatterplot Displayed Data" on p. 681 "Overlay Scatterplot Displayed Data" on p. 683 "Scatterplot Matrix Displayed Data" on p. 684 "3-D Scatterplot Displayed Data" on p. 684 "Histogram Displayed Data" on p. 685	Omitting or displaying series and categories
Series/Transpose Data	"Transposing Data" on p. 686	Transposing series between the category axis and the legend
Attributes (Also pushbuttons on the icon bar)	"Palettes" on p. 688	Changing fill patterns, colors, markers, line styles, bar styles, bar label styles, line interpolation, text styles
Attributes/Explode Slice	"Exploding Pie Chart Slices" on p. 699	Exploding pie slices
Attributes/Break Line at Missing	"Handling Missing Data in a Line Chart" on p. 699	Missing values in a line chart
Attributes/Swap	"Swapping Axes in Two-dimensional Charts" on p. 701	Swapping axes
Attributes/Spin Mode	"Rotating a 3-D Chart" on p. 702 "Using Spin Mode" on p. 702	Rotating or spinning a 3-D scatterplot

33 Printing

This chapter describes how to print files. You can print:

- Text files from syntax or output windows.
- Data files from the Data Editor window.
- Chart files from chart windows and the Chart Carousel.

Printer Installation

Before you can print a file or set printer options, you must install an appropriate printer driver for your printer. (Refer to your Microsoft Windows documentation for more information.)

Files and Windows

In SPSS, files appear within windows. While you can scroll, reduce, or enlarge a window that contains a file, changes in the dimensions of the window do not affect the file.

Printing a Syntax or Output File

You can print a whole syntax or output file or a selected portion. To print a syntax or output text file:

1. Make the window containing the file the active window.

2. From the menus choose:

   File
     Print...

This opens the Print dialog box, as shown in Figure 33.1. The name of the file is shown in the dialog box. The printer name is also displayed.

Figure 33.1   Print dialog box

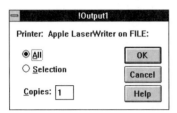

3. To print the file, click on OK.

The following print options are available:

❍ **All**. Prints the entire file. This is the default.

❍ **Selection**. Prints the selected area of the file. To select an area for printing, use the click-and-drag technique to highlight the area. If there is no highlighted area in the file, this option is disabled.

Copies. By default, one copy is printed. If you want multiple copies, enter the number of copies you want to print.

Determining the Correct Width and Length for Printed Output

In SPSS, output width and length are based on the number of characters per line and the number of lines per page as specified in the Preferences Output dialog box (see Chapter 36). Width and length selections generally should be consistent with font size and printer options, such as page orientation. For example, if you specify a font size or line length greater than the default values, you may need to change the page size or orientation in your printer setup to avoid truncating printed output (see "Setting Up Your Printer" on p. 710).

Printing a Data File

To print a data file, follow the same steps used to print a syntax or output file. The name of the file and the printer are shown in the Print dialog box. You can print the entire file or a selected area.

Options for Data Files

You can print or suppress grid lines that outline data cells. You can also print actual data values or value labels that have been defined.

A data file is printed as it appears on screen. Whether grid lines and value labels are printed depends on whether they appear in the Data Editor window.

Grid Lines

By default, grid lines are displayed. To turn grid lines off and on:

1. Make the Data Editor window the active window.

2. From the menus choose:

   Utilities
    Grid Lines

Value Labels

By default, value labels are not displayed. To turn value labels on and off:

1. Make the Data Editor window the active window.

2. From the menus choose:

   Utilities
    Value Labels

When value labels are turned on, all values for which a label is defined appear as the label. A label wider than the cell in which it appears is truncated.

Format of Printed Data Files

Printed data files are paginated from left to right and top to bottom. Page numbers in the form *row–column* are displayed. For example, page 1–1 contains the top rows of data in the first set of columns from the left. Page 2–2 contains data in the second set of rows from the top in the second set of columns from the left. Variable names and case numbers are printed on every page.

Printing a Chart File

To print a chart file:

1. Make the chart window or the chart carousel the active window.

2. From the menus choose:

File
  Print...

If the active window is a chart window, this opens the Print dialog box shown in Figure 33.2. If the active window is the Chart Carousel, this opens the Print dialog box shown in Figure 33.3. You can print only the entire chart, not just a selected portion.

Figure 33.2   Print dialog box for chart windows

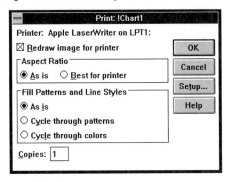

Figure 33.3   Print dialog box for Chart Carousel

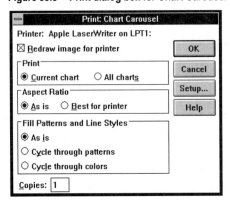

The following options are available for printing charts:

❑ **Redraw image for printer**. Redraws chart to adjust for printer fonts. If your chart uses fonts or font sizes that are not loaded in the printer, the printer uses the closest available font and size, and text may be truncated or may not be aligned properly with the chart unless the chart is first redrawn for the printer. This option produces the best printed results, but it can be slow. Deselect this default option if you want only a quick draft or if your chart uses only printer fonts.

Redrawing a chart for printing also allows you to adjust the following chart features:

Aspect Ratio. The width-to-height ratio of the outer frame of the chart. You can choose one of the following alternatives:

○ **As is**. Uses the chart aspect ratio as it appears in the chart on the screen. (Chart aspect ratio is controlled from the Preferences Graphics dialog box. See Chapter 36.)

○ **Best for printer**. Makes full use of an 8 1/2 × 11-inch page in landscape (horizontal) mode.

Fill Patterns and Line Styles. You can choose one of the following alternatives:

○ **As is**. Uses the colors and/or patterns as they appear on the chart. If you are using a black-and-white PostScript printer, colors appear as shades of gray.

○ **Cycle through patterns**. Substitutes patterns for colors in graphic elements, such as bars, lines, and pie sectors. For line charts, the cycle includes four line styles within four line weights to make 16 possible combinations. For bar charts, area charts, and pie charts, the cycle includes seven fill patterns (including solid). For scatterplots, the cycle includes 28 available marker types. Any existing patterns, line styles, or marker types in the chart are ignored. This option also converts all text to solid black and backgrounds to white.

○ **Cycle through colors**. Substitutes colors for patterns, line styles, and marker styles. The default palette of 14 colors is used. If more than 14 colors are required, patterns are added to colors. Any existing colors or patterns are ignored. This option also converts all text to solid black and backgrounds to solid white.

Copies. By default, one copy is printed. If you want multiple copies, enter the number of copies you want to print.

If you are printing from the Chart Carousel, the following option is also available:

Print. You can select one of the following alternatives:

○ **Current chart**. Print only the chart currently displayed in the Chart Carousel. This is the default.

○ **All charts**. Print all charts that are in the Chart Carousel. If you are printing to a file, all charts in the Chart Carousel are printed to the same file, with each chart on a separate page.

Setting Up Your Printer

This section describes how to control some of the various printer settings, such as page size and orientation. The available options vary for different printers. To modify printer settings, from the menus choose:

File
  Printer Setup...

This opens the Windows Print Setup dialog box, as shown in Figure 33.4.

Figure 33.4   Print Setup dialog box

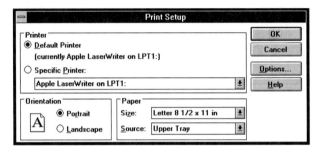

Printer. There are two alternatives:

○ **Default Printer**. The current default printer, based on the setting in the Windows Printer dialog box (accessed through the Windows Control Panel).

○ **Specific Printer**. To use a printer other than the default printer, select one from the drop-down list of installed printer drivers.

Orientation. There are two alternatives:

○ **Portrait**. The page is taller than it is wide. This is the default for PostScript printers.

○ **Landscape.** The page is wider than it is tall.

Paper. You can change both the selected paper size and source (tray). The available options depend on the selected printer.

Options. Other printing options include scaling of the printed document, printing to an encapsulated PostScript file, and assigning font substitution for fonts in your document that aren't available on the selected printer.

See your Windows documentation for more information on setting up your printer.

Production Mode Printing

Automatic printing of output and charts is available in production mode, using the /p command line switch. For more information, see Appendix C.

34 Utilities

This chapter describes the functions found on the Utilities menu, as well as several other capabilities: reordering target variable lists, accessed from system menus; stopping the SPSS processor, on the File menu; and accessing Microsoft Mail, available on the File menu if you are using Windows for Workgroups.

Command Index

If you are familiar with SPSS command syntax, you can quickly find the corresponding dialog boxes using the Command Index. From the menus choose:

Utilities
  Command Index...

This opens the Command Index dialog box, as shown in Figure 34.1.

Figure 34.1 Command Index dialog box

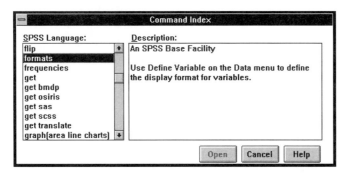

SPSS Language. Displays a complete list of SPSS commands in alphabetical order. To search for a particular command, use the scroll bar or type the first letter of the command name. This scrolls through the list to the first command that starts with that letter. Repeatedly typing the letter will cycle through all commands that begin with that letter.

To go to the corresponding dialog box for a command, select the command from the list and click on Open... (or double-click on the command name).

Description. Provides a brief description of the command and its availability. Some commands are not part of the Base system and require add-on options; others cannot be accessed through dialog boxes. The description identifies optional features and commands that can be run only by entering syntax in a syntax window.

Fonts

To change the type font used in a syntax or output window or in the Data Editor window, make the window the active window, and from the menus choose:

Utilities
  Fonts...

This opens the Font dialog box, as shown in Figure 34.2.

Figure 34.2   Font dialog box

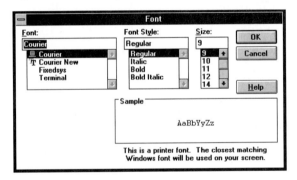

Font. Lists all the available fixed-pitch fonts for syntax and output windows. Lists all available fonts for the Data Editor.

Font Style. Lists available styles: regular, italic, bold, and bold italic.

Size. Lists available point sizes for the selected font.

Font changes are applied to all text in the active window. Fonts cannot be selectively applied to portions of a file.

Variable Information

To obtain information on individual variables, copy and paste variable names into command syntax, or go to a specific variable in the Data Editor window, from the menus choose:

Utilities
 Variables...

This opens the Variables dialog box, as shown in Figure 34.3.

Figure 34.3   Variables dialog box

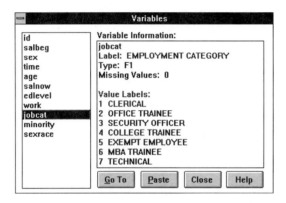

The Variable Information box displays variable definition information for the currently selected variable, including:

- Data format
- Variable label
- User-missing values
- Value labels

You can modify the definition of a variable using the Define Variable dialog box (see Chapter 3).

In addition to variable information, the following options are available:

Go To. To find the selected variable in the Data Editor window, click on Go To. This closes the Variables dialog box and makes the Data Editor the active window.

Paste. To paste variable names into command syntax:

1. If you have more than one syntax window open, make the syntax window into which you want to paste the variable names the designated syntax window.

2. Position the cursor where you want the variable names to be pasted.

3. Highlight the variables in the Variables dialog box and click on Paste. You can also paste individual variables simply by double-clicking on them.

Variable Sets

You can restrict the variables that appear on dialog box source variable lists by defining and using variable sets.

Defining Variable Sets

To define variable sets, from the menus choose:

Utilities
  Define Sets...

This opens the Define Variable Sets dialog box, as shown in Figure 34.4.

Figure 34.4   Define Variable Sets dialog box

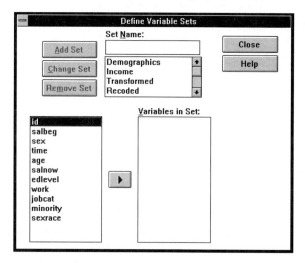

You can create new sets, modify existing sets, and remove sets.

- To create a new set, enter a set name, select the variables to include in the set, and click on Add Set.

- To modify an existing set or change the set name, select the set name from the list of sets, make the changes, and click on Change Set.

- To remove a set, select the set name from the list of sets and click on Remove Set.

Set Name. Set names can be up to 12 characters long. Any characters, including blanks, can be used. Set names are not case-sensitive. If you enter the name of an existing set, Add Set is disabled and Change Set is enabled, indicating that the new set definition will replace an existing set.

Variables in Set. Any combination of numeric, short string, and long string variables can be included in a set. The order of variables in the set has no effect on the display order of the variables on dialog box source lists. A variable can belong to multiple sets.

Using Variable Sets

To use variable sets, from the menus choose:

Utilities
  Use Sets...

This opens the Use Sets dialog box, as shown in Figure 34.5.

Figure 34.5   Use Sets dialog box

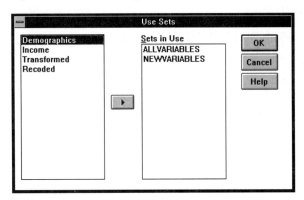

The source list contains any defined variable sets for the data file.

Sets in Use. Displays the sets used to produce the source variable lists in dialog boxes. Variables appear on the source lists in alphabetical or file order. The order of sets and the order of variables within a set have no effect on source list variable order. By default, two system-defined sets are in use:

- **ALLVARIABLES**. This set contains all variables in the data file, including new variables created during a session.

- **NEWVARIABLES**. This set contains only new variables created during the session.

You can remove these sets from the list and select others, but there must be at least one set on the list. If you don't remove the ALLVARIABLES set from the Sets in Use list, any other sets you include are more or less irrelevant.

File Information

To display complete dictionary information for every variable in the currently open data file, from the menus choose:

Utilities
 File Info

The following information is displayed in the output window:

- Variable name.

- Descriptive variable label (if any).

- Print and write formats. The data type is followed by a number indicating the maximum width and the number of decimal positions (if any). For example, F8.2 indicates a numeric variable with a maximum width of 8 columns, including one column for the decimal point and two columns for decimal positions.

- Descriptive value labels (if any) for different values of the variable. Both the value and the corresponding label are displayed.

Output Page Titles

SPSS can place a heading at the top of each page in output files. The default heading includes the date, page number, and the version of SPSS being used. To add a title or subtitle to the output page heading, from the menus choose:

Utilities
 Output Page Titles...

This opens the Output Page Title dialog box, as shown in Figure 34.6.

Figure 34.6   Output Page Title dialog box

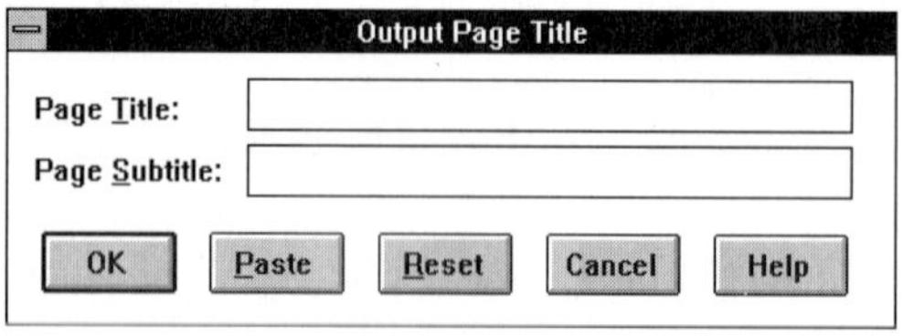

Page Title. The title can be up to 60 characters in length.

Page Subtitle. The subtitle can be up to 60 characters in length.

You can use quotation marks or apostrophes in your title or subtitle, but not both.

New titles and subtitles affect only new output and take effect on the next display page. If you want different titles for different analyses, enter a new title before running each analysis. Titles affect all output windows.

Displaying Output Page Titles

Output page titles and subtitles only appear on output pages if you choose to display full page headers. To turn on the display of full page headers, from the menus choose:

Edit
  Preferences...

This opens the Preferences dialog box. Click on Output... to open the Preferences Output dialog box, and click on Full in the Page Headers group to display page titles. For more information on output preferences, see Chapter 36.

Reordering Target Variable Lists

Variables appear on dialog box target lists in the order in which they are selected from the source list. If you want to change the order of variables on a target list—but you don't want to deselect all the variables and reselect them in the new order—you can move variables up and down on the target list using the system menu in the upper left corner of the dialog box, as shown in Figure 34.7.

Figure 34.7   System menu

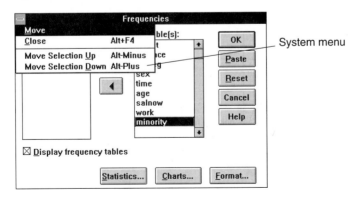

Move Selection Up. Moves the selected variable(s) up one position on the target list.

Move Selection Down. Moves the selected variable(s) down one position on the target list.

You can move multiple variables simultaneously if they are contiguous (grouped together). You cannot move noncontiguous groups of variables.

Stopping the SPSS Processor

If you inadvertently select a statistical analysis that you don't want, you can stop the SPSS processor. This is particularly useful if you are working with a large data file or have requested statistics for a large number of variables and the procedure takes a long time to execute. To halt the execution of a procedure, from the menus choose:

File
  Stop SPSS Processor

or press F3.

Microsoft Mail

If you are using Windows for Workgroups, you can access the Microsoft Mail facility. To send mail, from the menus choose:

File
  Send Mail...

This takes you directly to Microsoft Mail. For more information on Microsoft Mail, see your Windows for Workgroups documentation.

Other Utilities

The Utilities menu also contains the following features:

Grid Lines. Turns the display of grid lines in the Data Editor on and off.

Value Labels. Turns the display of value labels in the Data Editor on and off.

Auto New Case. Automatically creates new cases in the Data Editor.

Designate Window. Makes the active syntax or output window the designated window. Output is routed to the designated output window; command syntax is pasted into the designated syntax window.

35 Linking and Exchanging Information Between Applications

Windows supports two facilities for linking and exchanging files between applications: object linking and embedding, or **OLE**, and dynamic data exchange, or **DDE**. With OLE, you can link SPSS charts to other applications. If you are working in another application, you can use DDE to access and incorporate SPSS text, data, or charts.

When you use OLE to link SPSS charts to other applications, SPSS retains control of any changes made to the charts. Double-clicking on an SPSS chart linked to another application launches SPSS and opens the chart for editing. Any time you edit the chart in SPSS, the chart will be updated automatically in the other application if the file is open. If the file containing the linked chart is not open, the update will be automatic when you open the file.

When you access SPSS from another application and use DDE to incorporate SPSS text, data, or charts, control resides with the other application. You can edit or modify the transferred information without launching SPSS. If you edit that same information within SPSS, it remains unchanged in the other application until you request an update.

Object Linking and Embedding

Using the object linking and embedding facility, or OLE, you can link SPSS charts to other Windows applications that support this linking facility. Only SPSS charts, not text or data, can be linked. An SPSS chart can be linked to more than one document in a particular application and to more than one application concurrently. The information contained in the linked chart remains within SPSS, and SPSS controls any editorial changes. Any modifications made to the chart in SPSS are applied automatically in the other application if the file is open; if the file is not open, the changes are automatic when you open the file.

SPSS supports the linking, but not the embedding, capability of OLE. An alternate method of inserting an SPSS chart into another application is to copy and paste it.

Linking an SPSS Chart

Windows applications have slight variations in the exact commands used to link information. To link an SPSS chart to another application, follow these steps:

➊ Create and save the chart in SPSS. Make sure the chart is sized so that the text is readable, since the chart will be copied as a picture.

➋ Copy the chart to the clipboard by selecting Copy chart from the Edit menu.

➌ In the other application, select Paste Special... from the Edit menu. In some applications, you may need to press ⟨⇧Shift⟩ and hold it down while using the Edit menu.

➍ Select the Picture format (if there is a choice), and then select Paste Link. The size of the linked chart can vary depending on the requirements of the application receiving it.

To edit the chart, double-click on it in the other application. This starts SPSS (if it isn't already running) and opens the chart in an SPSS chart window. Changes to the chart in SPSS are automatically transferred to the linked chart in the other application.

Example of Linking

Suppose that in a report you want to include an SPSS chart that can be updated periodically. This example uses a report created in Microsoft Word for Windows 2.0. To link an SPSS chart to a Word document, follow these steps:

➊ Open SPSS and open the data file *bank.sav* (included with the SPSS Base system).

➋ Create a simple bar chart of job categories (*jobcat*).

➌ Edit and save the chart as *jobbars.cht*.

➍ From the menus choose:

Edit
  Copy Chart

This copies the chart to the clipboard.

➎ Minimize SPSS and open a new (or an existing) Word document.

➏ From the menus choose:

Edit
  Paste Special...

This opens the Paste Special dialog box.

➐ Select Picture and click on Paste Link.

The chart appears in the Word document.

Editing an SPSS Chart Linked to Word

To edit an SPSS chart linked to Word, follow these steps:

➊ Open the Word document containing the chart.

➋ Double-click on the chart. This launches SPSS (if it isn't already running) and opens the saved chart.

③ Edit the chart. For example, change the color of the bars in SPSS. The chart in Word also changes colors unless the field is locked (see the Word manual for information on locking and unlocking fields). You can observe the changes in both SPSS and Word by resizing the windows so that both are visible, or by pressing (Alt)-(Tab→) to switch between them.

④ In SPSS, save any changes you want to keep.

For more information on updating links or editing any linked object, consult the Word manual.

Alternative Method of Transferring Charts

You may want to use an SPSS chart in another application without creating a dynamic link to SPSS. When you select Copy Chart from the SPSS Edit menu, the chart is copied in picture format (MetafilePict). Some applications can read the picture format and separate it into meaningful editable objects.

Although you cannot embed an SPSS chart object in another application, you can paste a copied chart as a picture in Microsoft Word for Windows 2.0 and edit it using Microsoft Draw. For example:

① Open SPSS and open the data file *bank.sav*.

② Create a bar chart of job categories (*jobcat*) and click on Edit.

③ Double-click on the category axis. When the Category Axis dialog box opens, click on Labels....

④ From the Orientation drop-down list choose Staggered. Staggered axis labels will be easier to edit in Draw.

⑤ Save the chart as *jobstag.cht*.

⑥ From the menus choose:

Edit
  Copy Chart

This copies the chart to the clipboard.

⑦ Open a new (or existing) Word document.

⑧ From the menus choose:

Edit
  Paste Special...

This opens the Paste Special dialog box.

⑨ Select Picture and click on Paste.

This pastes the chart into the document. Since the pasted chart is not linked to SPSS, any changes made to the chart in SPSS will not be reflected in the Word document.

Editing an SPSS Chart Pasted into Word

If Microsoft Draw is installed (it comes with Word 2.0), you can edit a chart pasted into Word by following these steps:

1 Open the Word document containing the chart.

2 Double-click on the chart. This launches Microsoft Draw, with the chart ready to edit.

3 Edit the chart. For example, change the color of individual bars or change the type font and size. If you want to change the font of all the category labels at once, select them by holding down ⇧Shift while you click on each label.

4 When you are finished editing, choose:

File
  Exit and Return to [filename]

This returns the edited chart to the Word document.

Dynamic Data Exchange

If you are working in a Windows application, you can use the dynamic data exchange facility, or DDE, to request information from SPSS and instruct SPSS to execute commands. SPSS is available as a server for DDE—that is, another application (the client) can obtain information from SPSS through the DDE facility. SPSS supports the server, but not the client, capability of DDE. Without leaving the client application, you can use DDE statements to:

- Start SPSS (the *spsswin* directory must be on the DOS path).
- Open, close, and print files in SPSS.
- Perform SPSS procedures.
- Retrieve SPSS data, statistical output, and charts.
- Exit from SPSS, with the option to save open files.

If a DDE field in another application is linked to SPSS, any time you make changes in SPSS, you can update the links in the other application. In that way, you can avoid having to copy and paste the changes.

Using SPSS Results in a Report

Suppose you want to issue a periodic report that includes an SPSS analysis and employs the formatting capabilities of Microsoft Word for Windows 2.0. First, using the SPSS menu system, you run the analysis. Then, you write the report text in Word and insert DDE fields that link to the results of the SPSS analysis. At the end of the next time period, you can run an updated analysis in SPSS and include the results in the report simply by updating the links from Word.

If you are familiar with SPSS command syntax, you can produce a similar report by running all the SPSS commands directly from DDE fields in Word. If SPSS is not running when you insert the first DDE field connecting with SPSS, a dialog box asks if you want to open it.

To insert a DDE field in Word, you must specify an application name, a topic, and an item. The DDE application name of SPSS for Windows is spsswin. The DDE topics and items available for use with SPSS are discussed in detail in "DDE Specifications for SPSS" on p. 729. You may also need to set a DDETIMEOUT specification for Word in the *win.ini* file. See the Word manual or online Help for more information on DDE specifications.

An Analysis in SPSS

The following example illustrates the dynamic exchange of untabbed output, tabbed output, a chart, and part of a data file. It also illustrates how to run an SPSS command directly from Word. First, we will open SPSS and run several commands. If you paste each SPSS command before running it (see Chapter 4), you can save the syntax file and rerun the same commands periodically to update the report.

1 Start SPSS.

2 To select output preferences, from the menus choose:

Edit
  Preferences...

This opens the Preferences dialog box.

3 Click on Output.... in the Preferences dialog box.

This opens the Preferences Output dialog box.

4 In the Display group, make sure Commands and Resource messages are *not* selected. If they are currently selected, deselect them.

5 In the Page Headers group, select None.

6 In the Page Size group, select Infinite for Length.

Figure 35.1 Preferences Output dialog box settings for DDE

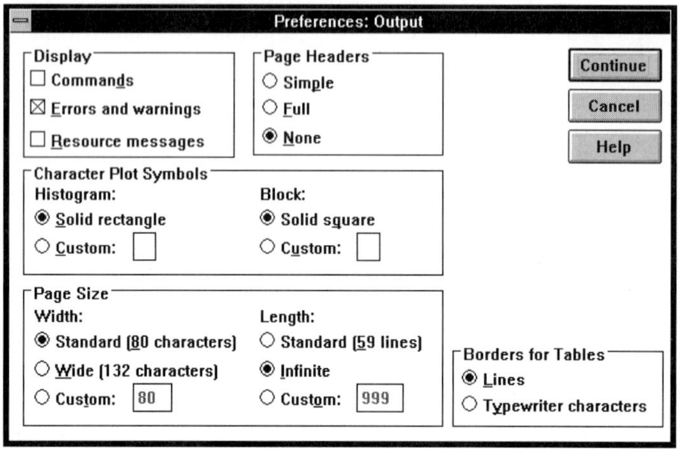

The settings shown in the Preferences Output dialog box ensure that the commands and resource messages will not be displayed in the output and that no page breaks will be transferred through DDE. Now you are ready to begin the analysis.

① Open the data file *bank.sav*.

② From the menus choose:

Statistics
  Summarize ▶
    Descriptives...

This opens the Descriptives dialog box.

③ Select variables *salbeg* and *salnow*.

④ Click on Options..., select Descending means, and click on Continue.

⑤ Click on OK. The results of the descriptive analysis appear in the !Output1 window.

⑥ To open a new SPSS output window, from the menus choose:

File
  New ▶
    SPSS Output

⑦ Click on the **[!]** pushbutton to make the new output window the designated output window.

⑧ From the menus choose:

Statistics
  Summarize ▶
    Frequencies...

This opens the Frequencies dialog box.

⑨ Select the variable *jobcat*.

⑩ Click on Charts..., select Bar Chart(s), and click on Continue.

⑪ Click on OK in the main Frequencies dialog box. A frequency table appears in the !Output2 window, and the chart appears in the Chart Carousel.

⑫ Click on Edit in the Chart Carousel. This places the chart in the window labeled Chart1, where you can change the color of the bars or other attributes of the chart.

⑬ Double-click on the label Clerical, and then click on Labels....

⑭ Change the label orientation to Staggered, click on Continue, and then click on OK.

⑮ Minimize the SPSS application window.

In SPSS, there are now four windows open: the Data Editor window, two output windows, and a chart window.

Transferring SPSS Results to Word

Now that you have generated output from your data in SPSS, you can transfer it to Word and include it in a report. To create a report in Word, follow these steps:

❶ Open a new document in Word, type some introductory text for the periodic report, and press ⏎Enter.

❷ Create a display style for untabbed SPSS output (which is formatted to be displayed in a fixed-pitch font). Base the new style on the Word style Normal, designate a fixed-pitch font, such as Courier, and assign it a name, such as *spss*.

❸ From the menus choose:

Insert
  Field...

This opens the Field dialog box.

❹ To get the frequencies output, highlight and replace the equals sign in the Field Code box with the following DDE command:

```
dde spsswin !output contents \*mergeformat
```

Do not type field characters { } before and after the DDE command; Word puts its own characters around the field. The DDE application name is spsswin, the topic is !output, and the item is contents. The specification *mergeformat allows you to make certain changes in the format that will be preserved when you update the link later. For more information about DDE syntax, see "DDE Specifications for SPSS" on p. 729.

⑤ Click on OK. Word brings the contents of the SPSS designated output window into the report text. The SPSS output will not be aligned in Word until you apply the display style created in step 2.

⑥ Highlight the text in the field, including the surrounding paragraph markers, and select spss from the drop-down list of styles. The resulting change into fixed-pitch font aligns the table of frequencies. Because you specified *mergeformat, updated output for the next periodic report should be formatted in fixed-pitch font.

⑦ Enter some more text of the report in Normal style and press ⏎Enter.

⑧ Insert another field and type the following in the Field Code box:

```
dde spsswin output1 tabbedcontents \*mergeformat
```

The topic output1 is the name of the window containing the output from the SPSS Descriptives procedure.

⑨ Click on OK. The tabbed Descriptives output is brought into the Word document in Normal style. Depending on your tab settings in Word, you may have to adjust the tabs. Because the text is tabbed, a fixed-pitch font is not necessary.

⑩ Insert a field and type the following in the Field Code box:

```
dde spsswin system "[means salbeg by sex]"
```

The brackets contain SPSS syntax that runs the MEANS command.

⑪ Click on OK. The results are returned to the Word document. (You may have to update the field by pressing F9.) Results are not written to an SPSS output window.

⑫ Insert a field and type the following in the Field Code box:

```
dde spsswin chart1 contents
```

SPSS returns the chart to the Word document. To adjust the size of the chart, click on it and drag the handles. To edit the chart, activate SPSS and make your changes. To update the link, click on the chart in Word and press F9. The changes will then take effect in the Word document.

⑬ Insert a field to bring the last four rows of data from SPSS, for variables *salbeg* through *age*. Type the following in the Field Code box:

```
dde spsswin !data "[salbeg age 470 474]"
```

The data are automatically in tabbed format and include data for the variables *salbeg*, *sex*, *time*, and *age*, for the last five cases in the data file. You might use this type of display to check on changes that were made to the data during the period between reports.

Updating the Links

The DDE links you have established allow you to update your periodic report as follows:

① Update your data file, rerun the same statistics in SPSS, and minimize SPSS.

② Open the report document in Word for Windows and update the links as described in the Word manual.

If you need the results of other procedures, you can run other SPSS commands directly from new fields inserted in Word.

DDE Specifications for SPSS

When you use DDE to exchange information with other applications, the code must have three elements: the application name, a topic, and an item within the topic. The DDE application name for SPSS for Windows is spsswin. The previous analysis illustrates several possible topics and items for use with DDE. The exact syntax format depends on the application. In Word, a DDE link has the following parts:

```
LinkType ApplicationName Topic Item
```

An example is shown in Figure 35.2.

Figure 35.2   Parts of a DDE command

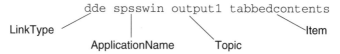

Whenever there is more than one word in an item, you must use quotation marks around the item, as in steps 10 and 13 on p. 728.

"TabbedContents" is useful for formatting output or other text containing columns so that you can use a proportional font. SPSS searches for a line that seems to have the most columns separated by more than two spaces and then uses it as a model to insert tabs. Data from the SPSS Data Editor are always tabbed.

Items Available When the Topic Is System

When you specify system as the DDE topic, you can request standard DDE information, such as available items or topics, by specifying one of the following three items:

sysitems. Lists available items.

formats. Lists available formats for file transfer.

topics. Lists available topics. You can use this item to find out which windows are open in SPSS.

When the DDE topic is system, you can also specify SPSS commands, surrounded by brackets and quotes. If this is a DDE REQUEST command, as in the Word example, the results of the command are sent to the other application and not written to an SPSS output window.

For a DDE EXECUTE command, the results are sent to an SPSS output window or a chart window. You can obtain the results by using a DDE REQUEST command with a window topic (see "Items Available When the Topic Is an SPSS Window," below). Some applications may require a WAIT command after the EXECUTE command so that SPSS can finish processing the command before the results are requested. See the documentation of the other application for specific requirements.

"[spss command]". Transfers text generated by the command in untabbed format. Use SPSS command syntax, with no period.

"[spss command]tabbedcontents". Transfers text generated by the command in tabbed format. Use SPSS command syntax, with no period.

The following system items execute SPSS commands. Each begins with an equals sign inside square brackets. The filename can be in either single or double quotation marks.

[=OpenFile('filename')]. Opens the named file within SPSS. The filename can be relative to the current directory, or you can specify a complete path. The current directory may be controlled by the other application. If you aren't sure what the current directory is, use the complete path. For data files, you can open files saved in any of the following formats: SPSS, SPSS portable, Excel, SYLK (symbolic link), Lotus 1-2-3, dBASE, or tab-delimited. The list of file types and recommended extensions for drag-and-drop files listed in Table 35.3 also applies to files opened with the DDE =OpenFile command.

[=Print('filename')]. Sends the named file to the printer. The file must be open in SPSS.

[=PrintAll('!Carousel')]. Sends all charts in the chart carousel to the printer.

[=Close('filename')]. Closes the file, asking first if you want to save it.

[=Exit()]. Exits from SPSS, asking first if you want to save each unsaved open file.

Items Available When the Topic Is an SPSS Window

In addition to the topic system, you can specify an open window in SPSS as a topic. You can specify either a designated window (with an exclamation point) or the name of the window. The topic names for designated windows and their associated items are listed in Table 35.1.

Open windows in SPSS can also be accessed by specifying as a topic a saved document name (such as *c:\spsswin\bank.sav*) or a window name (such as Chart1, Chart2, Output1, or Syntax2). The items and their results are shown in Table 35.2.

Table 35.1   Transferred information from SPSS designated windows

Topic	Item	Information Transferred
!output	contents	Contents of the designated output window
	tabbedcontents	Contents of the designated output window in tabbed format
!syntax	contents	Contents of the designated syntax window
	tabbedcontents	Contents of the designated syntax window in tabbed format
!data	tabbedcontents	Variable names and all data in the Data Editor, in tabbed format
	"tabbedcontents[range]"	Specified range of data (see "Range" on p. 732)
	"[range]"	
!carousel	contents	Chart currently displayed in Carousel
	chart number	Chart in the Carousel with the specified number, if the Carousel is open and the chart exists
	names	List of the charts in the Carousel, with chart numbers and descriptive labels

Table 35.2   Transferred information from saved documents or named windows

Type of Document	Item	Information Transferred
Chart	contents	Chart in picture format
Text (output or syntax)	contents	Text in untabbed format
	tabbedcontents	Text or data in tabbed format
Data	contents	Data in tabbed format
	tabbedcontents	
	"contents[range]"	Specified range of data in tabbed format (see "Range" on p. 732)
	"tabbedcontents[range]"	
	"[range]"	

If you specify the complete path for a saved document, you must enclose it in quotes. Some applications may have other requirements, such as special punctuation. In Word, for example, a field requesting the contents of an open data file can be specified as follows:

```
dde spsswin "c:\\spsswin\\bank.sav" tabbedcontents.
```

If you want a backslash included in a topic, Word requires a double backslash to distinguish it from other uses of the backslash.

Range

For data files, you can specify a range enclosed in brackets. The order is:

```
[StartVariable EndVariable StartRow EndRow]
```

The range of variables must be contiguous. The order of variables follows the order in the SPSS data file. If you specify a start variable and an end variable, the range includes those two variables and all the variables in between.

The range of cases must also be contiguous. Rows are specified by number. The row of variable names is row number 0 and the first row of data (first case) is row number 1. If you don't specify any rows, the variable names and all cases are included. For example, if the Data Editor window contains the file *bank.sav*,

```
dde spsswin !data "[salnow jobcat 0 5]"
```

returns the variable names *salnow*, *edlevel*, *work*, and *jobcat* (row 0) and data for those variables in cases 1 to 5. If you don't specify rows, all of the cases are returned. If you specify only a start row, all of the remaining cases are returned.

Dragging and Dropping Files

The drag-and-drop facility in Windows allows you to drag files out of the Windows File Manager and drop them onto the SPSS icon, an open SPSS window, or the running Print Manager icon.

Opening Files

Table 35.3 lists the file types that can be opened in SPSS using the drag-and-drop facility. The extensions listed for output (*.lst*) and syntax (*.sps*) files are required. The extensions listed for other file types are highly recommended since some other extensions can cause SPSS to identify the file type incorrectly.

Table 35.3   File types for drag and drop and DDE

File Type	Extension	SPSS Window
SPSS data	.sav	Data Editor
SPSS portable data	.por	Data Editor
Excel	.xls	Data Editor
SYLK (symbolic link)	.slk	Data Editor
Lotus 1-2-3, release3	.wk3	Data Editor
dBASE IV	.dbf	Data Editor
tab-delimited data	.dat	Data Editor
Syntax	.sps	Syntax
Output	.lst	Output
Chart	.cht	Chart

For Excel, SYLK, Lotus 1-2-3, and tab-delimited files, the first row of the data file should contain variable names or an error will result. To open spreadsheet and tab-delimited files that do not contain variable names in the first row, use the Open Data File dialog box on the SPSS File menu (see Chapter 2).

To open a file in SPSS, follow these steps:

1 Start SPSS. You can minimize SPSS or not.

2 Open the File Manager.

3 Use the mouse to select the document you want opened.

4 Holding down the mouse button, drag the document to the open SPSS window or the SPSS icon. As you drag it across the border of the File Manager, the file icon changes to the universal NO! symbol (a circle with a diagonal line through it). When it reaches the SPSS window or icon, it changes to a document symbol again (Figure 35.3). Release the mouse button to drop it on SPSS.

Figure 35.3   Drag-and-drop icons

In File Manager   Outside File Manager   On top of SPSS or
                                                       Print Manager icon

You can select several text or chart files at once and drag the group to SPSS. Hold down ⟨⇧Shift⟩ for contiguous files or ⟨Ctrl⟩ for noncontiguous files while selecting the files with the mouse. Multiple windows are opened in SPSS when you drop the files, one window for each file.

Another way to open a file with a registered extension is to double-click on its icon in the File Manager.

Printing Files

One way to print an SPSS file is to drop it on the running Print Manager icon. Follow these steps:

1 If the Print Manager is not running, open and minimize it.

2 Open the File Manager and select a directory.

3 Select the file you want printed.

4 Hold down the left mouse button to drag the file to the Print Manager icon and release the mouse button to drop it. As you drag the file across the border of the File Manager, the file icon changes to the universal NO! icon (a circle with a diagonal line through it).

When it reaches the Print Manager icon, it changes to a document symbol again. (See Figure 35.3.)

If SPSS is already open, the Print Manager prints the file. If not, SPSS opens, automatically requests a print, and then closes. For this to work, the file types must be registered with SPSS, as described in "Opening Files" on p. 732. You can print only one file at a time using this method.

36 Preferences

Many of the SPSS default settings can be replaced by user-specified values. Most of these changes remain in effect only for the duration of the session. However, some changes are persistent across SPSS sessions. These persistent default modifications are called **preferences**, and you can customize these preferences to meet your specific needs. These preferences include:

- Content and location of the SPSS journal file
- Working memory allocation
- Custom currency formats
- Plot symbols used in character-based charts and plots
- Colors, patterns, and other default preferences for high-resolution charts
- Output page width and length
- System information displayed in output windows
- Location of temporary files used during an SPSS session

The first time you start an SPSS session, the SPSS Startup Preferences dialog box opens automatically, as shown in Figure 36.1.

Figure 36.1   SPSS Startup Preferences dialog box

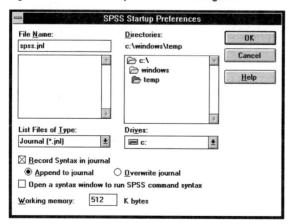

The startup preferences are a subset of the preferences available with the Preferences dialog box. Since you can modify the preference settings at any time and the new settings remain in effect across SPSS sessions, in most cases you can simply accept the default startup preferences.

To modify the SPSS preference settings during a session, from the menus choose:

Edit
  Preferences...

This opens the Preferences dialog box, as shown in Figure 36.2.

Figure 36.2 Preferences dialog box

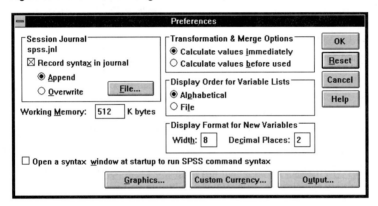

Session Journal

SPSS automatically creates and maintains a journal file of all commands run in an SPSS session. This includes commands entered and run in syntax windows and commands generated by dialog box choices. You can edit the journal file and use the commands again in other SPSS sessions.

❏ **Record syntax in journal**. Any SPSS command syntax generated in the session is recorded in the journal file. This is the default. You can turn the journal off and on during the session, saving selected sets of commands.

  ○ **Append**. Saves a journal of all SPSS sessions. The command syntax for each successive SPSS session is appended to the bottom of the journal file. This is the default.

  ○ **Overwrite**. Saves a journal of only the most recent SPSS session. Each time you start a new session, the journal file is overwritten.

Journal Filename and Location

By default, SPSS creates a journal file named *spss.jnl* in the *windows\temp* directory. To change the filename or directory location, click on File... in the Preferences dialog box. This opens the Preferences Journal File dialog box, as shown in Figure 36.3.

Figure 36.3   Preferences Journal File dialog box

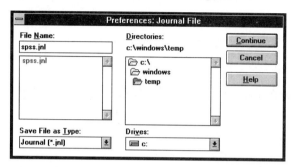

File Name. You can select a file from the list or you can type in a filename, a directory path and filename, or a wildcard search. By default, SPSS looks for all files in the current journal file directory with the extension *.jnl* and displays them on the list.

Save File as Type. Provides a wildcard search list of default file extensions for appropriate file types. The list contains the default extension for SPSS journal files (*.jnl*) and the wildcard search for all files (*.*).

Directories. To change the directory location, select the name of the directory on the Directories list. Directories below the current directory are denoted by closed file folder icons. Directories above the current directory are denoted by open file folder icons. The current directory is displayed above the list of directories and is also denoted by the last (lowest) open file folder icon.

Drives. To change the drive location, select a drive from the drop-down list of available drives.

Working Memory

You can allocate up to 16,000K bytes (16 megabytes) of virtual memory for workspace. The default is 512K. This is sufficient for most purposes. Unless SPSS tells you that there is insufficient memory to run a procedure, increasing the working memory allocation is usually not recommended, since this can actually decrease performance (make your computer slower) under some circumstances.

The new workspace allocation does not take effect until the next SPSS session. If the workspace allocation exceeds the available contiguous memory, SPSS allocates the available memory and indicates the amount in an alert box.

Open a Syntax Window at Startup

Syntax windows are text file windows used to enter, edit, and run SPSS commands. If you frequently work with command syntax, select Open a syntax window at startup to automatically open a syntax window at the beginning of each SPSS session. This is useful primarily for experienced SPSS users who prefer to work with command syntax instead of dialog boxes.

Transformation and Merge Options

Each time SPSS executes a command, it reads the data file. Some data transformations (for example, Compute, Recode) and file transformations (Add Variables and Add Cases) do not require a separate pass of the data, and execution of these commands can be delayed until SPSS reads the data to execute another command, such as a statistical procedure. There are two alternatives for the treatment of these transformations:

○ **Calculate values immediately**. Executes the requested transformation and reads the data file. This is the default. If the data file is large and you have multiple transformations, this may be time-consuming.

○ **Calculate values before used**. Delays execution of all transformations until SPSS encounters a command that requires a data pass. If the data file is large, this can save a significant amount of processing time. However, pending transformations limit what you can do in the Data Editor (see Chapter 3).

Display Order for Variable Lists

There are two alternatives for the display order of variables on dialog box source variable lists:

○ **Alphabetical**. Displays variables in alphabetical order. This is the default.

○ **File**. Displays variables in file order. This is the same order in which variables are displayed in the Data Editor window.

A change in variable display order takes effect the next time you open a data file. Display order affects only source variable lists. Selected variable lists always reflect the order in which variables were selected.

Display Format for New Variables

The default display format for new variables applies only to numeric variables. There is no default display format for new string variables.

Width. Total display width (including decimal positions) for new numeric variables. The maximum total width is 40 characters. The default is eight.

Decimal Places. Number of decimal positions for new numeric variables. The maximum number of decimal positions is 16. The default is two.

If a value is too large for the specified display format, SPSS first rounds decimal places and then converts values to scientific notation. Display formats do not affect internal data values. For example, the value 123456.78 may be rounded to 123457 for display, but the original unrounded value is used in any calculations.

Graphics

To specify new default setting for high-resolution graphics (charts and plots that appear in the Chart Carousel and chart windows), click on Graphics... in the Preferences dialog box. This opens the Preferences Graphics dialog box, as shown in Figure 36.4.

Figure 36.4 Preferences Graphics dialog box

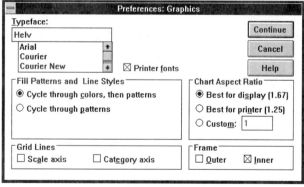

With the exception of changes in Chart Aspect Ratio, any changes you make in the default settings affect only new charts and charts still in the Chart Carousel. Charts in chart windows are not affected.

Note: Some chart modifications may cause some chart attributes to revert to the Preferences default settings. These modifications include changing chart types (Gallery menu) and transposing data (Series menu).

Typeface. The initial type font for new charts. Select a font from the list.

❑ **Printer fonts**. Displays only installed printer fonts on the list of available fonts.

Fill Patterns and Line Styles. The initial assignment of colors and/or patterns for new charts. You can choose one of the following alternatives:

○ **Cycle through colors, then patterns**. Use the default palette of 14 colors and then add patterns to colors.

○ **Cycle through patterns**. Use patterns only. Do not use colors. For line charts, the cycle includes four line styles within four line weights to make 16 possible combinations. For bar charts, area charts, and pie charts, the cycle includes seven fill patterns (including solid). For scatterplots, the cycle includes 28 available marker types.

Grid Lines. You can choose one or both of the following:

❑ **Scale axis**. Displays horizontal grid lines on the scale axis.

❑ **Category axis**. Displays vertical grid lines on the category axis.

Chart Aspect Ratio. The width-to-height ratio of the outer frame of charts. Charts displayed in chart windows, as well as new charts and charts in the Chart Carousel, are affected by a change in the Chart Aspect Ratio box. You can choose one of the following for the width-to-height ratio of charts:

○ **Best for display (1.67)**. This makes full use of the available space in a maximized window in VGA mode.

○ **Best for printer (1.25)**. This makes full use of an 8 1/2 × 11-inch page in landscape (horizontal) mode.

○ **Custom**. You can specify your own width-to-height ratio from 0.5 to 2.0. Values below 1 make charts that are taller than they are wide. Values over 1 make charts that are wider than they are tall. A value of 1 produces a square chart.

Frame. You can choose one or both of the following:

❑ **Outer**. Draws a frame around the entire chart, including titles and legends.

❑ **Inner**. Draws a frame around the graphic portion of the chart.

Custom Currency Formats

You can specify up to five custom currency display formats. To create a custom currency format, click on Custom Currency... in the Preferences dialog box. This opens the Preferences Custom Currency Formats dialog box, as shown in Figure 36.5.

Figure 36.5   Preferences Custom Currency Formats dialog box

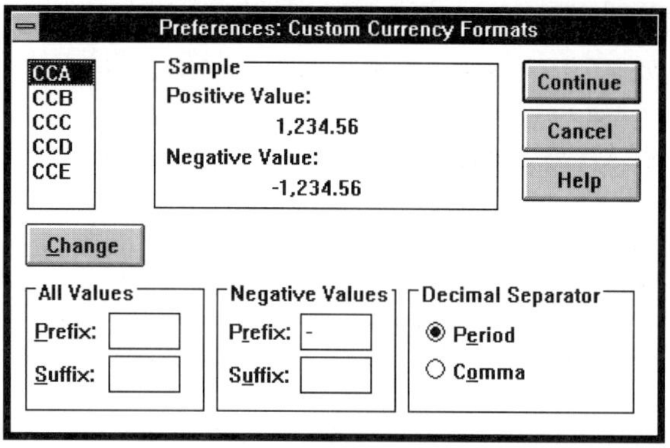

The five custom currency format names are CCA, CCB, CCC, CCD, and CCE. You cannot change the format names or add new ones. By default, all five custom currency formats use a minus sign for the negative prefix and do not have a negative suffix. To modify a custom currency format, select the format name from the source list, make the desired changes, and then click on Change.

All Values. Prefix and suffix specifications appear with both positive and negative values.

Negative Values. Prefix and suffix specifications appear only with negative values. For example, you may want to indicate negative values with parentheses instead of a leading minus sign.

Decimal Separator. The decimal indicator can be either a period or a comma.

Output

Output preferences affect the text-based results of your SPSS session displayed in the output windows. Changes to output preferences affect all output windows. Changes to output preferences affect only output generated after the modification is made; output generated earlier in the session is not affected.

To modify the display of system information, page-size specifications, symbols used in character-based plots, and borders for tabular data, click on Output... in the Preferences dialog box. This opens the Preferences Output dialog box, as shown in Figure 36.6.

Figure 36.6   Preferences Output dialog box

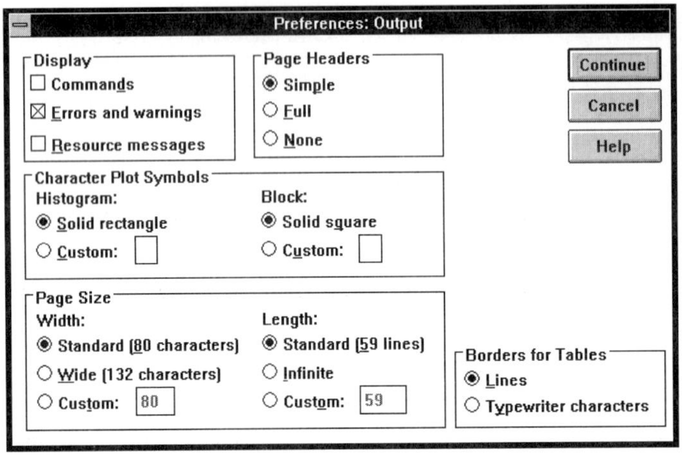

Display. In addition to the results of statistical procedures, SPSS can also display a variety of system information in the output windows.

❏ **Commands**. Displays SPSS command syntax in the output window. Most dialog box choices generate underlying SPSS command syntax, and it is often helpful to have a record of how certain results were obtained.

❏ **Errors and warnings**. Displays all SPSS error and warning messages in the output window. These are displayed by default. Deselect this item to suppress the display of error and warning messages.

❏ **Resource messages**. Displays resource utilization messages, including elapsed time, available memory, and memory required to run each statistical procedure.

Page Headers. This controls the display of page markers, titles, and subtitles in output windows.

○ **Simple**. Inserts page markers between output pages and starts output from each procedure on a new page. Output page titles are not displayed. This is the default.

○ **Full**. Inserts page markers between output pages, starts output from each procedure on a new page, and displays output page titles and subtitles.

○ **None**. Turns off page headers. Page markers are not inserted between output pages, new output blocks can start anywhere on a page, and output page titles and subtitles are not displayed.

Character Plot Symbols. For low-resolution, character-based charts and plots, you can select the plot symbols used in the output display.

Histogram. You can choose one of the following alternatives for histogram plot characters:

- ○ **Solid rectangle**. Uses graphical characters to display a solid rectangle. This is the default.

- ○ **Custom**. User-specified, standard typewriter character. Only one character can be specified. For example, each bar of the histogram can be represented by a string of asterisks.

Block. You can choose one of the following alternatives for block characters used in bar charts and icicle plots:

- ○ **Solid square**. Uses graphical characters to display solid squares for bar charts and icicle plots. This is the default.

- ○ **Custom**. User-specified standard typewriter character. Only one character can be specified. For example, each bar can be represented by a string of pound signs (#).

Use the Custom options for plotting symbols to specify standard typewriter characters if you want to open the output file later in another software application.

Page Size. In SPSS, page size is defined by the number of characters per line and the number of lines per page. The default settings of 80 characters per line and 59 lines per page are based on the default font size (10 pt) and the default paper size and orientation (8 1/2 × 11, portrait). For more information on fonts and printing, see Chapter 33.

Width. You can choose one of the following alternatives for width:

- ○ **Standard**. 80 characters per line. This is the default.

- ○ **Wide**. 132 characters per line.

- ○ **Custom**. User-specified number of characters per line. The minimum is 80. The maximum is 255.

Length. You can choose one of the following alternatives for length:

- ○ **Standard**. 59 lines per page. This is the default.

- ○ **Infinite**. Output appears as one continuous page.

- ○ **Custom**. User-specified number of lines per page. The minimum is 24. The maximum is 9999.

Borders for Tables. You can use either extended ASCII characters or standard typewriter characters to create borders around crosstabulations and other tabular output.

- ○ **Lines**. Uses graphical characters to create solid horizontal and vertical lines for tables. This is the default.

○ **Typewriter characters.** Uses standard typewriter characters to create horizontal and vertical borders for tables. The dash (–) is used for horizontal lines, the vertical bar symbol (|) is used for vertical lines, and the plus sign (+) is used for the intersection of vertical and horizontal lines. Select this option if you want to open the output file later in another software application.

Using SPSS Graphical Characters

SPSS uses a special graphical character set not available with other software applications. If you copy output that contains graphical characters from SPSS into another application via the Windows clipboard, SPSS automatically converts these graphical characters to standard typewriter characters.

• Table borders are converted to a dash (–) for horizontal lines, a vertical bar symbol (|) for vertical lines, and a plus sign (+) for the intersection of vertical and horizontal lines.

• The solid rectangle used in character-based histograms is converted to an asterisk (*).

• The solid square used in character-based bar charts and icicle plots is converted to a capital letter X.

If you save an SPSS output file with special graphical characters and then open it in another application (rather than cutting or copying and pasting), no conversion takes place, and you'll probably end up with something that looks like hieroglyphics.

Preferences File (spsswin.ini)

Preferences are stored in the *windows* directory in a file named *spsswin.ini*. This file contains all the user-controllable settings that are used in all SPSS sessions, including:

• Any selections made in the Preferences dialog boxes

• Font selections from the Font dialog box

• Utilities menu settings for grid lines, value labels, and status bar

• Chart color palette settings from the Colors dialog box

Figure 36.7 shows the initial settings in the *spsswin.ini* file the first time you start SPSS.

Figure 36.7   Initial contents of spsswin.ini file

```
[SPSSWIN]
Journal=c:\windows\temp\SPSS.JNL
Append=1
WorkSpace=512
OpenInput=0

[SET]
Journal=ON
```

Figure 36.8 shows a modified *spsswin.ini* file after various changes to settings during an SPSS session.

Figure 36.8   Modified spsswin.ini file

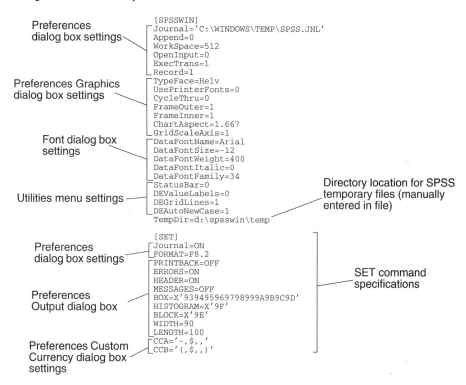

Editing the spsswin.ini File

The *spsswin.ini* file is a simple text file that can be edited with any text editor (for example, the Windows Notepad). Most settings can be easily modified by making dialog box and menu selections in an SPSS session, which is the recommended method for changing those settings. The only valid additional settings are SET subcommand specifications not available in dialog boxes and the directory location for SPSS temporary files.

SPSS is fairly tolerant of invalid specifications in the *spsswin.ini* file, either ignoring them or ignoring the entire file and using the initial default settings. If you somehow manage to alter the file in a manner that makes it impossible for SPSS to run, simply delete the file and restart SPSS. If there is no *spsswin.ini* file, SPSS opens the Startup Preferences dialog box and creates a new *spsswin.ini* file.

SET Command Specifications

The [SET] section of the *spsswin.ini* file contains any settings from the Preferences dialog boxes that also have SET command equivalents. You can add any additional SET subcommands that are valid in SPSS for Windows. Each subcommand must appear on a separate line (without a preceding slash).

Location of SPSS Temporary Files

SPSS creates various temporary files during a session. Depending on the size of your data file and the type of analysis you perform, these files may require a considerable amount of disk space. By default, SPSS temporary files are placed in the *windows\temp* directory. If the disk partition or drive containing the *windows\temp* directory does not have sufficient space, you can specify another location for the SPSS temporary files by adding the following line anywhere in the [SPSSWIN] section (*not* in the [SET] section) of your *spsswin.ini* file:

`TempDir=[directory path]`

For example, to place the SPSS temporary files in the *temp* directory of the D drive, you would specify:

`TempDir=D:\temp`

The directory must already exist (SPSS will not create a new directory). If SPSS can't find the directory, the *windows\temp* directory is used.

37 Window Control

The Window menu controls the placement and appearance of windows that are already open. The first two menu items, Tile and Cascade, place windows in visual arrangements that allow you to identify and activate any one of them easily. The other items apply to individual windows. To open additional syntax, output, or data windows, use the File menu.

Tile

To tile the display of open windows, from the menus choose:

Window
 Tile

This rearranges and resizes the open windows with no overlap so that you can see all of them at once, as shown in Figure 37.1. The active window is placed in the upper left corner of the SPSS application window.

Figure 37.1   Tiled windows

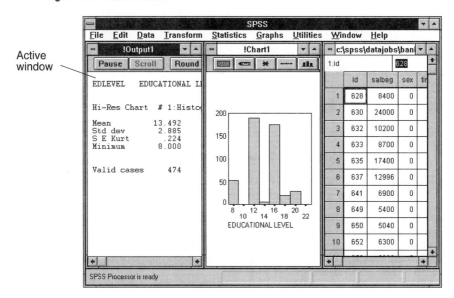

To activate another tiled window, click anywhere within it. If you activate a window and then click on its Maximize button, it expands to fill the SPSS application window. Clicking the Restore button sends the window back to its place in the tiled set. You can also resize tiled windows by dragging the sides or corners.

Cascade

To cascade the display of open windows, from the menus choose:

Window
  Cascade

The windows overlap so that you can see the title bar of each window, as shown in Figure 37.2. The active window appears in front of the others. To activate another window and bring it forward, click anywhere on the visible portion.

Figure 37.2   Cascaded windows

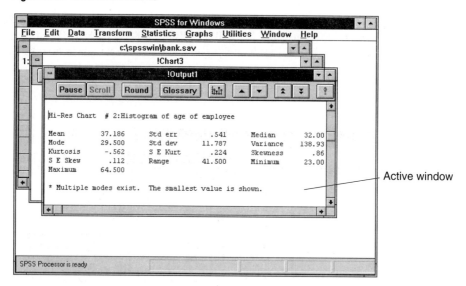

Icon Bar

Most windows have icon bars that contain pushbuttons or drop-down menus that provide quick access to special features of the windows. By default, windows display their icon bars. If you want more room in a window for the text or chart display, you can hide the icon bar. To hide or display the icon bar in the active window, from the menus choose:

Window
  Icon Bar

When the icon bar in the active window is displayed, there is a check beside it on the Window menu.

Status Bar

The status bar at the bottom of the SPSS application window indicates the status of the SPSS Processor, current command, number of cases processed so far, and whether a filter, weight, or split-file command has been turned on. To hide or display the status bar, from the menus choose:

Window
  Status Bar

When the status bar is displayed, a check mark appears beside it on the Window menu. In Figure 37.3, the status bar is displayed at the bottom of the screen. The chart window in the middle has its icon bar displayed, while the output window on the left has a hidden icon bar.

Figure 37.3 Window menu, icon bars, and status bar

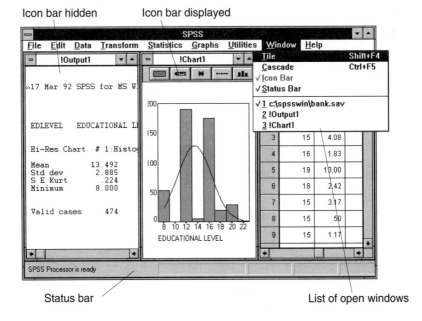

Selecting a Window from the Menu

At the bottom of the Window menu is a list of open windows, whether iconized or not. The active window has a check mark beside it. You can activate and display one of the other windows by selecting it from the menu. When you do so, the menu bar at the top of the SPSS application window changes to match the type of window activated.

38 Getting Help

SPSS for Windows uses the standard Windows Help system to provide information you need to use SPSS and to understand the results. This chapter contains a brief description of the Help system and the kinds of help provided with SPSS for Windows.

The best way to find out more about the Help system is to use it. You can ask for help in any of these ways:

- Click on the Help pushbutton in an SPSS dialog box.
- Select a topic from the Help menu in an SPSS window.
- Press [F1] at any time in SPSS.
- For specialized help, click on the Glossary pushbutton in an SPSS output window or the Syntax button in a syntax window.

Windows Help

When you ask for help, SPSS calls the Windows Help application *winhelp.exe*, which displays information from the Help database that was installed with SPSS. The menus and controls in the Help window are managed by Windows Help. SPSS for Windows and Windows Help run concurrently, along with any other applications that you have opened. You switch back and forth between them with a mouse click, the Task Manager, or any of the other standard Windows techniques.

Inside Windows Help

When a Help window (see Figure 38.1) is active, you can move from topic to topic with the pushbuttons across the top of the window: Contents, Search, Back, History, << (browse backward), and >> (browse forward).

Figure 38.1   Help window

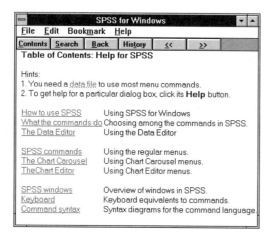

Within the text of a Help topic, there are hypertext links to other topics. These appear as underlined words and may be in color. Some of them cause Windows Help to display another topic (you can return with the Back button). Others cause another topic to "pop up" in front of the current one until you click the mouse or press a key.

For more information on Windows Help, use the Help menu in the Help window.

Copying Help Text

The Windows Help application allows you to copy some or all of any Help topic to the Windows clipboard. To copy Help text, from the Help menu choose:

Edit
  Copy...

This opens the Copy dialog box, as shown in Figure 38.2.

Figure 38.2   Copying Help text

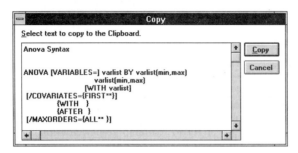

Highlight the text you want to copy and then click on the Copy pushbutton. From there, you can paste the text into an output window, a syntax window, the Windows Notepad, or a word processor.

Types of Help Available

The SPSS Help system provides the following types of assistance:

Help for dialog boxes. Each SPSS dialog box has a Help pushbutton that takes you directly to a topic describing the use of that dialog box. This is the fastest way to learn how to use a dialog box.

Help menu. The Contents selection on the SPSS Help menu takes you to the table of contents of the Help system. Each topic listed there functions as a menu from which you can choose other topics. In this way, you can reach any topic in the Help system, although you may need to navigate through several menus on the way.

Information on what menu commands do. To find out what a menu command does, press ⇧Shift-F1, release, and then select the command from the menu. (If you use a mouse, the pointer will change into a distinctive question-mark pointer as you move it onto the menu bar.) When you select the command, SPSS does not execute it. Instead, it displays a brief description of what the command does. The same Help topic also describes other commands on that menu so that you can compare related commands.

You can also get this information by selecting What Commands Do from the Help menu.

Output glossary. The SPSS Glossary contains definitions of terms that appear in the statistical output displayed by SPSS for Windows. Click on the Glossary pushbutton in an SPSS output window, and then select the term from the scrolling menu. The Search pushbutton in a Help window speeds up this process, since there are more than 1000 terms in the glossary.

You can also select Glossary from the Help menu.

SPSS Command Syntax Charts

Syntax diagrams for the SPSS command language are available to assist you if you work with command syntax in a syntax window. Press the Syntax pushbutton, and then select a command from the scrolling list. If the window already contains command syntax, the Syntax pushbutton takes you directly to the diagram for the command you are working on.

You can also select Syntax from the Help menu.

Figure 38.3 Syntax Help window

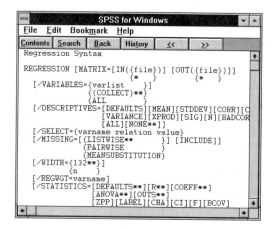

To see a syntax diagram as you work in a syntax window, you must reduce the main SPSS application window so that the Help window fits beside or below it. If you prefer, you can copy a topic (use the Edit menu in Windows Help) and paste it into the SPSS syntax window for reference. Don't try to run the syntax diagram, though!

Appendix A
Command Syntax

This appendix provides an overview of SPSS command syntax. For detailed information on specific commands, see the *SPSS Base System Syntax Reference Guide*.

A Few Useful Terms

All terms in the SPSS command language fall into one or more of the following categories:

- **Keyword**. A word already defined by SPSS to identify a command, subcommand, or specification. Most keywords are, or resemble, common English words.
- **Command**. A specific instruction that controls the execution of SPSS.
- **Subcommand**. Additional instructions on SPSS commands. A command can contain more than one subcommand, each with its own specifications.
- **Specifications**. Instructions added to a command or subcommand. Specifications may include subcommands, keywords, numbers, arithmetic operators, variable names, and special delimiters.

Each command begins with a command keyword (which may contain more than one word). The command keyword is followed by at least one blank space and then any additional specifications. For example:

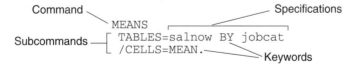

Syntax Rules

Keep in mind the following simple rules when editing and writing command syntax:

- Each command must begin on a new line and end with a period (.).

- Most subcommands are separated by slashes (/). The slash before the first subcommand on a command is usually optional.
- Variable names must be spelled out fully.
- Text included within apostrophes or quotation marks must be contained on a single line.
- Each line of command syntax cannot exceed 80 characters.
- A period (.) must be used to indicate decimals, regardless of your Windows international setting.
- Variable names ending in a period can cause errors in commands created by the dialog boxes. You cannot create such variable names in the dialog boxes, and you should generally avoid them.

SPSS command syntax is case insensitive, and three-letter abbreviations can be used for many command specifications. You can use as many lines as you want to specify a single command. You can add space or break lines at almost any point where a single blank is allowed, such as around slashes, parentheses, arithmetic operators, or between variable names. For example:

```
FREQUENCIES
 VARIABLES=JOBCAT SEXRACE
 /PERCENTILES=25 50 75
 /BARCHART.
```

and

```
freq var=jobcat sexrace /percent=25 50 75 /bar.
```

are both acceptable alternatives that generate the same results.

Include Files

For SPSS command files run via the SPSS INCLUDE command, the syntax rules are slightly different:

- Each command must begin in the first column of a new line.
- Continuation lines must be indented at least one space.
- The period at the end of the command is optional.

If you generate command syntax by pasting dialog box choices into a syntax window, the format of the commands is suitable for both INCLUDE files and commands run in a syntax window.

Commands Available Only with Syntax

The commands in Table A.1 cannot be obtained through the dialog box interface and can be obtained only by typing command syntax in a syntax window.

Table A.1   SPSS commands available only with command syntax

Command	Alternative
ADD VALUE LABELS	Data menu: Define Variable
BEGIN-END DATA	Enter data in Data Editor
BREAK	
CLEAR TRANSFORMATIONS	
COMMENT	
DO IF	
DO REPEAT	
DOCUMENT	
DROP DOCUMENTS	
END CASE	
END FILE	
ERASE	
EXECUTE	
FILE HANDLE	
FILE LABEL	
FILE TYPE	
FIT	
FORMATS	Data menu: Define Variable
GET SAS	
INCLUDE	
INPUT PROGRAM	
LEAVE	
LOOP-END LOOP	
Macro facility (!DEFINE)	
MATRIX DATA	
MCONVERT	
MODEL NAME	
N OF CASES	Transform menu: Select Cases
NUMERIC	Data menu: Define Variable
PLOT	Graph menu: Scatter
PRESERVE	
PRINT	
PRINT EJECT	
PRINT FORMATS	Data menu: Define Variable
PRINT SPACE	

Table A.1   SPSS commands available only with command syntax (Continued)

Command	Alternative
PROCEDURE OUTPUT	
READ MODEL	
RECORD TYPE	
REFORMAT	Data menu: Define Variable
RENAME VARIABLES	Data menu: Define Variable
REPEATING DATA	
REREAD	
RESTORE	
SAVE MODEL	
SET	Edit menu: Preferences
SHOW	Edit menu: Preferences
STRING	Data menu: Define Variable
TEMPORARY	
TSET	
TSHOW	
UPDATE	
VECTOR	
WRITE FORMATS	Data menu: Define Variable
XSAVE	

Appendix B
Commands Not Available in SPSS for Windows

Table B.1 and Table B.2 list the SPSS commands and SET subcommands not supported in SPSS for Windows.

Table B.1   Unsupported commands

EDIT	HOST	POINT
GET BMDP	INFO	SAVE SCSS
GET SCSS	KEYED DATA LIST	UNNUMBERED
HELP	NUMBERED	

Table B.2   Unsupported SET subcommands

ENDCMD	SCRIPTTAB	TB2
DUMP	TBFONTS	XSORT
NULLINE	TROFFTAB	
MXERRS	TB1	

Appendix C
Production Mode

<hr>

When you start an SPSS session by double-clicking on the SPSS icon in the Program Manager, SPSS opens in **manager mode**. In manager mode, you interactively analyze data using menus or SPSS command syntax. Based on examination of results, you can perform additional analyses in the same session.

In **production mode**, you submit a syntax file containing command syntax, and SPSS produces an output file and any charts requested. SPSS runs unattended and terminates after executing the last command, so you can perform other tasks while it runs. Production mode is useful if you often run the same set of time-consuming analyses, such as weekly reports. Production mode requires some knowledge of SPSS command syntax (see Appendix A).

Running SPSS in Production Mode

To run a command syntax file in production mode:

1. Change the extension of the command syntax file to *.inc*. For example, if the filename is *prodjob.sps*, rename the file *prodjob.inc*.

2. Double-click on the file in the File Manager, as shown in Figure C.1.

Figure C.1   Starting production mode from the File Manager

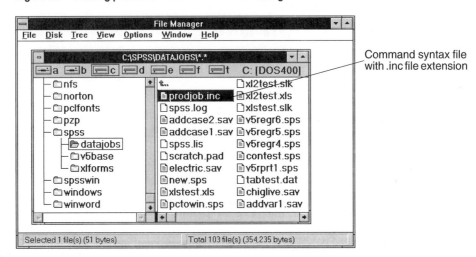

Command syntax file
with .inc file extension

Output File

SPSS creates an output file with the same name as the command syntax file and the file extension *.lst*. For example, for the command syntax file *prodjob.inc*, the output file is *prodjob.lst*. The output file is saved in the same directory as the command syntax file. If an output file with that name already exists, SPSS appends the results to the end of the file.

Chart Files

Chart names are assigned by adding a sequential number and the extension *.cht* to the first five characters of the command syntax filename. For example, for the command syntax file *prodjob.inc*, SPSS would assign the chart filenames *prodj1.cht*, *prodj2.cht*, *prodj3.cht*, etc. The extension of an existing chart file with the same filename as a chart created during the SPSS run is changed to *.bak* to prevent accidental overwriting.

Running Production Mode with Options

Production mode also provides options for changing the directory for output files, specifying data files, overwriting output files, and changing the SPSS working memory (virtual memory) allocation.

To run SPSS in production mode with optional specifications, from the Windows Program Manager choose:

File
  Run...

This opens the Run dialog box, as shown in Figure C.2.

Figure C.2   Run dialog box

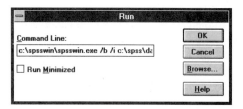

1. Enter the directory path and name of the SPSS program file (*spsswin.exe*) on the command line. The directory containing *spsswin.exe* is the directory in which SPSS was installed. The command line in Figure C.2 indicates that the SPSS program file is in the directory *c:\spsswin*.

2. After the directory path and SPSS program filename, enter /b to signal production mode.

3. After /b, enter /i followed by the directory path and filename of the command syntax file.

For example, to run the same command syntax file as in Figure C.1, you would enter

```
c:\spsswin\spsswin.exe /b /i c:\spss\datajobs\prodjob.inc
```

These are the minimum specifications to run SPSS in production mode from the Run dialog box. Optional specifications are discussed in the following sections.

Changing the Output Directory

By default, the output file and any chart files are saved in the same directory as the command syntax file. You can change the directory for output and chart files by specifying a directory path after the /b switch and before the /i switch.

Overwriting an Existing Output File

By default, if the output file already exists, results are appended to it. To overwrite an existing file, enter /r on the command line.

Overriding the Default Working Memory Allocation

By default, the working memory allocation defined in the Preferences file is used (see Chapter 36). To use a different allocation, enter /s followed by a number and the letter k (for kilobytes) or m (for megabytes) on the command line. If the letter is omitted, k is assumed. For example, /s 1.5m allocates 1.5 megabytes of workspace for the SPSS run.

The default 512K allocation is enough workspace for running most procedures on a moderate-size data file. In some circumstances, SPSS requires more workspace. For example, you may want a large number of transformations or crosstabulations. SPSS sometimes displays messages to indicate that you must allocate more memory to run a particular job. If you are doing a large number of transformations and you get a message that the job cannot be completed because of insufficient memory, you can estimate how much space is needed. For example, if about half the transformations were done before the message appeared, you can double the amount of workspace. Some messages tell you how much more workspace is needed.

Opening an SPSS Data File

By default, SPSS assumes that the command syntax file contains commands for opening or defining an SPSS data file (for example, GET, IMPORT, or DATA LIST). Optionally, you can specify the data file to be opened on the command line instead of in the command syntax file. Enter /d followed by the directory path and filename of the data file on the command line. If the file is not found or is not an SPSS data file, the SPSS run terminates. If command syntax in the syntax file requests that a different data file be opened, that data file is used in the SPSS run.

Printing Results

To automatically print the results from your production run, use one of the following command line switches:

/p   *Prints all results.*

/po   *Prints only character-based output.*

/pg   *Prints only high-resolution graphics.*

If your Windows Printer Setup is set to print to a file, all high-resolution charts are printed to a single file, with each chart on a separate page. If your Printer Setup is set to print to a specific filename, the /p switch will only create one print file, and any high-resolution charts will overwrite any character-based output.

Building a Syntax File

A syntax file containing SPSS command syntax is required to run SPSS in production mode. One way to build a syntax file is to manually enter syntax and save the syntax file. You can do this in a syntax window in an SPSS session or using any text editor or word processing software that saves files in text format.

There are three ways in which SPSS can help build your syntax file. These methods are usually faster than manually entering command syntax, and they minimize the chance of syntax errors. Each method involves running SPSS in manager mode and saving and editing the command syntax generated in the session.

Pasting Syntax from Dialog Boxes

The easiest way to build command syntax is to paste dialog box selections into a syntax window in an SPSS manager session. To do so, make dialog box choices for the analyses you want to perform. When you click on Paste, command syntax based on your dialog box choices is pasted into a syntax window (for more information on pasting command syntax, see Chapter 4). Save the text file from the syntax window and specify it as the syntax file on your command line in production mode.

Editing Syntax in an Output File

You can also save command syntax in an output file from an SPSS session that performs the analyses you want. To use this method, display of command syntax in the output must be selected in the Preferences dialog box (see Chapter 36). When SPSS runs your dialog box choices, it writes command syntax to an output file along with the results of your analyses. For example, Figure C.3 shows command syntax and output for descriptive statistics and bivariate correlations procedures.

Figure C.3   Unedited output file

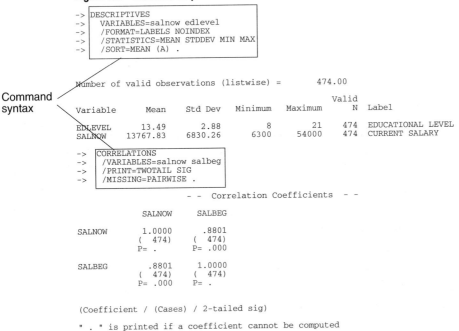

To create a syntax file, save only the command syntax to a file. You can do this by cutting and pasting the command syntax to another file or deleting everything but the command syntax from the output file. Make sure to remove any headers, titles, error and warning messages, and the right arrows (–>) that precede command syntax. Note, however, that any errors in the output must be resolved prior to the production mode run or the run will not complete successfully.

Figure C.4 shows an edited version of Figure C.3 that can be used as a syntax file in a production mode run. Since Figure C.4 does not contain syntax that opens a data file, a data file must be specified on the command line.

Figure C.4   Edited output file

```
DESCRIPTIVES
  VARIABLES=salnow edlevel
  /FORMAT=LABELS NOINDEX
  /STATISTICS=MEAN STDDEV MIN MAX
  /SORT=MEAN (A) .

CORRELATIONS
  /VARIABLES=salnow salbeg
  /PRINT=TWOTAIL SIG
  /MISSING=PAIRWISE .
```

Editing Syntax in a Journal File

By default, SPSS records all commands executed during a session in a journal file named *spss.jnl*. (See Chapter 36 for more information on name, location, and contents of the journal file.)

The journal file is a text file that can be edited like any other text file, and you can create a syntax file by editing the journal file. Remove any error or warning messages. Note, however, that any errors must be resolved prior to the production mode run or the run will not complete successfully.

Save the edited journal file with a different filename. Since SPSS automatically appends or overwrites the journal file for every session—including production mode sessions —attempting to use the same filename for a syntax file and the journal file may yield some unexpected and unwanted results.

Figure C.5 shows a journal file for an SPSS run that opens a data file, creates a variable *y* based on the values of variable *x*, and displays descriptive statistics for each variable. In addition to the SPSS command syntax, there is a data-specific warning message.

Figure C.5   Unedited journal file

```
GET FILE='c:\programs\mydata.sav' .
EXECUTE .
COMPUTE y = 10 / x .
EXECUTE .
>Warning # 511
>A division by zero has been attempted on the indicated command.  The result
>has been set to the system-missing value.
DESCRIPTIVES
 VARIABLES=x y
 /FORMAT=LABELS NOINDEX
 /STATISTICS=MEAN STDDEV MIN MAX
 /SORT=MEAN (A) .
```

The warning message has been deleted in Figure C.6. Only SPSS command syntax remains in the file, which can be specified as the syntax file on the command line.

Figure C.6   Edited journal file

```
GET FILE='c:\programs\mydata.sav' .
EXECUTE .
COMPUTE y = 10 / x .
EXECUTE .
DESCRIPTIVES
 VARIABLES=x y
 /FORMAT=LABELS NOINDEX
 /STATISTICS=MEAN STDDEV MIN MAX
 /SORT=MEAN (A) .
```

Appendix D
Working with Large Data Files

There is no defined limit to the number of variables that can be contained in an SPSS data file. Using command syntax, the system has been tested with up to 32,000 variables in a data file. However, there is a Windows limitation that effectively restricts the number of variables that can be accessed from dialog boxes to approximately 4500 (depending on the length of variable names). If your file contains a larger number of variables, only the first 4500 will appear on dialog box source lists.

If you need to work with data files that contain more than 4500 variables, you can either enter and run SPSS commands in a syntax window or you can use command syntax to create a subset of variables for use in the dialog box interface.

This appendix provides a brief overview of commands that you can use to read or save a subset of variables from a data file. For information on how to enter and run commands in a syntax window, see Chapter 4. For detailed information on individual commands, see the *SPSS Base System Syntax Reference Guide*.

Using Command Syntax to Create a Subset of Variables

The SPSS commands GET, SAVE, IMPORT, EXPORT, GET TRANSLATE, and MATCH FILES all have two optional subcommands for specifying variables to include or exclude:

- KEEP indicates variables that you want to keep. The order of variables on the KEEP subcommand determines the file order of variables in the working data file.

- DROP indicates variables that you want to drop.

For example, the command

```
GET FILE='bigfile.sav'
 /KEEP id age income index01 TO index99.
```

creates a working data file with only the specified variables and ignores any other variables that may be contained in the data file *bigfile.sav* (the keyword TO indicates consecutive variables in file order).

If it's easier to specify the variables you *don't* need, use the DROP subcommand, as in:

```
SAVE FILE='notsobig.sav'
 /DROP shoesize favcolr.
```

Adding Variables and Combining Subsets

There are at least two reasons why you might want or need to add variables from the original data file or combine subsets of variables in the working data file:

- If you create any new variables in the working data file, the only way to use those new variables with other variables not included in the subset is to add the other variables from the original data file or merge the subset with another subset that contains the necessary variables.

- If you split your data file into many, much smaller data files, you can use variables from more than one file by combining the subsets in the working data file.

The MATCH FILES command can handle both of these situations. The following example adds variables from the original data file to the working data file:

```
MATCH FILES FILE=* /FILE='bigfile.sav'
 /BY id
 /KEEP id TO index99 bigvar1 bigvar3 bigvar5.
```

- The first FILE subcommand indicates the working data file with an asterisk (*).

- The BY subcommand indicates a key variable that is used to match cases.

- The KEEP subcommand lists all variables from both files to keep in the new working data file.

- The keyword TO with the names of the first and last variables in the current working data file includes all the variables from the current working data file.

If you are combining files that each contain a small subset of variables, and the combined total number of variables in those subsets is less than 4500, you can use the dialog box interface to combine the files. From the menus choose:

Data
  Merge Files ▶
    Add Variables...

See Chapter 6 for more information on the Add Variables procedure.

Key Variables and Case Order in Combined Files

The MATCH FILES command assumes that cases appear in the same position in all the files that are being combined together. If cases are not in the same order or if some cases are present in some files but missing in others, data will be matched incorrectly. To avoid mismatched data, it is strongly recommended that you always use the BY subcommand with one or more **key variables** that uniquely identify each case. The key variables must be present in all the files being combined, and the files must be sorted in the order of the key variable values.

Appendix E
Application Program Interface

With the SPSS application program interface (API), you can start another application from SPSS, automatically read the contents of the working data file into the other application, and then automatically return to SPSS when you quit the other application.

The SPSS API uses the Windows registration database to add program items to the SPSS menus. This appendix provides a list of SPSS API keys and an overview of the Windows Registration Info Editor, which is used to add the keys to the registration database.

SPSS API Registration Database Keys

All SPSS API keys in the registration database must be located in the SPSSOtherApps path. Beneath the SPSSOtherApps key, you need a key that identifies each application. The name of the key can be any descriptive word (but cannot contain spaces). Beneath that key, there are two required keys:

- Launch identifies the program name and directory location.
- Menu identifies the SPSS menu location and menu item text.

For example, Figure E.1 shows the minimum database registration information required to launch Microsoft Excel from SPSS.

Figure E.1   Database registration information

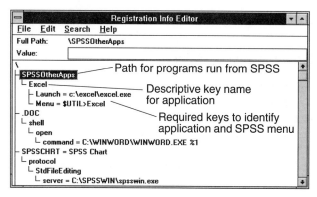

In this example, the menu item Excel will appear on the SPSS Utilities menu and selecting it will start Microsoft Excel.

SPSSOtherApps

The SPSSOtherApps key identifies the registration database path that contains all information on other applications run from SPSS. If this key/path does not exist in the registration database, you will need to create it (see "Editing the Registration Database" on p. 776).

Application Group Name Key

The keys for each application that you want to start from SPSS must be contained in a separate group in the SPSSOtherApps path. The key name that identifies each application key group can be any descriptive word or abbreviation, but it cannot contain blank spaces. For example, the key group name in Figure E.1 could be Spreadsheet instead of Excel, but it could not be Microsoft Excel.

Launch

The Launch key specifies the application name and directory location, as in:

```
Launch=c:\excel\excel.exe
```

The maximum length of the value is 255 characters. For some applications, you may need to append %1 to the end of the Launch value, as in:

```
Launch=c:\excel\excel.exe %1
```

If you have any doubts, always include %1 at the end of the Launch value.

ReExec

The ReExec key specifies the action to take in the event that the application is already running. There are two alternatives for the ReExec value:

0   Issue an alert and do not open another instance of the application.

1   Launch another instance of the application without issuing an alert. This is the default.

MenuType

The MenuType key specifies the SPSS menu bar with the menu that contains the selection used to run the application. There are three alternatives for the MenuType value:

0   Menu is on the main menu bar. This is the default. The main menu bar is the menu bar for the Data Editor and output and syntax windows.

1   Menu is on the chart window menu bar.

2   Menu is on the Chart Carousel menu bar.

Menu

The Menu key specifies the menu and/or submenu that contains the selection used to run the application and the text that is displayed on the menu for the selection. You can put new menu selections on existing menus or create new menus for your other applications.

Menus, submenus, and the text for the menu selection are separated by the greater than symbol (>), with the text for the menu selection appearing last. Existing SPSS menus and submenus are identified with special tags that begin with a dollar sign ($). For example,

```
Menu=$UTIL>Excel
```

specifies that the selection is on the Utilities menu and that the text displayed for the selection is Excel. Table E.1 contains a list of all valid SPSS menu and submenu tags.

You can also create your own menus and submenus. For example,

```
Menu=Applications>Spreadsheets>Excel
```

creates an Applications menu with a Spreadsheets submenu that contains the Excel selection.

The following restrictions apply to new menus:

- New menu names must be unique; they cannot duplicate existing menu names.
- New menu specifications cannot duplicate the tags (see Table E.1) reserved to identify existing SPSS menus.
- New menu names cannot contain the greater than symbol (>).

Table E.1   SPSS menu and submenu tags for Menu keys

Menu Bar	MenuType	Menu -> Submenu	Tag
Main	0	File	$FILE
		File -> New	$NEW
		File -> Open	$OPEN
		Edit	$EDIT
		Data	$DATA
		Data -> Merge	$MERGE
		Transform	$TRANS
		Transform -> Recode	$RECODE
		Statistics	$STAT
		Statistics -> Summarize	$SUM
		Statistics -> Custom Tables	$TABLE
		Statistics -> Compare Means	$MEAN
		Statistics -> ANOVA Models	$ANOVA
		Statistics -> Correlate	$CORR
		Statistics -> Regression	$REGR
		Statistics -> Loglinear	$LOGLIN
		Statistics -> Classify	$CLASS
		Statistics -> Data Reduction	$REDUCT
		Statistics -> Scale	$SCALE
		Statistics -> Nonparametric Tests	$NPAR
		Statistics -> Time Series	$TIMESERIES
		Statistics -> Survival	$SURV
		Statistics -> Multiple Response	$MULTRESP
		Graphs	$GRAPH
		Graphs -> Time Series	$GRAFTIME
		Utilities	$UTIL
Chart Window	1	File	$FILE
		File -> New	$NEW
		File -> Open	$OPEN
		Edit	$EDIT
		Gallery	$GALLERY
		Chart	$CHART
		Series	$SERIES
		Attributes	$ATTRIBUTES
Chart Carousel	2	File	$FILE
		File -> New	$NEW
		File -> Open	$OPEN
		Edit	$EDIT
		Carousel	$CAROUSEL

MenuSeparator

The MenuSeparator key specifies the display or suppression of a solid line to separate selections on the menu. There are two alternatives for the MenuSeparator value:

0 Do not display a separator line above the menu selection. This is the default.

1 Display a separator line above the menu selection.

Minimize

The Minimize key can be used to minimize (iconify) SPSS or the other application when the other application is started. There are three alternatives for the Minimize value:

0 Do not minimize either application. This is the default.

1 Minimize SPSS when the other application is started.

2 Minimize the other application after starting it.

MenuEnable

The MenuEnable key specifies the conditions required to enable the menu selection for the other application. There are two alternatives for the MenuEnable value:

0 Menu selection is always enabled.

1 Menu selection is enabled only if a working data file exists. This is the default.

ReadFile

The ReadFile key specifies the file format to use to write the working data file to the other application. The available file formats and key values are:

0 Other application initiates DDE conversation to read the working data file.

1 Working data file is not written to the other application. This is the default.

2 Working data file is written in SPSS data file format.

3 Working data file is written in XLS (Excel) format.

4 Working data file is written in SYLK (symbolic link) format.

5 Working data file is written in Lotus 1-2-3 Release 3 format.

6 Working data file is written in tab-delimited format.

7 Working data file is written in dBASE IV format.

CloseApp

The CloseApp key can be used to automatically close the other application or leave it running when you exit SPSS. There are two alternatives for the CloseApp value:

0   Do not close the other application on SPSS exit.

1   Close the other application on SPSS exit. This is the default.

Editing the Registration Database

To specify other applications to start from SPSS, you need to edit the Windows registration database using the Advanced Interface Registration Info Editor. To start the Advanced Interface:

1. From the Windows Program Manger menus choose:

    File
      Run...

2. In the Run dialog box, type `regedit /v` and click on OK.

This opens the Registration Info Editor, as shown in Figure E.2.

Figure E.2   Registration Info Editor

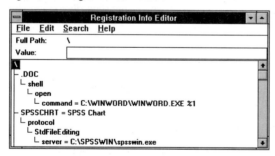

The registration database is displayed as a hierarchical path, similar to a directory path.

Adding Keys

To add a key to the registration database:

1. Highlight the key to which you want to add a subkey.

2. From the Registration Info Editor menus choose:

Edit
    Add Key...

3. In the Add Key dialog box, enter the key name and, if necessary, a key value.

When adding new keys to run other applications from SPSS, you start by adding a sub-key to the SPSSOtherApps key. This subkey is used to create a path for the group of keys used to run a particular application. All other SPSS API keys are added as subkeys to this application group name key. You can assign virtually any name to the application group name key. The only restriction is that key names cannot contain blanks.

If the SPSSOtherApps key is not in the registration database, you will need to create it before you can add subkeys to run other applications from SPSS (see the following example).

Example

This example creates a registration database entry to start Microsoft Excel from SPSS and read the contents of the working data file into an Excel spreadsheet.

① Open the Advanced Interface Registration Info Editor following the steps outlined in "Editing the Registration Database" on p. 776.

② If the SPSSOtherApps key is already in the registration database, skip to step ⑥.

③ If the SPSSOtherApps key is not in the registration database, highlight the backslash (\) at the top of the registration database hierarchy.

④ From the menus choose:

Edit
    Add Key...

⑤ In the Add Key dialog box, enter SPSSOtherApps in the Name text box and click on OK.

⑥ Highlight the SPSSOtherApps key.

⑦ Open the Add Key dialog box (see step ④ above).

⑧ In the Add Key dialog box, enter Excel in the Name text box and click on OK.

⑨ Highlight the Excel subkey directly under the SPSSOtherApps key.

⑩ Open the Add Key dialog box (see step ④ above).

⑪ Enter ReadFile in the Name text box and 3 in the Value text box and click on OK.

⑫ Highlight the Excel subkey again.

⑬ Open the Add Key dialog box (see step ④ above).

⑭ Enter Menu in the Name text box and $UTIL>Excel in the Value text box and click on OK.

⑮ Highlight the Excel subkey again.

⑯ Enter Launch in the Name text box and c:\excel\excel.exe in the Value text box and click on OK. (If Excel is in a different directory, substitute the appropriate directory location.)

The Excel key group in the SPSSOtherApps path should look like the one shown in Figure E.3.

Figure E.3   Key group to start Excel from SPSS

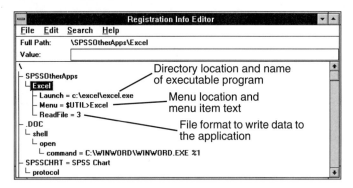

- Launch=c:\excel\excel.exe tells SPSS to start the executable program *excel.exe*, located in the *excel* directory.

- Menu=$UTIL>Excel adds a menu selection labeled Excel to the bottom of the Utilities menu.

- ReadFile=3 tells SPSS to write the contents of the working data file in XLS (Excel) format.

Sending Results Back to SPSS from Other Applications

You can send the modified data file back to SPSS via the SPSS DDE (Dynamic Data Exchange) Server. The basic steps for creating a DDE link to open the modified data file in SPSS are:

1. Write out (save) the data in one of the following formats: SPSS, SPSS portable, Excel, SYLK (symbolic link), Lotus 1-2-3, dBASE, or tab-delimited.

2. Connect to the SPSS DDE Server from the other application.

3. Use the SPSS DDE Server to send the =OpenFile command.

Figure E.4 is an example of an Excel macro that uses a DDE link to open an Excel file in SPSS. For more information on DDE, see Chapter 35.

Figure E.4   Excel macro with DDE link to SPSS

	A	B
	TEST.XLM	
1	Formulas	Comments
2	SendToSPSS()	Macro name
3	=INPUT("Name to save file to:",2)	Opens a dialog box that asks for filename
4	=SAVE.AS(A3,1,"",FALSE,"",FALSE)	Saves the current file as the name entered in dialog box
5	=EXEC("c:\spsswin\spsswin.exe")	Makes sure SPSS is running
6	=INITIATE("spsswin","system")	Opens the DDE channel
7	="[=OpenFile(""&A3&"")]"	Opens the file named in cell A3 in SPSS
8	=EXECUTE(A6,A7)	Passes the DDE commands to SPSS
9	=TERMINATE(A6)	Closes the DDE channel
10	=RETURN()	Returns to the Excel spreadsheet
11		
12		
13		

Appendix F
OEM-ANSI Translation

SPSS for Windows provides a program for translating text files containing high-order ASCII characters, such as letters with accent marks, between OEM (DOS) format and ANSI (Windows) format. This program is intended only for text files, not formatted data files.

The SPSS installation procedure automatically places an icon for the OEM-ANSI translation program in the SPSS program group (see Figure F.1). To use the program, simply double-click on the SPSSTran icon in the SPSS program group. If you don't have an SPSS program group or if the SPSSTran icon is not in the group, you can start the program by typing c:\spsswin\spsstran.exe (substitute the appropriate directory path if different) in the Run dialog box, accessed from the Program Manager File menu.

Figure F.1   SPSS program group with SPSSTran icon

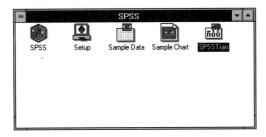

This opens the SPSS File Translation dialog box, as shown in Figure F.2.

Figure F.2   SPSS File Translation dialog box

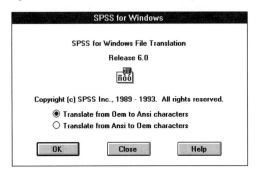

Choose the direction of translation and click on OK. This opens a dialog box similar to the one shown in Figure F.3.

Figure F.3   File selection dialog box

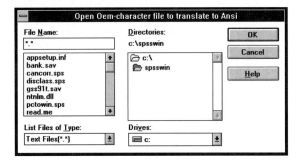

Choose the file you want to translate and click on OK.

Text File Translation

Numbers and unaccented characters in text files do not require translation. Translation should be necessary only for text files containing accented or other high-order ASCII characters that were created in DOS and will be used in Windows, or for text files that were created in Windows and will be used in DOS. Line-drawing characters in tabular output from SPSS are also translated. You can disable conversion of line-drawing characters if you are using this program in an environment that uses multi-byte characters or that does not support the (single) line-drawing characters.

Character data and labels in SPSS/PC+ data files are automatically converted when you read or write them in SPSS for Windows. This program does not translate characters in other data files unless they are saved in text format.

Disabling Conversion of Line Characters

To prevent the SPSSTran program from attempting to translate the line-drawing characters in tabular output from SPSS:

1. Exit SPSSTran.

2. Edit the *spsswin.ini* file, located in the *windows* directory, using any text editor.

3. At the bottom of the *spsswin.ini* file, starting on a new line, enter the following:

```
[SPSSTRAN]
TranslateLines=0
```

4. Save the modified *spsswin.ini file*, exit the file, and restart the SPSSTran program.

Disabling the conversion should not normally be necessary in languages with a roman character set. The conversion should be disabled before you translate any output files from SPSS in an environment where DOS uses a multi-byte character set, or where the DOS character set is from a code page that does not include the (single) line-drawing characters.

Appendix G
Keyboard Movement and Accelerator Keys

Although a mouse is recommended, you can accomplish most tasks in SPSS with the keyboard. This appendix provides a summary of accelerator and navigation keys.

Menus

Action	Keys
Move to the menu bar	F10 or Alt
Move between menus and submenus	→ ←
Move up and down a selected menu	↑ ↓
Select the highlighted menu item	↵Enter
Select a menu from the menu bar	Alt + underlined letter in menu name
Select an item from an open menu	Underlined letter in item name
Cancel selection, close menu	Esc
Use sets	F7
Stop SPSS Processor	F3
Help	F1

Dialog Boxes

Action	Keys
Select an item	`Alt` + underlined letter in item name
Move between items	`Tab→` / `⇧Shift`+`Tab→`
Select highlighted item	`Space`
Select OK or Continue	`↵Enter`
Select Cancel	`Esc`
Move up and down variable list or list box	`↑` `↓`
Move in a check box or radio button group	`↑` `↓`
Select multiple items in list box	`⇧Shift` + up and down arrow keys
Select multiple noncontiguous items in list box	`⇧Shift`+`F8`
Select all items in list box	`Ctrl` + /
Cancel current multiple selection in list box	`Ctrl` + \
Move selected variables up one position on list	`Alt` + minus sign (–)
Move selected variables down one position on list	`Alt` + plus sign (+)
Open the system menu	`Alt`+`Space`
Help	`F1`

Data Editor

Action	Keys
Move and select one cell down	⬇ or ⏎Enter
Move and select one cell up	⬆
Move and select one cell right or left	➡ ⬅ or Tab→ / ⇧Shift+Tab→
Select first cell in case (row)	Ctrl+⬅
Select first cell in case or selected area	Home
Select last cell in case	Ctrl+➡
Select last cell in case or selected area	End
Select first cell in variable (column)	Ctrl+⬆
Select last cell in variable	Ctrl+⬇
Select entire case (entire row)	⇧Shift+Space
Select entire variable (entire column)	Ctrl+Space
Select first cell in the data file	Ctrl+Home
Select last cell in the data file	Ctrl+End
Extend selection	⇧Shift + arrow keys
Scroll up or down the height of the window	PgUp PgDn
Scroll left or right the width of the window	Ctrl+PgUp / Ctrl+PgDn
Copy from selected cells	Ctrl+Ins / Ctrl +C
Cut from selected cells	⇧Shift+Del / Ctrl +X
Paste into selected cells	⇧Shift+Ins / Ctrl +V
Display value label list for data entry	⇧Shift+F2
Search for data	Alt+F5
Help	F1
Edit Mode	
Switch to Edit Mode	F2
Move one character right or left	➡ ⬅
Extend selection	⇧Shift + arrow keys
Move to beginning of value	Home
Move to end of value	End
Select to beginning of value	⇧Shift+Home
Select to end of value	⇧Shift+End

Syntax and Output Windows

Action	Keys
Move one character right or left	`→` `←`
Move one word right or left	`Ctrl`+`→` / `Ctrl`+`←`
Move up or down one line	`↑` `↓`
Move to start of line	`Home`
Move to end of line	`End`
Move to start of file	`Ctrl`+`Home`
Move to end of file	`Ctrl`+`End`
Move to next output block in output window	`Ctrl` + >
Move to previous output block in output window	`Ctrl` + <
Select text	`⇧Shift` + arrow keys
Select output page down	`Ctrl` + }
Select output page up	`Ctrl` + {
Search for text	`F5`
Replace text	`⇧Shift`+`F5`
Copy selected text	`Ctrl`+`Ins` / `Ctrl`+`C`
Cut selected text	`⇧Shift`+`Del` / `Ctrl`+`X`
Paste selected text	`⇧Shift`+`Ins` / `Ctrl`+`V`
Designate window	`Ctrl` + !
Help	`F1`
Output Window Icon Bar	
Pause	`Ctrl`+`S`
Scroll	`Ctrl`+`Q`
Round	`Ctrl`+ 0 (zero)
Glossary	`Ctrl`+`G`
Go to chart	`Ctrl`+`J`
Syntax Window Icon Bar	
Run	`Ctrl`+`A`
Syntax	`Ctrl`+`N`

Chart Carousel

Action	Keys
Open chart selection drop-down list	Ctrl+P
Discard selected chart	Ctrl+D
Edit selected chart	Ctrl+E
Go to next chart	Ctrl+F
Go to previous chart	Ctrl+B
Go to output	Ctrl+J

Chart Window[1]

Action	Keys
Refresh chart	Ctrl+R
Rotate 3-D chart on x plane	Ctrl+X
Rotate 3-D chart on y plane	Ctrl+Y
Rotate 3-D chart on z plane	Ctrl+Z

Window Control

Action	Keys
Tile windows	⇧Shift+F4
Cascade windows	Ctrl+F5
Cycle through open windows	Ctrl+Tab→ or Ctrl+F6
Close active window	Ctrl+F4

---

1. A mouse is required for some features of the Chart Editor.

Bibliography

Anderson, R., and S. Nida. 1978. Effect of physical attractiveness on opposite and same-sex evaluations. *Journal of Personality*, 46:3, 401–413.

Beard, C. M., V. Fuster, and L. R. Elveback. 1982. Daily and seasonal variation in sudden cardiac death, Rochester, Minnesota, 1950–1975. *Mayo Clinic Proceedings*, 57: 704–706.

Belsley, D. A., E. Kuh, and R. E. Welsch. 1980. *Regression diagnostics: Identifying influential data and sources of collinearity*. New York: John Wiley and Sons.

Benedetti, J. K., and M. B. Brown. 1978. Strategies for the selection of log-linear models. *Biometrics*, 34: 680–686.

Berk, K. N. 1977. Tolerance and condition in regression computation. *Journal of the American Statistical Association*, 72: 863–866.

_____. 1978. Comparing subset regression procedures. *Technometrics*, 20: 1–6.

Bishop, Y. M. M., S. E. Fienberg, and P. W. Holland. 1975. *Discrete multivariate analysis: Theory and practice*. Cambridge, Mass.: MIT Press.

Blalock, H. M. 1979. *Social statistics*. New York: McGraw-Hill.

Blom, G. 1958. *Statistical estimates and transformed beta variables*. New York: John Wiley and Sons.

Borgatta, E. F., and G. W. Bohrnstedt. 1980. Level of measurement once over again. *Sociological Methods and Research*, 9:2, 147–160.

Cedercreutz, C. 1978. Hypnotic treatment of 100 cases of migraine. In: *Hypnosis at Its Bicentennial*, F. H. Frankel and H. S. Zamansky, eds. New York: Plenum.

Chambers, J. M., W. S. Cleveland, B. Kleiner, and P. A. Tukey. 1983. *Graphical methods for data analysis*. Belmont, Calif.: Wadsworth, Inc.; Boston: Duxbury Press.

Churchill, G. A., Jr. 1979. *Marketing research: Methodological foundations*. Hinsdale, Ill.: Dryden Press.

Cleveland, W. S. 1979. Robust locally weighted regression and smoothing scatterplots. *Journal of the American Statistical Association,* 74: 829–836.

Cleveland, W. S., and R. McGill. 1984. The many faces of a scatterplot. *Journal of the American Statistical Association*, 79: 807–822.

Cohen, J. 1960. A coefficient of agreement for nominal scales. *Educational and Psychological Measurement*, 20: 37–46.

Conover, W. J. 1974. Some reasons for not using the Yates continuity correction on 2×2 contingency tables. *Journal of the American Statistical Association*, 69: 374–376.

_____. 1980. *Practical nonparametric statistics*. 2nd ed. New York: John Wiley and Sons.

Cook, R. D. 1977. Detection of influential observations in linear regression. *Technometrics*, 19: 15–18.

Daniel, C., and F. Wood. 1980. *Fitting Equations to Data*. Rev. ed. New York: John Wiley and Sons.

Davis, H., and E. Ragsdale. 1983. Unpublished working paper. Graduate School of Business, University of Chicago.

Davis, J. A. 1982. *General social surveys, 1972–1982: Cumulative codebook.* Chicago: National Opinion Research Center.

Dillon, W. R., and M. Goldstein. 1984. *Multivariate analysis: Methods and applications.* New York: John Wiley and Sons.

Dineen, L. C., and B. C. Blakesley. 1973. Algorithm AS 62: A generator for the sampling distribution of the Mann-Whitney U statistic. *Applied Statistics*, 22: 269–273.

Draper, N. R., and H. Smith. 1981. *Applied regression analysis.* New York: John Wiley and Sons.

Duncan, O. D. 1966. Path analysis: Sociological examples. *American Journal of Sociology*, 72: 1–16.

Everitt, B. S. 1977. *The analysis of contingency tables.* London: Chapman and Hall.

Fienberg, S. E. 1977. *The analysis of cross-classified categorical data.* Cambridge, Mass.: MIT Press.

Fox, J. 1984. *Linear statistical models and related methods.* New York: John Wiley and Sons.

Frane, J. W. 1976. Some simple procedures for handling missing data in multivariate analysis. *Psychometrika*, 41: 409–415.

_____. 1977. A note on checking tolerance in matrix inversion and regression. *Technometrics*, 19: 513–514.

Goodman, L. A., and W. H. Kruskal. 1954. Measures of association for cross-classification. *Journal of the American Statistical Association*, 49: 732–764.

Haberman, S. J. 1978. *Analysis of qualitative data.* Vol. 1. New York: Academic Press.

Hansson, R. O., and K. M. Slade. 1977. Altruism toward a deviant in city and small town. *Journal of Applied Social Psychology*, 7:3, 272–279.

Hoaglin, D. C., and R. E. Welsch. 1978. The hat matrix in regression and ANOVA. *American Statistician*, 32: 17–22.

Hoaglin, D. C., F. Mosteller, and J. W. Tukey. 1983. *Understanding robust and exploratory data analysis.* New York: John Wiley and Sons.

Hocking, R. R. 1976. The analysis and selection of variables in linear regression. *Biometrics*, 32: 1–49.

Hogg, R. V. 1979. An introduction to robust estimation. *Robustness in Statistics*, 1–18.

Judge, G. G., W. E. Griffiths, R. C. Hill, H. Lutkepohl, and T. C. Lee. 1985. *The theory and practice of econometrics.* 2nd ed. New York: John Wiley and Sons.

Kendall, M. G., and A. Stuart. 1973. *The advanced theory of statistics.* Vol. 2. New York: Hafner Press.

King, M. M., et al. 1979. Incidence and growth of mammary tumors induced by 7,12-dimethylbenz(a) anthracene as related to the dietary content of fat and antioxidant. *Journal of the National Cancer Institute*, 63:3, 657–663.

Kleinbaum, D. G., and L. L. Kupper. 1978. *Applied regression analysis and other multivariable methods.* Boston, Mass.: Duxbury Press.

Kleinbaum, D. G., L. L. Kupper, and H. Morgenstern. 1982. *Epidemiological research: Principles and quantitative methods.* Belmont, Calif.: Wadsworth, Inc.

Kraemer, H. C. 1982. Kappa coefficient. In: *Encyclopedia of Statistical Sciences*, S. Kotz and N. L. Johnson, eds. New York: John Wiley and Sons.

Lee, E. T. 1992. *Statistical methods for survival data analysis.* New York: John Wiley and Sons.

Lehmann, E. L. 1975. *Nonparametrics: Statistical methods based on ranks*. San Francisco: Holden-Day.

Loether, H. J., and D. G. McTavish. 1976. *Descriptive and inferential statistics: An introduction*. Boston: Allyn and Bacon.

Lord, F. M., and M. R. Novick. 1968. *Statistical theories of mental test scores*. Reading, Mass.: Addison-Wesley.

Mantel, N. 1974. Comment and a suggestion on the Yates continuity correction. *Journal of the American Statistical Association*, 69: 378–380.

Mantel, N., and W. Haenszel. 1959. Statistical aspects of the analysis of data from retrospective studies of disease. *Journal of the National Cancer Institute*, 22: 719–748.

Meyer, L. S., and M. S. Younger. 1976. Estimation of standardized coefficients. *Journal of the American Statistical Association*, 71: 154–157.

Neter, J., W. Wasserman, and R. Kutner. 1985. *Applied linear statistical models*. 2nd ed. Homewood, Ill.: Richard D. Irwin, Inc.

Nunnally, J. 1978. *Psychometric theory*. 2nd ed. New York: McGraw-Hill.

Olson, C. L. 1976. On choosing a test statistic in multivariate analysis of variance. *Psychological Bulletin*, 83: 579–586.

Overall, J. E., and C. Klett. 1972. *Applied multivariate analysis*. New York: McGraw-Hill.

Paul, O., et al. 1963. A longitudinal study of coronary heart disease. *Circulation*, 28: 20–31.

Rabkin, S. W., F. A. Mathewson, and R. B. Tate. 1980. Chronobiology of cardiac sudden death in men. *Journal of the American Medical Association*, 244:12, 1357–1358.

Roberts, H. V. 1979. An analysis of employee compensation. *Report 7946*, October. Center for Mathematical Studies in Business and Economics, University of Chicago.

———. 1980. Statistical bases in the measurement of employment discrimination. In: *Comparable Worth: Issues and Alternatives*, E. Robert Livernash, ed. Washington, D.C.: Equal Employment Advisory Council, 173–195.

Siegel, S. 1956. *Nonparametric statistics for the behavioral sciences*. New York: McGraw-Hill.

Sigall, H., and N. Ostrove. 1975. Beautiful but dangerous: Effects of offender attractiveness and nature of the crime on juridic judgment. *Journal of Personality and Social Psychology*, 31: 410–414.

Smirnov, N. V. 1948. Table for estimating the goodness of fit of empirical distributions. *Annals of Mathematical Statistics*, 19: 279–281.

Snedecor, G. W., and W. G. Cochran. 1967. *Statistical methods*. Ames: Iowa State University Press.

Somers, R. H. 1962. A new symmetric measure of association for ordinal variables. *American Sociological Review*, 27: 799–811.

Speed, M. F. 1976. Response curves in the one way classification with unequal numbers of observations per cell. *Proceedings of the Statistical Computing Section*, American Statistical Association.

SPSS Inc. 1991. *SPSS statistical algorithms*. 2nd ed. Chicago: SPSS Inc.

Stevens, S. S. 1946. On the theory of scales of measurement. *Science*, 103: 677–680.

Tatsuoka, M. M. 1971. *Multivariate analysis*. New York: John Wiley and Sons.

Theil, H. 1967. *Economics and information theory*. Chicago: Rand McNally.

Tukey, J. W. 1962. The future of data analysis. *Annals of Mathematical Statistics*, 33: 22.

Velleman, P. F., and R. E. Welsch. 1981. Efficient computing of regression diagnostics. *American Statistician*, 35: 234–242.

Winer, B. J., D. R. Brown, and K. M. Michels. 1991. *Statistical principles in experimental design*. 3rd ed. New York: McGraw-Hill.

Wright, S. 1960. Path coefficients and path regressions: Alternative or complementary concepts? *Biometrics*, 16: 189–202.

Wynder, E. L. 1976. Nutrition and cancer. *Federal Proceedings*, 35: 1309–1315.

Wyner, G. A. 1980. Response errors in self-reported number of arrests. *Sociological Methods and Research*, 9:2, 161–177.

Index

This is a combined subject index for the *SPSS for Windows Base System User's Guide* and the *SPSS Base System Syntax Reference Guide*. Information located in the *SPSS Base System Syntax Reference Guide* is denoted with the prefix R before the page number.